THE BACK DOOR
GUIDE TO
SHORT-TERM
JOB ADVENTURES

THE BACK DOOR GUIDE TO

SHORT-TERM JOB ADVENTURES

INTERNSHIPS, EXTRAORDINARY EXPERIENCES, SEASONAL JOBS, VOLUNTEERING, WORK ABROAD

by Michael Landes

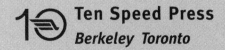

Ten Speed Press
Berkeley Toronto

Dedication

To my mom and dad, who not only opened my eyes to so many things while growing up but who also provided me with the tools I needed to develop into the person I am today. I feel very fortunate: it's comforting to know that someone encourages and has faith in your abilities no matter what.

Ten Speed Press

Box 7123

Berkeley, California 94707

www.tenspeed.com

Distributed in Australia by Simon & Schuster Australia, in Canada by Ten Speed Press Canada, in New Zealand by Southern Publishers Group, in South Africa by Real Books, in Southeast Asia by Berkeley Books, and in the United Kingdom and Europe by Airlift Book Company.

Cover and interior design by Toni Tajima

Cover illustration by Tony D'Agostino

Library of Congress Cataloging-in-Publication Data

Landes, Michael.

  The back door guide to short-term job adventures: internships, extraordinary experiences, seasonal jobs, volunteering, work abroad / by Michael Landes.—
Rev. and updated.

        p. cm.

  Includes index.

  ISBN 1-58008-147-9 (pbk.)

  1. Job hunting. 2. Interns. 3. Volunteers. 4. Overseas employers. I. Title: Short-term job adventures. II. Title.

HF5382.7.L352 2000

650.14—cd21   99-059529

Printed in Canada

First printing this edition, 2000

1 2 3 4 5 6 7 8 9 10 — 05 04 03 02 01 00

Acknowledgments vi

Preface vii

About Your Guide 1

1 Beginning the Climb 5

2 Your Path 20

3 Finding Your Way 35

4 Adventure Careers 43

5 Camps, Ranches, and Resorts 77

6 The Great Outdoors 109

7 The Environment 143

8 Back to Basics 177

9 Artistic and Learning Adventures 203

10 Work with Heart 233

11 Abroad Adventures 259

12 Indexes: Your Compass to the Guide 293

Alphabetical Listing of Programs 294

Category 300

Geographical Listing of Programs 309

Program Length 317

General 325

CONTENTS

Acknowledgments . . . .

As I reflect on how my life's work has developed and evolved over time, it has boiled down to two key ingredients—people and place—ingredients that have colored every aspect of my writing. The very nature of this guidebook has allowed me to transplant myself to many new environments; however, this component has also challenged me in many ways. Leading an adventurous life is definitely an invigorating lifestyle, but I have also struggled with the balance of transition and stability. This means creating a home base that I could find comfort in and an environment that would allow me to explore and take part in all the world has to offer—a factor that you must look at very carefully as you begin your own adventurous pursuits. As I began revising and rewriting the pages of this second edition, I've been very fortunate to have dear friends and family who have helped me to balance this sense of place.

Reach for the highest

Strive for the best . . .

Live day by day

And to God leave the rest.

I started and finished my writing and research in Boston, Massachusetts, while living in my great aunt's triple-decker home on the third floor. I can't thank Aunt Bea enough for providing me with a sense of home, along with teaching me about "the way things once were" and the importance of family. Conversations with her were the catalyst for me in writing my new Back to Basics chapter.

Most of the research and writing of this edition was done over a seven-month period in one of the most beautiful spots to write a book: San Diego, California. My dear friends, Rob and Robyn Caringella (and Mason!), opened their home and hearts to me and my passion. The times we shared and the gifts they provided me go beyond the word magical—it was these experiences alone that allowed my thoughts to turn into some of my best writing.

Beyond the sense of place that was created and nurtured, it was my connections with an amazing group of people (my "back door" team) that helped my words come alive. I feel very blessed for the following people who have influenced and added their gifts to this book:

Sue Schmid, whose spirit, soul, and sunshine is present on every page of your guide. I cannot thank her enough for her weekly inspirational quotes, her constant support and invaluable suggestions, and enriching and stretching my life in ways I never imagined. Yes, too much of a good thing is *beyond* wonderful—thank you for sharing your heartfelt gifts with me and the world (and helping me to turn my inspiration into action).

Brian Kean for his outbursts of wit and wisdom (and all his hard work that went into the development of page 43). His sense of humor and contagious laugh added so much to my writing and life.

Craig Dunkin for his friendship and for allowing me to share his "story" with the world (he's one amazing sports broadcaster now!).

Mike and Dorrie Williams for their creativity, great stories, and incredible support for so many years.

Scott Lewis for his wacky spirit and computer wizardry (which helped me to keep track of all the great information contained in your guide).

Sonia Borg for being such a positive influence in my life and opening my eyes to new places and a health-filled lifestyle.

For the special angels in my life: Nancy Conn, Renate D'Arcangelo, and Frances Lithgow.

Matthew and Kristin Landes and Grandma Siok for all their encouragement and love over the years.

Everyone who has helped me in "spreading the word" about my work, especially Jim Williams (not to mention his generosity and hospitality at his hostel in New York City); Patrick Combs (you never cease to amaze me!), Dick Bolles (and his influential writings that have truly inspired mine), Alison Doyle (and the great things she's doing with About.com), all the web sites that promote my book (especially Amazon.com), and all the Career Center and Internship Directors across the nation who support and connect their students to my work.

My team of contributing writers: Elizabeth Kruempelmann, David Lyman, Michele Gran, and Bill Borrie, along with all the program directors who year after year provide me with information and invaluable insights about their short-term job opportunities.

My talented team at Ten Speed Press who amazingly turned my words into this beautiful book: Jean Blomquist for her unbelievably thorough copyedit, Toni Tajima and Linda Davis for their creative design, Tony D'Agostino for his marvelous illustrations on the covers, Barbara King for her careful proofread, Dotty Hollinger and Libby Oda for keying in corrections, Ken DellaPenta for his incredible job on the final proofread and indexes, and finally, my editor, Julie Bennett, for putting her magical touches on the entire project.

And finally, many many thanks go to each of you for believing in and supporting all my hard work. Thank you for keeping my passion alive!

Stumbling upon a New Path . . . .

remember when you thought about "what I want to be when I grow up"? Not there now? Well, think about it again, because this time you have plenty of options to choose from. At first glance at your guide, you may think that it is solely an encyclopedia of unique short-term job opportunities. Undoubtedly, this may be the most alluring ingredient. However, I don't believe that a book of opportunities makes much sense without first questioning your existence and your purpose—you know, the who, what, where, how, and why. My hope is to challenge your "mind, body, and soul" as you begin to explore the pages of your career and life.

As Mark Twain so thoughtfully suggests, it's time to push past the things that you think have limited you, and begin to actively uncover a life that is happier, more meaningful, and prosperous. I say: Never be afraid to do what feels natural to you. Societal norms—professional achievement, wealth, power, and fame—dictate so many people's lives already. I believe these traits, which have been regarded as admirable and desirable, are merely incidental, extraneous, and self-defeating. There is no need to be seduced by this lure. What matters the most is the person you are becoming, the sort of life you are living, and the work that will complement both. It all begins with you—by looking at the world through curious eyes and exploring what's on the other side of the mountain.

Understanding what's important in your life and what is not will allow you to make decisions based on the bigger picture of your life—your tentative outline of adventures that will help to promote your dream career over the long haul. Some figure out this direction right away, others take a lifetime to get there. My direction has slowly evolved over time; however, I would like to share one incident with you that helped to push me in the right direction.

Most of my formative years can be coined my "circling about" years. This meant going from job to job and place to place, along with thinking that I was engaging in the right opportunities to manifest my life and career. An education gave me knowledge and confidence; internships—with organizations such as Gallo Winery, Apple Computer, and MTV—provided the foundation and practi-

Twenty years from now you will be more disappointed by the things you didn't do than by the things you did do. So throw off the bowlines. Sail away from the safe harbor. Catch the trade winds in your sails. Explore, dream, discover. —Mark Twain

vii

PREFACE

The secret to enjoying life is to be thankful for what each day brings.

cal training for my world of work. At this point in my life, I was cunning in my pursuits and took the initiative on every opportunity presented to me. I was financially secure and viewed by others as "successful." However, something was missing. It finally dawned on me that even though I seemed to be doing the "right" things, I wasn't really getting anywhere. What I lacked was vision.

Unfortunately, it wasn't until a tragic event occurred in my life that I began to develop this vision and see more clearly. Simply stated, I was hit by a car. The real impact of this tragedy didn't take hold until the doctors told me that I might not be able to ever walk again. Not walk again? That I could not accept. Looking at the situation, I had two choices: to look at myself as a victim or to look at the situation with positive eyes. I opted for the latter. What seemed like a tragedy at the time soon became a blessing in disguise and proved to be a very pivotal point in the person I was becoming.

The next six months of my life were dedicated to rehabilitating my legs and proving my doctors wrong—I would, indeed, walk again. However, my time of healing became more of a mental, emotional, and spiritual healing rather than a physical one. The simple things in life—the comfort of family and friends, the delights of tasting a fresh tomato, the sounds of a child's spontaneous laughter, or the sights of the ever-changing shapes and colors of clouds hovering over a magnificent sunset—soon became the things that were most important to me. As I initiated my quest in taking my first steps again (a miracle in itself), a new world seemed to bloom around me.

I realized I needed to build a foundation that would allow me to create a life that would harmonize my work with my natural gifts, abilities, and skills. This was an exciting realization. The decisions I made were now based on the bigger picture that I had created, rather than through a random process that I once pursued. This didn't mean that life became any easier; however, it did allow me to approach it with new eyes—relishing in every good and challenging moment.

The things I have experienced since this "revelation"—from coordinating an internship program at a university, venturing to Europe on a solo backpacking and cycling adventure, self-publishing the first edition of this book, or trying my hand at professional speaking and developing new friends and colleagues because of the work through my book—have provided the necessary ingredients to not only fuel my mission but also provide you with insights on uncovering yours. My hope is that the many "voices" that speak to you throughout the pages of your guide will not only encourage you to find your place in the world but also allow you to realize that life is truly a miraculous event. So explore, dream, and discover, and turn those dreams into reality. You'll find this to be one of the best decisions you'll ever make.

Writing, researching, and updating a guidebook involves an enormous amount of information gathering and exacting attention to the nitty-gritty details. This also means corresponding and communicating with thousands of people and programs, sifting through the important stuff, and presenting you with a unique blend of information and inspiration.

The heart of the book—the opportunities—has constantly evolved over time. Each year I'm presented with new programs, new resources, new ideas, new stories, and new quotes. To give you an idea of what I mean, take, for example, the new section called "Back to Basics" (found on page 177). This section evolved out of my own desire to work on an organic farm and connect more with the earth. My first step in the creation and development of this section began with a phone call to an association called Alternative Farming Systems Information Center (page 200) that I had found while searching for opportunities on the Internet (which proved to be a very discouraging process). After conversing with the association about what I was after, I was informed that they published a free directory of organic farms that offer internships and apprenticeships. I wasn't overly excited at that point, as I have queried many associations who produce internship directories, only to find out the last revision was done years ago.

Upon receiving their publication, I quickly thumbed through their listings (which were crafted by the farmers themselves) and highlighted the ones I thought had potential for my book (and for my quest to work at a farm). I then wrote to each potential farm and asked if they would like to become involved with my work. Many responded and many did not. Those who did sent me additional information through mail or e-mail. From this initial correspondence, I then began to make phone calls to the actual owners and staffing directors about their opportunities. I even visited a handful of farms so I could get a better feel of life on the farm. These experiences proved to be invaluable.

From my initial phone call to Alternative Farming Systems, I was able to generate twenty solid programs for this new section. Additionally, the conversations I conducted with owners and staff

1

ABOUT YOUR GUIDE

generated hundreds of other leads, ideas, and resources that would allow me to develop this section further. After months of hard work, I was able to present to you the best programs that were available, along with the realities of working on an organic farm.

This is how the book evolves: by gathering information, talking to people, showing up at their back door, and finding out what really goes on. One thing leads to the next. You can do the same. It takes just one phone call and a lot of determination on your part to get the information you need.

Beyond my own research, readers have also proved to be a valuable asset in providing me with the realities of working for a particular organization. Any comments I receive from readers on their experiences, I somehow integrate into the respective listing. Many times you'll find a direct quote at the bottom of the listing that captures this essence.

Whatever the way I've uncovered the information, every fact is always verified with the organization prior to inclusion in the guide. This also serves as my "weeding-out" process. Researching, updating, and rewriting each listing so that it reflects the spirit and soul of each program is probably the most important task of the book; however, when you correspond with hundreds and hundreds of programs over a very short period of time, it becomes a daunting assignment. As with any job, there are always elements that are more repetitive and exhausting than the rest. However, being the most important component of the guide, I put the most energy into this phase. My formative years taught me that you should do a job to the best of your ability or not do it all. I hope that you will find that my work reflects this very philosophy.

Using Your Guide . . . .

With so many opportunities presented in your guide, the challenge may well be picking one to do. To ease this challenge, each section has been set up so that you first have an overview of what's tucked away in it. This introductory material also includes information on a variety of opportunities in the section, along with special stories and other insights that you don't want to miss. Each section concludes with my recommendations on other resources—books, newsletters, web links—for further exploration.

UNDERSTANDING THE LISTINGS

each listing is visually laid out in the same fashion, so at first glance you can get the bigger picture of the program. The header information includes important facts about the program—the category (or "buzzword") it represents, the specific state or country where you will work, and the time commitment that is needed from you. These three elements also make up three of the five indexes found at the end of your guide. Note that when an organization has its work assignments evenly spread throughout many states, it is listed as USA. On the same note, if the program covers many regions throughout the world, it is listed as Worldwide. The header information also contains up to four icons that represent compensation, room and board, and eligibility requirements. The "Key to Icons" legend outlines these specifics.

Key to Icons

 Compensation is provided.

 A program fee is charged.

 Volunteer opportunity.

 Room and/or board is provided.

 The program is geared specifically for college students or recent graduates.

(Note that if this icon is not present, it generally means the program considers anyone over the age of eighteen. Read on for more details.)

 International applicants are also eligible to apply.

AMELIA ISLAND PLANTATION

Resort • Florida • 16 Weeks
www.aipfl.com

Barbara Ross, Internship Coordinator
P.O. Box 3000
Amelia Island, FL 32035-3000
(904) 277-5904 • (904) 277-5994 (fax)
intern@aipfl.com

● ●

NOTED FOR THEIR environmentally conscious development, Amelia Island Plantation is known in Florida for being the greenest resort. This 1,350-acre gated resort and residential community offers miles of sandy beach in a preserved natural setting, along with many amenities. Internships have been offered at the resort for nearly twenty years, with many former interns now in various management positions (including the Internship Coordinator!).

The Experience: Internships are offered in the following areas: Aquatics, Club Management, Commercial Recreation, Culinary, Golf and Tennis, Graphic Design, Lodging, Marketing, Nature Science, Promotions, Public Relations, Recreation Rental and Retail, Rooms Management, Staff Development, Theme Parties, and Turf Management.

Commitment: Internships are offered throughout the year (spring, summer, and fall), and a sixteen-week minimum commitment is preferred (although some interns stay as long as forty-eight weeks).

Perks: A housing stipend of $225 per week and two meals per shift is provided for most positions. Other positions receive an hourly wage in lieu of the stipend and meals. Other perks include assistance in locating housing, extensive training, and use of the amenities at discounted rates.

Ideal Candidate: The resort recruits junior and seniors at universities and colleges who must be receiving academic credit. Previous related experience (paid or unpaid) is a plus and a clean driving record is a requirement for many areas to even be considered. In addition, all candidates must be fluent in conversational English and provide their own transportation.

Getting In: Applicants can request information through e-mail or by calling. Be sure to indicate your area of interest and the semester you are required to intern so that the appropriate information may be sent. It's best to apply at least two months before the start date.

It's a funny thing about life; if you refuse to accept anything but the best, you very often get it. —W. SOMERSET MAUGHAM

Once you have glanced at this pertinent header information, the contact information and program details follow. I think you'll find this information to be self-explanatory. Each listing covers an overview of the organization, the experience, commitment, perks, the ideal candidate, getting in, and any insider tips that have been uncovered. In some listings this information is broken down by specific fields, while others are merely condensed into a paragraph or two. No matter the length, each will hopefully provide you with the "spirit and soul" of each program.

Although every effort has been taken to ensure that the most up-to-date contact and program information is provided, invariably some of the facts change over time. The most current information can generally be found through the program's web site; however, I suggest verifying all the specific details with the contact person.

Connecting with the Author.......

Simply stated, I'd love to hear from you. Your adventurous (and not-so-adventurous) tales, experiences, suggestions, and feedback help to fuel my passion and make each edition better than the last. Since my journeys take me to different locales throughout the year, the best way to contact me is through e-mail. Send me a note at mlandes@backdoorjobs.com, visit my companion web site at **www.backdoorjobs.com**, or write to me at 2054 N. Palm Avenue, Upland, CA 91784. **Happy adventures!**

The Climb

A small boy heard the mountain speak,
"There are secrets on my highest peak;
but beware, my boy, the passing of time.
Wait not too long to start the climb."

So quickly come and go the years,
and a young man stands below—with fears.
"Come on—come on," the mountain cussed.
"Time presses on—on, climb you must."

Now he's busied in middle-aged prime,
and maybe tomorrow he'll take the climb.
Now is too soon—it's raining today;
Gone all gone—years are eaten away.

An old man looks up—still feeling the lure.
Yet, he'll suffer the pain—not climb for the cure.
The hair is white—the step is slow.
And it's safer and warmer to stay here below.

So all too soon the secrets are buried,
along with him and regrets he carried.
And it's not for loss of secrets he'd cried,
But rather because he'd never tried.

—PHYLLIS TRUSSIER

for those who already know they want to excavate an archaeological dig in Peru or teach kids about the wonders of the Atlantic Ocean and don't need to do extensive soul searching, taking a peek at this section can't hurt. Finding yourself, deciding what brings meaning to your life, and determining your destiny all take time. This section will give you some creative ideas about the bigger picture in life and start your climb off on the right foot.

This section will help you to:

- Uncover who you are and what naturally motivates you.

- Find balance in your life.

- Map out the big picture of your life.

- Understand the power of people and place.

- Begin the decision-making process.

BEGINNING
THE CLIMB

How can you get very far,

If you don't know who you are?

How can you do what you ought,

If you don't know what you've got?

And if you don't know which to do

Of all the things in front of you,

Then what you'll have when you
 are through

Is just a mess without a clue

Of all the best that can come true

If you know what and which and who.

—Winnie the Pooh

We could all use an emptying out of identity every now and then. Considering who we are not, we may find the surprising revelation of who we are.

—Thomas Moore

Everyone has his own specific vocation or mission in life . . . therein he cannot be replaced, nor can his life be repeated. Thus, everyone's task is as unique as is his specific opportunity to implement it.

—Viktor Frankl

Who Are You?. . . . .

f you want to become an extraordinary person, it's time to stop being vague. Now is the time to take inventory of your talents, your personal quirks, and the careers that might resonate with your skills and abilities. With the work you are about to engage in, you will gain the ability to promote your uniqueness with passion and vigor when the time comes. Think of your life as a long, never-ending pathway stretching out ahead of you, with many pathways leading off to either side. The path you are on now represents the lifestyle you are now living (whether it be good or "bad"); the offshoots from this pathway represent new directions you might take—new jobs, new places to live, new relationships, and new experiences. However, in giving yourself many options, you'll always come to a signpost on the road presenting you with two or three (or four . . .) attractive possibilities. Which one should you take? Which one will help you with your long-term goals? Of course, some of these paths might have huge doors in front of them, and to get through these doors, you must do certain things before they swing open for you. A particular door might need a certain skill, a degree, a well-connected friend or family member, a unique personal characteristic, or a past experience as a key. So, let's start from the beginning and uncover the unique you.

Setting the Stage. . . . .

ave you ever been to a play? If not, make plans to see a production for the sheer enjoyment of it. Now, take a few minutes and ponder all the things that went into the play's production: the directors, producers, writers, the cast, set designers, costuming, acting, rehearsals, development, fund-raising, program design, publicity, and so forth. It's amazing to think of all the steps necessary to create one production. Have you thought about what will make your very own "production" incredible? Have you thought about the things you want to (or may want to) accomplish to create an incredible story for yourself? Are you the director and author of your story, or are you letting societal norms or others dictate or shape your story? Are you actively taking the time to develop your plot and create the things that are the most important? Think of all the "players" who are involved in your story: the scenery, the things that happen on a daily basis, the decisions that are made, the highs and the lows.

I dare you to think differently and to take your potential seriously. It's time to call on all your resources—to stretch them and challenge them. Your life is now. It's time to trade in your days of "getting by" and begin to work toward a life that brings fulfillment in everything you do. This journey must begin with an understanding of what's happening in your life right now—behind the scenes and on center stage. A powerful way to visualize the big picture of your life is by explicitly writing out all the important details. The details in your writing will give you something to work with along with something to act upon.

> It's very important to fall in love with what you're doing. To be able to get out of bed and do what you love for the rest of your day is beyond words. It'll keep you around for a long time.
>
> —George Burns

MAKE TIME THIS WEEK TO ANSWER THE FOLLOWING QUESTIONS:

- What kind of person do you want to be?
- What (and to whom) do you gravitate toward naturally?
- What are your values?
- What are your unique qualities?
- What are your likes and dislikes?
- What are five skills you enjoy using?
- What three words best describe you?
- What are your dreams and fears?
- Where do you need improvement?
- What do your friends say you are good at?
- Whom do you admire?
- What traits of those you admire would you make your own?
- Putting money aside, what job would give you the most satisfaction?
- If you could begin any hobby, what would that be?

Working through these questions (and additional ones you might have) will set the tone for the events and experiences that are now taking shape. You might also uncover some very interesting facts about yourself. But don't be alarmed if you don't. You might just need to think, explore, and do more. Once you begin to understand who you are and what is unfolding in your life, it will be easier to set goals, make decisions, and push past any barriers that might come your way. If you don't know yourself and the tools you have to work

I can play the piano. I speak two languages. I can juggle. I love teaching kids about the wonders of the world. I hate snakes. I love frogs. I'm a so-so painter. I love thunderstorms and crazy weather. I'm afraid of not having enough money, going into debt, or being dependent on my parents or another person. I'm a pretty good baker. I'm a rotten city driver and really don't care for big cities. I really want to be a writer, photographer, teacher, and speaker! I'm not very organized. I love Italian music and food. A lot of money is not important to me. I want to travel in my work. I enjoy helping others out. I want to be settled somewhere. I just want to goof off for a couple of months. I'd like to try living on a boat or on a remote island. One day I'd like to have my own business—maybe open a coffee shop. I want to work on an organic farm in another country. I like a lot of change and stimulation. I've always wanted to visit every national park in the U.S. (and even work at one!).

Do not try to do extraordinary things, but ordinary things with intensity. —Emily Carr

with, you'll certainly have a "mess without a clue." It's important not to overlook this important step in your journey.

Every man has two educations—that which is given to him, and the other, that which he gives to himself. What we are merely taught seldom nourishes the mind like that which we teach ourselves. Indeed, all that is mostly worthy in a man, he must work out and conquer for himself.

—EDWARD GIBBON

For further reading and extensive exercises on the self-development process, I suggest the book *What Color Is Your Parachute?* by Richard Bolles or *The Pathfinder* by Nicholas Lore.

HOT TIP

The Balancing Act . . . .

a s you uncover who you are, it's equally important to strive for balance in all you do. This means stimulating your mind, exercising your body, viewing the world as an integrated whole, and understanding that life is not a series of random, meaningless events. When you strive to reach this balance in your life, you'll harmonize your actions with the way life is and make the will of nature your own. Remember, it's not what you do once in a while that will shape your life, it's what you do on a consistent basis. Make the time each day to work on the whole you!

To explore the connection of the whole, check out the opportunities presented in the special section on Holistic Learning Centers on page 182.

Nurture your mind with great thoughts, for you will never go any higher than you think.

—BENJAMIN DISRAELI

MENTALLY

b ecoming mentally active means becoming aware of the world around you. Every relationship, experience, mishap, or good fortune in your life is making an impact on who you become. The information you take into your mind, whether it be from a conversation with a stranger, news on television, concepts you learned from a workshop, or an idea from a book, is a continual process. Although some experiences are beyond your control, you must realize that you have the ability to influence what you decide to take into your mind or not. Are the turmoil and mishaps from the evening news helping to shape your life or detract from it? Are the people you interact with on a daily basis adding a positive component to your life or inhibiting it? Since we generally "find ourselves" in other people and events, it's important to be aware of these associations.

What, then, are ways to include positive stimuli in your mind? For instance, make a list of friends and colleagues who make you feel more alive, happier, and more positive about life. Make it a point to spend more time with these people. Pay close attention to the book recommendations I have made throughout your guide (as well as recommendations from other friends). The words found in books will help you to think better and to become a more discerning and reflective person. Books will help you exercise the mind—learn a new skill, uncover new places to explore, be introduced to a new philosophy, and open your world to new concepts and ideas that will help to shape your life. In addition to reading the words of others, you might decide to create your own. I've had an ongoing journal for most of my life, which has included my thoughts, insights, experiences, or lessons I've learned. I generally carry my journal everywhere I go—you never know when a great idea might come your way! My journal has also served as the basis for much of the writing that has been included in your guide.

> The best of all things is to learn. Money can be lost or stolen, health and strength may fail, but what you have committed to your mind is yours forever.
>
> —LOUIS L'AMOUR

Keeping a Journal

Make time in your life to reflect upon your experiences. You don't have to start a new job or partake in a new experience to begin. Start today! Journals can help you discover new ideas, take action on these ideas, sort out difficulties with others, invent new ways of seeing things, plan new adventures, and help you to relive your experiences later in life. Books with blank pages seem to work the best. It's up to you to fill them with pictures, inspiring quotes, collages, or whatever is on your mind. You might just find the answers you were looking for.

> If you stuff yourself full of poems, essays, plays, stories, novels, films, comic strips, magazines, and music, you automatically explode every morning like Old Faithful. I have never had a dry spell in my life, mainly because I feed myself well, to the point of bursting. I wake early and hear my morning voices leaping around in my head like jumping beans. I get out of bed to trap them before they escape.
>
> —RAY BRADBURY

PHYSICALLY

all right, put your guide down and give me fifty—fifty push-ups, that is. Being physically balanced means making a commitment to taking care of your body. For one, this means adding positive behaviors that promote good health, as well as strengthening habits you've already created for yourself. It also means making a commitment to exercise every day. You'll find that when you look and feel your best, you tend to be a happier person, with more confidence propelling everything you do.

For some it will take breaking old habits and starting out fresh. Changing habits is especially hard at first, because it requires deter-

Each day comes to me with both hands full of possibilities, and in its brief course I discern all the verities and realities of my existence: the bliss of growth, the glory of action, the spirit of beauty. —HELEN KELLER

We are what we repeatedly do. Excellence, then, is not an act, but a habit.

—ARISTOTLE

Optimum Health. It's about creating healthy habits for eating, exercising, breathing, using your mind, and nourishing your spirit. It's about wholeness and balance. It's about making health choices on a daily basis that allow you to meet the demands of living without being overwhelmed. Holistic guru Dr. Andrew Weil, with his book **Eight Weeks to Optimum Health** (Fawcett Books, $13.95), provides a week-by-week program that will help shape and strengthen behaviors for becoming naturally healthy throughout your life.

Walking is the best exercise. Habituate yourself to walk very far.

—THOMAS JEFFERSON

mined efforts and time to make the changes stick. If you are just beginning your journey with exercise, walking is truly the best activity because it provides you with a complete workout. My preference is to walk in beautiful surroundings during the morning hours (there is something magical about the world waking up). I either walk with a companion to converse with, or by myself, so I can be alone with my thoughts and nature. Begin with ten minutes each day; then, gradually increase the duration so that you are walking at least thirty to forty minutes per day. Daily stretching, which improves the flexibility of your body, is another healthful component to include in your exercise program. The more flexible your body is, the better it can meet the demands of life. You might also explore yoga as a formal way of stretching your body (and mind). Yoga helps to tone every muscle in your body and will assist in balancing all parts of your body, along with helping you to relax.

Make exercise a daily ritual and vary it every so often so you find it refreshing and invigorating. Those who are more active can find a variety of activities that can help get the heart going, along with sweating out all the daily toxins of life. If you're not a fan of active sports, such as mountain biking, sea kayaking, or surfing, joining a fitness center will provide varied activities to keep your routine fresh. I especially like the energy that comes from step aerobics or a spinning class, or the spiritual connection that yoga provides. One key to exercise is making time for it, but the most important key is listening to your body. It will tell you if you've had too much or too little, so don't overdo. Sometimes curling up with a good book is all you really need to recharge your batteries. So listen. Getting sufficient sleep and relaxation is just as important as pushing your body.

Along with your exercise prescription, healthy eating habits are just as important. Those who are creating and eating well-balanced and healthful meals that include whole grains, fresh vegetables and fruits, fish, and minimal amounts of meats, are off to a great start. It's especially beneficial to seek out people whose lifestyle promotes healthier eating habits, as you are more apt to mirror their habits. What you take into your body will largely affect how you feel throughout the day. It takes time to figure out your balance. Because we need food to sustain us, it's exciting to explore the possibilities that will not only bring ample energy to all we do, but will also enhance and protect our healing abilities. Those of you who work hard at maintaining a proper diet, daily exercise, and proper relaxation will find an energy that will invigorate everything you do.

SPIRITUALLY

the point of bringing a spiritual perspective into your life is a simple reminder that you are more than just your physical body. I also believe it's accepting in childlike faith that a Supreme Being exists. I was born and raised Catholic, so my parents provided a solid foundation in my spiritual growth. It was not until college that I questioned just about everything—especially my existence and the meaning of life. I took classes on Buddhism and existentialism, and began exploring different types of organized religions. After years of agonizing over this area in my life, I realized it didn't really matter what everyone called this Being from above, so long as I reaffirmed that he did exist and that I needed to live my life with this knowledge. Life didn't really get any easier with this knowledge; however, my existence has become more meaningful, more magical, and more heartfelt by nourishing this spiritual side.

The way we spiritually connect to the world will be different for each person, but once you find this connection, the everyday problems of life (when we feel helpless, confused, or resentful) become more tolerable, and everyday occurrences become more purposeful. Nourishing your spirituality might include reading inspirational quotes, immersing yourself in nature, listening to the rhythms of a particular song, bringing fresh flowers into your home, lighting candles and being silent, praying, meditating, or listening to a sermon each Sunday. Whatever you do to get in touch with your core, it's very important to view the world as an integrated whole and live your life with faith. Religious leader David McKay taught, "The greatest battles of life are fought out daily in the silent chambers of the soul." Once you deal with these inward battles (and realize you cannot anticipate or control events), you will find that life is not a

Slow me down, God, and inspire me to send my roots down deep into the soil of life's enduring values, so I may grow toward the stars and unfold my destiny.

—WILFRED PETERSON

HOT TIP

Before you indulge in your next meal, take a moment and feel gratitude for the food you are about to eat. This will help to raise your spiritual awareness and provide a firmer sense of your dependence on other living things.

Far away there in the sunshine are my highest aspirations. I may not reach them, but I can look up and see their beauty. Believe in them and try to follow where they lead. —LOUISA MAY ALCOTT

series of random, meaningless episodes. Set aside a small part of your day to spiritually connect and become familiar with the complexities of your inner life.

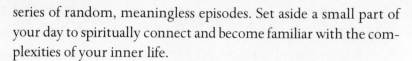

> *If you can dream it,*
> *you can do it.*
> —WALT DISNEY

Dreams

Listen to yourself and listen through your dreams. Dreams can help you understand your inner workings, solve life's problems, and see what your unconscious mind is working on at the moment. Dreams can point you in the right direction, whether you are lost or on the right track. You'll also find that your unconscious mind loves to guide you and answer questions you're not ready to ask your conscious mind.

EMOTIONALLY

life is continually filled with emotions tied to daily occurrences in your life. What happens in these everyday situations can also affect the way you feel. Staying emotionally balanced is the ability to be secure enough within yourself to handle life's ups and downs and not allow these things to control your life. Realize some things are within your control and others are not. You always have a choice about the content and integrity of your own life; however, external events and circumstances are beyond your control. When things don't go as you planned or people don't react the way you had hoped, you have the choice to allow feelings of hurt, anger, and inner turmoil to spread throughout your body or not.

You also have the choice to fill yourself with thoughts and actions that make you feel inspired, happy, excited, passionate, magical, energized, and enthusiastic. Positive results generally follow positive actions. Even though you may find yourself in challenging or difficult situations, these occurrences, approached with positive eyes, all help to make you a stronger and happier person. Tom Dennard, in his book *Discovering Life's Trails,* puts it this way: "We all have a tendency to want to label events in our lives as being good or bad because that's how we perceive them at the time. But bad can blend into good and good can blend into bad. We need to alter our perception of life's happenings as being good or bad and realize that every occurrence is necessary to make us who we are."

As you begin to understand your emotions, I encourage you to

CREATE A HAPPY BOX

Find an old shoe box and fill it with your favorite quotes. When you're feeling dispirited, pull one out at random and see what words of wisdom will help to inspire you, change your way of thinking, and move you in a new direction.

enjoy life's simple pleasures: compliment a stranger, hug a friend, laugh hysterically, scream at the top of your lungs, cry until the tears run dry. Remember you're human; do what you need to balance your emotions.

Understanding Your Needs. . . . .

now that you have a better picture of who you are, your desires, and how to maintain balance in all you do, it's time to focus on your needs. The most basic of human needs are food, shelter, and the ability to make enough income to meet your financial obligations. Once these essentials have been fulfilled, you can take strides to include more in your life—the path of self-actualization. Everyone will have different levels of each need as well as different ways to meet them. Up to this point, much of the focus has been on your wants. Wants are, well, anything. If you can figure out what you really want to do and what your basic needs are, you can be creative and resourceful about meeting both of them.

Often people attempt to live their lives backwards: they try to have more things, or more money, in order to do more of what they want so that they will be happier. The way it actually works is the reverse. You must first be who you really are, then, do what you need to do, in order to have what you want.

—MARGARET YOUNG

MASLOW'S HIERARCHY OF NEEDS

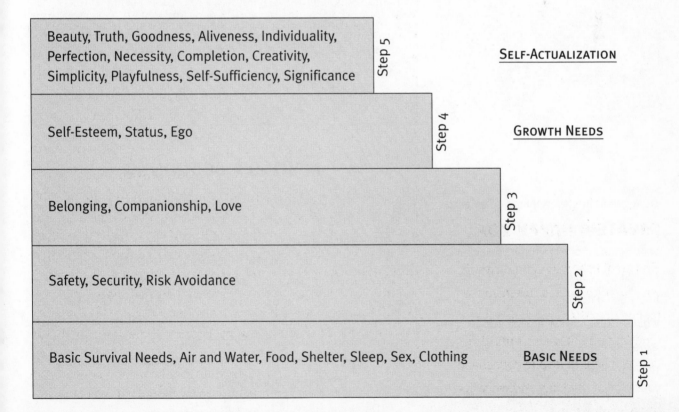

Beauty, Truth, Goodness, Aliveness, Individuality, Perfection, Necessity, Completion, Creativity, Simplicity, Playfulness, Self-Sufficiency, Significance (Step 5)	SELF-ACTUALIZATION
Self-Esteem, Status, Ego (Step 4)	GROWTH NEEDS
Belonging, Companionship, Love (Step 3)	
Safety, Security, Risk Avoidance (Step 2)	
Basic Survival Needs, Air and Water, Food, Shelter, Sleep, Sex, Clothing (Step 1)	BASIC NEEDS

Real development is not leaving things behind, as on a road, but drawing life from them, as from a root. —G.K. CHESTERTON

EXPLORE SIMPLICITY

to explore simplicity involves thinking about how your actions affect the earth, yourself, and others in this world. Simplifying your lifestyle is a continual process of choosing to focus on what is most important mentally, physically, emotionally, and spiritually. This may mean learning to become more self-reliant (such as planting your own garden or learning a new skill), seeking out entertainment that involves creativity and community growth, cooking from scratch to minimize waste, or volunteering your skills for a cause that helps to make the world a better place. The process of simplifying enables you to reexamine your wants and needs, and to shed the burdens of the unnecessary. You might also be pleasantly surprised that happiness goes beyond the material things in life.

> The people I consider successful are so because of how they handle their responsibilities to other people, how they approach the future—people that have a full sense of the value of their lives and what they want to do with it.
>
> —RALPH FIENNES

RECOMMENDED READING

Living simply need not translate into becoming poor, but rather making the wisest use of time and resources to live a richer and more joyful life. **The Simple Living Guide** by Janet Luhrs brings all the key elements together—from money, working, and travel to exercising, housing, and health—and is rich in resources and real-life examples to help you explore the possibilities of a simpler lifestyle. (Broadway Books, $20)

MAKING A BEGINNING

your connections with people and places, which have provided a definition of who you are, are now changing. Change requires a release of these connections. The times of transition—changing jobs, changing eating habits, changing partners, changing where you live—all require you to give something up in order to gain. Definitely not an easy process! When you hold onto what used to be, it inevitably blurs your reasons for change in the first place. The only way you can grow is by pushing past your old way of thinking and creating the things that are important to you.

> During your life, everything you do and everyone you meet rubs off in some way. Some bit of everything you experience stays with everyone you've ever known, and nothing is lost. That's what's eternal, these little specks of experience in a great and enormous river that has no end.
>
> —HARRIET DOERR

THE HUMAN CONNECTION

Once you've focused on what is important, whether this means becoming a more balanced person or turning your dream job into a reality, that "fire in your belly" will take hold and bring energy and enthusiasm to everything you do. The things you thought you could not do become visions of the past. Undoubtedly you will have periods of discouragement or times when progress appears to be at a standstill. To push past these fleeting moments, it is important to seek out people, teachers, and mentors who will not only encourage you but who will also enable you to develop your initial enthusiasm over the long haul.

I believe in the old adage—when the student is ready, the teacher will come. Of course, this does not mean that someone will appear at your back door or your phone will magically ring with your "teacher" ready to guide you. However, it does mean that your commitment, your hard work, and your enthusiasm toward your passion will promote this ability to uncover people who will take your passions to a new level. For instance, when I made the decision to write this book, I began calling other "like-minded" authors who could provide me with insights on their journey. Over a period of a couple years, I soon developed a network of people that I could bounce ideas off and share my enthusiasm with, and people who would keep me focused when I had lost momentum or felt discouraged. With their support and words of wisdom, I have been able to grow in ways I never thought imaginable when I first started out. The key to developing relationships such as these was putting myself out there, with the realization that some people would be willing to help and others would not. It's those who did that have made all the difference in the world.

LESSONS FROM GEESE

(BASED ON THE WORK OF MILTON OLSON)

FACT: As each goose flaps its wings, it creates an uplift for the bird that follows. By flying in a "V" formation, the whole flock adds 72 percent greater flying range than if each bird flew alone.

LESSON: People who share a common direction and sense of community can get where they are going quicker and easier because they are traveling on the thrust of one another.

continued on page 16

FACT: When a goose falls out of formation, it suddenly feels the drag and resistance of flying alone. It quickly moves back into the formation to take advantage of the lifting power of the bird immediately in front of it.

LESSON: If we have as much sense as a goose, we stay in formation with those headed where we want to go. We are willing to accept their help and give our help to others.

FACT: When the lead goose tires, it rotates back in the formation and another goose flies to the point position.

LESSON: It pays to take turns doing the hard tasks and sharing leadership. As with geese, people are interdependent on each other's skills, capabilities, and unique arrangement of gifts, talents, and resources.

FACT: The geese flying in formation honk to encourage those up front to keep up the speed.

LESSON: We need to make sure our honking is encouraging. In groups where there is encouragement, the production is greater. The power of encouragement (to stand by one's heart or core values and encourage the heart and core values of others) is the quality of honking we seek.

If you always do what you've always done, you'll always get what you've always got.

— LARRY WILSON

If we are always arriving and departing, it is also true that we are eternally anchored. One's destination is never a place, but rather a new way of looking at things.

— HENRY MILLER

THE POWER OF PLACE

along with the importance of people, our surroundings also shape our thoughts, emotions, and actions. We need places that support, rather than fragment our lives. Many times your growth is limited by sitting around in your old haunts, which promotes the way things used to be. Again, it's important to break past these associations, so you may respond to the positive stimulation of new things and places, which, in turn, promotes new directions and possibilities. When you are in an environment that offers few distractions and allows you to experience things you weren't sure you could do, it's much easier to figure out what matters and what doesn't, and to make the necessary changes in your life.

On the other hand, the current home environment that many of you have created often provides structure, a connection to family and friends, and familiar surroundings. There is also a certain aspect of yourself that resides in this place and that needs to be embraced. But, like it or not, we all have to leave home to find ourselves. The self you may be seeking is not "out there" in the literal sense but always within; often it reveals itself through your journey. To leave is to grow through adventure, risk taking, and excitement. Understand that a "coming home" can also provide you with stability and strength. As you stumble in your quest for self-discovery and growth, you will find that leaving and staying are necessary components. The secret is to heed the wisdom that emanates from your soul and find the balance between each path.

Making Choices. . . . .

as you begin to take action in your new beginning, you will be faced with many choices that will lay the foundation for your adventure and how you live your life. When you face the difficulties of making conscious choices, you will grow stronger, more capable, and more responsible to yourself. Choices are never easy; however, with a little planning, you can map out a tentative course of action, realizing that the outcome may or may not work. By understanding that either a positive or a negative outcome may result, you'll save yourself a lot of grief when unforeseen or unwanted consequences follow. That's why choices must first begin with a commitment attached to your choices. Tentative efforts always lead to tentative outcomes. Consider the real nature of your aspirations, begin making decisions based on these aspirations, then fully give yourself to these endeavors. It's only when you fully commit that the world responds in magical ways.

AUTOBIOGRAPHY IN FIVE SHORT CHAPTERS

BY PORTIA NELSON

ONE

I walk down the street. There is a deep hole in the sidewalk. I fall in. I am lost. I am helpless. It isn't my fault. It takes forever to find a way out.

TWO

I walk down the same street. There is a deep hole in the sidewalk. I pretend I don't see it. I fall in again. I can't believe I am in the same place. But it isn't my fault. It still takes a long time to get out.

THREE

I walk down the same street. There is a deep hole in the sidewalk. I see it is there. I still fall in. It's a habit. My eyes are open. I know where I am. It is my fault. I get out immediately.

FOUR

I walk down the same street. There is a deep hole in the sidewalk. I walk around it.

FIVE

I walk down another street.

And the day came when the risk to remain tight in a bud was more painful than the risk it took to blossom. —ANAÏS NIN

Don't Travel Down That Big River in Egypt . . . .

the college years—a time of exploration, excitement, discovery, and learning. Should I study architecture or maybe engage in the field of psychology? Like many of us navigating through this period in our life, Craig Dunkin was presented with a handful of tough questions—questions he had to answer without much direction. At that age, who really is aware of what we want our life to develop into? Unfortunately, most of us opt for the easy route, allowing the hand of society to push us in certain directions, instead of making the big decisions for ourselves. Craig was really interested in sports broadcasting; however, smart people go to law school, so that's what he did.

Twelve years later, Craig sits in his office at a very reputable law firm in Los Angeles. He's very successful and makes good money, but on this day, mindless lawyer tasks are par for the course. Then, the epiphany hit: "There is more to life than what I'm doing." This thought consumed him for the rest of the day. The "Inner-Craig" whispered, "What are you doing practicing law? What are you working toward?" This day changed his life.

While still acting as a lawyer, Craig decided to take a class at a local community college on sports broadcasting. A professor soon became his mentor, helping him to answer many of the tough questions he ignored in college. With excitement and passion as his guides, Craig spent the next few years revitalizing his inborn talents. He spent his evenings and weekends at any sporting event he had time to experience. However, he didn't sit there like any other ordinary fan, he was there on a mission.

I was raised to sense what someone wanted me to be and be that kind of person. It took me a long time not to judge myself through someone else's eyes.

—SALLY FIELD

Positioning himself in the centerfield bleachers or away from the crowds, a sports broadcaster was soon born.

Using a microphone and tape recorder as his "tools of the trade," he began giving play-by-play action of the games. Although he did not actually engage an audience on the details of the event (except for a few fans sitting near him), these "demo tapes" soon doubled as a key component of his sports broadcasting portfolio. Shortly thereafter, he began scouting out ball teams to expose his talents to the world. "I called every minor league baseball team across the nation and asked if they needed a broadcaster. If they said 'yes' or 'maybe,' I sent those tapes."

Months (which seemed like years) went by until he finally got a break from a ball team in the South who thought he had potential. A deal was made and this ex-California lawyer made his way to the small town of Clarksville, Tennessee.

Although he would spend extra time on weekends and at night figuring out the small details that make a ball game exciting, the extra work became a labor of love, rather than just laboring (as he had done as a lawyer). "That's what drew me to it all. This was my chance to be really good at something." He looks back at all his lawyer years as "floating down that big river in Egypt." Confused by what he meant, he continued, "You know, the Nile?" You see, the Nile was a constant reminder that he had been living in a world of **denial**—denial of what he really felt and wanted to do with his life.

Craig's thoughtful advice for anyone looking to make sense of their career is this: "If you don't like being a lawyer, but it allows you to have season tickets to the opera or a beautiful home on five acres—and that's what brings meaning to your life—then so be it. But if that's not enough for you, then why do it? You have to figure out what's important and then fill that aspect in your life. No matter how difficult it is to get into something, don't let that stop you. If you feel you are a talented actor, go do that. But, most importantly, just don't visit that river out in Egypt."

The important thing is to strive toward a goal that is not immediately visible.
That goal is not the concern of the mind, but of the spirit. —ANTOINE DE SAINT-EXUPÉRY

2

Each path is only one of a million paths. Therefore, you must always keep in mind that a path is only a path. If you feel that you must now follow it, you need not stay with it under any circumstances. Any path is only a path. There is no affront to yourself or others in dropping it if that is what your heart tells you to do. But your decision to keep on the path or to leave it must be free of fear and ambition. I warn you—look at every path closely and deliberately. Try it as many times as you think necessary. Then ask yourself and yourself alone one question. It is this—does this path have a heart? If it does, then the path is good. If it doesn't, it is of no use.

—CARLOS CASTANEDA, *The Teachings of Don Juan*

This section will help you to:

- Explore your options and gather information.
- Be successful in getting the right job based on your passions.
- Fund your adventure and think about money.
- Make the most of your short-term job adventure.

the work you have done in Section 1—understanding who you are, accepting yourself at every level, becoming your best, and uncovering what motivates you—has provided the foundation and structure for building your path. With this foundation, you will be able to uncover your passions more easily and make choices that affect the bigger picture of your life. This process takes time and will undoubtedly change as your life evolves. This section is about putting your ideas into action, knocking on the right doors, and making your dreams a reality.

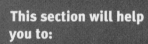

YOUR PATH

THE TOP TEN SECRETS TO ACHIEVING YOUR DREAM CAREER

10. What would you attempt to do if you knew you could not fail?

9. "Whatever you can do, or dream you can, begin it. Boldness has genius, power, and magic in it. Begin it now." —JOHANN VON GOETHE

8. Plan ahead! It wasn't raining when Noah built the ark.

7. Don't spend a lifetime exploring possibilities and do nothing. Action requires courage.

6. Don't put all your eggs in one basket. Always have an alternate plan.

5. To get what you want in life, you've got to ask others for help.

4. The shortest route to your life's work is not necessarily a straight line.

3. "Never let the fear of striking out get in your way." —BABE RUTH

2. "Perseverance is a great element of success. If you only knock long enough and loud enough at the gate, you are sure to wake up somebody." —HENRY WADSWORTH LONGFELLOW

1. "Never, never, never give up!" —WINSTON CHURCHILL

Never look down to test the ground before taking your next step. Only he who keeps his eye fixed on the far horizon will find the right road.

—DAG HAMMARSKJÖLD

Profound joy of the heart is like a magnet that indicates the path of life. One has to follow it, even though one enters into a way full of difficulties.

—MOTHER TERESA

Exploring . . . .

With so many opportunities presented throughout the pages of your guide, the challenge may well be picking one to explore. Each section not only provides plenty of options to choose from, but also offers recommended books, newsletters, associations, and web site links for further exploration and guidance. Realize that your guide is only one of many resources that will help you along in your journey. Don't cut any corners at this stage. Make an investment in every resource that piques your interest. Join an association in the field you are pursuing. Attend a conference with "like-minded" people who can help to facilitate your endeavors. By immersing yourself

Don't follow the path. Go where there is no path and begin the trail. When you start a new trail equipped with courage, strength, and conviction, the only thing that can stop you is you!

—RUBY BRIDGES

Go around asking a lot of damn fool questions and taking chances. Only through curiosity can we discover opportunities, and only by risking can we take advantage of them.

—CLARENCE BIRDSEYE

Thank You!

Send short, handwritten thank-you notes to all who help you in your quest. You'll realize at a later point how important these people were in getting you where you are today.

completely in this "information gathering" stage, you will be able make sound decisions on the direction of your life.

Collecting information also means talking to anybody and everybody who might help you to see more clearly and present you with ideas to fuel your fire. Think of all the possibilities: family and friends, career counselors and professors, colleagues, and even strangers. One of the best ways to get more information about a career that you are exploring is to talk to someone who is actually in the job you desire. For instance, if you want to write a book, talk to other authors; if you want to be a raft guide, talk to other raft guides; if you want to work for the Peace Corps, talk to other volunteers. Find role models who are acting in ways you are gravitating toward; then, make time in your day to talk to these people.

This week I challenge you to seek out another person who might help you in your pursuits. For those who are extroverts, this might be a simple task; however, for others, pushing yourself out of your "comfort zone" can be quite a daunting exercise. Enter risk taking. Risking is about moving from the fear of the unknown to the excitement of what is about to happen. Without risks, you'd never move away from home, find a great job, make a new friend, or fall in love. By learning how to take small risks, you'll begin to feel more comfortable about asking for anything that you want to help you in your journey.

To help you in the challenge I presented, you might begin your efforts by calling a friend and asking them how they found their summer job. Then, depending on your situation, you might make an appointment with a career counselor at school or through work. These initial strides will help to broaden your comfort zone, so you will be able to approach just about anyone. The worst-case scenario in asking for help is rejection. This just means you made contact with the wrong person, so you move on to the next person until you find someone who will help.

Never be scared to ask. Ask and keep asking. Communicate your needs to others. Call people out of the blue. Take people to lunch. Open yourself up to others. You'll find success is usually a team effort. Asking is powerful. It can work magic. It sure isn't easy and it doesn't work every time. It will, however, if you persist. So ask, and it shall be given to you!

Connecting . . . .

after you have uncovered specific organizations throughout your guide that appear to be strong work possibilities, narrow down your first round of prospective leads to ten or so (so you don't get overwhelmed at first). Out of this ten, pick the one program that interests you the least, and call them for more information. This call serves as your training ground, allowing you to get all your "phone talk" kinks worked out prior to conversing with the program that is on top of your list. Within time, you will feel more comfortable and confident about talking with recruiters and asking the right questions.

Casual inquiries cost the organization time and money, especially for nonprofits or service organizations that are underfunded, overworked, and understaffed. If your inquiry is not genuine, think twice before requesting more information.

Your guide includes contact names for many of the programs listed, so be sure to ask for this person; however, sometimes you'll find that the contact name has changed. Don't let that throw you off. Generally, someone will just transfer you to the right person; other times you'll have to explain who and what you're after. Eventually, you will talk to the right person.

This initial call is the first impression you will make on both the recruiter and the organization, so make sure it is a good one. Something that happens in this conversation just may be the link that eventually gets you the job. Some program contacts are receptive to talk; others don't have the time. At this point, you are mainly gathering information and promoting your enthusiasm as a potential candidate. During your conversation, you might ask for program brochures and an application, inquire about upcoming deadlines or the number of applicants that are hired, and uncover what they are specifically looking for in a candidate. Most of the information can be gathered through your guide and the organization's web site, but it's also a good idea to verify any specific facts with the person you are talking to (largely because the nitty-gritty details can change from year to year).

Half the time you won't be speaking to a real person; you'll be talking to their voice mail. Be prepared. If you stumble here, there's no way to erase what you've said. Prior to calling, it is a good idea to loosely script out what you want to say. It might go something like this: "Hello, my name is Sue Schmid and I read in *The Back Door Guide to Short-Term Job Adventures* that you offer a summer internship program. Could you please send me an informational brochure and application?" At this point, provide them with your mailing address, e-mail address (if

Enjoy your achievements as well as your plans. Keep interested in your own career, however humble;
it is a real possession in the changing fortunes of time. —DESIDERATA

23

you have one), and phone number. It's also important to speak slowly and clearly, and spell out any words that are difficult to understand. Remember someone is writing down your message to get you the information you need. Conclude with any enthusiasm you may have about the possibility of joining their program.

Many of you will also be requesting information through a simple e-mail note. Although e-mail seems to be the most efficient way to get the information you need, many programs are generally bogged down by all the notes they receive in a day's time. So be patient in receiving a response. Prior to clicking on your send button, be sure you have crafted a professionally written letter that has been spell-checked, grammar-checked, and proofread several times. Remember, you are not e-mailing your friend across the country to say hello. Think of this note as your initial cover letter to the program, which means putting effort into what you write. Although e-mail serves as an easy way to communicate, keep in mind that it also lacks in the human ingredient. Anytime I want to make an impression on a new client or am seeking out a new work assignment, I either call the person over the phone or schedule a meeting in person. **Never overlook the power of the human connection.**

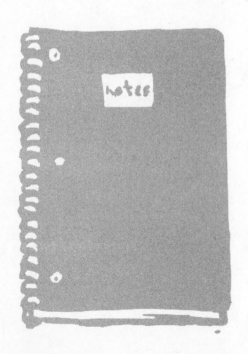

STAYING ORGANIZED

What works best for you? Whether it be with index cards or a notepad, or through your computer, you need to keep track of all the information you'll be collecting. For starters, create a "Notes Log" of all your correspondence. Write down everything, from the date of your initial phone call to the details of your conversation. Especially if you are applying to a handful of programs, your log will keep you focused on the needs of each. Make notes of important dates: deadlines, follow-up phone calls, or when you need to send off a thank-you letter. I also jot down personal tidbits about the person after talking with them. These tidbits serve as great conversation starters the next time you talk with the person, as they generally are surprised you remembered something so personal.

The Application Process . . . .

Once you receive the program's application packet in the mail, act upon it right away. Many times positions are filled as soon as applications have been reviewed. "The early bird gets the worm" saying generally holds true when applying for seasonal-type jobs. Although each program wants the best person for a specific job, many recruiters are concerned about filling the position before it is too late.

You'll also find that putting together your application seems to take longer than you anticipate, especially if the program has a four-page application to fill out and desires a couple of short essays and three letters of recommendation (along with a personalized cover letter and your updated resume). Yes, many programs ask a lot from you, but this is their first opportunity to weed out candidates who haven't taken this step seriously. Keep in mind the payoff for all your hard work: the possibility of working with a program that will forever change your life. Whatever you're asked to do in the application process, be sure that your skills, interests, and abilities are very apparent in the packet you send them.

HOT TIP

Before sending off your completed application, make a copy of it. In case it gets lost in the mail, you'll have a spare copy. This will also serve as your master for doing other applications.

YOUR RESUME AND COVER LETTER

Your resume might be the most important document that will assist you in your job search. The resume is your marketing brochure and selling tool—information that will hopefully paint a very clear picture of your talents and abilities. What kind of person are you? What kind of skills do you have? What are some of your life's experiences? What do you do in your spare time? What hobbies do you have? What are some major things that you have accomplished? If you've done your homework in Section 1, answering these questions will come easily and naturally.

The best resumes are those that are filled with the entire you. Along with your academic record and work experiences, be sure to

---

We are cups, constantly and quietly being filled. The trick is knowing how to tip ourselves over and let the beautiful stuff out. —RAY BRADBURY

include your skills, accomplishments, volunteer service, and any other unique attributes that make you stand out. I even put my favorite quote at the bottom of my resume.

As you create and develop your resume, it's very helpful if a team of people look it over for ideas, spelling errors, and areas you could improve on. If at all possible, have a career counselor or recruiter provide you with feedback; otherwise, there are plenty of resume books that are filled with great ideas. No matter what advice is given, the beauty of creating your resume is that anything goes—you get to make all final decisions!

Set your resume aside for a few days before you come back to it for revisions. This will give you time to work on a personalized cover letter (also known as a letter of interest). Many people think that cover letters are the same as a Post-it note that says: "Hey, check this out—I'd really like to work for you!" Unfortunately, you'll find these cover letters lying in the bottom of recycle bins. Your cover letter is the icing on the cake and is just possibly as important as the resume itself. It serves as an expansion of your resume and answers these key questions: what you are applying for, why you want to work for this particular organization, what your skills and abilities are (as they relate to the job opportunity), and why they should hire you.

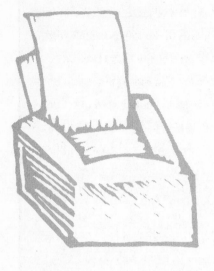

Your cover letter also describes your potential to the employer. Let your personality shine in your writing. You might not have all the necessary skills, but your cover letter might demonstrate that you're trainable for the job. Remember, many applicants aren't necessarily hired based on skill, but more for enthusiasm and energy. Job-specific skills and responsibilities, in general, can always be taught.

LETTERS OF RECOMMENDATION

Unless you've planned ahead, and have copies of letters of recommendation from former bosses, professors, or colleagues, this task might take some work on your part. First off, I need to emphasize how important it is to develop relationships with your professors or people who might serve as mentors in your career development. This means reaching out to others, asking for help, and seeing what develops and what doesn't. These people will serve as allies in all you do, especially when it comes to developing your future.

For those who haven't developed a network of support and "sideline cheerleaders," it's best to ask former bosses, teachers, or anyone who can provide a sincere impression of your talents and abilities. Query your list of possible "candidates" to see who is comfortable in sharing with others about your skills and abilities. To help the person in writing your letter, provide them with information about the program, the position you are applying to, and strengths that should be highlighted. Another nice touch is to provide them with a postage-paid envelope, so they can either send it to you or directly to the employer. After all is said and done, be sure to thank these people who have taken time out of their lives to help you along in your path. A handwritten letter makes a nice touch.

FOLLOW-UP

although each step in getting your dream job is important in itself, following up on your application might make the difference in who gets the job and who does not. One to three weeks after sending in your application materials, pleasantly surprise your contact with a phone call. In this phone call, verify that they have received your application, and at the same time, ask if there is anything else you can provide or any other questions that concern you. Once again, promote your enthusiasm about the program and job prior to ending your conversation.

HOT TIP — Even though a program might not ask for letters of recommendation, include them anyway. They will make your application packet stand out.

YOUR INTERVIEW

Congratulations! Once you've made it this far, all your preliminary hard work has paid off (and impressed the hiring team). This final step of landing the job is where you get to show off what you're all about and how you'll make a difference in their program. Whether you are interviewing in person or over the phone, it's best to prepare a "loose" script prior to your interview. Your script should include various trigger words that will help your brain connect your thoughts. These words are simply reminders of items (skills, unique stories, and strengths) you need to cover as you talk about yourself and the position. Moreover, if the work you want to do is really something you believe in, the feeling of enthusiasm will come across naturally.

RECOMMENDED READING:

If you are fresh out of college or are trying to put together a resume at age seventy, Yana Parker will assist you with all the details in her book, **Resume Catalog: 200 Damn Good Examples** (Ten Speed Press, $15.95). Yana's collage of resume ideas and inspiring advice will help you craft a resume that will not only paint a clear picture of your talents and abilities but also help you land more interviews. Not only do I highly recommend her book, but her web site is "damn good" too (www.damngood.com).

Think of Katharine Hansen as your personal cover letter coach. Her book **Dynamic Cover Letters for New Graduates** (Ten Speed Press, $9.95) will guide people of all ages and experiences through a step-by-step process of crafting an irresistible cover letter for any situation. Not only will you learn how to make any employer sit up and take notice of your words, you'll also feel more confident and enthusiastic about your job hunt. Quintessential Careers (www.quintcareers.com), a companion web site masterfully created by her husband, Randall, includes heaps of career resource links, ranging from job-hunting sites and career articles to cover letter and resume sites.

You gain strength, courage, and confidence by every experience in which you really stop to look fear in the face. —ELEANOR ROOSEVELT

You have a unique message to deliver, a unique song to sing, a unique act of love to bestow. This message, this song, and this act of love have been entrusted exclusively to the one and only you.

—JOHN POWELL

To grapple with any uneasiness prior to your interview, I suggest working with a friend who can act as your interviewer. Come up with a list of typical interview-type questions and challenge yourself to answer them out loud. By speaking out your answers, you are connecting your thoughts and ideas with actual words and stories. With practice, you'll be able to answer any question that comes your way. Remember, your goal is to paint a very real and sincere picture of who you are, what skills you have obtained over the years, and your potential for future growth. You should have the ability to talk about anything mentioned in your resume, along with supporting examples. If a question ever catches you off guard, don't be afraid to pause while you think about the question posed—silence many times works to your advantage. Those who have successful interviews are those who have done plenty of preparation and anticipate what questions the interviewer might ask. Just like anything, the more you interview, the better you will become.

Your interview also serves as your time to ask those all-so-important questions that will help you make important decisions about your future. Just as your prospective employer is studying everything about you during the interview, you should be doing the same. You're both sizing each other up to see if there is compatibility for a budding work relationship. Think of it in the same light as dating. Here are some key questions that you want to ask of your prospective employer:

- **What investment will the program make in directing and enhancing your natural learning process in exchange for your work and energy?**

On-the-job training is inherent in every position that you will be considering; however, the amount of training you will receive is an important consideration—especially if this is your first job in the field. Those that offer intensive training programs, informal and formal discussions, workshops, seminars, or lectures as part of your learning experience should make a big impact on your decision-making process.

That which we persist in doing becomes easier—not that the nature of the task has changed, but our ability to do so has increased.

—RALPH WALDO EMERSON

- **What staff members will you be working with and what are their backgrounds?**

The permanent staff will serve as your mentors, your teachers, and your guides. These people will also help you network in the field and connect you to possibilities that will enhance your career. You must decide whether you'll get the guidance you need given the staffing arrangement that exists.

• **What are the criteria for hiring short-term staff members?**

You'll find that your peers will provide some of the best sources of inspiration, learning, sharing, and friendship during your experience. Will your peers be likely to have a level of schooling and experience that will ensure that you are surrounded by a strong support group?

• **What kind of living conditions will be provided?**

A nice benefit for short-term work opportunities is that many offer room and board as part of your compensation package. If not, be sure to ask what type of housing assistance they provide, if any. Don't be the person that arrives at their new job only to find out that they will be sharing a room with three others and eating meals that don't do much for a healthy lifestyle. Will you have a private room? Will you share a bathroom? What types of meals are served? Are there kitchen facilities available for your use? Whatever is important to you, find out these important details.

• **What kind of experience did past interns have with the program?**

I always suggest talking candidly to others who have participated in the program to get their impression of the experience. You'll find that many programs also provide the names and phone numbers of past participants—so be sure to ask. In addition to talking with former participants, you might find it to your advantage to schedule an on-site interview (if one isn't provided), so you can talk with various staff members and interns who are currently working there, along with getting a feel for your work environment.

If a man is called to be a street sweeper, he should sweep streets even as Michelangelo painted, or Beethoven composed music, or Shakespeare wrote poetry. He should sweep streets so well that all the hosts of heaven and earth will pause to say, here lived a great street sweeper who did his job well.

—Martin Luther King, Jr.

• **What kind of job opportunities will exist after completion of your assignment?**

The beauty of a short-term work opportunity is that it can naturally evolve into a lifelong career with the organization. Many times the permanent staff is made up of former interns. It's important to see if there will be opportunities for future growth within the organization along with any career assistance that will be provided upon conclusion of your experience.

Originality is not doing something no one else has ever done, but doing what has been done countless times with new life, new breath. —Marie Chapian

ASK AND YOU SHALL RECEIVE!

f you have gathered enough information during your interview to make a sound decision about joining their program, be sure to tell them so. Many applicants leave this open-ended as their interview comes to a close, allowing the recruiter to make his or her own judgment. If you feel that you can make an impact on their program, and that they offer an experience that will enhance your talents and abilities, let them know so! Most often, you won't get a job offer on the spot, but it will definitely leave an impression of your enthusiasm.

After you've had a chance to digest your interview, take the time to send a handwritten letter to the person who interviewed you (once again). Reiterate your enthusiasm for the program (and position), expand on anything that you felt was left open-ended in the interview, and again, let them know that you want the job. Often, recruiters interview a handful of super applicants for only one position. Your persistence will often help influence their decision to hire you!

REJECTION SHOCK

fter all the hard work, time, and energy that you put into landing what you thought was the ideal job, there may be a time the mail brings a thin letter that states (in so many nice words) that you will not be offered a position. Enthusiasm and excitement quickly turn to feelings of failure. Nobody likes rejection; however, you must realize that this component will be part of your life no matter how hard you try. In fact, what has been thought of as a failure, often turns into a blessing in disguise, even though it's not very apparent at the time. It's like falling off your bike for the first time. You simply get on it and try again. Life is constantly like this—especially for those who are willing to go after what they truly believe in and take risks.

That's why it's very important not to "put all your eggs in one basket." It's easier to set yourself up for success by opening yourself up to many opportunities. By applying to many programs that pique your interest, you are bound to receive an offer or two—many times, more than you anticipated!

As I'm sure you are well aware, it takes time for careers, opportunities, and relationships to develop in your life. There is a process to everything you do. Again, try to think of what you are doing right now as your never-ending journey. A long-haul mentality approach will help you understand that the things you

> Life is not easy for any of us. But what of that? We must have perseverance and above all confidence in ourselves. We must believe that we are gifted for something, and that this thing, at whatever cost, must be attained.
>
> —MARIE CURIE

> If you're not rejected ten times a day, you're not trying hard enough.
>
> —ANTHONY COLEMAN

> Everyone has a talent. What is rare is the courage to follow that talent to the dark place where it leads.
>
> —ERICA JONG

do now entirely affect the opportunities that are presented in your future. Overnight success is rare (and is usually because of the hard work that led up to that point). Don't rush the process. Each step in your journey takes time.

Those who have planted a vegetable garden or have spent time on a farm know that there are certain steps that are necessary to turn a seed into something that is life sustaining. Mother Nature will additionally challenge this process every step of the way. That's why life should be approached with a long-haul mentality. Enjoy every good and challenging step along the way. Good things come to people who work hard to get what they're after. You might not see the results today or next week or even a month from now, but they'll hit you when you least expect it, and you'll be very happy to know that all your hard work has paid off.

SKEPTICS

Watch out for skeptics who want to divert you from your destiny. Cling to what you know in your heart is best.

If I had thought about it, I wouldn't have done the experiment. The literature was full of examples that said you can't do this.
—Spencer Silver, originator of Post-it notepads

Guitar music is on the way out.
—Decca Records turning down the Beatles in 1962

TV won't hold on to any market it captures after the first six months. People will soon tire of staring at a box every night.
—Darryl Zanuck, head of 20th Century Fox, 1946

Everything that can be invented has been invented.
—Charles Duell, Office of Patents Commissioner, 1899

Louis Pasteur's theory of germs is ridiculous fiction.
—Pierre Pachet, Professor of Physiology, 1872

Don't forget Columbus who was looking for India, or the fact that Edison knew 1,800 ways not to build a light bulb. It was Mark Twain who once said, "Let us be thankful for the fools—but for them the rest of us could not succeed!" Although many will like you to fail (misery loves company), don't you ever give up. You'll find that success is generally just around the corner.

DON'T QUIT

When things go wrong, as they sometimes will; when the road you're trudging seems all uphill; when the funds are low and the debts are high, and you want to smile, but you have to sigh; when care is pressing you down a bit—rest if you must but don't you quit.

Life is queer with its twists and turns, as every one of us sometimes learns; and many a fellow turns about when he might have won had he stuck it out. Don't give up though the pace seems slow—you may succeed with another blow.

Often the goal is nearer than it seems to a faint and faltering man; often the struggler has given up when he might have captured the victor's cup; and he learned too late when the night came down, how close he was to the golden crown.

Success is failure turned inside out—the silver tint of the clouds of doubt; and you never can tell how close you are. It may be near when it seems afar; so stick to the fight when you're hardest hit—it's when things seem worst that you mustn't quit.

The greatest mistake you can make in life is to be continually fearing that you will make one. —ELBERT HUBBARD

Money and Funding Your Adventure ....

Once you realize that your self-worth has nothing to do with your net worth, money will not be the only source of richness and fulfillment in your life. Obviously money can constrain us from doing the things we really want to do, especially if we're burdened by school loans, credit card debts, or making just enough to meet our daily financial obligations. Those in this situation will learn to become resourceful; there is always another way to make your dreams come alive, no matter the roadblocks that lay ahead. Once you've committed to a goal, whether it be working as a seasonal employee at a national park, starting a business, participating in a service learning adventure, or funding an experience abroad, opportunities will start taking shape. By broadcasting your intentions to the world, the world usually responds back in amazing ways (and if it doesn't, this might tell you that you've walked down the wrong path or, perhaps, you just need to try a little harder).

So how do you survive in the world while funding your passion in life? Although some of the ideas below might seem ludicrous, being resourceful and creative will help you create a livelihood that will blossom over time.

SELL LEMONADE!

Many of us had the chance to become young entrepreneurs as we grew up—selling lemonade, mowing lawns, washing cars—experiences that taught us the value of money. Apply this same philosophy to your current situation. What skill do you have that could benefit others, and at the same time, bring in some extra cash? Are you a budding artist? Perhaps a local business in town might need your help in designing a few brochures for a fee. Or possibly the local health club wouldn't mind offering you a membership in their club for your creativity? Whatever your goal, bartering your unique skills will definitely help in funding your passion.

TEMP JOBS

This is a great way to provide structure in your life while searching out what really matters, and at the same time, keeping a steady stream of money to meet your financial obligations. Many people have developed a complete lifestyle engaged in temporary work because of the diversity in job

One of the main reasons wealth makes people unhappy is that it gives them too much control over what they experience. They try to translate their own fantasies into reality instead of tasting what reality itself has to offer.

—PHILIP SLATER

We are very short on people who know how to do anything. So please don't set out to make money. Set out to make something and hope you get rich in the process.

—ANDY ROONEY

The man who does not work for the love of work but only for money is not likely to make money nor find much fun in life.

—CHARLES SCHWAB

assignments and varied time commitments. You'll also find that more and more temp agencies are offering health insurance and other services, which are benefits you don't want to overlook. Once you've built a reputation with a few organizations who like your work, many turn mundane work assignments into challenging work projects. Often this leads into permanent or consulting work that pays more and provides more freedom. Temp agencies abound in urban and suburban areas. Kelly Services (www.kellyservices.com/getajob) and Manpower (www.manpower.com) are two agencies that you might check out as you explore this option.

POSSESSION DOWNSIZING

most of us have garages or closets filled with possessions that have been sitting around for years—these make up all the key ingredients in conducting a profitable garage sale. The old adage of "one man's trash is another man's treasure" can bring you enough money to make a dent in your fund-raising efforts. A successful garage sale takes planning on your part: all your items should be priced, an ad should go in the local paper, and huge signs should be put up around the neighborhood the night before. I even conduct a pre-garage-sale for neighbors and friends the night before. Many people, who know you are fund-raising to support your passion, might even provide a monetary donation. Whatever the case, it's a good way to clear out clutter and make some extra cash on the side.

GRANTS AND LOANS

many seeking to participate in worthy causes can raise money through philanthropic groups (like Kiwanis), campus/alumni groups, community organizations, civic/religious groups, local businesses, colleagues, or even your current co-workers. There are also plenty of grants that major nonprofits give out each year. (Check out your library's reference area for books that cover grant possibilities.) In addition, don't be afraid to ask your family for help. A small loan might be the helping hand you need until you get on your feet.

SPARKLETT'S JUG THEORY

find yourself an old Sparklett's jug at your local thrift store. (You usually can spot one for about a dollar.) Set it somewhere in your house and start dropping in your spare change. I find that it's more exciting if you attach a goal to the money you're saving prior to putting in your first coin. Just recently I funded a trip to Europe from two years' worth of coin dropping!

RECOMMENDED READING

Spreading the "frugal gospel," Amy Dacyczyn's *The Complete Tightwad Gazette* includes 900 pages worth of sensible advice, recipes, tips, tricks, and strategies to save money. (Random House, $19.99)

DO WITHOUT

Simply stated, live within your means. The next time you go shopping, ask yourself, "Do I really need this?" More than likely, you don't. Remember the financial goal you've set up for yourself and don't stray from that path.

The grand essentials to happiness in this life are something to do, something to love, and something to hope for. —Joseph Addison

Happy Adventures . . . .

the day will come when you've packed your car and your short-term job adventure begins. It will undoubtedly bring you a wealth of experience, a firmer sense of who you are and where your career is going, and a supportive network of friends and colleagues in the field. Before you rush off, here are some ideas to help you make the most of your adventure:

Be prepared to work in areas not related to your main responsibility. Be willing and excited to chip in wherever needed. Look at every job you're given as an opportunity to learn more about the field you've chosen and a chance to contribute to the overall success of the program.

Make it a goal to acquire as many skills, in as many areas, as you can. Attend every class and seminar that is offered and immerse yourself in every aspect of the program.

Throughout the course of your adventure, talk to fellow staff members about their careers and lives. You'll be surprised at how much your peers enjoy giving advice and sharing "their story" with you. It's also flattering (to most) to be asked one's opinion—another person's insights might help you make better decisions in your life and further develop your career.

Make as many friends as possible. You never know when this newfound alliance will be able to help you in your path.

And finally, take the time to:

- Find your own retreat (and use it often).

- Give support, encouragement, and praise to others; and learn to accept it in return.

- Change your routine often and your tasks when you can.

- Focus on a good thing that happened during your day.

- Be creative and try new approaches.

- Use the "buddy system" regularly as a source of support, assurance, and redirection.

- Surprise someone with something.

- Find the child inside.

- Laugh, play, and smile.

- Be gentle with yourself and do the best job you can do.

- Follow those hunches, take risks, work and play hard, be flexible, and make plans—but also bend with life's flow.

- Fill the pages of your life with wonder and imperfection.

Work is about daily meaning as well as daily bread. For recognition as well as cash; for astonishment rather than torpor; in short, for a sort of life rather than a Monday through Friday sort of dying. . . . We have a right to ask of work that it include meaning, recognition, astonishment, and life.

—STUDS TURKEL

Happiness is like a butterfly. The more you chase it, the more it will elude you. But if you turn your attention to other things, it comes and softly sits on your shoulder.

Confidence comes from knowing that you have the talent to do a job. Confidence also comes from a good education, work and life experiences, and from a general belief in yourself and your abilities.

There is more treasure in books than in all the pirates' loot on Treasure Island . . . and best of all, you can enjoy these riches every day of your life.

—WALT DISNEY

i'm amazed at all the resources that people are continually creating to help us along in our journey. This section offers reviews of my favorite books, resources, and web links that have helped supercharge, guide, inspire, and shape my life—and I know many of these will do the same for you! These resources can also be found at the bookshop on my companion web site at www.backdoorjobs.com (with direct links to amazon.com for those who want to add a few books to their library). Read through and see what resources might help in shaping your life!

FINDING YOUR WAY

Life-Changing Fiction . . . .

The classic ***The Adventures of Tom Sawyer*** by Mark Twain takes us back to a dreamlike world of summertime, pleasantly reminding us that we were once boys and girls ourselves and should carry our childlike qualities into adulthood. (Viking Press, $5.95)

Santiago, a shepherd boy searching for his "treasure," teaches us about listening to our heart, acting upon the omens strewn along life's path, and realizing one's destiny is a person's only real obligation. Full of adventure, magic, and wisdom, ***The Alchemist*** by Paulo Coelho shares with us that the possibility of having a dream come true is what makes life interesting! (HarperSanFrancisco, $13)

Richard Bode's lifelong love affair with sailing provides a vivid metaphor on living life to the fullest. ***First You Have to Row a Little Boat*** is a wonderful book that teaches us to maneuver with patience around the obstacles we encounter in our own passage through life. (Warner Books, $11.95)

What would it be like if we were each given a life assignment? ***The Giver*** by Lois Lowry provides a somewhat eerie look at the way we might live someday. The story takes place in a utopian community where there is no hunger, no disease, no pollution, no fear—until a twelve-year-old boy rebels against the choices that have been denied him. (Laurel Leaf, $5.99)

Hope for the Flowers…The rush to get to the top will take new meaning after you read this touching and thought-provoking story about two caterpillars. Author Trina Paulus challenges us to believe in the butterfly inside. (Paulist Press, $14.95, splurge for the hardcover)

"I command that you be happy in the world, as long as you live!" What if someone demanded that of you? And is it really possible? A wonderful story (and quick read), Richard Bach's ***Illusions: The Adventures of a Reluctant Messiah***, takes you on a journey that explores your unique life and, possibly, answers the question of why we exist. This classic can be found at most used bookstores across the country. (Dell, $6.99)

While lying in a hospital bed some ten years ago, a dear friend of mine gave me a small book called ***The Little Prince*** by Antoine de Saint-Exupéry . . . and within a few hours my entire perspective of life changed—yours will too, as "what is essential is invisible to the eye." (Harcourt Brace, $16, splurge for the hardcover)

Dr. Seuss opens the door to all the exciting possibilities that lie ahead and earnestly warns of the potential pitfalls. You'll find

Oh, the Places You'll Go! to be the perfect send-off for your new adventure. (Random House, $17, splurge for the hardcover)

Benjamin Hoff's ***The Tao of Pooh*** is the perfect read for anyone wanting to learn the basic principles of Taoism, but through the eyes of the beloved character Winnie the Pooh, who "wanders around asking silly questions, making up songs, and going through all kinds of adventures, without ever accumulating any amount of intellectual knowledge or losing his simpleminded sort of happiness." Maybe Pooh has something, huh? (Viking Press, $11.95)

New Beginnings and Becoming Your Best . . . .

How do I live a happy, meaningful, and flourishing life? How can I be both a noble and effective person? Answering these bedrock questions was the single-minded passion of Epictetus, the venerable philosopher who was born a slave about A.D. 55 in the eastern outreaches of the Roman Empire. Both of his works, ***The Art of Living*** and ***A Manual for Living*** (a condensed version) provide a day-by-day, down-to-earth life of virtue. (HarperSanFrancisco, $16/$9)

Most people don't fully appreciate the fact that no matter who you are, if you want something in life, you've got to learn to ask for it. ***Ask for the Moon—and Get It*** by Percy Ross focuses on this most neglected secret to success and happiness. (Find this one in used bookstores.)

Building a deeper life of spirituality begins many times with the development of a personal prayer life. ***Beginning to Pray*** by Anthony Bloom offers practical guidelines on the power of prayer for people at all spiritual levels. (Paulist Press, $6.95)

"Excitement wears orange socks, faith lives in the same apartment building as doubt. . . ." ***The Book of Qualities*** by Ruth Gendler challenges you to look at your emotions and unique character in new and inspiring ways. (HarperCollins, $12)

Your dream job doesn't have to be just a dream. There are millions of fulfilling and interesting jobs out there for folks that don't seem to fit the "norm." Being different, unconventional, and hard-to-categorize can be a big asset if you know how to use it. After all, do you really want to do what everybody else does? ***The Career Guide for Creative and Unconventional People*** by Carol Eikleberry gives you a boost to make your dreams a reality. (Ten Speed Press, $11.95)

Career counselor Rick Jarow challenges each of us "to create a life work that will reflect our own nature, and to develop the courage

---

Are you looking for books that focus on alternative methods of making life better, freer, and safer? Contact ***Loompanics***, (360) 385-7471, loompanx@ olympus.net

Taking Off works with students and adults (aged sixteen to seventy) by locating options that match their interests and budget to create a well-thought-out plan for taking time off. Along with a database of three thousand opportunities worldwide (ranging from internships and apprenticeships to volunteer and travel programs), ongoing consultation, planning, career counseling, and support are provided over a period of eighteen months for a fee of $1,000 (or $150 per hour). Taking Off, Gail Reardon, Director, P.O. Box 104, Newton Highlands, MA 02461; (617) 630-1606, (617) 630-1605 (fax), tkingoff@ aol.com

For a look at almost every career-related book available (ranging from alternative careers to travel), call for a copy of the ***Whole Work Catalog***. The catalog's goal is to help you find "whole" work—work that is personally satisfying as well as financially rewarding (and each book is backed by a one-year guarantee). The New Careers Center, Tom and Sue Ellison, ***Whole Work Catalog***, 1515 23rd St., P.O. Box 339, Boulder, CO 80306; (303) 447-1087

We read books to find out who we are. What other people, real or imaginary, do, think and feel is an essential guide to our understanding of what we ourselves are and may become. —URSULA K. LEGUIN

and wisdom to bring it into form." **Creating the Work You Love** offers a step-by-step and self-reflective process based on the seven chakras (the body's energy centers) that will challenge you to move past the daily struggles of life and push toward making your life a work of art. Also, visit Rick's "anti-career" web site at www.anticareer.com for more spirited words. (Inner Traditions, $14.95)

Do you need a whack on the side of the head . . . or maybe just a kick in the pants? Then indulge in Roger von Oech's **Creative Whack Pack**, a deck of cards that provides a brief story, hint, or insight that will keep your mind spinning for days to come. (U.S. Games Systems, $25)

Unfortunately, many of us look at money as an end, rather than as a means. Marsha Sinetar's **Do What You Love, the Money Will Follow** will help you realize that if you do what brings meaning to

your life, you'll pleasantly find that you'll have all the riches in the world. The book is filled with inspirational examples of people who have pursued what they love, rather than just the making of money. A must for those who are in jobs for the wrong reason or need a push in the right direction. (Dell, $12.95)

How many times have you talked yourself out of something because of self-sabotaging fears? **Feel the Fear and Do It Anyway** by Susan Jeffers will teach you to push past the negative chatter in your head, risk a little every day, and turn every decision into a "no-lose" situation. (Fawcett Books, $12.95)

Do you have the urge to strike out on your own and develop a career path that just might have the greatest job satisfaction and personal development? Let Paul Hawken show you the way. **Growing a Business** provides straight talk on what works and what doesn't, and why. You'll also learn that being in business is not about making money. It is a way to become who you are. (Fireside, $11)

Wouldn't it be nice to live a happier, more successful, and more peaceful life? **Happiness Is a Choice** is about believing in ourselves, having a positive attitude, and being hopeful about the events that shape our lives. And after reading Barry Kaufman's book, you might also want to take part in one of the many educational programs he (and his "happy" staff) offer through The Option Institute (see their listing on page 184). Whether you want to improve the quality of your life or overcome a challenging adversity, the program will help you actively explore a new way to live your life. (Fawcett Books, $9.50)

Just as it is important finding a career that brings meaning to life, so is finding a home with heart. *House as a Mirror of Self* by Clare Cooper Marcus explores the deeper meaning of home and the complex connections that each of us creates with our surroundings. (Conari Press, $16.95)

"Whether our gift is baking bread, assessing environmental hazards, teaching children, or powerhouse investing, it's never going to be enough to just dabble a little here and a little there. If you wish for full satisfaction, you must give yourself completely to this work, 100 percent." Complete with hands-on exercises, *How Much Joy Can You Stand?* by Suzanne Falter-Barns helps fuel, free, excite, and encourage the small dreams we keep like secrets and never do anything about. Her companion web site, www.howmuchjoy.com, might also reignite a few creative sparks. (Publishers Group West, $12.95)

If you need a swift kick in the rump to get you moving in the right direction, Barbara Sher might be someone you turn to. Whether you're looking to make improvements in your job or personal life, *I Could Do Anything If I Only Knew What It Was* will help you "recapture long lost goals, overcome the blocks that inhibit your success, decide what you want to be, and live your dreams." (DTP, $12.95)

For some reason, we have been brainwashed with the fact that the more we work, the better off we become. *The Joy of Not Working* teaches us how we can create a paradise away from the workplace—and develop our world of leisure (while making a living). Ernie Zelinski's down-to-earth writing is filled with great stories, cartoons, quotes, and plenty of exercises—all of which provide insights on how to get that "zest" back into your life and become excited about everything you do. (Ten Speed Press, $14.95)

Leo Buscaglia has to be one of my all-time favorite authors. His writings teach us to be human—to be who we are and what we feel, and how we can learn to be loving individuals and get the most out of life through love. Known for getting his students to hug trees (and each other) at the University of Southern California while teaching a class on love, Dr. Buscaglia will guide you to new levels of happiness (on this fantastic journey we're all on). *Love, Bus 9 to Paradise,* and *Personhood: The Art of Being Fully Human* are my favorites. (Fawcett Books, $10)

Based on the Myers-Briggs personality test, *Lifetypes* by Sandra Krebs Hirsh and Jean Kummerow gives you the tools to develop a

Web Links

About.com is one site provided by topic-specific experts that you'll have to visit for all your career planning and job search needs. Career planning expert Dawn Rosenberg McKay focuses on topics ranging from career change and exploration to relocating and temp work (www.careerplanning.about. com). Job searching expert Alison Doyle provides the best job links on everything from cool jobs to international internships (www.jobsearch.about.com).

The *Aboutjobs.com* network provides a searchable database for adventure seekers, with a focus on summer, resort, overseas, and intern jobs. Opportunities are posted by each program and can be viewed for free by visitors.

Are you "navigating" through your first year in college? *First Year Focus* (www.abacon.com/ firstyearfocus) provides support, information, and tips that will help get you on the right path. Included are some great ideas on internships and careers.

Jobweb.org (www.jobweb.org/ catapult) provides a comprehensive web site for college students and graduates seeking information on careers and jobs, including short-term work and internship experiences, career fairs, professional associations, career library resources, and employment centers.

It's never too late—in fiction or in life—to revise. —NANCY THAYER

If you were to start from scratch on finding a job on the Internet, you might start with *Rileyguide.com*. It's filled with link upon link of job resources, services, job listings, and information guides. The site also has a companion book called *The Guide to Internet Job Searching*. (VGM Career Horizons, $14.95)

For endless career link opportunities, all the major search engines on the web have career directories that are sure to give you more ideas. Some that you might want to explore include the *Go Network* (www.go.com/WebDir/Careers), the *4Anything Network* (www.4internships.com, www.4opportunities.com, and www.4volunteer.com), and *Alta Vista* (dir.altavista.com/Business/Jobs.shtml).

psychological self-portrait. After completing a series of questions (which is great fun with a group of friends), your "lifetype" emerges. The book then provides you with examples of each personality type as it relates to careers, relationships, and recreational activities that you should choose or avoid—and how to get the most out of your life by gaining a better understanding of yourself. (Warner Books, $12.99)

If you need a jolt of energy, check out Patrick Combs. He's a college career success speaker, author of *Major in Success*, and has a dynamo web site (which fills my mind with great ideas). Geared mainly to the college crowd, **Major in Success** will walk you through an inspirational journey, helping you to take a fresh look at your life and explore how to uncover your dream job (Ten Speed Press, $11.95). Once you've absorbed the information in his book, turn to his web site at www.goodthink.com for daily boosts of inspiration and information on success (especially look at his weekly column). Good Thinking Hot Tips can also be received through e-mail by sending a note to majordomo@po.databack.com with "subscribe pcombs" in the body of the e-mail.

Got the urge to throw in the towel at what you're currently doing and become joyfully jobless? Barbara Winters's book, **Making a Living Without a Job** ($13.95, Bantam Books), is for anyone who has always dreamed of becoming their own boss (and creating the work they love). She'll take you on a step-by-step journey that integrates the things you like to do with the things you're good at doing. She also self-publishes **Winning Ways**, a brilliant, bimonthly newsletter (six issues per year for $31), which is designed to share creative ideas about successful self-employment, along with thoughts on personal development. You can reach Barbara at babswinter@yahoo.com or by calling (612) 835-5647.

If you are looking for that perfect job but aren't sure how to find it, **The Pathfinder** will help you dispel those feelings of uncertainty and make a career direction your reality. Through extensive exercises such as goal setting, list making, self-tests, and other diagnostic tools, author Nicholas Lore shows you how to live a life you love, how to get there from here, and how to design your future career. (Fireside, $14)

If you are a manager or are about to become one, read John Marzetta's **PCC: How to Survive in Management, or Just Another Fish Story**. His inspiring words will change the way you manage people and work with others. You can receive a copy of his work by writing to him at John Marzetta, MARTEK, 505 Swift Ave., Oglesby, IL 61348; marzetta@ivcc.edu. There is no charge for the book; however, he asks for a donation of $5 (or whatever you can afford) to cover shipping and handling. All proceeds will be given to the St. Jude Children's Fund.

Why is it that some people thrive in the hustle and bustle of city life or choose to find comfort in the quiet of the countryside? Author Winifred Gallagher takes a hard look at how our physical place can delight us, deprive us, alter our moods, confine us, or influence everything we do. **The Power of Place** reveals the complexities between people and the places in which they live, work, and enjoy. A highly recommended read for those searching for a place that brings a sense of home. (HarperPerennial, $13)

What would your life be like if you never took risks? You'd never find a great job, make a new friend, fall in love, or . . . ! If you're having trouble making crucial choices in your life—moving from the fear of the unknown to the excitement of what is about to be—then read David Viscott's **Risking**. (Find this one in used bookstores.)

Stroll down the path of life with SARK and learn about her 250 jobs, how to relax about money, making friends with freedom and uncertainty, living juicy, drawing on the walls, and making your life an adventure. SARK's **Inspiration Sandwich** will inspire your creative freedom (Celestial Arts, $14.95), and **Living Juicy: Daily Morsels for Your Creative Soul** (Celestial Arts, $15.95) will challenge the way you look at your life and bring a refreshing new approach to "daily meditation." **Camp SARK,** her companion web site (www.campsark.com), provides all the details—with information ranging from subscribing to her **Magic Museletter** to tips on getting your own book published. For those who need a quick dose of inspiration, call her Inspiration Hotline at (415) 546-3742 for a three-minute recorded message.

The 7 Habits of Highly Effective People by Stephen Covey provides a step-by-step pathway for living principles that give us the security to adapt to change, and the wisdom and power to take advantage of the opportunities that change creates. (Fireside, $14)

If you've been dreaming of embarking on a life-transforming journey, one that will take you away from the office for a while, **Six Months Off** by Hope Dlugozima and James Scott can help you take your fantasies off the shelf and transform them into reality. The authors talked to more than two hundred sabbatical-takers who'd actually gathered the gumption to take time off of work and make their vagabond dreams come true. (Henry Holt, $12.95)

The higher you climb . . .
The more that you see.

The more that you see . . .
The less that you know.

The less that you know . . .
The more that you yearn.

The more that you yearn . . .
The higher you climb.

The farther you reach . . .
The more that you touch.

The more that you touch . . .
The fuller you feel.

The fuller you feel . . .
The less that you need.

The less that you need . . .
The farther you reach.

—DAN FOGELBERG

A practical and inspirational collection of profiles of more than thirty students, **Taking Time Off** by Colin Hall and Ron Lieber demonstrates how taking time off gives you a chance to explore career interests, gain practical experience, and develop a new perspective on your studies. (Noonday Press, $12)

Work, love, friendship, spirituality, living fully . . . how do we make sense of life's daily challenges as friends, parents, or leading a balanced lifestyle and achieving our best? **Touchstones: A Book of Daily Meditations for Men** by David Spohn and **Each Day a New Beginning: Daily Meditations for Women** by Karen Casey are great companions to begin each day with a thought-provoking meditation, helping you to ignite new possibilities and strengthen you on your path. (Hazelden, $11)

If you're going through a transition, whether it be a breakup, career change, or ending something and are unsure about your next step, I highly recommend **Transitions**. William Bridges takes you through the three stages of transition: Endings (that difficult process of letting go of an old situation), the Neutral Zone (that seemingly unproductive and confusing nowhere of in-betweenness), and the New Beginning (launching forth again in a new situation). To guide you through this transitional path, see his companion web site at www.wmbridges.com. (Perseus Press, $14)

What Color Is Your Parachute? Just the title of this book intrigues me. After reading it from cover to cover (and working through a dozen of Richard Bolles's flower exercises), I realized that it should be required reading for anyone who wants to successfully carve out their own career niche. Revised and updated annually, *Parachute* (a word coined by the author when he was referring to career transitions back in the late 1960s) is about taking chances, gaining confidence, and making changes in your career and life. Complete with exercises on self-assessment and career planning, it is perhaps most valuable to those who are securely employed but unhappy with what they're doing. As a companion for his wit, words, and wisdom, Richard Bolles has also crafted a magnificent web site—**JobHuntersBible.com**, which includes information (and lots of links) on one of his newest works—**Job-Hunting on the Internet**. (Ten Speed Press, $16.95)

The important thing is not to stop questioning. Curiosity has its own reason for existing. One cannot help but be in awe when he contemplates the mysteries of eternity, of life, of the marvelous structure of reality. It is enough if one tries merely to comprehend a little of this mystery everyday. Never lose a holy curiosity.

—ALBERT EINSTEIN

an adventurous lifestyle means to grow through excitement, challenge, and risk taking. It's about learning to look at the world through curious eyes—to wonder what's on the other side of the mountain—and allowing wanderlust to become your guide. The intimacy of your adventurous pursuits will allow you to see, hear, taste, and smell more intensely. You'll work hard and you'll play hard; however, by exploring your options in this section, you'll learn that work and play become the same thing. Push past your doubts and fears and let your journey to adventure begin!

Unique Opportunities to Explore in This Section:

▶ Clearwater's sloop flagship, a magnificent 106-foot replica of boats that sailed the Hudson River in New York over one hundred years ago, becomes a classroom of waves for sailing apprentices *(page 50)*.

▶ Is it true that the more risk you take, the more you can open yourself up to new adventures? Find out how Michael and Dorrie Williams left their "Corporate America" jobs and experienced an adventure of a lifetime by pedaling their bikes across America. This special cycling section also features seasonal employment opportunities with some of the best biking adventure programs in the United States *(page 53)*.

▶ How often do you find yourself taking extravagant pleasure in being alive? Learn about the Alaskan Inuit expression of Nuanaarpuq *(page 64)*.

▶ Experience the four pillars of self-reliance, fitness, craftsmanship, and compassion taught at Outward Bound, by participating in one of their rugged adventure programs throughout the United States *(page 66)*.

▶ This summer you might consider becoming a trip leader for Trailmark, while working with a team who fosters a genuine familylike atmosphere that can be felt throughout all their programs *(page 73)*.

I learned early that the richness of life is adventure. Adventure calls on all faculties of mind and spirit. It develops self-reliance and independence. Life then teems with excitement. But you are not ready for adventure unless you are rid of fear. For fear confines you and limits your scope. You stay tethered by strings of doubt and indecision and have only a small and narrow world to explore.

—WILLIAM O. DOUGLAS

A kayaker learns about the four pillars of self-reliance, fitness, craftsmanship, and compassion taught at Outward Bound.

43

Photo Credit: Jake Mills

ADVENTURE
CAREERS

THE ADVENTURE CENTRE AT PRETTY LAKE

Adventure Education • Michigan • Year-Round
www.net-link.net/ACPL

Jennifer Weaver, Assistant Education Director
9310 W. "R" Ave.
Kalamazoo, MI 49009
(616) 375-1664 • (616) 375-0735 (fax)
tcentre@aol.com

THE ADVENTURE CENTRE provides exposure to the many facets of adventure education, with clients who come from middle schools, high schools, colleges, universities, community agencies, the court system, alternative schools, social groups, and corporations. The Adventure Centre site includes five challenge ropes courses, seven low initiative areas, two fifty-foot climbing towers, and facilities for groups to camp out or stay indoors.

The Experience: Internships are designed to provide a wide range of experiences and exposure to many aspects of experiential education programming. The first phase of an internship generally includes participation in a five-day personal exploration workshop and/or three-day logistical workshops. Responsibilities may include group facilitation, maintenance of equipment and sites, preparation for incoming groups, and overnight supervision. Interns will receive instruction from highly experienced facilitators, first-hand experience facilitating groups and working with equipment, and an opportunity for certification at the Adventure Centre. Longer commitments may also include participation in program design, development, and marketing.

Commitment: Because of the pace and number of clients participating in the program, things can get hectic. As a result, the Centre relies heavily on seasonal staff to help out wherever necessary. Interns rarely work from 9 to 5, and many times the work experience can become emotionally and physically demanding.

Perks: A stipend is provided, along with housing if needed.

Ideal Candidate: Applicants must be at least twenty-one years of age with a background in psychology, social work, counseling, or other human services. They must have experience in experiential/adventure education, a high level of maturity, energy, flexibility, and enthusiasm.

The two most important requirements for prospective employees are a dedication to learning and a willingness to commit yourself to your own and others' personal growth. We are a process-focused experiential education organization. Because of this, in order to have a meaningful impact on the growth of our clients, we are looking for people who are ready to explore their personal issues and take a look at how their lives impact the facilitation of a group.

ADVENTURE CONNECTION

River Outfitter • California • April–October
www.raftcalifornia.com

Nate Rangel, President
P.O. Box 475
Coloma, CA 95613
(800) 556-6060 • (530) 626-7385 • (530) 626-9268 (fax)
getwet@raftcalifornia.com

ADVENTURE CONNECTION was created by a dedicated group of river enthusiasts who saw how river trips had the power to change lives. After working for, and with, some of California's finest professional river outfitters, they knew they could offer something different—a little more luxury, a tastier menu, a slightly higher-class trip—and still have competitive prices. They are now one of California's largest outfitters in the Mother Lode area.

The Experience: An annual white-water rafting workshop is offered each spring where Adventure Connection hires guides from among its best students (the course costs $800). A low student-to-instructor ratio is maintained in order to provide each participant with the best opportunity to develop their skills. Since Adventure Connection's hiring varies from year to year, the course also helps workshop participants apply to all outfitters in the area. Canoe and kayak instruction is also offered.

Perks: Pay varies by the river and the experience of the guide. Trip guides are paid by the day, generally $60 to $100 per day. Guides also receive generous tips, free meals and camping facilities, use of equipment for private trips, and a chance to work in the great outdoors.

Ideal Candidate: Those with great attitudes and good social skills make the best candidates. Applicants for guide positions with no prior experience should enroll in the company's annual river-guide school.

Getting In: Call for application materials (which are due by March 1). Prospective candidates should attend the white-water rafting workshop, generally held in early April of each year.

ADVENTURE PURSUITS

Adventure Education • USA/Canada/Mexico • Summer
www.apadventures.com

Farley Kautz, Program Director
31160 Broken Talon Trail
Oak Creek, CO 80467
(970) 736-8336 • (970) 736-8311 (fax)
info@apadventures.com

ADVENTURE PURSUITS offers wilderness adventure programs throughout the U.S., Canada, Mexico, and the Bahamas for young adults who desire an active and challenging outdoor experience. Personal achievement, teamwork, challenge, and fun are the underlying goals for each adventure. Groups work together to surpass individual expectations, whether it be climbing a 14,000-foot peak, negotiating a challenging section of white-water rapids, or sharing a great day's experiences with new friends around an evening campfire.

The Experience: Trip leaders, sharing responsibility with a coleader of the opposite sex, are responsible for up to thirteen teenage students. Leaders must be willing and prepared to sacrifice personal goals, if necessary, in response to the students' needs, and similarly, must be willing and able to adapt previous experiences to the goals of Adventure Pursuits.

Commitment: Trip leaders are typically hired for the entire duration of the season, which runs mid-June through late August. The position requires continuous duties for as long as twenty-eight days without time off. Time off varies from two to four days between trips.

Perks: Pay begins at a daily wage of $36 for first-year leaders, along with in-depth training, room and board, and outdoor gear pro-deals.

Ideal Candidate: Applicants must be at least twenty-one, certified in wilderness first aid, be physically and mentally able to lead extended trips in wilderness environments, and be able to hike, climb, bike, raft, kayak, and participate in and/or lead all activities on assigned trips. The average age of staff members and trip leaders is twenty-six.

We are looking for mature young adults with a proven ability to combine backcountry and teaching skills with solid experience working with teenagers.

ADVENTURES CROSS-COUNTRY

Adventure Education • Worldwide • Summer
www.adventurescrosscountry.com

Brian Danforth, Program Director
242 Redwood Highway
Mill Valley, CA 94941
(800) 767-2722 • (415) 332-5075 • (415) 332-2130 (fax)
arcc@slip.net

ADVENTURES CROSS-COUNTRY offers wilderness adventure travel programs for teenagers in a variety of outdoor settings in national parks and forests throughout the western United States, Canada, Australia, Fiji, and Costa Rica.

The Experience: Guides lead a group of thirteen teenagers, with a coleader of the opposite sex, through a rigorous wilderness trip, with activities that may include backpacking, rock climbing, mountain biking, rafting, kayaking, mountaineering, and scuba diving. The trips are both mentally and physically challenging for guides and participants, with adventures ranging from fifteen to thirty-nine days (twenty-four hours a day).

Commitment: Guides must be available starting in mid-June, and typically finish their assignments sometime between mid-July and late August.

Perks: A daily stipend of $25 to $35 is provided, along with room and board.

Ideal Candidate: Applicants must be at least twenty-one years of age, possess strong wilderness/backpacking skills, and experience working with teenagers, along with current certification in Wilderness First Responder. For those who are not WFR-certified, a WFR course is offered in early June.

We're looking for guides with fun personalities who are able to leap over tall buildings in a single bound!

ALABAMA SPORTS FESTIVAL

Sports • Alabama • 6–9 Months
www.alagames.com

Ron Creel, Chief Executive Officer
2530 East South Blvd.
P.O. Box 20327
Montgomery, AL 36120-0327
(800) 467-0422 • (334) 280-0065 • (334) 280-0988 (fax)
info@alagames.com

*Avoiding danger is no safer in the long run than outright exposure.
Life is either a daring adventure or nothing.* —HELEN KELLER

45

THE ALABAMA SPORTS FESTIVAL is a statewide Olympic-style competition for amateur athletes of all ages and abilities, including the physically challenged and seniors. The festival offers forty-two sporting events and has an annual participation of over seven thousand athletes in regional and state games competition. Internships provide individuals with experience in planning, management, marketing, fund-raising, recruiting, desktop publishing and graphic design, and sport development and management. Along with a monthly stipend of $100, lodging and meals are provided. Undergraduate and graduate students are encouraged to apply.

ALASKA WILDLAND ADVENTURES

Safari • Alaska • May–September
www.arctic.net/~coopland

Scott Thomas, Program Director
P.O. Box 389
Girdwood, AK 99587
(800) 334-8730 • (907) 783-2928 • (907) 783-2130 (fax)
info@alaskawildland.com

ALASKA WILDLAND ADVENTURES runs five- to twelve-day natural history safaris for adults and families, along with fishing and rafting programs. Part of the thrill is close-up views of wildlife such as bald eagles, brown bears, caribou, and seals. Summer seasonal positions include outdoor leadership (natural history trip leader, natural history guide, apprentice guide, rafting guide, and fishing guide), professional drivers (safari driver and shuttle driver), hospitality (assistant hospitality manager, cook, assistant cook, housekeeper, and dishwasher), and administrative (assistant safari manager, head raft guide, office assistant, and maintenance coordinator). Salaries range from $800 to $1,600 per month (plus gratuities). Tent housing is provided along with a payroll deduction for meals. Most positions run from mid-May through mid-September. Send a resume and cover letter requesting an application. The hiring begins in December.

AMERICAN ADVENTURES

Adventure Travel • USA • Summer
www.americanadventures.com

Staffing Manager
P.O. Box 1338
Gardena, CA 90249
(800) 873-5872 • (310) 719-9911

WITH OVER THIRTY ITINERARIES, AmeriCan Adventures offers active small-group camping and hostelling tours to foreign travelers (usually between the ages of eighteen and thirty-five) that cover most of North America, including Canada, Alaska, and Mexico.

The Experience: Tour leaders take their group in fifteen-passenger vehicles to national parks, cities, small towns, and everything in between. In a day's work, leaders must be prepared for driving, organizing activities, providing briefings and commentary, and leading a safe and enjoyable holiday for their passengers.

Commitment: Schedules are very flexible, but first-year leaders can normally expect to work from June through September. Longer seasons are possible in subsequent years. Each tour lasts from two to six weeks, and there are normally one to five days off between assignments.

Perks: The base pay ranges from $240 to $295 per week, along with tips. All en route and between trip accommodation is provided, and most meals are covered while on tour. The biggest perk, perhaps, is meeting interesting people from around the world and participating in a variety of adventure activities ranging from jeep tours to water sports on a complimentary basis.

Ideal Candidate: Applicants must be at least twenty-one with a clean driving record. The best applicants are outgoing, adventurous, and flexible, and have a considerable knowledge of North American history, geography, and culture. Knowledge of a foreign language is helpful, but not required. Leaders must participate in a two- to three-week training process before leading any tours. Although unpaid, most accommodations are provided during this time.

Getting In: Call for application materials. Applications are accepted throughout the spring and early summer, and training usually takes place sometime in June.

AMERICAN YOUTH FOUNDATION—MINIWANCA

Experiential Education • Michigan • 15 Weeks
www.ayf.com

"Poppy" Elizabeth Potter, Outreach Program Director
8845 W. Garfield Rd.
Shelby, MI 49455
(616) 861-2262 • (616) 861-5244 (fax)
wancapop@oceana.net

THE AMERICAN YOUTH FOUNDATION is a nonprofit organization founded in 1925 to help young people and those who serve young people achieve their personal best, lead balanced lives, and serve others. Programs include a residential summer camp, a four-trails program, and a high school leadership conference, along with year-round outreach programs to serve communities that house their sites and programs. Interns at Miniwanca assist in the facilitation of outdoor education, team building, leadership development, and service-learning programs for a variety of populations over a fifteen-week period. Interns will also gain training and experience facilitating the low ropes course and be given the opportunity to create and complete an individual project. Applicants must have experience working with youth programs, an ability to laugh easily, a positive attitude, and a willingness to put 110 percent energy into the program. A monthly stipend of $375 is provided, along with room and partial board.

APPALACHIAN MOUNTAIN TEEN PROJECT

Youth Development • New Hampshire • Year-Round

Program Director
P.O. Box 1597
Wolfeboro, NH 03894
(603) 569-5510

THE PURPOSE of the Appalachian Mountain Teen Project is to offer support to rural teens and their families as they face critical life transitions. Activities include a wide range of outdoor adventure programs, community service, and cross-cultural experiences. Interns assist with program planning, trip leadership, administration, fund-raising, and plan and execute projects of their own. Counseling opportunities and classroom experiences are also possible. Most of the experience involves working directly with youth aged twelve to eighteen. A stipend is generally offered. The Teen Project will also assist you in locating housing, and all outdoor clothing and equipment may be borrowed from the program.

In our program, you won't hang off the highest cliffs, speed down the fastest zip line, or paddle the biggest waves . . . but you might develop the deepest relationships and see the widest connections in an appreciative, small town community.

BCT.TELUS EMPLOYEE FITNESS PROGRAM

Health & Fitness • Canada • Year-Round

Susan Hui, Student Internship Coordinator
1-1795 Willingdon Ave.
Burnaby, BC V5C 5J2
Canada
(604) 893-3409 • (604) 298-1387 (fax)
susan_hui@bctel.com

SINCE ITS INCEPTION IN 1977, the BCT.TELUS (British Columbia-Telus Telephone) Employee Fitness Program with twelve fitness centers has developed into one of the largest and most comprehensive fitness programs of its kind in North America. Its mission is to provide all employees with an opportunity to adapt their living habits toward a state of optimal health through the provision of quality fitness and related lifestyle services. Fitness specialist interns provide fitness assessment, exercise prescription, fitness class instruction, facility supervision, special event planning, sports programming, and general administrative duties. There is a small honorarium of $300. Benefits include a free fitness membership, fitness apparel, professional library access, and training opportunities.

BOMBARD BALLOON ADVENTURES

Ballooning • Europe • May–October
www.bombardsociety.com

Mike Lincicome, Staffing Director
Château de Laborde
21200 Beaune
France
(011) 33 380 26 63 30 (phone)
lincicome@compuserve.com

BOMBARD BALLOON ADVENTURES engages guests in hot-air ballooning adventures throughout Europe each May through October. Along with balloon pilots, chefs, and guides, the ground crew facilitates all the details of each ballooning adventure—from preparing each trip to mapping out and retrieving the balloon once it has landed (and it's noted that there is a lot of driving over the course of a workday). Applicants must have a clean driving record and, for those who reside outside of Europe, must have a valid work permit prior to application. (See InterExchange or the Council on International Education Exchange in the Abroad Adventures section for more information on obtaining a work permit.) While fluency is not required, working knowledge of spoken French, Italian, and/or German is definitely helpful. Benefits include a small wage

Be not the slave of your own past. Plunge into the sublime seas, dive deep, and swim far, so you shall come back with self-respect, with new power, with an advanced experience, that shall explain and overlook the old. —RALPH WALDO EMERSON

47

along with lodging and meals. Send a resume, a copy of your driver's license, dates of availability, and your height and weight. For more information on staffing opportunities, visit their staffing web site at http://ourworld.compuserve.com/homepages/lincicome.

BOOJUM INSTITUTE FOR EXPERIENTIAL EDUCATION

Experiential Education • California • Year-Round
www.boojuminstitute.org

Joseph Scanlon, Program Director
P.O. Box 687
Idyllwild, CA 92549
(909) 659-6250 • (909) 659-6251 (fax)
info@boojuminstitute.org

BOOJUM INSTITUTE is a nonprofit educational organization whose mission is to promote self-discovery, constructive interaction with others, and a deeper understanding of nature through experiential, adventure, and environmental education. They primarily serve students, from sixth grade through college, but also provide programs for youth-at-risk. A full challenge course program is offered, along with backpacking, ropes courses, rock climbing, canoeing, hiking, and sea kayaking.

Environment: Joshua Tree National Park, the Sierra Nevadas, Lake Mead National Recreational Area, Yosemite National Park, and Point Reyes National Seashore all serve as the Institute's outdoor classroom.

The Experience: Interns must have clear goals of what they want to learn at Boojum. Formal training and other opportunities are then built into the internship experience. Training could range from working with a field instructor to assisting the logistician with menu planning, food buying and preparation, and movement of gear and people to course sites.

Commitment: Positions are available from February through November, with their busiest period from mid-August through mid-November. Interns can expect to work weekends and some holidays depending on course load.

Perks: A $100 per month stipend and comfortable housing are provided.

Ideal Candidate: Applicants must be at least twenty years old, hold current first aid and CPR certification, have an excellent driving record, a genuine interest in learning more about the outdoor experiential education field, and be able and willing to work hard.

Getting In: Send a resume and cover letter. Upon receipt, Boojum will send an application with three reference forms.

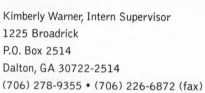

This is an entry-level position for someone who is interested in the experiential education field. We are looking for folks who are open, honest, have a sense of humor, and good self-assessment skills.

BRADLEY WELLNESS CENTER

Health & Fitness • Georgia • Year-Round

Kimberly Warner, Intern Supervisor
1225 Broadrick
P.O. Box 2514
Dalton, GA 30722-2514
(706) 278-9355 • (706) 226-6872 (fax)

LOCATED IN THE "carpet capital" of the world, Bradley Wellness Center offers experience in adult fitness, cardiac and pulmonary rehabilitation, corporate wellness, and educational programming. Assisting members in achieving "optimal well-being," interns provide assessments, exercise supervision and leadership, exercise prescription programs, and health/lifestyle education. A monthly stipend of $300 is provided, along with housing at Hamilton Medical Center (adjacent to facility) and a 50 percent discount in the cafeteria. Four positions are available every semester (or quarter) for undergraduate or graduate students with a background in exercise science or health education.

BRECKENRIDGE OUTDOOR EDUCATION CENTER

Therapeutic Recreation • Colorado • Winter/Summer
www.boec.org

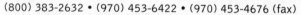

Internship Coordinator
P.O. Box 697
Breckenridge, CO 80424
(800) 383-2632 • (970) 453-6422 • (970) 453-4676 (fax)

SINCE 1976, the Breckenridge Outdoor Education Center (BOEC) has been dedicated to its mission of providing empowering outdoor experiences for people with a wide variety of physical and mental disabilities, serious illnesses, and other "at-risk" populations. The center's goal is to provide participants with the opportunity to learn new skills, experience pristine natural areas, challenge themselves, and work together to enhance the health and self-confidence necessary to expand human potential. BOEC offers wilderness/adventure programs in downhill and cross-country skiing, ropes course, rafting, rock climbing, camping, fishing, and other activities.

The Experience: Interns are the lifeblood of the center and are "where the rubber meets the road." Time and time again, BOEC's clients comment that the energy, professionalism, and expertise of the staff is the center's greatest asset. The bottom line on all intern work, whether in the Wilderness Program, Professional Challenge Program, or in one of the many offices, is that it can prove to be both difficult and rewarding. Winter interns focus on teaching lessons in the Adaptive Ski Program for people with disabilities and assist the course directors in leading multi-day programs in the great outdoors. Summer interns focus on the Wilderness Program, where they have the opportunity to develop the full range of skills necessary to become a top-notch wilderness instructor.

Commitment: Applicants must commit to working full-time for an entire season. The winter season runs from early November to May 1; and the summer, mid-May to mid-September. The initial training phase lasts three weeks. Expect few days off and long workdays.

Perks: A monthly stipend of $50 is provided, along with meals and housing in rustic and peaceful cabins. Perks include a ski pass during the winter, and of course, the invaluable training and great experience that come from participation in the internship. Interns are able to trade some of their time and wilderness expertise for membership at the Breckenridge Recreation Center, which has hot showers, hot tubs, swimming pools, and workout equipment.

Ideal Candidate: Group facilitation and strong supervisory skills are important. Other qualities, such as flexibility, willingness to work long hours, and the ability to live harmoniously with others in a community setting are just as important. However, they have hired interns with a limited experiential education background, basing their decisions largely on the applicant's commitment, good attitude, and enthusiasm for the BOEC and mission. Applicants must be over twenty-one years of age and have advanced first aid and CPR certification.

Getting In: Application deadlines: summer—March 15; winter—September 15.

CANADIAN BORDER OUTFITTERS

Canoe Outfitter • Minnesota • Summer
www.canoetrip.com

Patrick and Chickie Harristhal, Owners
P.O. Box 117
Ely, MN 55731
(800) 247-7530 • (218) 365-5847 (phone/fax)
cbo@cbo-ely.com

CANADIAN BORDER OUTFITTERS is a full-service wilderness canoe trip outfitter located in the northeast corner of Minnesota, just a few miles from the Ontario border. Most staff are hired not to work in one specific job but rather in an "area" of their business. Assignments may include work in the pack house, restaurant, or store, or in cleaning/maintenance, dock/canoe handling, or wilderness instruction. Limited lodging is available for staff at their base on Moose Lake. Some choose to rent apartments in the Ely area, share expenses, and commute to Moose Lake. Meals can be purchased at the base camp at a discount.

CHALLENGE ALASKA

Therapeutic Recreation • Alaska • June–October
www.challenge.ak.org

Program Director
1132 E. 74, Suite 107
Anchorage, AK 99511
(907) 344-7399 • (907) 344-7349 (fax)
challenge@arctic.net

PROVIDING SPORTS AND RECREATIONAL THERAPY opportunities to Alaskans with disabilities, Challenge Alaska believes that everyone, regardless of ability, should have an equal opportunity to engage in diverse recreational activities. Exhilarating physical recreation is a crucial aspect of early rehabilitation and lifelong well-being, an important track to improved mobility, increased self-confidence, and development of specific skills. These benefits, in turn, promote employment opportunities, social integration, spiritual peace, and physical independence. Activities include sea kayaking, fishing, camping, rafting, skiing, waterskiing, wheelchair racing, and a variety of other events. Interns assist in recreation, special events, volunteer coordination, administration, resource development, newsline production, and database operations. A ten- to twelve-week commitment from June through October is needed. Experience and/or a desire to work with people with a disability is a must! Benefits include a $50 per week stipend and some assistance with food.

CHINGACHGOOK YMCA OUTDOOR CENTER

Outdoor Education • New York • April–October

Kenis Sweet, Outdoor Center Director
1872 Pilot Knob Rd.
Pilot Knob, NY 12844
(518) 656-9462 • (518) 656-9362 (fax)

CHINGACHGOOK (PRONOUNCED CHIN-JA-COOK) YMCA, located on spectacular Lake George in the New York Adirondacks, provides year-round programs for over ten thousand children and young adults each year. More than 150 interns and seasonal staff keep things hopping at their outdoor education school and summer camp, where they teach environmental, recreational, and outdoor education as well as lead teen adventure trips (which focus on hiking, canoeing, rock climbing, mountaineering, rafting, ice climbing, kayaking, and camping). Benefits include a weekly stipend of $175, room and board, and extensive training. Candidates must be a minimum of twenty-one years of age with experience in the outdoor adventure field, and available to work the entire season. Send resume and four references (with phone numbers).

CHUCK RICHARDS' WHITEWATER

River Outfitter • California • Summer

Chuck Richards, President
Box W.W.
Lake Isabella, CA 93240
(619) 379-4444 • (619) 379-4685 (fax)
chuckrichards@lightspeed.net

HERE'S RAFTING Southern California style—blazing hot days, balmy starlit evenings, sizzling barbecues, great grins, no bugs, and no goosebumps. Raft guides will take adventure seekers on the Kern River, which provides class three to five rapids. In order to be a summer guide, applicants need to participate in three to five successive weekends of training in March and April (for a fee of $350). Along with lodging in their bunkhouse, guides receive $40 to $60 per day (plus tips).

CLEARWATER

Sailing • New York • 1–4 Months
www.clearwater.org

Gioia Blix, Captain
Hudson River Sloop
112 Market St.
Poughkeepsie, NY 12601-4095
(914) 454-7673 • (914) 454-7953 (fax)
office@clearwater.org

CLEARWATER CONDUCTS environmental education, advocacy programs, and celebrations to protect the greater Hudson River and to create awareness of the estuary's complex relationship with the coastal zone. Their flagship, the sloop *Clearwater* (a magnificent 106-foot replica of boats that sailed the Hudson over one hundred years ago), is a classroom of waves, carrying unique programs on history, biology, and environmental science to nearly twenty thousand adults and children every year.

The Experience: Becoming a sailing apprentice involves intense training in the tasks expected of *Clearwater's* deck crew and in leading groups during education sails. With the help of professional educators, education assistants study the ecology of the Hudson, the use of sampling gear, and learn how to engage and excite students in education activities. Everyone will participate in all crew activities, including education, sailing, and maintenance, with the opportunity to contribute your own special talents to the

Photo Credit: Chris Bowser

Sailing apprentices and their classroom of waves aboard Clearwater's sloop flagship.

overall effort. Crew positions are available as first, second, and third mate; bosun; engineer; and cook.

Commitment: The main sailing season begins mid-April and winds up in November, although positions are available year-round. Crew positions run four months; education assistants—two months; sailing apprentices—one month; and interns/volunteers—at least one week.

Perks: Apprentices and education assistants receive room and board on the sloop, plus a stipend of $25 per week (in the winter the stipend rises to $50 per week). Crew position stipends range from $140 to $300 per week, and weeklong interns/volunteers are asked to donate $40. The living quarters are rustic, featuring open bunks, no showers (except, of course, for the ocean), composting, and "unique" sanitary facilities. Meals are generally vegetarian.

Ideal Candidate: Candidates must be sixteen years or older, and willing and able to work outdoors eight to ten hours per day. Great strength and sailing skill are not as important as coordination, common sense, and an enthusiasm for learning. The ability to deal intelligently with the sloop's hundreds of passengers and casual visitors and to live and work cooperatively in a close and sometimes stressful environment is critical.

Getting In: Call for application materials and current deadlines. It's recommended you volunteer for one week to see what it's like before you commit to other positions.

CLIPPER CRUISE LINE

Cruise Ship • Worldwide • 1 Year
www.clippercruise.com

A. J. Bockelman, Recruiter
Human Resources
7711 Bonhomme Ave.
St. Louis, MO 63105
(800) 325-1933 • (314) 727-2929 • (314) 727-5246 (fax)
clipperhr@aol.com

CLIPPER CRUISE LINE'S fleet of small ships leads passengers and crew on several itineraries throughout the world. Each ship is equipped with motorized inflatable landing craft that can be launched in minutes for spontaneous landings on small islands and deserted beaches. Onboard crew members begin their assignments in entry-level positions, including housekeepers, servers, or deckhands. Applicants must commit for one year, be at least twenty-one years of age, have U.S. citizenship, be friendly and outgoing, and have the stamina to work long hours (most work a minimum of twelve hours per day). In addition to a salary and

tips, crew members receive room and board, transportation to and from the ship, and a full-benefit medical package.

CLUB MED

Adventure Travel • Worldwide • Year-Round
www.clubmed.com

Human Resources Director
4500 SE Pine Valley St.
Port St. Lucie, FL 34952
(800) 258-2633 • (407) 337-6660 (job hotline)

KNOWN FOR ITS GREAT LOCATIONS, interesting architecture, and carefree lifestyle, Club Med is the pioneer of the all-inclusive resort, attracting thousands of adventurous singles and families each year. Be it snorkeling, indulging in a gourmet meal, or being entertained, the "voice of Club Med" is their team of ten thousand GOs (gentils organisateurs)—those "young, bouncy, and good looking" men and women from all around the world who do everything they can to make their enthusiasm contagious to the flock of GMs (gentils membres)—the guests! The best deal at Club Med is to take your chances with their "wild card" option. You pick the week for a set, money-saving price; they pick the place (which evens out the numbers at various resorts).

The Experience: Each year Club Med recruits over thirty-five hundred new GOs in all areas of expertise. GOs work hard giving sports instruction, being sociable, leading group activities and tours, or putting on evening entertainment. Basically, from the moment the GMs arrive until their farewell cocktail party, their Club Med experience is defined by the GOs they meet along the way.

Perks: You don't work at Club Med to become a millionaire but rather to explore a different lifestyle. Still, you should be able to save most of your salary since Club Med covers almost all your expenses, including transportation from your home to the village, room and board (GOs are generally lodged two to a room), health, accident, and repatriation insurance, as well as use of the village's recreational facilities. Your salary will depend on your specific job and level of responsibility.

Getting In: A few common-sense tips: submit a complete application (resume, cover letter, and photo) by the deadline; pay careful attention to the qualifications requested (language requirements, degrees, experience, and availability); and most importantly, be sure you communicate all your enthusiasm and energy in the interview.

The pessimist complains about the wind; the optimist expects it to change; and the realist adjusts the sails. —WILLIAM ARTHUR WARD

CONTIKI HOLIDAYS

Tourism • USA • May–October
www.contiki.com

Marie Martin, Field Manager
2300 E. Katella Ave., #450
Anaheim, CA 92806
(800) 266-8454 • (714) 740-0808 • (714) 740-0818 (fax)
fieldmanager@contiki.com

TOUR MANAGERS with Contiki conduct city tours, give historical and practical information talks, and organize each day of a tour, including stops en route, meals, and excursions. Coach drivers work with a tour manager on most tours and are responsible for driving motor coaches with up to fifty-three passengers on board.

Commitment: Tours, which all depart from Anaheim, range in duration from three to twenty-three days and generally are conducted May through October. Tour managers are responsible for their clients twenty-four hours per day.

Perks: Tour managers receive $355 per week and drivers receive $66 to $73 per day depending on the duration of the tour. Accommodations, food, and some expenses are covered while on tour; however, the biggest perk while working for Contiki is travel!

Ideal Candidate: It's preferred that tour manager applicants have a college degree, a couple years of work experience, knowledge of U.S. history and geography, and a great personality. Mandatory training for tour managers begins mid-March with a tour manager training school. (A fee is charged, although it is reimbursed after four successful tours.) Drivers can be trained at any time to receive their Class B Commercial driver's license, free of charge. This particular office runs North American tours only and legal U.S. working status is required.

Getting In: Contiki accepts applications beginning in November. Interviews are generally conducted mid-January through March.

DELTA QUEEN STEAMBOAT COMPANY

Steamboat • Louisiana • Year-Round
www.deltaqueen.com/hr/hrintro.html

Seasonal Employment Director
Robin Street Wharf
1380 Port of New Orleans Place
New Orleans, LA 70130-1890
(800) 215-0805 • (504) 586-0631

THE DELTA QUEEN STEAMBOAT COMPANY, America's oldest passenger cruise line, was founded in 1890. Where once thousands of passenger steamboats—known as floating palaces—plied the nation's heartland rivers, today there are just three left, including the legendary Delta Queen, the magnificent Mississippi Queen, and the grand American Queen.

The Experience: Remember, steamboating's not an easy life, but it sure can be rewarding. Opportunities include food and beverage (from sous chefs to bartenders), housekeeping, porters, engineers, carpenters, mates, front desk coordinators, gift shop clerks, human resources coordinator, hotel management, concierge, entertainers, and band members.

Commitment: Steamboat's vessels operate year-round; thus they do not hire just for summer or seasonal employment. Steamboaters are not required to sign contracts, like many other cruise lines do. You start as a full-time staff member; they just request that you provide a two-week notice before you leave, to be eligible for rehire. Crew members work an average of twelve to fourteen hours per day for approximately forty-two days straight, but then have two weeks off to rest and relax.

Perks: All crew members are paid a daily wage, and some positions have added gratuities. Crew members will become a dues-paying member of the Seafarers International Union, and will receive benefits such as medical insurance through the union. In addition, room and board are provided, as well as a majority of transportation expenses (including airfare) to and from the steamboats. All three boats have washer and dryer facilities, a crew dining room, and crew lounges. A variety of social and sporting activities are planned for crew members, either onboard the steamboat or in ports along the rivers.

Ideal Candidate: Candidates must be U.S. citizens or hold a green card, be at least eighteen years old, have the stamina to work long hours, and be friendly and outgoing.

Cycling

OPEN YOURSELF UP TO THE POSSIBILITIES

It's those who take the risk and make that "left-hand turn in the road" who get the most from life.

—MICHAEL WILLIAMS

Michael and Dorrie Williams were living the "American Dream"—well-paying corporate jobs, benefits, a beautiful two-story home, security, and all the possessions that a lifestyle like this can bring. Yet, there was a downside to the world the Williams's created for themselves. They were married to their jobs, Uncle Sam was taking most of their loot, and another snow-filled winter in Philadelphia wasn't helping their mental state. All they could think of was a week's vacation that would recharge their batteries.

However, their plan for a one-week vacation soon turned into two weeks, which kept escalating the more they talked about it. "We got to thinking. Why are we living this sort of lifestyle? What were we really working toward? What would we do if we put all our respon-

sibilities aside?" Finally, it was an overnight decision. An overwhelming realization consumed them. Now was the time for them to walk away from the things that society dictated as being the right things to do. Their decision? To adventure around the United States on their bikes for not a week or two—but a whole year.

That night they talked about their trip. The next morning they worked out the details. Just like that. They soon broke the news of the new direction in their life to co-workers, family, and friends. At the same time, they started sifting through the material possessions in their home, soon to be peddled off and turned into funds for their trip. "It was the biggest garage sale we ever had. We sold everything except for the things that meant the world to us (and a couple bikes)."

What about security? What about money? What about the future? "That's why a lot of people don't want to make a change. They're scared about starting over, that they're not going to find a job again." Quite the contrary for Michael and Dorrie—"There will always

Michael and Dorrie Williams conquer the top of their third pass across the perilous Rockies on their bike adventure across America.

You can be anything you want to be, do anything you set out to accomplish if you hold to that desire with singleness of purpose. —ABE LINCOLN

be jobs out there. If you want something bad enough, you'll get it eventually."

And the adventure began! They hopped on their bikes and took off across America—from the hills of Kentucky, through the flatlands of the Midwest (milking a few cows along the way), across the perilous Rockies (conquering the tops of three mountain passes), all the way to the Pacific Ocean. To help them on their 3,700-mile journey, they used maps and guides purchased through Adventure Cycling (see below), which provided information on hostels, campgrounds, bike shops, where to get food, and distances between landmarks on the Trans-America Bike Trail.

The trip wasn't about covering a certain distance each day for the Williamses. Their philosophy: open yourself up to the experience and other people, and let anything happen; then deal with it, learn from it, and experience it as it comes to you. "We knew nothing about what to expect, and that's why we had such a great time. Without setting up a structure or any restrictions, you won't set yourself up for a letdown.

Some days we rode just a few miles because we loved where we were or the company we were with." The key—the more risk they took, the more they opened themselves up to new adventures.

What do you do when you finish a cycling adventure like this? Michael and Dorrie found themselves back in the small college town where they first met and created jobs that resonate with the simple things that are most important to them. Their trappings are fewer, and they live on less; but they live more happily and at a better pace. "It's nice to plant some roots, have a circle of friends, and balance adventure with the grounding we've created."

It's amazing how much more mental a long journey on a bicycle is than physical! It can be a group journey, but there is plenty of time on one's own, pedaling away. There's a lot of time to think and grow and look into yourself.

—SARAH WAGONER

The Adventure Cycling Association is America's largest nonprofit recreational bicycling organization. Since 1973 they have been helping their members use their bicycles for adventure, exploration, and discovery. They publish detailed bike maps for over 21,000 miles of scenic backroads and trails in the United States, which allow you to travel cross-country without ever seeing an interstate highway. The maps include information on bicycling conditions, local history, and services that cyclists need (such as location of bike shops, campgrounds, motels, and grocery stores). Membership (for $30 per year) provides discounts on all sorts of resources, including *Adventure Cyclist*, their member-only magazine, and *The Cyclist's Yellow Pages*, their annual guide to bicycle maps, books, routes, and organizations. Adventure Cycling Association, P.O. Box 8308, Missoula, MT 59807-8308; (406) 721-1776, (406) 721-8754 (fax), acabike@adv-cycling.org, www.adv-cycling.org

CYCLING

Cycling Adventures . . . .

are you thinking about creating your own cycling adventure? Not only can you pedal anywhere in the world, you might also consider leading others on a cycling trip by working seasonally for a bike adventure organization. Here's a handful of programs based in the United States that offer riding adventures and other work opportunities that will take you to all corners of the earth:

Backroads

Active Travel • Worldwide • April–October
www.backroads.com

Maribeth Hutson, Leader Applications–BDG
801 Cedar St.
Berkeley, CA 94710-1800
(800) 462-2848 • (510) 527-1889 • (510) 527-1789 (fax)
humanresources@backroads.com

BACKROADS offers more than 150 different types of "active-travel" vacations, including bicycling, walking, hiking, and multisport journeys in more than eighty-five destinations around the world. Traveling actively means traveling under your own power and at your own pace—not watching the world go by from behind the window of a car or tour bus. It means getting out there by foot, bicycle, water or ski—seeing, touching, feeling, and experiencing. It means trying out the native greetings, meeting the locals, making new friends, and having a whole lot of fun.

The Experience: As a leader, you're the catalyst for a fun, interesting, safe, and personally rewarding experience for your guests. This means being able to think on your feet and display total confidence when unusual situations arise. It also means displaying infinite compassion and patience at all times, and maintaining a positive attitude and sense of humor. You'll become involved in every aspect of the adventure, ensuring that all equipment is in optimal working condition; buying and preparing food; delivering luggage at each night's accommodations; acting as a representative at hotels, restaurants, campgrounds, and with the general public; and keeping accurate financial records and complete written reports.

Perks: First-year leaders receive $55 per day for hotel trips and $73 per day for camping trips, plus gourmet meals, accommodations in some of the best inns or campgrounds the region has to offer, and transportation costs. The pay scale and benefits increase in recognition of each year's experience. Backroads requests that you be at least a tem-porary resident of the Bay Area during the trip-leading season. All leaders are flown to and from trips out of either San Francisco or Oakland airports. If you are not living in the area, you are responsible for getting yourself to the Bay Area prior to your flight. All leaders are expected to attend events at Backroads' Berkeley headquarters to launch the summer season in April and celebrate its end in October.

Ideal Candidate: The staff is composed of high-energy individuals with varied backgrounds who enjoy people, travel, and the outdoors. To become a leader, candidates must be a minimum of twenty-one years of age, have a valid driver's license, and an excellent driving record. The ideal candidate is a master problem solver, effective public speaker, chef, area expert, translator (on trips to Europe), skilled driver, meticulous record keeper, a motivating force in group dynamics while being sensitive to individual needs, and in great physical shape. Foreign applicants must be citizens of the European Community.

Getting In: Write to request a detailed application packet or call the Backroads Job Hotline at (510) 527-1889, extension 560, for voice-recorded information twenty-four hours a day. Leader applications are evaluated starting in January with interviews conducted from February through April. The application deadline is April 1; however, it is to your advantage to submit your application as early as possible.

Bike–Aid

Cycling • USA • 2 Months
www.bikeaid.org

Laura McNeill, Program Director
Just Act—Youth Action for Global Justice
333 Valencia St., Suite 330
San Francisco, CA 94103-3547
(800) 743-3808 • (415) 431-4480 • (415) 431-5953 (fax)
laura@justact.org

BIKE–AID is a vibrant, innovative program that coordinates an annual cross-country cycling adventure sponsored by Just Act. With departures from Portland, San Francisco, and Seattle beginning in mid-June, eighty-five individuals from around the world will cycle to Washington, DC, over a two-month period. The adventure combines both physical challenge, community interaction, education, leadership, fund-raising, and community service in the empowering experience of a lifetime. Cyclists will raise $1 for every mile ridden, totaling $3,600 (and Bike–Aid will provide an endless source of creative ideas to help with your efforts). Three scholarships are also offered for those who are able to spend time organizing the ride during the spring prior to participation. Overnight lodging is donated

Choose a job you love and you will never have to work a day in your life. —CONFUCIUS

CYCLING

by community organizations, schools, and individuals, and will include some camping. Beginners to prize-winning racers have participated in Bike–Aid, and riders from the ages of sixteen to sixty have met the challenge. It is not a race, and it encourages the participation of people from all backgrounds, ages, and abilities. Cyclists are advised to apply by March 31 to save on registration fees.

Bike–Aid satisfied my quest for community. My interests lay in the cause—promoting environmental solutions—rather than in the physical challenge of the ride itself. To me, the group dynamics were more of a challenge than the actual pedaling. Each of us is part of the solution: it takes too much wasted energy to blame others for things that don't work right in our world. —Alona Jasik, participant

Bikes Not Bombs

Alternative Transportation • Massachusetts
• Year-Round
www.igc.org/bikesnotbombs

Outreach Coordinator
59 Amory St., Suite 103
Roxbury, MA 02119
(617) 442-0004 • (617) 445-2439 (fax)
bnbrox@igc.org

BIKES NOT BOMBS is a nonprofit organization working for alternative transportation and community development. The group operates the Bicycle Recycling and Youth Training Center near Boston and promotes environmental education, meaningful employment, and safe sustainable communities in places as far as the Dominican Republic, Haiti, and Nicaragua. Thousands of bicycles and tons (literally!) of bicycle parts and tools have been sent overseas to help groups do everything from start a small cargo bike manufacturing facility to cooperatively run a bike shop and training center. Volunteers—including experienced, bilingual mechanics, administrative and outreach interns, and fieldwork organizers for international efforts—are needed to fill a variety of roles in Massachusetts. Send a cover letter and resume.

The Biking Expedition

Cycling • USA • Summer
www.bikingx.com

Brent Bell, Program Director
P.O. Box 547
Henniker, NH 03242
(800) 245-4649 • (603) 428-7500 • (603) 428-3414 (fax)
brent@bikingx.com

THE BIKING EXPEDITION provides mountain bike and road tours through the United States and Canada for students, ages eleven to eighteen. More than just a travel organization, they seek to build community, heighten self-esteem, and foster independence, while having tons of fun playing in the outdoors. Each summer they hire bike trip leaders and interns. Leaders receive $238 per week while on a trip (veteran leaders receive $350 per week while on a trip, plus bonuses and trip preference) and interns work on a volunteer basis. All receive complimentary room, board, and travel to the best road-biking and mountain-biking areas in North America. You must be at least twenty-one years of age (the staff average is twenty-six), Wilderness First Responder certified, and it's preferred you have a history of working for reputable outdoor education programs.

Photo Credit: Lauren Hefferon

Bicycle leaders with Cisclismo Classico engage participants in Italy's hidden treasures.

Ciclismo Classico

Cycling • Italy • April–October
www.ciclismoclassico.com

Lauren Hefferon, Director and Founder
13 Marathon St.
Arlington, MA 02174
(800) 866-7314 • (781) 646-3377 • (781) 641-1512 (fax)
lauren@ciclismoclassico.com

EXPERIENCE ITALY'S hidden treasures, by pedaling, walking, or skiing with Ciclismo Classico. These cultural adventures offer educational and dreamy itineraries that celebrate the Italian landscape, art, language, music, folklore, and its beloved cuisine. As cultural liaisons, bicycling and walking leaders take small groups on nine- to fifteen-day tours from April through October. Leaders engage participants in musical evenings, Italian lessons, wine tastings, cooking demonstrations, and other authentic experiences with their extensive network of Italian friends and families. Applicants must be at least twenty-three years of age, fluent in Italian, and have travel and group leader experience, bike mechanic skills, and boundless energy. Benefits include all trip expenses, along with a $400 (and up) per week salary plus bonuses and tips. Call or e-mail for an application packet.

International Bicycle Fund
Bicycle Advocacy • Washington • Year-Round
www.ibike.org

David Mozer, Director
4887 Columbia Dr., South
Seattle, WA 98108-1919
(206) 767-0848
ibike@ibike.org

THE INTERNATIONAL BICYCLE FUND is dedicated to promoting sustainable transport and international understanding. Major areas of activity are nonmotorized urban planning, economic development, bike safety education, responsible travel and cycle tourism, and cross-cultural, educational bicycle programs. Their cross-cultural bicycle tours provide an opportunity for Westerners to learn more about Africa and Cuba at a person-to-person level not usually available to tourists. Itineraries highlight the cultural, historical, economic, and physical diversity of the area. Tours are generally two and four weeks long, and costs range from $900 to $1,290, not including airfare. Unpaid internships are also available at their office in Washington, with a majority of the work focused on grant writing, fund-raising, administration, and supporting bicycle advocacy organizations around the world. Call for the free newsletter, IBF News (or view it at their web site: www.ibike.org/ibfnews.htm), which includes information on grassroots cycling programs all over the world.

> Life is like riding a bicycle, you don't fall off unless you stop pedaling.
> — CLAUDE PEPPER

Student Hosteling Program
Cycling • USA/Canada/Europe • Summer
www.biketrips.com

Ted Lefkowitz, Program Director
1356 Ashfield Rd.
P.O. Box 419
Conway, MA 01341
(800) 343-6132 • (413) 369-4275 (phone/fax)
shpbike@aol.com

SINCE 1969, the Student Hosteling Program (SHP) has been offering one- to nine-week teenage bicycle touring trips through the countrysides and cultural centers of the United States, Canada, and Europe. SHP trips provide adventure, fun, outdoor education, and the opportunity for emotional growth, while providing one of the safest and most wholesome youth environments available. Their groups are small, usually eight to twelve trippers and two to three leaders, making possible a close and rewarding group experience. SHP groups travel by bicycle, at their own pace and close to the land, using public and private transportation when necessary. Groups live simply, using campsites, hostels, and other modest facilities. In the countryside, groups buy food at local markets and cook their own meals.

The Experience: Senior leaders and assistant leaders conduct bicycling tours for students, grades seven through twelve. Prior to becoming a leader, participants will complete a five-day training course to find out which age groups and types of trips are a good fit. From there, leaders receive further training for their particular trip during a four-day preparation and orientation period just before their trip departure date. Leaders are known to be firm in matters of safety, respect for others, and the SHP rule structure, and also have the warmth, the humor, and the enthusiasm to provide a rewarding group experience.

Commitment: The minimum leadership time commitment is four weeks. Employment begins in late June for part or all of the summer.

Perks: Senior leaders earn $728 to $1,932 depending upon the length of the work period; assistant leaders wages range from $520 to $1,380. In addition, all trip-related expenses are paid.

Ideal Candidate: Senior leaders must be at least twenty-one years of age (the average is about twenty-five) and are typically teachers, graduate students, and college seniors. Assistants must be at least eighteen years old and are usually college sophomores and juniors. Many are former SHP trip participants. All leaders must hold a valid Red Cross first aid certificate and many have advanced first aid training as well. Most importantly, the leader's personality is the most critical element in making a trip work.

Getting In: After a lengthy screening process, leaders are selected to complete one of the five-day training courses in Massachusetts before being assigned a trip.

> Life is a series of hills . . . know when to shift.
> — ADRIAN MACDONALD (AFTER PEDALING 1,150 MILES ON HER BICYCLE)

CYCLING

DENALI RAFT ADVENTURES

River Outfitter • Alaska • May–September
www.denaliraft.com

Jim and Val Raisis, Directors
Drawer 190
Denali Park, AK 99755
(888) 683-2234 • (907) 683-2234 • (907) 683-1281 (fax)
denraft@mtaonline.net

DENALI RAFT ADVENTURES offers two- and four-hour, full-day, and overnight raft trips on the Nenana River, which forms the eastern border of Denali National Park. The season runs from mid-May through mid-September, and seasonal staff work as reservations clerks, bus drivers, and river guides. Dormitory-style rooms cost $60 per month, and everyone gets a roommate.

EPLEY'S WHITEWATER ADVENTURES

River Outfitter • Idaho • Summer

Ted Epley, Owner/Operator
P.O. Box 987
McCall, ID 83638
(800) 233-1813 • (208) 634-5173

LEADING GREAT ADVENTURES since 1962, Epley's provides half- to five-day river float trips on the lower Salmon River. In addition to leading float trips, guides also get involved with maintenance of equipment, buildings, and grounds; food preparation; and kitchen cleanup. The all-expense-paid training period begins June 1. Upon proper certification, Epley's will obtain a guide license for guides at a cost of $105. Guides then work a six-day workweek and finish up about August 31. Beginning pay starts at $700 per month, plus room and board, free laundry service, and medical benefits. Guides live in group quarters with a bathroom, beds, refrigerator, and living room. They also have a VCR, trampoline, and a basketball hoop for after-work entertainment. Candidates must be at least eighteen years of age; completed applications must be turned in by February 1.

We are looking for guides who have high morals, a willing-to-learn attitude, who work well with people, and don't drink alcohol or smoke.

FOUR CORNERS RAFTING

River Outfitter • Colorado • Summer
www.fourcornersrafting.com/employment.htm

Karen and Reed Dils, Owners
P.O. Box 569
Buena Vista, CO 81211-1032
(800) 332-7238 • (719) 395-8949 • (719) 395-8949 (fax)
dils@csn.net

COLORADO'S ARKANSAS RIVER is home to the most popular mild to wild raft trips in the country. Since 1976, Four Corners has been operating white-water rafting and float-fishing trips. Guides run mostly half- and one-day trips on various stretches of the Arkansas River (primarily class three and some class four and five white-water), teaching paddlers about the local history, geology, plants, and animals.

Commitment: Applicants must be able to start guide training in mid-May, followed by additional training on a local river until competent. Some guides are ready in late May; most, the first week of June.

Perks: First-season guides can expect $1,800 to $2,000, plus $400 to $800 in tips (more for experienced guides). Benefits include use of equipment on days off, discounts on river gear and clothing, and for extended river trips, the opportunity to learn to kayak. Housing can be difficult to find, although they keep an eye out for you. Four Corners leases campsites or spaces in large, lockable tents for $50 to $150 per month.

Ideal Candidate: Applicants must be at least eighteen, have first aid and CPR certification, and be comfortable in water, a good swimmer, personable, well groomed, and able to work in hot, wet, or cold weather. Any river training or experience you can get on your own or in other guide schools, a higher level first aid certification, and ability to stay past mid-August help. Most of their guides are educators, college students or graduates, or ski personnel.

Getting In: Call for application materials or visit their web site. After a screening process and reference check, selected candidates are invited for their training trip (usually six days on the Dolores River in southwestern Colorado). Training is $300, with half refunded if you stay the whole season. Hiring is done after the six-day training trip. There is no guarantee you will be hired if you are selected to go on the training trip.

Get on a river with an outdoor club or check out nearby guide-training schools. Contact us early and do your paperwork correctly and neatly. Be complete and make sure your references have current contact information.

FOUR CORNERS SCHOOL OF OUTDOOR EDUCATION

Adventure Travel • Utah • 3–4 Months
www.sw-adventures.org

Janet Ross, Executive Director
Southwest Ed-Ventures
P.O. Box 1029
Monticello, UT 84535
(800) 525-4456 • (801) 587-2156 • (801) 587-2193 (fax)
fcs@igc.org

••

HERE IN THE RUGGED TERRAIN of the "four corners" where Arizona, Colorado, New Mexico, and Utah meet, participants join Four Corners School of Outdoor Education on unique learning vacations. Programs are by foot, van, and raft, and explore areas such as wilderness advocacy, archaeology, and research with the Bureau of Land Management, National Park Service, and U.S. Forest Service. The school's goal is low-impact adventures with a very healthy dose of education.

The Experience: Internships vary with the season, program content, special projects, and office load. Four Corners School is very conscious about maintaining a balance between office work and field work. Special skills may be put to use, such as public relations, computer programming, painting, and carpentry.

Commitment: Internships generally run in three sessions: March to mid-June, mid-June to mid-August, and mid-August to the end of October.

Perks: A small stipend is provided. Interns are also in the unique position to go on a number of outdoor field programs, which generally last five days. Their programs are so diverse that one week you may be out backpacking, the next on the San Juan River. You'll also have access to their world-class experts.

Ideal Candidate: Applicants must be at least eighteen years of age. No area of interest supersedes another, but some prior knowledge of the outdoors is very helpful.

Getting In: Call for application materials. Send in your completed application by December 15. Phone interviews will be conducted.

We like applicants who are excited about the outdoors and make good ambassadors for the school. Our participants like friendly, knowledgeable people. We all have to work hard, so it helps to have an intern who doesn't mind the work. It doesn't hurt to know about the office environment, as duties will include some office times.

GRAY LINE OF ALASKA

Adventure Travel • Washington/Alaska • Summer
www.graylineofalaska.com

Kari Quaas, Manager of Training
300 Elliott Ave., West
Seattle, WA 98119
(800) 976-3840 • (206) 281-0559 • (206) 281-0621 (fax)
kari_quaas@halw.com

••

ALASKA IS DEFINITELY the last frontier—an outdoor enthusiast's paradise and "playground" for Gray Line of Alaska's motor coach tours. Gray Line is a subsidiary of Holland American Line-Westours, which operates cruise ships, dayboats, Westmark Hotels throughout Alaska and the Yukon, and the McKinley Explorer railcars on the Alaska Railroad (running between Anchorage and Fairbanks through Denali National Park).

The Experience: A motor coach driver/guide doesn't just become a chauffeur—drivers must also learn and develop tour narratives in order to provide an enjoyable vacation experience for customers through informative and entertaining narration. Being in a customer service-oriented position, drivers must be willing to go that "extra mile" to meet the needs of their passengers.

Commitment: Guides must be able to relocate to Washington or Alaska for the thirteen-week training program that starts in early February. After training is complete, guides must be able to commit to a 100-day contract working in Alaska during the summer. Guides average fifty to fifty-five hours per week, with daily work loads varying between six and thirteen hours, depending on the tour assignment.

Perks: During the training period, guides receive minimum wage. First-year drivers generally make $6,000 to $8,000, plus gratuities. Gray Line also has a bonus program in which drivers can earn up to 12 percent of their total wages for the season. Housing varies with each location. All employees receive discounted or "comp" fares for travel on company "products," including McKinley Rail, Gray Line motor coaches, Westmark Hotels, and dayboats, and a free cruise (with guest) of up to fourteen days on a

Holland America Line ship after the completion of a second season.

Ideal Candidate: Guides must be self-confident, have the ability to speak well, present a professional image, and maintain a responsible attitude. All applicants must be twenty-one years of age, with no more than one moving violation on driving records in the last three years. Those who love working with and around people, are able to go with the flow, and have a work hard/play hard mentality will thrive in this program.

Getting In: Submit application materials by the end of January. An audition and interview is required.

GREEN VALLEY RECREATION

Recreation • Arizona • 8 Weeks
www.gvrec.org

Jeff Ziegler, Executive Director
P.O. Box 586
Green Valley, AZ 85622-0586
(602) 625-3440 • (602) 625-2352 (fax)
recreation@gvrec.org

GREEN VALLEY RECREATION is a nonprofit membership organization that operates twelve recreation centers within an active retirement community. The mild winter months, with temperatures averaging in the 70s during the day and above freezing at night, are what bring most visitors to the Green Valley area. Recreation interns assist the recreation department in the implementation of recreation activities, such as special-interest classes, dances, lectures, movies, concerts, parties, and special events like the Senior Olympics. Participants registered in an accredited internship program receive a $3,000 stipend. A commitment of eight weeks is required, with internships available from August through May.

GREENBRIER RIVER OUTDOOR ADVENTURES

Adventure Education • West Virginia • Summer
www.groa.com

Matthew Tate, Program Director
P.O. Box 160
Bartow, WV 24920-0160
(800) 600-4752 • (304) 456-5191 • (304) 456-3121 (fax)
groa@groa.com

GREENBRIER RIVER OUTDOOR ADVENTURES offers a wide variety of programs for young people between the ages of ten and seventeen. Programs are based on the development of self-esteem and leadership through adventure, challenge, and small-group experiences, including community service projects. Everything—playing, cooking, eating, and sleeping—is done outdoors. While not a survival program, a large part of the program is learning how to live comfortably outdoors while taking time to enjoy the experience.

Environment: The base camp is located on a 250-acre site, nestled in the mountains of the Monongahela National Forest, an excellent place for rock climbing, white-water rafting, mountain biking, caving, and backpacking.

The Experience: Summer staff (group leaders and specialists) and interns provide for the general safety and supervision of students, oversee program logistics and itinerary, teach outdoor living skills, and facilitate and develop group dynamics. Staff members participate in a weeklong intensive training session to kick off the summer.

Perks: An hourly wage or stipend is provided along with room and board. Pro deals are also available on outdoor clothing and equipment.

Ideal Candidate: Applicants must be at least nineteen years old and have certificates in CPR, first aid, and water safety. A sincere interest in working with youth in the outdoors, experience in the field, and competency in outdoor living are traits found in their staff.

Getting In: Send resume and cover letter requesting application.

GUIDED DISCOVERIES

Marine Science • California • Summer
www.guideddiscoveries.org

Ross Turner, Executive Director
343 N. Harvard
P.O. Box 1360
Claremont, CA 91711
(800) 645-1423 • (909) 625-6194 • (909) 625-7305 (fax)

FOUNDED IN 1978, Guided Discoveries is a nonprofit outdoor educational organization providing hands-on science learning experiences for public and private schools. The programs are based on discovery. They hope to make a difference in the lives of children by guiding them through unique opportunities of discovery in a fun and adventurous atmosphere. They take an environmentally conscious approach to operating their facilities and present this philosophy to the students who participate in the programs.

Environment: During the summer, the program is offered at the Catalina Island Marine Institute (CIMI) at Toyon Bay on Santa Catalina Island (teaching marine science and island ecology) and at the Astrocamp, located in the San Jacinto Mountains near Idyllwild (teaching astronomy and space technology).

The Experience: Marine Science Instructors are provided with a fun and challenging opportunity to teach eight- to seventeen-year-olds about marine science and island ecology curriculum. Instructors are responsible for implementing an active, hands-on, experientially oriented program including snorkeling, marine labs, hiking, kayaking, sailing, and a variety of evening programs. This is a high-energy program where instructors spend their days working and teaching in a unique environment. Other seasonal opportunities include summer counselors, scuba (NAUI instructors and divemasters) staff, and sail staff.

Commitment: Dates start in early June and continue through August. Transitioning into their year-round program in the fall is a possibility (as working many seasons seem to be contagious here with staff!).

Perks: All staff receive a weekly salary, plus room and board. Scuba instructors start at $1,750 (for a ten-week period), and also receive liability insurance and NAUI Scuba Liability Insurance for one year. Over the years, many employees have left their mark upon their programs through ideas and insights that improved the quality of instruction, food, facilities, and administration.

Ideal Candidate: A bachelor's degree in marine biology, biology, or related science. Excellent water skills, current certification in lifeguard training, first aid, and CPR are required at the start of the contracted period (although training may be conducted on-site). Teaching experience with youth, flexibility, and the ability to work with others as a team and to live in a rural setting are desired.

Getting In: Send cover letter, resume (references from former supervisors helpful), and copies of current certifications, credentials, and degrees.

> *We look for employees who take pride in their work and are capable of thriving in a residential situation. The work can be hectic and difficult, but it is highly rewarding. Because the mountains and the ocean are such integral parts of the facilities, our employees often bring a love for the outdoors with them, or they quickly develop one.*

HENRY CROWN SPORTS PAVILION

Health & Fitness • Illinois • 12–15 Weeks
www.nwu.edu/fitness-recreation

Nancy Tierney, Fitness/Wellness Director
Northwestern University
2379 N. Campus Dr.
Evanston, IL 60208-3600
(847) 491-4833 • (847) 467-1405 (fax)
n-tierney@nwu.edu

THE HENRY CROWN SPORTS PAVILION and Norris Aquatic Center is one of the most comprehensive health/fitness facilities in the nation. The center is uniquely designed to take advantage of its prime location on beautiful Lake Michigan. The east end of the jogging track has a glass rotunda that enables walkers and joggers to view the lake while getting fit. The second floor, containing the fitness/conditioning equipment and lounge area, has glass windows that allow one to view the beautiful beachfront area. Fitness/wellness internships offer extensively structured, hands-on, and professional experience in all areas of the center. Whether an intern's interest is fitness, nutrition, or working with elite athletes, the internship experience is designed to emphasize their career goals. Internships traditionally involve a twelve- to fifteen-week commitment, and a stipend of $25 to $100 is provided depending on experience and national certification status. Additional opportunities exist to earn extra income through personal training and group fitness classes. Call or e-mail for application materials.

HIOBS—SOUTHERN LANDS PROGRAMS

Wilderness Education • Florida • 3 Months

Alyse Ostreicher, Staff Developer/Recruiter
Adolescent Instructor Practicum
177 Salem Ct.
Tallahassee, FL 32301
(850) 414-8816 • (850) 922-6721 (fax)
AlyseO@aol.com

THE HURRICANE ISLAND Outward Bound School's (HIOBS) Southern Land Programs offers the Outward Bound experience and philosophy to both delinquent and at-risk youth throughout Florida. In 1994, the U.S. Department of Justice reported HIOBS as one of the top five most successful programs in the nation. The program serves over one thousand youths per year and is a leader in community service.

The Experience: The Southern Land Programs has seven programs located throughout Florida, with each program teaching the four pillars of Outward Bound (self-reliance, craftsmanship, physical fitness, and compassion) to young adults between the ages of twelve and eighteen. Programs are either exclusively wilderness based or a combination of wilderness and residential programming. Courses range from 10 to 180 days, and all programs work with teams of instructors and teachers. The internship experience includes a ten-day orientation/expedition along with 2½ months of experiential work in two program areas. Interns will receive lots of draining, exhausting, feel-good work, which is their training ground for wilderness instructors.

Perks: There is a cost of $250 per participant for the orientation, which includes all food and lodging for ten days. During the internship, a daily stipend of $15, food, lodging, and travel between bases is provided. Interns also have access to HIOBS staff trainings and pro-deal purchases.

Ideal Candidate: At the minimum, applicants must be at least twenty-one years of age and have current CPR and first aid certification. Preference is given to those who have participated in an Outward Bound course as a student, experience working with teenagers, and have an enthusiasm and interest to impact young adults.

HULBERT OUTDOOR CENTER

Experiential Education • Vermont • Year-Round
www.alohafoundation.org

Meredyth Morley, Wilderness Trips Director
The Aloha Foundation
2968 Lake Morey Rd.
Fairlee, VT 05045-9400
(888) 333-3405 • (802) 333-3405 • (802) 333-3404 (fax)
ellen_bagley@alohafoundation.org

ESTABLISHED IN 1978, the Hulbert Outdoor Center is a nonprofit educational institution that serves six thousand participants annually through programs designed to foster personal growth, self-reliance, cooperation, confidence, and a sense of community in people of all ages. Year-round programs range from school programs, wilderness trips, Elderhostel experiences, and a unique leadership training program that includes certifications in everything from Wilderness First Responder and Backcountry Search and Rescue to lifeguard training and the ACA Canoe Instructor's Course (which are available to staff members!).

Environment: The Center is located in Vermont's Upper Connecticut River Valley on the shores of Lake Morey,

surrounded by over five hundred acres of young forests, bluffs, and rolling countryside. Recreation opportunities include miles of mountain biking, hiking, backcountry skiing, and access to developed ski areas and water sports.

The Experience: Hulbert provides unique opportunities that combine elements of wilderness travel, outdoor skill development, teamwork, sensitivity to the environment, and personal growth experiences. The prime responsibility of school program staff is to work with middle-school-aged children in programs emphasizing team building, ropes course, natural history, and other curriculum areas. Trip leaders lead extended wilderness experiences for groups of eight to ten participants.

Commitment: Programs are offered year-round, and staff typically work between the hours of 7 a.m. and 9 p.m.

Perks: Dependent upon experience, wages begin at $160 per week, along with room, board, and training. Trip staff are contracted per trip.

Ideal Candidate: Applicants must be at least twenty-one years of age and have a bachelor's degree, certification in first aid and CPR (WFR or higher preferred), a valid driver's license, the ability to work long hours in the outdoors, and a demonstrated experience teaching (preferably in the experiential education field).

Getting In: Send a cover letter and resume. An application packet will be mailed upon receipt.

> *The staff at Hulbert form a unique community of educators that values dedication, creative problem solving, and hard work. In the course of our work, we put in long hours and fill diverse roles. Throughout, in work and in the residential environment, we strive to create and to maintain a positive sense of community.*

INTERLOCKEN INTERNATIONAL

Adventure Travel • Worldwide • 3–9 Weeks
www.interlocken.org

Bri Solomon, Staffing Manager
RR 2, Box 165
Hillsboro, NH 03244
(603) 478-3166 • (603) 478-5260 (fax)
bri@interlocken.org

SINCE 1961, more than ten thousand young people have explored the world Interlocken-style. Whether participants join the residential summer camp in New Hampshire or a travel or community service program throughout the world, Interlocken campers and students

"learn by doing." They enrich their lives with lasting friendships, new skills, self-discoveries, and increased environmental and cultural awareness.

The Experience: The International Summer Camp is a creative community of 160 boys and girls (ages nine to fifteen) and 60 staff members from all over the world. Counselor opportunities abound at Interlocken—from outdoor adventures, wilderness activities, and sports to the visual arts, theatre, and environmental studies. Travel leaders take to the road with small groups of twelve to sixteen students and explore new and unusual environments, learn new skills, and challenge themselves physically and intellectually. Leaders are needed for the following areas: performing arts (traveling theatre in New England and Europe), wilderness adventure, cycling, environmental studies, and leadership training.

Commitment: Camp counselors must make a nine-week commitment beginning in mid-June; travel leaders can opt for either the three- or six-week program.

Perks: Camp positions start at $1,200 for the summer; travel leader wages start at $200 per week. All staff members receive room, board, and extensive training.

Ideal Candidate: Summer camp applicants must be at least twenty years of age and have finished one year of college as well as have experience teaching children and expertise in one of the many activities Interlocken provides. Travel leader applicants must be at least twenty-four years of age, with expertise in teaching theatre, visual arts, outdoor adventure, language (French or Spanish), or environmental education, along with the ability to work with small groups of teenagers.

Getting In: Send cover letter and resume requesting staff application packet. It's best to apply by January.

INTERNATIONAL FIELD STUDIES

Sailing Adventure • The Bahamas • 1 Year
www.intlfieldstudies.com

Dr. Walter Bohl, Executive Director
709 College Ave.
Columbus, OH 43209
(800) 962-3805 • (614) 235-4646 • (614) 235-9744 (fax)
ifs@infinet.com

INTERNATIONAL FIELD STUDIES (IFS) is a nonprofit organization that operates Forfar Field Station and a Sailing Program on Andros Island in the Bahamas (a place where the world's third longest barrier reef can be found).

The Experience: Seasonal staff at the field station educate and lead high school- and college-age groups in natural science activities, including diving and snorkeling, along with doubling as general factotums. As a captain or first mate in their sailing program, staff live on the boat (and are responsible for maintaining it), as well as running trips and sailing. Classes are also offered to help prepare sailors for the captain's exam.

Commitment: A one-year commitment is required.

Perks: Benefits include a monthly stipend that ranges from $200 to $800, along with meals, rustic housing on the beach or on board sailboats, travel between Florida and the Bahamas, educational courses, permits, training, licenses in scuba and outboards, four weeks' paid vacation, and two free one-week trips to the station for family members.

Ideal Candidate: Applicants must be able to withstand bugs, heat, and the lack of a U.S.-style civilization. Especially needed are applicants who are great with people from all walks of life, hardworking, eager to learn, self-motivated, positive, patient, and flexible. Mechanical aptitude and a knowledge and love of nature are also highly desirable.

Getting In: Send a resume and letter of intent; wait a week, then call Dr. Bohl. Selected applicants will be scheduled for an interview week in the Bahamas. The only way IFS can get serious applicants is to charge $495 for the interview week (which will be reimbursed after a year of service).

LONGACRE EXPEDITIONS

Adventure Travel • Worldwide • Summer
www.longacreexpeditions.com

Meredith Schuler, Program Director
RD 3, Box 106
Newport, PA 17074
(800) 433-0127 • (717) 567-6790 • (717) 567-3955 (fax)
longacre@longacreexpeditions.com

EACH SUMMER LONGACRE EXPEDITIONS leaders and groups of ten to sixteen teenagers bicycle, backpack, rock climb, kayak, mountaineer, white-water raft, snowboard, snorkel, scuba dive, explore caves, and canoe across miles of the most beautiful territory in North and Central America as well as Iceland. Trips focus on group living, wilderness skills, cooperation, independence, and fun.

The Experience: Trip leaders and assistants coordinate different trips that emphasize different ability levels—from basic "kid" trips to challenging courses for teenagers. Besides leadership positions, there are other jobs that are just as essential, including base camp cook, kitchen assis-

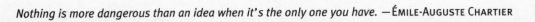

tant, nurses, and various specialists. All staffers are required to attend an eight- to nine-day staff training period, which begins around June 15.

Commitment: Seasonal staff have various work schedules to choose from, including leading a trip for four weeks, then acting as support staff for two to five additional weeks; working a two- to six-week trip; or arriving a few weeks early to help open the base camp before staff week, as well as scouting new routes and campsites.

Perks: Adventure leaders are paid $46 on up per day; base camp staff is paid $1,050 to $2,500 depending on position; and staffers who hold current certificates in EMT or WEMT are compensated an additional $100. There is no compensation for the staff training period; however, room and board are supplied. Perks include pro-deal purchases with outdoor manufacturers.

Ideal Candidate: Applicants must be twenty-one years of age, have a good driving record, and have certification in first aid, a water safety course, and CPR. Common traits include ability to communicate and be comfortable with teenagers, competence in a variety of outdoor activities, great physical condition, the ability to embrace Longacre's

trip-leading philosophy, and commitment to the group. Staffers come from all over the country and are often graduate students or college juniors/seniors who have taken a few years off to take a job or tour the world. Others are teachers who see the summer as an opportunity to be with kids in a non-classroom setting. Still others join Longacre each year, coming from seasonal positions at ski resorts, environmental centers, and other wilderness programs.

Getting In: Applications must be received by June 15. A personal interview is highly recommended.

NATIONAL OUTDOOR LEADERSHIP SCHOOL

Wilderness Adventures • Worldwide • 1–3 Months
www.nols.edu

Bruce Palmer, Director of Admissions and Marketing
288 Main St.
Lander, WY 82520
(307) 332-5300 • (307) 332-1220 (fax)
admissions@nols.edu

NUANAARPUQ

How often do you find yourself taking extravagant pleasure in being alive? As we hike over the crest of a snowy ridge in the heart of the vast wilderness, the world seemingly unfolds in front of us. At once, we can embrace endless miles of ridges, peaks, and valleys. An inner joy bubbles up within each of us. Overtaken with the beauty of the moment, one of us spontaneously shouts out, "Nuanaarpuq!"

Is it possible to express the feelings of such special moments in words? We used to be skeptical, feeling that the joy of the moment alone would suffice. That was until we learned of "Nuanaarpuq," the Alaskan Inuit expression. Those who live by this expression live with a deep respect for the natural world and have learned to appreciate and celebrate all the wonders of nature. It is expressed with both reverence and pleasure.

Are you aware of such moments of extravagant pleasure? Do you share this with others? Nuanaarpuq is about awareness, about finding and celebrating beauty in the simple things in life. It is the key word for opening up eyes and creating an excitement for life. It is a way to express our celebration of the present moment and for expressing deep joy.

Begin making this newfound awareness a daily part of your life and extend your joy to others. After all, excitement for life is contagious.

—Contributed by Christian Bisson and Julie Gabert, who work as outdoor educators at Hollins College in Virginia during the academic year and teach seasonally for the National Outdoor Leadership School in Wyoming. Through these experiences, they find many moments of Nuanaarpuq!

NOLS IS AN EDUCATIONAL ORGANIZATION with its roots in extended wilderness expeditions—believing that long stays in wild places are vital to understanding both the natural world and ourselves. Courses take students away from the distractions of civilization and into the mountains, deserts, and oceans to learn the skills they need to run their own expeditions. NOLS graduates are leaders who have an understanding of environmental ethics, a sense of teamwork, an appreciation of natural history, and overall competence and good judgment.

Environment: NOLS operates nine branch schools, including Alaska, the Pacific Northwest, Rocky Mountains, the Southwest, Teton Valley, and the Yukon in North America, as well as in Kenya, Patagonia (Chile), and Mexico.

The Experience: Most folks select their NOLS course by either concentrating on location or skills. Terrain, weather, expedition length, and specialized skills vary, but every course includes a core curriculum emphasizing leadership through the development of judgment and decision-making skills. Your choice will depend on your interests, experience, and time constraints. Course types include mountaineering, wilderness backpacking, ocean (sea kayaking and sailing), river (kayaking, rafting, and canoeing), winter (backcountry skiing and dogsledding), semester (a variety of skills over three months), outdoor educators (for practicing or potential outdoor educators), and shorter courses for people twenty-five years and older.

Commitment: Most courses run thirty days; however, there are ten-day courses and ninety-day semester courses.

Perks: Fees range from $750 to $8,300 depending on the location and the length of the educational expedition.

Ideal Candidate: Successful students come willing to learn and develop leadership skills and wilderness ethics. Prior outdoor experience is not a prerequisite for most NOLS courses, although being in good shape, a positive attitude, and the desire to learn wilderness skills in locations of incredible beauty are musts.

OFFSHORE SAILING SCHOOL

Sailing • USA • Year-Round
www.offshore-sailing.com

Kirk Williams, Director
16731 McGregor Blvd.
Fort Myers, FL 33908
(800) 221-4326 • (941) 454-1700 • (941) 454-1191 (fax)
sail@offshore-sailing.com

⋯⋯⋯⋯⋯⋯⋯⋯⋯⋯⋯⋯⋯⋯⋯⋯

IF YOU'RE ON A STARBOARD TACK and the wind veers, will you get lifted or headed? You'll learn the answer to this question, plus much more, by enrolling in Offshore's Learn to Sail Program. This program offers some invaluable experiences and unexpected lessons on the ABCs of sailing. When you finish this course, you should be able to day sail a sailboat of up to thirty feet without an instructor or paid skipper. The curriculum is based on seeing it, hearing it, and then going out and doing it. School locations include New Jersey, Connecticut, Rhode Island, Florida, Illinois, and Tortola in the Caribbean.

OUTDOOR ADVENTURE RIVER SPECIALISTS

River Outfitter • California • Year-Round
www.oars.com

Russell Walters, Director
P.O. Box 67
Angels Camp, CA 95222
(800) 346-6277 • (209) 736-4677 • (209) 736-2902 (fax)
russell@oars.com

⋯⋯⋯⋯⋯⋯⋯⋯⋯⋯⋯⋯⋯⋯⋯⋯

OUTDOOR ADVENTURE RIVER SPECIALISTS, commonly known as OARS, has been recognized worldwide as the industry model for river outfitters. They operate river trips on over twenty-five rivers, including Canadian and international waters. Choose the challenge of class five rapids or gentler trips with an "oar" option, meaning the guide does all the rowing while guests sit back and enjoy the ride. Internships are available in marketing, customer service, interpretation, and Internet development. Pay is $200 per week, with basic housing. Free trips are also available during days off.

The Outward Bound Experience

Outward Bound is a growing federation of Outward Bound schools and centers in twenty-six countries. In the United States, five wilderness schools make up the Outward Bound USA system. Since the first U.S. school was established in 1961, over 400,000 people have participated in their programs. Many people who sign up for Outward Bound see the experience as a sabbatical of sorts—a time to get away from the routine, assess their current situation, and set new goals. Well over a million people of all ages and backgrounds have benefited from Outward Bound around the world.

Photo Credit: Terry Moore

Outward Bound courses are designed to help people develop confidence, compassion, an appreciation for service to others, and a lasting relationship with the natural environment. Outward Bound is not a survival school. They do offer, however, a rugged adventure in the wilderness during which you will receive unparalleled training in wilderness skills. They provide a unique, rigorous curriculum, in which you will learn by doing and put your learning to the test daily. The four pillars of self-reliance, fitness, craftsmanship, and compassion are central to the Outward Bound experience.

Outward Bound will challenge you, both individually and as a member of a team, by taking you into unfamiliar territory and allowing you to apply your newfound knowledge and skills. Sometimes you may fail in your efforts. Facing failure and learning to overcome it through reasonable, responsible action is an essential part of the Outward Bound experience.

Teammates and instructors provide the emotional support for you to try and, if you fail, to try again. Perseverance is the basis for the Outward Bound motto, "to serve, to strive, and not to yield."

WORKING FOR OUTWARD BOUND

Many factors influence the quality and success of a group's Outward Bound experience, but none is more important than the quality of the staff. Staff members are sensitive, highly skilled, energetic outdoor leaders who are committed to the Outward Bound philosophy. The majority of staff are educators who are also mountaineers, climbers, and paddlers with solid life experience. Some work year-round; others only work two or three courses per year and work the rest of the year in education or other professions. Above all, staff members possess one important outdoor skill—good judgment, or the ability to make sound, safe decisions under challenging circumstances.

Positions include instructional staff, support staff, and volunteer positions. All staff receive room and board and are paid on a per diem basis. The pay generally ranges from $40 to $125 per day (but varies with school and position) with generous discounts on outdoor equipment and clothing. Most of the schools also have programs for corporate clientele. Facilitators are recruited to deliver these programs, some of which are classroom based, while others are more wilderness oriented.

Photo Credit: Brian Peterson

As a whole, Outward Bound does not offer a formal internship program. Occasionally an internship position is created for the "right" person who applies for the assistant instructor position and doesn't have all the necessary skills to assume the responsibilities of the position. Taking a course prior to working for Outward Bound is strongly encouraged and may be required, depending on the program to which you are applying. Wilderness Schools that have internship opportunities are noted below.

HEADQUARTERS

Outward Bound USA

100 Mystery Point Rd.
Garrison, NY 10524-9757
(888) 882-6863 • (914) 424-4000
national@outwardbound.org • www.outwardbound.org

WILDERNESS SCHOOLS

Colorado Outward Bound School

Sandy Esque, Staffing Director
945 Pennsylvania St.
Denver, CO 80203-3198
(800) 837-5211 • (303) 831-6970
sandy@cobs.edu • www.cobs.org/staff

KNOWN FOR BEING the first Outward Bound School in the United States, premier mountaineers, white-water boaters, desert "rats," and sea kayakers teach students the skills to tackle the rugged challenges of backcountry travel in Colorado, Utah, New Mexico, Baja California, and Alaska.

Hurricane Island Outward Bound School

Josie Howard, Human Resources Specialist
75 Mechanic St.
Rockland, ME 04841
(800) 643-4462 • (207) 594-1401
employment@hurricaneisland.org • www.hurricaneisland.org

ESTABLISHED INITIALLY as Outward Bound's landmark sailing program, the school now offers winter mountaineering, canoeing, backpacking, ice climbing, dogsledding, rock climbing, and sea kayaking from Maine to the Florida Keys, along with an urban and education system program providing initiatives and ropes/wall activities. Internships at Hurricane Island are offered throughout the year. Interns first attend a ten-day orientation and then participate as a trainee at several courses in Florida to gain experience. A small fee covers the cost of the orientation; thereafter, interns are provided with a small stipend. See Hurricane Island's Southern Lands Program on page 61 for details.

North Carolina Outward Bound School

Staffing Director
2582 Riceville Rd.
Asheville, NC 28805
(888) 756-2627 • (828) 299-3366
staffing@ncobs.org • www.ncobs.org

SINCE ITS BEGINNINGS in the rugged mountains of Appalachia, the school has expanded its programming to Costa Rica, the Everglades, the Bahamas, and Argentina/Chile. Students choose from a range of activities that include rock climbing, mountaineering, white-water paddling, sea kayaking, mountain biking, spelunking, and backpacking.

Internships and volunteer opportunities at NCOBS are structured to support students and staff in a variety of ways that are dependent on the needs of base camp. Work involves logistics, food and gear, vehicle, and clerical support in exchange for room and board. Other short-term opportunities that provide a monthly stipend (along with room and board) include assistant cooks and site support positions. Generally a three-month minimum commitment is necessary.

OUTWARD BOUND

Pacific Crest Outward Bound School

Staffing Coordinator
0110 S.W. Bancroft St.
Portland, OR 97201-4050
(800) 547-3312 • (503) 243-1993
www.pcobs.org

WHETHER IT'S WHITE-WATER RAFTING, alpine mountaineering, sailing, sea kayaking, or other exciting adventures, participants engage in adventures along the Pacific Crest Trail amid glaciers, canyons, rivers, and peaks.

Voyageur Outward Bound School

Staffing Director
111 Third Ave., South, Suite 120
Minneapolis, MN 55401-2551
(800) 328-2943 • (612) 368-0131
vobs@vobs.com • www.vobs.com

FROM THE REMOTE wilderness of Minnesota and Manitoba to the deserts and white-waters of Texas; from the Northern Rockies to the southern peaks of New Mexico, border-to-border adventures abound.

BEYOND THE UNITED STATES

Costa Rica Rainforest Outward Bound School

Staffing Director
SJO 829, Box 025216
Miami, FL 33102-5216
(800) 676-2018
info@crrob.org • www.crrob.org

COSTA RICA OUTWARD BOUND has various staff- and administration-type positions available throughout the year, including field instructor, surf instructor, student administrator, marketing intern, and web administrator. Candidates must have fluency in Spanish, general outdoor education/leadership experiences or knowledge, and make a commitment of eight to twelve months depending on position (although shorter-term possibilities may be available). Send your resume and philosophy statement to begin the application process. As a nonprofit foundation, they are able to obtain volunteer visas for foreign staff. This type of visa prevents them from paying volunteers a salary; however, it does allow them to cover airfare, room, board, and a cash stipend. Health insurance is provided under the ISIC card that is purchased for all foreign staff.

OUTDOORS WISCONSIN LEADERSHIP SCHOOL

Adventure Education • Wisconsin • Year-Round
www.augeowms.org

Cathy Coster, Associate Director
George Williams Lake Geneva Campus
P.O. Box 210
Williams Bay, WI 53191-0210
(414) 245-5531 • (414) 245-8549 (fax)
owls@idcnet.com

OUTDOORS WISCONSIN LEADERSHIP SCHOOL (OWLS) is one of the leading providers of adventure education in the Midwest. Thousands of participants have experienced a program at OWLS as a means of achieving personal and team growth in areas such as leadership, communication, creativity, trust-building, and problem solving.

The Experience: Adventure education interns facilitate team-building and leadership development programs for adolescents, colleges, and adult groups. The curriculum includes trust building, group initiatives, high and low ropes courses, team and individual climbing elements, and off-campus rock climbing. Outdoor/environmental education interns teach classes in natural awareness, wetlands, lake study, astronomy, and the weather, and coordinate school groups. Outdoor/guest recreation interns lead activities, including sports, games, natural awareness, and orienteering, and coordinate conference groups. Other seasonal positions range from arts and crafts teachers and lifeguards to bakers and groundskeepers.

Commitment: Adventure education internships and seasonal positions are available from March through November; outdoor/environmental education positions run September through May; and outdoor/guest recreation positions are available during the summer and winter.

Perks: Wages vary from $125 to $300 per week (depending on experience and position), along with room, board, and supplemental health insurance. Staff members live on the campus in comfortable, rustic cabins that include showers, toilet facilities, and single beds with linens. No more than two people share a room, and single rooms are assigned whenever possible. Wholesome and nutritious meals are served family- or buffet-style in their spacious dining room.

Ideal Candidate: For instructor positions, applicants should be college graduates with degrees in education or recreation with experience teaching in the outdoors. Interns should have at least college senior status, with coursework in related areas and experience working with people. A high energy level, good communication skills, and a strong commitment to creating powerful recreational and learning experiences for others are the most important qualifications for all positions.

Getting In: Send a cover letter, resume, and names and addresses of three references. Apply within four to six months of start date. Write or e-mail for more information.

OVERLAND TRAVEL

Adventure Travel • USA/Europe • Summer

Brooks Follansbee, Assistant Director
P.O. Box 31
Williamstown, MA 01267
(413) 458-9672 • (413) 458-5208 (fax)
overland@berkshire.net

OVERLAND TRAVEL provides a variety of adventure programs, with a focus on bicycling, hiking, or mountain biking (and canoeing, rafting, and rock climbing to complement the main focus). Trips are held in New England, the northern Rockies, Colorado, California, France, Spain, and Switzerland.

The Experience: Former participant and leader, Lisee Goodykoontz, says this about her experience: "Overland first showed me the outdoors, and how great it could be. Leading for Overland has given me the opportunity to share the gift I received as a teenager and to create for my Overland students the kind of positive, wholesome, and group-focused experience that was important to me growing up." Leaders go through extensive training prior to the start of their trips, including intensive sessions on safety, first aid, group dynamics, conservation, and fostering a community spirit.

Perks: A $150 per week stipend is provided, along with the benefit of traveling, working, and learning in some of the most spectacular places in the world.

Ideal Candidate: Candidates must be college graduates, have leadership experience (especially with thirteen- to eighteen-year-olds), and excellent people skills. Outdoor skills are sometimes less important than demonstrated leadership skills, especially in team sports (many Overland trip leaders have been team sports captains in high school and college).

Getting In: Send a resume and cover letter to begin the application process. There are rolling deadlines; however, most leaders are hired during the months of November through March. Finalists are invited out to Overland for a series of in-person interviews.

PHILLIPS CRUISES AND TOURS

Cruise Ship • Alaska • May–September
www.26glaciers.com

Carol Hugh, Personnel Officer
519 W. 4th Ave., Suite 100
Anchorage, AK 99501-2211
(800) 544-0529 • (907) 274-2723 • (907) 276-5315 (fax)
phillips@alaskanet.com

PHILLIPS OPERATES THE POPULAR "26 Glacier Cruise," giving thousands of people an opportunity to experience spectacular fjords, ice-blue glaciers, and the amazing wildlife of Prince William Sound.

The Experience: Passenger service crew members serve meals, bartend, and provide cruise narration, and other services to passengers. Reservation/sales agents work at their main office in Anchorage and are responsible for sales of Alaskan tour products, as well as providing communication between the cruise ship and sales office.

Commitment: The season runs from early May through mid-September, with a week of pre-season training. Applicants must be available for the entire season.

Perks: Salaries start at $1,600 per month. The only way to get to Whittier is via the Alaska Railroad. Because of Whittier's remoteness and the shortage of accommodations, Phillips Cruises rents housing facilities that crew members may live in for a nominal fee. Cable TV and all utilities are provided by the company.

Ideal Candidate: Applicants should be dynamic, enthusiastic, and have a service background. Candidates also must be at least twenty-one years of age, committed to working a full season, and be comfortable sharing accommodations in a remote location.

Getting In: Send a resume and cover letter requesting application materials.

PINE RIDGE ADVENTURE CENTER

Wilderness Adventures • Vermont • Summer
www.pineridgeschool.com

Cortney Cahill, Wilderness Program Manager
1079 Williston Rd.
Williston, VT 05495
(802) 434-5294 • (802) 434-5512 (fax)
adventurecenter@pineridgeschool.com

PINE RIDGE ADVENTURE CENTER is a nonprofit educational organization committed to providing experiential opportunities for personal growth and team development. Participants learn to take care of themselves and to share the responsibility for meeting the group's needs in an exciting and challenging environment. Trip leaders work as part of a gender-balanced leadership team on wilderness trips throughout the Northeast, building a sense of community on the ropes course, raising awareness, and developing new skills for participants. There is also a need for interns who have limited experience but want to learn to become wilderness trip leaders. A stipend, room, and board are provided. Send cover letter and resume by February 15.

PUTNEY STUDENT TRAVEL

Educational Travel • Worldwide • Summer
www.goputney.com

Ellen Stein, Director
345 Hickory Ridge Rd.
Putney, VT 05346
(802) 387-5885 • (802) 387-4276 (fax)
ellen@goputney.com

....

PUTNEY STUDENT TRAVEL provides unusual educational opportunities during the summer for small groups of students who venture off to the United States (Alaska and Montana), Latin America (Costa Rica and Ecuador), Mexico, Europe (Czech Republic, Italy, Switzerland, France, Holland, and England), and Africa (Tanzania). Having fun, getting off the beaten path, making friends, participating actively, and working together are part of the Putney way. After a three-day orientation in Vermont, leaders, who are given a high degree of independence and responsibility, guide groups of high school students to various locales. Trips focus on travel, language learning, and community service over a four- to six-week period. Applicants must be energetic, fun, creative, active, knowledgeable about the area they are visiting, and excited about spending time with high school students. Proficiency in the language of the host country is required (French, Spanish, German, Italian, Czech, or Swahili). There are no foreign language requirements for trips to the Caribbean and the United States. A weekly stipend of $400 along with trip expenses are provided (including airfare).

REACHOUT EXPEDITIONS

Outdoor Education Ministry • Washington • Year-Round
www.reachoutexpeditions.org

Paul Spence, Director
P.O. Box 464
Anacortes, WA 98221
(800) 697-3847 • (360) 293-3788 • (360) 293-8297 (fax)
rew@cnw.com

....

ARE YOU INTERESTED in and committed to helping lead youth and adults closer to Christ? Do you enjoy spending time adventuring in the outdoors? Do you have a heart for service? Are you willing to work long hours and go the extra mile for others? If so, Reachout may have a job for you. Reachout has been leading life-changing wilderness adventures since 1979, an alternative for kids who are looking for something real, whether they realize it or not.

The Experience: There are three ways you can get plugged into Reachout on a short-term basis: Resource staff are folks who Reachout can train to become raft guides or rock-climbing instructors and who run programs for kids. In general, they are semi-local volunteers who help out on weekends (mostly) during the busy spring and summer seasons; summer staff work and live on-site and minister full-time for three to four months with sixteen other summer staffers from all over the world; finally, three interns become involved in projects such as helping out during their winter season, lending a hand in the rafting department, or assisting their adventure combo coordinator.

Perks: Summer staffers are provided with room and board by host families. Beyond that, summer staff may choose to raise support, like a home-based missionary.

Ideal Candidate: Although Reachout offers programs requiring technical wilderness skills, extensive wilderness training is not a prerequisite. Maturity, a commitment to Christ, a heart for youth, self-motivation, and a willingness to serve are the qualities they are looking for.

RIVER ODYSSEYS WEST

River Outfitter • Idaho/Montana • Summer
www.rowinc.com

Peter Grubb, Owner
P.O. Box 579
Coeur d'Alene, ID 83816-0579
(800) 451-6034 • (208) 765-0841 • (208) 667-6506 (fax)
info@rowinc.com

....

RIVER ODYSSEYS WEST, commonly known as ROW, leads wilderness rafting and walking trips in Idaho, Oregon, and Montana, as well voyageur canoe trips, rafting adventures, and yachting and barge trips throughout the world. Guides lead one- to six-day white-water trips on the rivers of northern and central Idaho. Some trips paddle through deep gorges; others through beautiful valleys. Guides receive food, housing, and a daily wage. The ideal candidate has great people skills and previous river guiding and natural/cultural history interpretation experience. Those who play a musical instrument for campfire entertainment are also preferred. Initial contact is preferred through e-mail.

THE ROAD LESS TRAVELED

Wilderness Adventure • USA/Costa Rica/Nepal • Summer
www.theroadlesstraveled.com

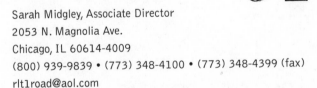

Sarah Midgley, Associate Director
2053 N. Magnolia Ave.
Chicago, IL 60614-4009
(800) 939-9839 • (773) 348-4100 • (773) 348-4399 (fax)
rlt1road@aol.com

THE ROAD LESS TRAVELED coordinates summer wilderness adventure, cultural awareness, and environmental education programs for teenagers. Participants venture to unique and culturally rich spots in the north and southwest regions of the United States (including Alaska), Costa Rica, and Nepal. Trip leaders begin their summer with ten days of staff training in Larkspur, Colorado; they then guide and engage participants in backpacking, ice and snow mountaineering, rock climbing, kayaking, white-water

rafting, and desert hiking. Candidates must be at least twenty-one years of age, WFR or WEMT certified, have experience in working with teenagers, and have solid wilderness skills. A mandatory personal interview and references are required.

ROADS LESS TRAVELED

Adventure Travel • Colorado • Year-Round
www.roadslesstraveled.com

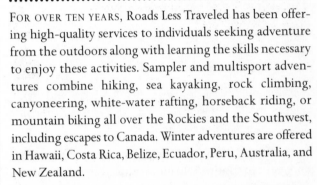

Brian Mullis, Director
2840 Wilderness Place
Boulder, CO 80301
(800) 488-8483 • (303) 413-0938 • (303) 413-0926 (fax)
fun@roadslesstraveled.com

FOR OVER TEN YEARS, Roads Less Traveled has been offering high-quality services to individuals seeking adventure from the outdoors along with learning the skills necessary to enjoy these activities. Sampler and multisport adventures combine hiking, sea kayaking, rock climbing, canyoneering, white-water rafting, horseback riding, or mountain biking all over the Rockies and the Southwest, including escapes to Canada. Winter adventures are offered in Hawaii, Costa Rica, Belize, Ecuador, Peru, Australia, and New Zealand.

The Experience: Guides lead backcountry biking and hiking adventures, which feature both inn-to-inn and camping retreats over a six- to eight-day period. Internships are also available for those who are interested in the programming aspects of their activities.

Commitment: In-depth guide training is held each April. A typical guide schedule is two to four weeks per month on tour, with time off in between trips.

Perks: Guide wages begin at $50 per day, along with room and board during each trip. Tips from guests can also be expected, ranging from $200 to $400 per trip. All staff are expected to find their own living arrangements between trips.

Ideal Candidate: Work as a guide is exciting and demanding. Those who have excellent people skills, genuinely enjoy people, and thrive in social situations fit the basic profile of their guides. Applicants must be at least twenty-five years old and, at a minimum, have Wilderness First Responder or equivalent certification. Guides must also provide their own mountain bikes, helmets, first aid kits, bike racks, panniers, and other personal gear (which can also be purchased through a discount program).

Success isn't something you chase. It's something you have to put forth the effort for constantly. Then maybe it'll come when you least expect it. —MICHAEL JORDAN

71

ROYAL PALM TOURS

Tourism • Florida • 10–16 Weeks

Ron Drake, President
P.O. Box 60079
Fort Myers, FL 33906-0079
(800) 296-0249 • (941) 368-0760 • (941) 368-7141 (fax)
rptours@aol.com

ROYAL PALM TOURS, located in a subtropical region of southwest Florida, provides customized tours, including wildlife- and nature-based themes, for both domestic and international groups coming to Florida.

The Experience: Tourism interns will gain hands-on experience in tour program research, destination development, copywriting, pricing, marketing, and operations. Visits to other tourism and recreation agencies will be provided, and a major project is assigned based on an intern's strengths and the agency's current needs. In a single word, they offer students a diverse internship experience.

Commitment: Internships are offered year-round, with length (usually ten to sixteen weeks) conforming to each student's curriculum requirements.

Perks: Royal Palms locates affordable housing (about $60 per week) in a private home. Flexible internship hours accommodate an agency-secured part-time job in a resort recreation department paying $100 or more per week. Other benefits include casual office attire (most of the time you will be wearing shorts and T-shirts!) and working with a member of the National Tour Association. Access to their membership provides travel, tourism, and leisure career opportunities with over four thousand fellow members.

Ideal Candidate: Royal Palm prefers students studying commercial recreation, leisure studies, tourism marketing, or destination development. Preference is given to those who are able to "color outside the lines," pay attention to detail, and have a compassion and sensitivity for the client's needs. A car is also necessary.

Getting In: Send cover letter (with preferred start and finish date) and resume. Interviews are conducted by telephone.

SAIL CARIBBEAN

Sailing • Caribbean • Summer
www.sailcaribbean.com

Michael Liese, Director
79 Church St.
Northport, NY 11768
(800) 321-0994 • (516) 754-2202 • (516) 754-3362 (fax)
sailcaribb@aol.com

SINCE 1979, Sail Caribbean has led teenagers from around the globe on adventures in learning and fun. Voyaging throughout the British Virgin and Leeward Islands in the Caribbean, students develop leadership skills and self-confidence taking turns each day as the skipper, navigator, first mate, chef, and crew of 51-foot sailboats with teens of their own age group (two- to three-week long sessions range from $2,800 to $3,700 plus airfare). Staff members, who serve as assistant skippers, have extensive sailing credentials and experience working with teenagers. One full week of intensive training is provided in leadership skills, teaching methods, and safety techniques specific to Sail Caribbean. Benefits include a salary along with room and board.

SPECIAL EXPEDITIONS MARINE

Sailing Adventure • USA • 6 Months

Carla Figliomeni, Human Resources
1415 Western Ave., Suite 700
Seattle, WA 98101
(206) 382-9594 (fax)
carlaf@specialexpeditions.com

KNOWN FOR THEIR expedition travel voyages, Special Expeditions Marine places a strong emphasis on in-depth exploration and discovery, where passengers (and the crew) learn about the environment, ecology, and natural history of a region through lectures, slide presentations, and guided walks. The vessels are small (just 152 feet in length), so the twenty-two crew members and seventy passengers are able to travel where the "big ships" cannot. Destinations include Baja California, the Sea of Cortez, the Columbia and Snake Rivers, and southeast Alaska. Shipboard staff include captains and mates, deckhands and pursers, chefs and stewards, expedition leaders and natural history staff. The work is demanding—averaging twelve hours a day—but time off is often filled with the chance to go hiking, snorkeling, kayaking, whale watching, or attending beach BBQs. Crew members earn on average

$2,000 per month and receive room and board. Along with an adventurous spirit and outgoing personality, applicants must make a six-month commitment, be at least twenty-one years of age, and be certified in CPR. On the basis of your cover letter and resume, applications are sent to those who they feel are a good match.

TOUCH OF NATURE ENVIRONMENTAL CENTER

Wilderness Education • Illinois • Year-Round
www.pso.siu.edu/tonec

Lisa Wait, Spectrum Wilderness Program Coordinator
Southern Illinois University
Mail Code 6888
Carbondale, IL 62901-6888
(618) 453-1121 • (618) 453-1188 (fax)
tonec@siu.edu

SINCE 1969, Touch of Nature's wilderness programs have provided outdoor education and recreation experiences for a wide variety of groups. Through wilderness settings, initiative courses, and adventure activities, the Spectrum Wilderness Program helps participants achieve self-confidence, self-reliance, cooperation, trust, and appreciation of the outdoors. Interns work and learn in most aspects of outdoor adventure programming, including backpacking, initiative courses, rock climbing, caving, and canoeing, including a thirty-day wilderness course with youth-at-risk. A monthly stipend along with basic living quarters is provided. College graduates (or those nearing completion) who have experience working with youth-at-risk and wilderness training (including first aid and CPR certifications) are encouraged to apply. This program works with a very challenging population in a wilderness setting. A strong desire to work with youth-at-risk is important.

TRAILMARK OUTDOOR ADVENTURES

Outdoor Adventure • USA • Summer
www.trailmark.com/staff

Rusty and Donna Pedersen, Directors
16 Schuyler Rd.
Nyack, NY 10960
(800) 229-0262 • (914) 358-0262 • (914) 348-0437 (fax)
staff@trailmark.com

FROM NEW ENGLAND to the northern Rockies, Trailmark runs summer adventure travel trips for teens ages twelve to seventeen—programs that foster a genuine familylike atmosphere. Each trip leader is responsible for four to six campers, engaging them in activities that encompass rafting, biking, backpacking, horse packing, climbing, mountaineering, windsurfing, sea kayaking, and canoeing over a two- to four-week period. Well before the Trailmark summer begins, leaders participate in an intensive pre-camp training session, to prepare and review the summer's activities and itineraries, as well as teen-counseling issues. All leaders, who average twenty-five years of age, must have first aid, CPR, and safety training. Many have been trained at Outward Bound and National Outdoor Leadership School (NOLS). A staff application can be downloaded from their web site.

Trip leaders are experienced, talented, high-energy, and supportive. We only select leaders who have extensive experience, and the sensitivity and maturity to handle the needs of teenagers.

U.S. ADAPTIVE RECREATION CENTER

Therapeutic Recreation • California • Winter/Summer
www.usarc.org

Kelle Malkewitz, Executive Director
P.O. Box 2897
Big Bear Lake, CA 92315-2897
(909) 584-0269 • (909) 585-6805 (fax)
usarc@bigbear.com

THE U.S. ADAPTIVE RECREATION CENTER (formerly California Handicapped Skiers) provides outdoor recreational opportunities to physically and cognitively challenged individuals. People with disabilities can now learn how to snow ski and waterski safely and well. Adaptive teaching techniques and equipment can overcome almost any disability—physical or mental. Adaptive ski instruction is available all season, with the summer program (Alpine

Challenge) focusing on waterskiing, sailing, fishing, canoeing, and kayaking. Volunteers may work as instructors or support staff, or participate in fund-raising activities. Alpine Challenge volunteers are trained in adaptive waterskiing and water safety procedures, adaptive camping, fishing, canoeing, and kayaking. All volunteers receive a complimentary ski pass.

U.S. OLYMPIC COMMITTEE

Sports • California/Colorado/New York • 13–21 Weeks
www.usoc.org/jobs

Student Intern Program
One Olympic Plaza
Colorado Springs, CO 80909-5760
(719) 632-5551 • (719) 578-4817 (fax)
internprog@usoc.org

THE U.S. OLYMPIC COMMITTEE is a nonprofit organization dedicated to providing opportunities for American athletes and to preparing and training those athletes for challenges that range from domestic competitions to the Olympic Games.

Environment: The majority of internships are at their headquarters in Colorado Springs; however, interns might work at either Lake Placid, New York, or Chula Vista, California.

The Experience: The internship program is designed to provide a quality work experience and a unique opportunity for exposure to the Olympic movement and spirit in the United States. The program offers internships in the divisions or areas of accounting, broadcasting, computer science, journalism, marketing, sports administration, and sport science (strength and conditioning, and testing).

Commitment: Winter/spring—twenty-one weeks; summer—thirteen weeks; and fall—fifteen weeks.

Perks: A $75 per week stipend is provided. Interns live at Olympic Training Centers (which house the athletes) on a double-occupancy basis, and eat meals at the athletes' dining hall. The complex in Colorado Springs is an athlete's paradise—gyms, weight room, pool, and recreational facilities.

Ideal Candidate: Applicants must be enrolled in an undergraduate or graduate program and have completed at least two years of college before the start of their internship. Most who get accepted into the program have a GPA of 3.0 or higher and have good writing skills. Work experience, volunteer experience, and college extracurricular activities are seriously considered in the selection process. Internships are very competitive.

Getting In: Operating twenty hours a day, the USOC Intern Information Line (at extension 2597) provides the latest information on internships. This is also a great way to have an application packet mailed to you. Applications must be received by these dates: winter/spring—October 1; summer—February 15; and fall—June 1. You will be notified four to eight weeks after submitting your application.

WILDERNESS INQUIRY

Adventure Travel • Worldwide • 4–5 Months
www.wildernessinquiry.org

Jeff Liddle, Program Director
1313 Fifth St. SE, Box 84
Minneapolis, MN 55414-1546
(800) 728-0719 • (612) 379-3858 • (612) 379-5972 (fax)
jeffliddle@wildernessinquiry.org

WILDERNESS INQUIRY is a nonprofit organization that focuses on getting people from all walks of life to personally experience the natural world in destinations all over the world. Whether by canoe, sea kayak, dogsled, horse pack, or backpack, trips are usually integrated to include lots of different folks. It's the unique mix of people and places that makes each trip a unique experience.

The Experience: Trail leaders are responsible for providing leadership on trips throughout the world, including the ability to organize, plan, and lead trips, and to maintain gear. Rigorous trips are par for the course, with groups usually traveling five to twenty miles per day. Over the course of a single trip, trail leaders may fill the roles of pack horse, teacher, rehabilitation specialist, folksinger, chef, personal relationship counselor, storyteller, attendant, disciplinarian, dishwasher, and bush doctor. Internships are also available in outdoor recreation/experiential education, therapeutic recreation, outreach and public relations, training, and fund-raising/development (these positions are offered year-round, from twenty to forty hours per week for a minimum of six weeks).

Commitment: Trip leader positions are seasonal, from December through April and June through September.

Perks: A $35 to $75 per day stipend is provided, amounting to $1,000 to $2,200 per season. Full-time also equals full benefits. The best perk has to be the opportunity to participate in outdoor adventures in locations across the globe.

Ideal Candidate: Individuals with previous experience in working with people with disabilities and the outdoors is desired. Applicants must have all certifications (Advanced First Aid, Lifeguard Training, CPR, and current driver's license) and be sensitive, responsible, have good judgment, a sense of humor, and be competent in providing training on all aspects of wilderness travel and living.

WILDERNESS WAY EXPERIENTIAL LEARNING PROGRAM

Experiential Education • New York • Summer

Bruce Matrisciani, Program Director
115 Post Rd.
Slate Hill, NY 10973
(914) 355-2624

WILDERNESS WAY EXPERIENTIAL LEARNING PROGRAM is committed to offering challenging activities for groups wishing to learn and grow in the outdoors. The noncompetitive "learn by doing" approach sparks excitement about the self, the group, and the environment. Staff will work with youth, ages three to fifteen, focusing on cooperative learning and experiential education through on-site activities (initiative games courses, challenge courses, zip lines, and climbing walls) and off-site activities (rock climbing, rappelling, and backpacking). Staff receives extensive training and $300 to $450 per week.

WOODS HOLE SEA SEMESTER

Educational Travel • Worldwide • 8–12 Weeks
www.sea.edu

Brian Hopewell, Dean of Enrollment
Sea Education Association
171 Woods Hole Rd., P.O. Box 6
Woods Hole, MA 02543
(800) 552-3633 • (508) 540-3954
admission@sea.edu

THE WORLD'S OCEANS cover upwards of 70 percent of the planet, but our understanding of the ocean as a physical system and as a vital element in human culture and history is still in its infancy. The mission of SEA is to give students the practical and theoretical experience necessary to contribute to our understanding of the ocean environment.

The Experience: This is a uniquely challenging program. SEA Semester students spend six weeks at the Woods Hole campus (the world capital of ocean science) receiving intensive classroom instruction in oceanography, nautical science, and maritime studies. Each student works closely with the oceanography faculty to design a research project, using the resources of the nearby Marine Biological

Laboratory. Upon successful completion of course work on shore, each student takes a berth as a member of the crew on one of SEA's two research vessels—120-foot blue-water "tall ships." Each vessel will then undertake its unique scientific mission during the second six weeks to places as far as the shores of Venezuela. On board, students become active members of the ship's crew and conduct oceanographic research and gather data for research projects.

Commitment: The semester program runs twelve weeks, five times per year. An eight-week summer class begins in early June.

Perks: The cost of SEA Semester is about the same as a semester at a private university—approximately $15,000 ($10,000 for the summer course). Financial aid is available. Housing is provided on shore; room and board are provided at sea. Students typically earn seventeen academic credits from Boston University, as well as 102 "sea days" toward the 180 days required to sit for a U.S. Coast Guard Able-Bodied Seaman's license.

Ideal Candidate: Previous sailing or marine science experience is not required. Sea Semester stresses problem solving, critical thinking, and teamwork. College-bound students seeking a rigorous academic experience prior to starting college, and college graduates seeking some practical experience before grad school or job hunting are welcome.

Getting In: Call or e-mail for materials and program video. Application materials are also available through their web site. Enrollment is limited to forty-nine spaces in each class. It's best to apply early.

WYMAN CENTER

Experiential Education • Missouri • Spring/Fall
http://stlouis.missouri.org/501c/wyman

Claire Wyneken, Program Administrator
600 Kiwanis Dr.
Eureka, MO 63025
(636) 938-5245 • (636) 938-5289 (fax)
wyman@stlouis.missouri.org

KNOWN FOR BEING THE OLDEST continuously operating youth camp west of the Mississippi (for over one hundred years), Wyman is an innovative experiential education center serving youth and adults from diverse backgrounds. Programs focus on youth development, environmental awareness, group dynamics, diversity, and enhancing self-esteem. Seasonal staff duties include instructing and facilitating groups in adventure, environmental, and life-skills programs. Along with extensive training, a competitive salary and potential housing is offered. Applicants

That is what learning is. You suddenly understand something you've understood all your life, but in a new way. —DORIS LESSING

must have interest in and experience working with children, excellent communication and leadership skills, flexibility, a strong work ethic, and a healthy sense of humor. Past staff members have said Wyman offers great training, a wonderful learning experience, and very rewarding work.

YOUTH ENRICHMENT SERVICES

Youth Development • Massachusetts • Year-Round
www.yeskids.org

Mary Crowther, Vice President
412 Massachusetts Ave.
Boston, MA 02118
(617) 267-5877 • (617) 266-6168 (fax)

YOUTH ENRICHMENT SERVICES (YES) is a nonprofit youth services agency with the mission to provide outdoor activity programs—such as skiing, mountain biking, and canoeing—for low- to moderate-income youth in the greater Boston area. Through YES programs, young people gain a sense of accomplishment and self-confidence, with the hope that these positive experiences will carry over to their education, family, community, and employment. While youth services is the mainstay of their agency, they also conduct Elderhostel programs during the summer at their lodge in the Berkshires of western Massachusetts. Intern duties include agency marketing and community outreach, equipment maintenance, database information management, assistance with youth/Elderhostel groups, and acting as a youth activity chaperone. Housing is offered during the summer.

Recommended Resources. . . . .

The **Alaska Wilderness Recreation and Tourism Association** serves as the statewide wilderness guide and ecotourism professional organization. For $10, they will provide you with the *Alaska Adventure Source Book*, a gold mine of resources for any mountain, naturalist, rafting, paddling, or ski guide who is interested in work in Alaska. Alaska Wilderness Recreation and Tourism Association, 2207 Spenard Road, Suite 201, Anchorage, AK 99503; (907) 258-3171, (907) 258-3851 (fax); info@awrta.org, www.awrta.org

Sailors and aspiring sailors can choose from over 150 **American Sailing Association** schools, sailing clubs, and charter companies throughout North America and the Caribbean (all of which are listed on their web site). In addition, many of these sailing schools offer weeklong courses and noninstructional trips to exotic locations throughout the world. American Sailing Association, 13922 Marquesas Way, Marina del Rey, CA 90292-6000; (310) 822-7171, (310) 822-4741 (fax), info@american-sailing.com, www.american-sailing.com

The **Eco-Source Network Center** (www.ecosourcenetwork.com) continues to create the world's most comprehensive, informative, fun, and useful site on ecotourism. A job and career information exchange connects visitors to the world of sustainable tourism, with job leads

ranging from ecolodge management and tour company operation to working as a guide or on a tourism board.

If your roots are grounded in adventure education, check out the Association for Experiential Education's **Jobs Clearinghouse Newsletter**. Hot off the presses each month, this newsletter provides contacts and job descriptions of professional jobs, seasonal positions, and internship opportunities in the experiential and outdoor education field. A three-month subscription runs $25 for members ($50 for nonmembers), or a year-round, monthly subscription is $50 for members ($95 if you're not). To keep in the know on issues related to experiential education, subscribe to their online discussion group by sending a message to listproc@lists.princeton.edu. In the body of the message write: subscribe aeelist<your name>. Association for Experiential Education, 2305 Canyon Blvd., Suite 100, Boulder, CO 80302-5651; (303) 440-8844, (303) 440-9581 (fax), info@aee.org, www.aee.org

The Outdoor Network (www.outdoornetwork.com) hosts an online forum for outdoor industry professionals. Visitors to their web site can search for outdoor education, outdoor recreation, and adventure travel jobs (written by each organization) and read up-to-the-minute news stories related to the outdoor industry.

5

getting paid for what you love to do is the common theme within the pages of this section. Whether you are guiding kids at a summer camp, teaching adults how to ski at a resort, or strumming your guitar at the nightly campfire of a dude ranch, this section will provide you with insights and options on taking part in unique opportunities in unique places.

The luckiest people in the world are those who get to do all year round what they most like to do during their summer vacation.

—MARK TWAIN

Unique Opportunities to Explore in This Section:

▶ For those who wish to blend a low-cost Caribbean vacation adventure along with some work, Maho Bay offers a unique work exchange program that promotes sustainable resort development in the Virgin Islands *(page 92).*

▶ Come explore the wonders of the Florida Keys, a place once inhabited by Indians and pirates and minutes from the only living coral reef in North America. Instructors and camp counselors at Seacamp help participants gain a better understanding of the natural features of the ocean and its ecosystems, along with instructing them in activities ranging from sailing to scuba *(page 95).*

▶ How about spending your winter months working at Royal Gorge, North America's largest cross-country ski resort? Peruse the seasonal work opportunities at forty-eight other ski resorts in this special "ski bum" section *(page 97).*

▶ Don your hat, mount your trusty horse, and ride into Wilderness Trails Ranch, where staff are hired each year to emulate the dude ranch experience for guests *(page 106).*

Photo Credit: Eagle's Nest Foundation

77

Fresh air, mountain music, laughter, love, and unique learning experiences abound at Eagle's Nest Camp. This summer counselor demonstrates the art of a raku firing to a camper at the natural arts arena.

CAMPS, AND RESORTS
RANCHES,

AMELIA ISLAND PLANTATION

Resort • Florida • 16 Weeks
www.aipfl.com

Barbara Ross, Internship Coordinator
P.O. Box 3000
Amelia Island, FL 32035-3000
(904) 277-5904 • (904) 277-5994 (fax)
intern@aipfl.com

. . . .

NOTED FOR THEIR environmentally conscious development, Amelia Island Plantation is known in Florida for being the greenest resort. This 1,350-acre gated resort and residential community offers miles of sandy beach in a preserved natural setting, along with many amenities. Internships have been offered at the resort for nearly twenty years, with many former interns now in various management positions (including the internship coordinator)!

The Experience: Internships are offered in the following areas: aquatics, club management, commercial recreation, culinary, golf and tennis, graphic design, lodging, marketing, nature science, promotions, public relations, recreation rental and retail, rooms management, staff development, theme parties, and turf management.

Commitment: Internships are offered throughout the year (spring, summer, and fall), and a sixteen-week minimum commitment is preferred (although some interns stay as long as forty-eight weeks).

Perks: A housing stipend of $225 per week and two meals per shift is provided for most positions. Other positions receive an hourly wage in lieu of the stipend and meals. Other perks include assistance in locating housing, extensive training, and use of the amenities at discounted rates.

Ideal Candidate: The resort recruits juniors and seniors, who must be receiving academic credit, at universities and colleges. Previous related experience (paid or unpaid) is a plus and a clean driving record is a requirement to even be considered for many areas. In addition, all candidates must be fluent in conversational English and provide their own transportation.

Getting In: Applicants can request information through e-mail or by calling. Be sure to indicate your area of interest and the semester you are required to intern so that the appropriate information may be sent. It's best to apply at least two months before the start date.

ASPEN LODGE RANCH RESORT

Dude Ranch • Colorado • Year-Round
www.aspenlodge.com

Dr. Boyd LaMarsh, General Manager
6120 Highway 7
Estes Park, CO 80517
(800) 332-6867 • (970) 586-8133 • (970) 586-8133 (fax)
aspen@aspenlodge.com

. . . .

ASPEN LODGE RANCH RESORT is a full recreation and sports facility bordering Rocky Mountain National Park and Roosevelt National Forest. Year-round seasonal positions include sports center attendant, children's counselors, waitstaff, bartender, housekeepers, wranglers, groundskeepers, and conference attendants. Wages start at $5.25 per hour (plus a season-end bonus), along with room and board (at a cost of $175 per month).

AUDUBON ECOLOGY CAMPS AND WORKSHOPS

Ecology • Connecticut/Maine/Wyoming • Summer
www.audubon.org

Program Manager
National Audubon Society
613 Riversville Rd.
Greenwich, CT 06831
(203) 869-2017 • (203) 869-4437 (fax)
aew@audubon.org

. . . .

SINCE 1936, the National Audubon Society has been offering summer work/learn opportunities to college students who have a strong interest in the environment. The student assistant program provides a combination of hard work, meeting interesting people, and, through attendance in the Audubon ecology camps and workshops program, a chance to study the many life-forms and physical aspects of forests, fields, ponds, streams, and seashore environments. As part of the program, each student assistant carries out a field study project. Past projects have included photography of seashore organisms, surveys of ferns, a study of frog vocalizations, and a study of bird nesting behavior. The summer is filled with learning opportunities, from stimulating, informational field classes to individual inquiry and consultation with a project advisor and professional staff. The program is offered in Connecticut, Maine, or Wyoming. Participants, as part of the work component of the program, will also assist in the kitchen or maintenance. A salary plus room and board are provided.

BRADFORD WOODS

Therapeutic Recreation • Indiana • Year-Round
www.indiana.edu/~bradwood

Kimberly Nunn, Administration
5040 State Road 67 North
Martinsville, IN 46151
(765) 342-2915 • (765) 349-1086 (fax)
knunn@indiana.edu

• •

BRADFORD WOODS, Indiana University's premier outdoor center, provides residential environmental education, challenge education (including leadership development, therapeutic programs, and adventure recreation), professional development and managerial training, and accessibility training and research programs. The campus is also home to Camp Riley, a summer residential camping program serving children and adults with disabilities. Environmental education/recreation interns during the fall and spring first participate in an intensive three-week training program, then teach in the residential environmental education program for elementary school students and facilitate challenge education programs for students of all ages (including college students). Summer positions at Camp Riley include activities coordinator, counselors, and instructors/assistants, with activities including adventure challenge, creative arts, nature, outdoor living skills, recreation, and waterfront. Stipends range from $50 to $200 per week, along with room and board, laundry services, and use of facilities and equipment. All candidates must be at least eighteen years old with a background in the outdoor education/adventure field.

CAMP CHATUGA

Camp • South Carolina • Summer
www.campchatuga.com

Kelly Moxley, Personnel Director
291 Camp Chatuga Rd.
Mountain Rest, SC 29664
(864) 638-3728 • (864) 638-0898 (fax)
mail@campchatuga.com

• •

CAMP CHATUGA is a small, independent camp for boys and girls from six to sixteen, with a focus on developing their potential intellectually, emotionally, spiritually, and physically in a fun and relaxed natural environment. A job at Chatuga is not a summer vacation—it is work. It is mentally and physically exhausting, but unbelievably rewarding. Can you live without alcohol, tobacco, perfect hair, privacy, a Walkman, air-conditioning, a VCR, a pre-

dictable schedule, and lots of money? If you answered yes, then this may be the job for you. Eight-week summer positions include counselor, nanny, dining hall supervisor, waterfront supervisor, horseback supervisor, outdoor program supervisor, health supervisor, health lodge counselor, mechanic, and maintenance crew. Pre-camp training helps staff members earn or renew certifications. Staff members receive $125 per week, plus free room and board. Salaries go up based on education, experience, and certifications. Other perks include free trips, laundry, and a staff T-shirt.

CAMP COUNSELORS/ WORK EXPERIENCE USA

Educational Travel • Australia/New
Zealand/Russia/Venezuela • 3–12 Months
www.campcounselors.com

Outbound Program Director
2330 Marineship Way, Suite 250
Sausalito, CA 94965
(800) 999-2267 • (415) 339-2727 • (415) 329-2744 (fax)
outbound@campcounselors.com

• •

CAMP COUNSELOR/WORK EXPERIENCE USA's outbound program affords the opportunity for independent and adventurous Americans to work and travel in Australia, New Zealand, Russia, or Venezuela for a couple months on up to a year (depending on the program). Work experiences range from youth camps to ski resorts with most opportunities available during the summer months. Each program also has specific age requirements that generally fall between age eighteen and twenty-five. Fees start at $365.

CAMP COURAGE

Therapeutic Camp • Minnesota • Academic Year/
Summer
www.lkdllink.net/~ccourage

Environmental Education Coordinator
8046 83rd St., NW
Maple Lake, MN 55358-9774
(320) 963-3121 • (320) 963-3698 (fax)
ccourage@lkdllink.net

• •

CAMP COURAGE, a nonprofit United Way organization, provides rehabilitation, enrichment, vocational, independent living, and educational services to empower children and adults with physical disabilities and sensory impairments to achieve their full potential.

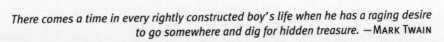

There comes a time in every rightly constructed boy's life when he has a raging desire to go somewhere and dig for hidden treasure. —MARK TWAIN

The Experience: Environmental education staff prepare the camp and provide teaching and hosting for Camp Courage environmental education and retreat groups. Duties include attending all training events, workshops, and staff meetings; teaching outdoor and environmental education programs (in a style attractive to and consistent with formal school educators); and hosting groups one evening per week.

Commitment: Positions are available during the summer or for nine months beginning in September.

Perks: A $150 per week stipend is provided during the summer (up to $275 per week for the academic year), along with room, board, holiday breaks, and work in a beautiful setting.

Ideal Candidate: Applicants must have at least two years of college, with classes in the natural sciences, recreation, or education fields. Consistent and appropriate leadership of children is vital, as are good communication skills. A qualified individual must be able to enthusiastically lead outdoor education activities one day, then clean cabins or help in the kitchen the next.

Getting In: Application deadlines: summer—March 15; September through May—August 15.

CAMP COURAGEOUS OF IOWA

Therapeutic Camp • Iowa • 3–19 Weeks
www.campcourageous.org

Jeanne Muellerleile, Camp Program Director
P.O. Box 418
Monticello, IA 52310-0418
(319) 465-5916 • (319) 465-5919 (fax)
Jeanne_Muellerleile@campcourageous.org

CAMP COURAGEOUS OF IOWA, surrounded by one thousand acres of state and county lands, is a year-round camp founded on the belief that children and adults with disabilities have the right to opportunities found in the world around them. Campers with mental and physical disabilities, hearing and visual impairments, autism, brain injuries, and other distinct groups are served. Counselors supervise the health, well-being, and personal care of groups of campers and ensure that they have a successful and enjoyable time. Activity specialists develop and implement everything from canoeing, camping, crafts, and nature activities to rock climbing, rappelling, caving, and the high and low ropes course. Full-time positions are offered from three to nineteen weeks, year-round. Interns and volunteers receive a salary of $100 per month; seasonal staff

receive $200 per week; and year-round staff receives $1,000 to $1,100. All receive room and board. Candidates should have flexibility and patience. A genuine desire to give your time, energy, and enthusiasm to others is required.

> *Working with children and adults with disabilities is an experience you will never forget.*

CAMP FRIENDSHIP

Camp • Virginia • Year-Round
www.campfriendship.com

Linda Grier, Director
P.O. Box 145
Palmyra, VA 22963-0145
(800) 873-3223 • (804) 589-5880 (fax)
info@campfriendship.com

CAMP FRIENDSHIP is located on 733 acres of woodlands, with the scenic Rivanna River on three sides and a small lake in the center. The summer camp program serves over two thousand children—coming from thirty-two states and twenty countries—each year. Facilities include a stable for eighty horses, gym, swimming pool, archery and riflery ranges, tennis courts, theater, ropes course (over sixty elements), and an environmental education center.

The Experience: Summer camp offers a diverse selection of elective activities: swimming, canoeing, gymnastics, riding, crafts, pottery, photography, ropes course, drama—over thirty choices. A specialized equestrian camp for girls is offered, as well as thirteen different challenge trips for teenagers, which include hang gliding, rafting, caving, rock climbing, kayaking, bicycling, and waterskiing. Counselors with instructional skills are hired for this season. The environmental education program is offered to school groups in the spring and fall, with weekend conferences and special program weekends for children. Program staff teach environmental education, orienteering, and ropes courses; lead canoe trips and campfires; and lifeguard for swimming.

Commitment: During the summer, most positions are a twenty-four hour responsibility with one day off per week. During the school year, staff usually work $5\frac{1}{2}$ days per week, averaging eight to ten hours per day.

Perks: All staff will receive a salary, housing, meals, and use of the camp's recreational facilities when they are not scheduled for use by guests.

Ideal Candidate: Applicants should be at least nineteen, with one year of college completed. Preference for positions during the school year is given to summer staff. A strong commitment to the environment and to the importance of each individual child is essential.

Getting In: Call for application. Interviews in person are preferred, although telephone interviews are possible.

CAMP HIGH ROCKS

Camp • North Carolina • Summer
www.highrocks.com

Hank Birdsong, Camp Director
P.O. Box 210
Cedar Mountain, NC 28718-0210
(828) 885-2153 • (828) 884-4612 (fax)
mail@highrocks.com

CAMP HIGH ROCKS is a relatively small boy's camp with a staff-to-camper ratio of approximately one to three, insuring a high degree of individual attention for each boy. Activities include hiking, backpacking, mountain biking, rock climbing, English horseback riding, and water activities (from swimming to an extensive river canoeing and kayaking program). Counselors must have completed one year of college, be competent in their teaching field, and have an understanding of and interest in children. An extensive counselor training program is offered to staff before the camp begins. Counselor salaries range from $1,530 to $2,000 for the nine-week season, depending on qualifications. Room, board, laundry, and a two-day Wilderness Medical Associates Wilderness First Aid course are provided.

CAMP HIGHLAND OUTDOOR SCIENCE SCHOOL

Outdoor Center • California • Spring/Fall
www.camphighland.net

Drizzt Cook, Director
P.O. Box 218
Cherry Valley, CA 92223
(909) 769-0442 • (909) 845-8090 (fax)
work@camphighland.net

CAMP HIGHLAND OUTDOOR SCIENCE SCHOOL is an innovative residential grade school science program in the foothills of the San Bernardino Mountains, just fifty miles from Joshua Tree National Park. Outdoor education field/cabin instructors have the opportunity to teach over twenty classes, including archaeology, botany, ecology (wildlife, forest, mountain, and desert), entomology, canoeing, climbing, archery, ropes course, team building,

and outdoor living skills. Wages start at $40 per day, plus room and board. Contracts become available each spring and fall. Send resume, cover letter, and three references.

CAMP LA JOLLA

Health & Fitness • California • Summer
www.camplajolla.com

Nancy Lenhart, Founder and Executive Director
176 C Ave.
Coronado, CA 92118
(800) 825-8746 • (619) 435-7990 • (619) 435-8188 (fax)
camplj@aol.com

Camp La Jolla is dedicated to providing children, as well as young and mature adult ladies, with a nationally acclaimed fitness and weight-loss program. Just a short walk from the sandy beaches of the Pacific Ocean, programs are held on the beautiful campus of UC San Diego, with boundless recreational and educational opportunities. Live-in resident counselors will provide sports and physical fitness activities in their $35 million complex, as well as nutrition education, behavior modification, field trips, and evening programs. Counselors receive $100 to $150 per week, along with room and board.

CAMP WOODSON

Therapeutic Camp • North Carolina • 5–15 Weeks

John McGee, Internship Director
741 Old U.S. Highway 70
Swannanoa, NC 28778
(828) 686-5411 • (828) 686-7671 (fax)

CAMP WOODSON is a year-round therapeutic, adventure-based wilderness program operated by the North Carolina Office of Juvenile Justice. Activities such as hiking, rock climbing, canoeing, urban exploring, and horseback riding are used to address issues of troubled youth (who have all been through the court system). The camp's approach is to challenge individuals and provide opportunities for success.

The Experience: Interns will conduct and process initiatives and perform both individual and group counseling for students, aged thirteen to seventeen, who have come from unstable family situations and have failed in the traditional school system (their range of offenses might include breaking and entering, assault, substance abuse and drug violation, auto theft, or sexual offenses, and their attendance at the camp is voluntary). Interns become role models and friends, with their goal to capture the magic from difficult and challenging situations and make that magic real for the students.

Commitment: Three five-week sessions and a training week between each session is recommended.

Perks: Although no compensation is provided, housing and food may be available. Perks include living in the beautiful western North Carolina mountains, where there are many opportunities for climbing, hiking, canoeing, and mountain biking. Interns should have their own transportation.

Ideal Candidate: Interns typically have backgrounds in human service fields and have experience in leading and facilitating outdoor adventure activities.

Getting In: Submit cover letter and resume, then call to arrange an interview.

CHRISTODORA-MANICE EDUCATION CENTER

Wilderness Education • New York • May–October
www.geocities.com/christodora

Program Director
One East 53rd St., 14th Floor
New York, NY 10022
(212) 371-5225 • (212) 371-2111 (fax)
christodora@prodigy.net

COORDINATING CAMPING programs since 1908, Christodora provides challenging and rewarding environmental learning experiences to motivate urban youths who generally come from economically or experientially disadvantaged families in New York City. The center is a small, high-quality residential center in the Berkshire Mountains, with a strong emphasis on environmental education and adventure programs.

The Experience: Field teachers educate and facilitate the growth, understanding, and development of students (ages eleven to eighteen) in program areas such as environmental sciences, wilderness, group initiatives, and leadership training. This might also include supervision of overnight trips and wilderness expeditions. Outdoor education interns assist field teachers in program areas while developing skills to teach their own lessons in a supervised setting. Wilderness leadership interns supervise and colead six- to nineteen-day courses with field teachers.

Perks: Field teachers receive a minimum stipend of $300 per week, while interns receive a minimum of $170 per

week. Room, board, equipment discounts, and insurance coverage are also provided.

Ideal Candidate: Field teacher applicants must have a college degree; outdoor education interns must have completed one year of college; and wilderness leadership positions require a minimum of two years of college. All candidates must have a strong interest in the wilderness, interpretation, and experiential education. CPR, first aid, and lifeguard certifications are preferred.

Getting In: Submit resume, cover letter, and three references.

CLEARWATER CANOE OUTFITTERS AND LODGE

Lodge • Minnesota • Summer
www.canoebwca.com

Marti and Bob Marchino, Directors
774 Clearwater Rd.
Grand Marais, MN 55604
(800) 527-0554 • (218) 388-2254 • (218) 388-2254 (fax)
info@canoebwca.com

THE MAIN LODGE OF Clearwater Canoe Outfitters and Lodge was completed in 1926 and is listed on the National Register of Historic Places. The largest remaining whole log structure in northeastern Minnesota, it has retained the look and feel of the pioneer days. A few secluded cabins and bed and breakfast rooms in the lodge itself offer an alternative to camping. The business prides itself on its wilderness preservation ethic and consists of six to eight staff members. Seasonal positions include front desk, housekeeping, waterfront, maintenance, cook, naturalist, and outfitting packer. (Most staff work in more than one position.) A salary along with room and board are provided.

COFFEE CREEK RANCH

Dude Ranch • California • Year-Round
www.coffeecreekranch.com

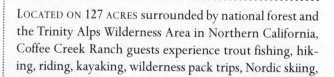

Ruth Hartman, Owner
HC2, Box 4940
Trinity Center, CA 96091-9502
(800) 624-4480 • (530) 266-3343 • (530) 266-3597 (fax)

LOCATED ON 127 ACRES surrounded by national forest and the Trinity Alps Wilderness Area in Northern California, Coffee Creek Ranch guests experience trout fishing, hiking, riding, kayaking, wilderness pack trips, Nordic skiing, health spa use, gold panning, and use of the rifle range. Seasonal staff is needed in the office, front desk, accounting, and the kitchen (including prep chefs and bakers). Pay depends upon the position and season chosen, but generally runs $850 to $1,000 per month. Room, board, and use of the facilities at the ranch (including the exercise room and hot tub) are provided.

> *The more versatile you are the better. We are looking for a person that never says, "Not my job!"*

COLLEGE SETTLEMENT—KUHN DAY CAMPS

Camp • Pennsylvania • Year-Round

Andrew Fielding, Program Director
600 Witmer Rd.
Horsham, PA 19044
(215) 542-7974 • (215) 542-7457 (fax)
camps@i-bob.com

THE COLLEGE SETTLEMENT OF PHILADELPHIA operates a day and resident summer camp and a residential outdoor school, mostly for seven- to fourteen-year-olds from economically disadvantaged families. Many of these children live in difficult situations and face challenging problems in their daily lives. The Teen Adventure Program offers a once-in-a-lifetime chance for urban youth to experience the thrill of camping, hiking, and adventuring on the East Coast. Trip leaders plan custom trips and activities and take their groups by van to West Virginia and New England (including Maine). Summer camp staff—from counselors to activity leaders—teach and share experiences with children in a fun and caring environment. Wages start at $1,600 for the season, along with meals and housing. Applicants should have experience in outdoor pursuits (climbing, backpacking, rafting, or kayaking preferred), be enthusiastic, work well with others, and have a sense of fun mixed with a great dose of common sense. Those who are open-minded and enjoy making a difference in others' lives are strongly encouraged to apply.

THE COLORADO MOUNTAIN RANCH

Dude Ranch • Colorado • Summer
www.coloradomountainranch.com

Mike, Lynn, and Gail Walker, Owners
10063 Gold Hill Rd.
Boulder, CO 80302-9770
(800) 267-9573 • (303) 442-4557 • (303) 417-9114 (fax)
office@coloradomountainranch.com

OWNED AND OPERATED BY the Walker family since 1947, The Colorado Mountain Ranch provides a warm, friendly environment where individual growth and learning occur through confidence-building activities in an active outdoor setting. Adventurous programming abounds at the ranch, where campers can participate in everything from a challenge ropes course to Western horseback riding, hiking, and camping.

Environment: Nestled in the pine and aspen forests and wildflower meadows of Colorado's Rocky Mountains, the ranch encompasses 180 acres at an elevation of 8,500 feet. The camp is bordered on the east by the mining town of Gold Hill; and to the west, Roosevelt National Forest rises to the magnificent snowcapped peaks of the Continental Divide.

The Experience: Summer seasonal staff are instrumental in creating and implementing every aspect of ranch programs, activities, facility use, food service, and maintenance. Every job involves inspiring and guiding campers, participating enthusiastically in all daily activities, and embracing the Native American philosophy of respect for self, others, and nature.

Commitment: Staff training begins in early June, with camp finishing in mid-August. Only applicants who are available for the entire season are considered.

Perks: Staff members receive a stipend of $1,400 per season, along with meals and housing. The mountain climate and setting are perfect for a full range of healthful, outdoor activities, from swimming and riding to hiking, camping, and playing in the high-country snow fields. Days are generally sunny and warm, nights cool, and the air is usually crisp and clear. Living with others and working together as a team, staff members grow in love and understanding of themselves, each other, and life.

Ideal Candidate: Applicants, who must be at least eighteen and have completed high school, are selected on the basis of abilities, enthusiasm, creativity, reliability, sincerity, sensitivity, and a commitment to guiding others toward their full potential.

> *The Ranch is a song; it is a song of happiness, of love, of peace, and of understanding. It is a song that had a beginning, but that can never die for too many people have heard this song. The intertwining of the melodies will continue until the song has become a part of everyone who has come here. That song will go out from here in the hearts and minds of those who know it and spread itself and become a part of all it touches. Let your song reflect that which you are and will become here, and carry it with you when you leave. —Colorado Mountain Ranch*

> *Dude and guest ranching is more than a vacation; it is a spirit, a tradition of Western hospitality, warmth, honesty, family, and natural beauty. It is, indeed, a ministry that touches lives and helps to make this a better world in which to live. —GENE KILGORE*

COLORADO TRAILS RANCH

Dude Ranch • Colorado • Summer
www.coloradotrails.com

Robin Williams, Manager
12161 Country Road 240
Durango, CO 81301-6306
(970) 247-5055 • (970) 385-7372 (fax)
cotranch@aol.com

• •

BEAUTIFUL MOUNTAIN SCENERY, hard work, and lots of fun are just a few of the elements that guest ranch staff experience every summer at Colorado Trails Ranch. Crew positions include chef, riding guide, housekeeping, server, floater, counselor, maintenance, and sports/utility staff. If you have a ready smile, are willing to work hard, love the outdoors, and enjoy working with people, they may have a job for you. An hourly wage (plus bonus) along with room and board is provided.

COLVIG SILVER CAMPS

Camp • Colorado • Summer
www.colvigsilver.com

Scott Kelley, Program Director
9665 Florida Rd.
Durango, CO 81301
(800) 858-2850 • (970) 247-2564 • (970) 247-2547 (fax)
colvigsilvercamps@compuserve.com

• •

LOCATED IN THE San Juan Mountains of southwest Colorado, Colvig Silver Camps is a residential, wilderness-oriented summer camp serving children seven to seventeen years of age. The camp is a short drive or hike from high alpine regions (14,000-foot peaks), desert canyon areas (including Anasazi ruins), low alpine regions, mountain lakes and streams, raging rivers, and ponderosa pine forests. Their program is unique in that they offer a mix of traditional summer activities along with backcountry wilderness trips.

The Experience: Program coordinators organize and implement the camp's daily schedule, with input from both staff and campers; counselors are responsible for planning and leading in-camp activities and wilderness trips and living with a group of four to six campers; arts and crafts coordinators develop crafts programs for all age levels; wranglers are responsible for planning and teaching Western-style riding and tack care; and the expedition coordinator packs food and equipment for all expedition trips leaving camp.

Commitment: The season begins in early June (with mandatory staff training) and continues through late August.

Perks: A salary of $800 to $1,000 is provided, along with room, board, laundry, and wilderness first aid training for head counselors.

Ideal Candidate: All applicants must be over eighteen, with one year beyond high school. Current lifeguarding certificate is very beneficial.

Getting In: Call for application materials. After your application is received, they follow up on your references, then schedule an on-site or phone interview. Positions are filled on a first-come, first-served basis.

> *I have been intimately associated with Colvig Silver Camps for seven years. I saw it in your book and just wanted to let you know that I think it is a wonderful place to work. I was a camper there for five years beginning when I was eleven; and later went back to work there as a counselor for two years. This camp was my initial introduction to outdoor recreation and obviously had some pretty amazing influences on me, being that I now want to pursue a career in that field.*
> —Amie Podolsky, summer staff

COSTA AZUL ADVENTURE RESORT

Resort • Mexico • 9–12 Months
www.costaazul.com

Human Resources Director
U.S. Headquarters
224 Avenida Del Mar, Suite D
San Clemente, CA 92672-4011
(800) 365-7613 • (949) 498-3223 • (949) 498-6300 (fax)
getaway@costaazul.com

• •

LOCATED THIRTY MINUTES north of Puerto Vallarta, Mexico, Costa Azul sits on its own white, sandy beach in the tiny fishing village of San Francisco. The resort includes everything from a pool with swim-up bar and an open air restaurant, to programs that specialize in ecology and adventure trips out of the resort.

The Experience: Adventure guide/guest services staff lead trips ranging from kayaking, surfing, and snorkeling to hiking, bird watching, and botany. Other responsibilities include attending to guests, activity and trip planning, on-site promotion of activities, working with several employees, and implementing recommendations for their tour program.

Commitment: Applicants must be able to relocate to Mexico for at least nine months, although a commitment of one year is preferable. Start dates begin every month.

Perks: Benefits include a $200 to $400 per month stipend (depending on experience), on-site housing, all meals and beverages, and complimentary hotel rooms for visiting family or friends.

Ideal Candidate: Applicants must be at least age twenty-one, have an outgoing personality, enjoy working and serving the public, have current CPR certification, the ability to relocate to Mexico for at least nine months, and have course work in and a working knowledge of Spanish. Other qualifications and experiences that would make the applicant stand out include a background in environmental studies; knowledge of or interest in plants and wildlife; service-industry background; mountain biking, snorkeling, or scuba diving skills; first aid/lifesaving training; prior resort experience; ocean kayaking experience; knowledge of horses; and recreation management experience.

Getting In: To be considered, send resume, thorough cover letter, and references.

COULTER LAKE GUEST RANCH

Dude Ranch • Colorado • Year-Round
www.guestranches.com/coulterlake

Susan and Russ Papke, Managers
P.O. Box 906
Rifle, CO 81650
(800) 858-3046 • (970) 625-1473
coulterlake@sopris.net

LOCATED ON THE scenic western slopes of the Rockies, with a sparkling blue lake for swimming, fishing, and boating, Coulter Lake Guest Ranch has eight cabins scattered along the lakefront, among the aspen trees. Horseback riding, fishing, boating, square dances, bonfires, and sing-alongs keep guests busy throughout the day. Seasonal positions, which are available throughout the year, include housekeepers, food and beverage staff, wranglers/trail guides, and maintenance staff. Staff members receive $100 or more per week, along with a tip pool, housing, meals, necessities, laundry, and horseback riding. The staff is also encouraged to "play guest" on days off. Coulter Lake prefers a healthy, wholesome, active, organized, responsible, and tactful person. The ability to play the guitar is also a plus. Send resume and a cover letter describing job desired and a brief rundown on experience. A snapshot is appreciated. Phone interviews are conducted after your application is received.

EAGLE'S NEST FOUNDATION

Experiential Learning • North Carolina • Year-Round
www.enf.org

Paige Lester-Niles, Assistant Director
633 Summit St.
Winston-Salem, NC 27101
(336) 761-1040 • (336) 727-0030 (fax)
Summer: (828) 877-4349 • (828) 884-2788 (fax)
page@enf.org

WITH THE MISSION OF promoting the natural world and the betterment of human character, Eagle's Nest is an experiential outdoor education foundation coordinating the Eagle's Nest Camp for boys and girls (celebrating more than seventy years) and the Outdoor Academy of the Southern Appalachians, a semester program for tenth graders. This school-away-from-school focuses on environmental education, regional studies, and the arts, and centers students and faculty in a close community life. Pure and simple, the Eagle's Nest Foundation is about teaching and nurturing.

Environment: Nestled at the base of the Shining Rock escarpment, Eagle's Nest is situated on 180 acres of wooded land, where there are many places to rock climb, white-water paddle, and soak up the culture of the southern Appalachians. Evenings are cool; summer days are warm.

The Experience: There are two facets to Eagle's Nest: (1) Eagle's Nest Camp staff members teach activities in the arts, music, and drama (batik, West African drum and dance, pottery, musical instrument making, raku—not your everyday arts and crafts classes), wilderness (whitewater canoeing on a handful of rivers, rock climbing, and backpacking), and athletics (emphasizing skill and teamwork, not competition). Staff members also double as trip leaders, where they develop, plan, and set goals for the courses; then take teenagers on intense wilderness experiences that range from hiking one hundred miles of the Appalachian Trail and biking the Blue Ridge Parkway to service projects and cultural exchange in Mexico or paddling the chilly waters of northern Ontario. (2) Outdoor Academy teachers emphasize a broad spectrum of knowledge, skills, and attitudes in a college preparatory curriculum of English, history, natural science, fine arts, foreign languages, and mathematics. It combines classroom activities inside and out, with experiential learning as its strength.

Commitment: The hours are long but very rewarding, as the staff works with kids who are eager to learn and do. Staff

Every job should be looked at as an education and an adventure.
The satisfaction must come from your work. —RICHARD N. BOLLES

85

have one 24-hour day off per week and at least 2 hours off per day.

Perks: A $145 to $250 per week salary, plus room and board from their wonderful whole-foods kitchen (which includes meals for vegetarians and vegans) is provided for camp staff; Outdoor Academy benefits vary. Fresh air, mountain music, laughter, and love abound at Eagle's Nest, and most thrive and live vivaciously in this community-empowering environment.

Ideal Candidate: Applicants with experience in outdoor and experiential education and who have a strong desire to teach and play in the outdoors are desired. A high energy level and creativity are a must.

Getting In: Call for a staff application. Applications are reviewed December through January. If you can't reach Paige, ask for Noni Wiate-Kucera (the director).

> The most important aspect of Eagle's Nest is the community itself. Being responsible to the community is at the heart of life at ENF. Consequently, attitude is the most important attribute at Eagle's Nest, that is, a willingness to be a jack-of-all-trades, have patience and love of children, a sense of goodwill and support of others, and a desire to develop one's own potential. It is a place that allows one to reap his or her own rewards.

EBNER CAMPS

Camp • Connecticut • Summer
www.awosting.com

Barb Ebner, Director
Route 202
Bantom, CT 06750
(800) 662-2677 • (860) 567-9678 • (860) 868-0081 (fax)
camps@netrax.net

EBNER CAMPS runs two children's resident summer camps: Awosting Camp (for boys), the oldest private boys' program in the country, and Chinqueka Camp (for girls). Campers range from age six to fifteen and are from all over the world—as is the staff.

The Experience: Summer camp counselors will have the shared responsibility of running a group cabin as cocounselors as well as working as instructors in selected activity areas. Teaching positions range from ceramics and photography to martial arts and canoeing (and everything in between).

Commitment: Their camp season operates for eight weeks, usually the third week in June until the third week of August. Counselors report five days earlier than the campers for a five-day intensive orientation period. You will receive one day and three or four nights off per week.

Perks: Salaries range from $1,200 to $1,800 for the eight-week camp season. Perks include free lodging, meals, a uniform shirt, laundry, a complimentary suntan, and a busload of memories. A bonus of 10 percent of contract salary is given for a "job well done!" Tipping is allowed, which could net an additional $300 to $500.

Ideal Candidate: Candidates must have some basic skill in one of the camp's teaching positions, and a knowledge of other languages is helpful when dealing with campers and staff that originate from all over the world.

Getting In: Submit cover letter stating your interest and requesting an application, along with your resume. There is a late-April deadline, but it's best to apply in January or February.

Photo Credit: Eagle's Nest Foundation

Summer instructors at Eagle's Nest Camp get their bearings prior to leading a group of campers on a three-week adventure along the Appalachian Trail.

FAIRVIEW LAKE YMCA CAMPS

Environmental Education • New Jersey • 3–4 Months
www.fairviewlake.org

Christina Henriksen, Environmental Education Director
1035 Fairview Lake Rd.
Newton, NJ 07860
(973) 383-9282 • (973) 383-6386 (fax)

FAIRVIEW LAKE YMCA CAMPS provide environmental education and conference programming for students in first through twelfth grades, as well as adult groups. The camp's mission is to improve the quality of life in the community by fostering healthful living, developing responsible leaders and citizens, strengthening the family, promoting the equality of all persons, protecting the environment, and utilizing community members and organizations to solve contemporary problems.

Environment: Located on 600 acres of mountains and forests, the center offers miles of trails for hiking, a 110-acre lake, athletic fields, a lighted tennis and basketball complex, cross-country skiing, boating, and canoeing.

The Experience: Intern responsibilities will include participation in staff training; planning and teaching environmental lessons on a variety of subjects that range from aquatic ecology to survival skills; providing instruction on the Action Socialization Experience Course; leading evening activities; assisting at dining hall orientation and meal service when needed; assisting housekeeping and office staff; providing environmental education and recreational programming and services to conference groups; and completion of a project chosen in consultation with the director.

Commitment: Internships are available in two sessions: March through June, and September through November.

Perks: Interns are paid a stipend of $150 per week, plus room and board. Staff housing includes a semiprivate room with kitchen/living room complex.

Ideal Candidate: Lifeguard training, first aid, and CPR certifications preferred, but training may be provided by the camp. People are considered based on their love of the outdoors, the desire to influence young minds, and flexibility of their work schedule.

Getting In: Submit resume and cover letter.

FARM AND WILDERNESS FOUNDATION

Camp • Vermont • 10 Weeks
www.fandw.org

Martha McPheeters, Program Head
263 Farm and Wilderness Rd.
Plymouth, VT 05056
(802) 422-3761 • (802) 422-8660 (fax)
fandw@fandw.org

FARM AND WILDERNESS is a nonprofit educational organization that operates five sleepaway camps for children (ages nine to seventeen), a day camp, a family camp in late August, outdoor education programs in the spring and fall, a retreat center, and a spring and fall work crew. The essence of Farm and Wilderness can be found in the Quaker values of simplicity, honesty, self-reliance, and respect for all persons. These values are woven into the fabric of the Farm and Wilderness community, creating an environment where people develop a deep regard for one another and explore a style of life that is simple, rugged, and exciting.

The Experience: Each year, nearly 300 staff members are hired for seasonal work (250 of them in the summer). Jobs include camp counselors and administrators, carpenters, cooks, drivers, farmers, gardeners, maintenance workers, nurses, outdoor educators, special event coordinators, and trip leaders. There are no sharp lines between work and play in their camps, because a cooperative group spirit enriches all the experiences of swimming and hiking, building and farming, dancing and music, crafts and cooking, and sharing thoughts and emotions.

Perks: Salaries range from $900 to $5,500, plus room and board for a season (approximately ten weeks of work) depending on the position.

Ideal Candidate: The staff is made up of "doers." They have backpacked in the Sierras, run food drives for the homeless, worked to clean up the environment, promoted the concept of world peace, played with bands, built houses, operated farms, and climbed the Himalayas. In any given year, more than half return for another summer.

FOOD SERVICE MANAGEMENT INTERNSHIP

Food Service • USA • Summer
www.nacufs.org

Sarah Johnson, Committee Chair
105 Smalley Center
West Lafayette, IN 47906-4205
(765) 494-1000 • (765) 494-0718 (fax)
sarah.c.johnson.1@purdue.edu

THE FOOD SERVICE MANAGEMENT INTERNSHIP PROGRAM, cosponsored by the National Association of College and University Food Services and the Association of College and University Housing Officers International (www.acuho.ohio-state.edu), is an educational program that introduces aspiring young professionals to the food service industry. Spanning eight weeks over the summer, interns will receive on-the-job experience that will better qualify them to assume the responsibilities related to college and university food service. Interns participate in all areas of kitchen production and sanitation, testing and sampling new food products, quality control of food production and recipes, purchasing procedures, and ordering techniques. College students in their junior or senior year who are pursuing a degree in hotel and restaurant management or food service administration are preferred; however, students with food service work experience are also welcome. A stipend of $1,200, along with room, board, and uniforms is provided.

GUNFLINT LODGE AND OUTFITTERS

Canoe Outfitter • Minnesota • Winter/Summer
www.gunflint.com

Shari Baker, Assistant Manager
143 S. Gunflint Lake
Grand Marais, MN 55604
(800) 328-3325 • (218) 388-2294 • (218) 388-9429 (fax)
shari@gunflint.com

GUNFLINT LODGE is a seasonal fishing resort and canoe outfitter (without TV or radio reception) and is surrounded by over one million acres of wilderness in the Superior National Forest. Guests come from all over the country to relax in the north woods atmosphere, fish, swim, canoe, and explore. Seasonal winter and summer opportunities may include activities leader, baker, trail guides, food and beverage staff, front desk, dock staff, dog musher, wilderness canoe guide, general helpers, and housekeepers. Resort

and outfitting work means long, hard, and sometimes irregular hours. Although you may be hired for a specific position, there are times when you may be called upon to fulfill other job duties. Most positions pay $1,065 per month and recreational equipment is available for use in off-hours. Bunkhouse-style accommodations (with shared kitchen facilities) are available for $115 to $130 per month.

HIDDEN CREEK RANCH

Dude Ranch • Idaho • February–October
www.hiddencreek.com

Staffing Director
7600 E. Blue Lake Rd.
Harrison, ID 83833
(800) 446-3833 • (208) 689-3209 • (208) 689-9115 (fax)
hiddencreek@hiddencreek.com

HIDDEN CREEK RANCH engages their guests in an adventure vacation with a Native American philosophy: "generating joy and excitement through the celebration of life."

The Experience: When you begin working at Hidden Creek Ranch, you become part of their ranch family. Whether working as a wrangler, kid's wrangler or counselor, baker or chef, waitstaff, housekeeper, or maintenance staff, you will have only one responsibility: to truly make each guest feel at home. To ensure that the staff has a frequent change of scenery, everyone will be cross-trained to help in other aspects of the ranch operation. Besides your main job, you might also be helping in the kitchen; serving the meals and

Whether working as a wrangler, baker, or counselor, each staff member at Hidden Creek Ranch is cross-trained in all aspects of ranch operation.

caring for the guests; assisting in some outdoor cooking; helping in the care of their animals; helping unload and stack the hay; airport transportation; and general errands and maintenance chores.

Commitment: The guest season starts in the beginning of May and ends in October. Some positions start as early as February or begin as late as June, although you must be available to work June through August. Preference is given to those who can work the entire season.

Perks: Along with a base salary, all staff have the chance to earn a bonus for successfully completing their contract. Benefits include three all-you-can-eat gourmet meals per day and housing in Wrangler's Haven (which Hidden Creek boasts is "the finest employee housing in the business"). Everything is provided, including fully furnished rooms (shared with one other person), laundry, recreation room, satellite television, and trading post purchases at 5 percent above wholesale—a place that provides that home-away-from-home feeling.

Ideal Candidate: Applicants must be at least eighteen years of age and have current standard first aid and CPR certification.

Getting In: Send a resume and cover letter, denoting your earliest start and finish dates. An application, which you can submit through e-mail, is also available on their web site. It is advised to get your application in as early as possible (over eight hundred are received each year); the hiring process begins in November.

HILTON OCEANFRONT RESORT

Resort • South Carolina • 3–12 Months
www.hiltonheadhilton.com

Marcie Robinson, Director of Recreation
P.O. Box 6165
Hilton Head Island, SC 29938
(800) 445-8667 • (843) 842-8000 • (843) 842-8033 (fax)

A SHELTERED PART of Palmetto Dunes Resort, Hilton Oceanfront Resort is a 2,000-acre retreat on the Atlantic Ocean.

The Experience: Known for being one of the largest recreation internship programs in the country, interns will be cross-trained in all aspects of the operation, with special projects ranging from convention, fitness, recreation, and special events. Food and Beverage and Rooms Division interns are provided with an extensive training program that covers the gamut of hospitality and culinary services.

Commitment: Recreation internships are available throughout the year for sixteen weeks; Food and Beverage and Rooms Division internships range from six months to one year.

Perks: Wages begin at $5.25 per hour. For a monthly fee of $300, housing in fully furnished condominiums and two meals in the employee cafeteria are provided per day.

Ideal Candidate: The program is designed for college students who are required to do an internship for their college degree. Interns should be energetic, service- and guest-oriented, thoughtful, dedicated, and self-motivated.

Getting In: Call for application materials. For nonrecreation internships, contact Mary Rieger, employment manager, at (843) 341-8099.

THE HOME RANCH

Dude Ranch • Colorado • Year-Round
www.homeranch.com

Will Hardly, Manager
P.O. Box 822
Clark, CO 80428
(970) 879-1780 • (970) 879-1795 (fax)
hrclark@homeranch.com

THE CALL OF THE WEST has always been strong in the hearts of Americans. No matter if they were raised on the romantic tales of Zane Grey, thrilled by the heroics of matinee idols like Roy Rogers, or laughed at the antics depicted in *City Slickers*, it is a safe bet that people of every generation have longed for the opportunity to ride the range and conquer the mountains. Working at The Home Ranch is a chance to heed that "call," if only for a little while. The 1,500-acre ranch accommodates over forty-two guests per week, with activities including wilderness hikes, horseback riding, or fly-fishing on the Elk River in the summer, and cross-country skiing, snowshoeing, and downhill skiing in the winter. Seasonal staff positions include children's counselors, kitchen helpers, cooks, dishwashers, waitstaff, housekeepers, front desk and maintenance personnel, hiking and cross-country ski guides, and wranglers. All positions are offered with a graduated salary starting at $900 per month, plus room, board, and laundry facilities.

HORIZON CAMPS

Camp • Maine/New York/Pennsylvania • Summer
www.horizoncamps.com

Staff Coordinator
3 W. Main St.
Elmsford, NY 10523
(800) 544-5448 • (914) 345-2086 • (914) 345-2120 (fax)
staff@horizoncamps.com

THE HORIZON CAMPS consist of four unique camps that work together to celebrate the growth and development of children. Both Camp Echo Lake and Echo Lake Southwoods are located in the heart of the Adirondack Mountains; Kamp Kohut is located on magnificent Lake Thompson in Maine; and Indian Head Camp is found in the Endless Mountains of northeast Pennsylvania. All are in spectacular settings with hundreds of acres to enjoy.

The Experience: Being a camp counselor is a demanding and often a difficult job. Counselors live, work, eat, sleep, and play with campers nearly all day, everyday. Cabin specialists spend a majority of their time with their group of campers and benefit from a variety of activities throughout the course of a day. Activity specialists also live with campers, but their daytime focus is on a specific activity area. Additionally, there are some positions that afford staff members to become a "jack-of-all-trades."

Commitment: The camp season runs roughly from mid-June through mid-August.

Perks: All staff receive an unforgettable, powerful experience with children, along with a salary, room, board, and travel.

Ideal Candidate: Young adults who are most successful at camp have high energy, are hardworking, and committed to working with children. The average age of the staff is twenty-one; some are college students, some teachers, others have graduated and are looking for a fulfilling way to spend a summer. If you are looking for a quiet, relaxed, "laid-back" environment, that's not what you'll find at these camps.

Getting In: Applications are accepted from October through April, although early applications are encouraged (as positions fill quickly).

HUNEWILL GUEST RANCH

Dude Ranch • California • May–October
www.hunewillranch.com

Betsy Hunewill Elliott, Personnel Director
200 Hunewill Ln.
Wellington, NV 89444
(775) 465-2201 • (775) 465-2056 (fax)
hunewillranch@tele-net.net

HUNEWILL RANCH is situated in Bridgeport Valley (California) in the heart of the eastern Sierras, at 6,500 feet. Directly behind the ranch are snow-covered crags that mark the boundary of Yosemite National Park. Staff members come back year after year to work hard and meet vacationers from all over the world while spending free time in the Sierras, breathing fresh, clean air. Seasonal staff, who must be at least eighteen years of age, are hired from the end of May to early October, with duties that may include maintenance, child care, work in the kitchen, cleaning cabins, or as wranglers. Applicants must be wholesome, robust, and cheerful employees who are willing to pitch in where needed. Benefits include $5.75 to $7 per hour (plus any tips), housing in employee cabins, and meals for a nominal fee (no cooking facilities are available in the cabins). Send a cover letter and resume to begin the application process.

INCLINE VILLAGE GENERAL IMPROVEMENT DISTRICT

Resort • Nevada • Winter/Summer
www.ivgid.org

Laurie Gwinn, Human Resources Manager
Recreation and Public Works Dept.
893 Southwood Blvd.
Incline Village, NV 89451
(775) 832-1205 • (775) 832-1122 (fax)
ivgid@sierra.net

IVGID FACILITIES include a ski resort, two 18-hole golf courses, a recreation center, beaches, and parks, with employment opportunities in each of these areas. Paid seasonal positions range from day camp leaders and recreation hosts to food and beverage and ski staff. In addition, recreation internships are available, where participants spend half their time in paid work assignments and the other half in volunteer work. Applicants should possess a good work ethic, enjoy the outdoors and beautiful mountain settings, have flexible schedules, and most of all, be customer-service focused.

KALANI OCEANSIDE RETREAT

Ecotourism • Hawaii • 3 Months
www.kalani.com/volunteer.htm

Resident Volunteer Coordinator
RR2, Box 4500, Pahoa-Beach Rd.
Kehena Beach, HI 96778
(800) 800-6886 • (808) 965-7828
kalani@kalani.com

SURROUNDED BY thermal springs, orchid farms, snorkeling tidal pools, steam bathing, waterfalls, botanical gardens, historic villages, and spectacular Volcanoes National Park, Kalani treats you to Hawaii's aloha comfort-offering personal retreats, annual events, and a three-month resident volunteer program. Throughout the year, twenty resident volunteers provide services to guests, working thirty hours per week in food service, grounds/maintenance, or housekeeping. A participation fee of $300 includes meals, shared lodging, and a week-long vacation during your three-month stay. Ongoing offerings include volcano and native plant treks, dolphin swims, snorkeling, hula, massage, Hawaiian mythology and language classes, shiatsu, and yoga.

> *If I could have my way about it, I would go back there and remain the rest of my days. It is paradise! If a man is rich, he can live expensively and his grandeur will be respected as in other parts of the earth. If he is poor, he can herd with the natives and live on next to nothing; he can sun himself all day long under the palm trees, and be no more troubled by his conscience than a butterfly would. When you are in that blessed retreat, you are safe from the turmoil of life. The past is a forgotten thing, the present is forever, the future you leave to take care of itself.*
> —Mark Twain, on Hawaii

LEGACY INTERNATIONAL

Experiential Learning • Virginia • Summer
www.legacyintl.org

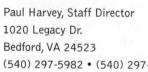

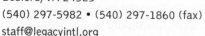

Paul Harvey, Staff Director
1020 Legacy Dr.
Bedford, VA 24523
(540) 297-5982 • (540) 297-1860 (fax)
staff@legacyintl.org

EVERY SUMMER SINCE 1979, a dynamic learning environment has been created at Legacy's Global Youth Village that emphasizes experiential learning, and challenges young people and staff to turn cross-cultural theory and skills into practical action. Each person contributes their own thread of education, thought, personality, and dreams to Legacy. Legacy's aim is to transform the legacy of prejudice, fear, confusion, and misunderstanding into a legacy of hope and to help future generations realize their capabilities.

The Experience: Summer staff live and work with people from all over the world, while developing a deeper understanding of community development issues, discovering the broader implications of daily actions and choices, and exploring the complexity of political and social situations. Very different from an academic environment, this experience is an intensive and fulfilling learning opportunity that requires active, responsible participation. A two-week pre-program training enhances the diverse skills and perspectives represented within the staff team. The Global Youth Village experience offers a hodgepodge of staff positions—from ESL instructors and global awareness trainers to lifeguards, art studio staff, and counselors.

Commitment: The program extends from mid-June through mid-August, with many positions involving a 6 1/2-day workweek (including 24-hour on-site responsibility as live-in cabin counselors).

Perks: Benefits include a stipend, housing, meals, medical benefits, and laundry service. Accommodations are in cabins with youth and/or other staff. In addition, Legacy offers a healthful rural environment including a whole-foods, vegetarian diet.

Ideal Candidate: Whether you are finishing college or preparing for graduate school, the Global Youth Village experience offers an amazing learning opportunity. All applicants must have previous youth work experience, be at least twenty-one years of age, and seek to enhance professional youth work or teaching experience. Smoking and alcohol use are not allowed during the term of employment.

Getting In: Visit their web site for details on the experience, a listing of available positions, and an on-line application. It is suggested you contact them by April 1 at the very latest.

> *We look for people who are really excited about the program and show the flexibility and maturity to work in an intense, multicultural setting with lots of challenges. With these qualities, we'll sometimes overlook a person's lack of experience just because of their openness and excitement, and we'll train them.*

LIFE ADVENTURE CAMP

Therapeutic Camp • Kentucky • Summer

Kathleen Reese, Program Director
1122 Oak Hill Dr.
Lexington, KY 40505
(606) 252-4733 • (606) 225-5115 (fax)
lifeadventurecamp@juno.com

••

SPONSORED BY the United Way, Life Adventure Camp is a primitive wilderness camp, concerned primarily with providing a successful and positive camping experience for children with emotional and behavioral problems. The program is designed around decentralized camping; campers and staff live in small groups in a primitive outdoor setting. Groups consist of eight to ten campers and three counselors.

Environment: Their campsite is located sixty miles southeast of Lexington on five hundred acres of rugged, undeveloped land in Estill County. The land is densely forested and offers wildlife, creeks, caves, rock outcroppings, and other natural areas for exploring.

The Experience: After extensive training, camp staff provide opportunities and activities that enhance a positive self-concept; provide a group living setting that encourages and teaches appropriate social-interaction skills among peers and adults; and teach basic and advanced low-impact camping skills, with the hope of increasing each camper's awareness and appreciation for the natural environment. There are no permanent facilities at the campsite; thus, campers and staff must build their campsites, using natural materials and plastic tarps. Water is supplied by a well and must be carried by hand to all campsites. This is the perfect opportunity for anyone wanting to lead outdoor programs or work with children.

Commitment: The season begins in mid-May and continues through early August.

Perks: A stipend of $1,000 to $3,000 is provided, along with room and board. Housing is provided in Lexington during in-town staff training sessions and during time off between sessions for those staff members who do not live in the Lexington area. First aid and CPR certifications will be provided at no cost.

Ideal Candidate: Applicants must be at least nineteen years of age, and those with experience working or volunteering with children and seeking a career in social work, counseling, or outdoor education are preferred.

Getting In: Call or write for application materials (which are due by March 30).

We are looking for open-minded men and women who want to learn to live a simple lifestyle and share this with children. People who are excited about living in the woods, cooking meals over a fire, exploring caves and creeks, carrying water from a well, and being with children will thrive in our program.

LOST CREEK RANCH

Dude Ranch • Wyoming • May–October
www.lostcreek.com

Mike and Bev Halpin, Owners
P.O. Box 95
Moose, WY 83012
(307) 733-3435 • (307) 733-1954 (fax)
ranch@lostcreek.com

••

LOST CREEK RANCH is nestled between Grand Teton National Park and Bridger Teton National Forest at an elevation of 7,000 feet. Seasonal positions include administration, wranglers, guides, chefs and bakers, waitstaff, facilities attendants, and ranch hands. The dress "code" at Lost Creek is Western, so be prepared to bring your jeans, boots, and denim shirts. A weekly wage, room, board, and laundry facilities are provided. Employee housing is fairly rustic and most employees will have one or two roommates. Those who complete their employment agreements receive a season-end bonus (consisting of $5 for each day worked during the nonguest season and $10 for each day worked during the guest season). Preference is given to individuals who are twenty-one or older and can work the entire season (May through October). All applicants must also be certified in CPR and first aid.

MAHO BAY CAMPS

Sustainable Resort • Virgin Islands • 1–6 Months
www.maho.org/summer.html

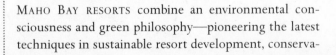

Roland Kravatz, Director
4-Hour Worker Program
Box 310
Cruz Bay, VI 00831-0310
(800) 392-9004 • (340) 776-6504 (fax)
mahobay@maho.org

••

MAHO BAY RESORTS combine an environmental consciousness and green philosophy—pioneering the latest techniques in sustainable resort development, conservation, recycling and site restoration, along with close-to-nature experiences and economy. Tent-cottages and architecture, which are surrounded by Virgin Islands National Park and the turquoise waters and white sandy beaches of the Caribbean, provide plenty of creature comforts without disturbing the creatures that were there before we were. Activities on the premises range from sailing and snorkeling to educational programs and yoga. For those who wish to blend a vacation adventure along with some work, Maho provides a work exchange program. Volunteers contribute four hours per day of work to the Maho community, and in return, receive a low-cost Caribbean vacation, with free lodging and a nonoptional meal plan at $55 per week. No experience is necessary; however, volunteers must be at least eighteen years of age, and stay a minimum of one month during the time frame of May 1 to November 15. Work assignments might include housekeeping, maintenance, food services, store assistance, or guest registration.

MOUNTAIN TRAIL OUTDOOR SCHOOL

Outdoor Center • North Carolina • March–November
www.kanuga.org

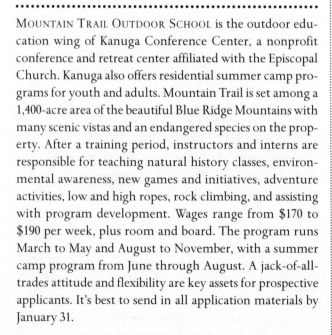

Paul Bockoven, Outdoor Education Director
Kanuga Conference Center
P.O. Box 250
Hendersonville, NC 28793-0250
(828) 692-9136 • (828) 696-3589 (fax)
mtos@kanuga.org

MOUNTAIN TRAIL OUTDOOR SCHOOL is the outdoor education wing of Kanuga Conference Center, a nonprofit conference and retreat center affiliated with the Episcopal Church. Kanuga also offers residential summer camp programs for youth and adults. Mountain Trail is set among a 1,400-acre area of the beautiful Blue Ridge Mountains with many scenic vistas and an endangered species on the property. After a training period, instructors and interns are responsible for teaching natural history classes, environmental awareness, new games and initiatives, adventure activities, low and high ropes, rock climbing, and assisting with program development. Wages range from $170 to $190 per week, plus room and board. The program runs March to May and August to November, with a summer camp program from June through August. A jack-of-all-trades attitude and flexibility are key assets for prospective applicants. It's best to send in all application materials by January 31.

NORTH FORK GUEST RANCH

Dude Ranch • Colorado • May–September
www.northforkranch.com

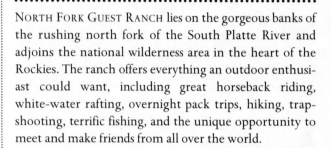

Dean and Karen May, Owners
Box B
Shawnee, CO 80475
(800) 843-7895 • (303) 838-9873 • (303) 838-1549 (fax)
northforkranch@worldnet.att.net

NORTH FORK GUEST RANCH lies on the gorgeous banks of the rushing north fork of the South Platte River and adjoins the national wilderness area in the heart of the Rockies. The ranch offers everything an outdoor enthusiast could want, including great horseback riding, white-water rafting, overnight pack trips, hiking, trapshooting, terrific fishing, and the unique opportunity to meet and make friends from all over the world.

The Experience: Because the ranch is a people-serving business, they do not hire people merely to get a job done. You will be expected to give totally of yourself, sharing with and caring for their guests. Positions include cook, kid's counselor, office/kitchen, wrangler, maintenance, and housekeeper/waitress.

Commitment: The season starts in early May and does not end until the second week in September. They are primarily interested in those who can stay through the end of August or later.

Perks: Staff members receive $550 per month, plus room and board. On your day off and after daily duties, you can enjoy all ranch activities.

Getting In: Call for application materials. They begin their review of applications starting in January and try to have their entire staff hired by April 1.

> *Do you love people? Do you love to work? Are you willing to learn and do new things? Are you flexible and willing to help out anytime, anywhere, and do anything? Are you enthusiastic and excited about other people enjoying their vacation? Would you involve yourself in the basic ranch objective of making the guests' stay at North Fork Ranch a great experience? If you answered yes to these questions, you are the type of person they are looking for!*

Don't settle for less than your potential. Remember, average is as close to the bottom as it is to the top. —ABIGAIL VAN BUREN

93

OAKLAND HOUSE SEASIDE INN AND COTTAGES

Guest House • Maine • 8–11 Weeks
www.oaklandhouse.com

Jim and Sally Littlefield, Innkeepers
RR1, Box 400
Brooksville, ME 04617
(207) 359-8521 • (207) 359-9865 (fax)
jim@oaklandhouse.com

LIFE AT Oakland House Seaside Inn and Cottages is more "like it used to be," with creative use of time and leisure hours spent by their guests and staff. At the turn of the nineteenth century, the first guests were the "Rusticators," who arrived on steamships from Boston, New York, and places beyond. They were writers, artists, and educators seeking respite from city bustle. Today Oakland House offers a half-mile of prime oceanfront, ocean and lakeside beaches, hiking trails, a dock, rowboats, and, of course, relaxation.

The Experience: No matter the position, the staff's goal at Oakland House is to make guests feel welcome in a family-style atmosphere. Positions include waitstaff, office assistants, kitchen assistants, grounds people, cabin stewards, and housekeepers. Due to the general long-term nature of guest visits (one-week minimum in cottages), there are many opportunities for friendships and cordial staff relationships.

Commitment: Positions extend for eleven weeks during the summer and eight weeks during the fall.

Perks: The pay varies with each position. Staff members will live in the 200-year-old hotel and are encouraged to the enjoy the surrounding area on days off. The owners also offer complimentary boating excursions and many perks throughout the season.

Ideal Candidate: Applicants must be at least eighteen years of age, and staff members often return year after year as they work through college. Because of its rural location, it's helpful if employees bring a car.

POINT REYES NATIONAL SEASHORE ASSOCIATION

Camp • California • Summer

Scott Wolland, Education Programs Director
Point Reyes National Seashore
Point Reyes, CA 94956
(415) 663-1200 • (415) 663-8174 (fax)

POINT REYES offers a six-week residential Science Camp for kids aged seven to twelve, who explore the rich coastal environment and diverse habitats of the region, as well as a six-day Adventure Camp for teens, aged thirteen to sixteen, who are led on a four-day backpack trip on the seashore focusing on self-esteem, teamwork, and backpacking skills.

The Experience: Naturalist intern/counselors primarily assist with guided natural history and environmental education programs, mealtime supervision, free-time activities, and cabin supervision for children attending the Science Camp. Not only will interns work with experts in the field of environmental and outdoor education, they will also have the chance to obtain training in educational and behavior management techniques, natural history interpretation, and recreational leadership skills. Other summer staff positions include six naturalists, a director, and three kitchen workers.

Commitment: Summer positions start in late June (with staff training) and end in mid- to late August.

Perks: A $150 per week stipend, plus room and board, is provided. This is a great way to experience the warmth and camaraderie of living and working with other staff members in a residential camp environment.

Ideal Candidate: Applicants should enjoy working with children and the outdoors, have a knowledge of ecological concepts/communities, and be first aid and CPR certified. Preference is given to those who are in college; who are willing to work and live with campers in a rustic setting; and who are creative, enthusiastic, flexible, self-motivated, and have a sense of humor. Experience in supervising or teaching students is a bonus.

Getting In: Call for application materials (which are due by April 1). On-site interviews are preferred, but phone interviews are acceptable.

RAMAPO ANCHORAGE CAMP

Therapeutic Camp • New York • Summer
www.ramapoanchorage.com

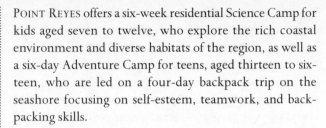

Tom Decker, Director
P.O. Box 266
Rhinebeck, NY 12572
(914) 876-8403 • (914) 876-8414 (fax)
info@ramapoanchorage.com

RAMAPO ANCHORAGE CAMP fosters the development of positive social and learning skills for children who have a wide range of emotional, behavioral, and learning problems.

Counselors work individually with each child through educational and outdoor adventure programming, helping them to develop their school readiness and the communication skills necessary for healthy development. The staff consists mostly of college students and recent graduates who have strong leadership and caring qualities that enable them to motivate and relate to young people. A stipend along with room and board are provided. Application forms can be found through their web site.

REDFISH LAKE LODGE

Lodge • Idaho • Summer

General Manager
P.O. Box 9
Stanley, ID 83278
(208) 774-3536 • (208) 774-3546 (fax)

ESTABLISHED IN 1929, Redfish Lake Lodge is a family-oriented rustic lodge located in the rugged Sawtooth Mountains. The area is known for its incredible backpacking, horseback riding, white-water rafting, rock climbing, mountain bike riding, and fishing. Summer positions include food service staff, service station attendants, housekeepers, marina staff, store assistants, front-desk clerks, and maintenance people. Along with room and board, a $772 per month salary is provided.

ROCKY MOUNTAIN VILLAGE

Therapeutic Camp • Colorado • Summer
www.easterealsco.org

Christine Newell, Camping and Recreation Director
Easter Seals Colorado
P.O. Box 115
Empire, CO 80438
(800) 692-5520 • (303) 569-2333 • (303) 569-3857 (fax)
campinfo@cess.org

ROCKY MOUNTAIN VILLAGE, owned and operated by Easter Seals Colorado, serves as a residential camp for children and adults with physical and/or cognitive disabilities. Seasonal positions include activity director, registered nurse, cabin counselors, kitchen/cooks, maintenance, and specialists in these areas: trips/travel, ropes course, outdoor education, arts and crafts, aquatics, horseback riding/animals, and media. Those who have a desire to work with children and adults with disabilities are preferred. A weekly stipend of $125 is provided (along with a $200 bonus if you work the entire season).

ROSE RESNICK LIGHTHOUSE FOR THE BLIND

Therapeutic Camp • California • Summer
www.lighthouse-sf.org

Volunteer Coordinator
214 Van Ness Ave.
San Francisco, CA 94102-4508
(415) 431-1481 • (415) 863-7568 (fax)
volunteers@lighthouse-sf.org

ROSE RESNICK LIGHTHOUSE FOR THE BLIND serves blind, visually impaired, and deaf/blind persons of all ages by providing rehabilitation, social services, and recreational opportunities. During the summer volunteers provide practical support services at Enchanted Hills Camp, located in the wine country of Northern California. Volunteers assist with arts and crafts, hiking, swimming, horseback riding, and a variety of special activities. Fun is the common theme for the camp experience; however, the most important goal is for campers to achieve independence and develop confidence in their abilities. Sessions run from mid-June through the end of August for three days to two weeks. Volunteers receive room and board, training in sensitivity to blindness, and the ability to test their own boundaries of giving and caring.

SEACAMP

Camp • Florida • Summer
www.seacamp.org

Grace Upshaw, Camp Director
1300 Big Pine Ave.
Big Pine Key, FL 33043
(305) 872-2331 • (305) 872-2555 (fax)
seacamp98@aol.com

ESTABLISHED IN 1966, Seacamp is dedicated to the study of marine communities and island habitats, with courses led by academically trained marine science instructors. Over 7,500 teenagers have attended one of Seacamp's eighteen-day programs, which focus on everything from sailing, scuba, and kayaking to photography and arts and crafts. Although their backgrounds vary, each participant shares at least one common interest: the importance of oceans and marine life to their world.

Environment: With its beautiful location at Newfound Harbor, Seacamp is minutes from the only living coral reef in North America. Opportunities abound to explore the exciting waters of the Florida Keys, both in the Atlantic

Ocean and the Gulf of Mexico. Indians, pirates, and Flagler's Railroad all contribute to the heritage of this subtropical area.

The Experience: A variety of instructor positions are available, including those in arts and crafts, boardsailing, photography, sailing, science, and scuba, as well as other positions as counselors and kitchen and maintenance staff. Whatever the position, each staff member participates in all camp activities. The camp experience is a unique learning environment that combines the living and working aspects of the staff member's life, and many times it becomes hard to distinguish between learning and teaching experiences.

Commitment: The summer season runs from late May through late August. For those who would like to continue to teach young people about the sea, Newfound Harbor Marine Institute (a Seacamp program) provides workshops and residential programs from early September through late May. See their listing on page 162 for more information.

Perks: Benefits include a weekly salary, lodging, meals, and health insurance. A four-week pre-camp training program provides American Red Cross lifeguarding, first aid, and CPR certification, NAUI skin-diving instruction, a forty-hour workshop in seamanship and boat handling, and if scuba certified, rescue diver training.

Ideal Candidate: The minimum age for employment is nineteen years, and most candidates are either in college or have just graduated. With the heart of Seacamp's program focused on marine science education, the best applicants possess an interest in working with teenagers in a water-oriented setting.

Getting In: Call for application materials. Phone interviews begin in March and continue through April.

SNOW MOUNTAIN RANCH

Family Resort • Colorado • Year-Round
www.snowmtnranch.org

Jeni Fuqua, Assistant Human Resources Director
YMCA of the Rockies
P.O. Box 169
Winter Park, CO 80482
(970) 887-2152 • (303) 449-6781 (fax)
jfuqua@snowmtnranch.org

SNOW MOUNTAIN RANCH, a conference center and family resort accommodating up to 1,700 guests per day, offers hiking, horseback riding, mountain biking, snowshoeing, roller-skating, an indoor pool, basketball/volleyball courts, and groomed cross-country ski trails. Camp Chief Ouray, a summer resident youth camp, is located at Snow Mountain and serves youth from ages eight to sixteen. Seasonal job opportunities are available throughout the year and include administration and front desk, food services, housekeeping, craft shop and maintenance staff, adventure education and Nordic ski instructors, and youth counselors. A weekly stipend of $145 is provided, along with meals and housing. Applicants must be at least eighteen years of age and enjoy meeting new people, the Rocky Mountains, and living in a Christian environment.

Seacamp instructors help participants gain a better understanding of the natural features of the ocean and its ecosystems.

Skiing

WORKING AT A SKI RESORT

Photo Credit: David Madison

Seasonal ski instructors at Royal Gorge Cross Country Ski Resort help novices fine-tune their cross-country skiing abilities.

The popular saying among employees at the Village at Breckenridge Resort is "you move here for the winters, but end up staying for the summers." This appears to be the common theme for thousands of snow enthusiasts who work seasonally at ski resorts all over the country. Beyond a work environment that provides breathtaking scenery, one of the biggest perks of becoming a "ski bum" for the winter is the coveted ski pass (along with free ski rentals and lessons, as well as discounts on just about everything offered at the resort).

Most ski resorts generally offer the same types of seasonal jobs, which fall under the categories of administration, food and beverage, hospitality services, mountain operations, and ski services. So whether you want to become a snowboard instructor, teach children how to ski, serve meals to guests, or assist with marketing efforts, opportunities abound. In general, people from all walks of life are hired, and many have recently finished their college studies or are looking for a lifestyle change.

For those interested in ski instructor positions, it's not enough to be an excellent skier. Certification by the Professional Ski Instructors of America (www.psia.org/education/certification.htm) is often a hiring requirement. For ski patrol positions, the National Ski Patrol (www.nsp.org) provides courses and certification. Similarly, the American Association of Snowboard Instructors (www.aasi.org) provides snowboarding certification.

—Contributed by About.com's job searching expert, Alison Doyle (www.jobsearch.about.com)

The following are some of the best ski resorts around the country for seasonal job opportunities:

CALIFORNIA

Alpine Meadows

Human Resources Department
P.O. Box 5279
Tahoe City, CA 96145
(530) 581-8212
info@skialpine.com • www.skialpine.com

Bear Valley Ski Company

Personnel Department
P.O. Box 5038
Bear Valley, CA 95223
(209) 753-2301 • (209) 753-6421 (fax)
work@bearvalley.com • www.bearvalley.com/employment.html

Boreal Mountain Playground

Spin Shaffer, Human Resources Director
P.O. Box 39
Truckee, CA 96160
(530) 426-3666 • (530) 426-3173 (fax)
hr@borealski.com • www.borealski.com

BOREAL MOUNTAIN PLAYGROUND includes both Boreal and Soda Springs Ski Areas, which are located at the top of historic and scenic Donner Summit Pass in the Lake Tahoe region. Cleverly timed, Boreal opens on Halloween; Soda Springs on Thanksgiving. Boreal is best known for its night skiing and radical terrain parks and half pipes. Soda Springs was the first ski area in Tahoe to offer lift access tubing as an added snow sport. Typical seasonal snow jobs are offered, and employees can work one of two shifts, up to forty-eight hours per week, to accommodate day and night skiing. Along with a weekly wage, food is discounted at 50 percent, and merchandise from the sport shop is discounted at 25 percent. Along with complimentary ski rentals, employees can also ski free at Alpine Meadows, and Park City, Utah, which are owned by the same corporation. A pass-exchange program allows employees to check out Donner Ski Ranch, Royal Gorge, and Sugar Bowl midweek, and a new summer Sports Action Park makes it possible to work seasonally during the summer months.

Kirkwood Resort

Human Resources Department
P.O. Box 1
Kirkwood, CA 95646
(209) 258-6000 • (209) 258-8899 (fax)
www.skikirkwood.com

Mammoth California

Bill Medove, Recruiting Staff Trainer
P.O. Box 24
Mammoth Lakes, CA 93546
(800) 472-3160 • (760) 934-0654 • (760) 934-0608 (fax)
personnel@mammoth-mtn.com • www.mammoth-mtn.com

LOCATED IN THE eastern Sierras in central California, Mammoth is a four-season mountain resort with facilities at Mammoth Mountain and June Mountain ski resorts, as well as operations at the Tamarack Lodge, Sierra Star Golf Club, Sierra Meadows stables, the Mammoth Mountain Inn, and the Juniper Springs Lodge. Seasonal positions are offered in one of four areas, including skier services, outside operations, food services, and hotel operations. Along with a weekly wage, winter housing is provided for first-year seasonal employees who are part of the Mammoth entry-level staff or those participating in the Foreign Exchange Program. Housing varies from private rooms to bunkbeds at a cost of $9 to $15 per night (with a payroll deduction).

Northstar-at-Tahoe

Employee Services
P.O. Box 129
Truckee, CA 96160
(530) 562-3510 • (530) 562-2217 (job hotline) •
(530) 562-2214 (fax)
northstarjobs@boothcreek.com •
www.skinorthstar.com/employ.html

Resort at Squaw Creek

Human Resources Department
400 Squaw Creek Rd.
Olympic Valley, CA 96146
(800) 327-3353 • (530) 583-6300 • (530) 581-6632 (fax)
www.squawcreek.com

Royal Gorge Cross Country Ski Resort

Carol Smith, Director of Operations
9411 Hillside Dr.
P.O. Box 1100
Soda Springs, CA 95728
(800) 500-3871 • (530) 426-3871 • (530) 426-9221 (fax)
info@royalgorge.com • www.royalgorge.com

WITH OVER nine thousand acres of private lands and a network of eighty-eight trails, Royal Gorge is the largest cross-country ski resort in North America. Guest services include two overnight lodges, a day lodge, and ten warming huts sprinkled throughout the track system in historic Donner Summit. From mid-November through mid-April, seasonal employees are hired in administration, mountain operations, resort services, the ski school, and the wilderness lodge. As in any ski area, work hours are entirely dependent upon the weather. Along with a weekly wage, perks include a free season ski pass, use of rental equipment, and ski school lessons, as well as discounted meals. For those who need housing, Royal Gorge has several furnished houses that are usually within walking (or skiing) distance of the resort, with rents ranging from $75 to $150 per month plus utilities. Bunkhouse-style accommodations are also available for part-time employees. Send a resume and cover letter to begin the application process or join them at their job fair in mid-October.

Ski Homewood

Human Resources Department
5145 W. Lake Blvd.
P.O. Box 165
Homewood, CA 96141
(530) 525-2992 • (530) 525-0417 (fax)
smile@homewood.com • www.skihomewood.com

Snow Summit Mountain Resort

Cheryl Hightower, Personnel Director
880 Summit Blvd.
P.O. Box 77
Big Bear Lake, CA 92315
(909) 866-5766 • (909) 866-6806 (fax)
personnel@snowsummit.com • www.snowsummit.com

WITH AN AVERAGE snowfall of seventy-five inches, Snow Summit Mountain Resort is located in Southern California's pristine Big Bear Lake area. Over one thousand winter seasonal positions are available in all areas of operation, ranging from the ski school and rental shop to food and beverage and marketing. Entry-level wages range from $5.75 to $7 per hour (with generous allowances for previous work experience). Benefits include complimentary lift tickets and lessons and discounted ski and snowboard rental, meals, and retail purchases, along with employee mixers and a family Christmas and ski party. Most of the seasonal staff is hired at their October job fair, where managers and supervisors from every department will be on hand to conduct personal interviews and make job offers to qualified individuals. Those who cannot make it to the job fair must submit their applications in person to the personnel department.

Squaw Valley USA

Personnel Department
P.O. Box 2007
Olympic Valley, CA 96146
(530) 581-7112 • (530) 581-7117 (job hotline) •
(530) 581-7202 (fax)
personnel@squaw.com • www.squaw.com

Sugar Bowl Ski Resort

Jim Brady, Personnel Department
P.O. Box 5
Norden, CA 95724
(530) 426-6730 • (530) 426-6731 (job hotline)
personnel@sugarbowl.com • www.sugarbowl.com

HOME TO THE first chairlift in California and first gondola in the country, Sugar Bowl is known for its rich history and deep powder—over 1,500 acres of challenging terrain, four picturesque mountain peaks, and three day lodges. Those who come to work for Sugar Bowl are lured by the mountains, an enjoyable working experience, and an enriching lifestyle. Benefits include a season pass and complimentary lift tickets for friends and family, discounts on just about everything, flexible schedules, and housing assistance. It's recommended that you join them at their job fair, which is normally conducted the last two Saturdays of October.

COLORADO

Aspen Skiing Company

Human Resources Department
P.O. Box 1248
Aspen, CO 81612-1248
(970) 920-0945 • (970) 923-0499 (job hotline) •
(970) 920-0771 (fax)
jbeck@skiaspen.com •
www.skiaspen.com/asc/employment.html

Beaver Run Resort

Personnel Director
620 Village Rd.
P.O. Box 2115
Breckenridge, CO 80424-2115
(800) 288-1282 • (970) 453-6000 • (970) 453-9351 (fax)
work4brr@colorado.net • www.beaverrun.com

Copper Mountain Resort

Human Resources Department
P.O. Box 3001
Copper Mountain, CO 80443
(970) 968-2318 • (970) 968-6339 (job hotline)
cmr-hr@ski-copper.com • www.ski-copper.com

Crested Butte Mountain Resort

Kariin Berkland, Student Employee Coordinator
12 Snowmass Rd.
P.O. Box A
Mt. Crested Butte, CO 81225
(970) 349-2312 • (970) 349-4777 (job hotline) •
(970) 349-2250 (fax)
jobs@cbmr.com • www.crestedbutteresort.com

SKIING

Spirit has fifty times the strength and staying power of brawn and muscle. —MARK TWAIN

KNOWN FOR ITS extreme skiing and its funky Victorian architecture, Crested Butte remains one of the last undiscovered ski towns in the West. It is also the site for the U.S. Extreme Skiing and Snowboarding Championships. Crested Butte's College Student Employee Program is a winter filled with fun while learning about resort operations. You'll ski like crazy and live in a resort community with about sixty other college students from around the world. Seasonal employment, available from mid-November through mid-April, is offered in many different departments, including lift operations, children's ski school, hotel operations, and guest services. Benefits include an hourly wage of $6.25 per hour, affordably priced housing, an unlimited ski pass, and a $500 academic scholarship (by working the entire season). Student employees are housed in a new apartment complex on Mt. Crested Butte, which is walking distance from the base area. Applicants must either be students or recent graduates with a passion for the snow and lots of enthusiasm. Call to receive an application packet (or you can download it from their web site). Telephone interviews may be conducted for those unable to travel to Crested Butte for a personal interview.

Purgatory Resort

Human Resources Department
#1 Skier Place
Durango, CO 81301
(970) 247-9000 • (970) 385-2119 (fax)
purghr@frontier.net • www.ski-purg.com/hr.htm

Silver Creek Resort

Human Resources Director
1000 Village Rd.
P.O. Box 1110
Silver Creek, CO 80446
(970) 887-5130 • (800) 448-9458 (job hotline)
staff@silvercreek-resort.com • www.silvercreek-resort.com

Steamboat Ski and Resort Corporation

Human Resources Department
2305 Mt. Werner Circle
Steamboat Springs, CO 80487-9023
(970) 879-6111 • (970) 879-7844 (fax)
personnel@steamboat-ski.com •
www.steamboat-ski.com/hr.html

Telluride Ski and Golf Company

Missy Sallee, Manager of Human Resources
565 Mountain Village Blvd.
Telluride, CO 81435
(800) 728-6900 • (888) 754-1010 (job hotline)
www.telski.com

IN ADDITION TO the typical ski resort seasonal jobs available throughout the year, Telluride offers a twelve-week internship program that allows interns to work in different departments and perform varied tasks. A $1,000 stipend is provided, along with a free ski pass if working during the winter months. To begin the application process, send a resume and a letter detailing your skills and internship goals.

Vail/Beaver Creek

Human Resources Department
P.O. Box 7
Vail, CO 81620
(970) 845-2460 • (970) 479-3068 (job hotline) •
(970) 845-2465 (fax)
www.snow.com/vail

Village at Breckenridge Resort

Sarah Ziesmer, Human Resources Specialist
P.O. Box 8329
Breckenridge, CO 80424
(888) 754-5621 • (970) 453-3120 • (970) 453-3127 (fax)
breckjob@colorado.net • www.breckresort.com/job.cfm

IN THE WINTER MONTHS at the Village at Breckenridge Resort, guests enjoy skiing, snowmobiling, cross-country skiing, sleigh rides, and ice-skating, while the summer is filled with white-water rafting, mountain biking, hiking, and a summer music festival on Maggie Pond. This is a great opportunity for snow enthusiasts to advance their careers in the resort and hospitality field—and to merely have fun! Employees will work at either the Breckenridge Mountain Lodge, Rocky Mountain Resort Lodging, Tannhauser Condominiums, or the Village at Breckenridge. Positions range from food and beverage, front desk, reservations, and housekeeping to internships and career-track positions. Wages range from $7.25 to $12 per hour. Limited housing is available in condos spread throughout Breckenridge for $300 per month. Perks include a complimentary ski pass (which can be used at Breckenridge, Beaver Creek, Keystone, and Vail), free group ski/snowboard lessons, and discounted meals and room nights. A comprehensive health insurance plan is also offered. A personal interview is required and applicants are encouraged to come to their job fair, held in late October of each year.

Winter Park Resort

Human Resources Department
P.O. Box 36
Winter Park, CO 80482
(888) 562-4525 • (970) 726-1536 • (303) 892-5823 (fax)
wpjobs@skiwinterpark.com •
www.skiwinterpark.com/employment

"COME ENJOY the year-round beauty of the Rockies—and don't forget to bring your adventurous spirit with you." Winter Park is the fifth largest ski area in Colorado although it manages to avoid the mainstream crowds of the "rich and famous." Popular activities at Winter Park include skiing, snowboarding, snowshoeing, snow biking, ice-skating, snowmobiling, tubing, mountain biking, rafting, hiking, camping, fishing, stargazing, hunting, and beautiful scenery. For applicants with a limited skiing or snowboarding background, positions are available in food service, facilities, grounds crew and parking, ticket and lesson sales, reservations, and children's center staff. For applicants with some basic skiing or snowboarding ability, there are numerous openings for lift attendants. Advanced skiers and snowboarders may apply for positions as race-crew members, ski and snowboard instructors, and ski patrol. Wages start at $7.50 per hour for entry-level positions, along with a free season pass, complimentary lift passes for friends, free ski and snowboard lessons, group health insurance, and food and beverage discounts. Employees can also use the Sports Science Fitness Center or the Early Education Center (employee daycare) for a nominal fee. Winter Park also offers a limited amount of subsidized employee housing in nearby condos.

IDAHO

Lookout Pass Ski Area

Dean Cooper, General Manager
P.O. Box 108
Wallace, ID 83873
(208) 744-1301 • (208) 744-1227 (fax)
dean@skilookout.com • www.skilookout.com

Sun Valley Resort

Personnel Director
P.O. Box 10
Sun Valley, ID 83353
(800) 894-9946 • (208) 622-2082 (fax)
www.sunvalley.com

MAINE

Sugarloaf/USA

Human Resources Office
RR1, Box 5000
Carrabassett Valley, ME 04947
(207) 237-2000
info@sugarloaf.com • www.sugarloaf.com

Sunday River Ski Resort

Human Resources Department
P.O. Box 450
Bethel, ME 04217
(207) 824-3000
hjordan@sundayriver.com • www.sundayriver.com

MONTANA

Big Mountain Ski and Summer Resort

Human Resources Department
P.O. Box 1400
Whitefish, MT 59937
(800) 858-3930 • (406) 862-2911 • (406) 862-2955 (fax)
bigmtn@bigmtn.com • www.bigmtn.com

Big Sky Ski and Summer Resort

Human Resources Department
1 Lone Mountain Trail
P.O. Box 160001
Big Sky, MT 59716
(800) 548-4486 • (406) 995-5812 • (406) 995-5001 (fax)
jobs@bigskyresort.com • www.bigskyresort.com

NEVADA

Diamond Peak Ski Resort

Staffing Director
1210 Ski Way
Incline Village, NV 89451
(800) 468-2463 • (775) 832-1126 • (775) 832-1281 (fax)
info@diamondpeak.com • www.diamondpeak.com

DIAMOND PEAK SKI RESORT is located in Lake Tahoe's showcase community—Incline Village. You will experience spectacular alpine and cross-country skiing, with incomparable views of Lake Tahoe. Winter seasonal positions include all your typical resort positions, from ski instructors and ski patrol to food and beverage staff and shuttle drivers. Most winter positions commence in the beginning of December and continue through mid-April (depending on the snow conditions). Hourly wages range from $6.50 to $13.50 per hour and perks include free skiing/snowboarding, free basic ski equipment rental, free lessons, food and beverage discounts, and access to the Incline Village Recreation Center. Call for a job description brochure. The best way to learn about employment opportunities is by attending their annual job fair held in mid-October.

SKIING

There is no shortcut to life. To the end of our days, life is a lesson imperfectly learned. —HARRISON E. SALISBURY

101

Heavenly Ski Resort

Human Resources Department
P.O. Box 2180
Stateline, NV 89449
(775) 586-7000
humres@skiheavenly.com • www.skiheavenly.com/employ

NEW HAMPSHIRE

Attitash Bear Peak Resort

Janice Sullivan, Personnel Director
Route 302
Bartlett, NH 03812
(603) 374-2611 • (603) 374-1960 (fax)
jsullivan@attitash.com • www.attitash.com

Loon Mountain Resort

Human Resources Department
RR1, Box 41
Kancamagus Highway
Lincoln, NH 03251-9711
(603) 745-6281
rberkeley.lm@boothcreek.com •
www.loonmtn.com/winter/jobs.html

NEW MEXICO

Angel Fire Resort

Human Resources Department
P.O. Drawer B
Angel Fire, NM 87710
(800) 633-7463 • (505) 377-6401 • (505) 377-4240 (fax)
www.angelfireresort.com/employ.html

OREGON

Hoodoo Ski Area and Recreation Services

Human Resources Department
Box 20, Hwy 20
Sisters, OR 97759
(541) 822-3799 • (541) 822-3398 (fax)
hoodoo@hoodoo.com • www.hoodoo.com

Inn of the Seventh Mountain

Human Resources Department
18575 SW Century Dr.
Bend, OR 97702-1950
(800) 452-6810 • (541) 382-8711 • (541) 382-3517 (fax)
www.innofthe7thmountain.com/jobs.html

Mt. Bachelor Ski and Summer Resort

Pat Gerhart, Human Resources Manager
335 SW Century Dr.
P.O. Box 1031
Bend, OR 97709-1031
(800) 829-2442 • (541) 382-2442 • (541) 382-6536 (fax)
work@mtbachelor.com • www.mtbachelor.com

Mt. Hood Meadows Ski Resort

Human Resources Director
P.O. Box 470
Mt. Hood, OR 97041
(503) 337-2222 • (503) 337-2232 (fax)
hr@skihood.com • www.skihood.com

Mt. Hood Meadows features 2,150 acres of rugged terrain, complete with mogul-filled bowls, chutes, ridges, and outback skiing in Heather Canyon. Winter positions (from early November to late April) include lift operators, ski patrol, snow groomers, rental technicians, cashiers, ticket checkers, bus drivers, and food service staff. Wages range from $6.50 to $10 per hour. Perks include a free season ski pass, lessons, and shuttle bus transportation. Discounts on food and ski shop purchases are also available. Applicants should be gregarious, neat, and have previous service-oriented experience and the tenacity to work in a mountain environment. They conduct a job fair the first week of October. It's highly recommended you attend this fair.

Timberline Lodge

Human Resources Director
Timberline Ski Area
Timberline Lodge, OR 97028
(503) 622-0730 • (503) 622-0710 (fax)
jobs@timberlinelodge.com • www.timberlinelodge.com

YOU'LL RECOGNIZE a "sense of place" (and some of nature's most scenic country) at Timberline Lodge. Constructed of mammoth timbers and native stone, the lodge, registered as a National Historic Landmark, stands today as tribute to the rugged spirit of the Pacific Northwest. Seasonal positions are available in lift operations, skier services, front desk, rental shop, lodge services, kitchen and banquets, and the ski school. Hourly wages range from $6.50 to $16, plus tips, depending on position. Employee housing is located nearby.

UTAH

Park City Mountain Resort

Human Resources Department
P.O. Box 39
Park City, UT 84060
(435) 647-5421
hr@pcski.com • www.parkcitymountain.com

SKIING

Snowbird Ski and Summer Resort

Kent Boam, Human Resources Recruiting Manager
7350 S. Wasatch Blvd.
Salt Lake City, UT 84121
(801) 947-8240 • (801) 947-8244 (fax)
kboam@snowbird.com • www.snowbird.com

WITH A MID-MOUNTAIN average annual snowfall of more than five hundred inches, Snowbird attracts more fresh powder snow than almost any other resort in the country. Snowbird's mountain trails cover more than two thousand skiable acres. Seasonal staff positions include food service personnel, front desk clerks, reservation clerks, sales clerks, security officers, switchboard operators, valets, tram operators, ski hosts/hostesses, housekeeping, parking attendants, warehouse laborers, ski school, and mountain operations. Wages start at $7.50 per hour, with perks featuring a generous ski privilege program that includes dependent passes, group health/hospitalization, life insurance, free transportation, and discounts on food, ski lessons, and lodging. Most Snowbird employees live in and commute from the Salt Lake City area. Snowbird not only hires seasonal employees for winter and summer but also has many year-round positions.

VERMONT

Okemo Mountain Resort

Human Resources Department
77 Okemo Ridge Rd.
Ludlow, VT 05149
(802) 228-4041
jobs@okemo.com • www.okemo.com

Stowe Mountain Resort

Human Resources Coordinator
5781 Mountain Rd.
Stowe, VT 05672-4890
(802) 253-3541 • (802) 253-3543 (job hotline) •
(802) 253-3406 (fax)
info@stowe.com • www.stowe.com/infocenter/jobs.html

Stratton Mountain

Human Resources Department
RR1, Box 145
Stratton, VT 05155
(802) 297-4107 • (802) 297-4104 (job hotline) •
(802) 297-4300 (fax)
www.stratton.com

Sugarbush Resort

Human Resources Department
RR1, Box 350
Warren, VT 05674
(802) 583-6400 • (802) 583-6495 (fax)
hr@sugarbush.com • www.sugarbush.com

Topnotch Resort and Spa

Personnel Director
P.O. Box 1458
Stowe, VT 05672
(800) 451-8686 • (802) 253-8585 • (802) 253-9263 (fax)
topnotch@sover.net • www.topnotch-resort.com

WASHINGTON

Stevens Pass Ski Area

Personnel Department
P.O. Box 98
Skykomish, WA 98288
(206) 812-4510 • (206) 812-4517 (fax)
personnel@stevenspass.com • www.stevenspass.com

WYOMING

Grand Targhee Ski and Summer Resort

Joni Dronen, Human Resources Department
Ski Hill Rd.
Box SKI
Alta, WY 83422
(800) 827-4433 • (307) 353-2300 • (307) 353-8148 (fax)
jdronen.gt@boothcreek.com • www.grandtarghee.com

GRAND TARGHEE is a small, family-oriented resort nestled in the pines at eight thousand feet on the west side of the spectacular Teton Mountain range. Over five hundred inches of annual snowfall provide some of the best skiing conditions during the winter, with miles of mountain-bike trails and terrain available during the summer. For music lovers, Targhee is known for their great summer music festivals. Targhee offers typical resort jobs in these departments: mountain, guest services, accounting/administrative, maintenance, lodging, food and beverage, retail, and rental. The summer season runs from June 15 to October 1; winter—November 15 to April 15. Seasonal employees receive an hourly wage, a free season ski pass with skiing privileges in Jackson Hole and Big Sky, and employee meal and retail discounts. Reasonable housing is available nearby, and the resort's free employee bus accommodates most work schedules. They begin hiring employees for the winter starting in August; for the summer, in March.

SKIING

SOL DUC HOT SPRINGS

Resort • Washington • May–September
www.northolympic.com/solduc

Andrew Bales, Human Resources Manager
Olympic National Park
P.O. Box 2169
Port Angeles, WA 98362-0283
(360) 327-3583 • (360) 327-3593 (fax)
sdrjob@aol.com

. . . .

THE QUILEUTE INDIANS called it Sol Duc—a land of sparkling water. The original resort was built in 1912 and was conceived as a health spa in the European tradition. The main attraction to the area is the three hot spring mineral pools. These soaking pools are man-made circular pools supplied with all natural, mineral rich, hot spring water. Staff opportunities during the summer months include your typical resort-type positions. They also have internship opportunities for those who want to be immersed in all aspects of resort management. Wages start at $6.50 per hour, with coed, dormitory-style housing and three meals provided at $7 per day. The rooms vary in size, with the largest housing up to six staff members at peak season. The employee lounge has games, books, a VCR, and over two hundred videos to choose from. Accommodation for married couples is limited. The biggest perk is a lively family atmosphere and work environment, not to mention free use of the hot spring mineral pools and swimming pool. Those who have previous hotel or restaurant experience are preferred; however, positive energy and attitude, with a willingness to learn and put forward your best effort is even better. Few on-site interviews are conducted due to their isolated location.

STANFORD SIERRA CAMP

Resort • California • Spring/Fall

Chad Smith, Conference Staff Director
P.O. Box 10618
South Lake Tahoe, CA 96158-3618
(530) 541-1244 • (530) 541-2212 (fax)
chad.smith2@stanford.edu

. . . .

STANFORD SIERRA CAMP provides full-service lodging and meeting facilities to conferences, business retreats, and social events of thirty to two hundred people. Thankfully, they are not the Ritz-Carlton and do not offer valet parking or room service or wear uniforms or demand uniformity. However, they do provide their guests with four-star meals, comfortable lodging, a beautiful environment, and—above all—professional, efficient, and friendly service. They are in the service industry, whether they host a scientific conference or a wedding with a live band.

Environment: The camp is located at Fallen Leaf Lake, a clear, deep lake with a breathtaking mountain backdrop, next to South Lake Tahoe, California. Behind the resort is Desolation Wilderness, a national wilderness area with some of the best hiking and scenery in the Sierras. The solitude of nature will be right outside your "back door."

The Experience: Conference staff positions include kitchen, fountain, office assistants, host/hostess, housekeeping, assistant head of housekeeping, evening manager, night watch, and accounting staff. Most staff members spend their time housekeeping and working in the dining room. Everyone shuttles guests to the airport, monitors the boat dock, washes dishes, and cleans the main lodge. You will gain valuable experience in resort management, work hard, play hard, make new friends, and help guests enjoy their stay.

Commitment: The spring conference season begins mid-April and ends mid-June; while the fall conference season begins the first week in September and ends mid-November. The workload varies widely according to conference size and demands (anywhere from thirty to fifty hours per week, with shifts spread throughout the day).

Perks: Wages start at $5.75 per hour, plus room and board, gratuities, and a season-end bonus of $200 to $400. Housing is in rustic cabins (all have power; some have bathrooms; most staff have roommates; and all cabins are in an amazing locale), and the food is healthful and plentiful, with vegetarian options available (you will often eat what the guests do—meaning salmon, prime rib, salad bar, and such). Perks include full use of the facilities, including waterskiing, sailing, tennis, volleyball, basketball, and miles of hiking trails.

Ideal Candidate: Self-motivated, hardworking, and reliable people who have an excellent sense of professionalism, a warm personality, and a high level of maturity make the best candidates. Applicants also must be able to handle the responsibilities of living and working in a diverse community. The staff comes from all walks of life—college students, professionals between jobs, experienced workers in the service industry, travelers, or people taking time off. At a minimum, two years of college or more is preferred.

Getting In: Call for application materials. Phone interviews and hiring will occur during the week following the application deadline. (The spring deadline is mid-March and the fall is mid-August.) Face-to-face interviews, if possible, usually work to the applicant's advantage.

SUNRIVER RESORT

Resort • Oregon • Year-Round
www.sunriver-resort.com

Human Resources Director
P.O. Box 3609
Sunriver, OR 97707
(503) 593-4600 • (503) 593-4411 (fax)

WITH OVER 3,300 ACRES in and around the Cascade mountain range (and including Mt. Bachelor), Sunriver Resort offers numerous recreational opportunities, including white-water rafting, canoeing, fishing, and swimming. The resort is surrounded by golf courses, tennis courts, pools, thirty miles of bike paths, a marina (with canoe, kayak, raft, and fishing rentals), a bike shop with over 450 bikes, and a complete stable operation.

The Experience: Resort internship positions focus on social activities, youth programs, bike shop, and the marina. Each intern will gain exposure to various departments to complete a well-rounded internship (such as sales and marketing, special events, recreation department, management, and tours, just to name a few). Each intern will also be responsible for completing and presenting a special project beneficial to both the intern and Sunriver. In addition, over 250 seasonal positions are available, including youth program leaders, bike shop mechanics, marina program leaders, food and beverage, front desk, recreation, housekeeping, and golf staff.

Commitment: Some year-round positions are available, and limited positions are available in May and June. Most positions are twelve weeks, mid-June through Labor Day, with varying work schedules.

Perks: Interns receive a stipend of $950 per month; seasonal employees receive $6.50 to $7 per hour. Housing is not provided; however, efforts are made to help employees find adequate housing. In addition to your wages, employees are welcome to take part in numerous free recreation amenities. Discounts in all their restaurants and resort shops are available, as is a 50 percent discount on accommodations for your immediate family. Your summer work attire is provided—Sunriver shirts and shorts. Oh, and don't forget your bike. It's the best way to get around.

Ideal Candidate: Applicants must be friendly and outgoing, enjoy working with people, and physically able to meet the demands of the job. Intern candidates must be juniors or seniors studying recreation, physical education, elementary education, sports management, or hotel management. First aid and CPR certifications are required for all recreation employees. For those wanting a full-time job at Sunriver, get your foot in the door by working a summer seasonal job. The best employees get to stay on through winter.

Getting In: Call for application materials. (The best time to apply is sometime in February or March.) A personal interview is a prerequisite to employment.

SUPERCAMP

Camp • Worldwide • 3–6 Weeks
www.supercamp.com

Kevin Irvine, Director
1725 South Coast Highway
Oceanside, CA 92054-5319
(800) 285-3276 • (760) 722-0072 • (760) 722-3507 (fax)
info@supercamp.com

SUPERCAMP is an academic and personal-growth camp for teenagers. Each program teaches academic skills that help campers succeed in any subject, at any level, and it also addresses life skills, to help develop friendships, resolve conflicts, and communicate more clearly. Camps are held on academic campuses across the country, including the Claremont Colleges, Colorado College, Emory University, Hampshire College, and Stanford University. They also have international programs in Bangkok, England, Hong Kong, Malaysia, Mexico, Singapore, and Thailand.

The Experience: Team leaders head up SuperCamp activities, supervise students, facilitate team meetings, and create camp spirit, as well as serving as a role model for teens. A team usually consists of two or three team leaders, plus eleven to fourteen students. Facilitators set camp direction, inspiration, guidance, and tone, and are the most visible leaders at camp. The curriculum they present consists of personal growth (communication, team building, relationships, and motivation) and academic growth (memory, creativity, power writing, quantum reading, and academic strategies). Other staff personnel include medical personnel, counselors, and office managers.

Commitment: Staff usually work three to six weeks during the summer; dates vary with each position and camp location. Most staff work two to four camp sessions.

Perks: An honorarium of $250 to $2,700 per camp session is provided, along with room and board. All staff members will attend a four- to five-day staff training session and learn accelerated learning philosophies and techniques, communication and leadership skills, and gain experience working with teens.

Ideal Candidate: Applicants must be at least eighteen years of age, physically fit and energetic, comfortable relating to teenagers, highly committed to others, self-motivated, full of playful energy, willing to work long hours, and do whatever it takes to get the job done!

> I started with SuperCamp on a whim, looking for something fun to do with my summer, and it was the most profound, life-changing experience ever. The benefits I've received from this experience are priceless. I've been working with SuperCamp for five years, and have had the opportunity to travel and work in places like Colorado, Texas, Illinois, Massachusetts, Singapore, and Hong Kong—yes, I worked at a summer camp in Southeast Asia! These experiences not only boosted my self-confidence and self-esteem, but also gave me the satisfaction that I truly had made an impact on young people's lives (along with helping me carve out my own career path).
>
> If you care about making a difference for people by inspiring them to live up to their potential; if you want an experience that will have a life-long impact on you; if you are interested in learning skills that will take your life to the next level, personally and academically, then grab on to this opportunity. You will come home not only with an incredible experience, but also with a fresh, new outlook on life.
>
> —Contributed by Troy Stende, who spends his summers with SuperCamp, and in the off-season, as a professional college speaker with the Good Thinking Company (www.goodthink.com). Troy would love to hear from you at tstende@yahoo.com.

WILDERNESS CANOE BASE

Outdoor Education Ministry • Minnesota • 2 Weeks
http://wcb.godsnetwork.net

Jim Wiinanen, Director
12477 Gunflint Trail
Grand Marais, MN 55604
(218) 388-2241 • (612) 522-2519 (fax)
fishhook@boreal.org

•••

LOCATED IN A rustic and remote wilderness setting on two islands, Wilderness Canoe Base serves youth-at-risk and church youth groups year-round. A youth hostel is also located on the premises.

The Experience: As a wilderness volunteer, you will live in a vital, diverse community, helping young people to better know themselves, to live creatively with others, and to experience "the greatness of God's love." Volunteers contribute energy and talents in all areas of camp ministry. Positions include camp grandparent, composting gardener, guest theologian, kitchen staff, housekeeping, logger, maintenance/construction, naturalist, nurse, photographer, sewing specialist, and trips assistant.

Commitment: Applicants must commit for at least two weeks. Volunteers are especially needed in late April and the month of May.

Perks: Room, homemade meals, health and accident insurance, and a $10 credit per week of service from the camp store are provided.

Ideal Candidate: Applicants must have a basic commitment to the Christian faith and be willing to participate in the community process of work, worship, fellowship, affirmation, empowerment, and responsibility.

Getting In: Call for application packet. Apply at least one to two months prior to start date.

WILDERNESS TRAILS RANCH

Dude Ranch • Colorado • Summer
www.wildernesstrails.com/jobs

Jan Roberts, Owner
23486 CR 501
Bayfield, CO 81122
(800) 527-2624 • (970) 247-0722 • (970) 247-1006 (fax)
jobs@wildernesstrails.com

•••

EXPERIENCE THE American West where the lifestyle of the American cowboy still lingers. Don your hat, mount your trusty horse, and ride into Wilderness Trails Ranch, where guests experience everything from learning how to speak to horses in their own language to participating in Western dance and sing-alongs (along with some great wilderness adventures). Seasonal staff are hired to emulate the dude ranch experience and are encouraged to participate fully in all that they have to offer. Whether you are working as a wrangler or as a cabin supervisor, the entire staff works as a team and plays an extremely important role in the operation of the ranch. Applicants must be available to work the entire season, which runs from mid-May to the end of August, and be at least eighteen years of age. In addition to a monthly salary ranging from $750 to $1,000, meals and dormitory-style accommodations are provided. Applications can be downloaded from their web site.

Y.O. ADVENTURE CAMP

Camp • Texas • Year-Round
www.yoadventure.com

Dan Reynolds, Director
HC-01, Box 555
Mountain Home, TX 78058-9705
(830) 640-3220 • (830) 640-3348 (fax)
dreynold@ktc.com

Y.O. ADVENTURE CAMP, located on the historic 40,000-acre Y.O. Ranch, is an environmental education camp during the school year and a private residential camp during the summer. The ranch itself is home to the world's largest herd of registered longhorn cattle and also boasts one of the largest herds of free-roaming exotic animals.

The Experience: Staff will be trained to lead all activities conducted at the ranch, including Y.O. safari, reptiles, insect study, orienteering, ropes course, group initiatives, climbing, overnight camp-outs, and more. School groups range from fourth to twelfth grade. A comprehensive training program is provided, which covers all of their activities, teaching techniques, and child behavior.

Commitment: Positions available year-round; consecutive seasons are available.

Perks: A $350 to $650 per month stipend is provided, along with dormitory-style housing and meals.

Ideal Candidate: Applicants must be at least nineteen years of age, have completed one year of college, hold a valid driver's license, and must be first aid and CPR certified. Summer season applicants must be certified in lifeguard training.

Getting In: Call for an application packet, or you can fill it out on their web site. Interviews are conducted over the telephone.

YMCA CAMP SURF

Camp • California • Year-Round
www.ymca.org/camp

Mark Thompson, Camp Director
106 Carnation Ave.
Imperial Beach, CA 91932
(619) 423-5850 • (619) 423-4141 (fax)
campsurf@ymca.org

YMCA CAMP SURF (in sunny San Diego) hires seasonal instructors to teach surfing, body boarding, and kayaking along with leadership development and low ropes courses. Wages range from $30 to $50 per day, along with room and board. Send a cover letter and resume. See their web site for work opportunities at other YMCA camps in San Diego.

YMCA WILLSON OUTDOOR CENTER

Outdoor Center • Ohio • Year-Round
www.ymcacolumbus.com

Outdoor Education Director
2732 County Rd. 11
Bellefontaine, OH 43311-9382
(800) 423-0427 • (937) 593-9001 • (937) 593-6194 (fax)
ywillson@bright.net

WITH A FOCUS ON outdoor education activities, YMCA Willson Outdoor Center provides programs that include a summer camp, weekend retreats, and horseback riding. The camp sits on 409 acres of land, with a 40-acre glacial kettlehole lake, a 1860s log cabin, and a 35-foot climbing wall. Interns teach classes about the environment to school children and lead recreational activities. In addition, camp director, trip leader, and counselor positions are available. A stipend of $170 per week is provided along with room and board.

To put one's thoughts into actions is the most difficult thing in the world. —JOHANN VON GOETHE

Recommended Resources. . . . .

Each January, the **American Camping Association** publishes the *ACA Summer Camp Employment Booklet*, a free guide to nationwide job listings for day and resident camps. Detailed descriptions, salary ranges, and employment benefits are listed for most camps. Their web site also provides information on job fairs, careers at camps, and education and training programs. American Camping Association, Business Center, 5000 State Rd., 67 North, Martinville, IN 46151-7902; (800) 428-2267, (765) 342-8456, (765) 349-6357 (fax), customerservice@aca-camps.org, www.acacamps.org/jobs.htm

The Colorado Dude and Guest Ranch Association publishes a directory of approved ranches in Colorado. Although the directory really acts as a vacationer's guide, it lists thirty-eight ranches (all of whom hire seasonal employees), complete with contact information and phone numbers. Call or write for your complimentary copy. Colorado Dude and Guest Ranch Association, Charles Henry, Executive Director, P.O. Box 2120, Granby, CO 80446; (970) 887-3128, (970) 887-1229 (fax), coloranch@compuserve.com, www.coloradoranch.com

To assist individuals seeking employment at a ranch, the **Dude Ranchers' Association** provides a couple of great services. First off, they publish *The Dude Rancher Directory*, listing contact information, amenities, and services for more than one hundred member dude ranches in twelve western states and two Canadian provinces. Dude ranches vary from working cattle ranches to more luxurious resort-type facilities. Although it doesn't list seasonal jobs at each ranch, it's a great resource for contact information—plus it's free. In addition, they publish a biweekly in-house newsletter that is sent directly to all member ranches. For a $5 fee, they will place an "employment wanted" ad in the newsletter. Simply send them your name, address, phone number, dates of availability, type of positions preferred, and two to three sentences describing your experience or qualifications. Many ranchers do use these ads when hiring. Of course, there are no guarantees, but it is a good and inexpensive way to contact all the ranchers at one time. Dude Ranchers' Association, Bobbi and Jim Futterer, Executive Directors, P.O. Box 471, LaPorte, CO 80535; (970) 223-8440, (970) 223-0201 (fax), duderanches@compuserve.com, www.duderanch.org/employ.htm

Looking for a job at a summer camp? Or maybe you would like to re-create the experience you once had as a kid by participating in a grown-ups' camp? **Kidscamps.com** will provide some great leads.

The **Learning Disabilities Association of America** publishes *The Summer Camp Directory*, a great resource for those who want to work with children with learning disabilities in a camp setting (plus it's only $4). Although it doesn't provide a listing of jobs, it does serve as a source of contacts for your own job development. The association also publishes many other booklets and pamphlets on various subjects for the learning disabled. Contact them to receive a free packet of information. Learning Disabilities Association of America, 4156 Library Rd., Pittsburgh, PA 15234-1349; (412) 341-1515, (412) 344-0224 (fax), ldanatl@usaor.net, www.ldanatl.org

have you ever marveled at the geysers of Yellowstone, explored the verdant mountains of the Rockies, paddled a canoe in the Boundary Waters of Minnesota, or walked across a glacier in Alaska and wondered what it would be like to work in such magnificent places? These are the types of opportunities that thousands of seasonal workers enjoy with organizations such as the National Park Service, hospitality services within the parks, or those that maintain thousands of miles of hiking trails. From jobs as campground hosts and interpreters to trail maintenance laborers and wilderness specialists, you'll explore every conceivable assignment while working in the wild.

I only went out for a walk, and finally concluded to stay out until sundown; for going out, I found, was really going in.

—JOHN MUIR

Unique Opportunities to Explore in This Section:

▶ Chop, trim, shovel, and rake on your vacation? Each year the American Hiking Society looks for volunteers who will help with hundreds of trail miles to make hiking safer in America's national parks and forests *(page 110)*.

▶ Bill Borrie believes those who succeed in the future will be those who learn how to make wonderful things happen, regardless of what the naysayers are suggesting. Explore his get-up-and-go approach to landing a federal agency job *(page 119)*.

▶ From the architectural relics of the Anasazi in Mesa Verde to geysers bursting in Yellowstone, the National Park Service offers seasonal workers some of the most incredible places to work in the United States *(page 127)*. Also visit the details on other public agencies, including the Bureau of Land Management *(page 113)*, the U.S. Fish and Wildlife Service *(page 134)* and the U.S. Forest Service *(page 137)*.

▶ Can you see yourself patrolling a remote island wilderness in Alaska by kayak or playing the role of an 1800s resident of historic Ft. Laramie? These are just a few of the assignments participants enjoy with the Student Conservation Association *(page 132)*.

Photo Credit: John Spring

A conservation intern with the Student Conservation Association involved in a surveying assignment at Olympic National Park.

THE GREAT
OUTDOORS

ADIRONDACK MOUNTAIN CLUB

Conservation Education • New York • Year-Round
www.adk.org

Applications
P.O. Box 867
Lake Placid, NY 12946-0867
(518) 523-3441 • (518) 523-3518 (fax)
adkinfo@adk.org

• •

EDUCATIONAL WORKSHOPS, wildflower and birding field trips, guided hikes, kayaking, and winter cross-country skiing are among the programs of this venerable club for nature lovers. Duties may include assisting with the maintenance and reconstruction of backcountry hiking trails, working in a backcountry information center, interpreting Adirondack natural history, and/or operating two mountain lodges. Pay is based on position, and room and board may be provided. Applicants require a strong outdoor orientation and public service skills. Positions are often filled by outgoing, highly motivated, and independent individuals. Call for application form (or check out their web site). Applications are due by February 15 for the summer; other seasons have rolling deadlines.

ALASKA STATE PARKS

State Park • Alaska • Winter/Summer
www.dnr.state.ak.us/parks

Kathryn Reid, Volunteer Coordinator
3601 C St., Suite 1200
Anchorage, AK 99503-5921
(907) 269-8708 • (907) 269-8907 (fax)
volunteer@dnr.state.ak.us

• •

CREATED IN 1970, Alaska State Parks manages more than 130 state park units with more than six million visitors each year. These park units range in size and character from the half-acre Potter Section House State Historic Site to the 1.5-million-acre Wood-Tikchik State Park. In general, state parks are accessible by road and offer a host of visitor facilities including campgrounds, boat launches, hiking trails, and visitor centers.

The Experience: Typical positions include archaeological assistant, backcountry ranger assistant, natural history interpreter, park caretaker, ranger assistant, and trail crew. Almost half of the positions offered are campground hosts. Hosts stay in the campground (in their own RV or trailer) and assist the ranger with campground maintenance and visitor contact.

Commitment: Most positions are full-time; however, a few positions are part-time, and approximately ten positions are offered during the winter. Time off is usually given during the middle of the week.

Perks: Most positions offer an expense allowance ($100 to $300 per month), uniforms, rustic housing, and, of course, the state's beauty. Transportation to and from Alaska is the responsibility of the volunteer.

Ideal Candidate: Applicants must be eighteen years or older and have U.S. citizenship.

Getting In: Write or call for a current volunteer program catalog, which includes general information, specific position descriptions, and an application. The catalog becomes available each October, with applications accepted between November 1 and April 1 (with some exceptions). You may apply for as many positions as you like.

> *Many positions are filled before April 1st, so it is best to send your application in as soon as possible. Some of our rangers work seasonally, so do not be concerned if you do not receive an immediate reply, particularly from November through January.*

AMERICAN HIKING SOCIETY

Trail Maintenance • USA • 1–2 Weeks
www.americanhiking.org

Shirley Hearn, Volunteer Vacations Coordinator
1422 Fenwick Ln.
Silver Spring, MD 20910
(888) 766-4453 • (301) 565-6704 • (301) 565-6714 (fax)
info@americanhiking.org

• •

THE AMERICAN HIKING SOCIETY is a national nonprofit organization dedicated to establishing, protecting, and maintaining foot trails in America. Serving as the voice of the American hiker in our nation's capital, American Hiking works to educate the public about the benefits of hiking and trails, to increase the following for trails, and to foster research on trail issues.

The Experience: AHS Volunteer Vacations offers an inexpensive way to visit a new part of the United States, work with your hands, and help conserve and revitalize America's trails. Vacationers rake, shovel, trim, lop, and chop hundreds of trail miles in America's national parks, forests, and rangelands. Volunteering affords you an opportunity to whip some trail miles—and your mind and body—into shape. You'll spend your days performing rewarding trail work. During late afternoon and evening hours, you'll explore the countryside, photograph wildlife, relax by a mountain stream, or simply enjoy the fellowship of people who share your passion for the outdoors. Most projects require a hike into a remote base camp; some offer bunkhouse or cabin accommodations. For each project, American Hiking chooses an experienced volunteer team leader to serve as the liaison between your crew and the host agency. If you are interested in serving as a leader, just indicate that on your registration form.

Commitment: On a typical day, after a hearty breakfast, you will be on the trail at 9 a.m., work for six to eight hours, and return to base camp by 4 p.m., just in time to enjoy the long summer afternoons. On two-week vacations, you will get the weekend off.

Perks: Host agencies provide tools, safety equipment, workers' compensation, and project leaders. Most agencies also provide food; however, for some projects, volunteers may be asked to donate an additional $40 per week. Registration requires a nonrefundable $75 registration fee, which includes first-year membership to American Hiking ($10 savings). AHS members pay $60 for the first trip, and each additional trip costs $40.

Ideal Candidate: Participants should possess a desire to improve America's trails, and be in good physical condition (the ability to hike five miles or more a day) and at least eighteen years of age. Volunteers supply their own camping equipment (tent, sleeping bag, personal items) and arrange their own transportation to and from the work site (although many agencies provide pickups at major airports near the work sites).

Photo Credit: American Hiking Society

Volunteers with the American Hiking Society help construct a footbridge.

Getting In: Call to receive a project schedule and registration form (or check out their web site). American Hiking also publishes *Helping Out in the Outdoors*, an annual directory of more than two thousand volunteer positions and internships on America's public lands. The cost is $7 (add $3 to receive by first-class mail or if you're overseas).

> *I have no right to set foot on any trail that someone else worked and sweated over if I don't work and sweat over some trail that someone else will hike on.*
> —Joe Burton, AHS member and volunteer

ANASAZI HERITAGE CENTER

Museum • Colorado • Summer

Curator
Bureau of Land Management
27501 Highway 184
Dolores, CO 81323
(970) 882-4811 • (970) 882-7035 (fax)

COME SPEND eight weeks during the summer in beautiful southwestern Colorado working in a "hands-on" museum committed to the preservation and interpretation of the northern San Juan Anasazi. Interns in collections management and cultural resources management are provided with a realistic and well-rounded experience in a federal museum setting. Interns are expected to be self-motivated and able to work with a minimum amount of supervision once the task is understood. Interns receive a $50 per week stipend, plus communal housing. Send a resume and cover letter before April 1.

APPALACHIAN MOUNTAIN CLUB

Conservation Education • New Hampshire • Year-Round
www.outdoors.org

Staffing Director
Pinkham Notch Visitor Center
P.O. Box 298
Gorham, NH 03581
(603) 466-2721 • (603) 466-2822 (fax)

APPALACHIAN MOUNTAIN CLUB (AMC), the nation's oldest and largest recreation and conservation organization, offers a smorgasbord of projects for volunteers and seasonal workers. Seasonal crews work in the White Mountain National Forest in base camps, shelters, huts, visitor centers, or a youth hostel, with positions ranging from backcountry staff, trail crew, and educational instructors.

Now I know the secret of making the best persons; it is to grow in the open air and to eat and sleep with the earth. —WALT WHITMAN

The average weekly pay for seasonal workers ranges from $250 to $340 after deductions for room and board. Volunteers for AMC help maintain more than 1,300 miles of recreational trails, including 350 miles of the Appalachian Trail. However, it's not all hauling rocks and clearing brush; volunteers also lead nature hikes, fill in for hut crews, and give public information talks. For more information, call for a copy of their annual *Trail Volunteer Opportunities* catalog, which lists more than seven hundred opportunities.

APPALACHIAN TRAIL CONFERENCE

Trail Maintenance • Maine/Pennsylvania/Vermont/ Virginia • 1–6 Weeks
www.atconf.org

Susan Daniels, Crew Program Director
799 Washington St.
P.O. Box 807
Harpers Ferry, WV 25425
(304) 535-6331 • (304) 535-2667 (fax)
crews@atconf.org

HELP BUILD a piece of the Appalachian National Scenic Trail, one of the most famous footpaths in the world. Winding along the peaks of the Appalachian chain from Georgia to Maine, this trail exists thanks to countless dedicated volunteers who planned, constructed, and now maintain and manage the trail by participating in ATC's Volunteer Trail Crew Program. Operated in cooperation with the U.S. Forest Service, National Park Service, and trail-maintaining clubs, a professional crew leader directs the crews in designing and building new trail segments, shelters, and bridges, rehabilitating damaged trails, improving wildlife habitat, and preserving open areas. Food, accommodation, equipment, and on-the-job training are provided, and participants must be at least eighteen years of age. Crews operate from May through October from base camps in southern Virginia, south-central Pennsylvania, Vermont, and Maine. Participants may volunteer for up to six weeks.

BADLANDS NATIONAL PARK

Natural Resources • South Dakota • Year-Round
www.nps.gov/badl

Marianne Mills, Resource Education Chief
P.O. Box 6
Highway 240
Interior, SD 57750
(605) 433-5245 • (605) 433-5248 (fax)
marianne_mills@nps.gov

BADLANDS NATIONAL PARK consists of 244,000 acres of eroded sedimentary formations and mixed grass prairie. The weather is hot and dry in the summer (up to 110 degrees), cold and icy in the winter (down to −30 degrees), and always windy. It was just voted as having the best sunrises/sunsets in the world by International Nature Photographers (just a hint of its beauty). Seasonal employees staff the visitor center; provide interpretive walks, children's hikes, and slide-show presentations; patrol the backcountry; or engage in research and writing programs. Applicants must be friendly and social people who can work in a high-stress environment and/or extremely remote setting. Benefits include a weekly stipend of $50, along with housing.

CANYONLANDS NATIONAL PARK

National Park • Utah • Year-Round
www.nps.gov/cany/home.htm

Katie Juenger, Volunteer Coordinator
2282 S. West Resource Blvd.
Moab, UT 84532-3298
(435) 259-3911 • (435) 259-8628 (fax)
canyinfo@nps.gov

CANYONLANDS features a 337,570-acre wilderness area that offers spectacular scenery, great trails for hiking, mountain biking, and off-road four-by-four exploring. It is now part of a group of parks located in southeast Utah that includes Arches National Park as well as Hovenweep and Natural Bridges National Monuments. Seasonal volunteer positions, which typically last three to four months, include campground hosts, resource management, interpretation, backcountry, archives, archaeology patrol, visitor information services, and maintenance staff. Housing, uniform, and a $7 per day stipend are provided, dependent on funding. Positions are available both in Canyonlands and Arches National Parks.

Bureau of Land Management

I look forward to an America which will not be afraid of grace and beauty, an America which will protect the beauty of our natural environment. . . .

—JOHN F. KENNEDY

The Bureau of Land Management (BLM) is responsible for managing about one-eighth of the land in the United States. Most of these public lands are located in the western United States, including Alaska, and are dominated by extensive grasslands, forests, high mountains, arctic tundra, and deserts.

VOLUNTEERING AND CAREER OPPORTUNITIES

Volunteers help the BLM educate others and instill a pride in the public lands that is crucial if these lands are to be held in trust for future generations. Volunteers improve the health of the public lands by restoring riparian areas across the West, building and repairing fences to protect special areas, planting trees, pulling weeds, and helping in many other ways.

Many students—from high school through college—participate in one of two paid seasonal programs offered by the BLM: the Student Career Experience Pro-

gram and the Student Temporary Employment Program. Positions include natural resources, wildlife, cultural resources, recreation, information resources, and administration.

Fire-fighting jobs are mostly seasonal positions during the months between May through September, depending upon the fire season in a particular area. Jobs include not only fire fighting (hand crews, engine crews, smoke jumpers) but also many fire support positions in dispatching, warehousing, and equipment operations. Once experienced wildland firefighters, many opt for the coveted smoke jumper position (a wildland firefighter who parachutes into remote areas to provide initial attack on wildfires). Smoke jumpers usually travel for 100 days out of a 120-day fire season (and it's noted that candidates should keep up a year-round physical fitness program to complete four weeks of rookie training—one of the hardest training programs to go through to get a job).

Information for any of these programs can be obtained through the BLM headquarters or one of the state offices around the country.

Headquarters/Career Opportunities

BLM—Office of Public Affairs
1849 C St., Room 406-LS
Washington, DC 20240
(202) 452-5125
www.blm.gov/careers

Volunteer Inquiries

Bureau of Land Management
Environmental Education and Volunteers Group
1849 C St., Suite 406-LS
Washington, DC 20240
(202) 452-5078
jrolfes@wo.blm.gov
www.blm.gov/education/volunteer.html

National Interagency Fire Center

3833 S. Development Ave., FA-106
Boise, ID 83705
Volunteer opportunities: Pam Johansen, (208) 387-5457,
Pam_Johansen@blm.gov

National Training Center

9828 N. 31st Avenue
Phoenix, AZ 85051
Volunteer opportunities: Sherry Smith, (602) 906-5679,
sdsmith@az.blm.gov

The wonder of the world, the beauty and the power, the shapes of things, their colors, lights and shades.
These I saw. Look ye also while life lasts. —FROM AN OLD GRAVESTONE IN ENGLAND

BLM STATE OFFICES

Alaska State Office

222 W. 7th Ave., Suite 13
Anchorage, AK 99513-7599
(907) 271-5043
www.ak.blm.gov
Volunteer opportunities: Don Pino, (907) 267-1231,
dpino@ak.blm.gov

Arizona State Office

222 N. Central Ave.
Phoenix, AZ 85004-2203
(602) 417-9200
www.az.blm.gov
Volunteer opportunities: Christine Tincher, (602) 417-9504,
Christine_Tincher@blm.gov

California State Office

2135 Butano Dr.
Sacramento, CA 95825-0451
(916) 978-4400
www.ca.blm.gov
Volunteer opportunities: Tony Staed, (916) 978-2835,
tstaed@ca.blm.gov

Colorado State Office

2850 Youngfield St.
Lakewood, CO 80215-7093
(303) 239-3600
www.co.blm.gov
Volunteer opportunities: Helene Aarons, (303) 239-3669,
haarons@co.blm.gov

Eastern States Office

(including Arkansas, Iowa, Louisiana, Missouri, Minnesota, and
all states east of the Mississippi River)

7450 Boston Blvd.
Springfield, VA 22153
(703) 440-1713
www.blm.gov/eso
Volunteer opportunities: Joy Pasquariello, (703) 440-1719,
jpasquar@es.blm.gov

Idaho State Office

1387 S. Vinnell Way
Boise, ID 83709-1657
(208) 373-4000
www.id.blm.gov
Volunteer opportunities: Shelley Davis-Brunner,
(208) 373-4019, s1davis@id.blm.gov

Nevada State Office

P.O. Box 12000
Reno, NV 89520-0006
(775) 861-6586
www.nv.blm.gov
Volunteer opportunities: Nancy Adams, (775) 861-6427,
nadams@nv.blm.gov

New Mexico State Office

(including Kansas, Oklahoma, and Texas)

1474 Rodeo Rd.
Santa Fe, NM 87502-0115
(505) 438-7400
www.nm.blm.gov
Volunteer opportunities: Shirley Baker, (505) 525-4308,
sbaker@nm.blm.gov

Montana State Office

(including North Dakota and South Dakota)

222 N. 32nd St.
Billings, MT 59101-6800
(406) 255-2885
www.mt.blm.gov
Volunteer opportunities: Lorrene Schardt, (406) 255-2827,
lschardt@mt.blm.gov

Oregon State Office

(including Washington)

1515 S.W. 5th Ave.
Portland, OR 92208-2965
(503) 952-6002
www.or.blm.gov
Volunteer opportunities: Mick Cronin, (503) 375-5612,
mcronin@or.blm.gov

Utah State Office

324 S. State St., Suite 301
Salt Lake City, UT 84145-0155
(801) 539-4001
www.blm.gov/utah
Volunteer opportunities: Sherry Foot, (801) 539-4195,
sfoot@ut.blm.gov

Wyoming State Office

5353 Yellowstone Rd.
Cheyenne, WY 82003
(307) 775-6256
www.wy.blm.gov
Volunteer opportunities: Terri Trevino, (307) 775-6020,
ttrevino@wy.blm.gov

BUREAU OF LAND MANAGEMENT

CARLSBAD CAVERNS NATIONAL PARK

Caving • New Mexico • 2 Months
www.nps.gov/cave

Paula Bauer, Volunteer Coordinator
3225 National Parks Hwy.
Carlsbad, NM 88220
(505) 785-2232 • (505) 785-2302 (fax)
caca_interpretation@nps.gov

ESTABLISHED TO preserve Carlsbad Cavern and numerous other caves within this Permian fossil reef, the park contains close to ninety separate caves. Carlsbad Cavern, with one of the world's largest underground chambers and countless formations, is also highly accessible, with a variety of tours offered year-round. Special opportunities are available for people interested in caves, natural resources, and working with the public. Volunteer positions include park interpretation, visitor services, maintenance, environmental education, history and curatorial, resource management, and cave restoration. A minimum commitment of thirty-two hours per week for at least two months is needed. In return, the park provides dormitory-style housing or an RV site with full hookups.

COLORADO TRAIL FOUNDATION

Trail Maintenance • Colorado • Summer
www.coloradotrail.org

Trail Crew Coordinator
710 10th St., Suite 210
Golden, CO 80401-5843
(303) 384-3729 • (303) 384-3743 (fax)
ctf@coloradotrail.org

THE COLORADO TRAIL FOUNDATION recruits and trains volunteers to help maintain five hundred miles of trails stretching from Denver to Durango—and across eight mountain ranges and seven national forests! Volunteers can participate in weeklong trail crew work with teams made up of seventeen individuals. Trail crews are highly participatory, and all volunteers are encouraged to join in daily camp life. The fee of $35 includes meals, housing, and supplies. Crews generally fill by April, so it's best to get on their mailing list by February 1. It's also noted that participants should establish an exercise program prior to their arrival on the crew to minimize sore muscles. Application materials and registration forms can be obtained through their web site.

CRATER LAKE COMPANY

Hospitality Services • Oregon • May–October
www.crater-lake.com/work.htm

Personnel Director
1211 Ave. C
White City, OR 97503
(541) 830-8700 • (541) 830-8514 (fax)
renee@crater-lake.com

CRATER LAKE COMPANY provides the hospitality services for Crater Lake National Park, known for having the deepest lake in the United States and the seventh deepest in the world. "Team member" positions are available in lodging (front desk clerks to campground registration staff), food and beverage (chefs to bartenders), retail (assistant managers to store clerks), administrative (office managers to activities coordinators), tour boats (boat pilots to ticket sales), cave tours, and maintenance. The season runs from May through October, with two-, four-, and six-month contracts. Most seasonal positions start at $7 per hour, plus a season-ending bonus (supervisory and skill positions pay more). Dorm-style housing is provided for $2 per day (with free laundry facilities) and RV spaces are also available. (RVers are encouraged to apply!) Full and partial meal plans are also available for a nominal cost. Call or write for application materials. (Also inquire about seasonal positions at Oregon Caves.)

CRATER LAKE NATIONAL PARK

National Park • Oregon • Year-Round
www.nps.gov/crla

Chief Park Naturalist
P.O. Box 7
Crater Lake, OR 97604
(541) 594-2211 • (541) 594-2299 (fax)

WITH A DEPTH of 1,932 feet, Crater Lake is the deepest lake in the United States and the seventh deepest lake in the world. Interpretive interns have a variety of duties, including leading guided walks, giving campfire talks and junior ranger programs, providing information at visitor center desks, issuing backcountry permits, and other related assignments. Topics of programs include geology, limnology, winter ecology, and history. Training includes a minimum of eighty hours in visitor center duties, principles and techniques of interpretation, radio and correspondence procedures, and the natural and cultural history of the park. Interns receive a $10-per-day work stipend, plus housing.

CUSTER STATE PARK RESORT COMPANY

Hospitality Services • South Dakota • April–November
www.custerresorts.com

Human Resources Department
HC 83, Box 74
Custer, SD 57730
(800) 658-3530 • (605) 255-4541 • (605) 255-4706 (fax)
email@custerresorts.com

IN THE SUMMER OF 1874, Major General George Custer led a scientific expedition through the Black Hills of South Dakota. When word spread that the expedition had discovered gold near the present-day city of Custer, prospectors and settlers soon followed. After the turn of the twentieth century, visionaries like South Dakota Governor Peter Norbeck realized that our environment was more precious than gold. In 1919, he urged the South Dakota State Legislature to preserve our natural resources and designate 48,000 acres near Custer as a permanent state park. Today Custer State Park spreads across a total of 73,000 acres. Seasonal employees have the opportunity to work in one of four resorts that are managed by Custer State Park Resort Company: the State Game Lodge and Resort, Blue Bell Lodge and Resort, Legion Lake Resort, or Sylvan Lake Resort. Typical seasonal positions are available; the more unique positions include entertainers, jeep drivers, interpretive guides, and wranglers. They also have a management trainee internship program. Interns are introduced and trained in all areas of resort operations. A monthly salary is provided, along with meals (and housing, if needed). An end-of-season bonus is also available to all who finish their agreements.

DENALI NATIONAL PARK AND PRESERVE

National Park • Alaska • Year-Round
www.nps.gov/dena

Janie Lasell, VIP Coordinator
Box 9
Denali Park, AK 99755
(907) 683-2294 • (907) 683-9623 (fax)
Janie_Lasell@nps.gov

DENALI NATIONAL PARK AND PRESERVE features North America's highest mountain, Mount McKinley, and encompasses more than six million acres filled with spectacular scenery and large mammals (such as grizzly bears and moose). Seasonal volunteer positions include interpretive naturalists, campground hosts, backcountry patrol, and resource management assistants. Housing is provided; however, campground hosts must provide their own RV or trailer. A subsistence stipend of $50 per week may be provided.

DENALI PARK RESORTS

Hospitality Services • Alaska • May–September
www.denalinationalpark.com

Carol Mehler, Human Resources Director
Aramark
241 W. Ship Creek Ave.
Anchorage, AK 99501
(907) 279-2653 • (907) 264-4680 (fax)
hrcarolm@mtaonline.net

DENALI NATIONAL PARK has more than six million acres of pristine wilderness, including some of the most awe-inspiring scenery and wildlife in North America, including Mt. McKinley, which rises over 20,000 feet into the Alaskan sky. Denali Park Resorts operates four properties as well as Alaska Raft Adventures and Tundra Wildlife Tours. The Denali National Park Hotel is located just inside the park entrance, and the McKinley Chalets, McKinley Village, and Lynx Creek complexes are located just outside the park entrance.

The Experience: Seasonal positions include dinner theatre performers, food and beverage staff, housekeeping, maintenance workers, retail services, and tour and river guides. Employees should expect a busy work environment with extensive guest contact. Those who want to gain experience in the hospitality industry, use professional skills, enjoy the Denali wilderness, and meet a diverse group of people will thrive in this environment.

Commitment: The season runs from May through mid-September, with preference given to those who can work the entire season.

Perks: Most first-year employees earn $5.50 to $8.00 per hour and a bonus of approximately $300 for the season. Room and board are available for $11 per day, and all employees have free use of laundry facilities. A variety of rustic, dormitory-style company housing units with a central bathhouse exists. In general, you will live with one or two other people. Besides the overall beauty of this region, perks abound in Denali National Park. There are many employee activities, free rafting, and discounted tours, flight-seeing, and retail purchases—not to mention fishing, kayaking, biking, and hiking.

Ideal Candidate: Applicants must be at least eighteen for housing, although many jobs require that you be at least twenty-one. Local services are limited in Denali, which is

120 miles from Fairbanks, the nearest city. Therefore applicants should have a strong desire to enjoy and discover the wilderness.

Getting In: Applications are accepted from December through August.

FLAGG RANCH RESORT

Hospitality Services • Wyoming • Winter/Summer
www.flaggranch.com

Priscilla Sanchez, Human Resources Coordinator
3207 S. Hardy Dr.
Tempe, AZ 85282
(800) 224-1384 • (480) 829-7600 • (480) 829-7460 (fax)
flaggranch@worldnet.att.net

•••

LOCATED TWO MILES SOUTH of Yellowstone National Park and three miles north of Grand Teton National Park, Flagg Ranch is a privately owned company that operates visitor services under a concession agreement with the National Park Service. Summer and winter seasonal positions are available in these areas: lodging, food and beverage, gift shop, front desk/reservations, auditor, campground, gas station, grocery store, maintenance, river guide, naturalist/activities coordinator, security, dorm assistant, snowcoach driver, and management/supervisory positions. An hourly wage is provided, along with room and board for a nominal cost deducted from your paycheck. The ranch also has a limited number of full hookup sites for employees with their own trailers or motor homes. Note that Flagg Ranch conducts its recruiting efforts from Tempe, Arizona.

FLAGSTAFF AREA NATIONAL MONUMENTS

National Monument • Arizona • Year-Round

Anita Davis, Volunteer Coordinator
Route 3, Box 149
Flagstaff, AZ 86004
(520) 526-0502 • (520) 714-0565 (fax)
anita_davis@nps.gov

•••

IMAGINE PRESERVING the remains of an ancient dry-farming community, the cliff dwellings of the Sinagua, or teaching people about the cinder cone volcano that erupted over nine hundred years ago. The Flagstaff Area National Monuments offers volunteer opportunities in a variety of programs including interpretation, visitor services, resource education, volunteer coordination, cura-

torial work, photography, and graphic design. Along with training and volunteer uniform, a trailer pad or shared housing may be available. A three-month commitment is necessary.

FLAMINGO LODGE IN EVERGLADES NATIONAL PARK

Hospitality Services • Florida • Year-Round
www.flamingolodge.com

Human Resources Office
Amfac Parks & Resorts
#1 Flamingo Lodge Highway
Flamingo, FL 33034-6798
(941) 695-3101 • (941) 695-3921 (fax)
everglad@ix.netcom.com

•••

AMFAC PARKS & RESORTS provides the hospitality services in Everglades National Park. Seasonal positions at Flamingo Lodge range from food and beverage and hotel services to marina staff and accountants. The summer season runs from May 1 through the end of October, with the winter season spanning from November 1 through the end of April. Generally, the earlier you can start and the later you can stay, the better your chances will be of receiving an offer of employment. Wages for most positions start at $5.25 per hour and include free dormitory-style housing or full RV hookup (in the winter, there is a nominal charge). Other benefits include complimentary Florida Bay and Back Country Boat Cruises, and rental of canoes, kayaks, and skiffs. Applicants must be at least eighteen years of age.

FLORISSANT FOSSIL BEDS NATIONAL MONUMENT

National Monument • Colorado • Summer

Volunteer Coordinator
Field Internship Program
P.O. Box 185
Florissant, CO 80816-0815
(719) 748-3253 • (719) 748-3164 (fax)

•••

FLORISSANT FOSSIL BEDS NATIONAL MONUMENT sits at an elevation of 8,400 feet and preserves fossil remains and geologic evidence of a far different world, from thirty-five million years ago. The fossil beds are named after a nearby small town, Florissant, which takes its name from the French word for flowering or blooming.

Be glad of life, because it gives you the chance to love and to work and to play and to look at the stars. —HENRY VAN DYKE

The Experience: Interpretative interns provide information on natural and cultural resources, explain area significance, and communicate National Park Service philosophy to the visiting public. Paleontology interns are involved with projects relating to the geological or paleontological resources of the park, including resource management, museum collection curation, and technical assistance with excavating and monitoring of paleontological sites. All interns participate in a one-week orientation training session, including standard first aid and CPR. Training in other park operations, basic wildland fire fighting, and natural and paleontological resources monitoring is scheduled throughout the twelve weeks (beginning in late May).

Perks: A $12 per day stipend is provided, along with housing and uniforms.

Ideal Candidate: Interpretive applicants must have effective communication skills, the ability to work comfortably with a variety of people of all ages, ability to work independently and as part of a team, and an interest and ability to work outdoors. Paleontology applicants must have completed basic undergraduate course work in geology or biology. Since there is no public transportation in the area, and housing may be several miles from the park, a personal vehicle is highly recommended.

Getting In: Send a cover letter, stating your interest in the position, and a resume with two references (with contact information) by mid-March.

FREDERICKSBURG AND SPOTSYLVANIA NATIONAL MILITARY PARK

Military Park • Virginia • Year-Round
www.nps.gov/frsp/volunteers

Gregory Mertz, Supervisory Historian
120 Chatham Ln.
Fredericksburg, VA 22405
(540) 373-6124 • (540) 371-1907 (fax)
greg_mertz@nps.gov

FREDERICKSBURG WAS the scene of four major Civil War battles, resulting in more than 100,000 casualties. No other area of similar size witnessed such heavy losses. The boundaries encompass more than eight thousand acres, making the park the largest military preserve in the world. The park has a visitor center on the Fredericksburg battlefield, where interpreters conduct tours of the Sunken Road battleground, and a library where research regarding the Union army can be done. Another visitor center on the Chancellorsville battlefield is also the starting point for conducted tours of the site where Stonewall Jackson was mortally wounded. Research on the Confederate army and cultural resource management tasks all occur at the historic structure Chatham, an eighteenth-century manor house.

The Experience: Various seasonal, volunteer, and internship positions are available: historical interpreters provide information and conduct walking tours for park visitors; historical researchers complete projects to help the staff access specific information easily; education coordinator assistants develop lesson plans and visuals for the park staff or teachers to use for student programs; curatorial assistants help with cataloging museum artifacts; cultural resource management assistants help to identify and preserve military and civilian landmarks of the Civil War era; restoration assistants properly protect and repair monuments, historic buildings, and other cultural resources; and administrative assistants may learn various federal personnel, budgeting, or purchasing practices.

Commitment: Most volunteers must make a commitment of at least 100 hours and internships range from 120 to 480 hours for the term. Schedules vary with each position.

Perks: Housing is provided when available. Seasonal wages vary.

Getting In: Request application materials and specific descriptions of jobs. It's best to apply at least three months before your desired start date.

FURNACE CREEK INN AND RANCH RESORT

Hospitality Services • California • Year-Round
www.furnacecreekresort.com

Kathleen Bankston, Human Resources Director
Death Valley National Park
P.O. Box 187
Death Valley, CA 92328
(760) 786-2311 • (760) 786-2396 (fax)
hr@furnacecreekresort.com

AMFAC PARKS & RESORTS operates four properties in Death Valley: Furnace Creek Inn, a 68-room historic inn; Furnace Creek Ranch, a 224-room resort; Stove Pipe Wells Village, an 82-room motel; and Scotty's Castle. These properties provide everything from lodging and restaurants to tennis and swimming. Guest service and hospitality positions of all types are available throughout the year. Besides an hourly wage, benefits include low-cost employee meals and housing (including linens, utilities, and cable TV) as well as free golf, tennis, and swimming facilities. Applicants must be at least eighteen years.

A GET-UP-AND-GO APPROACH
TO LANDING A FEDERAL AGENCY JOB

We live in a world where there is more and more
information and less and less meaning.

—BILL BORRIE

I think I am going to take a contrary stance concerning getting hired into government jobs. I do not think that it is as hopeless as some of you are being told. Now, don't get me wrong—it is never easy to get the job that you want. But I think the negative attitude that is now spreading throughout many agencies is self-destructive. Be very careful with your career decisions!

Briefly put, I believe that the federal agencies will always find a way to hire good people. And that means you, folks. The leaders of these agencies know that long-term effectiveness depends on the creativity and enthusiasm of its personnel. True leadership requires constantly energizing and reinventing the agency. This requires younger, competent people with the drive to provide true public service and stewardship of the national estate.

I do, however, believe that you will have to work harder to get to where you want to be. This may require you to shift some of your expecta-

tions. You may have to change your sights as to what you can achieve in the short term. For instance, you may have to think again about the hope of immediately working in your favorite state. Instead, you may have to go somewhere new, such as Georgia, which has some wonderful wilderness areas! Similarly, you might not get to live in the size of town that you like. Instead, you might have to consider living in Washington, DC, or Sacramento or Glendive. You might also have to work on projects that are not your obvious choice. But the more you learn about the agency and all of its missions, the more effective you become. You may even get to work for a different agency (for instance, the Bureau of Land Management). In each case, you should view each of these as stepping stones, learning opportunities, and necessary experiences. And, you never know, you might like what you see!

You guys and gals are training for careers that

will require different skills than what many current employees have. You will have new perspectives, new experiences, and new ideas. This is threatening to older employees, and one of their strategies for coping with this is to discourage or disparage you. But you will be the ones guiding the agency in the future—with your abilities, knowledge, and get-up-and-go. Those who succeed in the future, I believe, will be those who learn how to make wonderful things happen, regardless of what the naysayers are suggesting. A can-do attitude will win in the long run.

So, if you really, really want to work for a particular agency, then I say go out and work for them! Don't let anybody tell you that you can't! If you believe that what you should be doing is working for the government, and that that is the best use of your skills and enthusiasm, then you are a good prospect to hire. And any manager worth their salary will go out of their way to find a way to help you. They will give you a chance to show your worth, and if they like what they see, they will want to keep you on. The decision they face is how many chips to spend on your behalf— how much are you worth? So, work hard, be reliable and energetic, and show how much the public lands and public service mean to you.

Part of what I think older employees are communicating to you is that some of the old assumptions within the agencies no longer hold. For instance, it could be said that you no longer have a job for life. Others will tell you that it is no longer who you know that matters. And it is no longer reasonable to expect the government to look after your career. In short, YOU now have much more responsibility for your career. It is no longer an automatic rise through the levels. This is unsettling for people who still believe in the old ways, and one way of communicating that is to warn new people not to enter into the organization.

So, set your sights high and work hard toward getting there. These are magnificent places to manage and important benefits to provide to the American public. You should be honored to have the opportunity to serve but also congratulated on your decision to do so. Be proud of the small contributions you can make—those contributions will grow.

—Contributed by Dr. Bill Borrie, who recently received the Faculty Member of the Year Award in the School of Forestry at the University of Montana. Montana Public Radio also channels his voice across the airwaves of western Montana. Dr. Borrie welcomes readers to his web site at www.forestry.umt.edu/people/borrie.

THE GLACIER INSTITUTE

Natural Resources • Montana • 2–7 Months
www.digisys.net/glacinst

R. J. Devitt, Program Director
P.O. Box 7457
Kalispell, MT 59904
(406) 755-1211 • (406) 755-7154 (fax)
glacinst@digisys.net

THE GLACIER INSTITUTE is based at two facilities in and adjacent to Glacier Park in northwest Montana and is governed by a working board of directors who aren't afraid to get dirty. Outdoor enthusiasts will enjoy that most of their work is conducted outside in beautiful country. The institute courses often bring in local natural resource specialists and employees from Montana Fish, Wildlife, and Parks; Flathead National Forest; Flathead Valley Community College; Glacier Natural History Association; and Glacier National Park.

Environment: Both their facilities are rustic, historic sites in spectacular settings. Opportunities for river floating, hiking, wildlife viewing, and backcountry camping abound. During time off, the towns of Columbia Falls, Kalispell, and Whitefish are close enough for movies, restaurants, and shopping.

The Experience: As an intern, you are a full-fledged staff member, acting as a primary teacher of youth programs and an assistant during adult classes. At Big Creek, you will help with all organizational, programmatic, and facility aspects concerning on-site operations of the program. This includes cooking with students, teaching evening programs, creating and implementing curriculum, and helping with facility upkeep. At the field camp, you will fill a similar role. Responsibilities include staffing the office, accompanying instructors on field trips, trail/first aid support, and developing and teaching youth programs. As a teacher/naturalist at Big Creek, your responsibilities increase as you serve as a mentor to interns.

Commitment: Programs run from the spring until fall (and interns work two to four months, up to seven months). The work schedule is very irregular and busy. There may be times with no programs and times when programs run nonstop.

Perks: Interns receive $175 per month; teacher/naturalists earn $375 per month. Housing as well as food or a food stipend is also provided. Because they are a small organization, they rely heavily on staff creativity and input, so there are many opportunities to become involved in program enhancement and development.

Ideal Candidate: Applicants should be at least nineteen years old and have two years of college or more, and some prior experience teaching or working with youth. Interns must have CPR/first aid certification, and teacher/naturalists and the assistant to the director must have at least an advanced first aid certification.

Getting In: Call for job descriptions and application. Most interviews are done over the phone, but they prefer personal interviews if at all possible. Deadlines: spring and summer—January 31; fall—February 15.

> *Staff members really enjoy working and living with people of all ages, are enthusiastic and energetic, love learning and being outside, and are creative and flexible. We need people who can be happy working and living in a residential, remote setting with rustic accommodations. Self-directed people who can work without much supervision and are willing to do anything will do very well in our program.*

GLACIER PARK

Hospitality Services • Montana • May–September
www.gpihr.com

Jeff Graybill, HR Recruiting
P.O. Box 147
East Glacier Park, MT 59434
(406) 226-9311
jobs@gpihr.com

RISING FROM THE PLAINS of northwest Montana and southern Alberta, the jagged peaks of the Rocky Mountains make up the heart of Waterton-Glacier International Peace Park. Glacier Park operates seven historic hotels, nine restaurants, five retail gift shops, a pro golf shop, four camp stores, and thirty-three famous 1930s red tour buses.

The Experience: Seasonal positions include food and beverage, rooms division, retail, maintenance/engineering, warehouse, property services, and transportation from May through September each year. Employees with a performing arts background will have the opportunity to be part of a full-scale nightly production. Singers, musicians, dancers, choreographers, stage technicians, and full support personnel are all a part of traditional evening performances at both Glacier Park Lodge and the Many Glacier Hotel.

Perks: Wages range from $5.15 to $7.25 per hour, depending on the position and whether you work in the United States or Canada. Housing in Glacier is EXTREMELY

When you work, you fulfill a part of earth's fondest dream assigned to you when that dream is born. —KAHLIL GIBRAN

rustic. The "structures" are located in remote Rocky Mountain settings, weathering extreme winter elements and hundreds of new tenants each season. All housing is dormitory-style, with triple or quad accommodations. There is also limited trailer/RV space. Housing is charged at $2.50 per day, and meals are $6.50 per day.

Ideal Candidate: The minimum working age is eighteen years old (although waitstaff, bartenders, and drivers must be at least twenty-one). Applicants will be considered based on their work availability dates (a full season is preferred), qualifications, and experience in the respective position.

Getting In: Call for application materials. Most positions are filled by May 1, although midsummer opportunities, which begin as early as June 1 or as late as August 15, are available. From October through April, you can reach Glacier Park at Viad Tower, Station 0924, 1850 N. Central Ave., Phoenix, AZ 85077-0924; (602) 207-2612.

GLACIER PARK BOAT COMPANY

Tour Boat Outfitter • Montana • Summer
www.montanaweb.com/gpboats

Susan Burch, Director
P.O. Box 5262
Kalispell, MT 59903-5262
(406) 257-2426 • (406) 756-1437 (fax)
gpboats@montanaweb.com

A BANK TELLER turned boat builder started a family legacy in Glacier National Park. In the summer of 1937, Glacier Park Boat Company launched its first boat tours in the park with two classic-style wooden boats. Four generations later, this family-run operation has five locations throughout the park and boats that now carry from forty-five to eighty passengers. Seasonal staff captain the tour boats from June 1 through September 15, while giving commentaries on the historic and natural aspects of "America's little Switzerland." Extensive pre-season training in tour boat operation and history of the region is provided (which also prepares each staff member for boat certification exams). Applicants must be at least eighteen years of age, possess current CPR/first aid certificates, pass a physical exam and drug test, enjoy working with the public, and have good communication skills—especially public speaking. Benefits include minimum wage pay, along with family-style housing and meals (for $6 per day). It's suggested you apply by January or February.

GRAND CANYON NATIONAL PARK LODGES

Hospitality Services • Arizona • Year-Round

Employment Office
Amfac Parks & Resorts
P.O. Box 699
Grand Canyon, AZ 86023
(888) 224-0330 • (520) 638-0143 (fax)
gcnpljobs@gcnpl.grand-canyon.az.us

GRAND CANYON NATIONAL PARK LODGES, located on the South Rim of Grand Canyon, is the authorized concessionaire providing hospitality services for the park. There are no "easy jobs" at Grand Canyon—the staff are known to work hard and play ferociously. Positions include food and beverage, retail sales, housekeeping, front desk, and accounting. Many employees start in entry-level positions and advance during the season. Positions are offered year-round or on a seasonal basis, beginning as early as March and ending as late as mid-October. Preference is given to those who can work at least a three- or four-month period. Wages range from $5.75 to $7.00 per hour and higher, depending on position and experience. Dormitory-style housing (two to a room) is provided for $16 per week, and RV spots are available for $90 per month. A low-cost employee meal plan is also offered. Applicants must be eighteen years of age to live in company-provided housing. Deadlines are rolling; however it's best to apply in early January.

GRAND TETON LODGE COMPANY

Resort • Wyoming • May–October
www.gtlc.com

Personnel Manager
P.O. Box 250
Moran, WY 83013
(800) 350-2068 • (307) 543-3068 • (307) 543-3139 (fax)

GRAND TETON LODGE COMPANY manages three unique resorts—Jackson Lake Lodge, Colter Bay Village, and Jenny Lake Lodge—all located in the heart of Grand Teton National Park. Jackson Lake Lodge is a full-service resort hotel, with 385 guest rooms, situated on a bluff overlooking Jackson Lake and the skyline of the Tetons; Colter Bay Village, on the shores of Jackson Lake, is a family resort offering cabins, tent cabins, and RV park accommodations; and Jenny Lake Lodge is a small, elegant resort located in the shadow of the towering Tetons.

The Experience: Whether for a summer or many seasons, employment in Grand Teton provides a unique and gratifying experience in one of the most beautiful and rugged areas in the world. While the work is demanding and the summer cannot be considered a vacation, Grand Teton Lodge Company offers employees an opportunity to live in an area that annually attracts well over three million visitors. Seasonal jobs are available in these departments: accounting, employee services (including recreation staff and personnel clerks), food and beverage, guest activities (wranglers, river guides, and van/bus drivers), hotel services, maintenance, and retail.

Commitment: The Grand Teton season runs from May through October. Depending on the position, various starting and ending dates can be accommodated. Preference will be given to applicants who can work until the end of the season, and positions beginning in July and August are also available. Work schedules vary but in most cases are six days, forty-eight hours per week.

Perks: Entry-level salaries begin at $6 per hour, and dormitory-style housing is provided at no charge (RV sites are $4 per day). There is a $42.50 per week fee for employee services, which include cafeteria meals, laundry facilities, and laundered linens. Employee recreational activities, such as dances and sporting events, are also scheduled throughout the summer.

Ideal Candidate: Applicants must be at least eighteen years of age.

HOPEWELL FURNACE NATIONAL HISTORIC SITE

Historic Site • Pennsylvania • 3–4 Months
www.nps.gov/hofu

Frank Hebblethwaite, Supervisory Historian
National Park Service
2 Mark Bird Ln.
Elverson, PA 19520-9535
(610) 582-8773 • (610) 582-2768 (fax)
hofu_superintendent@nps.gov

••

HOPEWELL FURNACE is one of the finest examples of a restored charcoal-burning iron furnace, which once dominated life in southeastern Pennsylvania and provided the foundations for the industrial development of this country. Hopewell Furnace operated from 1771 until 1883, spanning several generations of our industrial history, from its infancy in the colonial period to the giant steel and railroad industries at the turn of the last century. As an active living history site, Hopewell features first-person interpretation of colliers, blacksmiths, farmers, housewives, servants, cooks, and members of the ironmaster's family. The interpretive program also includes an active farm with horses, sheep, and cows. In addition, Hopewell conducts its own charcoal burn twice a year in an effort to preserve the otherwise lost skill of producing charcoal from cord wood. The charcoal produced in these burns is used as fuel in molding, casting, and blacksmithing demonstrations.

Environment: Located in southeast Pennsylvania, Hopewell is surrounded on three sides by 7,000-acre French Creek State Park and is close to Amish country.

The Experience: Seasonal staff positions may include museums and cultural resource preservation, historical interpretation, living history, and visitor center operations. Duties are determined by the needs of the site and interest of the intern.

Commitment: Internship dates are variable, full- or part-time. In general, positions last three to four months at a minimum of twenty hours per week.

Perks: Although no stipend is available, shared housing and reimbursement for miscellaneous expenses are provided.

Ideal Candidate: Applicants must show a willingness to work with and get along with a wide variety of co-workers and visitors. A genuine desire to insure that each visitor has an enjoyable experience at Hopewell is essential.

Getting In: A National Park Service volunteer application may be obtained through the Volunteers in Parks web site at www.nps.gov/volunteer. Completed applications should be sent through e-mail to Hopewell. Those who do not have web access should send a cover letter and resume.

ISLE ROYALE NATIONAL PARK

National Park • Michigan • Summer
www.nps.gov/isro

Volunteer Coordinator
800 E. Lakeshore Dr.
Houghton, MI 49931
(906) 487-7153 • (906) 487-7170 (fax)

••

IN LAKE SUPERIOR'S northwest corner sits a wilderness archipelago, a roadless land of wild creatures, unsoiled forests, refreshing lakes, and rugged, scenic shores accessible only by boat or floatplane. Volunteer positions are available in the park library, photo darkroom, resource management, backcountry campground, interpretation, and assistance with monitoring projects on park wildlife and vegetation. A stipend of $60 to $70 per week is provided

I frequently tramped eight or ten miles through the deepest snow to keep an appointment with a beech tree, or a yellow birch, or an old acquaintance among the pines. —HENRY DAVID THOREAU

as well as meals and comfortable dormitory-style housing on Mott Island, the park's summer headquarters.

LAKE POWELL RESORTS AND MARINAS

Hospitality Services • Arizona • Summer

Inta Bingham, Staffing and Placement Specialist
Glen Canyon National Recreation Area
P.O. Box 1597
Page, AZ 86040
(520) 645-1081 • (520) 645-1016 (fax)
bingham-inta@aramark.com

LAKE POWELL RESORTS AND MARINAS, managed by Aramark Corporation, operates five marinas and resort properties as well as Wilderness River Adventures, a river guide company. The vermilion ridges, towering mesas, long and twisting canyons, deep and clear mirrors of water, arching rainbows, and the play of light and shadow in Glen Canyon that inspired Zane Grey in 1915 will instill similar feelings of supernatural awe in you. Positions are available in the marina (marina utility, fuel attendant, boat rental attendant, boat instructor, marine mechanic, truck driver, maintenance, and rental clerk), food and beverage (food and cocktail servers, bus people, bartender, cook, cashier, dishwasher, and food and beverage utility), hotel (front desk clerk, night auditor, housekeeper, bellhop, maintenance, utility, laundry, van driver, and bus driver), and retail (sales clerk). Seasonal wages start at $5.70 per hour and dormitory-style housing (single and double occupancy options) is offered for a monthly fee.

LAKE TAHOE BASIN MANAGEMENT UNIT

Natural Resources • California • Year-Round

Michael St. Michel, Visitor Center Director
U.S. Forest Service
870 Emerald Bay Rd., Suite #1
South Lake Tahoe, CA 96150
(530) 573-2600 • (530) 573-2600 (fax)

COORDINATED BY THE U.S. Forest Service at Lake Tahoe, the interpretive services program provides informational and interpretive materials through a visitor center, stream profile chamber, self-guided trails, brochures, displays, and guided activities. Year-round opportunities abound for seasonal interpretive naturalists. Summer naturalists assist with campfire programs, environmental education activities, living history programs, exhibits for display, natural history information, recreational activities, and various special projects; fall naturalists teach third and fourth

graders about the life cycle of the Kokanee salmon, which spawn in a creek near the visitor center; and winter naturalists serve fifth and sixth graders, interpreting Lake Tahoe's winter environment in a classroom setting and outdoors on snowshoes. A subsistence allowance, training, and complimentary government housing (on the shores of Lake Tahoe in a historic estate) is provided.

A summer naturalist with the Lake Tahoe Basin Management Unit helps children collect aquatic insects on a creek walk.

MAINE APPALACHIAN TRAIL CLUB

Trail Maintenance • Maine • May–October
www.matc.org

Tom Lohnes, Corresponding Secretary
P.O. Box 283
Augusta, ME 04332-0283
simt@somtel.com

VOLUNTEER OPPORTUNITIES abound in the club. More than five hundred members and volunteers help maintain 261 miles of the Appalachian Trail in Maine, from Mt. Katahdin to Route 26 in Grafton Notch, including thirty-seven lean-tos and tent sites. Trail crew leaders, assistants, and interns provide everything from logistical support to path reconstruction. Positions begin as early as May and include a travel grant, stipend, and room and board. Caretaker positions are available at various campsites throughout Maine from mid-May to late October. Duties include greeting and registering hikers, performing maintenance tasks and providing overnight backpacking hikes. A $220 to $255 per week stipend is provided along with housing, cook stove, work tools, and some personal gear. Applications are accepted as early as late fall for the following season. Call or see their web site for a complete listing of positions and where to send your application materials.

MINNESOTA CONSERVATION CORPS

Conservation Education • Minnesota • Summer
www.dnr.state.mn.us/forestry/mcc

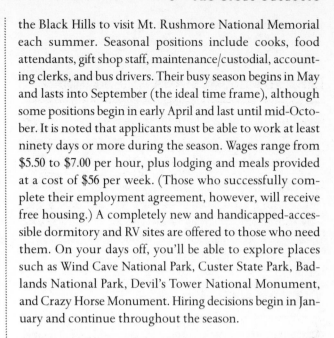

Staffing Director
500 Lafayette Rd.
St. Paul, MN 55155-4004
(651) 296-6195 • (651) 296-5954 (fax)
karen.nelson@dnr.state.mn.us

THE MINNESOTA CONSERVATION CORPS'S summer program provides the chance for Minnesota youth, ages fifteen to eighteen, to work on various natural resource projects while learning basic work skills. The summer staff, ranging from site directors, work project coordinators, crew leaders, and education coordinators, supervise and work with the youth corps members, along with instructing them in environmental awareness, life skills, and career development. Past projects have included erosion control, building and maintaining hiking trails, historical restoration, timber stand improvement, and tree planting. Depending on the position, a weekly stipend of $290 to $440 is provided, along with room, board, and transportation while on the job. Applicants who thrive in these positions aren't afraid of mosquitoes, rain, heat, and other challenges that the outdoors presents. Individuals who are sign language interpreters and/or skilled in American Sign Language are encouraged to apply. In addition, those who are deaf or hard-of-hearing are needed for leadership roles. Application materials must be received by April 1.

MT. RUSHMORE NATIONAL MEMORIAL

Hospitality Services • South Dakota
• Summer
www.mtrushmoregiftshop.com

Russ Jobman, Human Resources Director
Amfac Parks & Resorts
P.O. Box 178
Keystone, SD 57751-0178
(800) 827-9323 • (605) 574-2515 • (605) 574-2495 (fax)
fharvey@mtrushmoregiftshop.com

AMFAC PARKS & RESORTS provides all the hospitality services (including a cafeteria, ice cream and fudge shops, and gift shop) for the millions of people who travel through the Black Hills to visit Mt. Rushmore National Memorial each summer. Seasonal positions include cooks, food attendants, gift shop staff, maintenance/custodial, accounting clerks, and bus drivers. Their busy season begins in May and lasts into September (the ideal time frame), although some positions begin in early April and last until mid-October. It is noted that applicants must be able to work at least ninety days or more during the season. Wages range from $5.50 to $7.00 per hour, plus lodging and meals provided at a cost of $56 per week. (Those who successfully complete their employment agreement, however, will receive free housing.) A completely new and handicapped-accessible dormitory and RV sites are offered to those who need them. On your days off, you'll be able to explore places such as Wind Cave National Park, Custer State Park, Badlands National Park, Devil's Tower National Monument, and Crazy Horse Monument. Hiring decisions begin in January and continue throughout the season.

NORTHWEST YOUTH CORPS

Conservation Education • Oregon • Summer
www.nwyouthcorps.org/staff.html

Jeff Parker, Program Director
2621 Augusta St.
Eugene, OR 97403
(541) 349-5055
work@nwyouthcorps.org

NORTHWEST YOUTH CORPS (NYC) is a summer education and job training program for high school youth. Youth crews work on projects for government agencies and private landowners in a format stressing environmental education and development of basic job skills. Crews typically live and work in remote locations throughout Oregon and in parts of Washington and Idaho. During the week, crews set up primitive camps near their job sites, live in tents, and cook their own meals over a campfire or Coleman stove. On weekends, three to four crews rendezvous for recreational outings and educational activities. NYC is the only fully mobile conservation corps in the country.

The Experience: Crew leaders and assistants work shoulder to shoulder with their crew while supervising the successful completion of a wide variety of manual labor projects and providing environmental education programs. If you're aged sixteen to nineteen, you might consider participating in this unique program. More than four hundred youth crew members will build fences, pull debris from creeks, brush ski trails, restore wildlife habitat, plant

Climb the mountains and get their good tidings. Nature's peace will flow into you as sunshine flows into trees. —JOHN MUIR

125

trees, enhance fisheries, or work to save endangered species. NYC also has a special program for fourteen- and fifteen-year-olds.

Commitment: The program requires long days, high energy, and a love for challenge. Time off is limited.

Perks: Crew leaders average $4,700 to $5,300 per summer, plus meals and rustic housing. Crew members earn $6.50 per hour, with a $5.75 per day deduction for meals.

Ideal Candidate: The ideal candidate has a youth leadership background, experience in professional positions, a solid environmental ethic, and a diverse set of conservation skills. Current first aid and CPR certifications are required, and lifesaving certification is desirable.

OLYMPIC NATIONAL PARK

National Park • Washington • Year-Round

Maurie Sprague, Information Specialist
600 East Park Ave.
Port Angeles, WA 98362-6798
(360) 452-4501 • (360) 452-0335 (fax)
maurie_sprague@nps.gov

OLYMPIC NATIONAL PARK occupies over 900,000 acres in Washington State, established to preserve primeval forests and the largest natural herd of Roosevelt elk. In 1976, it was designated a Biosphere Reserve, and soon thereafter, it was designated a World Heritage Site. The park consists of a rugged and spectacular glacier-capped mountainous core penetrated by deep valleys, some with lush temperate rainforests, a separate 57-mile-long coastal strip, and some one hundred offshore islands.

The Experience: Hurricane Ridge interns work as interpretive rangers, preparing and presenting talks and walks during the summer, and in the winter, leading interpretive snowshoe walks and short indoor talks; Lake Crescent interns engage in visitor services and interpretation; Wilderness Information Center interns provide wilderness information and camping permits; wilderness resource/ vegetation interns monitor wilderness conditions, revegetation, and greenhouse work; Olympic Park Visitor Center interns work as interpretive rangers; and VIP (Volunteers in Parks) positions include interpretation, resource management, backcountry ranger, natural sciences, maintenance, and campground host. A two-week training program is provided for all positions.

Commitment: Positions are generally available throughout the year. Visitor center internship positions vary season-

ally, although plan on two or three months or longer. A minimum commitment of 2 1/2 months is generally needed.

Perks: Interns receive a $50 to $100 stipend per month, plus shared housing (with one other park employee) in a modern one-bedroom apartment.

Ideal Candidate: Applicants should have a strong background in natural science, park management, or interpretation. Some knowledge of ecological processes and natural history is desirable. The ability to work independently and with people is required.

Getting In: Call for application materials (or get more information at www.nps.gov/volunteer). Phone calls are welcomed, and it is suggested you send your application one to three months before the season begins.

OREGON DUNES NATIONAL RECREATION AREA

Forest Service • Oregon • 1–6 Months

Volunteer Coordinator
Siuslaw National Forest
855 Highway 101
Reedsport, OR 97467
(541) 271-3611 • (541) 271-6019 (fax)

THIS IS SAND DUNE COUNTRY! Oregon Dunes is unique in that it is one of only a few areas where windswept open dunes, some towering over four hundred feet, are bordered by the beach to the west and the coastal forest to the east. Volunteer and intern positions include overlook hosts, headquarters hosts, guided field trip and nature walk interpreters, campground hosts, recreation (including off-road vehicle) assistants, fish and wildlife assistants, writers, illustrators, photographers, graphic designers, and office help. If you have a special skill or talent you think is valuable in managing the Oregon Dunes, let them know. Work one month or six, a few hours a week or full-time! Help is generally needed most from May through September. A $12 per day stipend and uniforms are provided. Housing is available to volunteers who work at least twenty-four hours per week. Housing is located two miles north of where you will be working, complete with kitchen, bathroom, and laundry facilities. Campground hosts receive a campsite with hookups.

The National Park Service

Many Americans have had love affairs with the national parks since Yellowstone, the first national park, was created in 1872. Today the National Park Service preserves and manages more than 360 national sites across the United States. From the architectural relics of the Anasazi in Mesa Verde, the historical treasures of Gettysburg Battlefield, the fossil reefs of Carlsbad Cavern, the geysers bursting in Yellowstone, or, say, the awesome coastal redwood forest in Redwood National Park, the National Park Service personnel are there to protect these awe-inspiring places and to teach and educate the millions of people who visit. All national park employment opportunities can be found at their web site at www.nps.gov/personnel.

SEASONAL JOBS

Seasonal workers are hired every year to help permanent staff, especially during peak visitation seasons. Jobs range from carpenters, campground hosts, fee collectors, firefighters, historians, laborers, landscape architects, naturalists, law enforcement rangers, lifeguards, park rangers, tour guides, visitor use assistants, and so much more. Seasonal jobs are very competitive, although competition is usually less keen at smaller, lesser-known parks and for seasonal jobs in the winter season. Application forms, including a list of parks hiring for a particular season, are available from any regional office or the Seasonal Employment Program, Human Resources Office, National Park Service, P.O. Box 37127, Mail Stop 2225, Washington, DC 20013-7127; (202) 208-5074, waso_pers_seasonal@nps.gov. The filing period for winter employment is June 1 through July 15 (postmarked); the summer employment filing period is November 15 through January 15 (postmarked). Applicants are encouraged to use the seasonal employment web site at www.sep.nps.gov.

VOLUNTEERS IN PARKS (VIP) PROGRAM

VIPs work in almost every park in the National Park System and perform varied duties that might include working at information desks, presenting living history demonstrations in period costume, serving as campground hosts, leading guided nature walks and evening campfire programs, or maintaining and patrolling trails. All VIPs are given special training, and some parks reimburse volunteers for some out-of-pocket expenses, such as local travel costs, meals, and uniforms. Visit www.nps.gov/volunteer on the web, or call the VIP coordinator at the national park where you would like to volunteer. Be sure to ask for the Volunteers in Parks brochure, which provides a nifty map of all the national parks (with contact information) and application materials.

INTERNSHIP OPPORTUNITIES

Internships are available, but only administered at the park level or in various National Park Service centers and offices. Since there is no centralized list of internship opportunities, it's best to contact each park for specific information.

Whether you are a college student or a retiree, the Student Conservation Association (SCA) is one of the best ways to land a paid seasonal internship with the National Park Service (as well as other federal agencies, like the Bureau of Land Management and U.S. Forest Service). Throughout the year, SCA publishes a catalog of opportunities that range from educating people to save the Florida manatee to providing guided nature and historic talks at a national monument. More information on SCA can be found on page 132, or visit them on the web at www.sca-inc.org.

Undergraduate and graduate students who might be interested in an internship dealing with cultural

We sleep, but the loom of life never stops and the pattern which was weaving when the sun went down is weaving when it comes up tomorrow. —HENRY WARD BEECHER

resources in areas such as anthropology, archaeology, architectural history, architecture, history, landscape architecture, or museum work, should contact the National Council for Preservation Education. In conjunction with the National Park Service, the National Council sponsors a ten-week summer program ($10 per hour stipend; March 15 application deadline). They also represent more than fifty other institutions who are involved in historic preservation education and offer internships. More information can be received from Michael Tomlan, Project Director, National Council for Preservation Education, 210 West Sibley Hall, Cornell University, Ithaca, NY 14853; mat4@cornell.edu, www.preservenet.cornell.edu/intern.htm.

PARK CONCESSIONAIRES

Hotels, lodges, restaurants, stores, transportation services, marinas, and many other visitor facilities in the National Park System areas are operated by private companies who hire their own employees (which are listed in this section). These jobs are not federal government positions. Contact the National Park Service regional office covering the location in which you'd like to work, or the park itself, for names, addresses, and telephone numbers of the respective concessionaires.

The National Park Service puts out a free directory of service companies and concessionaires operating in our national parks, called *National Parks Visitor Facilities and Services*. It's a little outdated (last revised in 1994), but it's packed with all the contacts you'll need to start your search. To get your own copy, call any NPS field office; however, I suggest calling the Nebraska NPS office at (402) 221-3611. Their staff does a great job of answering all your questions and will get you the information you need quickly.

 HOT TIP The National Park Foundation provides a nifty web guide to national parks. Visitors can search by name, state regional tours, scenic and historical trails, or by special interest at www.nationalparks.org/guide.htm.

National Park Service Regional Contacts

The National Park Service preserves more than 360 sites, including national parks, national monuments, and historic sites. Following are the seven field offices with national parks denoted in parentheses (where most jobs come available). You may also want to contact a park directly for information on current positions at www.nps.gov/parklists/byname. htm.

Alaska Regional Office

National Park Service
2525 Gambell St., Room 107
Anchorage, AK 99503-2892
(907) 257-2574

Includes Denali, Gates of the Arctic, Glacier Bay, Katmai, Kenai Fjords, Kobuk Valley, Lake Clark, and Wrangell-St. Elias.

Inter-Mountain Regional Office

National Park Service
12795 W. Alameda Parkway
Denver, CO 80225-0287
(303) 969-2020

Includes Arizona (Grand Canyon and Petrified Forest), Colorado (Mesa Verde and Rocky Mountain), Montana (Glacier), New Mexico (Carlsbad Caverns), Oklahoma, Texas (Big Bend and Guadalupe Mountains), Utah (Arches, Bryce Canyon, Canyonlands, Capitol Reef, and Zion), and Wyoming (Grand Teton and Yellowstone).

Midwest Regional Office

National Park Service
1709 Jackson St.
Omaha, NE 68102-2571
(402) 221-3456

Includes Arkansas (Hot Springs), Illinois, Indiana, Iowa, Kansas, Michigan (Isle Royale), Minnesota (Voyageurs), Mississippi, Missouri, Nebraska, North Dakota (Theodore Roosevelt), Ohio, South Dakota (Badlands and Wind Cave), and Wisconsin.

National Capital Regional Office

National Park Service
1100 Ohio Dr., SW
Washington, DC 20242
(202) 619-7256

Includes Washington, DC, and nearby areas in Maryland, Virginia, and West Virginia.

Northeast Regional Office

National Park Service
U.S. Custom House
200 Chestnut St., Room 322
Philadelphia, PA 19106
(215) 597-4971

Includes Connecticut, Delaware, Maine (Acadia), Massachusetts, New Hampshire, New Jersey, New York, Pennsylvania, Rhode Island, Vermont, and most areas of Maryland, Virginia (Shenandoah), and West Virginia.

Pacific West Regional Office

National Park Service
600 Harrison St., Suite 600
San Francisco, CA 94101
(415) 427-1316

Includes California (Channel Islands, Kings Canyon, Lassen Volcanic, Redwood, Sequoia, and Yosemite), Guam (National Park of American Samoa), Hawaii (Haleakala and Hawaii Volcanoes), Idaho, Nevada (Great Basin), Oregon (Crater Lake), and Washington (Mount Rainier, North Cascades, and Olympic).

Southeast Regional Office

National Park Service
Richard B. Russell Federal Building
75 Spring St., SW, Suite 1130
Atlanta, GA 30303
(404) 331-5711

Includes Alabama, Florida (Biscayne and Everglades), Georgia, Kentucky (Mammoth Cave), Louisiana, North Carolina, Puerto Rico, South Carolina, Tennessee (Great Smoky Mountains), and the Virgin Islands (Virgin Islands National Park).

PACIFIC CREST TRAIL ASSOCIATION

Trail Maintenance • California/Oregon/Washington • Spring–Fall
www.pcta.org

Program Coordinator
5325 Elkhorn Blvd., PMB #256
Sacramento, CA 95842-2526
(888) 728-7245 • (916) 349-2109 • (916) 349-1268 (fax)
info@pcta.org

THE PACIFIC CREST TRAIL ASSOCIATION conducts volunteer trail maintenance projects in cooperation with the Bureau of Land Management, National Park Service, U.S. Forest Service, and private landholders throughout California, Oregon, and Washington. From hot dry deserts to cool high ridges, one- to ten-day projects offer the opportunity to give something back to the trail.

PARKS CANADA RESEARCH ADVENTURES

Conservation Education • Canada • 1–2 Weeks
www.worldweb.com/ParksCanada-Yoho/adventur.html

Donna Cook, Program Coordinator
Good Earth Travel Adventures
P.O. Box 8510
Canmore, AB T1W 2V2
Canada
(888) 979-9797 • (403) 678-9358 • (403) 678-9384 (fax)
info@goodearthtravel.com

JOIN COMPANIONS from around the world who share your passion for nature, national parks, and conservation; then roll up your sleeves and participate in an adventure you'll never forget. Volunteers choose from programs that range from tracking wolf packs to checking bluebird nesting success—programs that monitor the health of diverse mountain ecosystems. Research days will be spent outdoors working in the spectacular mountain landscapes of the Canadian Rockies. Projects last from one to two weeks, and often involve hiking, flatwater paddling, snowshoeing, or skiing. A participation fee ranges from $80 to $170 (Canadian funds) per day, which covers lodging (in rustic lodges, warden cabins, or field camps), food, local transportation, and some of the project research expenses. Anyone may participate as long as they are fit, in good health, and are a minimum of eighteen years of age. Apply at least two months prior to project commencement.

The world is a sacred vessel, which must not be tampered with or grabbed after. To tamper with it is to spoil it, and to grasp it is to lose it. —LAO TSU

POTOMAC APPALACHIAN TRAIL CLUB

Conservation Education • Virginia • Summer
www.patc.net/trails.html

Heidi Forrest, Trail Management Coordinator
118 Park St., SE
Vienna, VA 22180-4609
(703) 242-0693 • (703) 242-0968 (fax)
heidif@erols.com

THE POTOMAC APPALACHIAN TRAIL CLUB is a volunteer trails organization that provides upkeep and improvement of 970 miles of hiking trails, thirty shelters, and twenty-eight cabins in Virginia, Maryland, West Virginia, Pennsylvania, and the District of Columbia. Work on trails, shelters, and cabins is performed solely by volunteer "overseers," interns, trail crews, and ridge runners. Volunteers generally sign up for a one-week block in the months of May through September. Longer-term volunteers may receive a weekly stipend of $220. This is a great way to meet new people with outdoor interests and an outstanding way to make a real contribution to the hiking public.

PRIEST LAKE STATE PARK

State Park • Idaho • Summer

Park Manager
314 Indian Creek Park Rd.
Coolin, ID 83821-9706
(208) 443-2200

AT AN ELEVATION of about 2,400 feet, Priest Lake offers an abundance of beautiful scenery and recreational opportunities. Visitors enjoy the dense cedar-hemlock forests and have ample opportunity to observe nature's inhabitants such as whitetail deer, black bear, moose, and bald eagles. Noted for its clear water, Priest Lake extends nineteen miles and is connected to the smaller Upper Priest Lake by a placid two-mile-long thoroughfare. Priest Lake offers park visitors a diversity of outdoor enjoyment, ranging from boating and fishing to snowmobiling and cross-country skiing.

The Experience: Located either in the Indian Creek or Lionhead Unit, interns work as crew leaders, interpretation, maintenance crew, registration aides, and store clerk and manager. Interns will have the opportunity to observe and learn about park operational and administrative methods, and acquire skills and experience necessary to pursue a career in parks and recreation.

Commitment: The internship begins one week prior to Memorial Day weekend and lasts through the Labor Day weekend.

Perks: There are some paid and some nonpaid positions, with housing available at a nominal cost. Maintenance and clerical positions are paid $6 per hour, and interpretive positions are paid $6.50 per hour. All interns are required to purchase and wear a park-approved uniform.

Ideal Candidate: CPR and first aid training is required prior to starting employment.

Getting In: Write or call for further information and application procedure. Applications are accepted from January 1 through March 15 annually. Normally a personal interview with qualified applicants is required at the park.

SAGAMORE INSTITUTE

Historic Site • New York • May–November
www.sagamore.org

Internship Director
9 Kiwassa Rd.
Saranac Lake, NY 12983
(518) 891-1718 • (518) 891-2561 (fax)

BUILT IN 1897 as the wilderness retreat of the Vanderbilt family, Sagamore's twenty-seven rustic buildings include the architectural prototype for many National Park Service designs. Mostly a U.N.-designated Biosphere Reserve, the park is a historic laboratory for evolving land-use policy. Offered to the public during the summer and fall seasons, a two-hour, guided tour engages guests in a twenty-five-minute slide presentation followed by a walking narrative of the grounds and many of the buildings.

The Experience: After intensive training, interns conduct historic tours that interpret the institute's socioeconomic and architectural history in light of American cultural and land-use history, as well as the history and uncertain future of the Adirondack park. Other opportunities exist to participate in and help to shape lectures, seminars, and audiovisual presentations by Sagamore staff. Internships are available in history and public interpretation, environmental studies, visual arts and architecture, and public policy and planning. A weekly seminar with common readings and guest speakers is also provided.

Commitment: Summer interns are generally in residence sometime between May 1 and mid-June and continue through Labor Day; fall residencies are September through early November. Sagamore welcomes those who can work the entire season.

Perks: A weekly stipend of $75, along with room and board, is provided. Interns also have the opportunity to participate in residential programs, which might include workshops on Adirondack ecology, history, arts and crafts, or education and professional development, as well as engage in outdoor programs ranging from backpacking to llama trekking.

Ideal Candidate: Interns often come fresh out of college or on summer break, in the period of career change, on sabbatical, or are retired professionals who often have taken an Elderhostel course at Sagamore.

SHENANDOAH NATIONAL PARK

Hospitality Services • Virginia • April–November
www.visitshenandoah.com

Human Resources
Aramark—Virginia Skyline Company
P.O. Box 727
Luray, VA 22835
(540) 743-5108 • (540) 743-7883 (fax)

ARAMARK-VIRGINIA SKYLINE COMPANY is the concessionaire in Shenandoah National Park, operating lodges, dining facilities, craft and gift shops, camp stores, gas stations, and stables throughout the park. Shenandoah is located in northern Virginia, approximately one hundred miles southwest of the Washington, DC, area. Seasonal positions include hospitality and food service staff. The season runs from April through November, and most jobs require forty-plus hours per week. Weekends and holidays are the busiest times, and all employees must be able to work these days. Competitive wages are offered based on your experience along with health insurance benefits. A limited amount of dormitory-style housing is available, with shared bath or individual rooms with bath. Costs are $30 per room per week for single or $20 per room per week for shared. Trailer pads with electrical hookups are available at $20 per week. A special meal program ranges in price from $2 to $6. All applicants must be eighteen years of age or older.

SIGNAL MOUNTAIN LODGE

Lodge • Wyoming • May–October
www.signalmtnlodge.com

Megan Dorr, Personnel Manager
Grand Teton National Park
P.O. Box 50
Moran, WY 83013
(800) 672-6012 • (307) 543-2831 • (307) 543-2569 (fax)
signalmtnlodge@aol.com

SIGNAL MOUNTAIN LODGE is a privately owned company that operates visitor services under a concession agreement with Grand Teton National Park. Their operation includes seventy-nine guest units, two restaurants, two gift shops, a bar, a grocery/gas station, and a marina, along with Leek's Marina and Restaurant, just ten miles north of the lodge. Signal Mountain is located directly on Jackson Lake, just thirty miles from the town of Jackson Hole and twenty-five miles from the south entrance of Yellowstone National Park. Grand Teton covers 485 square miles and has over 200 miles of hiking trails and some of the best rock climbing in North America.

The Experience: Seasonal employment opportunities include lodging/laundry help, cooks, employee dining room cook, pantry, waiter/waitress, host/hostess, busperson, dishwasher, bartender, gift store sales, service station/grocery store attendant, front desk reservations office, marina attendant, management and staff positions, and day/night auditor.

Commitment: The summer season runs from early May until mid-October. Positions are full-time, and a normal work schedule is eight hours per day, five to six days per week, although schedules vary with the season.

Perks: Hourly wages vary, and all employees eat and live on the property. Meals are $225 per month, and dormitory-style housing is provided at no cost.

Ideal Candidate: Applicants with retail/food service, hotel experience, and a genuine, enthusiastic desire to work with the public are most likely to get hired. Those with the longest dates of availability will be given first consideration.

Getting In: Call or e-mail for application. It is suggested you apply early; most positions are filled by April.

The way we choose to see the world creates the world we see. —BARRY NEIL KAUFMAN

ST. MARY LODGE AND RESORT

Lodge • Montana • May–October
www.glcpark.com

Dustin Wyant, Assistant General Manager
P.O. Box 1808
Sun Valley, ID 83353
(208) 726-6279 • (208) 726-6282 (fax)
Summer: (406) 732-4431 • (406) 732-9265 (fax)
jobs@jlcpark.com

GLACIER NATIONAL PARK is a two-million-acre masterpiece of unsurpassed beauty. Conquer the challenge of biking the famous Going-to-the-Sun Highway, adventuring on a fifty-mile hike along the Continental Divide, or touring through this pristine wilderness. To guests visiting Glacier, the family-owned St. Mary Lodge and Resort offers the park's most complete guest facilities (and one of the most magnificent views in the world).

The Experience: Positions include food and beverage staff, housekeeping, sales and administration, front desk clerks, gas station attendants and mechanics, maintenance and grounds personnel, night security, and resident assistants, as well as internships in accounting, hospitality, retail management, and recreation. The work required is challenging both mentally and physically; however, the atmosphere of the Rocky Mountains and the companionship of fellow employees make it seem less strenuous than it would elsewhere.

Commitment: The lodge is open from May 15 to October 1, although staff members can begin their summer as early as May 1 and end it as late as October 15.

Perks: Most positions pay between $5.15 and $5.50 per hour. Food servers can gross about $2,700 for the summer. All employees receive room and board (three meals a day) for $8.95 per day (which is deducted from your biweekly paycheck). Employees are housed in dormitories and one-room cabins, by seniority and age. Be aware that their housing is very rustic and cabins share a central bathroom and shower facilities.

Ideal Candidate: St. Mary's attracts people who have high energy and are looking for the experience of a lifetime.

Getting In: Call for application materials. Late season help is always needed (from mid-August through October 15).

STUDENT CONSERVATION ASSOCIATION, INC.

Conservation Education • USA • 3–12 Months
www.sca-inc.org

Geoff Carter, Director of Recruiting
689 River Rd.
P.O. Box 550
Charlestown, NH 03603-0550
(603) 543-1700 • (603) 543-1828 (fax)
internships@sca-inc.org

CENTRAL TO THE Student Conservation Association's (SCA) mission is the goal of educating students and professionals of all ages about the need for active stewardship of the environment, and encouraging them to pursue lifelong careers focused on conservation and care of the earth's natural resources.

The Experience: Can you see yourself . . . patrolling a remote island wilderness in Alaska by kayak? Assisting with desert tortoise research in Southern California? Leading canoe trips and giving talks in northern Minnesota? Playing the role of an 1800s resident of historic Ft. Laramie? These are just a few of the assignments participants in the resource assistant or conservation associate programs enjoy. Participants will also have the chance to live and work in America's national parks, wildlands, and historic sites, ranging from California's Joshua Tree to the Great Smoky Mountains. For those age twenty-one and over, SCA also offers paid leadership positions, working with sixteen- to nineteen-year-old volunteers through their conservation work crew program.

Commitment: Depending on your availability and background, opportunities range from seasonal (twelve to sixteen weeks) to yearlong programs.

Perks: Benefits include a food allowance (which is generally $50 per week), free housing, travel to and from position site, and the chance to live and work in some of our nation's most beautiful places. Participants in the resource assistant program are also eligible for education awards of $1,180 from the Corporation for National Service.

Ideal Candidate: Participants are mostly college students or recent graduates, but some are teachers, career changers, or retirees (with no upper age limit). In general, applicants are seeking real-life experiences in the conservation field to further academic, career, or personal goals.

Getting In: SCA publishes *Make Contact*, a catalog of opportunities (including application materials) printed on a monthly basis. This information is also available online and updated weekly. After filling out an extensive application (along with a $10 fee), it is forwarded to various agencies (who do the hiring) based on your choices. There are no program deadlines; however, to enhance your chances of being selected, you should apply by these dates: spring— January 15; summer—March 1; fall—June 1; early winter- September 15; and late winter—November 15.

Need a job, career advice, or experience in the environmental field? Then bookmark the Student Conservation Association's Career Resource Center at www.sca-inc.org/adv/ adv.htm. Along with a conservation career bookstore and career advice area, many visitors opt for a subscription to **Earth Work Online,** a searchable database of jobs in the conservation field. However, if you're like me, I like to see everything in print. Don't worry. You can also receive all this great information by subscribing to their monthly publication, **Earth Work Magazine** (the printed format of their jobs and internship database). Over 1,500 jobs appear over the course of a year. A six-month subscription runs $25; one year is $48 (and those who subscribe for a year will also receive a free copy of **Earth Work Annual,** the SCA's yearly career planning handbook packed with job-finding and job- enhancing tips).

THEODORE ROOSEVELT NATIONAL PARK

National Park • North Dakota • Spring–Fall
www.nps.gov/thro

Bruce Kaye, Chief of Interpretation
315 Second Ave.
P.O. Box 7
Medora, ND 58645
(701) 623-4466 • (701) 623-4840 (fax)
bruce_kaye@nps.gov

THEODORE ROOSEVELT National Park, which memorializes the twenty-sixth president for his contribution to conservation, preserves the colorful North Dakota badlands along the Little Missouri River, the surrounding prairie, and a variety of wildlife. Interpreters staff information desks at visitor centers, prepare and present campfire programs, and give guided tours (on foot and by bus). Campground hosts are available in two campgrounds. Resource management volunteers work with the biological control program and Geographical Information Systems (GIS). Depending on length of volunteer work, housing and/or campground space may be provided.

U.S. ARMY CORPS OF ENGINEERS

Conservation Education • USA • Year-Round
www.orn.usace.army.mil/volunteer

Volunteer Clearinghouse
P.O. Box 1070
Nashville, TN 37202-1070
(800) 865-8337
ornvol@usace.army.mil

THE U.S. ARMY CORPS OF ENGINEERS, the steward of almost twelve million acres of land and water, offers many volunteer opportunities in recreation and natural resources management. These include trail building and maintenance, park attendant, campground hosting, wildlife habitat construction, educational interpretation, visitor center staffing, photography, and dozens of other unique and challenging opportunities. Benefits vary with the position and may include reimbursement for out-of- pocket expenses and free camping. To learn of these opportunities, the corps offers a volunteer clearinghouse, a nationwide, toll-free hotline number for those interested in volunteering their time with the corps. Before you call, you should be ready to provide information about your interests, talents, and the locations where you may want to volunteer. The clearinghouse, in turn, will provide you with contact information for the area you have requested, as well as written information about volunteer opportunities there.

Why should we live with such hurry and waste of time? We are determined to be starved before we are hungry. Men say a stitch in time saves nine, and so they take a thousand stitches to save nine tomorrow. —HENRY DAVID THOREAU

U.S. Fish and Wildlife Service

Imagine banding birds at a national wildlife refuge, raising fish at a national fish hatchery, conducting wildlife surveys, leading a tour, or assisting in laboratory research. You can engage in these things by volunteering at national wildlife refuges, fish hatcheries, research stations, and administrative offices. The work may be hard, the conditions harsh, and living quarters primitive, but it is well worth the experience—a commitment made by more than seven thousand personnel.

The Fish and Wildlife Service manages more than five hundred wildlife refuges and nearly eighty national fish hatcheries that raise more than two hundred million fish each year, from the arctic north coast of Alaska to tropical Caribbean islands. These sites cover over ninety million acres and include virtually every kind of habitat necessary for survival of America's wildlife. As our world forges into the twenty-first century, U.S. Fish and Wildlife personnel are challenged by pollution, deforestation, and the continued loss of wetlands and other vital wildlife habitat.

For information on specific volunteer positions in certain geographic locations or for general information on employment, contact the volunteer coordinator at the nearest regional personnel office listed below. Most volunteers receive room and board, and sometimes travel expenses. Summer employment applications generally need to be submitted sometime between January and April.

U.S. FISH AND WILDLIFE SERVICE FIELD OFFICES

Service Headquarters

U.S. Fish and Wildlife Service
SCEP Coordinator
4040 N. Fairfax Dr.
Room 300, Webb Building
Arlington, VA 22203
(703) 358-1724 • www.fws.gov

Alaska Region

U.S. Fish and Wildlife Service
SCEP Coordinator
1011 E. Tudor Rd.
Anchorage, AK 99503-6199
(907) 786-3328 • www.r7.fws.gov

Great Lakes/Big Rivers

U.S. Fish and Wildlife Service
SCEP Coordinator
BHW Federal Building, 1 Federal Dr.
Fort Snelling, MN 55111-4056
(612) 713-5316 • www.fws.gov/r3pao
(Iowa, Illinois, Indiana, Michigan, Minnesota, Missouri, Ohio, and Wisconsin)

Northeast

U.S. Fish and Wildlife Service
SCEP Coordinator
300 Westgate Center Dr.
Hadley, MA 01035-9589
(413) 253-8315 • www.fws.gov/r5fws
(Connecticut, Delaware, Maine, Maryland, Massachussetts, New Hampshire, New Jersey, New York, Pennsylvania, Rhode Island, Vermont, Virginia, and West Virginia)

Mountain Prairie

U.S. Fish and Wildlife Service
SCEP Coordinator
Denver Federal Center
P.O. Box 25486
Denver, CO 80225
(303) 236-7903 • (303) 236-4733 (Job Information Line)
www.r6.fws.gov
(Colorado, Kansas, Montana, Nebraska, North Dakota, South Dakota, Utah, and Wyoming)

Pacific

U.S. Fish and Wildlife Service
SCEP Coordinator
Eastside Federal Complex
911 N.E. 11th Ave., 6th Floor West
Portland, OR 97232-4181
(503) 231-2260 • (503) 231-2018 (Job Information Line)
www.r1.fws.gov
(California, Hawaii, Idaho, Nevada, Oregon, Washington, and the Pacific Islands)

Southeast

U.S. Fish and Wildlife Service
SCEP Coordinator
1875 Century Center Blvd., NE
Atlanta, GA 30345
(404) 679-7077 • www.fws.gov/r4eao
(Alabama, Arkansas, Florida, Georgia, Kentucky, Louisiana, Mississippi, North Carolina, South Carolina, Tennessee, Puerto Rico, and the Virgin Islands)

Southwest

U.S. Fish and Wildlife Service
SCEP Coordinator
500 Gold Avenue, SW
Albuquerque, NM 87102
(505) 248-7838 • www.southwest.fws.gov
(Arizona, New Mexico, Oklahoma, and Texas)

VEGA STATE PARK

State Park • Colorado • Year-Round
www.coloradoparks.org/vega

Kevin Tobey, Park Manager
P.O. Box 186
Collbran, CO 81624
(970) 487-3407 • (970) 487-3404 (fax)
vega@csn.net

• •

VEGA STATE PARK, located at an elevation of 8,000 feet on the eastern edge of the spectacular Grand Mesa, is one of forty state parks in Colorado. Vega Reservoir and the meadows that surround it are rich in history and natural beauty; the area was originally a mountain meadow where cattle ranchers grazed their herds from the late 1800s until 1962. "Vega" is the Spanish word for "meadow."

The Experience: Year-round seasonal positions include rangers, maintenance workers, and gate attendants, along with volunteer campground hosts. Internships are offered in collection and management of revenues, interpretation/environmental education, general maintenance, special projects, administration, and law enforcement. With a relatively small staff, all workers, regardless of the position, help each other in completing tasks. As a result, job duties can be highly variable, and employees find it nearly impossible to be bored.

Perks: Seasonal workers and interns receive a wage of $5.41 to $7.44 per hour, along with low-cost housing and training. Volunteers receive free housing (or RV site) and an annual pass to forty Colorado state parks after volunteering forty-eight hours. This is an excellent opportunity to learn about park management, meet wonderful people, and make lifelong friendships.

Ideal Candidate: Applicants must be highly energetic, friendly, outgoing, and motivated, and able to work independently with little supervision. Good public relations skills are a must.

Getting In: Applications are accepted year-round; however, summer applications must be received by March 31. Top applicants will be interviewed by phone.

A great flame follows a little spark. —RALPH WALDO EMERSON

VERMONT YOUTH CONSERVATION CORPS

Conservation Education • Vermont • April–October
www.vycc.org

Jenna Potash, Recruitment Coordinator
92 S. Main St.
Waterbury, VT 05676
(800) 639-8922 • (802) 241-3699 • (802) 241-3909 (fax)
ycorps@together.net

THE VERMONT YOUTH CONSERVATION CORPS (VYCC) is a nonprofit organization that hires teams of teenagers who work and study under adult leadership while completing conservation and park management projects in Vermont state parks and national forest recreation areas. Youths in the program participate in a daily integrated cycle of reading, discussion, writing, and team-building activities. Assignments might include trail construction and maintenance, footbridge construction, timber-stand improvement, creek and watershed restoration, park management, or facility improvement. A diverse crew team is a key component of the VYCC experience. Crew members may be economically disadvantaged, college-bound, high school dropouts, or learning-disabled youth. This extraordinary diversity helps break down traditional social and economic barriers and provides a rich and challenging environment for participants to learn from one another.

The Experience: Crew leaders supervise the work projects, facilitate the daily learning and discussion program, conduct a daily environmental education program, and build teams that communicate well, respect one another, and are fun and productive. The residential camp director manages all aspects of various centers and supervises a staff of four leaders. Park corps managers are responsible for operating a park with a crew of two to ten youths aged seventeen to twenty-four years and one or two assistant managers (couples are encouraged to apply). Park assistant managers work with the park corps managers in all areas.

Perks: Crew leader pay ranges from $2,700 to $3,456 per season; camp director—$4,224 to $4,950; park corps assistant—$4,200 to $4,700; and park corps manager—$6,500 to $13,000. All positions include room and board, paid staff training, and reimbursement for travel to Vermont. Qualifying staff will also receive an AmeriCorps Educational Award of between $1,000 and $2,500.

Ideal Candidate: Candidates should have experience with at-risk youth; a background in education, environmental studies, or a related field; excellent organizational and communication skills; cooking skills and enthusiasm for health and tasty food; and standard first aid and CPR certifications.

WIND CAVE NATIONAL PARK

National Park • South Dakota • 3–4 Months

Kathy Steichen, Assistant Chief Interpreter
Route 1, Box 190
Hot Springs, SD 57747-9430
(605) 745-4600 • (605) 745-4207 (fax)

LOCATED IN THE SOUTHERN BLACK HILLS, Wind Cave National Park features some of the most pristine mixed grass prairie found in the United States, including a world-renowned cave with over eighty-four miles of passages. Large herds of free-roaming bison, elk, pronghorn, and deer inhabit the grasslands and forest. Seasonal positions are available in interpretation/visitor services, campground hosts, and resource management. Three- or four-month positions are available year-round. Benefits include training, park housing/campsite, and a stipend.

WOLF CREEK OUTDOOR SCHOOL

Environmental Education • California • Spring/Fall
www.nps.gov/redw

Jay Moeller, Education Coordinator
Redwood National Park
P.O. Box 7
Orick, CA 95555
(707) 822-7611 • (707) 488-2861 (fax)
jay_moeller@nps.gov

WOLF CREEK OUTDOOR SCHOOL is a residential environmental education facility, including a new shower house, amphitheater, and craftsman-style lodge as well as two new staff houses and six student cabins. Nearby old-growth redwood forests and freshwater streams serve as outdoor classrooms. Environmental education interns teach fourth through sixth grade students about old growth and stream ecology, as well as engage them in prairie treks, values clarification activities, and campfire programs. Positions are available during the spring and fall, and applicants must have a vehicle and a valid driver's license. Housing, a uniform, and a food stipend are provided. Applications are available from Redwood National Park or from the Student Conservation Association (603) 543-1700.

U.S. Forest Service

If you've heard of Smokey Bear or Woodsy Owl, you're familiar with the U.S. Forest Service. With 29,000 permanent employees and a temporary workforce that typically exceeds 15,000 workers in the summer, the Forest Service is one of the government's major conservation organizations. The agency manages 191 million acres of federal lands, assists state and private landowners, conducts research, and works with international organizations and other countries to build a better world. Employees are stationed at more than nine hundred separate work locations—most of which are in national forests; however, many work on college campuses, at research laboratories, or in office buildings in cities or towns.

Although the largest number of jobs are in forestry, there's something for everybody. Here's a snapshot of some of the most sought-after volunteer positions:

- Archaeologists help inventory national forest lands for prehistoric and historic sites (Indian burial grounds, hunting sites, old mining camps, or homesteads). Fieldwork varies but may involve inventory surveys, photography, mapping, and test excavation.

- Backcountry rangers are jacks-of-all-trades. They educate the public to practice sound land ethics, as well as practice fire prevention, camping ethics, assist in clearing and maintaining trails, maintain fire lookouts, inventory campsites, and record wildlife observations.

- Campground hosts serve as picnic ground or campground patrons—greeting visitors, providing information, and maintaining the camp.

- Wilderness rangers meet wilderness visitors and provide information on proper wilderness use and ethics. These rangers are usually in the field for one-week to ten-day periods.

- Other seasonal and volunteer opportunities include positions in administration, cartography, education, fire fighting, guard stations, historical research, human resources, hydrology, interpretation, range management, recreation, research, visitor centers, and wildlife and fish management.

As many Forest Service employees reach retirement age, employment opportunities will increase over the next couple years, especially in the fields of conservation, wildlife, and communications.

TIPS ON GETTING IN WITH THE FOREST SERVICE:

- Contact local Forest Service offices to learn what types of seasonal positions are available, how best to find out about them, and what skills and abilities you need to develop. Although the regional offices are the forest hubs, there are more than nine hundred separate work locations across the United States. Most regional offices publish volunteer opportunity directories that you can obtain for free.

- Summer job opportunities begin approximately mid-May and end September 30th. Applications are typically accepted from December through April 15th. Applicants must be at least sixteen years of age and qualify for a position based on work experience and/or education. Beyond the summer, positions can last a couple months or as long as four years.

The whole soul is composed into a kind of real harmony the instant one sets oneself to work. —THOMAS CARLYLE

U.S. FOREST SERVICE REGIONAL OFFICES

National Headquarters

U.S. Forest Service
P.O. Box 96090
Washington, DC 20090-6090
(202) 205-1760 • (202) 205-0885 (fax)
oc/wo@fs.fed.us • www.fs.fed.us

Region 1—Northern Region

U.S. Forest Service
Federal Building
P.O. Box 7669
Missoula, MT 59807
(406) 329-3511
(Montana, northern Idaho, North Dakota, northwestern South Dakota)

Region 2—Rocky Mountain Region

U.S. Forest Service
740 Simms St.
PO Box 25127
Lakewood, CO 80225
(303) 275-5350
(Colorado, Kansas, Nebraska, South Dakota, and eastern Wyoming)

Region 3—Southwestern Region

U.S. Forest Service
Federal Building
517 Gold Ave., SW
Albuquerque, NM 87102
(505) 842-3292
(Arizona and New Mexico)

Region 4—Intermountain Region

U.S. Forest Service
324 25th St.
Ogden, UT 84401
(801) 625-5297
(southern Idaho, Nevada, Utah, and western Wyoming)

Region 5—Pacific Southwest Region

U.S. Forest Service
630 Sansome St.
San Francisco, CA 94111
(415) 705-2874
(California, Hawaii, Guam, and Trust Territories of the Pacific Islands)

Region 6—Pacific Northwest Region

U.S. Forest Service
333 SW 1st Ave
P.O. Box 3623
Portland, OR 97208-3623
(503) 326-3816
(Oregon and Washington)

Region 8—Southern Region

U.S. Forest Service
1720 Peachtree Rd., NW
Atlanta, GA 30367
(404) 347-4191
(Alabama, Arkansas, Florida, Georgia, Kentucky, Louisiana, Mississippi, North Carolina, Oklahoma, Puerto Rico, South Carolina, Tennessee, Texas, Virgin Islands, and Virginia)

Region 9—Eastern Region

U.S. Forest Service
310 W. Wisconsin Ave., Suite 500
Milwaukee, WI 53203
(414) 297-3693
(Connecticut, Delaware, Illinois, Indiana, Iowa, Maine, Maryland, Massachusetts, Michigan, Minnesota, Missouri, New Hampshire, New Jersey, New York, Ohio, Pennsylvania, Rhode Island, Vermont, West Virginia, and Wisconsin)

Region 10—Alaska Region

U.S. Forest Service
Federal Office Building
P.O. Box 21628
Juneau, AK 99802-1628
(907) 586-8863

U.S. FOREST SERVICE

YELLOWSTONE NATIONAL PARK LODGES

Resort • Wyoming • Year-Round
www.ynpjobs.com

Tim Baymiller, Human Resources Director
Amfac Parks & Resorts
P.O. Box 165
Yellowstone, WY 82190
(307) 344-5324 • (307) 344-5627 (job hotline)
(307) 344-5441 (fax)
info@ynpjobs.com

••

BIGGER THAN THE STATES of Delaware and Rhode Island combined, Yellowstone National Park contains the world's largest concentration of thermal features. Here visitors and employees alike can take advantage of hiking on thousands of miles of maintained trails among geological phenomena, wildlife, forests, lakes, and rivers (filled with rainbow trout for fly-fishing enthusiasts). You'll also find that patiently waiting for a geyser to erupt becomes very addicting, and like many, you may fall victim to becoming an official "geyser gazer." Amfac Parks & Resorts operates the major visitor services concession facilities in Yellowstone, including lodging, restaurants, shops, boat and horse activities, campgrounds, and transportation services.

The Experience: Yellowstone must be approached with a "work hard, play hard" mentality. You'll definitely work hard in the position you take on; however, you'll also have the opportunity to play hard in your own backyard. More than three thousand employees are hired each season in practically every conceivable resort-related field, ranging from lodging services to employee recreation. A majority of the staff works at one of six major locations around the park, which include Mammoth Hot Springs, Roosevelt Lodge (the "dude ranch" of Yellowstone), Canyon Village, The Lake Area, Grant Village, or Old Faithful, each with its own unique charm and features. For many, a summer in Yellowstone is an unforgettable and once-in-a-lifetime experience.

Commitment: Seasonal positions are typically filled from May 1 through November 1, although many employees come on board starting April 1. Yellowstone also offers positions during the winter months (with many filled by summer employees).

Perks: The pay for entry-level positions begins at $5.75 per hour. Cafeteria-style meals, shared lodging, and laundry facilities are provided at a cost of $61.25 per week. Employee residence facilities range from rustic cabins to a typical dorm complex. (Note that you can request to live with a friend or, perhaps, someone that you meet in your

orientation seminar.) The biggest perk includes an employee recreation program, with activities that range from outdoor adventure programs (from white-water rafting trips to fly-fishing trips), outdoor equipment rental, slide shows and seminars, live bands, line dancing, sports leagues, video rental, a photography and T-shirt design contest, a year-end talent show, and a program especially for those over the age of forty.

Ideal Candidate: People who are willing to work hard, who enjoy working with and for others, and who take pride in a job well done make the best employees.

Getting In: Call for an application packet or get the details from their web site. Positions fill very quickly, so it is best to apply by early February. Note that applications are accepted into the summer, especially for those who can arrive in August (when many students go back to college) and work through September/October. Call three weeks after you send your application.

> *After spending twenty years working in corporate America, I realized that my most rewarding experiences inside work were guiding, educating, and mentoring others. Those outside of work were my artistic pursuits, travel, health and fitness, and environmental projects. Changes in my personal life have made it possible for me to change direction now and integrate my career with the real passions in my life. My resume outlines specific skills, but cannot possibly convey the positive energy, enthusiasm, and creativity I bring to my work. Coming to Yellowstone was just a step in breaking away from the mind-set that money and possessions are the measure of a person and their success in life. Being here has shown me that some people value other things and live a totally different way. Now I seek people who are doing what they really love, filled with creative force, shaping their own lives, and having a positive influence on the lives of others.*
> —Sandra Aldrich, a reader working at
> Old Faithful in Yellowstone National Park

I shall tell you a great secret, my friend. Do not wait for the last judgment, it takes place every day. —ALBERT CAMUS

YELLOWSTONE PARK SERVICE STATIONS

Gas Station • Wyoming • Summer

Hal Broadhead, General Manager
P.O. Box 11
Gardiner, MT 59030-0011
(406) 848-7333 • (406) 848-7731 (fax)
ypss@ycsi.net

••

WHATEVER HAPPENED to full-service gas stations? You know, when the service attendant comes out of the office in overalls and a blue baseball cap, stops by your car to greet you, then fills your tank, washes the windows, and checks under the hood? Nowadays it's "pay at the pump" and you are off (with gas-covered hands)—that is, unless you are cruising through Yellowstone National Park and need a fill-up. Yellowstone Park Service Stations still relies on traditions of years past where service attendants take first-rate care of you. Summer seasonal employees, from service station attendants to automotive technicians, earn $6 per hour (and a season-end bonus). A payroll deduction of $8.75 per day is made for dormitory-style housing, with meals served in employee dining rooms.

YOSEMITE CONCESSION SERVICES CORPORATION

Hospitality Services • California • Year-Round
www.yosemitepark.com/jobs

Lisa Abbott, Human Resources Director
P.O. Box 578
Yosemite, CA 95389
(209) 372-1236 • (209) 372-1050 (fax)
hr@ycsc.com

••

YOSEMITE CONCESSION SERVICES CORPORATION is the primary concessionaire in Yosemite National Park and provides a variety of guest services to the park's four million annual visitors. The lodging division operates all guest accommodations, ranging from rustic tent cabins to the impressive National Historic Landmark Ahwahnee Hotel. The food and beverage division hosts a variety of opportunities for their guests' dining needs. Fast food, cafeterias, fine dining, and family-oriented restaurants are available on a year-round basis. Alternate ways to enjoy Yosemite are offered through the guest recreation division, with guided tram and horseback tours, rafting along the Merced River, or bicycle rentals. The renowned Yosemite Mountaineering School offers rock-climbing lessons, guided climbs, and backpacking trips in both Yosemite Valley and

the High Sierra of Tuolumne Meadows. Winter snowfall brings both Nordic and alpine skiers to Badger Pass.

The Experience: Positions are available in the front office, housekeeping, kitchen, cafeteria, bicycle stands, warehouse, accounting, general offices, gift shops, golf course, pool, refreshment stands, restaurants, transportation, security, maintenance, stables, grocery division, rafting, High Sierra camps, Badger Pass, and the ice rink. Employees can also participate in Yosemite's employee recreation program in their time off. This program offers a variety of activities and facilities, including a fitness center and wellness program; numerous organized sports, such as softball, volleyball, and basketball; organized hikes to some of the most spectacular areas in Yosemite; arts and crafts classes; barbecues, rafting trips, dances, movies, and so much more.

Commitment: Seasonal and year-round schedules are available, most of which are available during the spring and summer. A commitment of at least ninety days is needed, although in special situations, ten weeks is allowed.

Perks: Wages begin at $5.87 per hour. Employee housing consists of double- or (voluntary) triple-occupancy, canvas tent or hard-sided cabins, or dormitory rooms. Rent ranges from $13 to $17 per week, which includes blankets, pillows, towels, and linen. Employees receive a 70 percent discount at all cafeterias, a 50 percent discount at other various eating establishments in the park, and a 10 percent discount at all retail shops, including the grocery store. In addition, all housing areas have a community kitchen where employees may prepare their meals. Other perks include half off on all guest activities, including tours, rafting, ice-skating, ski rentals, lift tickets, and horseback rides.

Ideal Candidate: Employees must be at least eighteen years of age to room in employer-provided housing. Foreign applicants must possess the right to work in the U.S. prior to applying.

YOSEMITE NATIONAL PARK

National Park • California • Summer
www.nps.gov/yose/intern.htm

Kathy Dimonte, Student Intern Coordinator
Wawona Ranger Station
P.O. Box 2027
Wawona, CA 95389
(209) 375-9505 • (209) 375-9525 (fax)
kathy_dimonte@nps.gov

••

YOSEMITE'S INTERNSHIP PROGRAM is sponsored by the Yosemite Association, a nonprofit organization that raises money to be used for special projects in the park. Natural resource interpretation interns will work in one of three district visitor centers and provide walks, talks, and campfire programs, as well as "rove" a specific area discussing upcoming activities, park policies, and natural and cultural history with visitors. Wilderness management interns will spend time in a wilderness permit office, issuing backcountry permits and discussing weather conditions, equipment, and trail conditions with day hikers and overnight backpackers.

Commitment: Internships are full-time and run twelve weeks during the summer (mid-June through Labor Day). In addition, they generally hire one student during the spring and another in the fall.

Perks: The Yosemite Association provides each intern with a $10 per day stipend to defray the cost of food during the working day, along with a $1,000 tax-free scholarship upon successful completion of the twelve-week commitment. Shared housing, ranging from canvas-covered tent cabins to large houses, is also provided. Perks include one Yosemite Association seminar during the summer, a packet of books, maps, and other materials about Yosemite, and a privilege card for discounts with the park concessionaire.

Ideal Candidate: The program is limited to upper-level undergraduates, recent graduates, or graduate students with above-average scholastic records. Applicants should have a strong interest in resource preservation and management, a solid academic base in the natural or physical sciences, and have an ability to communicate ideas effectively, a genuine liking for people, and enthusiasm for

sharing knowledge with others. Maturity, a sense of responsibility, creativity, and a willingness to work hard are essential attributes.

Getting In: Call for application materials or visit their web site. All applications must be postmarked by February 1.

ZION AND BRYCE CANYON NATIONAL PARK LODGES

Lodge • Utah • March–December

Mark Wascher, Human Resources
Amfac Parks & Resorts
Zion Lodge
Springdale, UT 84767
(435) 772-3213 • (435) 772-2001 (fax)
zionbryce@redrock.net

AS YOU HIKE TO THE RIMS, wade the narrows, and explore slot canyons, unspoiled backcountry serves as your playground at Zion, while Bryce Canyon boasts multihued rock spires, pillars, and rocky temples. Amfac Parks & Resorts operates the hospitality services in these two national parks. The Zion Lodge season begins March 1 and continues through December 1 (Bryce Lodge opens one month later and closes a month earlier). Resort-type positions abound in both lodges. Along with an hourly wage, dormitory-style housing and meals are provided at $8.25 per day. Applicants must be at least eighteen years of age.

Thunder is good, thunder is impressive; but it is lightning that does the work. —MARK TWAIN

Recommended Resources. . . . .

The National Association for Interpretation publishes the biweekly *Jobs in Interpretation* newsletter, which provides listings of internships, seasonal jobs, and career opportunities in the natural and cultural interpretation field. Members of the association ($15 for students, $45 for professionals) receive five issues for free. Subscriptions, either through regular mail or e-mail, are also available for nonmembers. The National Association for Interpretation, P.O. Box 2246, Fort Collins, CO 80522; (888) 900-8283, (970) 484-8283, (970) 484-8179 (fax), jobsnai@ aol.com, www.interpnet.com

Passport in Time Clearinghouse, commonly known as PIT, invites you to share in the thrill of discovery through archaeological and historical research on national forests and grasslands throughout the United States.

U.S. Forest Service archaeologists and historians guide volunteers in activities ranging from excavating sites to historic building restoration. Many projects involve backcountry camping in which volunteers supply their own gear and food. Some projects offer meals for a small fee; others might provide hookups for your RV. Project length ranges from a weekend up to a month, and there is no registration fee or cost for participating. The *PIT Traveler*, a free newsletter/directory, announces current projects every March and September (however, see their web site for late-breaking project opportunities). Passport in Time Clearinghouse, Carol Ellick, Project Manager, P.O. Box 31315, Tucson, AZ 85751-1315; (800) 281-9176, (520) 722-2716, (520) 298-7044 (fax), pit@sricrm.com, www.volunteeramerica.com/usfs/pit_home.htm

VolunteerAmerica.com provides information on volunteer opportunities and vacations at public lands across America, including state parks, the U.S. Forest Service, National Park Service, and the Bureau of Land Management. While visiting their site, be sure to sign up for their free biweekly newsletter.

Each April **Volunteers for Outdoor Colorado** publishes *Hands On Colorado Volunteer Opportunities*, a wonderful guide profiling more than seven hundred opportunities around Colorado with agencies such as the U.S. Forest Service, the Bureau of Land Management, Colorado state parks, and various other state programs. The projects, which take place during the months of April through October, include trail construction and maintenance, wildlife studies and surveys, fieldwork, botany, backcountry monitoring, urban projects, environmental education, and administrative support. Call for your free copy, or for the most up-to-date listing of projects and opportunities, check the "clearinghouse" section of their web site. Volunteers for Outdoor Colorado, Volunteer Clearinghouse, 600 S. Marion Parkway, Denver, CO 80209-2597; (800) 925-2220, (303) 715-1010, (303) 715-1212 (fax), voc@voc.org, www.voc.org

RESOURCES

those who have a deep care for the earth will find endless opportunities in this section. Whether you'll be leading educational canoe trips in a swamp forest, teaching children about native wildlife of the area, or developing programs that help to protect the integrity of the earth's natural systems, your adventures will help to promote a personal responsibility for our natural world.

Unique Opportunities to Explore in This Section:

▶ Located in the culturally rich and historic Brandywine Valley of Pennsylvania, Longwood Gardens offers six different work programs that provide training in everything from greenhouse production to the performing arts *(page 158)*.

▶ Each year, hundreds of men and women from across the country spend months at a time aboard commercial fishing vessels operating off the Alaskan coast as fisheries observers, all made possible by the North Pacific Fisheries Observer Training Center *(page 163)*.

▶ As an intern naturalist at River Bend Nature Center, you can help people discover, enjoy, understand, and preserve the incredible natural world that surrounds us *(page 165)*.

▶ Interns with the School for Field Studies head off to places such as Australia, the British West Indies, and Yungaburra, while teaching and engaging others in environmental problem solving *(page 167)*.

▶ If you are a birding enthusiast looking for an interesting life experience or a new way to spend your vacation, explore the volunteer possibilities with the American Birding Association *(page 174)*.

Use the talents you possess, for the woods would be very silent if no birds sang except for the best.

—HENRY VAN DYKE

143

Participants learn more about the streams and ponds at Schuylkill Center for Environmental Education.

Photo Credit: Schuylkill Center for Environmental Education

THE
ENVIRONMENT

4-H ENVIRONMENTAL EDUCATION PROGRAM

Environmental Education • Georgia • 3–9 Months

Diane Davies, State 4-H Specialist
Rock Eagle 4-H Center
350 Rock Eagle Rd., NW
Eatonton, GA 31024-6104
(706) 484-2872 • (706) 484-2888 (fax)
ddavies@uga.edu

THE 4-H ENVIRONMENTAL EDUCATION PROGRAM, the largest residential environmental education program in the nation, is part of Georgia's 4-H and Youth Program (first implemented at Rock Eagle 4-H Center in 1979). More than 400,000 students from 500 different schools have participated in the program.

The Experience: Environmental education and teacher/naturalist interns teach interdisciplinary morning and afternoon outdoor and environmental education classes, provide leadership to schools participating in the program, conduct evening programs, and maintain teaching laboratories and classes. Extensive training in environmental education is provided. Interns will work at one of four 4-H state facilities, including Rock Eagle (central Georgia piedmont), Jekyll Island (coastal barrier island), Wahsega (north Georgia mountains), or Tybee Island (coastal barrier island).

Commitment: Most programs run through the school year (September through May); however, some positions are available for a semester's length.

Perks: Stipends range from $160 to $200 per week, depending on location. Interns receive housing and food and have use of educational materials and contacts with school and state officials.

Ideal Candidate: Applicants should have a genuine interest in children, a dynamic personality, well-developed communication skills, creativity, and leadership abilities. A bachelor's degree in education, natural science, environmental education, outdoor recreation, or a related field is preferred.

Getting In: Submit resume, including references and a cover letter. Contacts for each location include Rock Eagle, Steve Dorsch, 350 Rock Eagle Rd., NW, Eatonton, GA 31024-6104, (706) 484-2862, 4henved@uga.edu; Wahsega, Environmental Education Coordinator, 77 Cloverleaf Trail, Dahlonega, GA 30533, (706) 864-2050, eeewah@stc.net; Jekyll Island, Donna Stewart, 201 S. Beachview Dr., Jekyll Island, GA 31527, (912) 635-4117, donnast@uga.edu; and Tybee Island,

Naomi Gomillion, P.O. Box 1477, Tybee Island, GA 31328, (912) 786-5534.

Be aggressive. If you are interested in working at one of our centers, call the above contacts. We hire between forty and fifty seasonal instructors.

AMERICAN HORTICULTURAL SOCIETY

Agriculture • Virginia • Year-Round
www.ahs.org

Internship Coordinator
7931 E. Boulevard Dr.
Alexandria, VA 22308
(800) 777-7931 • (703) 768-5700 • (703) 765-8700 (fax)
gardenahs@aol.com

THE AMERICAN HORTICULTURAL SOCIETY is located at River Farm, a historic twenty-six-acre property along the Potomac River. Interns assist with renovation, restoration, and maintenance of gardens and grounds, and help with the children's gardening program and other special projects. Interns also participate in society programs and projects, such as their annual seed program, open house events, lectures, and seminars. Interns receive $8 per hour, and AHS will help arrange housing in a local neighborhood.

ANITA PURVES NATURE CENTER

Nature Center • Illinois • 3–12 Months
www.urbanapark.org

Judy Miller, Environmental Program Manager
Urbana Park District
1505 N. Broadway Ave.
Urbana, IL 61801
(217) 384-4062 • (217) 384-1052 (fax)

DEDICATED IN 1979, the nature center is named in honor of Anita Parker Purves, a concerned citizen who initiated interest in environmental awareness in Urbana. The center provides environmental recreation programming for all segments of the community, promoting appreciation, understanding, and responsible use of the earth.

The Experience: The assistantship and internship program is designed to provide an opportunity to develop programming and leadership skills in environmental education activities by working with students, park district staff, and cooperating organizations. Duties include developing curricula for environmental programs; providing leadership for programs; recruiting and training volunteers; participating in the planning, implementation, and evaluation of workshops and special events; assisting with development of displays and exhibits; and preparation and administration of program budgets.

Commitment: Programs run for a minimum of three months and a maximum of twelve months.

Perks: Assistants receive a stipend of $350 per month; interns receive $150 per month.

Ideal Candidate: Assistantship candidates must have either a bachelor's or master's degree in environmental education/science, while intern applicants must have at least junior status. All applicants must also have a genuine interest in working with people of all ages; have an interest in environmental education, interpretation, and resource management; and intend to pursue a career in environmental education or a related field.

Getting In: Call for more information. After reviewing applications, selected applicants are invited for an interview. Phone interviews are conducted for out-of-state candidates. Interviews include a panel interview, tour of the facilities and programs, and a written exercise.

ASPEN CENTER FOR ENVIRONMENTAL STUDIES

Nature Center • Colorado • Summer
www.aspen.com/aces

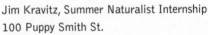

Jim Kravitz, Summer Naturalist Internship
100 Puppy Smith St.
Aspen, CO 81612
(970) 925-5756 • (970) 925-4819 (fax)
acesone@rof.net

SINCE ITS FOUNDING in 1968 by Aspen resident Elizabeth Paepcke, the nonprofit Aspen Center for Environmental Studies has been educating people to be environmentally responsible. Managing the 25-acre Hallam Lake sanctuary and another 175-acre natural area, the center offers hikes and nature classes to children and adults. It also runs the Environmental Learning Center, which houses the Scott Field Laboratory, Pinewood Natural History Library, Gates Visitor Center, and a bookstore informally known as "the Den."

The Experience: Summer naturalist interns get involved in just about everything that has to do with maintaining the center—landscaping, giving talks on the birds of prey program, rehabilitating injured animals and birds, teaching natural-history classes to children and adults, and leading

nature walks. Interns teach all the summer programs, from leading a troop of adults on a sunset walk by the lake to teaching children about the rich diversity of insects in the area. After spending a summer leading interpretive walks, learning animal rehabilitation, and teaching children about the environment, interns are sure to leave with a newfound appreciation of nature.

Perks: A weekly stipend of $125 and free accommodations are provided. Interns often cook and eat dinners together, forming friendships that the center's communal atmosphere encourages. Interns are also allowed to take at least one class for free from the center's naturalist field school.

Ideal Candidate: College juniors, seniors, graduate students, and recent graduates are eligible, although the bulk of interns have received college degrees by the start of the internship. The center strongly prefers students who have studied the natural sciences or environmental studies and have experience working at other nature centers. First aid certification is required.

Getting In: Submit a completed application (which can be found on their web site), a resume, and three letters of recommendation (the letters are suggested, but not required) by March 1. Top candidates are interviewed over the phone.

AUDUBON NATURALIST SOCIETY

Natural History • Maryland • Year-Round
www.audubonnaturalist.org

Education Program Coordinator
8940 Jones Mill Rd.
Chevy Chase, MD 20815
(301) 652-9188 • (301) 951-7179 (fax)
hq@audubonnaturalist.org

FOUNDED IN 1897, the Audubon Naturalist Society (not to be confused with the National Audubon Society) pioneered the linking of natural history studies with conservation activities. Interns serve as coteachers of children's classes (ages four to ten) for twelve weeks during the summer. In seasons other than the summer, part-time positions are available. Full-time interns receive a $200 per week stipend along with room and kitchen privileges. Perks include a 20 percent discount at the bookshop and free (or at cost) participation in most programs. First aid and CPR certification is required, as is a car or bike. Send off a cover letter, resume, and two letters of recommendation three months prior to your start date.

AULLWOOD AUDUBON CENTER AND FARM

Education/Farm • Ohio • 13 Weeks
www.audubon.org/local/sanctuary/aullwood

John Wilson, Environmental Education Specialist
1000 Aullwood Rd.
Dayton, OH 45414-1129
(937) 890-7360 • (937) 890-2382 (fax)
aullwood@gemair.com

AULLWOOD AUDUBON CENTER AND FARM is one of the original five environmental education centers in the United States owned and operated by the National Audubon Society. With over 75,000 visitors per year, they reach far with their message about promoting awareness of the relationships within natural and agricultural systems, with humans as an integral element. Environmental education/interpretation interns are involved in an extensive orientation and then gradually assume the same kinds of responsibilities as full-time staff, with a concentration on education or farming activities. All facets of an environmental education center and organic farm are explored, meaning "the good, the bad, and the ugly!" over a thirteen-week period. A $70 per week stipend is provided, along with furnished housing and utilities on the Aullwood property.

BARRIER ISLAND ENVIRONMENTAL EDUCATION CENTER

**Environmental Education • South Carolina
• Academic Year**
www.stchristopher.org/bi_home_page.htm

Jim Koenig, Program Director
St. Christopher Camp and Conference Center
2810 Seabrook Island Rd.
Johns Island, SC 29455-6219
(843) 768-1337 • (843) 768-0918 (fax)
barrisld@stchristopher.org

DEVELOPED WITH the guidance and support of the Episcopal Diocese of South Carolina and St. Christopher Camp and Conference Center, Barrier Island provides a residential environmental education program for schoolchildren. The facilities include everything from an arts and crafts building and recreation hall to beachfront cabins and a health center.

The Experience: From leading groups seining (dragging nets through the estuary to catch and learn about fish) to introducing participants to a "touch tank" (with touchable saltwater creatures), intern naturalists teach day and evening programs to more than 260 students about the coastal ecosystems. Most classes are held outdoors for a truly hands-on approach to the ocean, salt marsh, beach, forest, and sand dune habitats.

Commitment: Positions extend from August through the following May, full-time. Staff training begins at the end of August and the first school group visits the first week of September.

Perks: A weekly stipend of $180 is provided, along with a private room with shared bath, meals, and temporary health insurance.

Ideal Candidate: An undergraduate degree in education, biology, or environmental sciences is required. Teaching interest and ability with elementary-aged students, as well as a strong desire to learn about plants, animals, insects, and habitats of the coastal environment, is of utmost importance.

Getting In: Send cover letter, resume, and references. Due to the large number of applicants, personal interviews are desired but not always possible. A videotape recording of yourself will give you an edge on the competition. Phone calls are always welcome.

BERRY BOTANIC GARDEN

Botanical Garden • Oregon • Summer
www.berrybot.org

Gael Varsi, Garden Manager
11505 SW Summerville Ave.
Portland, OR 97219-8309
(503) 636-4112 • (503) 636-7496 (fax)
bbg@rdrop.com

IN ANY SEASON, the Berry Botanic Garden is a wonderful place to browse and learn. Located in Portland, the garden's six acres are designed around slopes, natural springs and creeks, open meadows, and towering Douglas firs. Horticulture interns work with the garden staff maintaining and developing areas of the garden, propagating, and various special projects. The program generally runs for ten weeks, through the summer, full-time. Internships may start any time between April 15 and July 1. A stipend of $2,400 is provided (and housing may be available for one intern). Applicants should be enthusiastic and excited about plants, horticulture, and working in public gardens. Someone who needs experience for their career is the most likely to get hired.

BRUKNER NATURE CENTER

Environmental Education • Ohio • 3–9 Months

Debbie Brill, Administrative Director
5995 Horseshoe Bend Rd.
Troy, OH 45373
(937) 698-6493 • (937) 698-4619 (fax)
brukner@juno.com

SURROUNDED BY 165 acres of rolling hills, accessed through six miles of hiking trails, Brukner Nature Center endeavors to provide meaningful experiences that emphasize natural history and the environment. Over sixty permanently injured native Ohio animals and birds are housed on the property and used for educational programming.

The Experience: Interns assist in planning, preparing, and conducting natural history, historical, and native wildlife programs for school-age children and the public. Extensive work is also done with the wildlife, including daily husbandry and care of their forty permanent residents as well as work with injured and orphaned native wildlife in the wildlife rehabilitation unit. This is a great program for those who want an in-depth experience at a nature center.

Commitment: A commitment of three months is required; however, longer terms, from six to nine months, are preferred.

Perks: Housing and a $75 per week food stipend are provided.

Ideal Candidate: A background in natural history or animal husbandry and previous experience working with wildlife, planning educational programs, and guiding interpretive hikes are preferred.

Getting In: Send cover letter and resume. Opportunities are offered year-round; however, openings are less competitive during the school year.

CALLAWAY GARDENS

Botanical Garden • Georgia • March–August
www.callawaygardens.com

Intern Director
Education Department
P.O. Box 2000
Pine Mountain, GA 31822-2000
(800) 225-5292 • (706) 663-5146 • (706) 663-6720 (fax)
education@callawaygardens.com

CALLAWAY GARDENS, a man-made landscape in a unique natural setting, provides a wholesome family environment where all may find beauty, relaxation, inspiration, and a better understanding of the living world.

The Experience: Education interns conduct and assist with education programs in home horticulture and natural history, and lead horticulture interpretation, walks, hikes, demonstrations, and workshops. Horticulture interns are involved in the practical, day-to-day maintenance of the gardens, including the grounds, conservatories, greenhouses, trails, and the vegetable garden (all assigned on a rotational basis). All interns attend weekly classes and field trips, and complete intern projects and journals.

Commitment: Internships begin either in March or May, and run through the end of August.

Perks: A biweekly salary along with housing and utilities are provided. Benefits include free gardens and beach admission, access to recreation and sports facilities on a space-available basis, employee discounts in the restaurants and shops on the property, and use of the education department library for research, reading, and work in progress. Many interns find bicycles ideal for commuting to work and for recreation in the gardens.

Ideal Candidate: Education candidates must speak and write well, enjoy meeting and teaching a variety of people, and possess enthusiasm, flexibility, and a love of the outdoors. Education applicants come from a variety of backgrounds, ranging from education and natural history to agriculture and landscape design. Horticulture candidates have a background in landscape design, horticulture, entomology, botany, or forestry.

Getting In: Send a resume and cover letter describing career goals, professional interests, and reasons for seeking employment with Callaway. An application, which should be returned with three letters of recommendation, will then be mailed back to you. Deadlines: spring—January 15; summer—February 15.

CAMP MCDOWELL ENVIRONMENTAL CENTER

Outdoor Education • Alabama • 4 Months
www.campmcdowell.com/cmec/job.html

Heather Martin, Director
105 Delong Rd.
Nauvoo, AL 35578
(205) 387-1806 • (205) 221-3454 (fax)
cmec@campmcdowell.com

SHARE CAMP MCDOWELL'S seven hundred acres of secluded forests, streams, waterfalls, and canyons in northwest Alabama with groups of twelve students (ranging from grades four through eight). Teach hands-on classes with subjects and activities including forest ecology, earth and water science, insects and wildlife, canoeing, map and compass, low and high ropes, Native American history, arts and crafts, astronomy, fishing and field games. Programs run from February through May and late August through November. Staff receive a $190 per week stipend, meals, and shared rooms in a newly renovated house, complete with kitchen, living room, laundry, and screened porch with rocking chairs! To apply, send a cover letter, resume, and references.

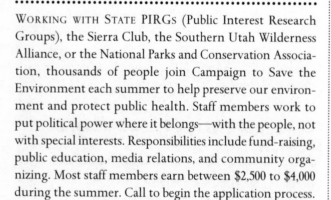

We're seeking applicants who have maturity, enthusiasm, initiative, a sense of humor, flexibility, and team spirit. In addition, applicants must have a demonstrated respect and affinity for children and a desire to help them learn and grow, as well as a desire to work outside and to be a member of a friendly and supportive team.

CAMPAIGN TO SAVE THE ENVIRONMENT

Environmental Advocacy • USA • Summer
www.pirg.org/jobs/campaign/index.htm

National Coordinator
29 Temple Place, 5th Floor
Boston, MA 02111
(800) 753-2784 • (617) 292-8057 (fax)
summerjobs@juno.com

WORKING WITH STATE PIRGs (Public Interest Research Groups), the Sierra Club, the Southern Utah Wilderness Alliance, or the National Parks and Conservation Association, thousands of people join Campaign to Save the Environment each summer to help preserve our environment and protect public health. Staff members work to put political power where it belongs—with the people, not with special interests. Responsibilities include fund-raising, public education, media relations, and community organizing. Most staff members earn between $2,500 to $4,000 during the summer. Call to begin the application process.

THE CENTER FOR HEALTH, ENVIRONMENT, AND JUSTICE

Environmental Advocacy • Virginia • Year-Round
www.essential.org/cchw

Barbara Sullivan, Intern Coordinator
150 S. Washington St., Suite 300
Falls Church, VA 22046-6806
(703) 237-2249 • (703) 237-8389 (fax)
barbaras@essential.org

THE CENTER FOR HEALTH, Environment, and Justice has been assisting disenfranchised communities struggling for environmental justice since 1981. Through their organizing, leadership development, research, and technical assistance, they empower individuals with skills and sound information to start local environmental groups, strengthen existing groups, and develop networks that reach beyond the limits of class and race to protect public health and the environment. Volunteer interns work on such topics as environmental racism, children and toxins, nonprofit management, fund-raising, incineration of landfills, sludge disposal, corporate greenwashing, and medical waste incineration. Because their national office is small and utilizes team-based work techniques, interns are likely to have a more diverse experience than interns at organizations with larger staff and rigid departmental structures.

CENTRAL WISCONSIN ENVIRONMENTAL STATION

Environmental Education • Wisconsin • Year-Round
www.uwsp.edu/acad/cnr/affil/cwes

Sterling Strathe, Assistant Director
10186 County MM
Amherst Junction, WI 54407
(715) 824-2428 • (715) 824-3201 (fax)
cwes@uwsp.edu

SPONSORED BY the University of Wisconsin, Stevens Point's College of Natural Resources, the Central Wisconsin Environmental Station is a K–12 environmental learning center serving more than ten thousand children annually. Through hands-on environmental education activities, the station provides a foundation for the study of ecological principles and concepts as they relate to people and their environment.

The Experience: Environmental education/interpretation interns serve as regular staff members and provide instruction in environmental studies for groups of K–12 students.

Summer staff counselors and specialists are responsible for carrying out overall camp operation, with an emphasis on environmental education in the residential camp setting. Types of activities conducted vary with the type of camp offered, which includes the nature adventure (seven- to thirteen-year-olds), natural resource careers workshop (fifteen- to eighteen-year-olds), or a two-week camp for children with learning disabilities.

Perks: A $1,800 stipend, plus a $300 living allowance is provided for spring and fall interns. On-site housing may be available, and some meals are provided. Summer staff pay ranges from $125 to $165 per week along with room and board.

Ideal Candidate: Intern applicants must have reached at least their junior year in college and have completed course work in methods of environmental education or interpretation. Previous practical experience in environmental education, outdoor education, or natural history interpretation is desirable. Summer staff applicants should have training or experience in one or more of the following areas: recreation, environmental education, water or field sports, backpacking, canoeing, or arts and crafts. Preference will be given to applicants with a college background.

CHESAPEAKE WILDLIFE SANCTUARY

Wildlife • Maryland • Year-Round
www.chesapeakewildlife.org

Internship Coordinator
17308 Queen Anne Bridge Rd.
Bowie, MD 20716-9053
(301) 390-7010 • (301) 249-3511 (fax)
cheswild@erols.com

THE CHESAPEAKE WILDLIFE SANCTUARY is a nonprofit wildlife rehabilitation center surrounded by eighty-five acres. It is the only organization in Maryland that provides free medical treatment to sick and injured wildlife and hand-rearing care to orphaned wildlife on a year-round basis. The main goal of the sanctuary is to provide intensive hands-on training and experience to individuals who wish to pursue a career in wildlife, veterinary medicine, or related fields. Internship positions are available in small mammals, large mammals, avian, wildlife education, and administrative areas. Interns should be prepared to work hard, get dirty, and perform routine and repetitive duties. On-site and off-site housing is provided at a nominal charge. Merit-based scholarships, ranging from $350 to $1,000, are offered upon completion of the internship.

CHICAGO BOTANIC GARDEN

Botanical Garden • Illinois • 3–12 Months
www.chicago-botanic.org

Aviva Levavi, Intern Coordinator
1000 Lake Cook Rd.
Glencoe, IL 60022-8264
(847) 835-8263 • (847) 835-1635 (fax)
alevavi@chicagobotanic.org

RECOGNIZED FOR the most diverse botanic garden internship in North America, the Chicago Botanic Garden strives to stimulate an interest in and appreciation for gardening, horticulture, botany, and conservation. Just a half-hour drive from downtown Chicago, its unique design of islands and water attracts more than a half-million visitors annually and provides a dramatic setting for the interaction of plants and people.

The Experience: The garden offers two types of internships for college students: a horticulture rotating program, where interns rotate through different work areas each month, and a specialized program, where interns focus their professional experience in one area. In addition to gaining horticultural expertise, interns will gain experience in the administration of botanic gardens. Opportunities are available in every conceivable area of operation—from greenhouse and nursery crop production and environmental education to community gardening and visitor programs.

Commitment: Internships range from three to twelve months beginning each spring.

Perks: A $6.50 per hour wage is provided for most positions (graphic design and education interns are volunteer), and the garden will assist in finding affordable housing in the

A garden intern participates in the Chicago Botanic Garden's horticulture internship program.

The old Lakota was wise. He knew that man's heart, away from nature, becomes hard; he knew that lack of respect for growing, living things soon led to lack of respect for humans too. —LUTHER STANDING BEAR

149

area. Interns have the use of library and research facilities and may attend seminars, classes, and field trips. A car or bicycle is recommended.

Ideal Candidate: Applicants should be enthusiastic, energetic, positive thinking, and willing to "grow" with the gardens. Preference is given to those with some experience and a background in horticulture, botany, ecology, or conservation.

Getting In: Call or write for application materials (which must be received by March 1 for all positions and time frames).

DAHLEM ENVIRONMENTAL EDUCATION CENTER

Nature Center • Michigan • Year-Round
www.jackson.cc.mi.us/dahlemcenter

Diane Valen, Program Coordinator
7117 S. Jackson Rd.
Jackson, MI 49201
(517) 782-3453 • (517) 782-3441 (fax)

KNOWN FOR ITS award-winning elementary education curriculum, the Dahlem Environmental Education Center strives to bridge the gap between humans and the natural environment. Operating on Jackson Community College property as a nonprofit organization, the center generates its own revenue via memberships, user fees, gifts, grants, fund-raising projects, and special events. A professional staff, supplemented with seasonal interns and trained community volunteers, provides educational services for more than 26,000 visitors annually, including more than 400 school and youth groups.

The Experience: Naturalist interpretive interns primarily teach in the center's school program. Along with exposure to all aspects of nature center operations, interns will have the opportunity to engage in exhibit design, assist in program development, write for nature center publications, provide animal care, participate in special events, and work with volunteers. Summer ecology camp counselors develop and implement their own activity plans for ten to twelve elementary school–age campers each week, and summer wildlife biologist interns coordinate research and work with staff in the center's countywide bluebird recovery project.

Perks: On-site housing, staff training, and a weekly stipend of $206 are provided.

Ideal Candidate: Applicants should have college-level training in an environmental field and previous teaching/

programming experience, especially with children in an outdoor educational setting. The ideal applicant is responsible, flexible, creative, and enthusiastic, with a "do and discover," rather than a "show and tell," teaching style.

Getting In: Call or write for application materials and deadlines. Telephone interviews are provided for qualified applicants.

DEEP PORTAGE CONSERVATION RESERVE

Environmental Education • Minnesota • 3–9 Months
www.deep-portage.org/jobs.html

Molly Malecek, Program Director
RR 1, Box 129
Hackensack, MN 56452-9720
(218) 682-2325 • (218) 682-3121 (fax)
portage@uslink.net

EACH YEAR thousands of students from Midwest schools explore conservation and environmental education activities at Deep Portage Conservation Reserve. In addition, Deep Portage serves area residents and visitors with weekly classes, interpretive programs, wildflower garden displays, land-use demonstrations, and recreational opportunities for birding, hiking, hunting, and skiing.

The Experience: Staff duties include preparing and presenting interpretive and environmental education programs for school groups and the general public, hosting visitors in the interpretive center, assisting professional staff in curriculum development and assessment, and special project work. The recreation program teaches every kind of outdoor recreation skill for appreciating lake and forest country. Participating in this program will help each staff member to become a forester, wildlife manager, recreation leader, or a K–12 formal-education teacher.

Commitment: Positions are offered year-round (beginning in January, June, or September) and last from three to nine months.

Perks: A weekly stipend of $125 to $200 is provided, along room and board.

Ideal Candidate: Along with enthusiasm, applicants should have a variety of skills and, whenever possible, certifications in these skills.

Getting In: Submit cover letter, resume, and three letters of reference at least twelve weeks before your requested start date.

DELAWARE NATURE SOCIETY

Nature Center • Delaware • Year-Round
www.delawarenaturesociety.org

Karen Travers, Member Programs Coordinator
Ashland Nature Center
P.O. Box 700
Hockessin, DE 19707
(302) 239-2334 • (302) 239-2473 (fax)
karen@dnsashland.org

CREATED BY A HANDFUL of concerned people in 1964, the Delaware Nature Society fosters understanding, appreciation, and enjoyment of the natural world. Interns teach and coteach children's classes at the Ashland Nature Center. Along with training workshops and programs, interns will have the opportunity to work with people of all ages and interests, design curriculum, work with live farm and wild animals, and develop their own special skills and interests. A stipend of $2,000 helps to alleviate the costs of housing, food, and transportation. Applicants must have completed their junior or senior year in college and be pursuing a career in environmental education or natural sciences. Send a cover letter, resume, and two letters of recommendations by March 15 for summer positions. For other times during the year, applications are accepted on a rolling basis.

EAGLE BLUFF ENVIRONMENTAL LEARNING CENTER

Environmental Education • Minnesota • 9 Months
www.eagle-bluff.org

Beth Turnbull, Internship Coordinator
Route 2, Box 156A
Lanesboro, MN 55949
(507) 467-2437
intern_program@eagle-bluff.org

EAGLE BLUFF ENVIRONMENTAL LEARNING CENTER is a nonprofit environmental school dedicated to developing and fostering educational opportunities that will create universal awareness, enhance respect, and promote personal responsibility for the natural world. Participants in the naturalist fellowship program spend nine months (beginning in late August) developing teaching, public relations, and many other skills related to residential environmental education. Fellows kick off the program with a two-week training period, then coordinate, teach, and lead residential and day-use naturalist programs for visiting groups.

Fellows live in private rooms with communal living, dining room, and kitchen areas. In addition to room and board, a monthly stipend of $350 is provided. Applicants must have a bachelor's degree, experience working with children, and CPR and first aid certification.

FERNWOOD NATURE CENTER

Nature Center • Michigan • Year-Round
http://landtrust.org

Wendy Jones, Head Naturalist
13988 Range Line Rd.
Niles, MI 49120-9042
(616) 695-6491 • (616) 695-6688 (fax)

FERNWOOD IS A combined 100-acre nature center, botanic garden, and arts and crafts center that provides a sense of environmental awareness, cultural appreciation, and education for the community. They host 30,000 public visitors per year, and 8,000 local school children visit for environmental education programs.

The Experience: Intern naturalists conduct and lead nature walks and activities for children ranging from preschool to high school age, lead weekend programs for adults and families, develop displays, write articles, work on prairie reconstruction, and maintain nature trails. Seasonal naturalists develop and conduct natural history programs for school groups and weekend visitors, assist in supervision and training of interns, maintain and design educational displays, supervise care of animals, supervise and assist in the daily operations of the nature center, and provide grounds maintenance.

Commitment: Intern positions are available each spring and fall, for a duration of ten to twelve weeks, full-time. Seasonal naturalist positions last from late March through mid-November.

Perks: Intern naturalists earn $5.50 per hour, while seasonal naturalists earn $6 per hour. All interns receive housing, workshops, classroom training, and discounts in gift shops and the cafeteria.

Ideal Candidate: Applicants should have an interest and training in natural history, ecology, biology, or related subjects. Previous experience (paid or volunteer) in environmental education or work with children improves your chances tremendously. Also, a good knowledge of plant and animal identification is very helpful.

Getting In: Submit cover letter, resume, and references.

FIVE RIVERS METROPARKS

Natural History • Ohio • 3–12 Months
www.metroparks.org

Lyn Modic, Chief of Education and Programming
1375 E. Siebenthaler Ave.
Dayton, OH 45414
(937) 275-7275 • (937) 278-8849 (fax)
metroparks@dayton.net

INTERNSHIPS AND APPRENTICESHIPS at Five Rivers Metro-Parks provide practical on-the-job experience in outdoor education and park management. Positions are available in the following areas: Possum Creek Farm (lead school tours or youth groups through the barn and trails and care for farm animals), Carriage Hill (historical farm restoration and agriculture/farm maintenance), Cox Arboretum (horticultural education); Germantown MetroPark (natural history), North MetroParks (natural history); Wesleyan MetroPark (natural history and youth programming); and Wegerzyn Horticultural Center (horticulture and education). The program runs during the summer or nine to twelve months beginning in the fall. A $6 per hour wage is provided along with free housing at several work sites.

> *It is most difficult to obtain an internship during the summer due to the large number of applicants. I highly recommend considering an apprenticeship with us.*

FOOTHILL HORIZONS OUTDOOR SCHOOL

Outdoor Education • California • Academic Year
http://stan-co.k12.ca.us/foothill

Dan Webster, Head Naturalist
Stanislaus County Office of Education
21925 Lyons Bald Mountain Rd.
Sonora, CA 95370
(209) 532-6673 • (209) 533-1390 (fax)
foothill@sonnet.com

THROUGHOUT THE YEAR, classes of sixth-grade students, accompanied by their teachers, spend an entire week at Foothill Horizons Outdoor School. During this time, the students participate in a variety of activities to increase their knowledge and awareness of and sensitivity to nature. The students take part in nature classes, campfires, square dancing, free play, night hikes, and field trips.

The Experience: Interns begin the first three weeks of their ten-month internship experience (beginning in mid-August) participating in intensive training, observing naturalists, and team teaching. From the fourth week on, interns lead groups of students on hikes, teaching them about ecology, conservation, Native American history and culture, and sensory awareness. After several weeks of teaching, interns rotate through other support positions. The head naturalist will observe and evaluate each intern twice each semester, which is meant to further refine the intern's teaching technique. Interns are encouraged to use any and all resources available to improve their teaching, including Project Learning Tree and Project Wild workshops, regularly scheduled in-services, conferences, curriculum guides in the library and, of course, the knowledge of the naturalists.

Perks: A daily stipend of $40 is provided, along with room, board, and health fund.

Ideal Candidate: Applicants must be upper-division college students or graduates who have concentrated in the areas of natural and environmental sciences, resource management, parks and recreation, child development, or education. Beyond that, Foothill is looking for people who are passionate about making a positive impact on kids' lives.

Getting In: The application process requires either an on-site visit and mini-teaching demo by the applicant, or a phone interview and a videotaped lesson presented by the applicant to a group. Positions are filled between the months of March and June.

> *As a young teacher who isn't sure of the exact path I want to take, working at Foothill Horizons has given me the opportunity to teach outdoor education and help me with the decision of where I belong in the world. I am learning about science, nature, Miwuk Indians, and classroom management skills from experienced naturalists. I have never worked in an environment where I have received so much support and enthusiasm from co-workers who love their jobs. I can already feel that my experience is helping me to stay on a path with heart, guiding me to whatever comes next—whether it be teaching or doing something completely different. I consider it a great gift to spend the next year of my life at Foothill Horizons. I am already a better person because of the time I have spent here.* —Jacob Sackin, Intern

FRIENDS OF THE EARTH—U.S.

Environmental Advocacy • Washington, DC
• Year-Round
www.foe.org

Kevin Payne, Fellowship Coordinator
1025 Vermont Ave., NW, Suite 300
Washington, DC 20005-6303
(202) 783-7400 • (202) 783-0444 (fax)
foe@foe.org

••

FRIENDS OF THE EARTH—U.S. is a dynamic environmental advocacy organization that protects the planet from environmental disaster; preserves biological, cultural, and ethnic diversity; and empowers citizens to have an effective voice in decisions affecting their environment and their lives. Each fellow or intern works closely with project directors researching, writing, lobbying, and assisting with administrative support. Fellows make a six-month, full-time commitment and receive a stipend of $800 to $1,000 per month; interns make a three-month commitment, work part-time, and are unpaid.

GARDEN IN THE WOODS

Horticulture • Massachusetts • April–September
www.newfs.org/volunteers.html

Pattie Scheuring, Horticulture Internships
The New England Wild Flower Society
180 Hemenway Rd.
Framingham, MA 01701-2699
(508) 877-7630 • (508) 877-3658 (fax)
scheuring@newfs.org

••

ON A 45-ACRE landscape of rolling hills, ponds, and streams emerges Garden in the Woods, with over 1,600 kinds of plants grown in a naturalistic fashion. Sponsored by the New England Wild Flower Society, the garden offers educational programming and nature walks as well as operates a native plant nursery that produces over 30,000 plants for garden displays and sale to the public.

The Experience: For over twenty years, the New England Wild Flower Society has offered an internship program to train students in the practical aspects of native plant cultivation and propagation and to provide assistance to the horticulture staff. Interns can focus on one of three areas: propagation and nursery management, garden maintenance and development, or plant conservation. Regular on-site activities are supplemented by field trips to nearby gardens, arboreta, nurseries, and natural areas. In addition,

interns are assigned a small special project based on their area of interest, which might include nursery sales, interpretation, design, writing, or conservation.

Commitment: Internships run for six months beginning on April 1.

Perks: A weekly stipend of $200 and on-site/shared housing is provided. Perks include participation in selected field trips and a wide range of optional education classes provided by the education department.

Ideal Candidate: Preference is given to applicants who have career aspirations and at least two years of educational course work in plant-related fields, previous work experience, and the ability to engage in rigorous outdoor work.

Getting In: Call or download application materials and information from their web site. Applications, which include a $7.50 processing fee, are due by mid-February. Depending on distance, applicants may be interviewed in person or over the phone, with decisions made by the first week in March.

GLEN HELEN OUTDOOR EDUCATION CENTER

Environmental Education • Ohio • Year-Round
www.glenhelen.org

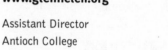

Assistant Director
Antioch College
1075 SR 343
Yellow Springs, OH 45387
(937) 767-7648 • (937) 767-6655 (fax)
ghelen@antioch-college.edu

••

THE GLEN HELEN OUTDOOR EDUCATION CENTER is a residential outdoor education program serving more than 3,000 elementary school–aged students annually. Six biotic communities and a raptor center encompass this 1,000-acre nature preserve owned and operated by Antioch College. Naturalist interns plan and lead small groups of residential environmental education programs, care for hawks or owls in their raptor center, and actively participate in a comprehensive training program. Interns also portray a living history character from the late 1700s during the fall and winter terms. Positions are offered from early January to early June or from mid-August to mid-December, with a possibility of summer work. A stipend of $250 per week, along with room and board is provided. In addition, interns have access to all the facilities at Antioch College and are able to receive undergraduate or graduate credit (with tuition waived). Applicants must have completed at least

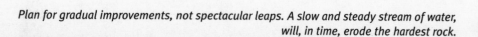

Plan for gradual improvements, not spectacular leaps. A slow and steady stream of water, will, in time, erode the hardest rock.

two years of college (though a degree is preferred), enjoy working with a close-knit staff, and have an interest in working with children in a residential outdoor education setting.

GREAT SMOKY MOUNTAINS INSTITUTE

Environmental Education • Tennessee • 1 Year
www.nps.gov/grsm/tremont.htm

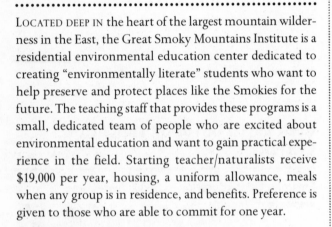

Director
9275 Tremont Rd.
Townsend, TN 37882
(423) 448-6709 • (423) 448-9250 (fax)
gsmit@smokiesnha.org

LOCATED DEEP IN the heart of the largest mountain wilderness in the East, the Great Smoky Mountains Institute is a residential environmental education center dedicated to creating "environmentally literate" students who want to help preserve and protect places like the Smokies for the future. The teaching staff that provides these programs is a small, dedicated team of people who are excited about environmental education and want to gain practical experience in the field. Starting teacher/naturalists receive $19,000 per year, housing, a uniform allowance, meals when any group is in residence, and benefits. Preference is given to those who are able to commit for one year.

HAWK MOUNTAIN SANCTUARY ASSOCIATION

Wildlife • Pennsylvania • Year-Round
www.hawkmountain.org

Dr. Keith Bildstein, Director of Research and Education
1700 Hawk Mountain Rd.
Kempton, PA 19529-9449
(610) 756-6961 • (610) 756-4468 (fax)
bildstein@hawkmountain.org

HAWK MOUNTAIN SANCTUARY ASSOCIATION is a private, nonprofit organization with programs in education, research, and conservation policy that are national and international in scope. Hawk Mountain, established in 1934, was the world's first sanctuary for hawks, eagles, and other birds of prey. Science education interns help guide field trips and present on-site and off-grounds interpretive programs to schoolchildren and the general public; ecological research interns help the sanctuary study raptors and Appalachian Mountain fauna and flora; and biological interns assist with censuses of songbirds, raptors, and other

flora and fauna, and maintain databases. Along with a monthly stipend of $500, interns receive free housing on the sanctuary grounds.

HEADLANDS INSTITUTE

Environmental Education • California • Year-Round
www.yni.org

Cleveland Justis, Education Director
GGNRA, Building 1033
Sausalito, CA 94965
(415) 332-5771 • (415) 332-5784 (fax)
yni@yni.org

HEADLANDS INSTITUTE, operating out of historic Fort Cronkhite in the Marin Headlands (north of San Francisco), is an educational nonprofit organization that provides field-based science programs in nature's classroom to inspire a personal connection to the natural world and responsible actions to sustain it. Educational adventures engage students in interactive learning through outdoor activities, learning games, team-building exercises, and classroom instruction.

The Experience: Field instructors develop a set of activities and hikes for ten to fifteen students (a majority are in the fourth through sixth grade) that meld the client's needs with the instructor's unique strengths and the institute's core themes. The three broad core themes are "sense of place," interconnections, and stewardship. In addition, each instructor is expected to attend weekly staff meetings and present a one-hour evening program once or twice a week for groups of up to eighty students. Education interns will have a rotating schedule that includes observing instructors in the field, working on administrative projects in the office, delivering promotional slide presentations, and developing an educational project.

Commitment: Positions begin in late August, early January, and early June. Positions are one semester in duration.

Perks: Education interns receive room, partial board, and a small stipend of $150 per week. Instructor positions start at $63 per day and include housing, partial board, medical/dental plan, retirement plan, paid training, and vacation benefits. Part-time and substitute instructor positions are also available.

Ideal Candidate: Candidates for either position must have at least a four-year degree in a related field and current first aid/CPR certification. Successful candidates for field instructor positions generally have two years' experience teaching in the outdoors. Intern applicants require demonstrated interest (education or experience) in natural science and experience working with children. Although not required, applicants are encouraged to complete a Wilderness First Responder, EMT, or other advanced first aid training.

Getting In: Applications are accepted on a rolling basis, but priority is given to those received by October 15 (for positions starting in January) and March 15 (for summer and fall positions). Top candidates are invited to Headlands for an interview and an opportunity to observe a field program.

HOLDEN ARBORETUM

Arboretum • Ohio • Summer
www.holdenarb.org

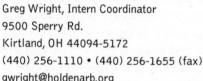
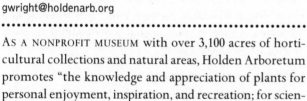

Greg Wright, Intern Coordinator
9500 Sperry Rd.
Kirtland, OH 44094-5172
(440) 256-1110 • (440) 256-1655 (fax)
gwright@holdenarb.org

· ·

As a NONPROFIT MUSEUM with over 3,100 acres of horticultural collections and natural areas, Holden Arboretum promotes "the knowledge and appreciation of plants for personal enjoyment, inspiration, and recreation; for scientific research; and for educational and aesthetic purposes."

The Experience: The internship program is designed to give a balance of hands-on experience and educational programming. The educational aspect of the program has four parts: an orientation that combines lectures and tours to help interns understand the arboretum, its grounds, and its purpose; educational sessions; field trips to eight other horticultural institutions in northeast Ohio and Canada, helping to broaden the interns' understanding of public horticulture; and demonstrations, which give interns an opportunity to learn additional skills on equipment they might not otherwise use during the summer. Internships are available in horticulture, horticulture maintenance, landscape gardening, conservation, horticulture therapy, and education.

Commitment: The internship is a full-time position offered during the summer. Interns spend between five and ten hours each week in educational programs—most of them taking place during work hours.

Perks: Along with housing, intern wages start at $6 per hour. The intern campus promotes bonding on a social level through activities including picnics, ball games, and nights out.

Ideal Candidate: Applicants must be studying horticulture,

natural history, or related fields. Current students and recent grads receive first consideration.

Getting In: Submit cover letter, resume, and names of three references by February 1.

HORIZONS FOR YOUTH

Environmental Education • Massachusetts
• Year-Round
www.hfy.org

Mike Dattilio, School Program Director
121 Lakeview St.
Sharon, MA 02067
(781) 828-7550 • (781) 784-1287 (fax)
outdoors@hfy.org

· ·

HORIZONS FOR YOUTH offers outdoor environmental education programs in the spring, fall, and winter, and a summer camp. Field teacher instructors and interns develop and teach lessons and activities in the outdoors, focusing on ecology, environmental science, conservation, and group dynamics. Adventure leaders plan and implement 23-day wilderness trips, and environmental camp leaders plan and implement a 5-day environmental camp experience. Most staff receive $200 per week, plus room and board. For more information on becoming a summer camp counselor, contact Julie Wiggins (camp@hfy.org).

A field instructor at Horizons for Youth teaches children about the buzzing world of bees.

For every thousand hacking at the leaves of evil, there is one striking at the root. —HENRY DAVID THOREAU

HUMANE SOCIETY OF THE UNITED STATES

Wildlife • Washington, DC • Year-Round
www.hsus.org

Intern Coordinator
Wildlife and Habitat Protection Section
2100 L St., NW
Washington, DC 20037
(202) 452-1100 • (202) 258-3079 (fax)
wildlife@hsus.org

KNOWN AS THE LARGEST animal protection organization in the United States, the Humane Society is dedicated to ending animal suffering in all areas by instituting changes through investigation, legislation, and public outreach. Most of their programs are focused on companion animals, laboratory animals, farm animals, wildlife, habitat protection, and the environment. Duties as an intern include research, writing, monitoring legislative hearings, and limited clerical responsibilities. Preference is given to college students with course work in biology, zoology, or ecology.

INTERNATIONAL CRANE FOUNDATION

Birding • Wisconsin • Year-Round
www.savingcranes.org

Scott Swengel, Curator of Birds
P.O. Box 447
Baraboo, WI 53913-0447
(608) 356-9462 • (608) 356-9465 (fax)
sswengel@savingcranes.org

THE INTERNATIONAL CRANE FOUNDATION is a nonprofit organization dedicated to conservation and preservation of the world's cranes and the natural wetland and grassland communities in which they live. Aviculture interns receive hands-on training in the care and management of endangered cranes. Most of the time will be spent caring for the birds, and each intern is responsible for developing and completing a research project with assistance from the staff. Internships start at all seasons and are available year-round. A stipend of $325 to $600 per month is provided along with housing. Senior undergraduates through recent college graduates may apply, and individuals seeking graduate training are especially encouraged. Send cover letter, resume, and three letters of recommendation.

KALAMAZOO NATURE CENTER

Environmental Education • Michigan • Summer
www.naturecenter.org

Sarah Reding, Adventure Program Director
Michigan State Parks
P.O. Box 127
Kalamazoo, MI 49004-0127
(616) 381-1574 • (616) 381-2557 (fax)

NATIONALLY RECOGNIZED for their outreach, education, and avian research programs, the Kalamazoo Nature Center, partnering with Michigan state parks, coordinates the Michigan State Parks Adventure Program. Within the system's 260,000 acres, over 140 miles of Great Lakes frontage; 460 miles of lakes, rivers, and streams; virgin timber stands; waterfalls; and plenty of recreational opportunities can be found. Summer staff develop and implement naturalist programs for adults and youth within one of ninety-six Michigan state parks, as well as schedule and promote all programs. A $220 to $240 per week stipend and assistance in securing housing is provided. Candidates must have degree work in environmental education, parks, or biology. Send a resume and cover letter (including three references with contact information).

KEEWAYDIN ENVIRONMENTAL EDUCATION CENTER

Environmental Education • Vermont • 5–10 Weeks
www.keewaydincamps.org

Tori Cleiland, Director
10 Keewaydin Rd.
Salisbury, VT 05769
(802) 352-1050 • (802) 352-7822 (fax)
keec@keewaydincamps.org

KEEWAYDIN ENVIRONMENTAL EDUCATION CENTER is a nonprofit organization that provides short-term residential environmental education programs for public school groups. Many students and their teachers raise the necessary funds to pay for their trip to Keewaydin, which not only allows the whole class to participate but also gives the kids a sense of ownership.

The Experience: The role of environmental education instructors at Keewaydin is challenging, fun, demanding, and rewarding. Throughout the fall and spring, instructors teach students about natural science, local history, human impact, and land issues; and during the winter, instructors focus on the adaptation of plants, animals, and humans as they weather (and survive) the winter months.

Commitment: Positions are available for ten weeks during the winter, eight weeks in the spring, and five to six weeks during the fall. Although positions are seasonal, instructors frequently stay on for more than one season.

Perks: A $195 per week salary is provided, along with room and family-style meals. During the spring and fall, instructors live in unheated wooden cabins close to the lake. A spacious hunting lodge serves as home for instructors during the winter. Unfortunately Keewaydin cannot accommodate instructors' dogs or other pets.

Ideal Candidate: Enthusiasm for learning, living, and working with children, as well as caring deeply for the earth and all its inhabitants, are qualities found in the Keewaydin staff. Smokers are suggested not to apply.

Getting In: Send resume and cover letter to begin the application process, and it's best to apply at least two to three months ahead of time. Telephone interviews are common for all positions.

KEWALO BASIN MARINE MAMMAL LABORATORY

Marine Science • Hawaii • Year-Round
www.dolphin-institute.com

Internship Program Coordinator
The Dolphin Institute
1129 Ala Moana Blvd.
Honolulu, HI 96814
(808) 593-2211 • (808) 597-8572 (fax)
participate@dolphin-institute.com

THROUGH A CAREFULLY designed full-time apprenticeship training program, interns work directly with the dolphins and researchers to learn effective dolphin and whale behavior teaching techniques and research skills. Projects include exploring dolphin perception, intelligence, and communication; assisting with dolphin husbandry and care; assisting the staff in the research laboratory; and orientating Dolphin Institute volunteers. Interns must provide their own transportation, living accommodations (the institute will assist in arranging group housing), and daily expenses. If you are no longer a student, inquire about their short-term projects and volunteer program.

LAKE COUNTY FOREST PRESERVE

Environmental Education • Illinois • 4–12 Months

Mark Hurley, Intern Coordinator
21950 Riverwoods Rd.
Deerfield, IL 60015
(847) 948-7753
forestpreserves@co.lake.il.us

INTERNS WORK AS "paraprofessional" naturalists, based at the 550-acre Ryerson Conservation Area (which is managed by the Lake County Forest Preserve). A large portion of time is spent developing, preparing, and presenting programs to youth and adults, and the completion of an independent project. Other responsibilities may include participation in volunteer and teacher training programs or special events. Internships include a sixteen-week program beginning in mid-August ($3,900 stipend); a six-month program beginning in late February ($5,850 stipend); or a yearlong program that begins in late August ($11,250 stipend). Furnished housing can be arranged for a fee of $100 per month.

LAND BETWEEN THE LAKES

Environmental Education • Kentucky • 3–12 Months
www.lbl.org/internships.html

Jo Travis, Intern/Apprentice Coordinator
Tennessee Valley Authority
100 Van Morgan Dr.
Golden Pond, KY 42211
(270) 924-2075 • (270) 924-2060 (fax)

LOCATED IN western Kentucky and Tennessee, Land Between The Lakes (LBL) offers 170,000 acres of wildlife, history, and outdoor recreation opportunities, wrapped by 300 miles of undeveloped shoreline.

The Experience: Interns and apprentices work closely with professionals to receive firsthand experience in recreation, environmental education, forestry, wildlife, history, graphic design, photography, public relations, environmental engineering, or health and safety. Work locations might be in a family campground, a resident group camp, a living-history farm, a nature center, or the LBL administrative office. More than fifteen hundred people have completed internships at LBL since 1964.

Commitment: Internships last from twelve to sixteen weeks. Apprenticeships are available up to one year.

A pond-frog cannot imagine the ocean, nor can a summer insect conceive of ice. Remember, you are restricted by your own learning. —CHUANG-TSU

Perks: Interns receive a $125 weekly stipend; apprentices receive a $175 weekly stipend. Housing in fully furnished houses or house trailers is also provided.

Ideal Candidate: Prospective interns must have completed at least two years of college course work. Apprentice applicants must have at least a bachelor's degree and cannot be currently enrolled in school. Someone with lots of enthusiasm and commitment has as good a chance as someone with all the experience in the world.

Getting In: Call for application materials. The summer deadline is January 15, with finalists interviewed by phone. Apprenticeships are filled as vacancies occur.

LASSEN COUNTY YOUTH CAMP

Natural Resources • California • Spring/Fall

Personnel Director
Lassen County Office of Education
472-013 Johnstonville Rd., North
Susanville, CA 96130-9710
(530) 257-2196 • (530) 257-2518 (fax)

THE LASSEN COUNTY YOUTH CAMP, located on the east shore of Eagle Lake, provides opportunities for groups of sixth graders who attend four-day sessions that uncover the study of plants, animals, water, and soil of the area. Naturalists and interns conduct field activities and teach natural history, physical science, and other environmental awareness–oriented subjects. A stipend of $90 per day ($40 per day for interns), along with room and board, is provided. All applicants must be certified in first aid and CPR; naturalists must possess a college degree.

LONG LAKE CONSERVATION CENTER

Experiential Education • Minnesota • 3–9 Months
www.llcc.org

Bob Schwaderer, Executive Director
Route 2, Box 2550
Palisade, MN 56469
(800) 450-5522 • (218) 768-4653 • (218) 768-2309 (fax)
llcc@mlecmn.net

ESTABLISHED IN 1963, Long Lake Conservation Center (LLCC) is Minnesota's original environmental learning center. Each year thousands of students and adults explore LLCC's 760-acre outdoor classroom and learn about the environment and conservation of natural resources through school year programs, a summer camp, and public programs.

The Experience: In a spirit of symbiosis, Long Lake views each fieldwork experience as an opportunity for the intern and the center to benefit equally. You'll help keep their teacher-to-student ratios to a more intimate level and bring in fresh ideas and a helping hand. At the same time, you'll gain teaching experience, leadership and discipline skills, a broadened range of activities, program planning and curriculum development experience, organizational skills, and an introduction to the Midwestern experiential education network. Depending on which season you join, you'll become proficient at teaching a number of topics, including aquatic biology, archery, canoeing, cross-country skiing, deer/wolf relationships, fire building and wilderness ethics, human ecology, initiative games, orienteering, simulation games, snow studies, and snowshoeing. Summer counselors will supervise, organize, and assist campers during junior naturalist sessions and ecology and wilderness river canoe expeditions.

Perks: Interns receive a $100 per week stipend (summer counselors receive $160 per week), room and board, liability coverage, and limited attendance at professional workshops and meetings. Each staff member has a private sleeping room in a new dorm built in 1999, and shares a kitchen, lounge, and two complete bathrooms.

Ideal Candidate: Intern candidates seeking experience in teaching and developing communications skills are ideally suited to this program. Applicants must be working toward a degree in a related field, or have already graduated and are seeking to gain experience. Nontraditional students (i.e., older adults seeking a career change or reentry into the workforce) are also welcome to apply. Counselor applicants must be at least a high school senior and enjoy working with adolescents and the outdoors. Swimming and/or lifesaving is highly desirable.

Getting In: Request an application packet. Applications are considered on a first-come, first-served basis, and many candidates apply nine to twelve months in advance.

LONGWOOD GARDENS

Horticulture • Pennsylvania • 3–24 Months
www.longwoodgardens.org

David Foresman, Student Programs Coordinator
Route 1, P.O. Box 501
Kennett Square, PA 19348-0501
(610) 388-1000 • (610) 388-2908 (fax)
studentprograms@longwoodgardens.org

LOCATED IN THE culturally rich and historic Brandywine Valley, Longwood Gardens is one of the world's premier display gardens, with nearly four acres of greenhouses and conservatories, flower gardens, fountain gardens, century-old trees, and natural areas encompassing one thousand acres. Longwood offers six training programs geared for high school and college students as well as professional gardeners. In general, interns and trainees specialize in one work area, such as curatorial, arboriculture, greenhouse display, greenhouse production, research, education, or performing arts, supplemented by seminars, workshops, continuing education courses, and field trips over a three- to twenty-four-month period. All participants receive a stipend and are able to live rent-free on the grounds of the former estate of industrialist Pierre S. du Pont. The student houses are furnished and include kitchen utensils and dishes, laundry facilities, study areas, and nearby garden space. Their web site provides all the details, including job openings and an application form.

Learning by doing is the best teacher for interns at Longwood Gardens.

MISSION SPRINGS CONFERENCE CENTER

Outdoor Education Ministry • California
• Year-Round
www.missionsprings.com

Mark McReynolds, Outdoor Education Director
1050 Lockhart Gulch Rd.
Scotts Valley, CA 95066
(800) 683-9133 • (831) 335-3205 • (831) 335-7726 (fax)
info@missionsprings.com

• •

THE MISSION SPRINGS CONFERENCE CENTER holds an outdoor education program for children in grades four to eight from both Christian and public schools. The program is affiliated with the Pacific Southwest Conference of the Evangelical Covenant Church and serves sixty schools with 2,700 students. The proximity to Santa Cruz, the beach, and many other natural attractions makes this a great place to work, live, and learn.

The Experience: Over sixty naturalist/counselors lead natural science classes, Bible studies, field trips, and other activities throughout the year. Naturalists will have the opportunity to gain work experience in outdoor education, Christian camping, and youth ministry; obtain training in educational techniques, natural history interpretation, recreational leadership skills, and camp ministry; and enjoy living in a tight-knit Christian community near the coast.

Perks: A stipend of $225 per week is provided, along with room, board, limited insurance, and laundry services. This is a superb community, teaching, and ministry experience.

Ideal Candidate: Individuals with emotional maturity, excellent physical health, enthusiasm, enjoyment of the outdoors, interest and ability to teach Bible classes, concern about environmental issues, and current Red Cross standard first aid certification are desired.

Getting In: Submit cover letter and resume, then follow up with a phone call.

I'm looking for solid Christians interested in teaching environmental education. Previous youth ministry, camp, and teaching experience sure helps.

MONTEREY BAY AQUARIUM

Aquarium • California • Summer
www.mbayaq.org

Internship Coordinator
Interpretive Programs Office
886 Cannery Row
Monterey, CA 93940-1085
(831) 648-7902 • (831) 648-4890 (job hotline)
llam@mbayaq.org

• •

MONTEREY BAY AQUARIUM envisions a world in which the oceans are healthy and people are committed to protecting the integrity of Earth's natural systems, which sustain us all. To help make this vision a reality, they create exhibits, programs, and publications that introduce people from all walks of life to the wonders of the marine world—from Monterey Bay to the vast oceans beyond. With increased visitation during the summer months, the aquarium adds

Some trees grow very tall and straight and large in the forest close to each other, but some must stand by themselves or they won't grow at all. —OLIVER WENDELL HOLMES

159

Photo Credit: L. Albee

special programs to help enhance the visitor experience and take advantage of additional program venues. Interpretive staff work outdoors conducting talks, interpreting for visitors waiting in line, telling stories, dressing up visitors in costumes and scuba gear, interpreting artifacts, or showing visitors live animals and seaweed from their Great Tide Pool. Inside, staff members deliver video presentations in the auditorium and interpret exhibits throughout the galleries. While there is minimal contact with the aquarium's live collections, there are daily opportunities to work with large and diverse audiences. Applications are accepted starting in January.

MONTSHIRE MUSEUM OF SCIENCE

Science Museum • Vermont • 15 Weeks
www.montshire.net

Amy Vanderkooi, Intern Coordinator
One Montshire Rd.
Norwich, VT 05055
(802) 649-2200 • (802) 649-3637 (fax)
montshire@montshire.net

••

LOCATED A STONE'S THROW from Dartmouth College, Montshire Museum of Science serves as a hands-on education center that creates its own changing natural history, physical science, and technology exhibits. The museum conducts a variety of programs, trips, and other activities for children and families, as well as courses, workshops, and forums for business leaders and community groups.

The Experience: Science education interns will have the opportunity to teach a variety of science concepts to preschoolers and schoolchildren, to develop curricula and design demonstrations for kids and families, to interpret exhibits, to work in day camps and other environmental education activities, and to assist with special events. Exhibit interns will be involved in the research, design, and construction of exhibits. Internet and education interns work with a nonprofit Internet access provider for schools and community organizations in the area. Membership and development interns work with varied membership programs and a strong development effort. Public relations interns work in the various avenues of communication, ranging from articles and media spots to advertising and graphic design.

Commitment: The fifteen-week, full-time internship program is held during all seasons of the year. Other schedules may be available to meet the needs of an individual intern, including part-time work.

Perks: A $600 stipend is provided, which is intended to help offset food and gas expenses. Local families welcome interns into their homes.

Ideal Candidate: Prerequisites include an interest in science and a desire to work with people. Familiarity with natural and physical science, communications, and education is useful.

Getting In: Call for an application materials. Upon receiving your application, they will call or send a letter to arrange an interview. In-person interviews are held with applicants who live nearby and telephone interviews with most distant applicants.

MOTE MARINE LABORATORY

Marine Science • Florida • Year-Round
www.mote.org

Andrea Davis, Volunteer/Intern Coordinator
1600 Ken Thompson Parkway
Sarasota, FL 34236
(800) 691-6683 • (941) 388-4441 • (941) 388-4312 (fax)
adavis@mote.org

••

MOTE MARINE LABORATORY is a nonprofit organization dedicated to research in marine and environmental sciences, with a focus on the southwest Florida coastal region. College interns have the opportunity to participate in scientific literature review, project development, data processing and analysis, and report writing. Internships are available in all research areas of the laboratory as well as such support areas as the aquarium, communications, and education. Although a volunteer position, interns receive all the benefits of membership, including free aquarium admission, gift shop and cafe discounts, special event discounts, and lecture and seminar admission. Housing is also available at $75 per week. It's best to apply by February 1 for summer internships.

NAGS HEAD WOODS PRESERVE

Conservation Education • North Carolina • Summer

Jeff DeBlieu, Preserve Steward
The Nature Conservancy
701 W. Ocean Acres Dr.
Kill Devil Hills, NC 27948
(252) 441-2525 • (252) 441-1271 (fax)
smithdeb@nhwoods.org

••

NAGS HEAD WOODS, managed by the Nature Conservancy, is filled with a mixture of maritime deciduous forest, maritime swamp forest, and several other biological communities. The naturalist intern designs and leads educational field trips for visitors to the preserve, including guided canoe trips, hikes, and weeklong day camps for children aged nine to twelve. The stewardship research internship is designed to link high-priority preserve research needs with the attainment of research requirements for a graduate degree in the natural sciences. A stipend along with housing is provided. All candidates require a strong interest in and commitment to conservation, the ability to work well with a variety of people, and the ability to work independently and conscientiously. Submit cover letter and resume by mid-February.

NATIONAL WILDLIFE FEDERATION

Wildlife • USA • 3–12 Months
www.nwf.org/nwf/jobopps/internships.html

Internship Coordinator
8925 Leesburg Pike
Vienna, VA 22184-0001
(703) 790-4545

THE NATIONAL WILDLIFE FEDERATION (NWF), the nation's largest member-supported conservation education and advocacy organization, offers an internship program for college graduates with an interest and knowledge in environmental issues. Each intern is given a responsible role and becomes an essential part of NWF's conservation and education efforts. Typical internships include animal tracks program, backyard wildlife habitats program, conservation, campus ecology, communications, legal, outdoor education, population and environment program, publications, and schoolyard habitats. The internship length varies from a summer on up to a year, with stipends ranging from $275 to $340 per week. Opportunities are available at their national headquarters in Virginia and at offices all over the U.S., with destinations as far as Anchorage, Alaska! This is a great way to make vital contacts with influential nature lovers.

THE NATURE CONSERVANCY

Natural Science • Virginia • Summer
www.tnc.org

Employment Specialist
4245 N. Fairfax Dr., Suite 100
Arlington, VA 22203-1606
(800) 628-6860 • (703) 841-5379 • (703) 247-3721 (job hotline)

THE NATURE CONSERVANCY, founded in 1951, is an international conservation organization committed to preserving natural diversity by finding and protecting lands and waters supporting the best examples of all elements of the natural world. Hands-on conservation internships at nationwide field offices and preserves include administrative, naturalist, preserve, and stewardship positions. Call for the latest line on opportunities and application materials. Each office conducts its own recruiting, so it's best to apply to the state office that interests you. (Their web site provides contact information.)

NATURE'S CLASSROOM ATOP LOOKOUT MOUNTAIN

Experiential Education • Alabama • Spring/Fall
www.naturesclassroom.com

Maria Luther, Director
P.O. Box 400
Mentone, AL 35984
(800) 995-4769 • (256) 634-4443 • (256) 634-3601 (fax)
natures@hiwaay.net

STARTED AS an experiential education program with an environmental foundation, Nature's Classroom is designed to support traditional classroom learning by teaching creative and practical applications of subjects taught in school. Students enjoy the informal, outdoor atmosphere, opening themselves to new growth experiences.

Environment: The program is located on the picturesque and rural Lookout Mountain, on the Little River (one of only two rivers that begin and end on a mountain), bordering Tennessee and Georgia.

The Experience: Teachers work with public- and private-school children from the fourth to seventh grade, teaching hands-on classes in all curriculum areas as well as leading field groups in the outdoors. Small group activities are designed to foster group cooperation, communication, and team-building concepts using group initiatives and a low ropes challenge course. A large-group activity may include a simulation of the Underground Railroad, an environmental hearing, or a night hike.

Commitment: Contracts are available from mid-February through end of May and/or mid-September through mid-December. Most staff work up to thirteen hours a day, three to four days a week.

Perks: Along with a private cabin or room, meals, training, access to canoes and climbing gear, and the chance to work with a diverse staff, teachers receive a weekly stipend of

If you give a person a fish, you feed him for a day. If you train a person to fish, you feed him for a lifetime. —CHINESE PROVERB

161

$190 (and up). Health insurance, up to $150 per year for incidental medical expenses, and use of a washer and dryer are also provided.

Ideal Candidate: Teachers must have a four-year degree and be at least twenty-one, creative, flexible, and motivated to have fun. A sense of humor is very helpful and appreciated, and being able to put the needs of the program and children first is a must. Although individuality and diversity are celebrated, a professional appearance (woodsy professional, that is) is just as important. Emotional maturity is needed to be a success and have fun.

Getting In: Call for application materials. Candidates are welcome to stay for a few days during their on-site interview.

NEW CANAAN NATURE CENTER

Nature Center • Connecticut • Academic Year/Summer

Camp Director
144 Oenoke Ridge
New Canaan, CT 06840
(203) 966-9577 • (203) 966-6536 (fax)

ESTABLISHED IN 1960, New Canaan Nature Center is a non-profit nature center serving a wide range of students and visitors, with a focus mainly on the education of students in grades K–8. Seasonal teacher/naturalist positions are offered during the summer or for the academic year. Applicants must have a heartfelt desire to teach, an interest in experiencing a nature center setting, and a fairly strong background working with kids. A weekly stipend of $250 is provided along with possible free housing.

NEWFOUND HARBOR MARINE INSTITUTE

Marine Science • Florida • Spring/Fall
www.nhmi.org

Judy Gregoire, Intern Coordinator
1300 Big Pine Ave.
Big Pine Key, FL 33043-3336
(305) 872-2331 • (305) 872-2555 (fax)
info@nhmi.org

NEWFOUND HARBOR MARINE INSTITUTE, sponsored by the Seacamp Association, offers programs in marine science and environmental education to school groups (from elementary to high school). Designed to awaken the senses and gain a better understanding of the natural features of the ocean and its ecosystems, participants can explore the dynamics of natural communities in a variety of habitats including the opportunity to snorkel and wade with instructors as they experience the wonders of the Florida Keys. More than eight thousand students participate in the program annually.

Environment: The institute is located 120 miles southwest of Miami—an ideal site for exploring the subtropical marine and terrestrial habitats of the Lower Keys—and is within the boundaries of the Florida Keys National Marine Sanctuary (where the year-round temperature averages 79 degrees).

The Experience: Instructor positions and internships are designed to provide college students and preprofessionals with a variety of experiences—from developing their ability to lead interpretive programs to snorkeling among coral reefs with visiting school groups. Over six to eight weeks of intensive training are provided; staff learn boat handling skills and U.S. Coast Guard boating rules to captain their twenty-six-foot oceanic research vessels. Seminars and hands-on training workshops are conducted on topics including mangrove ecology, reef fish ecology, coastal ecology, shark biology, coral reef ecology, and field techniques. Staff also participate in teaching techniques seminars, program observations, and team-teaching sessions. Other seasonal opportunities exist in photography, marketing, maintenance, food service, and support staff.

Commitment: Interns and instructors work eight to ten hours per day, five or six days per week throughout the academic year. For those who would like just a summer experience teaching youth about the sea, the Seacamp Association offers a residential program from late May through late August. See their listing on page 95 for more information.

Perks: A monthly stipend (interns start at $50 per week), room and board, a travel bonus, and access to staff boats are provided. American Red Cross certification in advanced first aid, CPR, and lifeguarding is also provided.

Ideal Candidate: Applicants should have an interest in marine environment and children, boating and waterfront experience, and a college degree (or current study) in biology or environmental science.

Getting In: Send cover letter, resume, transcripts, and three letters of recommendation to receive an application. Deadlines: fall—July 1; spring—October 15.

NORTH CASCADES INSTITUTE

Experiential Education • Washington • Year-Round
www.ncascades.org/nci

Program Coordinator
2105 State Route 20
Sedro-Woolley, WA 98284-9394
(360) 856-5700 • (360) 856-1934 (fax)
nci@ncascades.org

•••••••••••••••••••••••••••••••••••••••

NORTH CASCADES INSTITUTE is a nonprofit organization dedicated to increasing understanding and appreciation of the natural, historical, and cultural landscapes of the Pacific Northwest. Its primary focus is on field-based, experiential, and environmental education for children and adults. Volunteer internships are available at the Mountain School (room and board provided) and Mountain Camp, as well as positions in watershed education, field seminar, and administration. Perks include extensive training, participation in field seminars, and a free T-shirt.

NORTH PACIFIC FISHERIES OBSERVER TRAINING CENTER

Fish Observer • Alaska • Year-Round
www.uaf.edu/otc

Paula Cullenberg, Director
University of Alaska, Anchorage
707 A St., Suite 207
Anchorage, AK 99501-3600
(907) 257-2770 • (907) 257-2774 (fax)
anpjc@uaa.alaska.edu

•••••••••••••••••••••••••••••••••••••••

EACH YEAR HUNDREDS of men and women from across the country spend months at a time aboard commercial fishing vessels operating off the Alaskan coast as fisheries observers. Working independently alongside the fishermen, observers collect data on species and quantities of fish caught, fish lengths, weights and sex, and sightings of marine mammals and sea birds for federal and state agencies who manage Alaska's fisheries. Observers are hired by one of five private contractors. Once accepted by a contractor, a potential observer must successfully complete a two- to three-week training course that covers sampling responsibilities, fish identification, and safety at sea. Observers work generally under a ninety-day contract, although their actual time at sea can vary from three weeks to three months. It's noted that there is a very high demand for observers (the government employs about 375 people per year). Most observers can find work year-round if they want. Wages between $90 and $135 per day are pro-

An observer measures the width of a crab onboard a commercial crabbing vessel in Alaska with the North Pacific Fisheries Observer Training Center.

vided, along with transportation expenses and insurance. A bachelor's degree in biology, natural science, or environmental science is required.

NYS DEPARTMENT OF ENVIRONMENTAL CONSERVATION

Environmental Education • New York
• 12 Weeks

Anita Sanchez, Naturalist Intern Program Coordinator
Five Rivers EE Center
56 Game Farm Rd.
Delmar, NY 12054-9776
(518) 475-0291 • (518) 475-0293 (fax)

•••••••••••••••••••••••••••••••••••••••

THE NEW YORK STATE Department of Environmental Conservation runs three centers: Five Rivers Environmental Education Center, Rogers Environmental Education Center, and Stony Kill Farm Environmental Center. With programming for teachers, school groups, youth groups, conservation organizations, and the public, the three state-run centers promote an understanding of natural history, ecology, environmental science, and natural resources.

Earth gives life and seeks the man who walks gently upon it. —HOPI LEGEND

The Experience: Intern naturalists receive training in a wide variety of education center programs, the operations and activities of a nature center, and principles of environmental interpretation. Duties range from leading environmental activities to designing educational exhibits.

Commitment: In general, internships are twelve weeks in length, available year-round.

Perks: Along with a $100 per week stipend, interns receive a living space on the grounds, with a fully equipped kitchen, furnished living room, and private bedroom.

Ideal Candidate: Applicants must be eighteen and older, with at least two years of college experience in environmental education, science education, or natural resources/history. Enthusiasm, love of the outdoors, and a desire to work with people are required.

Getting In: Send completed application three months before your desired start date. It's noted that summer is ten times as popular as other seasons, and applicants are less likely to get accepted. Spring (April through June) is actually the most interesting season.

PEACE VALLEY NATURE CENTER

Nature Center • Pennsylvania • 10–12 Weeks

Craig Olsen, Assistant Naturalist
170 Chapman Rd.
Doylestown, PA 18901
(215) 345-7860 • (215) 345-4529 (fax)

PEACE VALLEY NATURE CENTER began in 1975 with a mission to educate schoolchildren and the general public about the natural world. The nature center features nine miles of trail, winding through five hundred acres of diverse natural communities, including fields, deciduous forests, thickets, streams, ponds, coniferous forests, and a portion of Lake Galena. The center is home to a solar building that houses displays, a shop, and a Clivus Multrum composting toilet.

The Experience: Interns are required to observe and teach programs, complete and present a project, write a natural history article, attend a board meeting, participate in bird walks, keep a daily diary, and attend staff meetings.

Commitment: The spring and fall internships run for twelve weeks. The summer internship is ten weeks. Interns must work every other weekend; Mondays are days off.

Perks: Interns receive $5.15 per hour, housing, and the opportunity to gain experience teaching and observing various teaching styles and methods.

Ideal Candidate: Preference is given to applicants with two years of college, who are studying environmental education, biology, environmental studies, or a related field. Applicants must be interested in teaching children of all ages about the natural world.

Getting In: Send a resume, references, and cover letter requesting an application. Candidates within a two-hour drive are interviewed on-site; others are interviewed by phone. Applying for the spring or fall internships increases the candidate's chances of employment.

POCONO ENVIRONMENTAL EDUCATION CENTER

Environmental Education • Pennsylvania • 6–10 Months
www.peec.org

Flo Mauro, Director
R.R. 2, Box 1010
Dingmans Ferry, PA 18328
(717) 828-2319 • (717) 828-9695 (fax)
peec@ptd.net

LOCATED IN the Delaware Water Gap National Recreation Area, Pocono Environmental Education Center's (PEEC) outdoor classroom consists of a 38-acre campus with access to over 200,000 acres of public land—fields, forests, ponds, waterfalls, and scenic hemlock gorges. Throughout the year, PEEC hosts school groups, religious organizations, universities, professional conferences, and workshops. PEEC also sponsors Elderhostel programs, family nature study vacations, and professional development workshops on topics ranging from ornithology and wildflowers to photography and Native American studies.

The Experience: Environmental education instructors provide programming, development, and service programs; program planning interns assist in scheduling, implementing, and coordinating educational programs; and public relations interns focus on the publications and marketing of PEEC.

Commitment: Six- to ten-month staffing assignments begin in February, June, or September.

Perks: A $500 to $800 per month stipend is provided, along with lodging in heated cabins with a private bath (usually shared with one roommate), a shared staff lounge, and meals served in the dining hall.

Ideal Candidate: Enrollment in or completion of a degree program in English, communications, environmental/outdoor education, natural sciences, or related fields is required. Applicants must demonstrate experience working with people and interest in working in a residential setting. Certification in lifeguarding, first aid, or CPR is preferred.

Getting In: Submit resume, cover letter, and two references. Selected candidates will have on-site interviews to observe the typical operation of the center.

RAINFOREST ACTION NETWORK

Environmental Advocacy • California • Year-Round
www.ran.org/vip

Adrienne Blum, Intern Program Director
221 Pine St., Suite 500
San Francisco, CA 94104
(415) 398-4404 • (415) 398-2732 (fax)
helpran@ran.org

RAINFOREST ACTION NETWORK is a nonprofit activist organization working to protect the earth's rainforests and support the rights of their inhabitants through education, grassroots organizing, and nonviolent direct action. Major education and advocacy programs include Africa campaign, Amazon oil campaign, old growth campaign, education outreach, fund-raising, grassroots organizing, Protect-an-Acre Program, and World Rainforest Week. Intern opportunities include media operations, database coordination, campaign administration and coordination, executive administration, development assistance, and writing, layout, and research. Internships are unpaid, although local commuting costs are reimbursed. RAN welcomes people of all backgrounds with an interest in environmental issues.

RICHARDSON BAY AUDUBON CENTER AND SANCTUARY

Natural Science • California • 3 Months

Meryl Sundove, Education Coordinator
National Audubon Society
376 Greenwood Beach Rd.
Tiburon, CA 94920
(415) 388-2525 • (415) 388-0717 (fax)

SURROUNDED BY eleven acres of land and nine hundred acres of tidal wetlands on San Francisco Bay, Richardson Bay is composed of a wildlife sanctuary (where thousands of waterbirds winter in the shallow bay) and a public education center.

The Experience: Environmental education interns participate in all aspects of the education center and sanctuary operations. Spring and fall interns teach natural science classes and programs for children—first as assistants, then as leaders after gaining experience. Other responsibilities include weekend nature walks and slide and film presentations. Summer interns primarily work in the children's program (for those aged three to twelve years), which includes three half-day workshops, with a variety of different natural history and environmental science themes, over a four-week period. All interns also help with office work, bookstore operations, and sanctuary maintenance projects.

Commitment: The internship requires a full-time commitment for at least three months.

Perks: A $500 food stipend (for three months) is provided. Housing is sometimes available.

Ideal Candidate: Candidates should deal effectively with people, be well organized, and have an interest in natural history. Experience working with children or teaching is helpful.

Getting In: Submit cover letter and resume.

RIVER BEND NATURE CENTER

Environmental Education • Minnesota • Year-Round
www.rbnc.org

John Blackmer, Chief Naturalist
100 Rustad Rd.
P.O. Box 186
Faribault, MN 55021-0186
(507) 332-7151 • (507) 332-0656 (fax)
blackmer@rbnc.org

HOME TO ACTIVE WETLANDS, maple and basswood forests, and restored prairies, River Bend helps people "discover, enjoy, understand, and preserve the incredible natural world that surrounds us." Intern naturalists develop and teach programs, providing hands-on teaching experiences for children from preschool through age twelve in environmental day camps during the summer and for school groups throughout the academic year. In addition, interns design and teach public weekend programs for all ages, including youth, families, seniors, and special needs groups. A $140 weekly stipend, plus housing, is provided. A minimum of three years of college study is required. Send off a cover letter, resume, and a list of three references.

Behold the turtle; he makes no progress unless his neck is stuck out. —JAMES CONANT

RIVER NETWORK

River Conservation • Oregon • 1 Year
www.rivernetwork.org

Coyote Days, Office Manager
520 SW 6th, Suite 1130
Portland, OR 97204
(800) 423-6747 • (503) 241-3506 • (503) 241-9256 (fax)
info@rivernetwork.org

RIVER NETWORK is a national river conservation organization dedicated to helping people save rivers. They support river conservationists in America at the grassroots, state, and regional levels, help them build effective organizations, and link them together in a national movement to protect and restore America's rivers and watersheds. They also work with river conservationists to acquire and conserve riverlands that are critical for wildlife, fisheries, and recreation.

The Experience: Conservancy interns research land ownership along specific rivers, research new markets with municipal watershed agencies and U.S. Army Corps of Engineers mitigation programs, and produce publications of rivers that they work on. Watershed interns work with online services, research and write about technical issues related to river protection, identify and recruit river experts, respond to requests for assistance from activists, and compile fund-raising information for river activists.

Commitment: A one-year, full-time commitment is preferred.

Perks: A $1,500 per month stipend, plus vacation and sick days are provided. Perks include attending work-related river-rafting trips, conferences and trainings, and meetings with people in the environmental/river protection fields.

Ideal Candidate: Applicants must have an interest in river protection or environmental issues. The ideal candidate is someone who has just graduated or will be graduating with a bachelor's or master's in environmental studies or a related field. Applicants must be well organized, work well both as team members and individuals, and be computer literate.

Getting In: Send a cover letter describing why and when you are interested in an internship and your major areas of interest, a resume, a nontechnical writing sample about an environmental issue you've researched, and a list of three personal references.

RIVERBEND ENVIRONMENTAL EDUCATION CENTER

Environmental Education • Pennsylvania • Summer
www.gladwynepa.com/riverbend

Stacy Olitsky, Educator Director
1950 Spring Mill Rd.
Gladwyne, PA 19035-1000
(610) 527-5234 • (610) 527-1161 (fax)
olitreec@aol.com

HOUSED IN A 1923 converted barn and surrounded by thirty-one acres of forest, fields, and streams, Riverbend provides a unique setting for educational activities designed to establish an awareness and understanding of the principles upon which our natural world is based. Spend time at Riverbend using your creative abilities and love of natural history while sharing the joy of discovery with children. Environmental education interns prepare and teach classes to schools, organized groups, and the public while gaining an orientation to environmental education, a working knowledge of ecological and environmental concepts, and experience developing and implementing educational goals and lesson plans. Environmental educator/camp staff work at the Exploration Camp and are directly responsible for the creation and implementation of hands-on, exploration-based activities. Benefits include $200 to $350 per week and housing if needed.

SALISH SEA EXPEDITIONS

Marine Science • Washington • Spring/Fall
www.amouse.net/~salish

Sophy Johnston, Program Director
P.O. Box 976
Kingston, WA 98346
(360) 297-2512
salish@amouse.net

SALISH SEA EXPEDITIONS provides boat-based research expeditions to groups of students, ranging from fifth to twelfth graders. Aboard the research ship, students rotate through tasks such as helping handle sail, cooking meals, launching and recovering scientific gear, evaluating data, plotting a course, or standing a night watch. In the classroom, science educators help students develop their itinerary and research plan; then, while aboard the ship, they double as watch leaders and scientific study teachers. Prior to working with students, staff participate in a seven-day training period that focuses on Puget Sound ecology, program methodology, safety procedures, and ship operations. Along with room and board, base salaries range from $200 to $300 per week. All positions require a college degree and a demonstrated ability to teach and design/implement scientific research projects. Basic first aid and CPR certificates are required; however, advanced certificates in EMT or WFR are highly encouraged.

SARETT NATURE CENTER

Nature Center • Michigan • Year-Round
www.sarett.com

Dianne Braybrook, Internship Coordinator
2300 Benton Center Rd.
Benton Harbor, MI 49022
(616) 927-4832 • (616) 927-2742 (fax)
sarett@sarett.com

MORE THAN 25,000 STUDENTS from preschool through college follow the Sarett Nature Center staff naturalists down the pathway to environmental education each year. The naturalists teach a wide range of environmental topics, including nature awareness, pond study, sand dune ecology, and cross-country skiing.

Environment: The center owns six hundred acres along the Paw Paw River, manages another twelve hundred acres of wooded dunes for the Nature Conservancy, and provides nature interpretation at Grand Mere State Park, a wilderness area along Lake Michigan.

The Experience: Intern naturalists teach a variety of natural history programs to school groups, primarily preschool through sixth grade. During these programs, interns lead interpretive nature walks, teach cross-country skiing (winter), lead sixth-grade students on an overnight wilderness camping experience (spring/summer), aid in developing educational programs and weekend activities for the public, and care for resident educational animals. Interns also complete a special project ranging from an interpretive program or display, writing a natural history article for publication, or engaging in field research.

Commitment: Positions are available year-round.

Perks: A $100 per week stipend is provided, plus housing.

Ideal Candidate: Biology or environmental science college graduates interested in sharing their knowledge of the natural world with children of all ages are ideal. Useful skills include bird, tree, insect, animal track, and woodland/wetland wildflower identification for the northeastern United States; cross-country skiing and snowshoeing; canoeing and lifesaving; and low-impact wilderness camping.

Getting In: Submit cover letter (including the season you wish to work), resume, and three or four references. Deadlines: winter/spring—October 1; summer—March 1; and fall—June 1.

THE SCHOOL FOR FIELD STUDIES

Environmental Studies • Worldwide • 1 Year
www.fieldstudies.org

Intern Coordinator
16 Broadway
Beverly, MA 01915-4499
(800) 989-4435 • (978) 927-7777 • (978) 927-5127 (fax)
jobs@fieldstudies.org

THE SCHOOL FOR FIELD STUDIES (SFS) is the country's oldest and largest educational institution exclusively dedicated to teaching and engaging undergraduates in environmental problem solving. Students will learn about environmental issues and work to solve them by actually living within the ecosystems and communities where they take place. For example, students at their Center for Rainforest Studies in Australia are engaged in rainforest restoration and have assisted the communities there in replanting more than twenty thousand trees.

The Experience: Participating in a practical education in environmental studies, interns will assist staff members with organizational and academic tasks, group dynamics, administrative support and logistics, site management, and the academic and research programs. Placements are offered in Australia, the British West Indies, Canada, Costa Rica, Kenya, and Mexico.

Commitment: Interns must make a commitment of one year. Start dates are late January, June 1, and September 1.

Perks: Benefits include a stipend of $750 for each semester and $500 for both summer sessions, along with room, board, and evacuation insurance. Half of the direct round-trip airfare is also reimbursed at the conclusion of service.

Ideal Candidate: Applicants must be college graduates (twenty-one years or older) and have valid certification in first aid and CPR (lifeguard certification preferred) as well as experience in group dynamics, leading groups, or teaching. Ideal candidates are energetic, motivated individuals who seek out new challenges and enjoy a group living environment. Some programs also require a specific language proficiency, and those who have been through an SFS summer or semester program are given preference.

The moment one gives close attention to anything, even a blade of grass, it becomes a mysterious, awesome, indescribably magnificent world in itself. —HENRY MILLER

167

SCHUYLKILL CENTER FOR ENVIRONMENTAL EDUCATION

Environmental Education • Pennsylvania • 15 Weeks
www.schuylkillcenter.org

Director of Education
8480 Hagy's Mill Rd.
Philadelphia, PA 19128-1998
(215) 482-7300 • (215) 482-8158 (fax)
scee@schuylkillcenter.org

FROM A NATURAL HISTORY and environmental education library to a computer learning center and hands-on discovery museum, the Schuylkill Center provides a hodgepodge of environmental facilities and programs.

The Experience: Interns become environmental educators-in-training, working closely with the professional teaching staff, then practicing newly acquired skills firsthand with the children and adults who visit the center. Duties include teaching daily environmental education programs for preschool level through twelfth grade; assisting with the center's daily operations; conducting weekend natural history programs; surveying environmental education curriculum materials; designing and constructing displays and exhibits for the discovery museum; and observing and assisting with adult workshops, teacher in-services, and college credit courses.

Commitment: The program is offered each spring and fall for fifteen weeks.

Perks: A $1,600 stipend is provided. Periodic teacher workshops in national environmental education curriculum and materials are available.

Ideal Candidate: Applicants must have a minimum of two years of college in the field of environmental education, biology, natural sciences, or elementary education, with an interest in the environment and desire to work with people. Those with a combined background of natural sciences and teaching experience are preferred.

Getting In: Call for application materials (which are due by December 1 for the spring and May 1 for the fall).

SCICON

Outdoor Education • California • Academic Year

Rick Mitchell, Administrator/Director
P.O. Box 339
Springville, CA 93265
(559) 539-2642 • (559) 539-2643 (fax)
rickmit@tcoe.k12.ca.us

EXPERIENCING NATURE and science firsthand, more than eleven thousand students each year participate at the Clemmie Gill School of Science and Conservation (SCI-CON), a residential outdoor education school operated by the Tulare County Office of Education. With community involvement as its backbone, every acre has been acquired through donations, and every building and facility built through volunteers and contributions. A museum of natural history, planetarium, observatory, raptor rehabilitation center, and over seventeen miles of trails are just some of the highlights of this beautiful 1,100-acre campus.

The Experience: The internship program kicks off with an in-depth orientation program, which includes guest speakers, field trips, and an intensive training workshop. Interns then gain experience in every facet of outdoor school operation, and learn to teach basic concepts of outdoor education in all areas of natural history. In addition, they gain skills in large-group management, program scheduling, and administration. There is also a California teaching credential program in which you can enroll concurrently with the internship.

Commitment: Internships begin in mid-August with three weeks of staff training and continue with program operation through the end of June (a ten-month commitment). Interns can expect long days with irregular hours, Monday through Friday.

Perks: A stipend of $46 per day is provided, along with room, board, and health insurance.

Ideal Candidate: Applicants with a bachelor's degree in science, education, or recreation are preferred (although upper-division students will also be considered). Applicants must have a high energy level, professional appearance, and a real love for children and the outdoors. The program is ideal for those considering careers and leadership roles in outdoor education.

Getting In: Send off your resume and cover letter before March 1; an application packet will be sent to you upon receipt.

THE SCOTT ARBORETUM OF SWARTHMORE COLLEGE

Arboretum • Pennsylvania • 3–12 Months
www.scottarboretum.org

Claire Sawyers, Director
Swarthmore College
500 College Ave.
Swarthmore, PA 19081-1397
(610) 328-8025 • (610) 328-7755 (fax)
csawyer1@swarthmore.edu

....

THE SCOTT ARBORETUM, which is uniquely situated on the campus of Swarthmore College (a small outstanding co-educational liberal arts college with a student population of 1,300), was established in 1929 for the purpose of cultivating and displaying trees, shrubs, and herbaceous plants suited to the climate of eastern Pennsylvania and which are suitable for planting by home gardeners.

The Experience: Summer internships offer a broad range of practical work experience to those interested in the ornamental horticulture field. Interns work with the staff and volunteers in gardening, plant propagation, plant records, educational programs, and special events. Two yearlong internships are also offered in their curatorial and education departments. The curatorial intern supervises and assists volunteers and summer interns who work in the garden along with assisting in educational events; and the education intern assists in planning and implementing education programs, develops educational exhibits, assists with interpretation of permanent displays, and is responsible for producing publicity for the arboretum.

Commitment: Summer internships are available for a minimum of ten weeks, April through September. Yearlong internships are full-time, beginning in June.

Perks: Summer interns receive $8 per hour; yearlong interns earn $1,250 per month plus benefits, including ten days' paid vacation and ten paid holidays. Assistance with locating housing will be provided; however, Swarthmore is a college community, so you shouldn't have a problem here. Other perks include free admission to college events like concerts and plays as well as free use of the college's sports facilities.

Ideal Candidate: Applicants must have a keen interest in horticulture and enjoy working with people and plants.

Getting In: Submit cover letter, resume, and three references (with contact information) by March 1.

SEA TURTLE RESTORATION PROJECT

Ecotourism • Costa Rica • 2 Weeks
www.seaturtles.org

Randall Arauz, Central American Director
Costa Rica Volunteer Project
P.O. Box 400
Forest Knolls, CA 94933
(800) 859-7283 • (415) 488-0370 • (415) 488-0372 (fax)
rarauz@sol.racsa.co.cr

....

VOLUNTEERS ARE NEEDED for beach patrols and sea turtle hatchery work from August 15 to January 15 at Punto Banco, on the Pacific coast of Costa Rica, which is surrounded by black sand, warm ocean waters, and a tropical rainforest. Volunteers work with a Costa Rican biologist and community members. Activities include walking the beaches at night searching for nesting turtles, moving turtle nests to the hatchery, and participating in environmental education programs in the community. Adult turtles will be tagged and measured, and data on hatching success will be recorded. Leisure activities include jungle hikes and snorkeling. Volunteers will stay in rustic cabins operated by the Tiskita Jungle Lodge along with local (and delicious) cuisine. One to four volunteers participate at a time, and a two-week commitment is required. Volunteers with some knowledge of Spanish and who are willing to participate in environmental education programs with local children are highly desirable. The program cost is $750 for two weeks with discounts for stays of one month or longer. (Transportation is additional.)

SHAVER'S CREEK ENVIRONMENTAL CENTER

Environmental Education • Pennsylvania • 3–6 Months
www.cde.psu.edu/shaverscreek

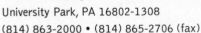

Doug Wentzel, Internship Coordinator
The Pennsylvania State University
508A Keller Bldg.
University Park, PA 16802-1308
(814) 863-2000 • (814) 865-2706 (fax)

....

SHAVER'S CREEK, administered by Penn State's Continuing Education program, is an environmental education laboratory seeking to enhance the quality of life by providing exemplary outdoor learning opportunities. This multifaceted center offers environmental education programs for group visits, natural/cultural history exhibits, live amphibians and reptiles, hiking trails, herb gardens, and more. The

How wonderful it is that nobody need wait a single moment before starting to improve the world. —ANNE FRANK

raptor center, providing perpetual care and housing for eagles, falcons, hawks, and owls, is one of the few federally and state-licensed raptor facilities in Pennsylvania.

The Experience: Environmental education interns become an integral part of the staff and are encouraged to participate in all aspects of the center's operation. A two-week orientation and training period is followed by seasonal program opportunities in both day and residential settings. Interns work with all ages, preschool to adult, as they lead natural and cultural history programs for school and community groups, families, and the general public. Interns also have the opportunity to contribute articles to the members' newsletter, lead adventure and team-building programs, participate in the care and handling of the live animal collection, and assist in the general operation of the center. Observations, recordings, and videotaping are used in evaluation, and interns are encouraged to keep a journal.

Commitment: Positions are available year-round, from three to six months, with the opportunity to work multiple seasons.

Perks: A weekly stipend of $125 and on-site housing (nestled in the woods away from park visitors, with a private sleeping room) is provided. Interns are encouraged to participate in professional development workshops and regional conferences, and each season includes a three-day staff trip to another environmental center or a facility of interest. Macintosh computers are used on-site, and access to the Internet is available. Career counseling, job listing resources, and assistance with resume writing are also provided.

Ideal Candidate: Successful candidates have a strong desire to teach and share their knowledge and enthusiasm for the natural world. A background in education or the natural sciences is helpful but not necessary. International students are encouraged to apply (as the center can assist with the J-1 visa application process).

Getting In: Interested candidates can call, fax, or write for an application. Deadlines: winter/spring—November 1; summer—March 1; and fall—July 1. Interviews with top candidates are conducted in person or by phone.

The most successful candidates have some experience in working with children. A site visit and meeting with the intern coordinator is beneficial but not necessary. Many first-time undergraduate candidates who are not accepted mistakenly fail to reapply for an upcoming season.

SQUAM LAKES NATURAL SCIENCE CENTER

Environmental Education • New Hampshire • Summer
www.sciencectrofnh.org

Amy Yeakel, Director of Education
P.O. Box 173, Route 113
Holderness, NH 03245-0173
(603) 968-7194 • (603) 968-2229 (fax)
scnh@lr.net

LOCATED IN a beautiful countryside in central New Hampshire, the Squam Lakes Natural Science Center is a unique outdoor classroom offering people of all ages the opportunity to discover and explore New Hampshire's natural world. Through the classroom and using the center's 200-acre site, teacher-naturalist interns teach and lead programs on natural history and environmental awareness. Interns are also involved in exhibit design and construction, care of the center's native wildlife collection, and the development of pre- and post-trip education materials. A $90 per week stipend is provided along with housing, including a private bedroom, shared bath, and kitchen use. College undergraduates with at least junior status or graduate students studying the natural sciences, education, environmental education, or a related field are most desirable. Enthusiasm, motivation, and a desire to work with people and animals are a must. Send resume and a cover letter (with three professional references). Applicants are encouraged to apply no later than March.

STARR RANCH SANCTUARY

Ecology • California • 3 Months
www.audubon.org/local/sanctuary/srs/intern.htm

Dr. Sandy DeSimone, Research Director
100 Bell Canyon Rd.
Trabuco Canyon, CA 92679
(949) 858-0309 • (949) 858-1013 (fax)
sandydes@exo.com

LOCATED IN the foothills of the Santa Ana Mountains in a mild and semiarid Mediterranean climate, Starr Ranch Sanctuary is a 4,000-acre preserve owned and operated by the National Audubon Society. Research interns participate in an independent research project while assisting researchers and leading nature walks during public events. Internships run for three months during the spring, summer, and fall. Interns must be undergraduate or graduate students with some ecological, biological, or conservation background. A $100 per week stipend is provided along with housing. Send cover letter stating career goals, resume, and two letters of recommendation.

STATEN ISLAND ZOOLOGICAL SOCIETY

Zoo • New York • Summer
www.statenislandzoo.org

Assistant Director of Education
614 Broadway
Staten Island, NY 10310
(718) 442-3174 • (718) 981-8711 (fax)

WHEN THE STATEN ISLAND ZOO opened in 1936, it was a Depression-era "modern miracle" with its eight-acre park setting and bylaws creating the first educational zoo in America. For over half a century, millions of people, second and third generations of families, have reaped the recreational and educational benefits of New York City's biggest little zoo.

The Experience: Zoofari day-camp instructors in art, science, and recreation coordinate the development, implementation, and evaluation of Zoofari sessions for preschool through sixth-grade age groups. Art instructors design student activities in which elements of art are explored, plan experiences with various media and methods, and focus on animal subjects. Outdoor recreation instructors plan and conduct noncompetitive activities, organize groups of fifteen to thirty children in both active and quiet activities, and develop and reinforce animal characteristics and behavioral concepts through use of games. Science instructors engage day campers in participatory learning, plan programs utilizing the zoo's exhibits and collections, and confidently handle and care for a variety of live animals in a group situation.

Commitment: Full-time positions are offered from June to late August.

Perks: A $250 per week salary is provided.

Ideal Candidate: Individuals experienced in environmental interpretation or elementary education with a concentration in science, art, or recreation are preferred. Instructors should possess appropriate skills for conducting learning activities in an informal setting (often outdoors) and the ability to structure curriculum on animal themes and examples. A strong background in learning theory, teaching strategies, curriculum/lesson planning, and evaluation is preferred.

Getting In: Submit cover letter and resume by April 1.

SURFRIDER FOUNDATION

Environmental Advocacy • USA • Year-Round
www.surfrider.org

John Hoskinson, Communications Coordinator
122 S. El Camino Real, PMB 67
San Clemente, CA 92672
(800) 743-7873 • (949) 492-8170 • (949) 492-8142 (fax)
info@surfrider.org

FED UP WITH Southern California's increasingly polluted waters, a circle of surfers banded together in 1984 to create a group dedicated to the preservation of coastal waters and beaches. Today Surfrider is an international organization with more than twenty-five thousand members. Its track record as a coastal watchdog is impressive: it stopped the California Coastal Commission from approving the building of a $200-million beach-destroying breakwater at Bolsa Chica State Beach and helped to divert storm-drain water from Santa Monica Bay to the city's sewage treatment system. Surfrider staff also spends time educating local students and lifeguard associations.

The Experience: The staff are a small, dedicated group of individuals sincerely trying to make a difference and have to perform a wide range of tasks to get the job done. Their program is informal, and it's what you make of it. Current projects that interns will participate in include Blue Water Task Force (assist in gathering water samples along seashores in an effort to demonstrate the severity and extent of near-shore pollution); Respect the Beach (a coastal educational program that includes videos and booklets designed to teach the basics about beach safety, marine ecology, and ocean stewardship); and Beachscape (a coastal mapping project). Positions are available in one of their forty-five local chapters (which generally border the coast) across the United States.

Perks: Although this is an unpaid position, you will receive industry exposure and contacts and an opportunity to interface with top-notch professionals.

Ideal Candidate: Surfrider looks for candidates who are outgoing and environmentally aware. Knowledge of the surf industry, flexibility, and a strong desire and commitment are valued assets. International applicants must speak English.

TREES FOR TOMORROW

Natural Resources • Wisconsin • Academic Year
www.treesfortomorrow.com

Sandy Lotto, Internship Coordinator
Natural Resources Education Center
P.O. Box 609
Eagle River, WI 54521-0609
(800) 838-9472 • (715) 479-6456 • (715) 479-2318 (fax)
trees@nnex.net

TREES FOR TOMORROW is one of the Midwest's oldest conservation education centers, with a "classroom" that includes miles of surrounding state and national forests, lakes and streams, and abundant wildlife. People of all ages learn by doing through firsthand observation of resource management techniques, preparing them to make their own informed decisions about how to manage our renewable resources.

The Experience: After an extensive training period, naturalist interns will give evening naturalist programs, teach a variety of indoor and outdoor classes, and develop an interpretive display or environmental education curriculum. The changing seasons offer additional duties ranging from teaching cross-country ski techniques to leading bog studies and orienteering classes.

Commitment: Four naturalists are hired from early September to early June.

Perks: A stipend of $500 to $550 per month is provided, along with full room and board. Perks include health insurance, paid holiday and vacation days, staff jackets and curriculum guides, and the chance to tour other nature centers and network with professionals in the field.

Ideal Candidate: A willingness to learn, coupled with good people skills and the ability to teach others about natural resources, are the key ingredients for the ideal intern. Recent graduates are preferred, although students at the junior or senior level are also welcome.

Getting In: Send cover letter, resume, and a list of three references by June 1. Telephone interviews are given to the most promising applicants.

UPHAM WOODS 4-H EE CENTER

Environmental Education • Wisconsin • Year-Round

Bob Nichols, Director
N194, County Highway North
Wisconsin Dells, WI 53965
(608) 254-6461 • (608) 253-7140 (fax)
bob.nichols@ces.uwex.edu

PART OF the University of Wisconsin system since 1950, Upham Woods provides environmental education programs for more than nine thousand adult and youth clients each year. Residential programs focus on animals, plants, water, and the unique geological formations of the region.

The Experience: Naturalists teach natural science and lead activities primarily for middle-school clientele. Other responsibilities include developing and leading challenge activities on-site, as well as planning, designing, and developing educational displays, activities, or curriculum.

Commitment: Positions are offered year-round, with a five-day, irregular workweek scheduled between the hours of 7 a.m. and 11 p.m.

Perks: A $250 per week stipend is provided, along with on-site staff-only housing and meals.

Ideal Candidate: Applicants must have completed introductory courses in either natural resources, recreation, or education (at least junior status for college students). Demonstrated success in working effectively with individuals and groups is preferred. Lifesaving, advanced first aid, and current CPR are required for summer positions.

Getting In: Call for application materials. Personal interviews are preferred, although phone interviews are acceptable.

VIRGINIA ROBINSON GARDENS

Botanical Garden • California • Summer

Tim Lindsay, Superintendent
1008 Elden Way
Beverly Hills, CA 90210
(310) 276-5367 • (310) 276-5352 (fax)

THE VIRGINIA ROBINSON GARDENS occupy over six hillside acres and include five distinctive gardens—the Italian terrace, formal mall, rose, kitchen, and tropical palm garden. Just seven miles from the Pacific Ocean, the facility offers many opportunities for the serious horticulturist. Interns receive hands-on training in nursery management, equipment maintenance, labeling, soil preparation, plant propagation, pruning and staking, and irrigation installation. Benefits include $8 per hour.

WIDGIWAGAN'S ENVIRONMENTAL EDUCATION PROGRAM

Environmental Education • Minnesota • Year-Round

Karen Pick, Program Director
2233 Energy Park Dr.
St. Paul, MN 55108-1533
(612) 645-6605 • (612) 646-5521 (fax)

LOCATED A HALF-MILE from the Boundary Waters Canoe Area Wilderness, Widgiwagan's wilderness-based environmental education program has offered high-quality outdoor experiential education for students since 1973. The program immerses youth in the outdoor classroom in small study groups (eight to twelve students with each instructor) and teaches about the environment, outdoor skills, and teamwork. Over 700,000 acres of wilderness are used for its classroom.

The Experience: The internship program, designed to develop the participant's abilities in natural history programming, wilderness skills, and youth leadership, includes pre-season staff training, seminars on instructing issues, and individual intern projects. Interns co-lead wilderness-based activities and all-day excursions for eight to twelve students, fourth through ninth grade. Two- to three-hour activities develop outdoor skills, encourage teamwork and cooperation, and create curiosity about the natural world. Four interns and seven naturalists are hired seasonally.

Commitment: Internships are offered each winter; naturalist positions are offered throughout the year, except during the summer.

Perks: Along with room and board, a $140 to $150 weekly stipend is provided.

Ideal Candidate: Applicants must have a desire to develop youth leadership skills, have confidence working in an outdoor setting, be pursuing (or have) a degree in an environmental field, and have certification in first aid, CPR, and lifeguarding.

Getting In: Request application materials. Inquire early as staff are hired on a rolling application basis.

WILDLIFE PRAIRIE PARK

Wildlife • Illinois • 12 Weeks
www.wildlifepark.org

Bonnie Cannon, Intern Coordinator
3826 N. Taylor Rd., RR2, Box 50
Hanna City, IL 61615-9617
(309) 676-0998 • (309) 676-7783 (fax)
wppnat@aol.com

WILDLIFE PRAIRIE PARK covers two thousand acres of grazing land, lakes, and forests, and presents wild animals native to Illinois in their natural habitats. It contrasts the rugged heritage and simple lifestyles of Illinois's past with the complex, energy-demanding society of the future, and provides a better understanding of our environment through education, conservation, and recreation.

The Experience: Student naturalist interns work under the direction of the park's education department, with duties that include special interpretive projects, trail monitoring and development, and presenting public educational programs. These varied duties will entail both indoor and outdoor tasks, physical and mental skills, and will provide working experience with park staff, volunteers, and the general public.

Commitment: Internships are offered year-round for a minimum of twelve weeks.

Perks: Spring, summer, and fall interns are provided with a minimum-wage salary, uniform shirts, and possible on-site lodging. Interns for the winter semester are on a voluntary basis.

Ideal Candidate: Candidates must be recent graduates or those pursuing a degree in outdoor/environmental education, interpretation, parks and recreation, or biology.

Getting In: Send a cover letter and resume.

WOLF RIDGE ENVIRONMENTAL LEARNING CENTER

Environmental Education • Minnesota • Academic Year
www.wolf-ridge.org

Julie Flotten, Naturalist Training Director
6282 Cranberry Rd.
Finland, MN 55603-9700
(800) 523-2733 (Wisconsin and Minnesota only)
(218) 353-7414 • (218) 353-7762 (fax)
mail@wolf-ridge.org

WOLF RIDGE Environmental Learning Center is an accredited residential school that provides all people with the opportunity to develop their understanding and appreciation of the environment and their responsibility for stewardship of the earth. Audiences include students of all ages, mostly school-age children. Wolf Ridge has trained naturalists since 1974; hundreds have graduated from this unique training program. In 1996, Wolf Ridge affiliated with the University of Minnesota in Duluth, providing a post-baccalaureate certificate in environmental education for the interns. This is an intense training program combined with a year of graduate study, designed for people interested in entering the naturalist field.

The Experience: Interns receive initial class training and begin teaching half-day environmental education classes within two weeks of arrival. This carefully designed program leads interns through a progression of methodologies and techniques to help develop a unique teaching philosophy and to make each an effective teacher in the environmental education field. Learning comes through direct experience, ongoing evaluations, seminars, workshops and field trips, and university classes.

Commitment: The intern positions begin in late August and end in June. No other work terms are available.

Perks: Interns receive a private room, partial board, a tuition scholarship paid directly to the University of Minnesota, a certificate in environmental education, special consultant weekends at cost, and occasional pro deals on equipment.

Ideal Candidate: Interns are required to have completed a four-year college degree with some general science coursework. Applicants should be interested in working with people, especially children, in the outdoors. A positive attitude and willingness to learn is essential. Basic first aid and CPR certification is required.

Getting In: Call for application packet. Applications are accepted through March 31. After telephone interviews, positions are offered in April.

> There are many applicants for this unique training program. Be careful with your application; be clear and communicate well about yourself and your experiences. This position demands a person who truly enjoys being with people, especially children, and is a hard worker with community focus.

Recommended Resources . . . .

Do you have a green thumb? Membership in the **American Association of Botanical Gardens and Arboreta** is one way to further your career goals and keep you in touch with what's happening at public gardens throughout the United States and Canada. Their annual internship directory, available for $10, lists more than one hundred summer jobs and internships in fields including horticulture, conservation, education, collections, children's programs, historic garden restoration, horticultural therapy, and zoo horticulture programs. American Association of Botanical Gardens and Arboreta, 351 Longwood Rd., Kennett Square, PA 19348; (610) 925-2500, (610) 925-2700 (fax), aabga@voicenet.com, www.aabga.org

If you are a birding enthusiast looking for an interesting life experience or a new way to spend your vacation, explore the possibilities with the **American Birding Association**.

Each January, they publish *Opportunities for Birders*, listing more than 650 volunteer projects for birders in the U.S., Canada, and an ever increasing list in other countries. Short- and long-term opportunities are available, and some offer a stipend. A copy of the directory is sent to each ABA member in February (membership is $20 for students, $40 for individuals), and listings can also be viewed through their web site, which is updated regularly. American Birding Association, Dr. Paul Green, Executive Director, 720 W. Monument St., P.O. Box 6599, Colorado Springs, CO 80934-6599; (800) 850-2473, (719) 578-9703, (719) 578-1480 (fax), paulgrn@aba.org, www.americanbirding.org/voldigen.htm

The Job Seeker is a biweekly newsletter that provides extensive listings of environmental and natural resource work opportunities—from internships to career track jobs—throughout the United States. The newsletter is a perfect compliment to your job search, and can be received either through regular mail or e-mail. E-mail subscriptions are available for three months ($19.50), six months ($36), or one year ($60), or you may want to invest in their *Summer Jobs Special*, which costs $10 for nine issues during the months of December through April (subscriptions through the regular mail are a little higher in price). *The Job Seeker,* Becky Potter, 28672 Cty EW, Warrens, WI 54666; (608) 378-4290, jobseeker@tomah.com, www.tomah.com/jobseeker

Environmental Career Opportunities provides job and internship opportunities for the environmental enthusiast throughout the United States. Especially look at parts five and seven of the publication for internship opportunities. More than seven hundred programs can be delivered to your doorstep every two weeks. A four-month subscription runs $49. (Shorter and longer subscriptions are available.) *Environmental Career Opportunities,* Betty Brubach, Brubach Publishing Company, HCR 4, Box 65, Leon, VA 22725; (800) 315-9777, (804) 985-2331 (fax), bbrubach@mindspring.com, www.ecojobs.com

At the heart of the **Environmental Careers Organization's** (ECO) dedication to solving environmental challenges is the Environmental Internship Placement Service. This program connects people with entry-level internships, helping them to become the next generation of environmental scientists and engineers, chemists and biologists, teachers, recycling coordinators, and environmental lawyers. Current listings can be found at their web site (which is updated periodically), with over 175 organizations sponsoring ECO associates. Positions vary from as short as three months to as long as two years, and typical stipends range from $300 to $600 per week. More than thirty thousand people apply to programs each year (no application deadlines) and about six hundred become ECO associates. ECO also offers national environmental career workshops and career development publications. The Environmental Careers Organization, Internship Placement Coordinator, 179 South St., Boston, MA 02111; (617) 426-4375, (617) 423-0998 (fax), www.eco.org

Environmental Opportunities, a monthly newsletter, lists environmental work opportunities in nonprofit organizations throughout the United States. A free sample copy will be sent upon request, or you can subscribe for six months ($28) or a year ($49). *Environmental Opportunities,* Sanford Berry, 103 Roxbury St., #5, Keene, NH 03431; (603) 357-5940 (phone/fax), ecosandy@cheshire.net

Each year the **Massachusetts Audubon Society** produces a directory of summer job opportunities in Audubon sanctuaries throughout the state—from the cape to the Berkshires. Typical assignments range from environmental education and naturalist internships to camp counselors and shorebird nesting monitors. Massachusetts Audubon Society, Claudia Bard Veitch, Human Resources Director, 208 S. Great Rd., Lincoln, MA 01773; (781) 259-9500, (781) 259-9506 (job hotline), (781) 259-8899 (fax), cveitch@ massaudubon.org, www.massaudubon.org

To the attentive eye, each moment of the year has its own beauty, and in the same field, it beholds, every hour, a picture which was never seen before, and which shall never be seen again. —RALPH WALDO EMERSON

Authors Joy Herriott and Betty Herrin have included over 250 jobs, internships, study and travel programs, and camps, all related to the natural science field, in their handbook, **Summer Opportunities in Marine and Environmental Science**. Although the guide is geared mainly to students, it provides a comprehensive list of resources and opportunities that are great information for anyone. The guide was last published in 1994; however, a special insert provides updates and new program listings. To pick up a copy, send $10.95 plus $2 shipping (checks made out to Summer Opportunities Guide). Summer Opportunities Guide, Joy Herriott, 85 Jennie Dugan Rd., Concord, MA 01742; (978) 369-7426

Outdoor and environmental enthusiasts will want to explore the information tucked away in **Taproot**, published by the Coalition for Education in the Outdoors. Known for its lengthy and comprehensive resources section, this magazine-style newsletter provides everything from networking ideas and a conference calendar to internship and job opportunities, as well as informative and refreshing feature stories written by professionals in the field. Single copies can be purchased for $8 or a yearly subscription (published quarterly) is available for $30. (For $20 more, you can join the coalition for the year.) *Taproot*—Coalition for Education in the Outdoors, Dr. Charles Yaple, Director, E331 Park Center, SUNY Cortland, P.O. Box 2000, Cortland, NY 13045; (607) 753-4971, (607) 753-5982 (fax), yaplec@cortland.edu, www.cortland.edu/ceo

In a world focused on technology and getting ahead at all costs, it might be time to look at life in a different way and focus on what's really important. This chapter is virtually about the simple life. It's for those who want to transform their world into something completely different—learning to become more self-reliant, connecting with the earth, integrating skills from the "good old days" that many of us take for granted, and leading a more balanced and harmonious lifestyle. It is the same spirit referred to by the poet Gary Snyder when he advised, "Find your place on the planet and dig in." This chapter will give you the tools to do just that.

> It is thus with farming; if you do one thing late, you will be late in all your work.
>
> —CATO THE ELDER

Unique Opportunities to Explore in This Section:

▶ The mind, body, and spirit connection—have you found your balance? From alternative education and retreat centers to yoga institutes and Zen centers, holistic learning centers are helping to enliven our souls. Make a personal commitment of self-exploration and growth by uncovering the unique opportunities presented in this special section *(page 182)*.

▶ Heartwood teaches the skills and knowledge it takes to build an energy-efficient house. Apprentices and workshop participants alike share a "clear determination to empower their hands, to train their eyes for quality and beauty in the design of things, and to question and explore the ways we might live in a more honest relation with our planet" *(page 189)*.

▶ With the philosophy of early to bed, early to rise, the Old Mill Farm School of Country Living familiarizes city folk with both the work and wonders of farm life. Apprentices take part in an alternative form of education by becoming familiar with and experiencing the chores required to maintain a general farm and rural lifestyle *(page 193)*.

▶ Working in exchange for your keep is the basis of Willing Workers on Organic Farms. As a short-term volunteer, you'll help with organic farming, gardening, homesteading, or other environmentally conscious projects, in exchange for room and three wholesome meals. Check out this special section to job-hop all over the world *(page 196)*.

Michaela Farms provides interns with the opportunity to experience all aspects of farm life, including a lifestyle that fosters simple and holistic living.

BACK TO BASICS

Before you dig into the organic farming opportunities in this section, here are some concepts you need to become familiar with:

Community Supported Agriculture (CSA) . . . .

CSAs link local people directly to farmers of fresh and sustainably produced food. Supporters purchase a share of the season's harvest for a fee (which generally amounts to $50 per month) and receive a weekly bag of vegetables, herbs, fruits, milk, eggs, meat, flowers, and/or crafts (many farms also include newsletters filled with recipes and activities at the farm). The CSA concept forms the framework for many internships at farms, including Claymont Farm CSA on page 186 and Michaela Farm on page 192. **Community Supported Agriculture of North America** provides listings of farms that offer CSA programs throughout the United States (www.umass.edu/umext/csa).

Biodynamic Agriculture . . . .

according to Stella Natura in her book *An Introduction to Biodynamic Agriculture*, biodynamics is a method of agriculture that seeks to actively work with the health-giving forces of nature. This means growing food with a strong connection to a healthy, living soil and recognizing the basic principles at work in nature. Farms such as Angelic Organics on page 179 and Davis Family Farm on page 186 provide hands-on training in these concepts. The **Biodynamic Farming and Gardening Association** provides an abundance of information on the biodynamic movement as well as a bimonthly magazine of opportunities for biodynamic apprenticeships. Single copies cost $3.50 or an annual subscription runs $35. Biodynamic Farming and Gardening Association, Building 1002B, Thoreau Center, The Presidio, P.O. Box 29135, San Francisco, CA 94129-0135; (888) 516-7797, biodynamic@aol.com, www.biodynamics.com.

The Community Supported Agriculture concept is a product of the turbulent 1960s in Japan. As the country faced a loss of farmland due to development, a growing amount of imported food, and the resulting exodus of farmers to cities, a group of Japanese homemakers approached a local farmer with the idea of making a financial commitment to the farm in exchange for fruits and vegetables. They entered into a contract, or *teikei*, which literally translates as "partnership," but philosophically means "food with the farmer's face on it." The concept took root and eventually spread. Today, more than six hundred CSA farms across the U.S. and Canada serve close to 150,000 participants.

—A bit of history about CSA, from "Buying the Farm," *Mother Jones*, March/April 1997.

In the seed we have an image of the whole universe. Each single time a seed is formed, the earthly organizing process is led to its end, to the point of chaos. And each time, within the seed-chaos, a new organism is built up out of the whole universe.

—RUDOLF STEINER, Austrian philosopher and forefather of biodynamic principles

ANANDA MARGA

Yoga Farm • California • Year-Round

Allen Thurm, Director
42310 Lake Hughes Rd.
Lake Hughes, CA 93532
(661) 724-1161
amurtla@igc.apc.org

SITUATED WITHIN the Angeles National Forest at an elevation of 3,250 feet, Ananda Marga is a nonprofit yoga/meditation, ecological, and social service organization. More than fifteen hundred peach trees and one hundred cherry trees are intercropped with Japanese and globe eggplants and melons. Apprentices are welcome year-round and participate in all activities of the farm. Benefits include a shared room in a large house, vegetarian meals, and a yoga/meditation lifestyle (including free instruction).

ANGELIC ORGANICS

Organic Farming • Illinois • 3–7 Months
www.angelicorganics.com

John Peterson, General Manager
1547 Rockton Rd.
Caledonia, IL 61011-9572
(815) 389-2746 • (815) 389-3106 (fax)
internship@angelicorganics.com

FOR THOSE WHO haven't worked on a farm before, Angelic Organics describes it this way: ". . . It's chaotic, messy, unpredictable, tiring, low-paying, uncomfortable, and unforgiving in ways that probably go beyond your normal understanding of these words." This is part of Angelic's "weeding out" process—with the hopes of hiring interns who realize farm life is not a pastoral paradise. For 5 1/2 days each week, interns practice the hands-on work of organic and biodynamic farming—everything from planting seed, field transplanting, mulching, trellising, irrigation, and harvest to packing and creating a beautiful presentation for market. The experience begins with a four-day training beginning mid-April, along with informal discussions, seminars, and visits to other farms throughout the course of the internship. Benefits include a $300 monthly stipend, shared furnished housing, paid utilities, workman's compensation, workday meals, and staples and produce from the garden for evening meals. Call for their internship booklet, which contains application materials and articles on farming practices. The best time to apply is late fall/early winter. (It's highly suggested that you visit the farm for a couple days to a week for a trial basis.)

APROVECHO RESEARCH CENTER

Sustainable Living • Oregon • Spring–Fall
www.efn.org/~apro

Internship Coordinator
80574 Hazelton Rd.
Cottage Grove, OR 97424
(541) 942-8198 • (541) 942-0302 (fax)
apro@efn.org

APROVECHO, which means "make best use of" in Spanish, is the central theme of the center—to learn how to live together sustainably and ecologically and to help others around the world to do the same. The center is located in the abundant ecosystem of Oregon's Willamette Valley. Culturally rich Eugene is just thirty minutes away.

The Experience: Groups of up to fourteen interns join ten resident staff members for an intensive ten-week learning experience. Daily classes and activities teach interns basic principles of sustainable forestry, organic gardening, indigenous skills, and appropriate technology. Classes combine a holistic approach of lecture and discussion formats with practical, hands-on activities. Readings, independent projects, and field trips supplement other course work. Applying newly learned skills, interns will cook with food from the garden, heat and build with wood from the forest, make use of native plant species for food, medicine, and crafts, and utilize resource-conserving technologies to build a solar oven.

Commitment: Internships span ten weeks, beginning in early March, June, and September. Classes typically run from 8 a.m. to 5 p.m., Monday through Friday. Weekends are open so interns can take advantage of Oregon's beautiful coastline, mountain ranges, and lakes and rivers.

Perks: The $1,800 tuition covers room, board, and instruction for the term. One full scholarship is offered each session, usually to a student from overseas. Interns generally need only a small amount of spending money, as most necessities are provided on-site. All interns live in an eco-friendly, straw-bale dormitory.

Ideal Candidate: Acceptance into the program is based on enthusiasm, a sincere interest in the subjects of study, and a willingness to join in a cooperative learning experience. Participants come from varied backgrounds and have ranged in age from seventeen to sixty-four. Interns who want to learn how to live in ways that are more ecologically and socially sustainable and to acquire specific practical and intellectual skills that will aid them on this path will thrive in this program.

Individuality is the salt of common life. You may have to live in a crowd but you do not have to like it, nor subsist on its food. You may have your own orchard. You may drink at a hidden spring. Be yourself if you would serve others. —HENRY VAN DYKE

Getting In: Call for a brochure and application. Internships are offered on a space-available basis to qualified applicants.

ARCOSANTI

Sustainable Living • Arizona • February–November
www.arcosanti.org

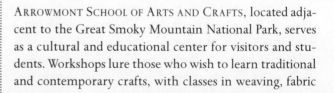

Workshop/Internship Coordinator
HC 74, Box 4136
Mayer, AZ 86333
(520) 632-7135 • (520) 632-6229 (fax)

BACK IN THE EARLY 1970s, an experimental town called Arcosanti emerged in the high desert of Arizona. Built as a model for how the world might build its cities in an energy-efficient way, Arcosanti intends to house seven thousand people living and working together. Designed with the concept of arcology (the synthesis of architecture and ecology), Arcosanti hopes to demonstrate ways to improve urban conditions and suburban sprawl, and lessen the destructive impact on the earth while simultaneously allowing interactions with the surrounding natural environment.

The Experience: Arcosanti's five-week workshop introduces participants to building techniques and an intensive look at Paolo Soleri's concept of arcology by incorporating independent, creative thinking and a "learn by doing" approach. The first week is dedicated to seminar topics ranging from exposure to drawings and plans and a surveying class, to site tours and discussions with Paolo Soleri. The rest of the time is spent working on projects, participating in cultural events, and a field trip to Phoenix to see sites of architectural interest. Completion of the Arcosanti workshop qualifies individuals to be considered for a three-month internship. Positions are available in permaculture/organic gardening, ceramics (creating windbells and planters that fund the Arcosanti project), construction, landscaping, planning and drafting, and woodworking.

Perks: The five-week program fee is $800. (The first week seminar costs $400.) The fee covers tuition, room and board, and use of the site facilities. Workshop participants generally stay in a camp that is equipped with electricity, toilets, showers, and simple living shelters. Interns only pay for meals and a weekly co-use fee.

Ideal Candidate: Although there is a need for skilled workers, most participants are novices. Individuals must be at least eighteen years of age (or be accompanied by a parent).

Getting In: Call for application materials. A nonrefundable registration fee of $50 is required with the application, which is applied to the workshop fee total.

While driving through Arizona, plan on a side trip to Arcosanti, an experimental town in the high desert, just seventy miles north of Phoenix. Learn about Paolo Soleri's concept of arcology (the synthesis of architecture and ecology), tour the grounds, or purchase one of their world-famous Soleri Bells. Concerts and other events in the Colly Soleri Music Center also allow visitors to experience Arcosanti. Shows include dinner and are often followed by a light show on the opposite mesa. Limited overnight guest accommodations are available by reservation. The simple guest rooms, beginning at $20 a night, provide "no frills" accommodations. The Sky Suite, at $75 a night, includes a kitchenette and a panoramic view of this beautiful valley.

ARCTIC ORGANICS

Organic Farming • Alaska • 6 Months

River and Sarah Bean, Owners
HC04 Box 9043
Palmer, AK 99645
(907) 746-1087
beans@alaska.net

ARCTIC ORGANICS, a ten-acre farm set at the base of the Chugach Mountains in Alaska, focuses on intensive organic vegetable production. Interns interested in small-scale organic farming are needed from mid-January through mid-September, with benefits including a stipend of $400 per month, along with bunkhouse living and kitchen privileges. (Meals are not included.)

ARROWMONT SCHOOL OF ARTS AND CRAFTS

Traditional Crafting • Tennessee • Year-Round
www.arrowmont.org

Program Coordinator
Work-Study Program
P.O. Box 567
Gatlinburg, TN 37738-0567
(423) 436-5860 • (423) 430-4101 (fax)
arrowmnt@aol.com

ARROWMONT SCHOOL OF ARTS AND CRAFTS, located adjacent to the Great Smoky Mountain National Park, serves as a cultural and educational center for visitors and students. Workshops lure those who wish to learn traditional and contemporary crafts, with classes in weaving, fabric design, quilting, jewelry making, wood turning, clay and metal working, enameling, photography, papermaking, drawing, and painting. Each spring and summer, Arrowmont sponsors a work-study program, where individuals assist the full-time support staff in the kitchen, housekeeping, maintenance, gardening, or office areas in exchange for room, board, and tuition. (If needed, course credit for classes is available through the art department at the University of Tennessee, Knoxville.) In addition, Arrowmont selects four to five artists each year to participate in their eleven-month artist-in-residence program, where artists work both in their private studios and in workshops, special media conferences, seminars, and Elderhostel classes. Applicants must apply by April 1 for both programs.

ATLANTIS YOUTH EXCHANGE

Farming/Au Pair • Norway • 2–24 Months
www.atlantis-u.no

Inbound Manager
Rolf Hofmos Gate 18
N-0655 Oslo
Norway
(011) 47 22 62 60 60 • (011) 47 22 62 60 61 (fax)
post@atlantis-u.no

ENJOY A FEW MONTHS living with a Norwegian host family on a farm, in the beautiful countryside of Vikings, trolls, high mountains, long fjords, and the midnight sun. Sponsored by Atlantis Youth Exchange, the working guest and au pair programs are a great way to get to know the Norwegian people, culture, customs, and lifestyle from the inside, rather than as an ordinary tourist.

The Experience: Working guests take part in the daily life on the farm, both in work and in leisure, as a member of the host family and the local community. During working hours participants are expected to help in the agricultural work on the farm, which might include haymaking, weeding, milking, picking berries and vegetables, painting, or light housework. As an au pair, participants will live as a member of the family, look after the children, and help with household duties.

Commitment: Most families invite working guests for two- or three-month stays (which are offered throughout the year) for up to thirty-five hours per week. The minimum stay as an au pair is six months (thirty hours per week), with a maximum stay of two years. The majority of families prefer to have an au pair for nine to twelve months.

Perks: A minimum wage of 700 Norwegian kroner per week is provided, along with a private room and meals with the family. Au pair participants also receive a travel card and are entitled to one week of vacation after six months of work. Each applicant is responsible for a work permit and travel arrangements to Oslo.

Ideal Candidate: Applicants must be between eighteen and thirty years old and have the ability to communicate in English. Successful applicants are open-minded and able to adapt to the host family's way of life. Life will often be quite different from what most participants are accustomed to at home.

Getting In: Applications, along with a fee of 1,300 Norwegian kroner (or equivalent in U.S. dollars), are due at least three to four months ahead of your preferred arrival date (which is generally plenty of time to obtain a visa). Applicants should provide a positive, honest, and smiling impression in their application.

AUGUSTA HERITAGE CENTER

Traditional Crafting • West Virginia • Year-Round
www.augustaheritage.com

Gerry Milnes, Apprentice Coordinator
West Virginia Folk Art Apprenticeship Program
Davis & Elkins College
Elkins, WV 26241
(304) 637-1209 • (304) 637-1317 (fax)
augusta@augustaheritage.com

AT THE HEART of Augusta emanates the "passing on" of West Virginia's traditional folk arts and the documentation of regional folkways. A five-week summer workshop program covers a broad spectrum of traditional arts and folklore, with more than two hundred classes and seminars as well as studio work. To encourage and sustain the practice of this tradition through one-on-one teaching from master artists, the West Virginia Folk Art Apprenticeship Program was created. Serving as mentors, master artists guide apprentices through hands-on instruction in a variety of folk and traditional arts at their studios. Instruction might include traditional music and song, woodworking and carving, fiber arts, basket making, blacksmithing, or musical instrument construction. Becoming personally involved with the master artist not only gives the apprentice a good grasp of the technical aspects of their art but also a feeling for the context in which the tradition has survived. Apprentices may apply for travel, phone, and material expenses. A panel meets twice each year to review applications, which are due April 1 and October 1.

The future must be seen in terms of what a person can do to contribute something, to make something better, to make it go where he believes with all his being it ought to go. —FREDERICK KAPPEL

Holistic Learning Centers

Along with a day filled with yoga, meditation, and healthful vegetarian meals, a volunteer with Kripalu shares her time and energy in an "off the mat" work assignment.

The journey to wholeness requires that you look honestly, openly, and with courage into yourself, into the dynamics that lie behind what you feel, what you perceive, what you value, and how you act. It is a journey through your defenses and beyond, so that you can experience consciously the nature of your personality, face what it has produced in your life, and choose to change that. Words lead to deeds. They prepare the soul, make it ready, and move it to tenderness.

—GARY ZUKOV

The importance of the whole—the balance of the mind, body, and spirit—is essential for anyone who wants to make a personal commitment to self-exploration and growth. From alternative education and retreat centers to yoga institutes and Zen centers, holistic learning centers provide a place for reflection, rejuvenation, and learning. Beyond the educational opportunities that exist, you might consider an extended stay by participating in special work-study programs that are available throughout the year. From holistic practices and meditation to creative arts and bodywork, these learning opportunities will undoubtedly reawaken your soul.

HOLISTIC WORK OPPORTUNITIES

Esalen Institute

Holistic Learning • California • 1 Month
www.esalen.org/workshops/work_study.shtml

Dorothy Thomas, Work-Study Program Coordinator
Highway 1
Big Sur, CA 93920-9616
(831) 667-3010 • (831) 667-2724 (fax)
dnt@esalen.org

FOUNDED IN the early 1960s, the world's first alternative education/holistic center has flourished, continually pushing the envelope of human potential. Once home to a Native American tribe known as the "Esselen," Esalen is situated on twenty-seven acres along the spectacular Big Sur coastline. Many first-timers opt for the "Experiencing Esalen" workshops, providing an introduction to holistic practices, such as Gestalt therapy, massage, sensory awareness, creative arts, and meditation. For those interested in a more intense and complete involvement in the center, Esalen offers a twenty-eight-day work-study program. Participants work thirty-two hours per week in one of Esalen's departments—kitchen, housekeeping, garden/farm, maintenance, or grounds—along with staff and long-term students. During most evenings and one weekend intensive, students are together in one of two groups exploring different practices and approaches available at the center, with assigned leaders who are with the group throughout the month. The fee of $795 also covers shared housing and healthful food.

Hollyhock

Holistic Learning • Canada • Spring–Fall
www.hollyhock.bc.ca

Work-Study Coordinator
Box 127, Manson's Landing
Cortes Island, BC V0P 1K0
Canada
(800) 933-6339 • (250) 935-6576 • (250) 935-6424 (fax)
hollyhock@oberon.ark.com

LOCATED ON an island north of Vancouver, British Columbia, Hollyhock offers a hodgepodge of workshops, one-month intensive programs, meditation retreats, and kayak and wilderness adventures—ranging from a writer's retreat and Esalen massage training to the alchemy of relationships and yoga teacher training. Those that wish to receive discounted room and board can participate in their work-

study program, which combines a structured learning component with service over an eight-week period. You'll spend fifteen hours each week on study, instruction, and practice, plus fifteen hours of work, mostly on outdoor projects.

Kripalu Center for Yoga and Health

Yoga Center • Massachusetts • 1–12 Weeks
www.kripalu.org

Volunteer Programs Manager
Box 793
Lenox, MA 01240-0793
(800) 546-1556 • (413) 448-3123 • (413) 448-3384 (fax)
kyadmin@kripalu.org

LOCATED IN a former Jesuit seminary in the Berkshires of Massachusetts, Kripalu serves up every possible permutation of yoga—ranging from yoga camp for grown-ups and Thai yoga massage to exploring your life's mission and meditation retreats. A day at Kripalu is filled with workshops, daily yoga, meditation, DansKinetics® classes, relaxing in whirlpools and saunas, and healthful vegetarian food choices—a sanctuary for your body and soul.

The Experience: Based on the yogic principle of "seva," or selfless service, Kripalu volunteers serve in "off the mat" karma yoga programs by sharing their time and energy—a lifestyle that supports the discovery of new ways to express each participant's energy and reveal his or her highest potential. With programs available throughout the year, the most popular is their one- to four-week Karma Yoga Program where participants live a balanced spiritual lifestyle while serving forty hours per week alongside the staff. Be prepared to engage in an active vigorous work-week that may involve chopping vegetables, cleaning bathrooms, or performing basic clerical tasks. Those who desire a more in-depth transformation at all levels (physical, emotional, mental, and spiritual) opt for the intensive, three-month Spiritual Lifestyle Program.

Perks: Volunteers receive dorm-style housing (with plenty of private space) and three healthy vegetarian meals per day (with a fresh salad bar and homemade breads). When not serving, volunteers can attend daily classes of yoga and meditation, workshops, evening concerts, and satsangas (spiritual gatherings), and have access to the sauna, whirlpool, and weight room.

Ideal Candidate: Although every age and professional background is represented in Kripalu programs, volunteers all have a strong personal intention to learn and practice the techniques that bring transformation and inner harmony. A willingness to serve others is essential.

HOLISTIC LEARNING CENTERS

Getting In: It's strongly recommend that you attend a guest program or two days of "rest and renewal" before volunteering. The Seva Program runs weekly from Sunday to Sunday; the Spiritual Lifestyle Program is offered each month. It's suggested that you apply at least two to three months prior to your anticipated start date.

Losang Dragpa Buddhist Centre

Buddhist Center • United Kingdom • Year-Round
www.losangdragpa.com

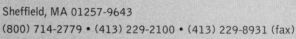

Working Holiday Program
Dobroyd Castle, Pexwood Rd.
Todmorden, West Yorkshire OL14 7JJ
United Kingdom
(011) 44-1706-812247 • (011) 44-1706-818901 (fax)
losangd@aol.com

LOSANG DRAGPA BUDDHIST CENTRE, located in an unusual and picturesque Victorian castle surrounded by twenty-four acres, is a college and retreat center that is home to thirty-five (and growing) lay and ordained Buddhists of all ages and backgrounds. The center provides a place where people can learn about the Buddhist way of life through meditation classes, study programs, and retreats. The activities of the community reflect the Buddhist principle of leading a pure and simple way of life. In exchange for thirty-five hours a week on projects including gardening, decorating, and building, participants receive food, warm and cozy dormitory-style accommodations, and meditation sessions and evening classes.

Omega Institute for Holistic Studies

Holistic Learning • New York • 7 Weeks
www.omega-inst.org/institutestaff.html

John Berryhill, Staff Development Manager
260 Lake Dr.
Rhinebeck, NY 12572-3212
(914) 266-4444 • (914) 266-8691 (fax)

OMEGA INSTITUTE began in the mid-70s when holistic health, psychological inquiry, and new forms of spiritual practice were just budding in American culture. Since then, they have become one of the country's largest alternative education and retreat centers, focusing on every imaginable aspect of body, mind, and spirit. Each year hundreds of staff join the institute to work and grow alongside "like-minded" people. The work itself is basic and rudimentary, with positions ranging from maintenance and housekeeping to food service and lifeguarding. Aside from the work component, staff members participate in the stimulating Holistic Studies Program, a collection of elective classes, workshops, and seminars in spirituality, health, community, and creativity. Topics range from bodywork and yoga to psychological and esoteric studies. During the season, more than one thousand classes taught by respected faculty are also available to choose from. Participants (ages eighteen and over) must commit to one work period (approximately seven weeks, full-time), and priority is given to those willing to make a full-season commitment. Benefits include a stipend of $50 per week, shared rooms, wholesome meals, educational programs, and use of the facilities.

The Option Institute

Happiness Center • Massachusetts • 2 Months
www.option.org

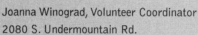

Joanna Winograd, Volunteer Coordinator
2080 S. Undermountain Rd.
Sheffield, MA 01257-9643
(800) 714-2779 • (413) 229-2100 • (413) 229-8931 (fax)
happiness@option.org

IMAGINE MAKING a conscious commitment to help yourself and others live happier, more successful, and more peaceful lives! The Option Institute offers a two-month residential volunteer program six times each year, where you'll work on various community service projects and at the same time experience a lifestyle that fosters personal happiness. The service component entails support staff work in the areas of food service, housecleaning, office support, and grounds maintenance. You'll also be serving people—oftentimes people who are having incredible difficulties and have come to the institute to reconstruct their lives. In weekly classes, you'll learn tools and ideas that participants have used to profoundly improve the quality of their lives, with the challenge of choosing how you want to be in this world. Volunteers also support the work of the Son-Rise Program, a unique method of working with children with special needs and their families. Room, vegetarian meals, weekly classes and seminars, and a personal "happiness coach" are the biggest perks, not to mention being located in one of the most beautiful regions of New England—the Berkshires in eastern Massachusetts.

We want people who have a good attitude, who want to wholeheartedly serve others, and who want to explore the idea of learning through service.

SET IN THE W_____
tains behind Big _____ Zen Mind Temple is a
working Zen Buddhist monastery that invites guests who
wish to participate in some Zen practice along with the
students and monks who live there. You'll rise with the residents and the sun (at around 5:30 a.m.), then join them
for a period of zazen meditation, morning service, temple
cleaning and breakfast, followed by 3 ½ hours of community work and lunch. Afternoons and evenings are free to
enjoy hiking, swimming, relaxing at the baths, and simple
vegetarian cuisine for dinner. The program also includes
an invitation to attend classes, lectures, and community
discussions. There is a fee of $50 per person per day (with a
minimum stay of three days). From April through September, Tassajara offers a work practice program, where
volunteers get the chance to assist with the maintenance
of the facilities and follow the daily resident schedule of
meditation and work. A minimum commitment of five
days is required and applicants must be at least eighteen
years of age. A $70 fee covers room and board, as well as
bodywork, yoga, lectures, and classes on Buddhism. For
those planning on staying at least five months, a small
stipend is available.

RECOMMENDED READING

For those who want to challenge the "mind,
body, and spirit," **Vacations That Can Change
Your Life** by Ellen Lederman provides listings of
more than two hundred soul-enriching vacations,
including meditation retreats, hypnotherapy
weekends, wilderness survival excursions,
and weeks spent swimming with dolphins.
(Sourcebooks, $16.95)

BLUE MOON FARM

Sustainable Farm • Illinois • May–November

Jon Cherniss, Owner
2184 County Rd. 1700E
Urbana, IL 61802
(217) 643-2031

. . . .

WITH A 360-DEGREE VIEW of the horizon, Blue Moon Farm
interns get quite a show while working the twenty acres of
organic vegetables, herbs, and flowers. Interns will be
involved in all aspects of production, including hands-on
experience with a wide variety of crops, growing methods
(from no-till planting to greenhouse production), and
marketing strategies (through a 130-member CSA, restaurants, and farmers' markets), and through informal
discussion of topics relevant to sustainable agriculture.
A $1,000 per month stipend and produce from the farm
is provided, as is assistance in finding local affordable
housing. Most interns live in the college town of Urbana-
Champaign, which is filled with active music and fine arts
culture as well as a wonderful farmers' market.

CASCADIAN HOME FARM

Organic Farming • Washington • 6–12 Months
www.cfarm.com/index.asp

Jim and Harlyn Meyer, Owners
P.O. Box 98
Rockport, WA 98283
(360) 853-8173 • (360) 853-7520 (fax)
meyer@cfarm.com

. . . .

A TWENTY-ACRE ORGANIC FARM located in the foothills of
the North Cascade Mountain Range, Cascadian Home
Farm grows a variety of berries, vegetables, herbs, and
flowers. A roadside stand serves as an outlet for their produce and on-farm educational programs include guided
tours, seminars, workshops, and an apprenticeship program. Rotating chores, focused areas of responsibility, and
special projects encompass the six- to twelve-month experience for each apprentice (beginning either in April or
October). All aspects of organic crop production will be
covered, along with greenhouse work, production of
added-value products (such as teas and leathers), marketing of farm products, providing hospitality for guests,
construction projects, and occasional workshops. Apprentices receive a $50 per week stipend, private bedroom,
shared bath, and laundry facilities. A farmhouse community kitchen provides whole food basics and harvested
crops, along with cooperative living, sharing of chores,

A talent is something given, that opens like a
flower, but without exceptional energy, discipline,
and persistence will never bear fruit. —MAY SARTON

and vegetarian cooking. Send a resume and a letter describing your desire to work at the farm, what experiences you can bring, what you hope to gain, and how long you are available to work.

CLAYMONT FARM CSA

Organic Farming • West Virginia • 3 Weeks–1 Year
www.claymont.org

Allan Bailliett, Internship Coordinator
P.O. Box 3047
Shepherdstown, WV 25443
(304) 724-6763
igg@igg.com

IN A CLASSIC horticultural setting covering nearly four hundred acres, Claymont Farm is located in the Upper Shenandoah Valley, which is filled with woods, streams and wetlands, food and ornamental gardens, and the Claymont Mansion, a two-room bed-and-breakfast. Interns participate in French biointensive and permaculture farming techniques for a small Community Supported Agriculture (CSA) program. Crop production is highly diversified and occurs both in the field and the passive solar greenhouse. Livestock is important in biodynamic agriculture; interns will have the possibility of working with free-range poultry, a small herd of Scottish Highland cattle, a small flock of heirloom Jacobs sheep, and a growing alpine dairy goat herd. Each year a seminar program features major figures in sustainable agriculture and transpersonal psychology; and every fall, the Mid-Atlantic Biodynamic Farming and Gardening Conference occurs at Claymont, with topics ranging from alternative agriculture to traditional nutrition. Housing is informal and will normally include a private room in the farmhouse (late arrivers may have a shared "retreat style" room in a nearby dorm), with three hearty organic communal meals served each day. A small stipend is available for those with experience. Two to four interns are needed throughout the changing seasons.

DAVIS FAMILY FARM

Horse-Powered Farm • New Hampshire • 1 Year

Barbara and Steve Davis, Owners
Apprentice Program
P.O. Box 95, Cold Pond Rd.
Acworth, NH 03601
(603) 835-2403

DAVIS FARM, a biodynamic, horse-powered farm in the hills of New Hampshire, offers a yearlong apprenticeship for singles or couples. A small rustic cabin, a share of all produce, and a stipend are provided in exchange for four days a week labor in the fields and wood lot. Activities include working with a CSA and market garden, maple syrup, honey bees, food preservation, orchard and berries, dairy cows, poultry, logging, woodshop, and pottery. Apprentices are involved in the year-round cycle of activities that the farm depends on for their own food and the income to meet expenses. The work is highly dependent on the seasons and the weather. The emphasis is on producing high-quality food and crafts for themselves and for their shareholders, and in developing an ecologically sustainable small farm that will continue to be productive in years to come. The farm is specifically looking for motivated and energetic individuals interested in learning the skills needed to work on sustainable farms and in farming in the future.

DODGE NATURE CENTER

Farm Education • Minnesota • 2–3 Months

Eloise Dietz, Internship Coordinator
365 W. Marie Ave.
West St. Paul, MN 55118
(651) 455-4531 • (651) 455-2575 (fax)

INSTILLING AN AWARENESS of and a sense of stewardship for the natural environment, the Dodge Nature Center places a heavy emphasis on environmental education programs for primary schools and the community family audience. Facilities include a model farm (with apple orchard, maple syruping, beekeeping), and a new education building. Available throughout the changing seasons of the year, internships include environmental education, natural resources management and restoration, agriculture, horticulture, and public relations/communications. A weekly stipend of $125 is provided. Send letter of interest (including relevant course work) and resume.

EMANDAL—A FARM ON A RIVER

Sustainable Farm • California • Year-Round
www.emandal.com

Clive and Tamara Adams, Owners
16500 Hearst Post Office Rd.
Willits, CA 95490
(707) 459-5439 • (707) 459-1808 (fax)
emandal@pacific.net

EMANDAL—A FARM ON A RIVER serves a [...] family home as well as an environmental educa[...] ity for school groups, a small children's camp for five weeks (during June and July), a family vacation farm during August, a weekend getaway for families in the fall, a varietal wine-grape vineyard, a working cattle and pig ranch, and producer of fine jams, jellies, pickles, and salsas. The philosophy is one of self-sufficiency, both mental and physical, as an individual and as part of a community, to ensure viability in our changing world.

The Experience: Emandal provides a learning environment and a chance to do something constructive while pondering life's choices. Explore the cycle of employment opportunities: January—gardener and farm workers; March—environmental education coordinator; April—naturalists, cook, and assistant gardeners; June—children's camp counselors, camp cooks, backpack counselor, program director, and teen programs director; July—family camp workers, pickle packers, and scrapbook editor; September through November—farm workers; November through December—mail-order workers. Typical job assignments include trail building, firewood gathering, painting cabins, fixing fences, planting seeds, washing clothes, making jam, labeling brochures, feeding animals, butchering chickens, building compost, teaching soap making, building rock walls, gardening, or creating meals.

Commitment: Positions are full- or part-time or any other times that can be negotiated. The days in summer are long—working up to twelve hours per day. A farmworker follows the sun. Days off and time off change dramatically with the seasons.

An organic farm instructor teaches participants about the wonders of growing vegetables at Emandal—A Farm on a River.

[...] cabins, the schoo[...] on the season.

Ideal Candidate: The farm is ideal for transitioning from one experience to another—whether the end of school, between jobs, prior to graduate education, before a trip around the world, or while making a decision about a career change.

We're always looking for good people, eager to learn and work, who are interested in others. We especially need grandparents for the summer camp!

GARDEN HARVEST

Sustainable Farm • Maryland • April–November
www.gardenharvest.com

Jim Dasher, Executive Director
14045 Mantua Mill Rd.
Glyndon, MD 21071
(410) 526-0698 • (410) 429-1991 (fax)
garharvest@aol.com

GARDEN HARVEST is a seventy-five-acre organic farm, which also doubles as an educational center that hopes to alleviate hunger and improve nutrition of the disadvantaged. One hundred percent of the organic fruit and vegetables grown are distributed fresh to soup kitchens and emergency food pantries in the area. Apprentices will receive extensive training and education in organic farming and sustainable agriculture, development of supervisory skills, experience in the operation of a nonprofit, and exposure to issues of hunger and homelessness. Duties range from growing, harvesting, and composting to beekeeping, delivery of produce, and supervision of volunteers. Positions are available from April through November (forty hours spread over six days), with a four-week minimum commitment. A small stipend, room, and board are provided. Applicants must have a college degree.

Work is not always required . . . there is such a thing as sacred idleness, the cultivation of which is now fearfully neglected. —GEORGE MACDONALD

GEORGE WASHINGTON'S MOUNT VERNON

Living History • Virginia • Summer
www.mountvernon.org/pioneer

Internship Coordinator
Pioneer Farmer Internships
P.O. Box 110
Mount Vernon, VA 22121
(703) 799-8611
mvinfo@mountvernon.org

MOUNT VERNON is a nonprofit organization created to preserve George Washington's home. Located just outside Washington, DC, the estate welcomes more than one million visitors each year.

The Experience: After completion of a short training program, which includes several field trips to related historic sites, interns act as living history guides, teaching visitors about Washington's innovative approach to farming and his stature as a progressive leader in early American agriculture. Interns also demonstrate Washington's farming practices, working with livestock (horses, mules, and sheep), using period-style farm tools, and discussing such things as Washington's crop rotation schemes, his use of fertilizers, and the diet of the field workers. Mount Vernon also offers unpaid four-week internships for retired agricultural teachers, who receive compensation for round-trip travel to Mount Vernon, as well as free housing on the estate. (Spouses are welcome!)

Perks: Interns are provided round-trip travel to Mount Vernon, a weekly stipend of $200, housing on the Mount Vernon estate, and period attire (eighteenth-century field-hand clothing).

Ideal Candidate: Mount Vernon recruits as many as six graduating high school seniors and undergraduate students (aged eighteen to twenty-two) who have a strong background in agriculture and good public speaking skills.

GOOD EARTH FARM SCHOOL

Organic Farming • Virginia • March–December

Andy Lee, Owner
1702 Mountain View Rd.
Buena Vista, VA 24416
(540) 261-8775
goodearth@rockbridge.net

LOCATED NEAR historic Lexington in the Blue Ridge Mountains, Good Earth Farm is a forty-one-acre research and development arm of Good Earth Publications. The farm school aims to help participants become more self-reliant in producing their own food and shelter through weekend and weeklong courses, including an internship program that runs from March through December. Internships focus on free-range poultry, organic market gardening, applied permaculture, ecological farm design, intensive rotational grazing, and composting. A combination of hands-on learning, self-designed study, and professional workshops ensures an exciting, well-rounded educational experience. Interns receive a small weekly stipend, housing, and food grown on the farm.

> With over twenty-five years of adventures to share in market gardening, house building, and organic gardening and farming, Andy Lee is the author of *Backyard Market Gardening: The Entrepreneur's Guide to Selling What You Grow*, a well-crafted guide, especially for those new to organic gardening. (Good Earth Publications, $19.95)

GREEN GULCH FARM AND ZEN CENTER

Organic Farming • California • April–October
www.sfzc.com

Program Coordinator
1601 Shoreline Hwy.
Sausalito, CA 94965
(415) 383-3134 • (415) 383-3128 (fax)
sf-zen@pacbell.net

GREEN GULCH FARM offers a residential apprenticeship in organic gardening and farming from April through October, with daily Zen meditation and study as a primary part of the program. Daily work includes harvesting, sowing, transplanting, compost making, tractor cultivation, raised-bed flower and vegetable gardening, fruit cultivation, craft production, and opportunities to market the produce at the farm and regional farmers' markets. Room, board, tuition, and weekly practicums and seminars with resident and visiting teachers are provided. Prior to applying, a three-week stay as a guest student is required before start of program.

HAWTHORNE VALLEY FARM

Sustainable Education • New York • Year-Round

Apprenticeship Director
327 CR 21C
Ghent, NY 12075
(518) 672-4790 • (518) 672-4887 (fax)
vsp@taconic.net

• •

HAWTHORNE VALLEY FARM was founded in 1972 by a group of experienced educators and farmers who recognized a growing need to create a place where children and young people might experience life in its wholeness and gain the inner strength and the practical abilities that they would need as adults. At Hawthorne Valley, farmers, artists, and teachers working out the insights of Rudolf Steiner have joined together to create such a place. The biodynamic dairy farm, bakery, and cheese-making operation offers apprenticeship training in agriculture; the Hawthorne Valley School, which provides a Waldorf education for local children, offers environmental education internships during the academic year and camp counselor positions during the summer; and the visiting students' program offers school classes and an experience of farm and country life. A ten-acre market garden supplies two Community Supported Agriculture programs, green market sales in New York City, and a retail health food store on the premises.

HEARTWOOD SCHOOL

Home Building • Massachusetts • 1–3 Weeks
www.heartwoodschool.com

Will and Michele Beemer, Workshop/Apprentice Coordinator
Johnson Hill Rd.
Washington, MA 01223
(413) 623-6677 • (413) 623-0277 (fax)
info@heartwoodschool.com

• •

HEARTWOOD teaches the skills and knowledge it takes to build an energy-efficient house as well as offering workshops on all aspects of the home-building crafts, including timber framing, cabinetmaking, and finish carpentry. Those who come to Heartwood range from students to retirees, and most have little or no previous construction experience; however, they all share a "clear determination to empower their hands, to train their eyes for quality and beauty in the design of things, and to question and explore the ways we might live in a more honest relation with our planet."

The Experience: In addition to attending a workshop as a participant, Heartwood invites four apprentices in residence who help with workshops and maintain tools and facilities in exchange for reduced rates in tuition. The main purpose of the apprenticeship is to train individuals who are interested in timber framing as a career. Apprentices must commit to ten weeks of residency (from early June through mid-August). This time period coincides with their entire timber framing curriculum and also includes the three-week house building workshop.

Commitment: One-week workshops are offered from early May through mid-October (enrollment averages ten students); the three-week home-building course begins in late July.

Perks: Those participating in one-week workshops pay a tuition fee of $475 ($850 per couple); the three-week house building course runs $1,200 ($2,100 per couple). The fee include materials and hearty lunches. Special weekly rates at nearby hotels, bed-and-breakfasts, and campgrounds are offered. Apprentices pay a fee of $2,250, which includes housing, lunch, and a one-year membership in the Timber Framers Guild of North America. Housing consists of use of a kitchen and bath and one of four sleeping areas: two lofts in the schoolhouse and two cabins behind it.

Getting In: Call for application materials. The apprentice application deadline is April 1 (with notification in early May).

HIDDEN VILLA ENVIRONMENTAL EDUCATION PROGRAM

Farm Education • California • 5–9 Months
www.home.earthlink.net/~hveep

Tammy Tiong, Intern Coordinator
26870 Moody Rd.
Los Altos Hills, CA 94022-4209
(650) 949-8643 • (650) 948-1916 (fax)
hveep@earthlink.net

• •

CONNECTING CHILDREN TO the earth and instilling a sense of responsibility for their environment, Hidden Villa engages participants (preschool to sixth grade) in hands-on, innovative programs promoting environmental awareness, multicultural understanding, and humanitarian values. Located in the foothills of the Santa Cruz Mountains on a 1,600-acre wilderness preserve and organic farm, Hidden Villa provides both a school-year environmental education program that services nearly fifteen thousand schoolchildren each year and a multicultural summer camp.

The world is moving so fast these days that the man who says it can't be done is generally interrupted by someone doing it. —HARRY EMERSON FOSDICK

189

The Experience: Environmental education interns spend one day each week working on the farm and studying agriculture and animal care with the ranch staff. The other four weekdays are dedicated to teaching. Duties include giving short tours of the farm for preschoolers, educating and working with elementary schoolchildren on the farm, or giving presentations to classrooms at surrounding schools. With an emphasis on fun and interactive education, interns will learn leadership skills as well as hands-on and creative teaching techniques (through the use of slides, puppets, music, role playing, and storytelling). They will also learn practical living skills, organic gardening, and the realities of life on a small farm.

Commitment: The program begins in September for an academic year. Participants have the choice to intern the full nine months or half a year.

Perks: A monthly stipend of $500, along with housing, partial board (food from the farm), and medical benefits is provided. Participants also have the ability to live in a beautiful place, meet inspiring people, and receive lots of experience with children, teaching, and farms.

Ideal Candidate: Those who have an interest in organic farming, the outdoors, and children, and can show how an internship might benefit their career path are preferred. It's also helpful to have experience in teaching, counseling, or working with children in other ways. Fun loving, maturity, and quality energy over the long haul are traits found in their interns.

Getting In: Call or write for application materials. Deadlines: mid-April for positions starting in September; mid-November for positions starting in January. All applicants are interviewed by telephone.

HOWELL LIVING HISTORY FARM

Sustainable Farm • New Jersey • 3–12 Months
www.livinghistory.com/howellfarm

Intern Coordinator
101 Hunter Rd.
Titusville, NJ 08560
(609) 737-3299

....

HOWELL LIVING HISTORY FARM is a 130-acre farm where the techniques that farm families used to feed and clothe themselves at the turn of the twentieth century are practiced and demonstrated to thousands of visitors each year. Hand, horse, ox, and steam- and gas-engine power are used to operate field, barn, and other equipment. As a working farm, Howell Farm offers recreational and educational

opportunities to its visitors, involving them in the work and play of a traditional family farm.

The Experience: The internship program at Howell Farm is designed to teach participants skills for their interpretation of turn-of-the-century farm life. These skills may be useful to those working with small farmers in developing countries, working at other living history farms or agricultural museums, or to the twenty-first-century homesteader. The internship program is integrated with the overall needs of a historical farm, which include cropping, equipment restoration and repair, site maintenance, an introduction to woodworking and metalworking, and educational programs for schools and the general public. The program is designed to involve participants in as many of the seasonal activities as possible.

Commitment: Program dates vary from year to year, but generally the twelve-week sessions start in March, June, and September. The yearlong program is designed as an advanced level program, so a college degree related to agriculture and/or farming experience is necessary.

Perks: A stipend, living quarters, hands-on training, and farm products are provided. Living accommodations are modest, with each intern having a private room and access to a shared kitchen, living room, and bathroom.

Ideal Candidate: Past interns have been returned Peace Corps volunteers looking to continue in the field of international agriculture, college students exploring careers related to agriculture, and people of all ages interested in sustainable agriculture.

INTERNATIONAL AGRICULTURAL EXCHANGE ASSOCIATION

Agriculture • Worldwide • 4–13 Months
www.agexchange.asn.au/~iaea

Program Coordinator
1000 1st Ave. South
Great Falls, MT 59401
(800) 272-4996 • (406) 727-1999 • (406) 727-1997 (fax)

....

DO YOU HAVE an agricultural or horticultural background? Have you always dreamed of working abroad? The International Agricultural Exchange Association (IAEA), along with a strong international network of past trainees and host families, connects participants to farming and agriculture jobs in the U.S., Canada, Australia, New Zealand, Japan, and Europe (Denmark, Germany, Ireland, Netherlands, Norway, Sweden, and the U.K.). There is more to life than what you can see out your back door.

The Experience: Experience the thrill of herding cattle in the outback of Australia, milking two hundred cows in less than two hours in New Zealand, or working in the flower market in Amsterdam—not to mention the adventures you can experience on your days off. IAEA is a great way to meet people from all over the world, to experience a different culture, and to live as a member with a host family.

Commitment: Departure dates are in March, April, July, August, September, October, and November, and range in program duration from four to thirteen months.

Perks: The up-front fee covers a "training allowance" paid to each participant that is approximately equal to the program cost ranging from $2,500 to $6,700. Host families generally pay allowances per month, plus room and board. Program fees cover a work visa, medical insurance, airline ticket, a stopover in Hawaii, Bangkok, or Singapore (for certain programs), an orientation in host country, transportation to site, and a two-year membership with IAEA.

Ideal Candidate: Candidates must be citizens of one of the member countries; have the desire to work overseas; be eighteen to thirty years old; have practical experience in agriculture, horticulture, or home management; have a valid driver's license; have no criminal record; have no children; be in good mental and physical health; and have a basic understanding of the English language.

Getting In: Call or write for information, application, and current program fees.

LOST VALLEY EDUCATIONAL CENTER

Intentional Community • Oregon • 2 Weeks–8 Months
www.lostvalley.org

Apprentice Coordinator
81868 Lost Valley Ln.
Dexter, OR 97431
(541) 937-3351 • (541) 937-3351 (fax)
info@lostvalley.org

••

STRUCTURED AS an intentional community, Lost Valley is a nonprofit educational center that organizes and hosts conferences, workshops, and retreats that focus on personal growth and sustainable living. Committed to the pursuit of a more sustainable lifestyle, seventeen adults and eleven children live on the grounds year-round.

The Experience: Apprentices receive specific training and supervision in various fields (from agroecology and sustainable food production to vegetarian cooking) while being fully immersed in a cooperative living lifestyle. In addition to the hands-on training, the experience is enhanced by field trips, guest instructors, salons, and

classes on a wide range of topics, including primitive skills, medicinal herbs, deep ecology, peer counseling, and appropriate technology. Community chores and weekly "well-being" meetings round out the week. In addition to training, coordinating, and supervising apprentices and volunteers, interns focus on a specific responsibility, which might include childcare, magazine publishing, program coordination and fund-raising, maintenance and building, permaculture and land stewardship, organic growing and production, gardening, or cooking.

Commitment: Intern positions are structured around a three- to eight-month period; apprentices may apply for a minimum commitment of two weeks, which may be extended by arrangement. All participants work forty hours per week.

Perks: All participants receive organic vegetarian meals and housing, consisting of indoor lodging for interns and tent camping for apprentices—complete with outdoor kitchen and solar showers. Apprentices pay $100 per month for food and lodging as well as a monthly instruction fee ranging from $100 to $200 per month. A handful of intern positions include a monthly stipend of $200. A swimming hole and a sweat lodge are available to rejuvenate the mind and body.

Getting In: Call or write for application materials. Qualified applicants are accepted on a first-come, first-served basis.

MAST INTERNATIONAL EXPERIENCE ABROAD

Agriculture • Worldwide • 3–12 Months
www.mast.agri.umn.edu

Susan Von Bank, Program Coordinator
University of Minnesota
1954 Buford Ave, Suite 240
St. Paul, MN 55108-6197
(800) 346-6278 • (612) 624-3740 • (612) 625-7031 (fax)
mast@coal.agoff.umn.edu

••

MAST INTERNATIONAL offers those between the ages of eighteen and thirty the opportunity to participate in three- to twelve-month training assignments in agriculture, horticulture, or forestry around the globe. Knowledge of the host country's language is preferred, except in France, Morocco, and Spain, where it is required. The program fee of $400 includes training placement, a small stipend, and room and board with a host family. (Airfare is additional.) Apply a minimum of three months prior to your preferred start date; four months for Germany and Denmark. Pre-departure orientations are held three times per year.

MERCK FOREST AND FARMLAND CENTER

Sustainable Farm • Vermont • Year-Round
www.merckforest.org

Program Director
Route 315 Rupert Mountain Rd.
P.O. Box 86
Rupert, VT 05768
(802) 394-7836 • (802) 394-2519 (fax)
merck@vermontel.com

••

MERCK FOREST AND FARMLAND CENTER, a 3,130-acre preserve located in the Taconic Mountains of southwestern Vermont, is a nonprofit conservation and education organization. Facilities include a small diversified organic farm, working forest, maple sugar operation, rustic cabins and shelters, group camping area, a solar-powered visitor center, and twenty-eight miles of trails for hiking and skiing. Depending on seasonal needs and intern interests, responsibilities may include forest and backcountry management, sugaring, livestock care, lambing and wool products, gardening and food preservation, pasture management, sustainable farming, environmental education, public and school programs, and visitor center administration. Interns receive a stipend of $65 per week, housing, and complimentary farm produce, maple syrup, and meats as available.

MICHAELA FARM

Organic Farming • Indiana • February–October
www.oldenburgfranciscans.org

Anita Brelage, Intern Director
P.O. Box 100
Oldenburg, IN 47036
(812) 933-0661 • (812) 933-6403 (fax)
michaelafarm@seidata.com

••

BEGUN BY the Sisters of St. Francis in 1854, Michaela Farm's three hundred acres provide a center for organic food production, ecological education, and spiritual renewal. Farm resources and facilities include everything from vegetable and flower gardens to greenhouses and a retreat cottage (which, by the way, is available for private retreats for one to ten days). Over seventy-five Community Supported Agriculture (CSA) members subscribe to a weekly box of produce from June through November.

The Experience: The CSA program forms the framework for an intensive nine-month intern program in sustainable agriculture beginning each February. This time frame affords interns the opportunity to experience all aspects of farm life, including organic and biodynamic food production, animal care and management, and a lifestyle that promotes more simple and holistic living. Interns will participate in practical work in the gardens and on the farm, technical demonstrations, farm management and marketing, and seminar discussions that range from soil fertility to holistic living. The practice of each intern's spirituality, religious beliefs, and creative expression is also encouraged, with opportunities available for nurturing an earth-centered spirituality.

Perks: Along with formal (and informal) instruction, a monthly stipend, meals (usually vegetarian), and housing is provided. Interns all live in one of two farmhouses in private rooms with a shared common space. Interns also get the chance to share in seasonal celebrations, biweekly community gatherings, and other events that contribute to community development.

Getting In: Call for application materials. Selected candidates are asked to come to the farm for a work experience and interview.

NATIONAL FUTURE FARMERS OF AMERICA CENTER

Agriculture • Worldwide • 3–12 Months
www.ffa.org/international

Jim Piechowski, International Activities Leader
6060 FFA Dr.
P.O. Box 68960
Indianapolis, IN 46268-0960
(317) 802-6060 • (317) 802-6061 (fax)
ffaintl@ffa.org

••

THE NATIONAL FUTURE FARMERS OF AMERICA (FFA) offers a handful of international programs that blend a cross-cultural and homestay experience with a practical, hands-on agriculture work component. World Experience in Agriculture participants, aged sixteen to twenty-four, observe, study, and participate in the agricultural operation of a farm. Placements are available throughout the world and can last anywhere from three to twelve months. In exchange for work assistance, participants usually receive lodging, meals, and a monthly stipend. Program fees range from $2,000 to $7,000 (depending on the country and length of stay), and include international airfare, land transportation, a two-day orientation, host arrangements, health and accident insurance (optional), and FFA administrative fees and support. For those with at least junior status in college, FFA also sponsors, in conjunction with the U.S. Department of Agriculture, an international internship program at U.S. embassies (in over 130 countries) over a nine- to twelve-week period. The $2,500 fee covers most expenses, including housing and a generous stipend.

NORTH COUNTRY FARMS

Organic Farming • Hawaii • 6 Months

Lee Roversi, Owner
P.O. Box 723
Kilauea, Kauai, HI 96754
(808) 828-1513 • (808) 828-0805 (fax)
ncfarms@aloha.net

· ·

LOCATED ON a "four-acre piece of heaven," North County Farm serves a seventy-five-member CSA, runs a co-op, and operates a bed-and-breakfast on the grounds of their organic farm. Each year they have a need for a hard-working couple interested in an apprentice lifestyle to help in a variety of tasks in exchange for a redwood studio cottage. A six-month commitment is necessary.

OLD MILL FARM SCHOOL OF COUNTRY LIVING

Alternative Farming • California • 6 Months
www.mcn.org/d/omf

Charles Hinsch, Director
P.O. Box 463
Mendocino, CA 95460
(707) 937-0244
omf@mcn.org

· ·

SINCE 1974, the Old Mill Farm School of Country Living has been familiarizing city folk with both the work and wonders of farm life. Surrounded by fifty thousand acres of state forests, the farm is an active, working homestead that places an emphasis on alternative energy, solar heat, and electricity; growing organic vegetables (biodynamic intensive raised beds), fruit trees, and herbs on forty acres; tending and utilizing black sheep, goats, and fowl; and forestry practices of log thinning and milling of redwoods and fir on an additional 280 acres. Also available on the property is a family guest cabin and hiker's hut.

The Experience: The farm offers an alternative form of education to apprentices desiring to become familiar with and experience the chores required to maintain a general farm and rural lifestyle as well as to become aware of the natural, organic relationship to the land and animals utilized. Working with guests, gardening, animal husbandry, and wood lot management will comprise most of the apprentice's time.

Perks: Room and farm-raised food with bulk grains and beans are provided. Apprentices live in a bunk cabin with a wood-heat cook stove and solar oven.

Ideal Candidate: The farm apprentice position requires a person who wants an organic homestead experience in gardening, small-scale animal care, and sustainable forestry; who is self-motivated and works well with others; and who is willing to make a six-month commitment. Prior to beginning the apprentice program, participants are expected to read the following books: *How to Grow More Vegetables* by John Jeavons (Ten Speed Press, $16.95), *Introduction to Permaculture* by Bill Mollison (Ten Speed Press, $16.95), and *The Complete Herbal Handbook for Farm and Stable* by Juliette de Baïracli Levy (Faber & Faber, $21.95). See the end of this section for additional information.

Getting In: To pursue an apprenticeship further, write a letter about yourself (your interests, experiences, skills, what time period you are interested to apprentice, and anything else they should know about you) and have two work character references sent to them. After your letter has had a chance to be reviewed (about two weeks), call them on a Wednesday morning.

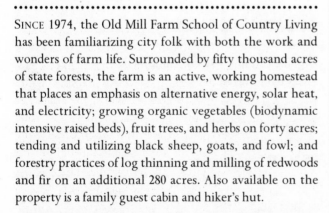

With the philosophy of early to bed, early to rise, we are a diversified farm expecting those with us to appreciate hard work along with good ideas to improve our sustainability and the environment.

THE RODALE INSTITUTE EXPERIMENTAL FARM

Experimental Farm • Pennsylvania • April–December
www.rodaleinstitute.org

Kim Frederick, Internship Coordinator
611 Siegfriedale Rd.
Kutztown, PA 19530
(610) 683-1409 • (610) 683-8548 (fax)
kfrede@rodaleinst.org

· ·

RODALE-STYLE FARMING has changed over the years—from organic and low-input to sustainable and regenerative—but the intent is unchanged: to provide more healthful food by creating and maintaining healthy soil. Each year more than 25,000 visitors see the results of health-based growing techniques firsthand in both the field crops and in the demonstration garden; it is hoped that each visitor will rediscover that the food they eat is a primary tool in achieving optimum health and avoidance of illness and disease. At the experimental farm, interns assist the staff in a variety of projects while gaining hands-on study and educational experience. Internships are generally available in the following departments (but may change due to funding): creative education team (library assistant and tour guides), farm operations, international programs, soil health, and a special work-study program in conjunction with Disney's flower and garden festival at EPCOT. Interns receive $6.50 per hour and generally work April/May through December. Priority will be given to applications received prior to February 15. Unpaid internships are available year-round and can be arranged in cooperation with a college or university for credit or with funding from a scholarship or other grant.

An intern at the Rodale Institute analyzes organic matter from the soil.

Photo Credit: The Rodale Institute

SLIDE RANCH

Sustainable Education • California • 7–11 Months
www.slideranch.org

Program Director
2025 Shoreline Highway
Muir Beach, CA 94965
(415) 381-6155 • (415) 381-5762 (fax)
slideranch@igc.org

SLIDE RANCH, a nonprofit education center, provides hands-on experiences by teaching respect for the human role in the web of life. Through participation in Slide Ranch programs, participants can make choices that are ecologically and agriculturally informed, take actions supporting the sustainable use of natural resources, and feel nourished by the natural world.

The Experience: Upon arrival, teachers-in-residence participate in a two-week intensive training program, and throughout the program, they receive ongoing support, supervision, staff development, and enrichment. Under

the guidance of a head teacher and program director, teachers gain valuable outdoor education teaching experiences by leading or team teaching groups of all ages. Beyond your responsibilities in the teaching programs, teachers-in-residence are also responsible for a chore area, which includes caring for the garden and compost or one of the many animals on the ranch.

Commitment: Positions begin in early February and last seven to eleven months. Living at the ranch is more than a nine-to-five job; it's a full-time commitment. Operating as a small community that works, lives, and plays together, all residents are expected to take part in the shared decision making and domestic responsibilities that go along with being part of a community.

Perks: A monthly stipend is provided. While each teacher is provided with an individual room and full board, cooking and dining space is shared, and all residents help in the preparation of food and the maintenance of the facilities. There is a five-day community trip scheduled, and each teacher is given several flexible vacation days to schedule during their tenure. Many former Slide Ranch teachers now teach professionally, while others work in the social services, community development organizations, sustainable agriculture, and environmental organizations.

Ideal Candidate: Candidates must have a keen interest in environmental education and community spirit.

Getting In: Call for a brochure and application guidelines. Speaking other languages or having experience working with low-income or special populations is pertinent information that should be included in your application.

SUSTENANCE FARM

Organic Farming • North Carolina
• February–November

Harvey Harman, Owner
1108 Callicutt Rd.
Bear Creek, NC 27207
(919) 837-5805

SUSTENANCE FARM is a diversified permaculture farm integrating vegetable and herb production, aquaculture, animals, tree and vine fruit, mushrooms, alternative buildings, education, and homesteading. Apprentices gain skills in basic farming, building, marketing, community building, and community development and are able to participate in educational workshops and classes on self-sufficiency and homesteading. In addition, apprentices can participate in the one-year Sustainable Farming Program offered through Central Carolina Community College, just fifteen miles from the farm. Room, board, and a stipend are provided.

TILLERS INTERNATIONAL

Traditional Farming • Michigan • 3–9 Months
www.wmich.edu/tillers

Dick Roosenberg, Program Organizer
5239 S. 24th St.
Kalamazoo, MI 49002
(800) 498-2700 • (616) 344-3233 • (616) 344-3238 (fax)
tillersox@aol.com

TILLERS TRAINING CENTER offers learning opportunities in traditional farming and crafting techniques, including classes in alternative energy, animal power, blacksmithing, farming, rope and broom making, and woodworking as well as old-time barn raising. Classes and activities are available year-round with fees ranging from free to $310. In addition to classes, Tillers offers internships in farming and woodworking. Two to four interns help with the farm, shop, and organizational work over a three- to nine-month period. While the pay is modest, most of the compensation comes from the opportunity to learn rare skills. On the farm, interns learn to drive oxen and horses in an array of tasks from manure spreading to haymaking. In the wood shop, interns learn to shape ox yokes, bend bows, and construct joinery for timber frames. An old abbey farmhouse serves as a guest house for students and interns working at Tillers. (Breakfast and lunches are provided; there is a kitchen to prepare evening meals.) Contact Tillers for their most recent catalog.

TREE OF LIFE REJUVENATION CENTER

Organic Garden • Arizona • Year-Round

Lawrence "Joaquin" Hershman, Master Gardener
P.O. Box 1080
Patagonia, AZ 85624
(520) 394-2060

IN EXCHANGE FOR ROOM, organic meals, and a small stipend, garden interns have the opportunity to learn biodynamic gardening, French intensive techniques, and permaculture design at this holistic healing center. Sitting atop a 4,100-foot mesa and surrounded by mountains, intern projects include work in the center's circle garden, solar greenhouse, the children's educational garden and park, two orchards, and vineyards. The seven-hour work day is shared with other interns and includes classes in yoga, meditation, and biodynamic gardening. Ample time is available for quiet reflection and development of a healthy, holistic, and sustainable lifestyle.

WALDEN FARM

Organic Farming • Tennessee • Year-Round

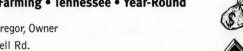

Alex McGregor, Owner
840 Murrell Rd.
Signal Mountain, TN 37377
(423) 886-6743

USING HAND LABOR, Walden Farm produces eight times more food per unit of land than the average organic farm through their integrated soil management techniques. Two to four apprenticeships are offered for those wishing to work full-time on a working farm, learning all aspects of commercial farming using an integrated system of organic methods. There is a three-month minimum commitment; however, only those who work a full season receive a small stipend. Apprentices share a living space in a barn loft (four bedrooms, living room, and bath with composting toilet) and receive three organic vegetarian meals a day (with a vegan option). Also inquire about the two weeklong workshops the farm sponsors in June, covering the topics of biointensive farming and gardening.

WOLLAM GARDENS

Flower Farm • Virginia • March–October
www.wollamgardens.com

Bob Wollam, Owner
5167 Jeffersonton Rd.
Jeffersonton, VA 22724
(540) 937-3222
wollam@summit.net

THREE APPRENTICES have the opportunity to learn all aspects of a cut-flower growing operation—from seeding, planting, and weeding to cutting and bouquet making. Most of the flowers are propagated in a small greenhouse and grown outdoors on almost four acres. Flowers are sold to florists and at two large farmers' markets in the Washington, DC, area. A private room in a historic colonial farmhouse, meals, and a $500 stipend for ten weeks is provided. Positions are available beginning mid-March through October. To begin the application process, contact by phone or e-mail.

The reason a lot of people do not recognize opportunity is because it usually goes around wearing overalls looking like hard work. —THOMAS EDISON

Willing Workers on Organic Farms

WWOOF (wuf), v. [O.E. woef, to travel in search of organic farms; to pull weeds in exchange for alms.]—From *The Shorter Oxford Dictionary*

Established in the United Kingdom in the seventies, Willing Workers on Organic Farms (commonly known as WWOOF) was initially designed to allow people from the city to experience rural areas of the U.K. Today its purpose is to promote the organic agricultural movement in the "global village" in which we live. Working in exchange for your keep is the basis of WWOOFing. As a short-term volunteer, you'll help with organic farming, gardening, homesteading (animal care, weeding, harvesting, and construction projects), or other environmentally conscious projects in exchange for room and board (usually three wholesome meals). A half-day's work for a full-day's keep seems to be a good rule of thumb, with the length of stay varying from a few days to several months (and sometimes longer). Of course, this varies with each country and farm.

This type of lifestyle affords the opportunity to obtain firsthand experience in organic/biodynamic growing methods by working with experts in the field; a chance to meet, talk, learn, and exchange views with others in the organic movement; the ability to learn about life in the host country by living and working as a family; and opening the door to travel in areas of a country that might have been overlooked.

GETTING INVOLVED

Details of farms registered with WWOOF in each country are available through the various programs listed on the following pages. Each organization publishes a directory of opportunities that you can obtain for a fee that generally ranges from $20 to $30 (cash), plus one or two International Reply Coupons (IRC). **Fees for each program are listed in U.S. currency unless otherwise noted.**

Once you have received the WWOOF listings, it's then your responsibility to contact the farm directly and arrange a mutually convenient time and period of work. Telephoning or e-mailing the host seems to be the most convenient method. For those with families, some farms are prepared to take children, with feeding and supervision arrangements agreed upon between the WWOOF member and host beforehand.

If you'll be working in a country other than your own, be sure to read through the visa requirements. According to most immigration departments, WWOOFing is seen as voluntary work and therefore permits it to be done by holders of a regular or tourist visa, provided that it is not the main reason for coming to a country.

WHAT IS AN IRC?

This acronym stands for International Reply Coupon, which serves as a form of payment for sending a twenty-gram letter anywhere in the world. IRCs are available at most post offices and cost slightly more than the cost of an international stamp (generally $1).

INDEPENDENT WWOOF PROGRAMS AND RESOURCES AROUND THE WORLD

United States/Canada

CityFarmer.org promotes the new and growing field of urban agriculture, which encompasses a wide variety of interests and concerns ranging from rooftop gardens and composting toilets to air pollution and mental/physical health. Information can be found on short- and long-term job openings (www.cityfarmer.org/jobs.html) and WWOOF-related opportunities (www.cityfarmer.org/wwoof.html) situated mostly in North America.

The Maine Organic Farmers apprenticeship program places individuals in one of forty working sustainable farms in Maine. Participants learn rural skills and gain firsthand experiences in market growing, livestock management, marketing techniques, food preservation, homesteading, and dairy farming. Opportunities are available year-round; however, most farmers look for apprentices from March through October. Room, board, instruction, practice, and a stipend are provided in exchange for your labor. There is a $20 application fee. Maine Organic Farmers and Gardeners Association, Rosey Guest, Coordinator, Apprentice Placement Program, P.O. Box 2176, Augusta, ME 04338-2176; (207) 622-3118, (207) 622-3119 (fax), mofga@mofga.org, www.mofga.org

Upon receipt of a **Northeast Organic Farming Association of Vermont** application, participants will receive the *Directory of Vermont Organic Farmers*, along with information on sponsored conferences and workshops. More than one hundred positions are advertised on sixty certified organic farms, which produce mixed vegetables, greenhouse tomatoes, maple syrup, hay, berries, apples, poultry, beef, flowers, herbs, Christmas trees, bread, sprouts, and dairy. A non-refundable fee of $15 ($20 for those who reside outside the U.S. or Canada) is required to cover the cost of the program. Northeast Organic Farming Association of Vermont, Kirsten Bower, P.O. Box 697, Richmond, VT 05477; (802) 434-4122, (802) 434-5154 (fax), www.nofavt.org/apprentice.htm

John Vanden Heuvel states that **WWOOF—Canada** continues to grow (organically and sustainably) and now has four hundred hosts all across Canada with two hundred of these in British Columbia and twenty in the western U.S. and Hawaii. Most opportunities are offered spring through fall; however, volunteers are needed year-round. Send a letter outlining when you'd like to come and possibly in what part of Canada (east, central, or west) you're thinking of going to. With your request include two International Reply Coupons (IRCs) if you are in the U.S., three IRCs if you are outside of North America, along with a membership contribution of $30 (cash only). As soon as they receive your materials, they will immediately send a booklet listing farms, descriptions, and contact information. WWOOF—Canada, John Vanden Heuvel, RR #2, S-18, C-9, Nelson, BC V1L 5P5; (250) 354-4417, wwoofcan@uniserve.com, www.members.tripod.com/~wwoof

WWOOF

Africa

WWOOF—Africa (Togo and Ivory Coast), Julien Venance, 12 BP 1235 Abijan 12-Port Bouet/Abidjan, Cote d'Ivoire, Africa. Send $40 to receive their directory.

WWOOF—Ghana, Ebenezer Nortey-Mensah, P.O. Box 154, Trade Fair Site, La Accra, Ghana, Africa. Send $25, plus three IRCs for their directory. (Listings also include information on bicycle workshops.)

Asia

WWOOF—Japan, Glenn and Kiyoko Burns, Akebono 5-Jo 3-Chome 19-17, Teine-Ku, Sapporo 006, Japan.

WWOOF—Korea provides a free listing that is available through the mail or its web site. Participants might engage in anything from growing grapes along with learning the techniques of making pottery on a Buddhist farm to growing herbs and vegetables on Cheju-Island, touted in travel magazines as Korea's Hawaii. The minimum work stay in Korea is one week. WWOOF—Korea, "Here We Go," Lee Chang Yul, K.P.O. Box 1516, Seoul, 110-601, Korea; (011) 82-2-723-4458, wwoofkr@netsgo.com, www.wwoof.com

Australia/New Zealand

WWOOF—Australia publishes a handful of organic farming lists that include their network of hosts in Australia and around the rest of their world. Their flagship list, *The Organic Farm and Cultural Experience List* (commonly known as the *AUSlist*, which costs $40AUS), includes more than 1,100 participating hosts who are mainly pursuing a simple, sustainable lifestyle. Also included are nurseries, schools, and people running home businesses such as guest houses, publishers, and writers, who have a willingness to host visitors for a cultural exchange experience. Other publications include the *WWOOF Worldwide List* (which includes more than 600 hosts in forty-eight countries for $25AUS) and the *WWOOF Organic Bed & Breakfast List*. Aimed mainly at the wealthier tourist, this list provides contacts of organic growers offering B&B or farm holiday accommodations for $10AUS. See their web site for payment methods in other currencies. WWOOF—Australia, Garry Ainsworth, WWOOF Pty Ltd, RSD, Buchan, Victoria 3885, Australia; (011) 61 3 5155 0218, wwoof@wwoof.com.au, www.wwoof.com.au

The Australian WWOOF Training Centre is primarily for students and travelers from non-English-speaking countries who need preparation for working and living on an organic farm in Australia (with training ranging from horse riding to sheep shearing). Australian WWOOF Training Centre, PO Box 60, Gulargambone NSW 2828 Australia; (011) 61 2 6825 1076, info@wwoof-australia.com.au, www.wwoof-australia. com.au

For $20, **WWOOF—New Zealand** provides a listing of more than five hundred properties, including farms, permaculture properties, market gardens, communities, and ventures in self-sufficiency in which organic growing plays some part. WWOOF—New Zealand, Andrew and Jane Strange, P.O. Box 1172, Nelson, New Zealand; (011) 64 3 544-9890 (phone/fax), wwoof-nz@xtra.co.nz, www.wwoof.co.nz

It's the good, the bad, and the ugly: accommodations can range from a bike shop to a retreat center to a biodynamic farm in the hills.

—ALONA JASIK ON HER EXPERIENCE AT
ORGANIC FARMS IN NEW ZEALAND

WWOOF

Europe/United Kingdom

The **European Centre for Ecological Agriculture and Tourism**, P.O. Box 10899, 1001 EW Amsterdam, The Netherlands. The centre provides WWOOF-type listings in Holland, the Baltic States, Czech Republic, Hungary, Poland, Portugal, and Slovakia.

WWOOF—Austria, Hildegard Gottleib, Langegg 155, 8511 St Stefan ob Stainz, Austria; (011) 43 46388-2270

Alternative Travel Club—Denmark (VHH), Bent and Inga Nielsen, Asenvej 35, 9881 Bindslev, Denmark. Membership is $10.

WWOOF—Finland, Anne Konsti, Luomutalkoovälitys, Partala Information Services for Organic Agriculture, Huttulantie 1, FIN-51900 JUVA, Finland; (011) 358-15 321 2380, anne.konsti@mtt.fi; Send two IRCs, $10, and some information about yourself to receive a list of forty organic farmers looking for summer volunteers.

WWOOF—Germany, Miriam Wittman, Postfach 210259, 01263 Dresden, Germany; info@wwoof.de, www.wwoof.de

Hungarian Association for Organic Farming, Biokultura Egyesulet, 1024 Budapest P. u. 4, Hungary

WWOOF—Ireland, Kieran and Rose O'Brien, Harpoonstown, Drinagh, County Wexford, Ireland

WWOOF—Italy, Bridget Matthews, Via Casavecchia 109, 57022 Castagneto Carducci, Livorno, Italy; (011) 39 0565-765001; wwoofitaly@oliveoil.net. The Italian list includes biodynamic and organic farms. Send an e-mail note or one IRC to receive their listing.

WWOOF—Norway, APØG, Norsk Økologisk Landbrukslag, Langeveien 18, N-5003 Bergen, Norway; (011) 47-55 32 04 80. Send $8 or ten IRCs for a listing of over fifty farms in Norway.

WWOOF—Spain, Integral, Agricultural Ecologica, Apdo 2580, E-08080, Barcelona, Spain

WWOOF—Switzerland, Postfach 59, CH-8124 Maur, Switzerland; wwoof@dataway.ch, www.dataway.ch/~reini/wwoof (or www.welcome.to/wwoof). Send $2 or two IRCs (for postage) and $15 to receive listing.

WWOOF—Sweden, Karin Hector, Urasa, Sodergard, 36014 Vackelsang, Sweden

WWOOF—United Kingdom (including England, North Ireland, Scotland, and Wales), Fran Whittle, P.O. Box 2675, Lewes, East Sussex BN7 1RB, England, United Kingdom; www.phdcc.com/wwoof. Annual membership is $20 or £15 plus one IRC.

WWOOF

Do not wish to be anything but what you are, and try to be that perfectly. —ST. FRANCIS DE SALES

Recommended Resources. . . . .

Each year the **Alternative Farming Systems Information Center** publishes *Educational and Training Opportunities in Sustainable Agriculture*, a sixty-page resource listing hundreds of opportunities in organic, alternative, or sustainable agriculture work, education, and training. The majority of listings are in the U.S. and Canada, although a handful are overseas. Call for your free copy or view the listings on their web site. (Click on the publication link.) Each listing is verified with the organization every year, with changes and additions added throughout the year on their web version. AFSIC, National Agricultural Library, 10301 Baltimore Ave., Room 304, Beltsville, MD 20705-2351; (301) 504-6559, afsic@nal.usda.gov, www.nal.usda.gov/afsic

Appropriate Technology Transfer for Rural Areas, commonly known as ATTRA, publishes a sixty-two-page listing of programs offering internships and apprenticeships on farms, sustainable living centers, and the like. Updated each January, the listing is accessible both through their web site (click on "Resources") or by calling for a complimentary copy. A gold mine of opportunities for the budding farmer, extensive program profiles are broken down by these regions: Northeast, South, North Central, West, Canada, and additional resources. ATTRA, P.O. Box 3657, Fayetteville, AR 72702; (800) 346-9140, (501) 442-9824, (501) 442-9842 (fax), webmaster@ attra.org, www.attra.org

The **Good Farming Apprenticeship Network** is designed to link future farmers with experienced handlers of working draft horses, mules, and oxen to ensure that animal-powered farming and logging practices are passed down through the generations. The participating farmers—ranging from British Columbia to Tennessee and from California to Nova Scotia—offer a broad range of learn-by-working experiences. For $5 you can obtain a printout (or e-mail list) of participating farms. Rural Heritage Good Farming Apprenticeship Network, Gail Damerow, Editor, 281 Dean Ridge Ln., Gainesboro, TN 38562-5039; (931) 268-0655, editor@ ruralheritage.com, www.ruralheritage.com

For a fee of $15, the **Ohio Ecological Food and Farm Association** links prospective apprentices and farmers seeking apprentices through a special matching service. After submitting application materials (by January 15), applicants will receive mailings of potential hosts. Farmer and apprentice applicants contact each other for mutual "sizing up," farm visitations, and making arrangements. Apprentices must be eighteen or older. Ohio Ecological Food and Farm Association, Sean McGovern, Apprenticeship Program Coordinator, P.O. Box 82234, Columbus, OH 43201; (614) 267-3663, (614) 267-4763 (fax), oeffa@iwaynet.net, www.greenlink.org/oeffa

RESOURCES

The **Seattle Tilth Association** promotes the art of organic gardening in an urban setting and maintains gardens at the Good Shepherd Center in Seattle's Wallingford district. A listing of Washington organic farms looking for seasonal workers is available through the association for a nominal fee. Call for more information or go to the "Work Opportunities" section on their web site. Seattle Tilth Association, Lisa Taylor, 4649 Sunnyside Ave. N, Room 1, Seattle, WA 98103; (206) 633-0451, (206) 633-0450 (fax), tilth@speakeasy.org, www.speakeasy.org/~tilth

Recommended Reading . . . .

We're living in a society where more and more people take things for granted and do not learn important skills for leading a self-reliant and simple lifestyle. **Back to Basics** from Reader's Digest provides practical and useful information that brings you back to the "old-fashioned" way of doing things—ranging from converting trees to lumber and building a home from them, growing and harvesting your own vegetable garden, learning traditional crafts and homesteading skills, or enjoyable activities that don't hurt your pocketbook. The pages are filled with building a new way of life. (Reader's Digest, $26.95)

Prior to beginning an apprenticeship at the **Old Mill Farm School of Country Living** (see page 193), participants are expected to read a handful of books to gear them up for their work experience. Here are three books that might be helpful before you apply to any organic farm: Nothing could be more fundamental to the needs of an increasingly crowded world than food. Based on Alan Chadwick's biointensive gardening techniques, **How to Grow More Vegetables** (Ten Speed Press, $16.95) will show you how to raise enough fresh, healthy, organic vegetables for a family of four on a parcel of land as small as eight hundred square feet. John Jeavons provides the ultimate how-to manual for sustainable gardening, with results that are more bountiful. Those investigating an ecologically responsible lifestyle might turn to the helpful advice provided in the **Introduction to Permaculture** (Ten Speed Press, $16.95). This self-sustaining philosophy promotes the interconnected relationship of plants and animals, from which people can reap a continual harvest. Bill Mollison also provides more in-depth insights in his book, **Permaculture: A Designers' Manual**. (Ten Speed Press, $45)

Remember that your work comes only moment by moment, and as surely as God calls you to work, he gives the strength to do it. —PRISCILLA MAURICE

A FARMER'S CREED

I believe a man's greatest possession is his dignity and that no calling bestows this more abundantly than farming.

I believe hard work and honest sweat are the building blocks of a person's character.

I believe that farming, despite its hardships and disappointments, is the most honest and honorable way a man can spend his days on this earth.

I believe my children are learning values that will last a lifetime and can be learned in no other way.

I believe farming provides education for life and that no other occupation teaches so much about birth, growth, and maturity in such a variety of ways.

I believe many of the best things in life are indeed free: the splendor of a sunrise, the rapture of wide open spaces, the exhilarating sight of your land greening each spring.

I believe true happiness comes from watching your crops ripen in the field, your children grow tall in the sun, your whole family feel the pride that springs from their shared experience.

I believe that by my toil I am giving more to the world than I am taking from it, an honor that does not come to all men.

I believe my life will be measured ultimately by what I have done for my fellow men, and by this standard I fear no judgement.

I believe when a man grows old and sums up his days, he should be able to stand tall and feel pride in the life he's lived.

I believe in farming because it makes all this possible.

—Written for the *New Holland America*,
originally published in 1975

no one can tell you how to live your life. You are the artist and must shape your experiences with your own hand. Whether you are an accomplished artist or seeking advanced learning in your field, as a creative-minded adventurer you will find a supportive arts environment in this section. So express those creative abilities and learn what it takes to do what you love and make enough money to support yourself!

A musician must make his music, an artist must paint, a poet must write if he is to ultimately be at peace with himself.

—ABRAHAM MASLOW

Unique Opportunities to Explore in This Section:

▶ Your locale? A cloud forest in Honduras. Your work site? A working art studio. The opportunity? Participating in structured weekly art classes and learning everything about art education and development with the Latin American Art Resource Project *(page 217)*.

▶ At some point in our life, we all come to a place where we long to uncover our mission—a lifelong "assignment" that evolves from deep within our soul. Join David Lyman, the founder of The Maine Photographic Workshops, in his journey of uncovering a deeper "calling" and building his place in the world *(page 220)*.

▶ Want to work with world-renowned musicians, play softball with the Tokyo String Quartet, and help produce a summer music festival? Check out the internship opportunities with the Northfolk Chamber Music Festival to begin your adventure *(page 223)*.

▶ The Smithsonian Institution is the world's largest museum and, quite possibly, the world's largest museum internship program. The Center for Museum Studies coordinates the central referral service for all internship programs, including sixteen museums and galleries, and the National Zoo *(page 225)*.

Photo Credit: La Sabranenque

Volunteers restore a medieval castle in an Italian hamlet with La Sabranenque.

203

ARTISTIC AND LEARNING

ADVENTURES

ACADEMIC STUDY ASSOCIATES

Art Education • Worldwide • Year-Round
www.asaprograms.com

Summer Staff Opportunities
P.O. Box 800
355 Main Street
Armonk, NY 10504-0800
(800) 752-2250
summerjobs@asaprograms.com

• •

ACADEMIC STUDY ASSOCIATES (ASA) offers opportunities in art appreciation, and work in the dramatic arts, design, and painting for students in grades seven through twelve. ASA's extensive summer arts program is conducted at the University of Massachusetts at Amherst, along with studio art courses at Stanford University and Oxford University, and language study programs in Spain and France. Resident advisors live with a group of six to twelve students (depending on the program) and are responsible for the general well-being of the students. Through social gatherings, floor meetings, and other activities, the advisors encourage their students to be independent and help to prepare them for the responsibilities of college. The ideal candidate has a tremendous amount of energy and a great deal of enthusiasm. Previous leadership experience and/or residence life experience is strongly recommended. A stipend of $300 along with room and board is provided. Those with teaching experience should inquire about short-term faculty openings.

ACADEMY OF TELEVISION ARTS AND SCIENCES

Media • California • Summer
www.emmys.org/eps

Price Hicks, Director of Education
Internship Program
5220 Lankershim Blvd.
North Hollywood, CA 91601-3109
(818) 754-2830 • (818) 761-2827 (fax)
internships@emmys.org

• •

THE ACADEMY OF TELEVISION ARTS AND SCIENCES (ATAS) is a nonprofit awards organization with a professional membership of nearly ten thousand representing the television industry. In addition to sponsoring the Emmy Awards and the internship program, ATAS runs the College Television Awards, faculty seminar and visiting artists programs, publishes *Emmy* magazine, sponsors industry-wide meetings, and maintains the ATAS/UCLA television archives.

The Experience: Opportunities are available in all areas of professional television production, including agency, animation, art direction, broadcast advertising and promotion, business affairs, casting, children's programming/development, cinematography, commercials, costume design, development, editing, entertainment news, episodic series, movies for television, music, network programming management, production management, public relations and publicity, sound, syndication/distribution, television directing and scriptwriting, and videotape postproduction. Each internship is hosted by an organization—children's shows, prime-time sitcoms, talent agencies, studios, and production companies. Interns receive in-depth exposure to facilities, techniques, and practices and are paired with past interns through the academy's mentor program.

Commitment: Internships last eight weeks, full-time in the summer.

Perks: Each intern receives a stipend of $2,000. Those residing outside Los Angeles County receive an additional $400 to offset travel expenses. Interns also receive free passes to first-run movie screenings and are honored at a large mid-season party.

Ideal Candidate: Any full-time college student can apply, although junior, senior, or graduate students are preferred. Successful candidates are typically pursuing degrees in liberal arts, theatre arts, business (advertising, marketing, or journalism), film, music, television, law, or English.

Getting In: Check with your on-campus career center for application materials; otherwise call ATAS or download the application from their web site. The entry period is from January 1 through mid-March (finalists will be notified by April 15). All finalists will then have to submit a videotaped interview for their final screening.

AMERICAN DANCE FESTIVAL

Dance Festival • North Carolina • Summer
www.americandancefestival.org

Jeannie Mellinger, Intern Program Coordinator
Box 90772
Durham, NC 27708-0772
(919) 684-6402 • (919) 684-5459 (fax)
internships@americandancefestival.org

• •

DON'T MISS THIS CHANCE to become part of an exciting community of dancers, students, choreographers, teachers, performers, critics, body therapists, dance medical specialists, scholars, and arts managers from all over the United States and around the world. Held for six weeks each summer at Duke University, the American Dance

Festival offers internships in the box office, central services, community development, development/hospitality, finance, merchandising, performances, press, school, and production. In addition to a $950 to $1,100 stipend, interns will receive one complimentary ticket to one night of all performances. Interns may also take one dance class per day and can observe panel discussions, seminars, and lectures by distinguished visitors as the work schedule permits. Apartments and shared housing are conveniently located near the festival site. Those needing housing assistance are encouraged to seek the festival's assistance. Interns also have full use of Duke facilities, including swimming pools, tennis courts, bookstores, and libraries. Applications must be received by February 1.

AMERICAN THEATRE WORKS

Theatre Festival • Vermont • Summer
www.theatredirectories.com

Jill Charles, Artistic Director
Dorset Theatre Festival
P.O. Box 510
Dorset, VT 05251-0510
(802) 867-2223 • (802) 867-0144 (fax)
theatre@sover.net

AMERICAN THEATRE WORKS presents the Dorset Theatre Festival each summer at the Dorset Playhouse, built from two prerevolutionary barns in the historic village of Dorset. The festival's apprenticeship program adheres to the traditional sense of the word "apprentice": learning a craft by working closely with professionals for an extended period of time. The program focuses on performance, production, a series of eight seminars, and contact with professionals. For those with more experience, internships are available in arts management, technical theatre, and the acting apprentice company. Both apprentices and interns receive housing, and interns also receive a small weekly stipend.

APERTURE FOUNDATION

Photography • New York • 6 Months
www.aperture.org

Maria Décsey, Work-Scholar Coordinator
20 E. 23rd St.
New York, NY 10010-4463
(212) 505-5555 • (212) 475-8790 (fax)
mdecsey@aperture.org

DEVOTED TO PHOTOGRAPHY and the visual arts, the Aperture Foundation promotes the development of photography as one of the most powerful forms of human expression helping to illuminate important social, environmental, and cultural issues.

The Experience: While working with a small, committed staff, and some of the greatest living photographers and photography writers, work-scholar program participants may choose to learn about writing and editing, design, exhibition planning and traveling, fund-raising, information systems, marketing of books and magazines, nonprofit business practices, production and manufacturing, or about archival and library work.

Commitment: Positions are full-time and require a six-month commitment, beginning in January or July.

Perks: A monthly stipend of $250 is provided along with discounts on books, magazines, and prints. Work-scholars also receive a limited edition print upon completion of their internship as well as letters of recommendation.

Ideal Candidate: Applicants are selected on the basis of interest and motivation in working for Aperture, the ability to contribute significantly to the program, and an openness to gain a meaningful work experience. Skills in the publishing business will enhance a candidate's application.

Getting In: Send a resume, two short writing samples, and cover letter describing your background, special skills, and personal objectives.

HOT TIP

Recognizing the need for writers to set aside periods of time to work intensively on projects away from the distractions of everyday life but still have a social connection, Dorset Colony for Writers provides a quiet working retreat for writers and other artists. Operating September through November and April through May, eight private rooms along with "public areas," where conversation and fellowship are encouraged, are available for a fee of $120 per week. Residency lengths vary and rooms are filled as requests come in. To apply, submit a letter with requested dates of residency, description of the project while in residence, and a resume of publications to John Nassivera, Executive Director, Dorset Colony for Writers, P.O. Box 510, Dorset, VT 05251.

Love is the spirit that motivates the artist's journey. The love may be sublime, raw, obsessive, passionate, awful, or thrilling, but whatever its quality, it's a powerful motive in the artist's life. —ERIC MAISEL

> Be concise in your letter; please let us know what positions you are most interested in and exactly when you can start. Enthusiasm and interest are the most important tips on getting accepted into the program. Staff members want to know that you are interested and that you will work hard once you arrive.

APPEL FARM ARTS AND MUSIC CENTER

Performing Arts • New Jersey • 3–9 Months
www.appelfarm.org

Matina Lagakos, Office Manager
P.O. Box 888
Elmer, NJ 08318-0888
(800) 394-1211 • (856) 358-2472 • (856) 358-6513 (fax)
appelarts@aol.com

APPEL FARM is renowned for its concerts and performing arts series, annual Arts and Music Festival, summer camp, and community arts outreach program—programs that provide people of all ages a supportive environment to study, appreciate, and present work in the creative and performing arts.

The Experience: Interns work side by side with Appel Farm staff in one or more of the following areas: festival management, arts administration, arts programming, marketing, and box office. Summer camp staff positions are available in theatre, music, fine arts, media, dance, or swimming and sports. Along with specific projects, interns will be expected, as is everyone at Appel Farm, to pitch in where help is needed. Everyone will do their share of envelope stuffing, data entry, filing, and other office work.

Commitment: Applicants should plan to make at least a three-month commitment, although internships may be extended up to six to nine months. Internship openings are available year-round; summer staff positions span from late June through late August.

Perks: Interns receive a $300 per month stipend; summer staff receive $1,000 to $1,400 for the summer. All staff receive room and board and live on-site in Appel's original farmhouse. Benefits include use of Appel Farm's arts facilities and encouragement of artistic freedom. Most staff bring along a car to explore the surrounding region, as the farm is located in a quiet country setting.

Ideal Candidate: If you want to gain administrative experience in the arts while being in a supportive atmosphere, contribute to a growing arts center, thrive on being given

responsibility and hard work, and if you genuinely like people, then this is the place for you. Camp staff must be at least twenty-one years of age, available for entire camp duration during the summer, and nonsmokers.

ARENA STAGE

Theatre • Washington, DC • 8–40 Weeks
www.arenastage.org

A. Lorraine Robinson, Intern Program Coordinator
1101 6th St., SW
Washington, DC 20024
(202) 554-9066 • (202) 488-4056 (fax)
arenastalr@aol.com

FOUNDED IN 1950, Arena Stage was an early pioneer in the resident theatre movement, which sought to establish living theatre in communities outside of New York. Today they present an expansive spectrum of dramatic literature that encompasses both classic and new American plays and musicals.

The Experience: Arena Stage offers practically every conceivable type of internship related to the theatre field. Interns will work with seasoned professionals in the areas of artistic and technical production, in arts administration, or at Living Stage (their social outreach theatre). The work experience is supplemented with seminars provided by Arena's directors, designers, and administrators.

Commitment: Administrative internships are available throughout the year. Directing, stage management, and technical production internships are available during the season (August through June) only. The duration of internships may vary from eight weeks (a production schedule) to forty weeks (a full season).

Perks: A $120 per week stipend is provided, along with complimentary tickets to Arena performances and regular informational seminars with Arena's staff of professionals and guest artists.

Ideal Candidate: The program is designed for people interested in pursuing a career in the professional theatre. Applicants should be serious-minded, highly motivated individuals who have basic training and experience in theatre and are willing to engage in the creative process and to test the limits of their own ingenuity.

Getting In: Call for their internship program brochure, which provides details on each position and application information. Deadlines: winter/spring—October 1; summer—March 1; and fall—May 1. An interview is mandatory and can be handled in person or by telephone.

Don't wait until the last minute to apply. Keep the coordinator abreast of the progress of your application if you are having trouble getting all of the materials in on time.

ART WORKSHOPS IN GUATEMALA

Art Workshop • Guatemala • 10 Days
www.artguat.org

Liza Fourre, Director
4758 Lyndale Ave., South
Minneapolis, MN 55409-2304
(612) 825-0747 • (612) 825-6637 (fax)
info@artguat.org

ART WORKSHOPS IN GUATEMALA offers a wide variety of ten-day workshops for those who want to add an educational component to their travel experience. Known as "the Land of Eternal Spring" (because of its year-round seventy-degree weather), Guatemala is the kind of place travelers fall in love with and never want to leave. The pace is slower, less hectic. Cobblestone streets and colorful bougainvillea spilling over rocks of century-old ruins provide daily inspiration. The range of workshops are perfect for those who want to expand their creative horizons, with classes that extend from creative writing and photography to backstrap weaving. The price for each educational travel package is approximately $1,750 and includes airfare from most major U.S. cities, lodging in a beautiful old colonial home, hearty breakfasts, ground transportation, and some pretty interesting field trips.

ASTORS' BEECHWOOD MANSION

Living History • Rhode Island
• May–December
www.astors-beechwood.com

Sheli Beck, Executive Director of Living History
580 Bellevue Ave.
Newport, RI 02840
(401) 846-3772 • (401) 849-6998 (fax)
astors@astors-beechwood.com

A VISIT TO the Astor summer cottage is a bit different than your ordinary mansion tour. Guests are transported back in time through interaction with members of the Beechwood Theatre Company, who portray the Astor family, society friends, and servants, re-creating the lifestyle of Newport's vivid Victorian past.

The Experience: An internship at the Beechwood Theatre Company is not your traditional theatrical experience. As a living history museum, intern staff members portray characters from the Victorian age (late 1800s), and take part in Victorian balls, teas, and murder mysteries. Interns also participate in classes focusing on audition skills, character development, and improvisation. Serving as role models for interns, five production team members perform in the Living History Museum as well as direct, teach, accompany, choreograph, and design costumes for the museum.

Commitment: The summer season runs from the beginning of May to late August; the fall season runs early August to late December.

Perks: A $90 per week stipend is provided (production staff make $200+ per week), along with housing. There are also opportunities to make extra income. All interns will be taught vintage dance, movement techniques, and Victorian etiquette.

Ideal Candidate: Applicants are expected to sing and have strong improvisational skills. Beechwood is an opportunity for the young actor to gain confidence in self and skills. Living in a mansion is also a lifetime highlight for many.

Getting In: Submit cover letter, resume, and photo. Auditions usually include two contrasting monologues and a song. (Videos are accepted.)

Photo Credit: Astors' Beechwood Mansion

Interns with Astors' Beechwood Mansion portray characters from the Victorian Age while entertaining guests.

It is the function of art to renew our perception. What we are familiar with we cease to see. The writer shakes up the familiar scene, and as if by magic, we see new meaning in it. —ANAÏS NIN

207

THE BANFF CENTRE FOR THE ARTS

Art Discovery • Canada • 1 Week–3 Months
www.banffcentre.ab.ca/cfa

Carol Phillips, Director
P.O. Box 1020, Station 28
107 Tunnel Mountain Dr.
Banff, Alberta T0L 0C0
Canada
(800) 565-9989 • (403) 762-6180 • (403) 762-6345 (fax)
arts-info@banffcentre.ab.ca

••

THE BANFF CENTRE FOR THE ARTS, surrounded by spectacular beauty and inspiration, is devoted to the professional development of accomplished artists as well as younger artists seeking advanced learning in their respective fields throughout the year. Some residencies allow learning through project creation, experimentation, and peer interaction, while others offer the more traditional workshop or master class environment. Career development workshops range from music and sound to the theatre arts and media production. Along with intensive training and classes, the participation fee (which begins at $325 per week) provides access to the entire facilities, including the library, practice areas, recreation complex, computer support, and counseling services. Accommodations and food service are also available for a nominal fee. A work-study program may assist some participants with the program fee, room and board, and an honorarium.

BERKELEY REPERTORY THEATRE

Theatre • California • 10 Months
www.berkeleyrep.org

Intern Coordinator
2025 Addison St.
Berkeley, CA 94704
(510) 204-8901 • (510) 841-7711 (fax)
press@berkeleyrep.org

••

SINCE ITS FOUNDING in 1968, Berkeley Rep has focused on the development of a resident company of theatre artists, including actors, playwrights, directors, designers, and theatre artisans. The sense of community and shared growth and knowledge that now exists within the Rep is one of its real strengths. The company mounts eight challenging productions each season, including two innovative Parallel Season productions and one fully produced school-touring production.

The Experience: Interns will work closely with an accomplished company of artists, administrators, guest directors, and designers. The program includes regularly scheduled informal seminars every month throughout the season as the production schedule allows. The partnership between the theatre and the intern is intended to fulfill as many career-building goals and objectives as possible and to provide the intern with a variety of professional contacts and craft-building experiences.

Commitment: Internships usually begin in August or September and span full-time over a ten-month period.

Perks: A $300 stipend per month is provided, plus local housing for most positions.

Ideal Candidate: Applicants should have already acquired basic training and experience in the theatre and are ready for the next step toward a career in professional theatre. Candidates should be willing to engage in the creative process and to test the limits of their own ingenuity. Serious-minded and highly motivated applicants are most often hired.

Getting In: Call for application materials. Applications are due by April 15 (March 15 for stage management candidates). If you have some solid experience, even if it's only in college, and you proofread your application, then you'll get an interview.

BOARSHEAD: MICHIGAN'S PUBLIC THEATER

Theatre • Michigan • Academic Year

Education Director
425 S. Grand Ave.
Lansing, MI 48933
(517) 484-7800 • (517) 484-2564 (fax)

••

BOARSHEAD PRODUCES six main-stage productions using professional actors, two main-stage children's theatre productions, and one touring production that tours throughout Michigan. Performance interns work and perform in all children's productions and usually perform in at least one main-stage production. Interns will also work on the technical aspects of all shows, from building scenery to running light and sound boards. Stage management internships are also available. An $85 per week stipend and housing is provided. Candidates should have some experience in theatre (even if it's community or school theatre) along with a strong desire to learn.

CAREER DISCOVERY PROGRAM, HARVARD UNIVERSITY

Design Discovery • Massachusetts • 6 Weeks
www.gsd.harvard.edu/cardisc

Program Coordinator
Graduate School of Design
48 Quincy St.
Cambridge, MA 02138
(617) 495-5453
discovery@gsd.harvard.edu

••

WHETHER YOU MIGHT BE considering a career in architecture, landscape architecture, or urban planning and design, the summer Career Discovery Program at Harvard University can help you experience what it's like to be in these professions. Students participate in a core program of morning lectures and panel discussions, with most of the time devoted to studio work. Short, intensive projects simulate typical first-year experiences in a professional design program. Drawing and computer workshops, one-on-one instruction, career advising, and field trips and tours throughout the Boston area round out this six-week intensive program. Along with a $30 application fee, the tuition of $2,000 also includes a kit of basic studio supplies. On-campus housing is available for a fee starting at $800, although you might look for shared living possibilities that might be less expensive. The Harvard Square subway stop makes it easy to live just about anywhere in the Boston area. The program is open to anyone that is seriously considering a career in the design professions. (At a minimum, applicants must be at least high school graduates.) Application materials are due in early May.

CENTER FOR AMERICAN ARCHEOLOGY

Archaeology • Illinois • Year-Round
www.caa-archeology.org/intern.htm

Karen Atwell, Education Program Manager
P.O. Box 366
Kampsville, IL 62053
(618) 653-4316 • (618) 653-4232 (fax)
caa@caa-archeology.org

••

NEAR THE CONFLUENCE OF the Mississippi and Illinois Rivers, the Center for American Archeology helps to unfold the unbroken record of nearly ten thousand years of human habitation in an area that has been called "The Nile of North America." Interns will teach various interactive museum education curriculum for students of all ages

and provide residential and tour-group learning experiences. Applicants must have experience in archaeological excavation and be able to supervise others in the field. Knowledge of human ecology, ceramic technology, an interest in settlement patterns and house construction techniques, and/or a bachelor's degree in anthropology or archaeology are preferred. Interns receive a salary, living accommodations, and some meals. Internships vary in length, depending upon the season.

CENTER FOR INVESTIGATIVE REPORTING

Journalism • California • 6 Months
www.muckraker.org

Internship Coordinator
500 Howard St., Suite 206
San Francisco, CA 94105-3000
(415) 543-1200 • (415) 543-8311 (fax)
cir@igc.org

••

THE CENTER FOR INVESTIGATIVE REPORTING serves as a base for journalists in pursuit of hidden stories about the individuals and institutions that shape our lives. Since the center's founding in 1977, the staff and associates have completed hundreds of major investigations and have become an important source of information for media outlets, community and public interest groups, and other journalists. Their stories have spurred interest and action in Congress, the courts, and the United Nations, and have forced changes in multinational corporations, government agencies, and other organizations. Media outlets such as *60 Minutes, 20/20*, CNN, and the *Washington Post* have relied on the center to produce similar types of stories for them.

The Experience: One of the center's most important functions is to teach investigative reporting skills to novice reporters. After a half-day orientation, six to eight interns are paired with senior reporters. Under the guidance of these senior journalists, interns follow the full cycle of a major project from concept to publication or broadcast. Interns will conduct interviews, gather information and search through public records, and often contribute to final stories with sidebars or other reporting. Research projects generally include investigations into the environment, public health, constitutional government, national security, the economy, and social justice. In exchange for training, the center requests that interns answer phones on a relief basis for one to two hours per week. In addition, interns participate in a series of seminars on investigative techniques, searching for public records, media ethics and law, and other issues.

Commitment: The duration is approximately six months, with a minimum commitment of fifteen to twenty hours per week. Start dates begin around January 15 for winter/spring and June 15 for summer/fall.

Perks: A $150 per month stipend is provided. Interns also interact with prominent local and national producers, reporters, and journalism instructors, as well as journalists visiting from foreign countries. For most participants, the internship launches a promising career in reporting.

Ideal Candidate: Students and career changers with good writing and research skills, as well as an interest in investigative reporting and a self-directed work style, are encouraged to apply.

Getting In: Call for application materials. Submit resume, cover letter (describing interests and background), and a few clips or writing samples. (If you haven't been published, make sure you send in vivid writing samples.) After a phone or on-site interview, two or three personal references will be requested. Deadlines: winter/spring—December 1; summer/fall—May 1.

CENTER FOR PHOTOGRAPHY AT WOODSTOCK

Photography • New York • Year-Round
www.cpw.org/interns.html

Kathleen Kenyon, Associate Director
59 Tinker St.
Woodstock, NY 12498
(914) 679-9957 • (914) 679-6337 (fax)
info@cpw.org

SINCE 1979, the center has presented the Woodstock Photography Workshops, an education series where national and international photographers serve as teachers. Workshop students come from all over the world to study with working photographers who have the skills and desire to share their experiences with a peer group.

The Experience: The intern experience is unlike traditional classroom education. In a matter of months, interns have the opportunity to meet an average of fifteen different guest teachers and hundreds of students. An entire range of topics, from teaching strategies to professional image making, is presented in a relatively short span. Fridays through Sundays are reserved for providing general hospitality and support for guest artists. In addition to the four workshop internships that are available, Woodstock also offers an arts administration internship with training opportunities ranging from exhibition design to fundraising strategies.

Commitment: Workshop internships are available from June through October; arts administration positions are available year-round (one to three days for three to six months).

Perks: Workshop interns have the opportunity to participate in workshops and the photography lecture series tuition-free (a $3,000 value). A small stipend is provided for arts administration interns. A fully equipped professional darkroom and use of the library are also available free of charge.

Ideal Candidate: Individuals who are curious, highly motivated, technically skilled, and able to handle a diverse audience and a fast-paced work environment are encouraged to apply.

Getting In: Workshop intern applicants may schedule a personal interview on Fridays at 2 p.m. during the months of March and April. A personal portfolio (ten prints), resume, and personal references (with phone numbers) are required for an appointment. Deadlines for arts administration interns are rolling.

CENTER STAGE

Theatre • Maryland • 9–10 Months
www.centerstage.org

Katharyn Davies, Internship Coordinator
700 N. Calvert St.
Baltimore, MD 21202
(410) 685-3200 • (410) 539-3912 (fax)
kdavies@centerstage.org

CENTER STAGE strives to explore a wide range of dramatic literature and production approaches, from fresh visions of the classics to active support of contemporary writing. Production internships are available in stage management, painting, properties, costumes, electrics, and sound. Administrative interns work in development/fund-raising, communications, marketing, dramaturgy, education, volunteer service, or company management. Positions begin in late August for a nine- to ten-month period. A stipend of $85 per week is provided along with a private room in one of three newly renovated row houses close to the theatre. Perks include tickets to all productions at Center Stage (and often to other local theatres and concerts) as well as participation in biweekly seminars. Applicants should have a proven ability in their area of specialization and a willingness to work hard. It's best to apply by March for the following season.

CENTRAL CITY OPERA HOUSE ASSOCIATION

Opera Festival • Colorado • Summer
www.centralcityopera.org

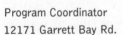

Curt Hancock, Artistic Administrator
621 17th St., Suite 1601
Denver, CO 80293-1601
(800) 851-8175 • (303) 292-6500 • (303) 292-4958 (fax)

BUILT IN 1878 by Cornish and Welsh miners, Central City Opera is one of the oldest opera festivals in the United States. The 552-seat theatre, a historic landmark in an old mining town, affords an intimate experience with grand opera and operetta. Summer festival staff positions include music librarian, public relations assistant, house management, switchboard, costume shop/wardrobe, gardening, gift shop, facility maintenance, production assistance, and general office positions. Stipends start at $180 per week, plus housing with a kitchen and laundry facilities. Travel reimbursement is also provided for those residing outside of Colorado. It's best to request an application by January; all materials are due by April 1. Applicants must be at least eighteen years of age, have an interest in opera, and exude a positive spirit.

THE CLEARING

Art Discovery • Wisconsin • Year-Round
www.theclearing.org

Program Coordinator
12171 Garrett Bay Rd.
P.O. Box 65
Ellison Bay, WI 54210
(920) 854-4088 • (920) 854-9751 (fax)
clearing@mail.wiscnet.net

AS AN "adult school of discovery in the arts, nature, and humanities," an experience at The Clearing is a unique combination of simplicity, small classes, and artistic surroundings, all taking place in a familylike atmosphere of living and learning together. Founded and designed by the renowned Danish landscape architect Jens Jensen, all buildings are log or native stone, blending with the rustic natural setting—a setting meant to provide a clearing of the mind. Offered as a summer residential program or autumn and winter day programs, courses range from "Career Development for the Best Work of Your Life" and "Recreating Body as Home" to watercolor, Navajo rug weaving, and writing classes.

COLONIAL WILLIAMSBURG FOUNDATION

Living History • Virginia • Year-Round
www.history.org

Peggy McDonald-Howells, Museum Professional Services Manager
P.O. Box 1776
Williamsburg, VA 23187-1776
(757) 220-7211 • (757) 565-8744 (fax)
phowells@cwf.org

COLONIAL WILLIAMSBURG—once the capital of England's richest and most populous colony in the "new nation" back in the eighteenth century—is now one of the world's largest outdoor living history museums. Volunteer internships are available in architecture, archaeology, archives and records, crafts programs, decorative arts administration, educational outreach programs, historic trades demonstrations, marketing, personnel, and public affairs. Tasks vary from one department to another but often include some research.

CREEDE REPERTORY THEATRE

Theatre • Colorado • 4 Months
www.creederep.com

Richard Baxter, Chief Executive Officer
P.O. Box 269
Creede, CO 81130
(719) 658-2541 • (719) 658-2343 (fax)
crt@creederep.com

SITUATED AT 9,000 FEET near the headwaters of the Rio Grande, Creede Repertory Theatre provides some spectacular scenery for their interns. Four-month internships are available in business, costume design, light and sound, shop set, and stage management. A $130 weekly stipend is provided along with housing.

CROW CANYON ARCHAEOLOGICAL CENTER

Archaeology • Colorado • Year-Round
www.crowcanyon.org

Melita Romasco, Laboratory Director
23390 County Rd. K
Cortez, CO 81321
(800) 422-8975 • (970) 565-8975 • (970) 565-4859 (fax)
interns@crowcanyon.org

CROW CANYON ARCHAEOLOGISTS have been carefully piecing together information that will help them understand the prehistoric people who once flourished in this majestic land of mesas, mountains, and canyons. Participants join archaeologists in their effort and learn the process of excavation, artifact identification, and interpretation by working on a dig site. The center's goal is to reconstruct the prehistoric cultural and natural environment in order to understand how the relationship between the two brought about a change in ancestral Pueblo life. With that knowledge, they may also recognize those dynamics in modern cultures and environments, including our own! The Crow Canyon campus is filled with adobe architecture, and hiking trails snake through the juniper-covered terrain.

The Experience: Field, laboratory, and environmental archaeology interns work closely with experienced professionals to assist them in excavating and recording archaeological contexts, in site surveying and mapping, in laboratory processing and analysis, or in studies of present and past environments. In addition, interns will be responsible for helping supervise small groups of program participants who are engaged in field or lab work. Interns may also be asked to give lectures or demonstrations to help participants prepare for fieldwork. Education interns work closely with experienced educators to assist them in preparation and teaching, including the development of a research project that assesses how and what students are learning.

Commitment: Positions are offered year-round; call for specific time frames. Interns will work a five-day week, normally Monday through Friday.

Perks: There is a modest stipend of $50 to $100 per week, plus meals at the center's dining hall and lodging in rustic cabins. Interns scheduled in the cold season will be provided with indoor housing. Everyone eats well at Crow Canyon; the resident chef serves up three delicious meals every day, including homemade salsas, luscious guacamole, gourmet tacos, and blue-corn chicken enchiladas! Interns will also attend research staff meetings where they may participate in discussions of research strategies, organization, and scheduling of work. Interns are welcome to attend evening educational programs and have the option of giving an evening lecture.

Ideal Candidate: Advanced undergraduate or graduate course work in archaeology, anthropology, or related fields, along with the ability to work as an effective member of a small research team with lay participants, and a strong interest in improving field, lab, and teaching skills is required. Experience either in archaeological field or lab/museum work is a must to be accepted for a research internship.

Getting In: It's recommended that you call for application materials by December for internships the following year. Deadlines vary and phone interviews may be conducted.

> *We do call references, so it's advisable to list people who have actually worked with you and are accessible by phone. Research internships are highly competitive; list any and all experiences that are applicable. Education internships are not as competitive, but a demonstrated interest in teaching is necessary.*

DIRECTORS GUILD—PRODUCER TRAINING PLAN

Television • California • Year-Round
www.dgptp.org

Kate Carroll, Administrator
14724 Ventura Blvd., Suite 775
Sherman Oaks, CA 91403
(818) 386-2545
trainingprogram@dgptp.org

ESTABLISHED IN 1965 and sponsored by the Directors Guild of America and the Alliance of Motion Picture and Television Producers, the Assistant Directors Training Program trains second assistant directors for the motion picture and television industry. Since its inception, more than 450 participants have graduated from the program and gone on to successful careers in the business.

The Experience: The program is designed to provide a basic knowledge of the organization and logistics of motion picture and television production, including set operations, paperwork, and the working conditions and collective bargaining agreements of more than twenty guilds and unions. Trainees are assigned to work projects on episodic television, television movies, pilots, miniseries, and feature films with various studios and production companies, and to learn to deal with all types of cast and crew members while solving problems in highly varied and sometimes difficult situations. The trainee work is physically demanding and is characterized by long hours.

Commitment: This is a 400-day trainee program, five to six days per week, twelve- to eighteen-hour days. Because of the freelance nature of production work, trainees may experience periods of layoff.

Perks: A salary of $487 to $598 per week is provided, plus medical benefits. Upon satisfactory completion of the program, trainees will be placed on the Southern California

Area Qualification List, providing eligibility for employment as a second assistant director.

Ideal Candidate: Applicant must be at least twenty-one years old and have either an associate's or bachelor's degree, or two years of paid work in film or television production.

Getting In: Applicants who meet the basic eligibility requirements must first take a written test ($75 fee). The test assesses job-related skills, including verbal, reasoning, and mathematical abilities, as well as organizational and interpersonal skills. The test is given once per year, usually in January, and is administered in Los Angeles and Chicago. The final selection of trainees is based on test scores and group and individual interviews. Deadline: mid-November for the following year.

DOW JONES NEWSPAPER FUND

Journalism • USA • Summer
www.dj.com/newsfund

Intern Program Coordinator
P.O. Box 300
Princeton, NJ 08543-0300
(800) 369-3863 • (609) 452-2820 • (609) 520-4124 (fax)
newsfund@wsj.dowjones.com

FOR COLLEGE STUDENTS interested in pursuing journalism careers, the Newspaper Fund offers a hodgepodge of summer internship programs. The Real-Time Financial Newswires Program places up to twelve students in financial news services as editors and reporters; the Newspaper Editing Program assigns eighty students to daily newspapers as copy editors writing headlines, editing copy, and designing pages; and the Online Program selects up to twelve students to work for online publications as producers and site designers. A $1,000 scholarship is provided for the summer. Be forewarned that the deadline for all programs (starting the following summer) is November 15. Each year Dow Jones also publishes *The Journalist's Road to Success*, which lists internships, training programs, and continuing education opportunities for journalists. For $3, this is a great resource for further research!

FLAT ROCK PLAYHOUSE

Theatre • North Carolina • Summer
www.flatrockplayhouse.org

Apprentice Director
2661 Greenville Highway
P.O. Box 310
Flat Rock, NC 28731-0310
(828) 693-0731 • (828) 693-6795 (fax)
frp@flatrockplayhouse.org

FROM BUILDING and running shows to attending classes, assisting patrons, or performing at the Sandburg Home and on the main stage, apprentices are constantly on the move. Flat Rock Playhouse believes that hands-on professional training is essential to any drama student's education. That's why they expose apprentices to as many facets of theatre as possible. Daily "master classes" range from acting and improvisation to costume design and professional preparation. Other opportunities exist in weekly technical crew assignments and performing in as many as five venues. The room and board fee of $1,000 (for a ten-week period starting in early June) includes three meals a day and on-site dormitory-style housing. Some scholarship and work-study money is available and is based on talent and financial need. Apprentices must be high school graduates with prior theatrical experience and committed to the development of the art form. Applications are due by April 15.

GEVA THEATRE

Theatre • New York • 1 Year
www.gevatheatre.org

Skip Greer, Director of Education
75 Woodbury Blvd.
Rochester, NY 14607
(716) 232-1366 • (716) 232-4031 (fax)
sgreer@gevatheatre.org

OCCUPYING A BUILDING that is on the National Registry of Historic Places, Geva Theatre offers a distinctive season that includes a wide variety of classics, revivals, musicals, and contemporary drama representing the whole body of American and international dramatic literature. Yearlong apprenticeships starting in August are available in administration, stage management, scenery/prop construction, electrics, and education. A stipend of $250 per week is provided. Send resume, cover letter, and three references.

You've got to dance like there's nobody watching; you've go to love like you've never been hurt;
you've got to sing like there's nobody listening; you've got to live like it's heaven on earth.

GREEK DANCES THEATER— DORA STRATOU

Performing Arts • Greece • Year-Round
http://users.hol.gr/~grdance

Alkis Raftis, President
8 Sholiou Str., Plaka
Athens, 105 58
Greece
011 (301) 3244395
grdance@hol.gr

• •

FOUNDED IN 1953 by Dora Stratou, Greek Dances Theater is based on the preservation of dances as a proof of the continuity of the Greek culture. It's an institution unique in the world, with varied activities all centered around Greek dance. As a theatre, it differs from all other theatres, and as a dance company it differs from other dance companies. Positions in dance, theatre management, ethnographic field research, and costume maintenance are available. This is an unpaid position, so interns must have their own financial resources.

HENRY FORD MUSEUM AND GREENFIELD VILLAGE

Museum • Michigan • Year-Round
www.hfmgv.org

Office of Workforce Development
20900 Oakwood Blvd., Lovett Hall
P.O. Box 1970
Dearborn, MI 48121-1970
(313) 982-6090 • (313) 982-6226 (fax)
employment@hfmgv.org

• •

HENRY FORD MUSEUM and Greenfield Village is the nation's largest indoor/outdoor museum complex with the goal of "inspiring people to learn from America's traditions of ingenuity, resourcefulness, and innovation to help shape a better future." Seasonal employment opportunities are available in virtually every facet of village operation, including historical presenter, blacksmith and glassblower, conservation technician, food service, visitor services, retail, and grounds maintenance. Along with a weekly wage, benefits include discounts on food and retail items, and the ability to admit up to four people into the village (at any time). The ideal candidate possesses outstanding hospitality and communication skills, enjoys dealing with the public, is flexible regarding scheduling, and exhibits pride and enjoyment in working for the village.

THE HERMITAGE

Archaeology • Tennessee • 2–5 Weeks
www.thehermitage.com

Internship Coordinator, Archaeology
4580 Rachel's Ln.
Hermitage, TN 37076-1331
(615) 889-2941 • (615) 889-9909 (fax)
info@thehermitage.com

• •

SINCE 1987 archaeological fieldwork has been performed on the grounds of the Hermitage. By exploring the foundations and other subsurface artifacts adjacent to President Andrew Jackson's family mansion, archaeologists and interns reconstruct what plantation life was like at the Hermitage of Jackson's time.

The Experience: After a brief orientation meeting and a welcoming barbecue, interns begin their two- or five-week adventure in historical archaeology during the summer months. With trowel in hand and sweat on brow, interns are fully immersed in archaeological excavation. The internship experience provides a full range of activities, including testing and model building as well as excavation and lab work. Interns will have the chance to unearth all sorts of artifacts, including pieces of pottery and glass, animal bones, rusty nails, glass beads, and coins from the 1850s. An integral part of life as a Hermitage intern is interaction with the public. Hundreds of tourists visit the grounds every day, and inevitably they encounter interns hard at work excavating. Although a sign explains the basics of the project, it's up to interns to answer any questions visitors have about the excavation. The Hermitage's current fieldwork focus is on investigations of slave dwelling sites in two different areas of Hermitage property.

Perks: Along with room and board, the two-week session carries a stipend of $500 and the five-week session provides a $1,250 stipend. Interns live in one of two 1930s-era farmhouses located on the Hermitage property, about a half-mile from the mansion. Each has a bathroom, a few pieces of furniture, and a fully equipped kitchen. Six people live in each house, with two or three to a bedroom.

Ideal Candidate: The five-week session is intended for advanced undergraduates and early-phase graduate students who have had some field training in archaeology and who are looking for more experience in a research-oriented setting. The two-week session is intended primarily for advanced undergraduates and graduate students who are interested in gaining exposure to the archaeological study of the recent past, but archaeological experience is not necessary.

Getting In: The application deadline is mid-April, with selections made by May 1.

THE HISTORY FACTORY

History • Virginia • Year-Round
www.historyfactory.com

Stacey Bender, Archival Services
14140 Parke Long Ct.
Chantilly, VA 20151
(800) 937-4001 • (703) 631-0500 • (703) 631-1124 (fax)
information@historyfactory.com

THE HISTORY FACTORY provides creative management of historical resources and records, and advises businesses on how to preserve and use their history for a variety of communications needs. An internship at The History Factory provides an excellent opportunity for college students to experience the entire scope of operation. Internships in the past have ranged from researching brand histories and compiling company chronologies to processing and cataloging archives and writing articles for company newsletters. Interns can expect to do research both at The History Factory and at Washington repositories, such as the Library of Congress and the Smithsonian. A small stipend or academic credit is provided; however, the biggest perk is the opportunity to work (in a casual dress environment) with rare and interesting historical materials from all over the country. Send your resume and cover letter (addressing your expectations of an internship and hours of availability) about three months prior to expected start date.

HORIZONS

Traditional Crafting • Massachusetts • Year-Round
www.horizons-art.org

Workshop Coordinator
108 N. Main St.
Sunderland, MA 01375
(413) 665-0300 • (413) 665-4141 (fax)
horizons@horizons-art.org

LOCATED MINUTES FROM the five-college communities of Amherst and Northampton in western Massachusetts, Horizons is a center for the visual arts. Two unique "campuses" serve as a forum for their workshops, with courses that include boat building, ceramics, fiber and book arts, fabric design, glassblowing, metals and jewelry, painting, photography, or woodworking. The three- to six-day Intensives Workshops take place at Horizons' studios; the Horizons to Go program allows participants to live and learn in places as far away as the villages of Tuscany or Provence, or as close as Casa Escondida in Santa Fe, New Mexico. Workshop tuition starts at $120, plus fees for lab materials, accommodations, and home-cooked, wholesome natural meals. Artist travel program fees range from $1,125 to $1,435 and include tuition, room, board, field trips, and entry fees. (Airfare is not included.)

JACOB'S PILLOW DANCE FESTIVAL

Dance Festival • Massachusetts • Summer
www.jacobspillow.org

Debbie Markowitz, Company Manager
P.O. Box 287
Lee, MA 01238
(413) 637-1322 • (413) 243-4744 (fax)

"HOW FITTING THAT many in the dance world refer to Jacob's Pillow as the Dance Farm, for it is indeed a place that nurtures." Jacob's Pillow is America's oldest dance festival, presenting ten weeks of dance performances and conducting a professional dance school each summer. Companies, students, and administrators from across the United States and around the world come together to create a unique and exciting environment.

Environment: Located in the Berkshire Hills of western Massachusetts, the campus includes 150 acres of woodlands, two theatres, four studios, and an outdoor stage.

The Experience: Working closely with staff members in all aspects of festival operation, interns receive extensive on-the-job training and experience. Visiting artists and professionals offer additional insights and the opportunity to make valuable contacts. Positions are available in archives/preservation, the business office, development, education, marketing/press, operations, programming, technical theatre/production, and video.

Commitment: All positions begin in late May and finish at the end of August.

Perks: A stipend of $100 per month is provided, along with housing at the Pillow's cottages and meals served in the Pillow's resident cafeteria.

Getting In: Send a resume and cover letter (indicating your primary area of interest, a brief statement describing your goals and expectations for the internship, and the names and phone numbers of two work-related references) by the beginning of March. Applicants for development, education, marketing/press, and programming positions should also include at least two writing samples.

JUILLIARD SCHOOL

Theatre • New York • Academic Year
www.juilliard.edu

Helen Taynton, Professional Intern Program Director
60 Lincoln Center Plaza
New York, NY 10023-6588
(212) 799-5000 • (212) 724-0263 (fax)
htaynton@juilliard.edu

THE JUILLIARD SCHOOL has various facilities that serve various types of theatre productions. The Juilliard Theatre, seating more than nine hundred people with a sixty-foot proscenium stage, houses Juilliard's opera and dance productions, concerts, recitals, and special events. The Drama Theatre contains a large thrust stage that supports drama productions ranging from classical Greek to modern avant-garde plays, as well as lectures, workshops, and spring repertory. Juilliard also has black box studios for performance, drama, and opera.

The Experience: Technical theatre internships are available in costumes, electrics, production, props, scene painting, stage carpentry, stage management, and wigs and makeup. The arts administration internship covers a variety of areas and departments including concert office, dance division, drama division, facilities management, orchestra library, performance activities, and vocal arts.

Commitment: Full-time internships begin in September and end in May. Although reasonable working hours are generally maintained, the interns' weekly schedules will vary with their duties and the requirements of the overall production schedule.

Perks: A stipend of $226 per week is provided. Keep in mind that you will be living in New York and may need more income in order to cover living expenses. Housing in New York City is expensive and requires careful consideration.

Getting In: Call for application materials (which are due by June 1).

THE KENNEDY CENTER

Performing Arts • Washington, DC • 3–4 Months
www.kennedy-center.org/internships

Danika Foster, Internship Program Coordinator
Education Department
2700 F St., NW
Washington, DC 20566
(202) 416-8821 • (202) 416-8802 (fax)
dcfoster@kennedy-center.org

THE KENNEDY CENTER is one of the country's foremost performing arts institutions. Founded in 1971 as a memorial to JFK, the center not only was a sorely needed addition to Washington's cultural scene but also quickly became an arts center of national and international importance. Today the center attracts the country's finest music, dance, and theatre companies, while also providing a home to the National Symphony Orchestra, the American Film Institute, and the Washington Opera. It also runs an admirable array of educational programs and competitions for students of all ages. The center's grand marble exterior is matched by a foyer, regal red carpet, and an eighteen-foot bust of JFK.

The Experience: Interns assist with the administrative, presentational, promotional, and/or technical aspects of the center. Special assignments may be available in administration, institutional relations, development, education, press, and with the National Symphony Orchestra. Each intern is also responsible for submitting a weekly journal, developing goals for his or her internship, maintaining a portfolio, and undertaking a project.

Commitment: Interns must make a full-time commitment of three to four months (available year-round).

Perks: A stipend of $650 per month is provided. Interns also may attend Kennedy Center performances free of charge, are welcome at special events (such as cast parties and the annual open house in the fall featuring performances by local artists), and may participate in educational events that provide opportunities to meet with prominent artists at the center. Interns are required to attend a weekly Executive Seminar Series (which involves presentations by executives of the center and other major arts institutions in Washington, DC) and participation in roundtable discussions about the performing arts and arts education.

Ideal Candidate: Internships are designed to offer meaningful learning experiences for people interested in careers in performing arts management and/or arts education. Upper-level undergraduate students (juniors and seniors), graduate students, and students who have graduated but have not been out of school for more than two years are eligible.

Getting In: Submit resume, cover letter (stating career goals, computer skills, and three internships of interest in order of preference), two current letters of recommendation, official transcripts, and one writing sample. Phone interviews may be conducted.

THE KITCHEN

Performing Arts • New York • 2–3 Months
www.thekitchen.org

Renée Danger-James, Director of Operations
512 W. 19th St.
New York, NY 10011
(212) 255-5793 • (212) 645-4258 (fax)
info@thekitchen.org

THE KITCHEN is a small nonprofit organization dedicated to the presentation and promotion of emerging artists and experimental art forms. Located in the Chelsea neighborhood of New York City, its performance season from September through the end of May annually features more than two hundred evenings of dance, music, performance, literature, and media. Their internship program is loosely structured around the interest, background, and schedule of each applicant, with internships available in curatorial, technical, marketing, fund-raising, administrative, and media services. Although financial remuneration is not offered, interns do receive free access to all Kitchen performances, an invaluable work experience, and contact with world-class artists. A two- to three-month commitment is necessary.

LA SABRANENQUE

Restoration • France/Italy • April–October
www.sabranenque.com

Jacqueline Simon, U.S. Correspondent
217 High Park Blvd.
Buffalo, NY 14226
(716) 836-8698
info@sabranenque.com

LA SABRANENQUE programs offer the chance to discover French village life "from the inside" through dynamic and genuine immersion in regional life and historic preservation. As a grassroots, nonprofit organization created in 1969, La Sabranenque has won several national awards for its restoration work and its international cultural activities.

Environment: Most activities are based in the restored old quarter (with full modern comfort) in the village of Saint Victor la Coste (near Avignon, southern France), listed as one of the "most beautiful villages in France." Projects are also conducted in various hamlets in Italy.

The Experience: Volunteers have the opportunity to become actively and directly involved in preservation and reconstruction work on sites and monuments often dating back to the Middle Ages. Volunteers learn the traditional construction techniques on the job from experienced technicians and, in a short period, experience the satisfaction of making a lasting contribution to the preservation of the villages of southern France. Work is shared with a diverse multinational team and can include stone masonry or cutting, tile floor or roof restoration, dry-stone walling, or vault construction. This is a different and unique way to see the beautiful villages of southern France and, at the same time, participate in creative experience.

Commitment: Projects range from a minimum of two weeks to three months in the months of April through October.

Perks: Participants cover the cost of room and board, along with a $535 program fee (for a two-week session).

Ideal Candidate: Applicants must be at least eighteen years of age.

LATIN AMERICAN ART RESOURCE PROJECT

Art Education • Honduras • 1–3 Months
www.hood.edu/academic/art/laarp

William and Sara Swetcharnik, Artists
7044 Woodville Rd.
Mt. Airy, MD 21771
(301) 831-7286 • (301) 694-7653 (fax)
swetcharnik@hood.edu

THE LATIN AMERICAN ART RESOURCE PROJECT (LAARP) is a unique development program that enables underprivileged artists and artisans to create work with low-cost, local resources. Under the direction of William Swetcharnik, an artist with extensive experience in traditional painting media of different cultures, the priority of this program is to provide opportunity through education.

Environment: The home base in Honduras is a great point of departure for Mayan ruins, tropical rain forests, and coral-reef islands. When the team takes off for workshop tours in remote areas of the isthmus, there are usually weekend opportunities for exploring as well.

The Experience: The LAARP internship program is an excellent opportunity for anyone interested in a firsthand experience of what it takes to run a development project in a poor country. A great deal of this experience consists of learning to navigate within a culture that operates very differently from, and not nearly as efficiently as, those of Europe and North America. Patience, love, and creativity are required to make things work. Some aspects of the work fit the training profile for any arts administrator: maintaining lines of communication and coordination of activities with collaborating institutions, presentations, and exhibitions. The fieldwork includes setting up regional workshops, researching local materials and methods at each site, and, of course, helping with the workshops themselves. To help effectively with the workshops, interns need firsthand experience with materials and methods, which entails a fair amount of studio work, particularly in the production of demonstration pieces for art and artisanry.

Commitment: The fee structure is designed to encourage a three-month internship (one month of training, one month of project development, and one month of project work).

Perks: The fee of $2,200 for one month, $3,800 for two months, or $4,800 for three months covers room and board, local transportation, Spanish tutorials, and art/development training. Interns live nearby with a local family in a quiet, safe area outside Tegucigalpa, with a regular supply of electricity, telephone, clean water, and an e-mail link with the outside world. Advice is provided for fund-raising efforts. After an initial exchange of information, there is a $100 fee to formalize the application.

Ideal Candidate: No special skills are required, only emotional maturity and an eagerness to learn, attested through good school records, work history, and letters of reference. A good working knowledge of Spanish is helpful but not necessary.

Getting In: Mail forwarded to Honduras takes a while, so it's best to communicate through e-mail. They will send you a list of current projects and the specifics of working and living in Honduras.

THE MAINE PHOTOGRAPHIC WORKSHOPS

Photography • Maine • Spring–Fall
www.meworkshops.com

David Lyman, Founder and Director
2 Central St.
P.O. Box 22
Rockport, ME 04856
(207) 236-8581 • (207) 236-2558 (fax)
info@meworkshops.com

THE PICTURE-PERFECT Maine coast village of Rockport serves as a backdrop for inspiration and subject matter for one of the nation's leading educational centers for photography, film and video, and creative writing. Referred to by students as the "Outward Bound School of Photogra-

phy," more than 250 one-week workshops, master classes, and expeditions are conducted by some of the most successful visual minds in the field. The curriculum is designed for budding enthusiasts to professional actors, filmmakers, photographers, storytellers, and writers.

The Experience: The Workshop hires nearly one hundred energetic people each summer to help run their "creative community of visual artists." Interns and staff members work as teachers and teaching assistants, technical and lab assistants, office and kitchen help, studio and darkroom assistants, video and computer technicians, gardeners, store clerks, drivers, administrative assistants, and publicity people. Another option you might consider is their highly praised seven-week work-study program (offered twice during the summer), which includes a comprehensive course in black-and-white photographic craft and vision, along with practical assignments, critiques, classes, field trips, lectures, slide presentations, and a term-end group exhibition in The Workshop's gallery. Students attend this course in exchange for twenty hours per week of work in a variety of roles.

Perks: Interns receive room and board, and paid staff start at $6 per hour. There is a fee of $2,195 for the work-study program, which covers tuition, lab fee, and shared room and board for seven weeks. All participants have access to darkrooms, editing suites, studios, and the library and gallery.

Ideal Candidate: In addition to practical skills of darkroom work, film and video training, and experience, characteristics of the summer staff include high energy, enthusiasm, responsibility, and punctuality; they are people who want to make a contribution as well as improve their career options.

Getting In: Write or call for a listing of openings and positions. A majority of the positions are filled at their three-day summer job fair, held the first weekend of April (provided it's not Easter).

MAINE STATE MUSIC THEATRE

Theatre • Maine • Summer
www.msmt.org

Rachel Clarke, Company Manager
14 Maine St., Suite 109
Brunswick, ME 04011
(207) 725-8769 • (207) 725-1199 (fax)
info@msmt.org

MAINE STATE MUSIC THEATRE, located on the Bowdoin College campus, is Maine's only professional resident music theatre where interns are put in the midst of some of the best professionals from around the country. Internships are available in performance and production (administration, box office, carpentry, costumes, house management, lighting, marketing, music direction, painting, props, stage management, and sound). All interns attend classes given by various members of the professional company and are overseen by an academic supervisor. Because team playing is essential for the summer, interns will also be required to work outside their particular concentration. A weekly stipend of $30 to $50 is provided along with room and board.

THE METROPOLITAN MUSEUM OF ART

Art Museum • New York • Summer
www.metmuseum.org

Internship Program Coordinator
Education Department
1000 Fifth Ave.
New York, NY 10028-0198
(212) 570-3710 • (212) 570-3872 (fax)
mma-ed@interport.net

• •

THE METROPOLITAN MUSEUM OF ART (The Met) is the largest and most diverse museum in the Western Hemisphere, containing two million pieces that cover nearly five thousand years of history. Summer interns are placed in conservation, library, education, administration, or one of their nineteen curatorial departments. The program begins with a two-week whirlwind orientation, where interns visit each curatorial department. This prepares them to give gallery talks and work at the visitor information center. Most interns also spend two full days each week in their respective departments. The Met also sponsors other programs, including a six- or nine-month internship program, the Graduate Lecturing Internship, fellowships, and an internship program at The Cloisters. Both paid and volunteer positions exist, and applicants must be college or graduate students.

THE NATION INSTITUTE

Journalism • New York • Year-Round
www.thenation.com/institute

Richard Kim, Assistant Director
33 Irving Pl.
New York, NY 10003-2332
(212) 209-5400 • (212) 982-4022 (fax)
instinfo@nationinstitute.org

• •

THE NATION INSTITUTE is a nonprofit foundation that supports research, conferences, seminars, educational programs, and other projects with an emphasis on social justice, civil liberties, and cultural politics. Editorial interns work on *The Nation*, America's oldest weekly magazine on politics and the arts; they do fact checking, research, reading and evaluating manuscripts, and are encouraged to write editorials, articles, or reviews for the magazine. On the publishing side, interns assist the advertising, circulation, and promotions staff with day-to-day business and in creating and carrying out developmental and research projects for the magazine and the institute. The internship carries a small stipend, along with participation in weekly seminars with distinguished authors, journalists, and politicians.

NATIONAL BUILDING MUSEUM

Museum • Washington, DC • Year-Round
www.nbm.org

Michael Kruelle, Volunteer/Visitor Services Coordinator
401 F St., NW
Washington, DC 20001
(202) 272-2448 • (202) 272-2564 (fax)
mkruelle@nbm.org

• •

THE MUSEUM'S EXHIBITIONS and educational programs interpret the world of engineering and architectural design, environmental and urban planning, building crafts and materials, and historic preservation. Volunteer interns work in exhibitions, collections, education, public affairs, development, or administration. All interns participate in an initial training program focusing on the history of the museum and its programs (along with specific information on their assignment) and sessions on communication techniques and learning styles.

Photo Credit: The Maine Photographic Workshops

David Lyman teaches creative people to become better at what they do at a total-immersion workshop.

IN SEARCH OF A MISSION—A DEEPER CALLING

At some point in our lifetime, we come to a place where we long to uncover our mission—a lifelong "assignment" that evolves from deep within our soul. Here's the story, as told by David Lyman, about his journey of uncovering a deeper "calling" and building his place in the world.

My father, the son of a New England minister, described one's mission in life as a "calling." However, a calling is not exactly a job. That was something you did to support your lifestyle. Nor was a calling exactly a profession, which is earning a living by doing something you like to do. A calling was more. It was something you had to do, loved doing, and loved doing for others.

For me, it began as photography. After a year covering the war in Vietnam as a Navy journalist, I went to work for a variety of adventure and sports magazines. By the age of thirty-two, I was feeling pretty good about my achievements, but I'd

become bored. I longed to make photographs and tell stories that made a difference. When I learned that Robert Gilka, then Director of Photography at *National Geographic* magazine, was to teach a workshop at The Center of the Eye in Aspen, I signed up, was accepted, and arrived at the workshop with portfolio in hand. To work for *National Geographic* and to travel the world making photographs of my adventures were lifelong dreams.

It was the summer of 1972, and I was thrilled to be among twenty other would-be photojournalists, all hoping to be discovered. Appearing before Gilka at the workshop, I presented my portfolio. He opened my book, turned a few pages, closed it, and pushed it back across the table. Then, in his famous drill sergeant's voice he said, "You earn a living with this stuff?"

I left the room in disillusionment and spent the remainder of the day in shock. I finished the workshop with thoughts racing through my mind about my future. However, I realized that if I am to make a statement with my photography, I will need to learn from the best. All fall I thought about what to do. The Center of The Eye went out of business. My research turned up only a few other workshops but none that fit my requirements. Jokingly I said to myself, "Why don't I start my own workshop right here on the coast of Maine?"

Soon thereafter, with the help of a photographer and designer, The Maine Photographic Workshops became a reality. One hundred and fifty students attended twelve workshops that first summer. It all started with $1,000 in my pocket and a $3,000 loan. I lost money the first summer, and again after the second, but the realization of what was happening drove me on. During the winters I recouped my losses by photographing ski races, sports personalities, and

resorts. Sooner than I could imagine, I was surrounded by the greatest minds in photography.

Twenty-five years later, we have a new campus with eight buildings, a summer enrollment of 2,700, and have become a well-established international center. As I look back over the years, I see that Gilka had given me just the right assignment after all—not the glamorous one I sought but an assignment that answered a deeper calling. It has been a gift to not only be able to build a place where creative people can come and learn but also a place that provides support and encouragement for those developing their own "calling." That is what I intended to do all along.

—Contributed by David Lyman, director and founder of The Maine Photographic Workshops (see listing page 218)

Photo Credit: The Maine Photographic Workshops

Work-study students learn new processes, tools, and techniques for mastering the craft of black-and-white photography.

NAVAL HISTORICAL CENTER

History • Washington, DC • Year-Round
www.history.navy.mil

Edward Furgol, Curator
The Navy Museum
901 M St., SE
Washington, DC 20374-5060
(202) 433-6901 • (202) 433-8200 (fax)
furgol.edward@nhc.navy.mil

TIRED OF CONDESCENDING INTERNSHIPS, the Naval Historical Center treats its interns well. (Admittedly, they must perform herculean amounts of work, but isn't that the nature of the position?) Internships here excite people about history. With a staff of less than one hundred, the center produces books, exhibits, and brochures. The museum and art gallery have less than a tenth of the National Air and Space Museum's annual visitors, but they provide their interns with greater insight into museum operations. The center serves a large branch of the federal government; it is the only organization dedicated to the history of all aspects of the U.S. Navy. Internships here consistently garner good reviews, and many former interns return as volunteers. It is no platitude to say that an internship at the center enhances one's academic and employment prospects.

The Experience: Each intern works on a personal project, with possibilities in archives, editing, design, historical research and writing, collections management, curation, education, publicity, documentary editing, and library science. Archival and collections management interns catalog new material and assist with accounting for items already in the collection. Editing interns help with their publication program. In design, interns work on invitation and exhibit layouts and silk-screening. Research and writing form the backbone of work in the branches dealing with post-1945 history, ships, and naval aviation, but interns also learn about museum curation. Library interns work in one of the oldest federal libraries. Everyone, just like the paid staff, turns to the more mundane pursuits: answering inquiries, addressing mass mailings, short bursts of office work, assisting with public programs, and organizing educational tour materials.

Commitment: Have your weekends free. Interning hours are Monday through Friday, excluding federal holidays. You won't make a fortune at the Naval Historical Center, but you will be able to arrange a schedule convenient for your academic or employment needs.

Perks: A small stipend is offered, and you will receive sound information on housing options. When intern numbers warrant (generally in the summer), the coordinator arranges field trips; and on the same note, intern T-shirts are designed and produced in-house. Interns have the social cachet of inviting their friends to public programs and private exhibit openings. In addition, each branch sends off its interns with a farewell lunch, and each intern will receive the services of excellent reference writers.

Ideal Candidate: The Naval Historical Center wants everybody to have the opportunity to work in naval history. Past interns have included history majors (naturally) but also those in museum studies, studio art, anthropology, English, French, political science, computer science, international relations, and geography.

Getting In: Call for application materials (or download them from their web site). Send a completed application along with a writing sample, unofficial transcripts, and an academic letter of reference. Design interns must submit a portfolio, which can be just slides in the mail. Interviews by telephone or in person form part of the application process.

> *Be enthusiastic and open to new experiences. It's hard sometimes, but try to submit a complete application packet. We love organizational skills.*

NEW STAGE THEATRE

Theatre • Mississippi • 9 Months

Education Director
1100 Carlisle St.
Jackson, MS 39202-2127
(601) 948-0142 • (601) 948-3538 (fax)

FOUNDED IN 1965, New Stage Theatre is the only fully professional theatre in the state of Mississippi. Under the leadership of its staff, the theatre operates year-round, offering an ambitious season that includes six main-stage productions, two second-stage shows, the premiere of a new play, and a main-stage production for young audiences.

The Experience: Acting intern company members tour the state of Mississippi with three arts-in-education productions for a variety of audiences. Interns also teach creative dramatics for children, conduct theatre workshops in area schools, assist with teacher workshops, and help coordinate equity auditions. When not performing or rehearsing, acting interns assist in the daily operation of the theatre, including technical and administrative duties as well as the strike of all productions. Technical interns participate in the building of all New Stage productions by assisting in the areas of design, carpentry, scenic painting, props, lighting, sound, and costuming.

Commitment: Internships run nine months, starting in mid-August. Interns usually work an average of fifty hours per week with one day off.

Perks: Stipends range from $5,000 to $6,000, and housing is available within walking distance of the theatre. Acting interns are given an opportunity to earn equity points toward their Actor's Equity Association card by being cast in understudy roles in equity productions.

Ideal Candidate: New Stage prefers recent college graduates with theatre experience, although others may apply. Applicants must have a good attitude, dedication to the theatre, as well as the ability to adapt and get along with others.

Getting In: Call for application materials (which are due in mid-March).

NORFOLK CHAMBER MUSIC FESTIVAL

Music Festival • Connecticut • Summer
www.yale.edu/norfolk/intern.htm

Elaine Carroll, Festival Manager
Yale Summer School of Music
P.O. Box 208246
New Haven, CT 06520-8246
(203) 432-1966 • (203) 432-2136 (fax)
norfolk@yale.edu

THE NORFOLK CHAMBER MUSIC FESTIVAL is known for its top-quality programs and serves as an international training institute for emerging professional musicians. From mid-June to late August more than thirty concerts are presented. This is definitely a foot in the door for those exploring the performing arts field. Seasonal staff have the opportunity to meet and work with leaders in performance, education, and presentation as well as world-renowned artists from all over the world. Positions for interns include artist liaison, box office manager, concert hall manager, facilities supervisor, housing coordinator, music librarian, and recording engineer, as well as administrative, recording, and production. A stipend of $1,000 to $1,500 is provided, along with room, board, and training. The ideal candidate loves the arts and wants to work at an insane pace to create one of music's truly exceptional summer events. Send resume, cover letter, and references. Phone interviews are acceptable for those residing out of town.

NORLANDS LIVING HISTORY CENTER

Living History • Maine • Year-Round
www.norlands.org

Internship Director
209 Norlands Rd.
Livermore, ME 04253
(207) 897-4366 • (207) 897-4963 (fax)

EMPHASIZING THE FRUGAL LIFESTYLE of the northern New England farm family as expressed in a "use it up, wear it out, make it do, or do without" philosophy, Norlands Living History Center offers the visitor an in-depth experience of eighteenth- and nineteenth-century rural life. The buildings include the Norlands mansion, home of the Washburns, a nationally prominent nineteenth-century family. After a thorough training period on local history and everyday lifestyles of the area (including an "adult live-in," a three-day experience of nineteenth-century rural New England life), interns portray a local character while educating visitors. A $200 per month stipend, plus housing, is provided.

THE PEARL THEATRE COMPANY

Theatre • New York • 6 Months
www.pearltheatre.org

Jessica Kroll, General Manager
80 St. Mark's Pl.
New York, NY 10003
(212) 505-3401 • (212) 505-3404 (fax)

THE PEARL is a resident acting company that produces five classical plays in its 160-seat theatre in Manhattan's East Village. Emphasis in put on the actor's craft, so audiences are transported to the world of the play rather than adapt the play to conform to modern idiom. Both administrative and production (stage management and costume) internships are available over a six-month period. Hours vary; however, most full-time interns can expect to work at least fifty hours per week and may work as many as seventy hours during load-in and tech week. A weekly stipend of $175 is provided ($225 for costume positions). Those receiving academic credit are unpaid. The Pearl is also one of the few theatres in New York authorized to grant Equity membership candidacy points to stage management interns.

The notes I handle no better than many pianists. But the pause between the notes—
ah, that is where the art resides. —ARTUR SCHNABEL

REPORTERS COMMITTEE FOR FREEDOM OF THE PRESS

Journalism • Washington, DC • 12–14 Weeks
www.rcfp.org

Rebecca Daugherty, Internship Coordinator
1815 N. Fort Myer Dr., Suite 900
Arlington, VA 22209
(703) 807-2100 • (703) 807-2109 (fax)
rcfp@rcfp.org

••••••••••••••••••••••••••••••••••

LOCATED ONE METRO STOP from Washington, DC, The Reporters Committee for Freedom of the Press is a voluntary association of reporters and editors dedicated to protecting the First Amendment interests of the news media by providing cost-free legal defense and research services to journalists throughout the United States.

The Experience: Journalism interns have the opportunity to report, write, and edit the committee's publications. These stories cover a broad range of issues, from the arrests of journalists to military press pool restrictions and access to executions. Interns also attend weekly seminars by prominent media and legal experts in the field, along with attending congressional hearings and media conferences relevant to the committee's work.

Commitment: Internships are offered three times a year for twelve to fourteen weeks.

Perks: Full-time interns receive a stipend of $650 to $1,000 per semester; part-time interns receive proportional shares, based on hours worked.

Ideal Candidate: Juniors, seniors, or graduate students are encouraged to apply. A strong background in journalism or political science is required.

Getting In: Submit resume, short writing sample (clips and/or a short research paper), and a cover letter describing interest.

> *Our interns go immediately to work here. They are very much a part of the committee's work in this small-staffed office. We generally consider those who are the best writers and are clearly professional in attitude and demeanor.*

SEATTLE REPERTORY THEATRE

Theatre • Washington • September–May
www.seattlerep.org

Andrea Allen, Director of Education
155 Mercer St.
Seattle, WA 98109
(206) 443-2210 • (206) 443-2379 (fax)
andreaa@seattlerep.org

••••••••••••••••••••••••••••••••••

THE SEATTLE REPERTORY THEATRE is one of America's largest professional, nonprofit theatres. The Professional Arts Training Program provides participants with a comprehensive work component along with exposure to the inner workings of the entire organization. Internships are offered in arts management, communications, costume shop, development, education, lighting design, production management, properties, scenic art, stage management, and technical production. Along with full-time requirements in each department, interns partake in a series of seminars and workshops that provide contact with theatre staff, guest artists, and members of the local arts community. A weekly stipend of $125 is provided. Send a resume, two letters of recommendation, and a brief personal statement about your goals and areas of interest (which must be received by March 15 for positions beginning in September).

SHAKESPEARE SEDONA

Theatre • Arizona • Summer
www.verdevalleyschool.org

Jill Patterson, Producing Director
3511 Verde Valley School Rd.
Sedona, AZ 86351
(520) 284-2080 • (520) 284-0432 (fax)
shakesedon@aol.com

••••••••••••••••••••••••••••••••••

SHAKESPEARE SEDONA is a five-week professional Shakespeare festival that takes place in the gorgeous red rock country of Sedona, Arizona. Internships are available in various areas, including stage management, lighting, set design, costume design, house management, technical theatre, and arts administration. A small stipend, room, and board are covered over the eight-week duration. In addition, students (age sixteen to adult) can participate in a three-week intensive study program that concentrates on classical acting techniques. Selected students will also get the chance to participate as actors and crew in the main-stage production.

SMITHSONIAN INSTITUTION

Museum • Washington, DC • 2–12 Months
www.si.edu/cms

Elena Piquer Mayberry, Experiential Programs Manager
Center for Museum Studies
900 Jefferson Dr., Suite 2235
Washington, DC 20560-0427
(202) 357-3102 • (202) 357-3346 (fax)
siintern@cms.si.edu

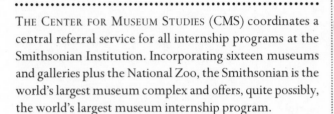

THE CENTER FOR MUSEUM STUDIES (CMS) coordinates a central referral service for all internship programs at the Smithsonian Institution. Incorporating sixteen museums and galleries plus the National Zoo, the Smithsonian is the world's largest museum complex and offers, quite possibly, the world's largest museum internship program.

The Experience: Interns at the Smithsonian develop job skills, expand expertise in academic disciplines, learn about museum careers, and see the workings of a major institution from the inside out. Smithsonian interns "learn by doing," working closely with an internship supervisor in a tutorial setting. Interns are placed in one of forty museums, administrative offices, and research programs—there is truly something for everyone. Remember that the Smithsonian Institution is more than just the science, art, and history museums. The great size of this cultural institution means that there are many interns here doing a wide variety of work, from exhibit design to research to conservation to public programs and education. There are also internships in areas not normally associated with a museum, such as photography, computer science, public affairs, administration, product development, and library science. Most museums also have enrichment programs for interns, which include career seminars, behind-the-scenes tours, and such.

Commitment: Most interns work at the Smithsonian for a period of two months to one year, for a minimum of twenty hours per week.

Perks: Unless otherwise noted, internships at the Smithsonian do not carry a stipend. CMS provides a resource guide to area housing opportunities. Other perks include a 20 percent discount at museum gift shops and a gym facility.

Getting In: Contact CMS for the booklet *Internships and Fellowships*, which contains program descriptions, contact information, and an application. The book *Internship Opportunities at the Smithsonian* may be purchased from the center for $5 (although this information is available at their web site for free). Submit one set of application materials for each museum/office where you wish to be considered for an internship. This includes a completed application form, a two- to three-page essay, two letters of reference, and transcripts. If you are not certain which program may be appropriate for you, submit five sets of application materials to CMS. Deadlines: spring—October 15; summer—February 15; and fall—June 15. No interviews are conducted.

> *The internships and fellowships brochure is very useful in answering initial questions and providing you with the names and numbers of intern coordinators for each specific program. Make sure you find out about the program you are applying for. A good way to get information is to contact the intern coordinator for each specific program; it is better to ask any questions you might have about the process before you apply. Don't ever think a question is stupid or irrelevant. Some of us were interns before and probably had the very same question. The most important thing to remember when applying is being yourself and letting you and your interests be apparent in your application. This way the project you may be selected for will truly match your interests and help you to fulfill your goals. The application essay gives you the opportunity to do this.*

SPOLETO ARTS SYMPOSIA

Arts Administration • New York • Summer
www.spoletoarts.com

Intern Coordinator
760 West End Ave., Suite 3A
New York, NY 10025
(212) 663-4440
clintoneve@aol.com

THE SPOLETO ARTS SYMPOSIA provides a series of summer programs including a writer's workshop, vocal arts symposia, and cooking and creativity classes. Each summer, beginning in July, interns are hired to assist with the administration of the programs, including a teen program coordinator and mother's helper. Applicants should be highly energetic and have some knowledge of Italian. In exchange for full-time work, room and board are provided.

SPOLETO FESTIVAL USA

Music Festival • South Carolina • May/June
www.spoletousa.org

Nunally Kersh, Producer
P.O. Box 157
Charleston, SC 29402-0157
(843) 722-2764 • (843) 723-6383 (fax)
nkersh@spoletousa.org

• •

THE SPOLETO FESTIVAL produces and presents world-class opera, dance, theatre, chamber music, symphonic and choral music, jazz, and the literary and visual arts—more than 120 events in seventeen days, playing to an international audience of more than 75,000 in a variety of theaters and other performance sites throughout historic Charleston.

The Experience: In what is called "a short-term, intensive, and exciting opportunity to learn about the world of the performing arts," apprentices work with arts professionals to produce and operate this extravagant event. Administrative apprenticeships are available in media relations, development, finance, box office, housing, general administration, merchandising, orchestra management, chamber music, and rehearsal. Production apprenticeships include stage carpenters, stage electricians, sound, properties, wardrobe, wigs and makeup, and administration.

Commitment: Employment period is from mid-May to mid-June, full-time.

Perks: A $225 per week stipend is provided along with housing at the College of Charleston. Out-of-town apprentices also receive $50 toward travel expenses. Other perks include a welcoming party, a participant badge (open access to all events), and excellent career training in the arts.

Ideal Candidate: Applicants should have excellent organization, communication, and administrative skills. Familiarity with the arts is also a plus.

Getting In: Call for application (which is due by mid-February). Secondary material or an interview may be required.

STAGE ONE

Theatre • Kentucky • Academic Year
www.stageone.org/intern.htm

Mary Mudd, Administrative Associate
Professional Theatre for Young Audiences
501 W. Main St.
Louisville, KY 40202-2957
(502) 589-5946 • (502) 588-5910 (fax)
mmudd@stageone.org

• •

STAGE ONE is an Equity theatre for young audiences, with a staff of professional actors, directors, administrators, designers, and educators dedicated to bringing quality live theatre to children and young people. Acting, development, education, public relations/marketing, and production/company management positions are available to students for an academic year, beginning in late August. A weekly stipend of $150 is provided.

STAGEDOOR MANOR PERFORMING ARTS CENTER

Performing Arts • New York • Summer

Konnie Kittrell, Production Director
651 Skyline Dr.
Gatlinburg, TN 37738
(423) 436-3030 • (423) 436-3030 (fax)

• •

EVERY SUMMER more than 240 talented kids and 117 staff members from all over the world travel to Stagedoor (in New York) to produce thirty-three full-scale productions in five on-site theatres. In addition to performance, Stagedoor offers a full program of classes in dance, TV, video production, directing, vocal training, acting technique, stage combat, technical skills—every facet of theatre and performance is covered. Staff and participants alike come to Stagedoor for experience and to fulfill professional and personal goals. They also come for fun, laughter, and friendships that last a lifetime. Their classrooms, video labs, dance studios, and costume and scenic shops are alive with the energy and enthusiasm of theatre.

The Experience: Positions at Stagedoor require great flexibility. The staff must have a commitment to teamwork and a true enjoyment of the energy and honesty of children. The days are long and the daily schedule of each staff member includes a variety of responsibilities and functions. Camp counselors double as stage managers, production assistants, dance captains, or sports personnel. Directors, musical directors, and choreographers teach classes in their craft and must hold professional credits. Technicians and designers have little interaction with campers, and focus most of their time with work behind the scenes. Stagedoor also hires office, housekeeping, and kitchen personnel, registered nurses, American Red Cross lifeguards, and swim and tennis instructors.

Commitment: The program lasts ten weeks, from mid-June to late August.

Perks: Salaries vary according to age and experience and range from $900 to $2,500 for the season. Dormitory-style housing, board, and transportation from New York City are also provided. Perks include working for an internationally famous training center with staff and children from all over the world. You'll have the chance to go to Broadway shows and meet visiting celebrities. This is a fast-paced summer stock environment.

Ideal Candidate: Staff members must be twenty-one or older, with previous experience working with children and the theatre. Most staff members are between the age of twenty-three and thirty.

Getting In: Call to request an application and brochure. Application materials are due by April 15, although it is best to apply by February because a high percentage of staff return each season!

THE THEATER AT MONMOUTH

Theatre • Maine • Summer
www.theateratmonmouth.org

Managing Director
P.O. Box 385
Monmouth, ME 04259-0385
(207) 933-2952 • (207) 933-2952 (fax)
tamoffice@theateratmonmouth.org

THE THEATER AT MONMOUTH, the "Shakespearean Theater of Maine," is a classical summer theatre that performs in the time-honored tradition of rotating repertory in an intimate Victorian opera house. The summer internship program provides the unique opportunity for interns to work side by side with the professional company on mainstage productions as staff members (rather than being relegated to a second stage or the classroom). Interns are the backbone of the summer staff and enjoy appropriate departmental responsibility while honing their skills under the supervision of seasoned professionals. The theatre offers internships in acting (performing on the main stage and in children's shows), costuming, technical theatre production, stage management, and theatre administration.

A modest stipend of $40 to $60 per week is provided along with room and board. Send cover letter, resume, and the names and phone numbers of at least three references by March 15.

UP WITH PEOPLE WORLDSMART

Educational Travel • Worldwide • 11 Months
www.upwithpeople.org

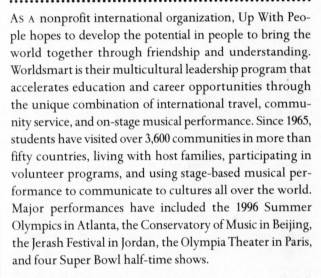

Admissions Counselor
One International Ct.
Broomfield, CO 80021
(800) 596-7353 • (303) 460-7100 • (303) 438-7301 (fax)
admissions@upwithpeople.org

AS A nonprofit international organization, Up With People hopes to develop the potential in people to bring the world together through friendship and understanding. Worldsmart is their multicultural leadership program that accelerates education and career opportunities through the unique combination of international travel, community service, and on-stage musical performance. Since 1965, students have visited over 3,600 communities in more than fifty countries, living with host families, participating in volunteer programs, and using stage-based musical performance to communicate to cultures all over the world. Major performances have included the 1996 Summer Olympics in Atlanta, the Conservatory of Music in Beijing, the Jerash Festival in Jordan, the Olympia Theater in Paris, and four Super Bowl half-time shows.

The Experience: Students begin their eleven-month Worldsmart assignment with a six-week training period in Denver, studying with professional songwriters, choreographers, and musicians. From there, 30,000 miles of foreign countries await for performance, learning, and living. Over the course of a Worldsmart experience, students might visit an elderly nursing home in Canada, paint a mural over graffiti in a small Danish town, sing to schoolchildren in Tokyo, or take part in an educational panel discussion in Oklahoma City. Simply stated, you'll see the world in a way you've never seen it before. Also inquire about intern positions and support/road staff.

Commitment: A one-year commitment is needed, with start dates every January and July.

Perks: The program fee of $13,700 covers most expenses while on tour, including ground and air transportation both nationally and internationally, accommodations, food, and educational program costs. Merit-based scholarships are also available; sixty percent of students receive an average award of $3,500.

Your diamonds are not in far distant mountains or in yonder seas; they are in your own backyard, if you but dig for them. —RUSSELL H. CONWELL

227

Ideal Candidate: Applicants must be seventeen to twenty-five years old, and have graduated high school or secondary school in order to travel. Music talent and/or performance experience is not required to interview or participate in the program. The ideal applicants are school- or career-bound people who want a unique travel experience. They are adventuresome and have a desire to learn, to give, and have an interest in other cultures.

Getting In: Call for application materials. A personal interview and written application materials are required. Interviews are generally conducted during a cast stay near your home.

WASHINGTON PERFORMING ARTS SOCIETY

Arts Administration • Washington, DC • Year-Round
www.wpas.org

Trish Shuman, Director of PR and Marketing
2000 L St., NW, Suite 510
Washington, DC 20036
(202) 833-9800 • (202) 331-7678 (fax)
wpas@wpas.org

BASED IN THE HEART of Washington, DC, the Washington Performing Arts Society is a fast-paced nonprofit that annually presents more than one hundred engagements and artist residency activities along with a variety of educational opportunities. The society's programs focus on the disciplines of classical European music, modern dance, world music, jazz, gospel, and performance art. Year-round internships are offered in public relations/marketing, development, and programming. A $100 per week stipend is provided during periods other than the summer.

WESTPORT COUNTRY PLAYHOUSE

Theatre • Connecticut • Summer

Julie Monahan, General Manager
P.O. Box 629
Westport, CT 06881
(203) 227-5137 • (203) 221-7482 (fax)

EACH SUMMER SINCE 1931, a series of plays and musicals has been presented in the Westport County Playhouse. One feels the history and charm of the theatre just by walking through the lobby, with walls covered with posters advertising shows dating from the beginning of the theatre's history. Each production is separately cast, often with well-

known stars from Broadway, film, and television. Actors, directors, designers, technicians, and managers are all union professionals with strong credits.

The Experience: Each intern will work directly under a department head, switching departments throughout the season, acquiring a full range of experience by the season's end. Areas of concentration include stage management, scenery, lighting, props, costumes, sound, administration, and public relations. Assignments are based on the needs of each show as well as the individual intern's aptitude for specialized work. Periodic seminars are conducted, each led by a director, designer, stage manager, actor, producer, or union representative.

Commitment: Internships begin in early June and continue through mid-September. A typical day for an intern: shop duty from 9:00 to 5:00, with a lunch break; dinner break between 5:00 and 7:30; then back to the theatre from 8:00 to 11:00 to run the current show.

Perks: Interns receive a $100 per week stipend, along with housing if needed. The Actor's Equity Association accepts the Westport Playhouse in its Membership Candidate Program. Upon application, an intern's work at the theatre may be credited toward membership in that union.

Ideal Candidate: The internship is best suited for those who are ready to begin a career in the theatre and need hands-on experience in a professional setting.

Getting In: Call for application materials (which are due by May 1). A personal interview is preferred, although a telephone interview may be substituted, if necessary.

Interns must be excited and enthusiastic about learning all about the world of backstage theatre, and must be willing to work long hours with only an occasional day off. In exchange, they will receive a wealth of experience in every area of theatre ranging from carpentry to wardrobe. Little, if any, acting or other performance experience is offered, yet acting students are welcome so they may learn the total universe of the theatre before specializing.

WILLIAMSTOWN THEATRE FESTIVAL

Theatre Festival • Massachusetts • Summer
www.wtfestival.org

Anne Lowrie, Company Manager
100 E. 17th St., 3rd Floor
New York, NY 01267-0517
(212) 228-2286 • (212) 228-9091 (fax)
alowrie@wtfestival.org

ONCE A SMALL SUMMER COMPANY, the Williamstown Theatre Festival (in northwest Massachusetts) has grown into a major theatrical event and has acquired a national reputation for the artists it attracts and the gifted young actors, designers, and directors it sends out into the world. Interns concentrate in one of the following areas: artistic, box office, design, directing, general/company management, literary management, photography, publicity, production management, publications management, stage management, or technical production. Interns work from early June through the end of August and are responsible for their own daily living expenses, including $500 for Williams College housing. An acting apprentice program is offered as well as a few fellowships and paid staff positions.

WOMEN'S STUDIO WORKSHOP

Art Studio • New York • Spring/Fall
www.wsworkshop.org/internship.html

Amy Ciullo, Program Director
P.O. Box 489
Rosendale, NY 12472
(914) 658-9133 • (914) 658-9031 (fax)
wsw@ulster.net

FOUNDED IN 1974, the Women's Studio Workshop (WSW) is a nonprofit artist's space founded and run by women to serve as a supportive working environment for all people interested in the visual arts. WSW staff artists coordinate grants, fellowships, internships, exhibition opportunities, and the Summer Arts Institute—WSW's primary education program for visual artists.

Environment: Located in the beautiful Hudson Valley, in the foothills of the Shawangunk and Catskill Mountains, WSW is surrounded by acres of marsh and woodlands. It is housed in the Binnewater Arts Center, a 100-year-old mercantile building that has been completely renovated to accommodate specialized studios in printmaking, papermaking, photography, and book arts. The five thousand square feet of studio space have been carefully designed, localizing work and printing areas, all with plenty of natural light and direct access to the outdoors.

The Experience: Interns work alongside the artists and staff, learning about papermaking, print media, book arts, and arts administration. Interns assist in the day-to-day running of the organization, including general maintenance and housekeeping. During the summer, interns spend half their time participating in the summer workshop series at no charge. In the spring and fall, WSW's studios are used by visiting artists who are working on their own projects or are working with WSW to produce a limited edition artist's book. One month each spring and fall is devoted to art-in-education projects with students from the local public schools.

Commitment: Interns have the option of working from February through July (Session I) or mid-August to mid-December (Session II).

Perks: A monthly stipend of $100 is provided along with housing. Interns are allowed unlimited access to studios after hours and may seek advice and/or instruction from staff concerning their own work.

Ideal Candidate: Applicants must understand that their internship experience does not serve as an artist's residency program. A car is recommended, and all serious candidates will be considered.

Getting In: Send a cover letter, resume, ten to twenty slides of your work, and three letters of reference. Postmark deadlines: Session I—November 1; Session II—March 1.

> *Do not send old recommendation letters. We would rather hear from a friend who knows you well than a professor who does not. In your cover letter, address why you want to come here, specifically how we will benefit from having you here, as well as how a WSW internship can help further your professional ambitions. A strong body of work is essential, as shown through good-quality slides.*

RESOURCES

WHAT DO MUSEUM PROFESSIONALS DO?

Not only are museums a powerful source of knowledge, they are also exciting places to work. Many who work in this environment find that many of the rewards come from disseminating their knowledge to others. The museum field encompasses a variety of opportunities that include interpretive specialists and docents, collections managers and exhibition researchers, writers and designers, along with administrative positions ranging from membership coordinators to public relations specialists. Potential employers are especially attracted to applicants who possess solid practical museum experience and can demonstrate a strong academic background. Many people secure practical, on-the-job training through internships or working as a museum volunteer. For a listing of museum-related web site links, visit www.aam-us.org/related.htm.

Recommended Resources.........

The **American Association of Museums** (AAM) represents the entire scope of museums, including art, history, science, military and maritime, and youth museums, as well as aquariums, zoos, botanical gardens, arboretums, historic sites, and science and technology centers. *AVISO*, AAM's monthly newsletter, provides listings for museum positions and internships as well as information on upcoming seminars, workshops, and other museum activities. AAM members receive it as part of their membership ($50 per year for students) or purchased as a yearly subscription for $40. AAM also sponsors a job placement center, resume review, and mentoring opportunities forum at its annual meeting. American Association of Museums, 1575 Eye St., NW, Suite 400, Washington, DC 20005; (202) 289-1818, (202) 789-1355 (fax), www.aam-us.org

Have you always wanted to participate in an archaeological dig? With the **Archaeological Fieldwork Opportunities Bulletin** in hand, you just might find the perfect project. Researched and edited by the Archaeological Institute of America (and updated for release each year in January), this comprehensive guide lists over three hundred excavations, field schools, and special programs with openings for volunteers, students, and staff throughout the world. The majority of the opportunities listed take place over the summer (which generally have late spring/early summer application deadlines). The guide can be purchased directly through Kendall/Hunt Publishing Company for $12 plus $4 for shipping and handling. For information, call them at (800) 228-0810 or visit the AIA web site at www.archaeological.org.

Established to provide a forum for the exchange of ideas among artists, **Art Papers Magazine** is a very small, nonprofit arts organization that publishes a bimonthly magazine about contemporary art and artists. Each issue of *Art Papers* brings timely reviews, critical features, and artist interviews to readers throughout the country. Subscriptions are $35 per year. *Art Papers Magazine,* P.O. Box 5748, Atlanta, GA 31107; (404) 588-1837, (404) 588-1836 (fax), info@artpapers.org, www.artpapers.org

Artists Communities details 3,600 residencies and retreats in the U.S. and abroad that are available to artists of every discipline, including seventy leading artists' communities. This is a must for those needing a creativity-stirring change of pace. (Allworth Press, $16.95)

"An organization of people who bring history to life," the **Association for Living History, Farm, and Agricultural Museums** (ALHFAM) has more than nine hundred members who work in living history sites as volunteers or paid staff. Their web site provides a listing of more than eighty international programs that provide living history programming. ALHFAM, 8774 Route 45 NW, North Bloomfield, OH 44450; (216) 685-4410, www.alhfam.org/alhfam.links.html

Whether you're interested in learning how to weave a rug or build a boat, or have the desire to spend your next vacation volunteering at a nature center, **Fodor's Great American Learning Vacations** provides the details on hundreds of programs offered inside and outside of North America. (Fodor's Travel, $17)

Each month, **The New England Conservatory of Music** publishes *Job Bulletin—Opportunities for Musicians Worldwide,* listing a wide range of music jobs and resources. The listings include work both in the U.S. and abroad, including performance, teaching, and arts administration positions—more than two hundred jobs each month, plus information on grants, competitions, conferences, fellowships, and festival auditions. Most of the positions profiled are career-track jobs, although they do provide listings of shorter-term work experiences. Mail subscription rates are $35 per year for U.S. and Canada ($49 per year for overseas); the e-mail version is $25. Contact the Conservatory for a complimentary copy prior to subscribing. New England Conservatory, Career Services Center Director, 290 Huntington Ave., Boston, MA 02115; (617) 585-1118, careerservices@newenglandconservatory.edu, www.newenglandconservatory.edu

Responding to artisans tired of the urban madness of the big cities, John Villani uncovers some of the most creative small-town communities in the United States in his book, **The 100 Best Small Art Towns in America**. The

RESOURCES

guide doesn't list any jobs for the budding artist, rather it serves as a great source of information on communities that support the arts, as well as encourages the lifestyle (and passion) of the artist. (John Muir Publications, $16.95)

If you're thinking of becoming an artist or craftsman (or wish to turn your hobby into a career), **Opportunities in Arts and Crafts Careers** will guide you in the right direction. Each artistic career path that Elizabeth Gardner profiles includes a brief history, a description of what's involved in the work, and discusses training options and job potential in the field. (VGM Career Horizons, $11.95)

ShawGuides.com provides continually updated information on educational travel and creative career programs throughout the world (and access to all the content is free). Their online database contains more than 3,500 programs ranging from cooking schools and writers' conferences to art and craft workshops and language vacations.

Theatre Directories, the publishing wing of American Theatre Works (see page 205), provides some great directories that include information on apprenticeship, internship, and short-term employment opportunities throughout the United States. The **Summer Theatre Directory** is filled with summer employment and training opportunities in summer stock theatres, Shakespeare festivals, theme parks, outdoor dramas, performing arts camps, and cruise ships. Or to find a job or an internship as an actor, designer, technician, or staff in a professional regional or dinner theatre across the U.S., the **Regional Theatre Directory** provides endless leads. ($18.95 for either book)

t he pay is modest. The work is important. The satisfaction is incredible. Your efforts may not immediately solve deep-rooted problems but will serve as the ongoing commitment to promote justice, peace, and the integrity of creation. If you have a heart for service and are willing to go the extra mile to help a good cause, it's time to start making a difference—the world needs you!

Unique Opportunities to Explore in This Section:

▶ Just because you've reached your golden years doesn't mean there isn't a world of opportunities to explore. It's only too late if you don't begin your journey now. Those who are beyond the age of fifty will uncover some unique opportunities and resources in this special section *(page 237)*.

▶ Did you know that more than one billion people throughout the world are denied the most basic of human rights—access to food? Help lead the fight against hunger by working in a yearlong fellowship sponsored by the Congressional Hunger Center and AmeriCorps*VISTA *(page 249)*.

▶ No one plans to grow old alone, but it happens. By focusing on friendship and celebrating life, interns can bring a sense of joy to the lonely and isolated elderly of Chicago with Little Brothers—Friends of the Elderly *(page 247)*.

▶ Traveling as a volunteer departs from conventional adventure travel and cultural immersion experiences in one very important way: the wondrous experience of giving. This special section provides insights on volunteering adventures and also lists the top ten volunteer programs listed in your guide *(page 256)*.

It is not by accident that the happiest people are those who make a conscious effort to live useful lives. Their happiness, of course, is not a shallow exhilaration where life is one continuous intoxicating party. Rather, their happiness is a deep sense of inner peace that comes when they believe their lives have meaning and that they are making a difference of good in the world.

—ERNEST FITZGERALD

233

Photo Credit: Global Volunteers

Global Volunteers participant Karen Fasimpaur walks with children in rural Tanzania.

WORK WITH HEART

A CHRISTIAN MINISTRY IN THE NATIONAL PARKS

National Park Ministry • USA • 3–15 Months

Rev. Richard Camp, Jr., Director
45 School St.
Boston, MA 02108
(617) 720-5655 • (617) 720-7899 (fax)
acmnp@juno.com

A CHRISTIAN MINISTRY IN THE NATIONAL PARKS is a special Christian movement recognized by over forty Christian denominations. It extends the ministry of Christ to the millions of people who live, work, and vacation in our national park, forest, and resort areas. This ministry serves government personnel and their families who live in these areas, students and professional resort workers who are employed to operate the resort facilities during the summer and winter vacation seasons, and the millions of tourists visiting the parks. This ministry cooperates with support committees in each area to provide regular interdenominational services, religious education, and Christian fellowship.

The Experience: Worship, work, and wilderness! This theme pervades the whole meaning of the ministry as it provides opportunities for Christian witness and service. Each member of the staff has a full-time job with either a park company or the National Park Service. Participants work as desk clerks, housekeepers, bellhops, store clerks, trail crew, rangers, tour guides, or food and beverage staff, along with work as a worship or music leader. An important aspect of the program is being a positive Christian witness in the workplace. All staff leaders are required to attend one of ten regional spring orientation conferences throughout the United States. Applicants must pay for transportation to and from the conference, although the expense of room and board is provided.

Commitment: A three-month commitment is necessary. Most participants arrive at the parks between late May and mid-June and stay through Labor Day, although some parks are open from May 1 through November 1. Year-round and winter placements are available for those who are able to commit themselves for periods of six to fifteen months, depending on the area assigned.

Perks: Participants are paid for their work by the park companies, with most earning between $1,200 to $2,000 (after room, board, and taxes) for a three-month period.

Ideal Candidate: The program seeks trained lay leaders who are least eighteen years of age, imaginative, dedicated, and open to creative service. The ministry demands maturity of thought and conduct, and applicants must have the ability to understand and live amiably with other people and other faiths.

Getting In: Applications are received year-round, although early applications are given first preference. Offers for summer positions are sent to qualified applicants starting in December, and applicants who wish to qualify for government jobs must apply by January 15.

ADVOCACY INSTITUTE

Public Advocacy • Washington, DC • 3–4 Months
www.advocacy.org

Internship Coordinator
1707 L St., NW, Suite 400
Washington, DC 20036
(202) 659-8475 • (202) 659-8484 (fax)
intern@advocacy.org

THE ADVOCACY INSTITUTE pursues a vision of the "just" society—where all people must be able to participate fully in public debate, public decision making, and the shaping of public values and policies. Such values and policies should include justice for those denied justice, economic equity for the poor and disadvantaged, public health and security for those at risk, and access to equal political power for those who have been denied a voice in the policy-making process. Interns, who will receive $7 per hour, work closely with professional staff in tasks that have included preparing curricula and materials to train public interest advocates, interviewing issue leaders, developing case studies of advocacy campaigns, monitoring congressional hearings and tracking legislation, and researching and writing action alerts and newsletter articles. Interns are expected to make a minimum commitment of three to four months, full-time. Send letter of interest (stating time frame available), resume, and one writing sample.

AMERICORPS

Service Learning • USA • 10–12 Months
www.americorps.org

Recruitment Administrator
Corporation for National Service
1201 New York Ave., NW, 9th Floor
Washington, DC 20525
(800) 942-2677 • (202) 606-5000 • (202) 565-2789 (fax)

AMERICORPS is a national service movement that engages thousands of Americans of all ages and backgrounds in a domestic Peace Corps—that is, getting things done across America by meeting our education, public safety, environmental, and human needs. The work will be tough and AmeriCorps members won't solve all of America's problems, but those who join this effort will definitely make a difference.

The Experience: AmeriCorps*VISTA has been helping to strengthen the needs of low-income communities since 1965, when it was first established as Volunteers in Service to America (VISTA). Members make a full-time, full-year commitment and are assigned to local public and private nonprofit organizations to work toward meeting the community needs determined by the community itself. VISTA members might mentor teens, teach elementary schoolchildren, walk the beat with community police officers, renovate low-income housing, help the homebound and disabled achieve self-sufficiency, or tackle one of the thousands of projects other VISTA members are conducting right now to help their communities.

AmeriCorps*NCCC, the National Civilian Community Corps, is a ten-month residential national service program for those between the ages of eighteen and twenty-four. The program takes its inspiration from the Depression-era Civilian Conservation Corps (CCC), which put thousands of young people to work restoring our natural environment. Today corps members in NCCC work on environmental projects but also in disaster relief, education, and public safety; they also help address other unmet human needs.

Commitment: VISTA members serve one year, with opportunities available year-round. NCCC members begin with a three-week training class starting in October and continue with a ten-month commitment.

Perks: All AmeriCorps members receive a modest living allowance, health coverage, travel expenses, and after completing one year of full-time service (from ten to twelve months), an education award of $4,725 ($2,362 for part-time service). NCCC members live on one of five campuses that serve five separate regions of the United States, ranging from a closed military base in San Diego to the Veterans Administration Medical Center in Maryland.

Ideal Candidate: Along with a deep desire to make a difference, VISTA applicants must be at least seventeen years of age and U.S. citizens or permanent residents; NCCC members must be between eighteen and twenty-four.

Getting In: Call for information and application materials. Joining AmeriCorps is a highly competitive process. Members are selected through a review process involving an initial screening of the application, an interview, and a review of references. Once an applicant qualifies for service,

a placement officer attempts to locate a suitable assignment, taking skills and preferences into account. This process may take a few months, so an early application is advised. The deadline for NCCC is March 15 for positions beginning in October.

BOSTON MOBILIZATION FOR SURVIVAL

Peace • Massachusetts • Year-Round

Wells Wilkinson, Internship Coordinator
11 Garden St.
Cambridge, MA 02138
(617) 354-0008 • (617) 354-2146 (fax)
mobilize@jps.net

••

Boston Mobilization for Survival is a leading grassroots peace and justice organization with tactics that include demonstrations, direct action, lobbying, petition drives, and public education through workshops and forums. Possible intern activities include outreach to religious, labor, campus, and community groups; writing campaign brochures and letters; speaking at public gatherings; promoting media coverage of issues; organizing meetings to plan and support campaigns; organizing public events, discussion groups, and demonstrations; or planning and holding fund-raising events.

BRETHREN VOLUNTEER SERVICE

Service Learning • Worldwide • 1–2 Years
www.brethren.org/genbd/bvs

Dan McFadden, Director
1451 Dundee Ave.
Elgin, IL 60120-1694
(800) 323-8039 • (847) 742-5100 • (847) 742-0278 (fax)
bvs_gb@brethren.org

••

"I slept and dreamt that life was pleasure, I woke and saw that life was service, I served and discovered that service was pleasure!" Sponsored by the Church of the Brethren, Brethren Volunteer Service (BVS) volunteers give their time and skills to help a world in need. It is a way for people to work at issues greater than themselves, recognizing that their efforts may not immediately solve deep-rooted problems but can be a part of ongoing work for justice, peace, and the integrity of creation.

The Experience: Volunteers choose from a variety of projects (more than 150 are available in twenty-four states in the U.S. and in seventeen nations abroad) including those involving children, young adults, senior citizens, farmworkers, disabled persons, general community services, agriculture, hunger/homelessness, prisoners and the prison systems, refugees, domestic violence, housing, health care, camping ministries, community organizing and development, education and teaching, the environment, and congregational placements. A booklet describes the specifics of each position. Volunteers begin their term of service with twelve to thirty other volunteers in a BVS three-week orientation (scheduled four times per year), which examines a wide range of topics, including peace and justice issues, hunger, stress management, Third World concerns, cross-cultural understanding, and poverty.

Commitment: Positions in the United States require a one-year commitment; overseas positions require two years.

Perks: Volunteers receive room, board, medical coverage, life insurance, transportation to and from the project, a monthly allowance of $45 to $55, and an annual retreat for those in the U.S. and Europe. Possible living environments include community style with other volunteers, in an apartment (sometimes shared), with a family, or on the project site. The financial costs include a $15 application fee, transportation to orientation, and an overseas travel fee ($400) for those going abroad.

Ideal Candidate: BVS seeks those who are willing to act on their commitment and values. BVS challenges individuals to offer themselves, their time, and their talents to work that is both difficult and demanding, rewarding and joyful. The minimum requirements: eighteen years of age, sound physical and mental health, high school education (or equivalent), willingness to examine and study the Christian faith, and commitment to the goals of BVS. A college degree or equivalent life experience is required for overseas assignment. In addition, there is a list of projects offered especially for married couples.

Getting In: Call for application materials. Applications are accepted year-round, although applicants are encouraged to apply four to six months prior to their availability.

> *It is essential that each volunteer bring a willingness to grow and a desire to serve. Important work toward peace, justice, and meeting the needs of humanity and the environment calls out for persons willing to serve.*

THE CARTER CENTER

Think Tank • Georgia • 12 Weeks
www.cartercenter.org/internships.html

Cynthia Hooks, Educational Programs Director
453 Freedom Parkway, One Copenhill
Atlanta, GA 30307
(404) 420-5151 • (404) 420-5196 (fax)
carterweb@emory.edu

IN 1982 JIMMY CARTER founded the Carter Center, a think tank to improve the quality of life for people around the world. Guided by Carter and staffed with distinguished professors, the Carter Center works with world leaders and dignitaries to promote democracy, resolve conflicts, protect human rights, eradicate disease, improve agriculture in developing countries, and tackle social problems in urban areas.

The Experience: Supervisors in each program (ranging from global development to urban revitalization) work with interns to establish weekly projects and long-term assignments. Interns are typically given a broad range of duties focusing on issues addressed by their program, but also indulge in office administration and issues cutting across other programs. To augment the intern's experience, a number of other educational and social opportunities are provided.

Commitment: Interns are required to commit a minimum of fifteen hours per week for at least twelve weeks.

Perks: Graduate/professional students may be eligible for a $3,000 stipend during the summer session (for a twelve-week, forty-hour per week term); otherwise positions are unpaid.

Ideal Candidate: The program is open to undergraduate juniors and seniors, recent graduates, and graduate/professional students who are interested in contemporary international and domestic issues. Foreign language ability and travel abroad are very helpful.

Getting In: Call for an application packet. Deadlines: spring—October 15; summer—March 15; and fall—June 15. Recognizing the need of some applicants to apply for funding or to make alternative plans, program staff strive to complete the process within a month.

The Golden Years

IT'S ONLY TOO LATE IF YOU DON'T START NOW

I think the most important thing is when we reach the point of acknowledging that we are aging, whether it's at retirement or after, that we pause for maybe a week or two and consult with people in whom we have confidence, to inventory every possible element of life that we in the past have enjoyed but had to put aside because we didn't have time to pursue it. We need to determine what things are interesting to us, and then constantly explore new ideas and be willing to take a chance.

—Jimmy Carter

Just because you're getting older doesn't mean that you have reached the end of the road. This life transition can serve as a challenging and exciting beginning—the chance to take advantage of opportunities that you never had time to explore. Obviously there are some restraints (Maslow's Hierarchy of Needs on page 13 comes to mind), but beyond these things, you have to determine if you'd like to look at the world through curious eyes or not. Realize that you have a lifetime of experiences and abilities that will assist you in a new career, volunteer work, learning a new trade, or making a difference in the world. It's only too late if you don't begin your journey now. It's your choice.

Beyond the opportunities presented throughout your guide, here are some special programs and resources specifically for those in their golden years.

Elderhostel offers those over the age of fifty-five inexpensive, short-term academic and volunteer opportunities around the world. Participants, known as "hostelers," participate in "lively and social" one- to four-week adventures ranging from a jazz course in New Orleans to experiencing the works of Michelangelo in Florence. Those that shy away from an academically stimulating experience might choose to participate in one of their many service projects, affording the opportunity to contribute energy and experience to important causes throughout the world. These short-term volunteer projects range from conservation work at national parks to building affordable housing with Habitat for Humanity. The all-inclusive program fee averages around $400; however, those participating in overseas experiences have fees that can push the $5,000 envelope. College dormitories, inns, rustic lodges, tents, and shipboard cabins serve as a home base and meals are served up in hotel dining rooms to neighborhood cafes. Add yourself to their mailing list, and three times a year you will receive their 175-page newspaper-sized catalog jam-packed with more than two thousand opportunities.

Elderhostel, 75 Federal St., Boston, MA 02110-1941; (877) 426-8056, (617) 426-7788, (617) 426-0701 (fax), www.elderhostel.org

Assuring "exotic adventures for the young at heart," **ElderTreks** offers off-the-beaten-path cultural experiences to destinations such as Sumatra, Bali, Thailand, and Morocco. The two- to three-week trips are geared for travelers who want to really explore and experience a country, from strolling through street markets and cycling through a tropical countryside to the human encounter of sharing dinner with a local family in their home. Nature is a key element to all itiner-

You must have been warned against letting the golden hours slip by.
Yes, but some of them are golden only because we let them slip. — J.M. Barrie

237

aries. An "adventure option" takes more intrepid travelers to remote areas either by foot, boat, or even on elephants, with accommodations that might be on the floor of a tribal headman's hut or under a canopy of trees in the jungle. Note that travelers must be fifty or over and the group size is limited to fifteen people. All inclusive fees start at $1,450.

ElderTreks, 597 Markham St., Toronto, ON M6G 2L7, Canada; (800) 741-7956, (416) 588-5000, (416) 588-9839 (fax), eldertreks@eldertreks.com, www.eldertreks.com

Photo Credit: ElderTreks

The trails aren't always dry when adventuring with ElderTreks, but the destination is definitely worth it.

reach out to adults who need extra assistance to live independently in their own homes or communities. They provide companionship and friendship to isolated frail seniors, assist with simple chores, provide transportation, and add richness to their clients' lives. Both these programs offer modest stipends and other benefits to help offset the cost of volunteering. *Retired and Senior Volunteer Program* volunteers choose how and where they want to serve—from a few hours to over forty hours per week. They might tutor children in reading and math, help to build houses, plan community gardens, or offer disaster relief to victims of natural disasters. Together these programs involve over a half-million seniors serving in tens of thousands of sites across the country. For the web-savvy, all the opportunities can be viewed through their web site.

Senior Corps, Recruitment Coordinator, Corporation for National Service, 1201 New York Ave., NW, 9th Floor, Washington, DC 20525; (800) 424-8867, (202) 606-5000, nsscresources@cns.gov, www.seniorcorps.org

The **National Senior Service Corps** helps people aged fifty-five and older engage in community-based service opportunities right in their own backyard. *Foster Grandparents* offer emotional support to child victims of abuse and neglect, tutor children who lag behind in reading, or, perhaps, assist children with physical disabilities and severe illnesses. *Senior Companions*

Much like home-exchange programs high school students enjoy, **Seniors Abroad** provides those over fifty with a unique international homestay experience. Participants, who are carefully matched, stay with locals in their own homes in places including Australia/New Zealand and Japan for three to four weeks (and those who are in the U.S. can provide voluntary hosting of people from these countries). A typical tour includes short homestays in several locations throughout the country. All-inclusive fees start at $2,600.

Seniors Abroad, Evelyn Zivetz, Director, 12533 Pacato Circle, North, San Diego, CA 92128; (619) 485-1696, (619) 487-1492 (fax), haev@pacbell.net

Name a beautiful place and chances are **Walking the World** will take you hiking there—that is, if you are fifty or older and still have that sense of adventure and curiosity about the world. Groups of twelve to sixteen hikers might explore the Anasazi ruins in Utah, hike the romantic islands of Hawaii, experience the cloud forests of Monteverde, or visit the famed Jungfrau in the Swiss Alps. Rather than simply being led through a beautiful place, participants learn about the natural and cultural histories as well as explore the area's plant and animal life, geology, weather, and human cultures. Trips extend from one to three weeks; land fees average $2,000. An online quarterly newsletter contains the latest line on travel opportunities as well as tips and in-depth articles on planning your trip.

Ward Luthi, Director, Walking the World, P.O. Box 1186, Fort Collins, CO 80522-1186; (800) 340-9255, (970) 498-9100 (fax), walktworld@aol.com, www.walkingtheworld.com

To the full-time RVer, home is where you park it. In years past, RVers were synonymous with retired folks, but there is a growing trend of people of all ages who have taken to the road seeking recreation, friendships, new opportunities, and exciting jobs, while traveling around in motor homes and travel trailers. **Workamper News**, published bimonthly, provides information on short-term jobs and opportunities in places all around the country, specifically for those who travel RV-style. Yearly subscriptions run $23, and a sampler of listings is provided on their web site (which includes a bookshop on other pertinent RV resources and guides).

Workamper News, Greg and Debbie Robus, 201 Hiram Rd., Heber Springs, AR 72543-8747; (800) 446-5627, (501) 362-2637, workamp@ arkansas.net, www.workamper.com

Working Options (www.aarp.org/working_ options/home.html), provided by the American Association of Retired Persons (AARP), serves as a resource center for midlife and older workers. The online guide explores information on everything from job searching, staying employable, and overcoming barriers to employment. You might also consider a membership with AARP, which is open to anyone age fifty or older (whether you are working or retired). Membership runs $8 per year. AARP, 601 E St., NW, Washington, DC 20049; (800) 515-2299, www.aarp.org

---

RECOMMENDED READING

Upon leaving the White House as president at age fifty-six, Jimmy Carter and his wife, Rosalynn, had to face the same questions many elder Americans encounter when retirement approaches: what are we going to do with the rest of our lives? In **The Virtues of Aging**, Jimmy Carter urges you to take charge of your life and explore the endless opportunities that this time affords. (Ballantine Books, $9.95)

It is a good idea to obey all the rules when you're young just so you'll have the strength to break them when you're old. —MARK TWAIN

THE GOLDEN YEARS

CHILDREN'S DEFENSE FUND

Child Advocacy • Washington, DC • 10–12 Weeks
www.childrensdefense.org/intern.html

Herman Piper, Internship Coordinator
Office of Interns and Volunteers
25 E St., NW
Washington, DC 20001
(202) 662-3797 • (202) 662-3680 (job hotline) • (202) 662-3570 (fax)
hpiper@childrensdefense.org

••

"DEAR LORD. BE GOOD TO ME. The sea is so wide, and my boat is so small." This quote captures the spirit of the Children's Defense Fund (CDF), a nonprofit, child advocacy organization that exists to provide a strong and effective voice for American children, who cannot speak, vote, or lobby for themselves. CDF's goal is to educate the nation about the needs of children and encourage preventative investment in children before they get sick, drop out of school, or get into trouble. Preventative investment in children—through carefully planned, long-term programs and policies—is a crucial investment in the nation's future well-being.

The Experience: Interns are assigned to one of four divisions, including child advocacy, nonprofit management, office of interns and volunteers, or legal; they then provide administrative and program support to CDF's professional staff of researchers, lobbyists, public interest lawyers, trainers, community organizers, media and communications specialists, fund-raising officers, event planners, administrative managers, and computer technology experts. Interns also have the chance to attend weekly brown-bag discussions on substantive issues, engaging in hands-on advocacy skills training, and participating in national grass-roots and mobilization efforts.

Commitment: Preference is given to those who can commit to a minimum of three days per week for ten to twelve weeks.

Perks: Commuter reimbursement costs are provided (and paid at the end of service).

Ideal Candidate: Candidates should have a passion for progressive social change, an interest in working on children's issues, and have a track record of activism or community involvement. Preference is given to college juniors, seniors, and graduate students.

CHOATE ROSEMARY HALL

Teaching • Connecticut • Summer
www.choate.edu/summer/interns/ti.html

Nancy Miller, Associate Director
Summer Program Teaching Internships
333 Christian St.
Wallingford, CT 06492-3800
(203) 697-2365 • (203) 697-2519 (fax)
nmiller@choate.edu

••

CHOATE ROSEMARY HALL, a secondary school spread over four hundred acres, offers one of the oldest summer enrichment programs in the country. Each summer thirty to thirty-five teaching interns are hired as members of the faculty, with senior teachers serving as mentors. Whether in the classroom, on field trips, or in the dorms, interns become engaged, stimulated, and supported in every facet of resident school life. Applicants must have completed three years of college and have a strong interest in exploring teaching as a potential career. A salary of $1,850 ($2,000 for graduates) is provided, along with room and board. It is advised that you submit application materials by the end of January; selected candidates will be invited to Choate Rosemary Hall for a campus tour and interviews.

CHRISTIAN APPALACHIAN PROJECT

Social Service • Kentucky • 3 Weeks–1 Year
www.chrisapp.org

Mary McNamara, Coordinator of Volunteer Recruitment
322 Crab Orchard St.
Lancaster, KY 40446
(800) 755-5322 • (606) 792-2219 • (606) 792-1761 (fax)
volunteer@chrisapp.org

••

THE CHRISTIAN APPALACHIAN PROJECT serves economically, socially, and/or physically challenged people in eastern Kentucky through programs ranging from adult education and teaching independent living skills to garden programs and home repair. Volunteers live together and share household duties, meals, and prayer as they support each other through their strong motivation to serve people. One-year volunteers receive room and board, a monthly stipend, health insurance, loan deferment information, and a potential AmeriCorps educational award. Summer camp counselors, who must be over eighteen, are needed to staff four summer camps in eastern Kentucky (room, board, orientation and training, and daily prayer are provided). A limited number of short-term opportunities are available for three weeks to eight months.

CITY YEAR

Service Learning • USA • 10 Months
www.city-year.org

Program Coordinator
National Headquarters
285 Columbus Ave.
Boston, MA 02116
(617) 927-2500 • (617) 927-2510 (fax)
info@city-year.org

CITY YEAR is an innovative service organization that unites diverse young leaders, ages seventeen to twenty-four, for a challenging year of full-time service, leadership, and civic engagement beginning each August. Corps members serve on the front line of America's most critical issues by eradicating racism and other social barriers that isolate our communities. Generally outfitted in distinctive red, tan, and black, corps members fan out in teams throughout communities in Boston, Chicago, Cleveland, Columbia, Columbus, Detroit, Philadelphia, Rhode Island, San Antonio, San Jose, and Seattle. Project work may involve mentoring and tutoring elementary school children, running after-school programs, building urban gardens, renovating housing developments, or teaching about AIDS/HIV and domestic violence to their peers. Corps members receive a weekly stipend of $150 and, upon graduation, are eligible for up to $4,725 in post-service awards for college tuition, job training, and other life-changing opportunities. The latest news can be found through their web site.

CO-OP AMERICA

Social Justice • Washington, DC • Year-Round
www.coopamerica.org/internships

Internship Coordinator
1612 K Street, NW, Suite 600
Washington, DC 20006
(800) 584-7336 • (202) 872-5307 • (202) 331-8166 (fax)
internships@coopamerica.org

CO-OP AMERICA is a nonprofit membership association of individuals and organizations working to build a more cooperative and socially responsible economy. They strive to educate their members to use their buying power more effectively to create change. Co-op America serves as a link between socially conscious consumers and responsible businesses by providing a variety of benefits, including a quarterly publication and the *National Green Pages* to their members.

The Experience: While at Co-op America, interns are exposed to the world of marketing and development in the nonprofit, social change sector. Internships are available in these departments: corporate accountability, executive, foundation fund-raising, Internet marketing, magazine and publications, marketing analysis, *National Green Pages* advertising, research, and socially responsible business research. All positions involve work in developing programs, research and writing, and general organizational strategy. Co-op America has a progressive office, treats interns as part of the team, and encourages interns to participate in all staff activities.

Commitment: Internships are offered year-round, although they prefer those who can work a minimum of two months. Schedules and length of internships vary depending on the project and intern's availability.

Perks: Interns receive a stipend of $100 per month, except for summer interns sponsored by the Everett Public Service Internship Program, which carries a stipend of $200 per week. All interns receive a two-year membership to Co-op America, a number of "intern appreciation lunches" (free food!), and every so often they close the office to do something fun together (such as tubing or bowling).

Ideal Candidate: They look for applicants who are interested in the environmental and social change movement, hardworking, able to work independently and as part of a team, and willing to work in a cooperative environment.

Getting In: Call for application materials. Send your resume and cover letter stating which position you are interested in and why.

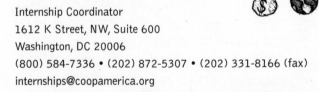
Let us know which internship you would like. Don't make us guess. Make sure there are no typos in your letter and resume. Be clear and concise about what you are looking for and what your skills are. Know something about the organization you are writing to. Let us know why you want to work at Co-op America rather than some other organization.

CONFRONTATION POINT MINISTRIES

Youth Development • Tennessee • Summer

Summer Staff Coordinator
P.O. Box 572
Crossville, TN 38557
(800) 884-8483 • (931) 484-7819 (fax)
cpoint@u-c.net

The greatest challenge of the day is how to bring about a revolution of the heart, a revolution which has to start with each one of us. —DOROTHY DAY

CONFRONTATION POINT MINISTRIES offers opportunities to lead weeklong mission trips with youth groups doing home repairs (on poverty-stricken homes) or outdoor adventure trips (which are designed to teach leadership development). The programs run from late May to early August, with training provided for the adventure staff. Besides having a solid Christian faith, applicants must have group leadership skills, maturity (not necessarily age, but twenty or over is better), a valid driver's license, and be hardworking, fun loving, and adventurous. Leaders receive a salary of $1,500, plus half of all partnerships that they raise (they provide a partnership-raising packet that will help you raise partners effectively), plus room and board.

CONGRESSIONAL YOUTH LEADERSHIP COUNCIL

Education • Washington, DC • Year-Round
www.cylc.org

Dr. Marguerite Regan, Education Director
1110 Vermont Ave., NW, Suite 320
Washington, DC 20005
(202) 638-0008 • (202) 638-4257 (fax)
mregan@cylc.org

THE COUNCIL is a nonprofit, leadership education organization committed to providing a hands-on learning experience for more than eight thousand outstanding high school students nationwide annually. In addition to inspiring young people to achieve their full leadership potential, the council provides internships for college students. Year-round opportunities include positions in conference, curriculum, enrollment and external relations, information systems, and public affairs. Interns work anywhere from twenty to forty hours per week at $7.50 per hour.

EDUCATIONAL CONCERNS FOR HUNGER ORGANIZATION

World Hunger • Florida/Haiti • 15 Months
www.echonet.org

Dr. Martin Price, Executive Director
17391 Durrance Rd.
North Ft. Myers, FL 33917
(941) 543-3246 • (941) 543-5317 (fax)
echo@echonet.org

EDUCATIONAL CONCERNS FOR HUNGER ORGANIZATION (ECHO) cultivates one of the largest collections of tropical food plants in the United States. Interns spend twelve

months in Florida engaging in experiential learning activities related to sustainable agriculture in the tropics, followed by three months in Haiti working with farmers or urban gardeners. Benefits include apartment-style dorms, a $350 per month stipend (for twelve months in Florida), health insurance, and travel expenses to Florida. Interns must raise their own support for the three months in Haiti, which is usually done through churches, friends, and relatives. A sincere Christian commitment is a must, as well as a strong body able to do manual work and a college degree. Completed applications must be received by September 15 for positions opening January through May, and by February 1 for positions opening June to December.

FARM SANCTUARY

Animal Rights • New York/California • 1–3 Months
www.farmsanctuary.org

Lorri Bauston, Education Coordinator
P.O. Box 150
Watkins Glen, NY 14891-0150
(607) 583-2225 • (607) 583-2041 (fax)
Or: P.O. Box 1065, Orland, CA 95963
(530) 865-4617 • (530) 865-4622 (fax)

DEDICATED TO ENDING the exploitation of animals used for food production, Farm Sanctuary (located both in the heart of upstate New York and in a small farming community in Northern California) serves as a refuge for abused or badly injured farm animals—a haven where "food animals" come to live, not die. More than three hundred animals reside in twelve shelter barns at the farm. A "People Barn" functions as a learning center where visitors can find out more about factory farming and the harsh realities of the "food animal" industry.

The Experience: The sanctuaries' well-established internship program allows volunteers to learn firsthand about the day-to-day responsibilities of farm work, farm animal care, and the practical applications of grassroots participation.

Commitment: Full-time positions are available year-round, so volunteers can join them any time. It's preferred that volunteers make a commitment of at least one month, and two- or three-month internships are encouraged.

Perks: Volunteers receive shared housing, with access to kitchen facilities.

Ideal Candidate: Anyone who has a strong commitment to animals and the joy of doing outdoor work is welcome.

FRONTIERS FOUNDATION

Community Service • Canada • 3–6 Months
www.amtak.com/frontiers

Volunteer Coordinator
2615 Danforth Ave., Suite 203
Toronto, ON M4C 1L6
Canada
(416) 690-3930 • (416) 690-3934 (fax)
frontier@globalserve.net

FRONTIERS FOUNDATION is a community-development service organization that works in partnership with communities in low-income, rural areas across northern Canada. Working on projects that are locally initiated, volunteers (who must be at least eighteen) build and improve housing, conduct training programs, and organize recreational activities in developing regions. Projects run year-round for three to six months. Accommodations, food, and travel inside Canada are provided.

FULBRIGHT TEACHER EXCHANGE PROGRAM

Teaching • Worldwide • 6 Weeks–9 Months
www.grad.usda.gov/International/ftep.html

U.S. Information Agency
USDA Graduate School
600 Maryland Ave., SW, Suite 320
Washington, DC 20024-2520
(800) 726-0479 • (202) 314-3520 • (202) 479-6806 (fax)
fulbright@grad.usda.gov

THE UNITED STATES INFORMATION AGENCY (USIA) is an independent foreign affairs agency that promotes U.S. national interests through a wide range of overseas information programs. One in particular for teachers is the Fulbright Teacher Exchange Program. This program provides opportunities for qualified educators to participate in direct exchanges of positions with colleagues from other countries for six weeks, a semester, or a full academic year. In general, exchange teachers are granted a leave of absence with pay and use their regular salary to cover daily expenses while abroad. A number of country programs provide full or partial transportation awards. Orientation costs, including one-way travel to orientation and two to three days of food and lodging at the orientation site, are paid by USIA. There is a deadline of October 15 for all programs that begin the following year.

GLOBAL EXCHANGE

Social Justice • California • 2–6 Months
www.globalexchange.org

Kirsten Moller, Internship Coordinator
2017 Mission St., Suite 303
San Francisco, CA 94110
(415) 255-7296 • (415) 255-7498 (fax)
info@globalexchange.org

ACTIVISM? EDUCATION? Travel? Other cultures? Justice? Human rights? Social responsibility? Sound interesting? Then this may be the internship for you. Global Exchange is a nonprofit research, education, and action center that works to build closer ties between U.S. citizens and citizens of developing countries who are working for greater social justice. Programs include study tours to developing countries, retail stores that promote alternative trade, educational resources development, media outreach, and human and labor rights campaigns. Interns work directly with a Global Exchange staff person while gaining real-life experience and working for a more equitable world. Candidates are expected to be self-motivated, creative, and willing to make a two- to six-month (part- or full-time) commitment based on project needs. Application materials can be viewed through their web site; send materials in at least one month prior to your requested start date.

GOULD FARM

**Therapeutic Community
• Massachusetts • 6–12 Months**
www.gouldfarm.org/staff.htm

Paula Snyder, Human Resources Manager
Box 157, 100 Gould Rd.
Monterey, MA 01245-0157
(413) 528-1804 • (413) 528-5051 (fax)
humanresources@gouldfarm.org

GOULD FARM is a compassionate, respectful family environment where people with mental illness learn to build more meaningful lives for themselves. The services at the farm remain rooted in the belief that every person has something valuable to contribute to the community despite mental or emotional limitations. Interns usually work in one area of the farm, which might include gardening, farming, forestry, dairy management, livestock, cooking, childcare, administration, or clinical work. Serving as informal counselors and role models, most interns lead a small group of people through a real-life task needed

When our eyes see our hands doing the work of our hearts, the circle of Creation is completed inside us, the doors of our souls fly open and love steps forth to heal everything in sight. —MICHAEL BRIDGE

243

to run the farm or community. A total of twelve positions are usually filled in May or September (lasting six to twelve months) with occasional summer opportunities (although a twelve-month commitment is preferred). Benefits include a monthly stipend of $250, a private bedroom in shared staff housing on the grounds, "farm fresh" meals, full health coverage, and the possibility of an AmeriCorps Education award. Your rural/community lifestyle will be filled with lots of work along with singing, dancing, music, art, weaving, and the celebration of nature and life!

GREEN CHIMNEYS CHILDREN'S SERVICES

**Therapeutic Community • New York
• 3–5 Months**
www.gchimney.org/~gchimney

Jackie Ryan, Internship Coordinator
400 Doansburg Rd., Caller Box 719
Brewster, NY 10509-0719
(914) 279-2995 • (914) 279-2714 (fax)
gchimney@gchimney.org

GREEN CHIMNEYS is dedicated to the development of basic education and daily living skills for children and adults to restore and strengthen their emotional health and well-being. The main campus is situated on a 150-acre farm where injured animals also have the chance for rehabilitation through the help from participants. The lessons learned from the animals become the stepping stone for a human connection and healing.

The Experience: A typical day at Green Chimneys includes special education classes, vocational education, life skills, therapy, therapeutic activities, and recreation. In responsibilities carried out with the residents, interns are offered the chance to participate in a variety of activities, along with participation in public programs and tours, teacher workshops, and weekend events.

Commitment: Programs vary in length from three to five months, with start dates beginning in January, June, and September.

Perks: A small stipend is provided, along with room and board. Interns are housed in shared rooms in a residence located across the street from the campus.

Ideal Candidate: Applicants must have a keen interest or background in children, animals, farms, and outdoor education, and must be at least twenty years of age (at least a junior in college or equivalent).

HABITAT FOR HUMANITY INTERNATIONAL

Service Learning • Georgia • 1 Week–3 Years
www.habitat.org

Volunteer Support Services
121 Habitat St.
Americus, GA 31709-3498
(800) 422-4828 • (912) 924-6935 • (912) 924-0641 (fax)
vsd@habitat.org

PUTTING FAITH INTO ACTION, Habitat brings people from all walks of life together to make affordable housing and better communities a reality for everyone. Habitat volunteers provide their construction and administrative skills for the vision of eliminating poverty housing from the face of the earth. Volunteer positions at the national office include administration, childcare, construction, fundraising, graphic arts, information systems, language translation, photography, or public relations. Internships are also available in the summer for college students. Furnished housing, a food stipend, and health insurance are provided.

HARTFORD FOOD SYSTEM

Sustainable Agriculture • Connecticut • Summer

Elizabeth Wheeler, Farm to Family Director
509 Wethersfield Ave.
Hartford, CT 06114
(860) 296-9325 • (860) 296-8326 (fax)
hfoods@erols.com

THE HARTFORD FOOD SYSTEM is a nonprofit organization that strives to increase the access to high-quality, affordable food for lower-income and elderly Hartford residents. In addition to its development and management of community food programs, such as farmers' markets, a Community Supported Agriculture (CSA) farm, and grocery delivery service, the Food System develops policy initiatives designed to influence the response of the local, state, and federal governments to food system issues. Food policy and CSA interns with a strong commitment to social justice and hunger issues, as well as an interest in sustainable agriculture, are needed throughout the year. All interns will receive a stipend of $200 to $250 per week.

HEIFER PROJECT RANCH

World Hunger • Arkansas/California/Massachusetts • Year-Round
www.heifer.org

Susan McKeon, Volunteer Coordinator
Route 2, Box 33
Perryville, AR 72126
(501) 889-5124 • (501) 889-1574 (fax)

••

HEIFER PROJECT is a Christian nonprofit development organization working in sixty countries (including the U.S.) to help alleviate world hunger. The ranch is a 1,200-acre educational facility, hosting twenty thousand people per year and modeling various approaches to ending world hunger, including sustainable agriculture practices. Volunteers are needed to work in the organic gardens and with the livestock, as well as to assist with the education program (including field trips for children, alternative spring break, tours, and the ropes course), office work, landscaping, maintenance, and construction. Volunteers receive a monthly stipend of $200, housing on the ranch, and hot meals with salad bar in the cafeteria Monday through Friday. Applicants must be at least eighteen, and applications are accepted year-round.

INNISFREE VILLAGE

Therapeutic Community • Virginia • 1 Year
http://monticello.avenue.org/innisfree

Recruitment Director
5505 Walnut Level Rd.
Crozet, VA 22932
(804) 823-5400
innisfree@prodigy.com

••

INNISFREE VILLAGE is a life-sharing community for adults with mental disabilities. Sixty-five people live and work together on a 600-acre farm in a model therapeutic environment, emphasizing empowerment, interdependence, and mutual respect of all community members.

The Experience: Volunteers and co-workers live together in family-style homes throughout the village. Generally two to four volunteers are assigned to each house and serve as houseparents. Responsibilities include cleaning, cooking, laundry, shopping, and finances of the house as well as caring for the personal needs of each co-worker. Volunteers are also engaged in therapeutic and meaningful work in the bakery, gardens, weavery, woodshop, and kitchens.

Perks: One-year volunteers receive a private room, board, a monthly stipend of $215, fifteen paid vacation days, and medical insurance.

Ideal Candidate: Fifteen to twenty people between the ages of twenty-one and sixty, all with various backgrounds and nationalities, are needed each year. Volunteers must be at least twenty-one years of age and able to commit for one year (although shorter-term positions are offered each year). Volunteers must have the desire to live with adults with disabilities in a rural community. A sense of humor, patience, flexibility, and common sense are also very helpful.

Getting In: Call for application materials (which are accepted year-round). There is a one-month orientation period.

THE INSTITUTE FOR THE ACADEMIC ADVANCEMENT OF YOUTH (IAAY) SUMMER PROGRAMS

Education • USA • Summer
www.jhu.edu/gifted/acadprog/jobs.html

Kimberley Theobald, Recruitment Coordinator
The Johns Hopkins University
3400 N. Charles St.
Baltimore, MD 21218
(410) 516-0053 • (410) 516-0093 (fax)
academic@jhunix.hcf.jhu.edu

••

THE INSTITUTE for the Academic Advancement of Youth (IAAY) is a comprehensive, university-based initiative that promotes the academic ability of children and youth throughout the world. The institute, which includes the Center for Talented Youth (CTY) and Center for Academic Advancement (CAA), holds summer residential and commuter programs that provide the opportunity for participants to take rigorous courses in the humanities (music/art, history, social sciences/philosophy, history/politics, language, and writing) and math/science (lab science, computer science, and mathematics). Residential programs are offered at sixteen sites around the country and held on beautiful college campuses in California; Maryland/Washington, DC; Massachusetts; New York; and Pennsylvania.

The Experience: This is a wonderful opportunity to work with unique and highly able youngsters in a dynamic setting. Positions include instructional (instructors, teaching assistants, laboratory assistants, and program assistants), residential assistants (similar to a college RA), and administrative (residential program assistants, health assistants, site nurses, office managers, academic counselors, academic deans, dean of residential life, and site directors).

We are here not to get all we can out of life for ourselves, but to try to make the lives of others happier. —WILLIAM OSLER

Commitment: Applicants must commit to two three-week sessions, beginning in late June and ending in early August.

Perks: A salary is provided, along with room and board at residential sites. All employees are responsible for the cost of travel to and from the residential site.

Ideal Candidate: Applicants are generally in college or are recent graduates. All candidates must be creative, energetic, and dynamic, and have the desire to work with children in an academic setting.

Getting In: Candidates whose application materials are completed by the end of January will be considered first. Some openings occur late in the hiring process, so qualified candidates are encouraged to submit and/or complete their application files through mid- to late June.

JUST ACT—YOUTH ACTION FOR GLOBAL JUSTICE

Global Justice • California • Year-Round
www.justact.org/volunteer

Sahar Khoury, Internship Coordinator
333 Valencia St., Suite 101
San Francisco, CA 94103
(415) 431-4204 • (415) 431-5953 (fax)
sahar@justact.org

JUST ACT (formerly called the Overseas Development Network) is a national, student-based, nonprofit organization. Since its creation in 1983, it has been a forum for thousands of young people to address global issues such as hunger, poverty, and social injustice. The staff at their headquarters is young, energetic, and committed to creating positive social change through hands-on learning experiences relating to international development, environmental education, and activism.

The Experience: Internships are available in alumni and donor relations, alternative opportunities clearinghouse, educational resources, *Global Links Newsletter*, office operations, and Bike-Aid public relations outreach. In addition, a unique fellowship combines an office internship during fall or winter/spring with participation in Bike-Aid, a cross-country bicycle ride during the summer. (For more details on Bike-Aid, see their special listing on page 55.)

Commitment: The time commitment for internships is somewhat flexible. They range from sixteen to twenty-four hours per week, although for summer positions an eight-week commitment is required from mid-June to mid-August.

Perks: No compensation is provided; however, the staff provides ongoing training and supervision as needed in basic Macintosh skills, nonprofit financing, publicity, event organizing, and research; forming partnerships with Asia, Latin America, and Africa; student mobilizing, leadership skills, teamwork, and community education. In addition, the summer program offers weekly brown-bag seminars given by grassroots development workers from around the world and free participation in their ongoing leadership trainings.

Ideal Candidate: Preference is given to young adults interested in working on global justice issues, especially those who enjoy being part of a small, grassroots-oriented, nonprofit organization.

Getting In: Their web site provides the specifics on internships as well as links and information on international and domestic volunteer and internship programs.

KELLOGG CHILD DEVELOPMENT CENTER

Child Development • Colorado • 3–12 Months
www.kellogg.org

Rebekah Dak, Assistant Program Director
2580 Iris Ave.
Boulder, CO 80304
(303) 938-8233 • (303) 938-5977 (fax)
kids@kellogg.org

THE KELLOGG CHILD DEVELOPMENT CENTER is a nationally acclaimed model childcare program. In addition, the center participates in research studies, writes articles for academic journals, helps in the creation of childcare-friendly legislation, and provides support services to other educators, families, and organizations. Interns at the center are given the chance to learn from some of the most influential child development educators in the world, along with becoming more successful and self-determined individuals. Internships are available in the comprehensive teaching program, administration, pediatric nursing, fundraising, nonprofit management, or marketing; however, each opportunity is based on the individual needs of each applicant. Typical assignments extend from three to twelve months on a part- or full-time basis. Full-time interns receive a monthly living stipend of $300 as well as a housing stipend of $350. Call for an application or visit their web site for more information. Applicants should be very clear about what their needs are and what it is they expect to gain from this opportunity.

LANDMARK VOLUNTEERS

Volunteer Service • USA • 2 Weeks
www.volunteers.com

Ann Barrett, Executive Director
P.O. Box 455
Sheffield, MA 01257
(413) 229-0225 • (413) 229-2050 (fax)
landmark@volunteers.com

• •

LANDMARK VOLUNTEERS is a nonprofit summer service organization for high school students who are looking for an opportunity to do something for others through community service. Under the supervision of an adult leader, volunteers are placed in teams of twelve at host organizations ranging from Burnt Island Lighthouse in Maine to the Grand Teton Music Festival in Wyoming. In return for lending a hand (primarily manual labor) over a two-week period, participants receive an exceptional learning opportunity and a chance to understand how voluntary service functions as an essential element of the American experience. Volunteers are admitted on a competitive basis with purpose, diligence, and responsibility as determining factors. A program fee of $650 covers the cost of placement as well as food and housing.

LITTLE BROTHERS—FRIENDS OF THE ELDERLY

Aging • Illinois • Summer/1 Year
www.littlebrothers.org/chicago

Christine Bertrand, Internship Coordinator
355 N. Ashland Ave.
Chicago, IL 60607-1019
(312) 455-1000 • (312) 455-9674 (fax)

• •

NO ONE PLANS to grow old alone, but it happens. Little Brothers—Friends of the Elderly serves lonely and isolated elderly over the age of seventy who live within the city of Chicago. These people most often lack a social network of family and friends, or have few social skills to build friendships, and identify themselves as lonely. Little Brothers—Friends of the Elderly's motto of "flowers before bread" points to their belief that hearts starve as well as bodies. Chicago is the original home of Little Brothers in the U.S., but programs also exist in six other U.S. cities and in Canada, France, Germany, Ireland, Mexico, Morocco, and Spain.

The Experience: Summer interns will be part of a team of helpers who, together with the elderly, organize and go to their vacation home, a fifteen-room house set on seven acres just two hours outside of Chicago. Interns will have constant interaction with the elderly, prepare and assist with various group activities, help with personal hygiene, assist with meal preparation, drive passenger vans, and help with house- or groundskeeping. Yearlong positions include human resources/volunteer management, nonprofit management, public relations assistant, and program site assistant. Spanish-speaking opportunities as well positions at other field offices are also available.

Commitment: Positions are offered during the summer or for one year, full-time, with a flexible schedule, including some evening and weekend work.

Perks: Along with room, board, health insurance, and a stipend of $600 per month, interns receive excellent training and experience in the field of aging while working under the guidance of experienced volunteers and staff.

Ideal Candidate: Applicants must have a sensitivity to the needs of elderly people who are growing old alone, a personal value system that emphasizes respect for the individual, a belief that friendship is essential in the lives of elderly people, and strong communication/interpersonal skills. Bilingual English/Spanish skills are welcomed.

> *Before I started volunteering with Little Brothers, I believed the world would be a better place if we focused on friendship and celebrating life, but now I am convinced. I realized that friendship takes time to develop but that everyone needs it. I learned that through celebrating life, chronic pain can disappear, at least for a second, and that even death loses its sting.*
> —David Scott, volunteer

LITTLE CHILDREN OF THE WORLD

Volunteer Service • Philippines • 1–3 Months

Dr. Doug Elwood, Volunteer Service Coordinator
361 County Road 475
Etowah, TN 37331
(423) 263-2303 • (423) 263-2303 (fax)
lcotw@conc.tds.net

• •

LITTLE CHILDREN OF THE WORLD is a nonprofit Christian service agency dedicated to helping create caring communities for children who are victims of poverty or abuse. Work is also done with other service agencies, including the Consuelo Foundation, Habitat for Humanity, and Teen Missions International.

People may make plans in their minds, but the Lord decides what they will do. —PROVERBS 16:9

Environment: Most of their work is concentrated in the central Philippines. Volunteers will work in Negros, a beautiful tropical island with sandy beaches and mountains climbing to 7,000 feet.

The Experience: Health workers assist in a special community-based health program; housing helpers assist in the construction of new houses and the repair of old ones; education helpers teach in one of the preschools or in a survival school; livelihood workers help with organic farming and biointensive gardening to promote self-reliance among indigent families; and peace workers help with the Sunday school, weekly Bible study groups, daily staff devotions, and training in the theory and practice of peaceful conflict resolution.

Commitment: Most volunteers stay for three months or more for a full experience, but shorter terms of at least one month are also welcome.

Perks: Housing is available, but volunteers are asked for a weekly contribution of $10 to help defray expenses for utilities and the use of facilities. Food expenses will be minimal; cooked meals generally cost about $5 per day.

Ideal Candidate: Candidates must have at least a high school diploma, but most are college students or recent graduates. Adaptability, flexibility, and ability to work with people of a different race and culture, as well as a love of children and a willingness to work with poor families, are trademarks of the best candidates.

Getting In: Call for an informational packet, which includes brochures, a newsletter, and an application form. It's best to apply a minimum of three months prior to your departure date.

Photo Credit: Little Children of the World

A volunteer with Little Children of the World assists in the construction of a new house in a poverty-stricken community in the Philippines.

LOCH ARTHUR COMMUNITY

Therapeutic Community • Scotland • 1 Year

Lana Chanarin, Volunteer Coordinator
Stable Cottage
Loch Arthur
Beeswing, Dumfries DG2 8JQ
Scotland
(011) 44 1387 760618

LOCH ARTHUR is a working community of seventy people in the southwest of Scotland, where volunteers live, support, and work with adults who have learning disabilities. The five hundred acres includes an organic farm (using biodynamic agriculture practices), market gardens, a large creamery (for cheese making), a bakery, weaving workshop, and six large households. A sense of home, community, spirituality, cooperation, emotional support, relationship building, and encouragement are the key ingredients of this shared lifestyle. The work component is about cooperation rather than competition, and provides a sense of responsibility and satisfaction. Most volunteers make a one-year commitment (although shorter stays are possible), with flexible schedules and time off for "holidays." Applicants must be at least eighteen, physically and mentally healthy, and willing and open to new challenges. A small stipend, lodging, and board are provided.

LUTHERAN VOLUNTEER CORPS

Service Learning • USA • 1 Year
www.lvchome.org

Dawn Longenecker, Recruitment Coordinator
1226 Vermont Ave., NW
Washington, DC 20005
(202) 387-3222 • (202) 667-0037 (fax)
staff@lvchome.org

THE LUTHERAN VOLUNTEER CORPS provides the opportunity for participants to work full-time in nonprofit agencies over the course of a year. Volunteers commit to exploring their spirituality while working for social justice, living in an intentional community, and simplifying their lifestyles. More than one hundred opportunities in a variety of organizations are available, including working with children and youth, counseling rape survivors and AIDS patients, organizing for better health care, advocating on behalf of refugees, staffing shelters for the homeless, tutoring adults, or working to preserve the environment. Life together with other volunteers includes sharing meals, chores, faith nights, and weekly community time. In addition, LVC schedules four regional retreats each year that provide time for personal reflection, recreation, and worship.

Commitment: The program year begins with a five-day orientation at the end of August, followed by the work placement that continues through late August of the following year. Positions are available in the inner cities of Baltimore; Chicago; Milwaukee; Minneapolis/St. Paul; Seattle; Tacoma (Washington); Washington, DC; and Wilmington (Delaware).

Perks: The biggest perks include a great work experience, new friends, urban living, and the opportunity to make a difference! Volunteers also receive a monthly stipend, room and board, medical insurance, transportation money, and two weeks of vacation. In addition, volunteers may be eligible for forbearance on student loans and education awards of up to $4,725.

Ideal Candidate: Applicants must be at least twenty-one years of age (with no upper age limit) and willing to commit to exploring their spirituality while working for social justice, living in an intentional community, and simplifying their lifestyles. Volunteers often find themselves in new and unexpected situations, so flexibility, openness, and a sense of humor are essential. Most volunteer placements can be done by people who have a general educational background and a willingness to learn new skills.

Getting In: Program information and applications are available upon request or through their web site. Applications are accepted from February 1 through July for positions beginning in the fall. Get your application in by February 1 for the best selection of cities and agencies.

MAKE-A-WISH FOUNDATION

Social Service • USA • Year-Round
www.wish.org

Volunteer Coordinator
100 West Clarendon, Suite 2200
Phoenix, AZ 85013
(800) 722-9474 • (602) 279-0855 (fax)
mawfa@wish.org

MAKE-A-WISH FOUNDATION fulfills the wishes of children between the ages of 2½ and 11 who have life-threatening illnesses. Only through the hard work and commitment of more than thirteen thousand volunteers in eighty-one chapters across the country is Make-A-Wish able to continue its work. Local chapters are always looking for volunteers to help in several areas, including wish granting, development and fund-raising, special events, marketing,

medical outreach, web site design, and administration. It's best to contact the local chapter for opportunities; their web site provides all of this information.

MERCY SHIPS

Ship Ministry • Worldwide • 2 Weeks–2 Years
www.mercyships.org

Don Stephens, Program Director
P.O. Box 2020
Garden Valley, TX 75771-2020
(800) 637-2974 • (903) 882-0887 • (903) 882-0336 (fax)
info@mercyships.org

MERCY SHIPS is a nonprofit Christian humanitarian organization committed to a threefold purpose of mercy and relief, training, and ministry. Mercy Ships has served the poor in over seventy-five port cities by providing medical care (surgeries along with medical, dental, and optical clinics and health care teaching), assisting through development projects, and fulfilling basic daily needs in order to demonstrate the message of hope through Jesus Christ. Whatever your interest or background, there could be a place for you in Mercy Ships—at sea or on land. Join Mercy Ships for as little as two weeks and up to two years (although many make a lifetime commitment). As a volunteer short-term crew member, you will have the opportunity to take a look at missions as well as at Mercy Ships. Openings are available in a wide variety of positions, both skilled and nonskilled. Applicants must be at least eighteen.

MICKEY LELAND HUNGER FELLOWS PROGRAM

Hunger Awareness • USA/Washington, DC • 1 Year
www.hungercenter.org

Jon McConnell, Director
Congressional Hunger Center
229½ Pennsylvania Ave., SE
Washington, DC 20003
(202) 547-7022 • (202) 547-7575 (fax)
mlhfp@aol.com

DID YOU KNOW that more than one billion people throughout the world are denied the most basic of human rights—access to food? In the U.S. (the richest country in the world), one in ten people suffer from hunger and malnutrition. The Mickey Leland Hunger Fellows Program, a joint partnership of the Congressional Hunger Center and AmeriCorps*VISTA, helps to make an impact by developing leaders in the fight against hunger.

The best and most beautiful things in the world cannot be seen or even touched. They must be felt with the heart. —HELEN KELLER

The Experience: Each year a select group of twenty participants are chosen to be fellows in this twelve-month program (beginning in late August). After an intensive ten-day orientation and training period in Washington, DC, fellows are placed for six months, in teams of two, in grassroots organizations at sites throughout the country to learn about hunger and poverty through hands-on experiences. The following six months are spent in Washington, DC, at national nonprofit organizations working on hunger and poverty policy. During this time, fellows meet weekly for professional development seminars.

Perks: Designed to experience living at the poverty level, fellows receive a modest living allowance that averages $8,000 for the year. Benefits include health insurance and an educational award of $4,725 for use toward further education, vocational training, or repayment of loans. Housing during the six-month field placement is provided (and assistance in finding housing is provided while in DC). Travel to and from training sessions and placements are also provided.

Ideal Candidate: Applicants are chosen on the basis of their commitment to social change, diversity of experience and perspective, vision for the future, demonstrated leadership potential, and willingness to learn and have their lives changed by this experience. All applicants over the age of eighteen will be considered.

Getting In: Call, e-mail, or visit their web site for application materials, which are due by January 30. Openings may occur late in the hiring process, so qualified candidates are encouraged to contact the center after the priority deadline.

MOBILITY INTERNATIONAL USA

Disability Awareness • Oregon • 3–6 Months
www.miusa.org

Melissa Mueller, Intern Coordinator
P.O. Box 10767
Eugene, OR 97440
(541) 343-1284 • (541) 343-6812 (fax)
info@miusa.org

MOBILITY INTERNATIONAL USA (MIUSA) is an innovative nonprofit organization that empowers people with disabilities around the world through international exchange, information, technical assistance, and training. MIUSA also serves as the National Clearinghouse on Disability and Exchange, which provides personalized information, referrals, and support for those who are disabled and interested in international exchange. Interns at MIUSA have the opportunity to develop skills and gain direct work experi-

ence in disability rights, international educational exchange, leadership, adaptive recreation, research, program development, public relations, and the day-to-day operation of a nonprofit organization. Internships generally last between three and six months, although those who commit for six months or longer receive a stipend of $125 per month.

The Experience: Interns will work directly with staff volunteers and have the opportunity to develop skills and gain direct work experience in disability rights, international educational exchange, leadership, travel and recreational opportunities, research, article and grant writing, program development, public relations, computer graphics and layout, and the day-to-day operation of a nonprofit organization. Interns are encouraged to work independently on their own projects as well as assigned and supervised projects.

Commitment: Internship programs usually last between three and six months.

Perks: For interns committed to six months or longer, a stipend of $125 per month is provided to help with living expenses.

Ideal Candidate: Interest in people with disabilities and promoting cross-cultural understanding is necessary. Preference will be given to applicants with international exchange or travel experience or who have career or master's project goals that mesh with the goals of MIUSA. Persons with disabilities are especially encouraged to apply.

RECOMMENDED READING

Are you about to go on your adventure with a disability? With adequate preparation, much of the world is accessible to a disabled traveler—especially with help from Mobility International. *Over the Rainbow* is MIUSA's quarterly newsletter that highlights international opportunities as well as resource and scholarship listings. The newsletter is free with membership or $15 for the year. From spending a study abroad year in Spain to working in Australia, *A World of Options* explores everything conceivable for the disabled. Six hundred pages worth of opportunities range from community service and travel to international educational exchange and personal accounts. The book is $30 (plus $5 shipping) and can only be purchased through MIUSA.

MY SISTER'S PLACE

Domestic Violence • Washington, DC • 1 Year
www.mysistersplace.com

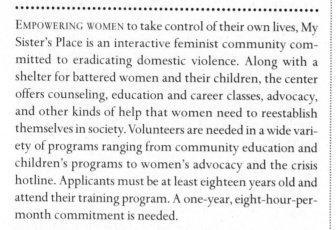

Jennifer Blomstrom, Volunteer Coordinator
P.O. Box 29596
Washington, DC 20017
(202) 529-5261 • (202) 529-5984 (fax)

••

EMPOWERING WOMEN to take control of their own lives, My Sister's Place is an interactive feminist community committed to eradicating domestic violence. Along with a shelter for battered women and their children, the center offers counseling, education and career classes, advocacy, and other kinds of help that women need to reestablish themselves in society. Volunteers are needed in a wide variety of programs ranging from community education and children's programs to women's advocacy and the crisis hotline. Applicants must be at least eighteen years old and attend their training program. A one-year, eight-hour-per-month commitment is needed.

NATIONAL 4-H COUNCIL

Youth Development • Maryland • 3–5 Months
www.fourhcouncil.edu

Patti Lucas, Conference Center Director
7100 Connecticut Ave.
Chevy Chase, MD 20815
(800) 368-7432 • (301) 961-2835 • (301) 961-2894 (fax)
plucas@fourhcouncil.edu

•••

RESEARCH AFFIRMS that our young people—the future citizens, workers, parents, and leaders of our society—face unprecedented challenges, making the business of "growing up" more complex than ever before. Obscured at times by statistics of youth violence, crime, substance abuse, and suicide is the equally tragic waste of our youths' creative talents and unique skills by the neglect or ineffective interventions of public and private institutions. The National 4-H Council embraces these challenges by offering community youth development, youth leadership, and experiential educational programs for the young citizens of our world.

The Experience: Program assistants (PAs) become licensed tour guides and facilitate the National 4-H Council's educational programs by leading groups of all ages through Washington, DC, and at the National 4-H Center. Using the city and its sites as a classroom for learning, PAs provide commentary and site interpretation, and also serve as role models for school groups and 4-H members. The Wonders of Washington (WOW) program gives groups the ultimate Washington experience, and includes study track options such as black heritage and science and technology. The Citizenship Washington Focus (CWF) helps teach youth how to become "better citizens today, better leaders tomorrow." When not escorting groups, PAs work with various center teams in sales, planning, billing, guest services, and education.

Commitment: The program extends from three to five months during the spring, summer, and fall. The workload averages between fifty to sixty hours per week, and may include evenings, weekends, and holidays.

Perks: A weekly stipend, on-campus dormitory-style living quarters, and cafeteria meals are provided. Interns will reside in Warren Hall, a large coed house with all the amenities of home. Warren Hall has nine bedrooms spread across three floors. Some bedrooms have private bathrooms, while others have community bathrooms on the floor.

Ideal Candidate: Applicants must be at least eighteen years of age and a citizen of the United States, and successfully complete a tour guide exam and three-week training period. Experience, interest, and the ability to work with youth is essential.

Getting In: Call for application materials or click on the Conference Center link through their web site.

> *My summer was about growing as a person. I moved out of Wisconsin to a place I knew nothing about to live with people I had never met. It was in this setting that I learned who I am and who I want to become. I know that when I return home I will never be the same, because I have worked and lived with twenty-four other people who have impacted my life in a way that cannot be described. It can only be experienced.* —Monica Monfre, participant

NETWORK: A NATIONAL CATHOLIC SOCIAL JUSTICE LOBBY

Social Justice • Washington, DC • 11 Months
www.networklobby.org

Linda Rich, Intern Coordinator
801 Pennsylvania Ave., SE, Suite 460
Washington, DC 20003-2167
(202) 547-5556 • (202) 547-5510 (fax)
lrich@networklobby.org

••

NETWORK: A National Catholic Social Justice Lobby educates, lobbies, and organizes to influence the formation of federal legislation to promote economic and social justice. NETWORK envisions a social, economic, and political order that ensures human dignity and ecological justice; celebrates racial, ethnic, and cultural diversity; and promotes the common good. Current issues include welfare reform, health care reform, affordable housing, and globalization of the economy.

The Experience: The associate program, which begins each September, is an eleven-month supervised program with two purposes: three participants receive continuing education in political ministry (faith-based advocacy) through the legislative process, and staff receive assistance in the ongoing work of citizen lobbying for economic and social justice. Associates experience lobbying on the federal level; learn how and when to impact legislation; communicate with NETWORK members about important legislation; and work in coalition with faith-based, nonprofit, and other organizations at a national level.

Perks: Associates are compensated with an in-depth learning experience, a stipend of $6,050, and a contribution to health benefits.

Ideal Candidate: Applicants must have excellent written and oral communication skills, and a willingness to do everything from analyzing legislation to stuffing envelopes is desired.

Getting In: Call or e-mail for application materials (which are due by February 1).

THE POPULATION INSTITUTE

Population Awareness • Washington, DC • 6 Months
www.populationinstitute.org

Devinka Peiris, Education Coordinator
107 2nd St., NE
Washington, DC 20002-7396
(800) 787-0038 • (202) 544-3300 • (202) 544-0068 (fax)
web@populationinstitute.org

THE POPULATION INSTITUTE is a small nonprofit organization working to increase public awareness of the world's constantly increasing population and to foster leadership that works on solutions to the overpopulation problem. Its headquarters are on Capitol Hill, with affiliates in Brussels, Belgium; Colombo, Sri Lanka; and Bogota, Colombia.

The Experience: The Population Institute offers leadership development opportunities through its Future Leaders of the World (FLW) Program. Public policy coordinators assist with legislative education projects, providing information to legislators and key staff, and following up on community leaders recruited during field trips across the nation. Field coordinators plan and implement educational tours around the nation for speakers of the institute. A media coordinator and special projects coordinator round out the list of opportunities.

Commitment: The program is a six-month, full-time position with sessions starting in January and July.

Perks: Participants receive a $1,200 per month stipend, plus medical benefits.

Ideal Candidate: Applicants must be able to demonstrate leadership qualities, international experiences and perspectives, a good academic record, and strong writing and oral skills. Knowledge of a foreign language is essential. Applicants must have completed at least two years of college, and be between twenty-one and twenty-five years of age. Foreign applicants must have valid authorization from the INS.

Getting In: Send resume, cover letter, an official transcript, and three letters of recommendation (two must be from academic sources). A personal interview in their DC office is required.

SPRING LAKE RANCH

Therapeutic Community • Vermont • 6 Months
www.spring-lake-ranch.org

Lynn McDermott, Personnel Director
Spring Lake Rd.
Box 310
Cuttingsville, VT 05738
(802) 492-3322 • (802) 492-3331 (fax)
springlakeranch@mindspring.com

SPRING LAKE RANCH is a small, therapeutic-work community founded in 1932. Residents decide to come to the ranch because stress, breakdown, or illness has interrupted the normal progress of their lives. All share a need for time to identify and work on problems and to assess and develop abilities that can be a foundation for future life. It is much easier to make friends and focus on what one can do rather than what one can't when working together on a common task.

Environment: The ranch is situated in a small, rural New England town located in the Green Mountains of Vermont. The ranch covers six hundred acres, most of which is either farmland or forest, with the Appalachian Trail crossing the property and major ski areas nearby.

The Experience: House advisor/work crew leaders are responsible for the residents with whom they share living space. They also lead or participate in a wide variety of manual tasks appropriate to the rural environment and dramatically changing seasons. This might include cutting wood, caring for animals, growing vegetables in their gardens for sale at the farmers' market in town, shoveling snow, maple sugaring, haying in meadows, and helping with ongoing chores of cooking, cleaning, sewing, and construction. The majority of people who have worked in the ranch community have found the experience both physically and emotionally demanding but intensely rewarding as well. Unlike many institutions for the chronically ill, the ranch program has little structure or job description and demands flexibility and emotional spontaneity from its staff.

Commitment: There is a minimum six-month commitment. The time spent at Spring Lake Ranch is an extremely demanding life experience, requiring balance, stability, and an ability to set limits on one's involvement and the use of one's energy to achieve a positive end.

Perks: Interns receive a $154 per week stipend, plus room and board. Acting as a house advisor, interns will live in one of nine cottages, supervising from two to nine residents. Perks include two weeks' vacation, comprehensive health insurance, and personal use of the auto shop, woodworking shop, computers, and laundry facilities. Interns also have the opportunity to attend seminars/workshops and other benefits that only come from working and living in a small community.

Ideal Candidate: Applicants must be twenty years of age or older, and show a willingness to share life with a community of diverse people. A basic knowledge of and experience in farming, gardening, carpentry, cooking, sewing, auto mechanics, landscaping, and recreational skills are not necessary but can be very helpful.

Getting In: Send resume and cover letter. A twenty-four-hour visit is strongly recommended as part of the interview process.

ST. ELIZABETH SHELTER

Homeless Shelter • New Mexico • 3–12 Months

Hank Hughes, Executive Director
804 Alarid St.
Sante Fe, NM 87501
(505) 982-6611 • (505) 982-5347 (fax)

THE ST. ELIZABETH SHELTER is a homeless shelter providing services to more than one thousand homeless individuals and families each year. Five live-in interns are responsible for most of the hands-on operation of the shelter, ranging from assisting homeless guests, organizing meals, processing donations, and maintaining the facilities. Past interns have noted that time spent with the guests is both the most rewarding and challenging aspect of the job. A modest stipend of $55 to $85 per week and a fully furnished, private suite above the shelter (with shared kitchen privileges) is provided, along with a hands-on experience in crisis resolution, mediation, and nonprofit management. Positions are available from three months to one year, forty hours per week. Those willing to make a commitment of nine months or more are eligible for health insurance and an exit stipend upon completion of the program. Spanish language ability and intercultural experience are a plus.

ST. VINCENT PALLOTTI CENTER FOR APOSTOLIC DEVELOPMENT

**Service Learning • Worldwide
• 1 Week–3 Years**
http://pallotti.cua.edu

John Driscoll, National Program Director
Cardinal Station, Box 893
Washington, DC 20064
(877) 865-5465 • (202) 529-3330 • (202) 529-0911 (fax)
pallotti01@aol.com

THE ST. VINCENT PALLOTTI CENTER promotes Catholic and Christian volunteer programs throughout the world. With various centers across the U.S., it provides support for volunteers before, during, and after their term of service.

The Experience: Their annual directory, *Connections,* profiles more than 120 social service programs that are available to volunteers. The majority of the programs are Catholic-sponsored, meaning the work generally includes a spiritual component in the service you do. Typical assignments might include work in AIDS ministry, agriculture, community outreach, campus ministry, carpentry and construction, education and teaching, legal services, medicine, homeless and social justice ministry, or volunteer coordination.

Commitment: Renewable assignments are generally six months to a year in the United States, and one to three years overseas; however, there are also short-term and summer programs available.

Perks: Depending on the program, volunteers usually receive a monthly living stipend that covers room and board (and sometimes a bit of spending money). Living arrangements are generally in a community setting that promotes a simple lifestyle. In addition, many opportunities offer health insurance, transportation costs, retreats, and spiritual direction and orientation.

Ideal Candidate: People of all ages, skills, and backgrounds—including married couples—are encouraged to become volunteers. The majority of programs have an age requirement of twenty-one, although some look for volunteers eighteen years and older. Some placements require a background specific to the work; others ask simply for people willing to do what they can. For placements overseas, language training is often required (although some programs include this training).

Getting In: Write or call for a copy of the *Connections* directory, which will provide you with the details of each program and their application process. Pallotti Centers across the U.S. include Boston (617-783-3924); Paterson, New Jersey (973-523-1544); Sacramento (916-454-4320); and St. Louis (314-367-5500). It's suggested that applicants always speak to a former volunteer, the work-site director, and a paid staff member to get a better idea of a particular opportunity.

STUDENT PUGWASH USA

Technology • Washington, DC • Year-Round
www.spusa.org/pugwash

Internship/Fellowship Coordinator
815 15th St., NW, Suite 814
Washington, DC 20005
(800) 969-2784 • (202) 328-6555 • (202) 797-4664 (fax)
spusa@spusa.org

STUDENT PUGWASH USA, a nonprofit education organization run by a staff of young professionals, provides university students with a range of programs to prepare them, as future leaders and concerned citizens, to make thoughtful decisions about the use of technology. They organize international conferences, coordinate a network of chapters on campuses nationwide, compile and publish an employment directory, and sponsor a number of national and regional events each year. Interns work as staff members, taking part in office discussions and decisions. Interns are encouraged to take individual initiative and responsibility and will be expected to work well as part of a team. All positions require energetic and creative individuals committed to sensitizing young people and the wider public to social issues posed by technology. Interns are paid $250 per week.

TEACH FOR AMERICA

Teaching • USA • 2 Years
www.teachforamerica.org

Admissions Director
315 W. 36th St., Sixth Floor
New York, NY 10108
(800) 832-1230 • (212) 279-2080 • (212) 279-2081 (fax)

EACH YEAR Teach for America places hundreds of corps members in K-12 positions in public school districts that traditionally have difficulty filling all of their teaching positions. These districts hire corps members at first-year teacher salaries ($22,000 to $32,000) for a two-year contract. Corps members can assume teaching positions in these shortage areas without meeting conventional licensure requirements, although they are usually required to work toward certification by enrolling in local university programs or in programs run by their school districts or states. Corps members are placed in urban sites in Baltimore, Houston, Los Angeles, New Jersey, New Orleans, New York City, the Mississippi Delta (including Arkansas), North Carolina, Phoenix, the Rio Grande Valley in Texas, San Francisco, southern Louisiana, and Washington, DC.

THIRD WORLD OPPORTUNITIES

Hunger Awareness • Mexico • 1 Week

Rev. M. Laurel Gray, Coordinator
1363 Somermont Dr.
El Cajon, CA 92021
(619) 449-9381 • (619) 449-9381 (fax)
pgray@ucsd.edu

THIRD WORLD OPPORTUNITIES is a hunger- and poverty-awareness program designed to provide opportunities for appropriate responses to human need. It seeks to encourage increased sensitivity to life in the Third World; intentional reflection on our relationships with Third World people; effective work projects that offer practical services to the hungry, the homeless, and the poor; and organized efforts to change existing conditions.

The Experience: As a "developmental response" to poverty (rather than through charity), volunteers become involved in work projects at Miracle Ranch Home for Boys, located on a 120-acre olive tree ranch. About ten boys, aged six to nineteen, live on this farm, most of whom have been abandoned by parents and later picked up off the streets of Tijuana, Mexico. Although there are many construction and maintenance tasks to perform, the most important part of volunteering is that of building relationships with the boys and community.

Commitment: Projects are generally for one week during spring break and summer.

Perks: For a fee of $200, participants are fed and housed at the project site. One of the highlights of the experience is the integration of work and worship, language development and play, and growth and fellowship with one another.

Ideal Candidate: The minimum age requirement is fifteen, and knowledge of Spanish and building experience are helpful but not necessary. Prospective candidates must have a keen interest in the Third World and a desire to learn about the root causes of hunger and poverty.

UNIVERSITY OF CALIFORNIA AT SAN FRANCISCO AIDS HEALTH PROJECT

AIDS Education • California • 12 Months
www.ucsf-ahp.org

Susan Sunshine, Staffing Coordinator
P.O. Box 0884
San Francisco, CA 94143-0884
(415) 476-3890 • (415) 476-3613 (fax)
ssunshi@itsa.ucsf.edu

THE UNIVERSITY of California at San Francisco (UCSF) AIDS Health Project (AHP) seeks to help people reduce the risk of HIV transmission, cope with the emotional challenges of HIV infection, and support friends and family who face the challenges of this epidemic. Since 1987, AHP has provided direct service to more than twenty thousand individuals and more than one thousand care providers annually.

The Experience: Interns become an integral part of the Health Project and are expected to take on many of the professional responsibilities of permanent staff. Encouragement and assistance whenever possible will be given for the individual intern's pursuit of academic and professional goals. Internships include publications, client support services, development, research, and HIV counseling/testing services over a twelve-month period (thirty-two hours per week).

Perks: Interns will receive a monthly housing stipend of $600 (which is paid directly to a landlord) along with a wealth of learning experience. Perks include student/staff privileges at UCSF, including reduced rate membership in the Milberry Union health and fitness program, use of the UCSF library, and other educational programs. Many interns get part-time paid work to supplement their internship experience financially.

Ideal Candidate: Applicants should have excellent interpersonal skills, including the ability and sensitivity to work with clinical and nonclinical staff; sensitivity to HIV-related needs and concerns; and the ability and sensitivity to work in a culturally diverse work setting that includes gays, lesbians, people of various ethnicities, persons with substance abuse problems, and people with HIV.

Getting In: Call for application materials (which are due by March 31). Acceptance into the program is provided no later than May 31.

Our deepest fear is not that we are inadequate.

Our deepest fear is that we are powerful beyond measure.

It is our light, not our darkness, that most frightens us.

We ask ourselves, Who am I to be brilliant, gorgeous, talented, and fabulous?

Actually, who are you not to be?

You are a child of God.

Your playing small doesn't serve the world.

There's nothing enlightened about shrinking so that other people won't feel insecure around you.

We were born to make manifest the glory of God that is within us.

It's not just in some of us; it's in everyone.

And as we let our own light shine, we unconsciously give other people permission to do the same.

As we are liberated from our own fear, our presence automatically liberates others.

—FROM NELSON MANDELA'S INAUGURAL SPEECH IN 1994

Both tears and sweat are salty, but they render a different result. Tears will get you sympathy; sweat will get you change. —JESSE JACKSON

VOLUNTEER ADVENTURES

Everybody can be great . . . because anybody can serve. You don't have to have a college degree to serve. You don't have to make your subject and your verb agree to serve. You only need a heart full of grace. A soul generated by love.

—MARTIN LUTHER KING, JR.

Traveling as a volunteer departs from conventional adventure travel and cultural immersion experiences in one very important way: the wondrous experience of giving. Volunteers live and work with local people who need assistance in fulfilling life's basic needs—food, shelter, clothing, education—development projects that help people to help themselves. Each volunteer's energy, creativity, and labor are put to use as they gain a genuine, firsthand understanding of other people.

First off, you must realize that volunteering costs money. Many volunteer organizations are underfunded and understaffed (and their staffs are often overworked). They keep their efforts alive by the contributions volunteers provide for the experience. Program expenses, transportation costs, meals, rent, health insurance, and the cost of developing and maintaining volunteer placements all add up. To put this "participation fee" into perspective, think about the costs associated with running a local animal shelter in your community. Creative funding and the work of volunteers makes it all possible. As you begin your search for a volunteer project, keep in mind that you will probably have to pay for many of these basic expenses.

Fees for volunteer projects can start as low as $300 for one- to three-week experiences and can grow to $4,500 or more for programs that take you to places further from the U.S. and that are longer in duration. Many programs offer all-inclusive fees, which include food, lodging, ground transportation, visas, and project materials.

Once you've compiled a list of volunteer programs that fit your criteria for volunteering, it's helpful to put together a list of questions that you can ask of each:

- Are there specific projects you'll be working on, or will you just get involved where help is needed?
- How many volunteers work on a particular project?
- Will you be living with a family in the community or with other volunteers?
- What types of food will be available?
- Does the village have running water?
- How long do the projects last?
- Is there time for additional travel once the project ends?
- What does the program fee include?

As you formulate your questions, it's best to call each program to get a feel for their organization. First impressions are a big deal to me. Talking to a knowledgeable and experienced program coordinator will outweigh any glossy catalog that you receive in the mail.

Volunteering should be fun and rewarding. It is a great way to get involved in a community, learn about a new place in our world, give something to a cause you believe in, and gain useful skills and experience. Go with an open mind and an open heart; you will return enriched with a better understanding of yourself and the world around you.

CHECK OUT THESE PROGRAMS

- Amigos de las Américas (page 260) • Brethren Volunteer Service (page 235)
- Concern America (page 266) • Global Citizens Network (page 268) • Global Service Corps (page 269)
- Global Volunteers (page 269) • Lutheran Volunteer Corps (page 248) • Peacework (page 280)
- SCI—International Voluntary Service USA (page 285) • Volunteers for Peace (page 287)

Recommended Resources. . . . .

Idealist.org (www.idealist.org) is a project of Action Without Borders, a nonprofit organization that promotes the sharing of ideas, information, and resources to help build a world where all people can live free and productive lives. Visitors can search (or browse) their online database for volunteer and internship opportunities at nonprofits (it includes more than twenty thousand organizations in 140 countries) as well as sign up for a daily job and internship "alert" or e-mail newsletter.

InterAction is a coalition of more than 150 U.S.-based nonprofits working to promote disaster relief, sustainable development, ethical standards, and public policy in 165 countries around the world. Volunteer, internship, and fellowship opportunities with these programs can be found in their ninety-seven-page publication, *Global Work* ($14, which includes shipping). In addition to the opportunities in the guide, *Monday Developments* lists dozens of job opportunities at international organizations (as well as in-depth articles and resources) on a biweekly basis. Sample copies are $4 or $65 for the year. InterAction, 1717 Massachusetts Ave., NW, Suite 801, Washington, DC 20036; (202) 667-8227, (202) 667-8236 (fax), publications@interaction.org, www.interaction.org/jobs

Known as the "Christian career specialists," **Intercristo** is a nonprofit ministry service dedicated to assisting Christians with their careers through career-building resources and a job referral program. After filling out an extensive application through their web site, you are provided with customized and up-to-date listings of short-term and career openings with nonprofit Christian organizations all over the United States and overseas. Most of the domestic job openings are salaried positions, and the majority of overseas positions require you to raise your own support. The fee of $59.95 is good for a three-month period. Intercristo, Career Specialist, 19303 Fremont Ave. North, Seattle, WA 98133-3800; (800) 251-7740, (206) 546-7330, (206) 546-7375 (fax), aab@crista.org, www.jobsinaflash.org

Sponsored by The National Assembly, the **Internships in Youth Development** database (www.nassembly.org) lists more than two thousand paid and unpaid internships in more than five hundred nonprofit human service and youth development organizations nationwide.

The **Quaker Information Center** provides a smorgasbord of Quaker and non-Quaker opportunities ranging from weekend work camps, volunteer service, internships, and alternatives to the Peace Corps, both in the U.S. and around the world. Detailed information and links on three hundred listings (for people of all ages) are available for free through their web site or can be sent through the mail for a donation of $10. Quaker Information Center, Peggy Morscheck, Director, 1501 Cherry St., Philadelphia, PA 19102; (215) 241-7024, (215) 567-2096 (fax), quakerinfo@afsc.org, www.afsc.org/qic.htm

The ultimate measure of a man is not where he stands in moments of comfort and convenience, but where he stands at times of challenge and controversy. —MARTIN LUTHER KING, JR.

Recruiting New Teachers publishes a variety of handbooks that offer guidance for prospective teachers. Recommended resources include *How to Become a Teacher*, a lively and comprehensive guide for those seriously considering the teaching profession, and *Take This Job and Love It!*, a guide and directory of programs for adults making a career change into teaching. Prospective teachers are encouraged to visit their web site for additional resources and information. Recruiting New Teachers, 385 Concord Ave., Suite 103, Belmont, MA 02478; (800) 458-3224, (617) 489-6000, rnt@rnt.org, www.rnt.org

The Catholic Network of Volunteer Service (CNVS) publishes **Response**, an annual directory of volunteer opportunities that includes 180 faith-based, full-time volunteer programs in the United States and in more than eighty countries worldwide. Volunteers of all ages, committed to social justice, spirituality, and a simple lifestyle, work in soup kitchens or family shelters, direct programs for at-risk youth, teach in schools, minister to the abused, provide health care, build houses, or offer service to refugees—to name just some of the many opportunities. Programs vary in length from a few weeks to a few years, although the average length of a domestic placement is one year and an international program, two years. Each program has its own combination of benefits and compensation; most include a stipend, room and board, and health insurance. All provide orientation and training, and some may offer retreats or language training. Call for your free copy of the directory, or view the most current listings on their web site. Long-term, full-time administrative volunteers are also needed at the CNVS office in Washington, DC. Benefits include a stipend, health insurance, and housing in a Christian community setting. Catholic Network of Volunteer Service, Gerry Lambert, Associate Director, 4121 Harewood Rd., NE, Washington, DC 20017-1593; (800) 543-5046, (202) 529-1100, (202) 526-1094 (fax), volunteer@cnvs.org, www.cnvs.org

RESOURCES

for many, working, learning, living, and traveling abroad for extended periods of time becomes the adventure of a lifetime. Many venture to unknown lands to fill a gap of time in their lives, improve their fluency in a foreign language, meet new and interesting people, and/or build self-reliance. Whatever your case, by traveling to a new land, you'll have the chance to immerse yourself in the culture and meet people on their own terms rather than experiencing it as a tourist would. This section will provide you with hundreds of working options to choose from along with the tools to shape your journey of self-discovery.

The world only exists in your eyes. You can make it as big or as small as you want.

—F. SCOTT FITZGERALD

Unique Opportunities to Explore in This Section:

▶ Whether you need the security of a prearranged job and living situation prior to going overseas or not, there are plenty of programs that will help you with your efforts. Alliances Abroad *(page 260)* or InterExchange *(page 272)* will take care of all your overseas arrangements, while BUNAC USA *(page 262)* or the Council on International Educational Exchange *(page 267)* will provide you with the coveted work permit to legally work in another country.

▶ Maybe you've heard before that a journey overseas is a journey of self-discovery. The nature of living and working in a foreign environment tests your formerly held beliefs and presents you with a whole new menu of life options. See what steps Elizabeth Kruempelmann took to transform her overseas idea into a rewarding international lifestyle *(page 264)*.

▶ Is it possible that a honeymoon adventure can bring out one's calling in life? Find out how the founders of Global Volunteers turned a two-week vacation into their life's work *(page 274)*.

▶ You'll find that many budget-conscious travelers who adventure overseas find their way to one of more than six thousand hostels tucked about the world. This special section focuses on everything you ever wanted to know about hostelling *(page 282)*.

Photo Credit: ElderTreks

Exchanging ideas about the world comes naturally when adventuring abroad.

ABROAD
ADVENTURES

ALLIANCES ABROAD

Work/Travel • Worldwide • 2 Weeks–1 Year
www.alliancesabroad.com

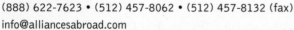

Nicole Rossi, Program Director
409 Deep Eddy Ave.
Austin, TX 78703
(888) 622-7623 • (512) 457-8062 • (512) 457-8132 (fax)
info@alliancesabroad.com

••

ALLIANCES ABROAD offers a mélange of programs that assist people of all ages to live, work, or study in more than seventy places all over the world (from Africa to Iceland). Specific programs include language classes; art, culinary, and cultural classes; volunteer and internship programs; au pair and homestay placements; and group tours. In general, you tell Alliances what you want to do, where you want to go, and when you want to go, and their "globally aware" and trained staff will turn your dream into reality. Programs last anywhere from two weeks to one year and previous language experience is not necessary. The placement fee (which ranges from $1,200 for a four-week language program to $7,000 for a one-year volunteer program) includes predeparture materials, placement in a program, orientation upon arrival, placement with a host family or student residence (which may or may not include board), support from a local staff representative, emergency insurance, and placement in a service project. Airfare and visa fees are additional. Call for an application packet.

AMERICAN INSTITUTE FOR FOREIGN STUDY

Educational Travel • Worldwide • Year-Round
www.aifs.org

Program Coordinator
River Plaza, 9 W. Broad St.
Stamford, CT 06902-3788
(800) 727-2437
college.info@aifs.com

••

THE AMERICAN INSTITUTE FOR FOREIGN STUDY (AIFS) and its affiliates organize cultural exchange programs throughout the world for more than fifty thousand students each year. The programs teach young people from around the globe to understand each others' qualities and differences as well as the ability to function in different cultures. For those residing in the U.S., AIFS coordinates summer educational travel programs for high school students and teachers who travel on one- to four-week educational trips in Europe, China, Mexico, Africa, Australia, and the Amer-

icas; other offerings include internships in London and study abroad programs. For those living in places other than the U.S., AIFS organizes au pair, academic year, and summer camp personnel placements in the U.S.

THE AMERICAN–SCANDINAVIAN FOUNDATION

Farming/Teaching • Finland • 2–10 Months
www.amscan.org/training.htm

Exchange Division Coordinator
15 E. 65 St.
New York, NY 10021
(212) 879-9779 • (212) 249-3444 (fax)
training@amscan.org

••

JOIN IN THE DAILY WORK on small family farms in Finland or teach English as a foreign language to Finns at public schools or private firms. Farming participants can work up to six months beginning in late spring/summer, and earn around $350 per month (after taxes and room and board deduction). English teachers work from two months up to an academic year starting in August and earn approximately $900 per month, although they are responsible for rent (which is generally $250 per month). Students or recent graduates who are U.S. citizens (or permanent residents) aged twenty-one to thirty are eligible to apply. There is an application fee of $50 (deadlines: farming—January 1; teaching—February 1). ASF can also assist with work permits for those who have a job offer in Scandinavia.

AMIGOS DE LAS AMÉRICAS

Service Learning • Latin America
• 8 Months
www.amigoslink.org

Glenn Bayron, Director of Domestic Programs
5618 Star Ln.
Houston, TX 77057
(800) 231-7796 • (713) 782-5290 • (713) 782-9267 (fax)
info@amigoslink.org

••

THROUGH THE UNPARALLELED "Amigos experience" more than eighteen thousand young volunteers have completed extensive leadership and community service training programs that prepare them to spend a summer as volunteers in ongoing community health and environmental development projects throughout Latin America (including Bolivia, Brazil, Costa Rica, Dominican Republic, Ecuador, Honduras, Mexico, and Paraguay).

The Experience: The program begins with an extensive experience-based training program both in the U.S. and Latin America. Once trained, volunteers are assigned to ongoing health and environmental programs partnered with sponsoring agencies in the host countries, ranging from community sanitation and nutrition education to home improvement and family garden projects. Participants typically live with families in small communities in rural and semi-urban areas and are supervised by more experienced volunteers and officials of the host agency. Amigos volunteers who have participated actively in training programs and who excel in the field program are always encouraged to apply for field staff positions.

Commitment: After a six-month training period, programs range from six to eight weeks during the summer.

Perks: There is a fee of $3,000 to $3,400, which includes round-trip international airfare, training materials, orientation, weekly training sessions, field project supplies, chapter support, host-country room, board, and transportation, and professional staff support. Many participants are able to cover program fees through fundraising efforts. Amigos has put together a fund-raising booklet that contains suggestions that have been proven successful by veteran volunteers. Participation fee scholarships and college tuition scholarships up to $1,400 are available to applicants with proven financial need.

Ideal Candidate: Volunteers must be at least sixteen years of age and have two years of Spanish or Portuguese completed before training. They must also successfully complete six months of Amigos training and several screenings or proficiency tests as well as actively participate in fund-raising and provide proof of health insurance.

> *Amigos volunteers are flexible, motivated, able to live and work independently and as team members, energetic, adventuresome, enthusiastic, and interested in public health, quality of life, and community service.*

AMITY INSTITUTE

Teaching • Latin America • 4–10 Months
www.amity.org

Karen Sullivan, Volunteer Teacher Coordinator
10671 Roselle St., Suite 101
San Diego, CA 92121-1525
(858) 455-6364 • (858) 455-6597 (fax)
mail@amity.org

••

Volunteers with Amity have the opportunity to teach English language classes at schools in Argentina, Costa Rica, Dominican Republic, Mexico, or Peru. One semester and full-year assignments are available, beginning either in March or late August. Applicants must be native English speakers and have a working knowledge of Spanish, an undergraduate degree, previous experience working or traveling abroad, and a personal commitment to international education and teaching. Volunteers receive a homestay experience with a host family, meals, and a weekly stipend of $15 to $20 provided by the host school. The candidate is responsible for round-trip transportation between the U.S. and the host school, international health insurance (about $50 per month), $150 per month for personal spending money, and an administration fee of $100 (payable upon placement).

AMIZADE

Community Service • Australia/Latin America/USA • 1–3 Weeks
www.amizade.org

Dr. Daniel Weiss, Executive Director
367 S. Graham St.
Pittsburgh, PA 15232
(888) 973-4443
volunteer@amizade.org

••

Amizade, the word for friendship in Portuguese, is a non-profit organization that provides one- to three-week volunteer programs in six sites around the world (the Brazilian Amazon, Bolivian Andes, Appalachia, the Korrawinga aboriginal community in Australia, and the Greater Yellowstone, and Navajo Nation in the United States). These short-term volunteer vacations offer a mix of community service, recreation, and the unique chance to participate in another culture. Past projects have included building a vocational training center for street children to doing historic preservation and environmental cleanup. Most projects are centered around the construction or renovation of schools, health posts, and environmental centers. Volunteers also have the opportunity to hike in the Andes, explore a rain forest, or possibly visit Inca ruins as part of their experience. The program fee ($595 for Yellowstone up to $5,750 for Latin American destinations) includes primitive room and board (and for Latin America, round-trip airfare from Miami).

The great thing in this world is not so much where we are, but in what direction we are moving. —Oliver Wendell Holmes

261

AU PAIR IN EUROPE

Au Pair • Europe • 3–12 Months
www.princeent.com/aupair

Corinne and John Prince, Program Directors
P.O. Box 68056
Blakely Postal Outlet
Hamilton, ON L8M 3M7
Canada
(905) 545-6305 • (905) 544-4121 (fax)
aupair@princeent.com

••

SINCE 1969, Au Pair in Europe has been offering au pair positions—today in more than twenty countries around the world—for those aged eighteen to thirty. Contracts range from three months (usually in the summer) to one year. Along with room and board, au pairs generally receive between $75 to $120 per week (for thirty hours' work per week). In most countries, the English language is quite acceptable with the exception of Germany, which requires that you have a good command of the German language. Programs in France and Italy require au pairs to attend a language course (usually one to three classes per week) in order to obtain a working visa. (The host family will help with the details.) There is a program fee of $425, which does not include airfare.

BERLITZ INTERNATIONAL

Language • Worldwide • Year-Round
www.berlitz.com

Study Abroad Director
400 Alexander Park
Princeton, NJ 08540-6306
(800) 457-7958 • (609) 514-3133 • (609) 514-9689 (fax)
bsa@berlitz.com

••

YOU MAY FIND YOURSELF speaking a new language before you know it. The Berlitz method is designed to teach you a new language the same way you learned your first one—naturally, through conversation. All day, even during meals, you'll be speaking, listening, and thinking in your new language with a team of instructors five to six days a week for almost eight hours a day. Through role plays, ranging from telephone conversations to making travel arrangements, you'll be exposed to just about every linguistic setting you'll encounter abroad. Or for those who want a full immersion in the language and culture, Berlitz offers the Study Abroad Program. Participants can study the language all day or just for four hours; stay with a host family, live in a short-term apartment, or stay in a hotel;

and visit for one to eight weeks in length. Study Abroad rates typically include tuition, materials, and accommodations with a host family that includes two meals per day.

BUNAC USA

Work/Travel • UK/Australia • 1–12 Months
www.bunac.org

Program Director
P.O. Box 430
Southbury, CT 06488
(800) 462-8622 • (203) 264-0901 • (203) 264-0251 (fax)
info@bunacusa.org

••

THE BRITISH UNIVERSITIES NORTH AMERICA CLUB—commonly known as BUNAC—provides U.S. full-time students aged eighteen and upward with the coveted Blue Card, allowing participants to obtain paid work experiences for a maximum of six months in England, Scotland, Wales, and Northern Ireland. An orientation is provided in BUNAC's London office, where you'll receive vital information on jobs and accommodations, maps and student guides, advice and counseling, and government paperwork. After filling out an application (which includes a $225 fee), you'll receive a program handbook outlining general living and accommodation information, general advice, and fifty pages of employer listings ranging from pubtenders to "career-type" positions. It's suggested participants bring along at least $1,000 to cover personal and living expenses prior to your first paycheck arriving. Just recently BUNAC started a pilot program to work and travel in Australia for up to twelve months for a fee of $550. Call for further details.

CASA XELAJÚ

Language/Community Service • Guatemala • 2–6 Months
www.casaxelaju.com

Julio Batres, Director
P.O. Box 3275
Austin, TX 78764-3275
(512) 416-6991 • (512) 416-8965 (fax)
info@casaxelaju.com

••

CASA XELAJÚ (pronounced "shay-la-hoo") provides Spanish and Mayan language study, internships and volunteer work experience, homestays, and tour and travel programs in Guatemala. Internships might include work in human rights, the medical field, education, social work, or vocational education. The internship and volunteer program has a fee of $68 to $75 per week, which includes supervision, homestay experience, and three meals per day. The language program tuition of $150 to $180 per week includes five hours of instruction five days per week, daily social and cultural activities, homestay, and three meals per day. Participants must make a minimum commitment of two months.

CDS INTERNATIONAL

International Education • Germany • 3–12 Months
www.cdsintl.org

Margaret Shonat, Program Officer, Special Projects
871 UN Plaza, 15th Floor
New York, NY 10017-1814
(212) 497-3500 • (212) 497-3535 (fax)
info@cdsintl.org

CDS INTERNATIONAL is a nonprofit organization dedicated to developing and enhancing opportunities for Americans to gain meaningful, practical training in Germany. While all programs contain an internship component, some have academic or language training elements as well.

The Experience: CDS offers three unique programs for those who want to broaden their professional and life experience while living, working, and learning in Germany. The Work Authorization Program provides participants with the necessary documents for employment in Germany once they have secured an internship position on their own. The Placement Program, for those up to age thirty, provides internship placement in Germany in the fields of business, graphic design, marketing, Internet/multimedia, engineering, or hotel management. The Scholarship/Fellowship Program is composed of two programs: Congress-Bundestag Youth Exchange for Young Professionals, intended primarily for young American adults aged eighteen to twenty-four in business, technical, vocational and agricultural fields, and the Robert Bosch Foundation Fellowship Program, which enables those from twenty-three to thirty-four with graduate training to acquire an in-depth understanding of the political, economic, and cultural environment of Europe.

Perks: Salaries vary depending on previous experience and training but average 1,500 deutsche marks (DM) per month, which is generally enough to cover basic living expenses. Round-trip transportation, related travel to seminars in Europe, and health insurance are provided for fellowship programs; internship placement participants must cover these costs. There is a participation fee of $200 to $400 for all programs.

Ideal Candidate: All programs require German language proficiency. A high level of interest for working in and acclimating yourself to Germany and its culture is necessary.

Getting In: Application deadlines vary with each program; however, most are generally five months prior to the departure date.

CENTER FOR GLOBAL EDUCATION

Educational Travel • Worldwide • 1–3 Weeks
www.augsburg.edu/global

Travel Seminar Coordinator
Augsburg College
2211 Riverside Ave., Box 307
Minneapolis, MN 55454
(800) 299-8889 • (612) 330-1159 • (612) 330-1695 (fax)
globaled@augsburg.edu

THE CENTER FOR GLOBAL EDUCATION takes participants around the world on short-term travel seminars, encountering the peoples and situations of Mexico, Central America, the Caribbean, and the southern Africa region. These one- to three-week educational trips will bring participants face to face with people of other cultures—people struggling for justice and human dignity. Each day consists of two to four meetings with community representatives, ranging from grassroots organizers to business leaders and representatives of the ruling and opposition political parties, as well as visits to key historical or archaeological sites. The program attracts a broad range of participants, from ages sixteen to eighty, from all ethnic backgrounds and from all professional areas. All have an interest in listening to and learning from people in the community. Seminar fees range from $1,495 to $3,995, which include meetings with community representatives, lodging, all meals, translation, local travel, and usually round-trip airfare.

A WHOLE NEW MENU OF LIFE OPTIONS

Elizabeth Kruempelmann

Maybe you've heard before that a journey overseas is a journey of self-discovery. Why is it that we have to physically and mentally immerse ourselves in a foreign culture in order to know who we really are and where we really come from? The nature of living in a foreign environment tests your formerly held beliefs and presents you with a whole new menu of life options. It's like seeing the world for the first time from the top of a mountain peak instead of the bottom of a valley. You realize there's a wider world of adventure, discovery, and opportunity waiting for you!

Going abroad for the purpose of gaining international experience is an indescribably unique and enriching opportunity that will undoubtedly have a positive influence on your personal and professional growth. But what does it really mean to have international experience in today's world? First and foremost, you'll attain a more balanced, less ethnocentric view of the world as you learn to

better understand yourself, your country, and world issues, using your host country as your new frame of reference. Second, language and travel experience will put you on par with your counterparts worldwide who grow up learning at least one foreign language, usually English, and who know how to navigate foreign countries with confidence. Third, the nature of living abroad will automatically open up an abundance of career and social opportunities as you continue to have more in common with others who have overseas experience.

For some people, taking part in an overseas work program revealed in this guide will mean an opportunity to gain international work experience and skills in order to have a wider choice of career possibilities and better financial benefits. For others, an overseas work experience will be part of a series of fun, exciting, and mind-expanding travel adventures to various areas of the globe. And for the few who get really hooked, participating in an overseas work adventure will be the first step to leading a very rewarding international lifestyle.

My experience falls into the last category. My story actually began in 1989 when I studied in Denmark and developed an insatiable desire to experience the world and become proficient in a few foreign languages. After I returned to the States from my year abroad, I was determined to find a way back to Europe—back to the daily intellectual stimulation of living in a foreign land rich in history, culture, and tradition. Of course, I knew quitting my job to pursue my international experience was a risk but a risk worth taking, and a risk that I can say has paid off in ways I never would have imagined!

In 1992 I took part in the Carl Duisberg Society's (CDS) exchange program to work in Germany, which proved to be a turning point for my personal and professional growth. CDS provided me with the proper work and residency permits, a one-month language course, and a homestay experience with a family. Finding an internship and a permanent place to live was my own problem. It was far from easy trying to secure a job with hardly any work experience; my rudimentary knowledge of the German language and a high unemployment rate in Germany made this difficult.

After several months of plugging away at the job search, I was happy to land an internship at a management consulting firm where I assisted with project presentations and proposal translations. As my internship came to an end and my German gradually improved, I decided to prolong my work and residency permits to get more out of my stay in Germany.

I had made it over the hardest part of adapting to the German culture and was finally starting to enjoy the language and social life. By securing a

flexible and well-paying job teaching English at the local language institute, I was not only able to extend my stay but also had more time and money to travel and make friends with other foreigners and Germans alike. Together we enjoyed bike tours around the countryside, German festivals, boat cruises on the Rhine, and weekends in Paris and Amsterdam, among many other unforgettable travel adventures.

At the time, the CDS program provided me with a window of opportunity to learn a language, get international work experience, and travel relatively cheaply around Europe. However, as I reflect now on my total experiences of studying and working in four foreign countries, learning three foreign languages, and traveling to thirty lands, the CDS program was my basic training for living out my dream of an international way of life. Some of the most important traits I learned included how to understand the world from a global perspective, how to take on a chameleon-like behavior to adapt to the local community, and how to become an opportunist by gaining something positive out of every situation. Whether you have a one-time experience abroad or continue to pursue international opportunities for the rest of your life, your overseas adventures will set you apart from the norm, uniquely shape your journey of self-discovery, and ultimately lead to a more fulfilling life!

—Elizabeth Kruempelmann currently lives with her husband in Portugal (and rumor has it she's working on a work abroad guidebook). Her international experience includes international business studies at the University of Copenhagen and teaching and marketing positions in Germany, Poland, and Portugal. You can reach her at ekruempe@hotmail.com.

Each friend represents a world in us, a world possibly not born until they arrive,
and it is only by this meeting that a new world is born. —ANAÏS NIN

CENTRE FOR INTERNATIONAL MOBILITY

International Education • Finland • 1–18 Months
http://finland.cimo.fi

Practical Training Coordinator
P.O. Box 343
FIN-00531, Helsinki
Finland
(011) 358-9-7747 7033
cimoinfo@cimo.fi

THE CENTRE FOR INTERNATIONAL MOBILITY arranges temporary practical training opportunities for those aged eighteen to thirty. Placements include agriculture and horticulture (farms and market gardens), hotels and restaurants, tourism, nursing, language teaching assistance program (teaching English, German, or French), and a family/working guest program. The training period normally takes place during the summer months; however, it is possible to extend the period up to eighteen months. A reasonable wage for your work can be expected (about $800 to $1,000 per month) along with accommodations. As a general rule, applications should be sent four to five months prior to your planned training period.

CHÂTEAU DE JEAN D'HEURS

Castle • France • April–November
www.chateaux-france.com/~jeandheurs

Fadel Mezian, Program Manager
55000, Lisle En Rigault
France
(011) 33 3 29 71 31 77
jeandheurs@chateaux-france.com

LIVE AND WORK in a French castle! Château de Jean d'Heurs is a superb example of eighteenth-century French château architecture. Officially classified as a national historic monument, it is noted for its majestic staircases and monumental ironwork. The castle is about a two-hour train ride from Paris (which will cost you about US$30). Housekeeper/gardener and assistant art restoration painter/plasterer positions are available, each with a flexible thirty-hour-per-week work schedule that gives you plenty of time to explore this beautiful region. In exchange for work, housing is provided in the castle (with complete use of the castle's kitchen and laundry). Program dates are flexible, however, the château is open April 1 through November 30.

CHINA TEACHING PROGRAM

Teaching • China • Academic Year
www.ac.wwu.edu/~ctp/info.htm

Todd Lundgren, Program Director
Western Washington University
Old Main 530A
Bellingham, WA 98225-9047
(360) 650-3753 • (360) 650-2847 (fax)
ctp@cc.wwu.edu

FOR A TUITION FEE of $1,200, the China Teaching Program provides a five-week training session at Western Washington University followed by a teaching placement at a Chinese institution for an academic year. The training, which begins in mid-July of each year, focuses on Chinese language development, an overview of the Chinese culture, preparation in living overseas, and teaching English as a foreign language. In early September, participants begin their assignment in China, teaching English speaking, listening, writing, and reading as well as contemporary American culture. The salary of $160 to $400 per month is adequate for buying food and other necessities in China. Housing and basic medical care are provided by the host institution.

CONCERN AMERICA

Refugee Aid • Latin America/Africa • 2 Years
www.concernamerica.org

Janine Mills, Recruitment Coordinator
2020 N. Broadway, Third Floor
P.O. Box 1790
Santa Ana, CA 92702
(800) 266-2376 • (714) 953-8575 • (714) 953-1242 (fax)
concamerinc@earthlink.net

CONCERN AMERICA is an international development and refugee aid organization that has staffed development projects in more than a dozen countries since 1972. Healthy children, appropriate sanitation systems, potable water, public health systems, and lasting employment opportunities are a few of the results from the work of Concern America.

The Experience: Through the work of volunteers, who are professionals in the fields of health, public health, nutrition, health education, adult literacy, sanitation, agroforestry, appropriate technology, and community organizing, Concern America assists impoverished communities and refugees in developing countries in their efforts to improve their living conditions. The program emphasizes empowering and training of community members in order to impart skills and knowledge that remain with the community long after the volunteer is gone. Volunteers currently serve in development projects in El Salvador, Guatemala, Honduras, Mexico, and Mozambique.

Perks: Concern America provides room and board, round-trip transportation, health insurance, a small monthly stipend of $250 per month, a repatriation allowance (first year—$50 per month, second year—$100 per month, third year—$150 per month), and support services from the home office.

Ideal Candidate: Applicants must have a degree/experience in public health, medicine, nutrition, nursing, agriculture, community development, education, or appropriate technology. Fluency in Spanish (except for the project in Mozambique, where Portuguese is required) or ability to learn Spanish at one's own expense is also required. All candidates must be at least twenty-one years of age.

The good we secure for ourselves is precarious and uncertain until it is secured for all of us and incorporated into our common life. —Jane Addams

COUNCIL ON INTERNATIONAL EDUCATIONAL EXCHANGE

Work Abroad • Worldwide • 1–6 Months
www.councilexchanges.org

Work Abroad
205 E. 42nd St.
New York, NY 10017-5706
(888) 268-6245 • (212) 822-2600 • (212) 822-2699 (fax)
info@councilexchanges.org

SINCE ITS FOUNDING IN 1947, the Council on International Educational Exchange (commonly known as Council) has been active in the development and administration of study, work, travel, and volunteer programs worldwide. Work abroad programs are available in Australia, Canada, Costa Rica, Ireland, France, Germany, and New Zealand; however, this list may change as new programs are developed each year. Council also has internship and seasonal staff employment opportunities at field offices in the U.S. and abroad.

The Experience: If you're a college student or recent graduate who has three to six months to enjoy an unforgettable travel experience, you can take advantage of Council's Work Abroad Program. Most participants find short-term or seasonal service industry positions, such as waiting

tables, bartending, office temping, and retail sales. Prior to departure, Council provides a handbook and general program information. An orientation, employment information, counseling services, and the use of a Council or a cooperating organization office from which to job-hunt is provided upon arrival.

Perks: There is a program fee of $300 to $400 (depending on country), which includes the highly coveted work permit to legally work in another country, along with all of Council's services. While working, most participants earn enough money to cover day-to-day expenses.

Ideal Candidate: Any applicant who is at least eighteen years old and currently in college (or recently graduated) is accepted into the program. There is no language requirement for most countries; however, for programs in France, Germany, and Costa Rica, candidates must have completed intermediate-level study in the appropriate language.

Council also sponsors International Volunteer Projects, a two- to four-week work-camp experience in Europe, Africa, Asia, and the Americas—from national parks and forests to inner-city neighborhoods and small towns. Volunteers may choose to build a playground, plant trees, restore a castle, organize a festival, or implement a recreation program for at-risk children. There is a $300 placement fee, which includes room and board. To learn more about these opportunities, a project directory is available in late March (for a fee of $20). Placements begin in April and continue on a first-come, first-served basis until July, by which time most summer projects have been filled. The average age of participants is twenty-one to twenty-five.

CROSS-CULTURAL SOLUTIONS

Service Learning • Africa/India/Peru/Kosovo
• 3 Weeks
www.crossculturalsolutions.org

Steve Rosenthal, Program Director
47 Potter Ave.
New Rochelle, NY 10801
(800) 380-4777 • (914) 632-0022 • (914) 632-8494 (fax)
info@crossculturalsolutions.org

CROSS-CULTURAL SOLUTIONS provides a unique three-week program in which volunteers work in health care, education, or social development projects in New Delhi or Rajgarh, India; Lima, Peru; eastern Ghana; or Macedonia/Kosovo. The program is entirely driven by each volunteer's contribution of $1,850 ($1,950 for Peru; $2,450 for Macedonia/Kosovo), which offsets the cost of food, lodging, and in-country transportation. (Airfare is additional.) All nationalities and backgrounds are welcome, and nearly every candidate is accepted into the program. Apply two months prior to projected start date.

GLOBAL CITIZENS NETWORK

Community Service • Worldwide • 1–3 Weeks
www.globalcitizens.org

Kim Regnier, Program Director
130 N. Howell St.
St. Paul, MN 55104
(800) 644-9292 • (651) 644-0960
gcn@mtn.org

GLOBAL CITIZENS NETWORK sends teams of six to twelve people to rural communities around the world, including Belize, Guatemala, Kenya, Nepal, St. Vincent, the Yucatan, and New Mexico and South Dakota in the United States. The teams, led by a trained team leader, spend one to three weeks in their chosen community and become immersed in the daily life of the local culture. Community projects are initiated by the local people and may include planting trees, digging irrigation trenches, setting up a schoolroom, or building a health clinic. Each day consists of both work and learning. Volunteers stay in local homes or as a group in a community center, and meals are shared with the host family or communally prepared and shared with project hosts. No special skills or experience are required—only an open mind, open heart, and willingness to experience and accept a new culture. The tax-deductible fee ranges from $550 to $1,600. (Airfare is additional.) Volunteers under eighteen years of age must be accompanied by a parent or guardian.

GLOBAL ROUTES

Service Adventures • Worldwide • 5–8 Weeks
www.globalroutes.org

Jessica Grant, Staffing Director
1814 7th St., Suite A
Berkeley, CA 94710
(510) 848-4800 • (510) 848-4801 (fax)
mail@globalroutes.org

THROUGH COMMUNITY SERVICE and cross-cultural exchange programs designed by Global Routes, North American high school and college students stretch their minds by living and working with people in small, rural communities throughout the world. Grassroots community development and homestays in Latin America, Africa, Asia, and the United States are at the heart of these experiences. Students work side by side with their host families on projects selected by the community, which might include constructing a community center, teaching local children, or reforesting surrounding areas. Experiential learning covers everything from cultural sensitivity to the history and language of the area.

The Experience: Adventure leaders (one man, one woman) will lead a group of up to eighteen high school students or provide support and coordination for college-level interns who live either singly or in pairs in villages. The leader is also responsible for organizing the group's in-country orientation and managing the debriefing process prior to their return. Preference is given to applicants who are able to lead two or more programs sequentially. The intention of

Photo Credit: Global Citizens Network

A Global Citizens Network volunteer and a local man from Kenya dig the foundation for a health clinic.

the programs is to place students in an environment radically different from their own where they can reflect on their own life and culture. Leaders must facilitate this process in a fun and creative way in addition to meeting the logistical demands of managing a group in a developing country.

Commitment: Positions are offered year-round and roughly correspond to summer vacation and academic terms. The positions generally involve a four- to seven-week commitment, as well as attending a five-day orientation prior to departure.

Perks: Group leaders receive $225 per week for four- to seven-week high school programs or $2,000 for 2 1/2-month-long college programs. All living expenses and round-trip travel to/from the program site are also covered. The biggest perk is the opportunity to see amazing places and meet interesting people.

Ideal Candidate: Leader applicants must be at least twenty-four years of age, have extensive experience working with high school and/or college students and travel experience in the region where you wish to lead (preference is given to those who have lived/worked in the region) as well as be certified in first aid and CPR. All Latin American program leaders must be fluent in Spanish, or French for the Guadeloupe program.

Getting In: Applicants are encouraged to visit their web site for more information and application materials.

GLOBAL SERVICE CORPS

Educational Travel • Worldwide • 2 Weeks–6 Months
www.globalservicecorps.org

Rick Lathrop, Executive Director
300 Broadway, Suite 28
San Francisco, CA 94133-3312
(415) 788-3666 • (415) 788-7324 (fax)
gsc@igc.org

••

GLOBAL SERVICE CORPS (GSC) creates opportunities for people, young and old, who want to share their time and experience to help make the world a better place. GSC participants live in developing countries and work on a wide range of projects designed to provide communities with the means to function sustainably. At the same time, participants gain a new perspective on the world we share.

The Experience: As a GSC volunteer, you may find yourself picking coffee beans in a Costa Rican rain forest community, teaching English to Thai Buddhist monks, or helping Kenyan women fight AIDS. The most rewarding aspect of this experience is spending time with the people of the host communities, sharing ideas, and breaking down cultural stereotypes. Many volunteers, in their spare time, visit nearby temples, rain forests, hot springs, or volcanic lakes, depending on the country. GSC also offers internships at their headquarters in San Francisco.

Commitment: Short-term (two to four weeks), long-term (two to six months), and student internship programs are available.

Perks: Program fees range from $1,695 to $2,895, which includes airport pickup, in-country transportation, accommodations (hotel, lodge, or homestay), meals, travel excursions, and project administration.

Ideal Candidate: Volunteers must be at least twenty years old, flexible, adaptable to the customs and culture of their host country, and willing to perform a valuable service to a community in need.

Getting In: Call for application materials. Apply at least two months prior to departure date.

GLOBAL VOLUNTEERS

Service Adventures • Worldwide • 1–3 Weeks
www.globalvolunteers.org

Volunteer Coordinator
375 E. Little Canada Rd.
St. Paul, MN 55117-1628
(800) 487-1074 • (651) 407-6100 • (651) 482-0915 (fax)
email@globalvolunteers.org

••

EACH YEAR GLOBAL VOLUNTEERS sends more than 150 teams of volunteers who live and work with local people on human and economic development projects identified by the community as important to their long-term development. "Travel that feeds the soul" sums up the volunteer experience, where each participant's energy, creativity, and labor are put to use as they gain a genuine, firsthand understanding of how other people live day to day. Development projects are available in twenty countries throughout Africa, the Americas, Asia, the Caribbean, Europe, and the Pacific.

The Experience: The work projects encompass six primary categories: English development, caring for children, teaching basic subjects, community infrastructure, health care, and business instruction and consultation. Volunteers might teach conversational English to elementary classrooms in Poland, work with mentally disabled children in Ecuador, assist with building houses or community gardens in Ghana, provide basic health services to com-

Unless one says good-bye to what one loves, and unless one travels to completely new territories,
one can expect merely a long wearing away of oneself. —JEAN DUBUFFET

munities in the Cook Islands, or teach the principles of business management and free enterprise in China. Volunteers on U.S. service programs have a unique opportunity to experience deeply rooted cultures that lend rich texture to the American fabric.

Commitment: Programs generally last one to three weeks, depending on the destination.

Perks: A tax-deductible program fee ranges from $400 to $2,395. Most of this fee pays for program costs such as food, lodging, ground transportation, team leader expenses, project materials, volunteer coordination, program development, volunteer materials and communication, and on-site consultants. Airfare, visas, and medical insurance are additional costs. Volunteers find community meals abundant, sometimes adventurous, and a refreshing change for the palate. Lodging is generally double occupancy in hotels, guest houses, community centers, or private homes.

Ideal Candidate: Volunteers typically share common characteristics, such as flexibility, compassion, a sense of adventure, and most important, the desire to work with and learn from local people in the host community. Volunteers are drawn from all occupations and backgrounds, and mostly from throughout the United States and Canada (generally between the ages of thirty and seventy-five). There are no language or professional requirements for participation in most programs.

Getting In: Call for the most current brochure or visit their web site for the latest news. Applicants must complete their application materials one to three months prior to their departure date.

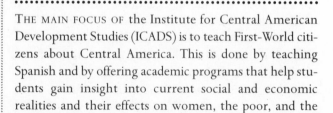

If our national anthem weren't "The Star-Spangled Banner," it would be an infectious symphony of Tex-Mex polkas, mystical Lakota drumming, Mississippi Delta blues, cowboy soliloquies, and Appalachian reels. You don't need to cross the oceans to explore new worlds. Unique and powerful service opportunities exist within U.S. borders. From coast to coast, we can help as developing communities fight the challenges of high unemployment, substandard living conditions, racism, and low per-capita income.

GLOBAL WORKS, INC.

Service Adventures • Worldwide • Summer
www.globalworksinc.com

Biff Houldin, Director
RD 2, Box 356-B
Huntingdon, PA 16652
(814) 667-2411 • (814) 667-3853 (fax)
info@globalworksinc.com

GLOBAL WORKS IS AN environmental and community service–based travel program (with language immersion and homestay options) for students ages fourteen to eighteen. Leaders and staff provide the backbone for these four-week summer adventures that take participants to places that range from small villages in the mountains of Fiji to castle ruins in the Czech Republic. With a work hard, play hard mentality, days are filled with meaningful projects, travel, and exposure to different cultures. Life-changing community projects may include building a new water system, constructing a playground, educating children about wolves, or rebuilding castles in ruins—all of which hope to positively affect the community. The working conditions are excellent and the pay quite good. Applicants must be at least twenty-three years old and have experience in leading groups and working with kids. Immersion program applicants require a true language proficiency.

INSTITUTE FOR CENTRAL AMERICAN DEVELOPMENT STUDIES (ICADS)

Language/Social Justice • Costa Rica • Summer
www.icadscr.com

Program Coordinator
Dept. 826
P.O. Box 025216
Miami, FL 33102-5216
(011) 506-225-0508 • (011) 506-234-1337 (fax)
icads@netbox.com

THE MAIN FOCUS OF the Institute for Central American Development Studies (ICADS) is to teach First-World citizens about Central America. This is done by teaching Spanish and by offering academic programs that help students gain insight into current social and economic realities and their effects on women, the poor, and the environment.

The Experience: Upon arrival in Costa Rica, participants are introduced to their homestay family and are provided with a rigorous orientation and tour of the San José area. The program then begins with three to four weeks of intensive Spanish training (depending on the ability of each student) for 4¹/₂ hours per day, five days per week. Students are taught in a class with no more than three other students. For the next six to seven weeks, students participate in an internship experience (and may have a new homestay family that is closer to the internship site). Students might work in orphanages or health centers, or with women's organizations, environmental organizations, or other community groups.

Commitment: The program extends for ten weeks, beginning in early June.

Perks: There is a program fee of $3,400, which includes airport pickup, intensive Spanish instruction and internship placement, room, breakfast and dinner (the main staple in Costa Rica is rice and beans), laundry service, e-mail service, and group field trips and activities. (Airfare, health insurance, and visa fees are additional costs.)

Ideal Candidate: High school graduates to working professionals (and everyone in between) have participated in an ICADS summer. Applicants must have a good working knowledge of Spanish upon arrival. ICADS also looks for those who feel they would like to provide their labor, energy, and expertise to help further the goals of oppressed groups and social justice organizations in Costa Rica.

Getting In: The "early" application deadline is April 1.

INSTITUTE FOR INTERNATIONAL COOPERATION AND DEVELOPMENT

Global Development • Africa/Latin America/India • 6–20 Months
www.iicd-volunteer.org

Program Director
P.O. Box 520
Williamstown, MA 01267
(413) 458-9828 • (413) 458-3323 (fax)
iicdinfo@berkshire.net

••

THE INSTITUTE FOR International Cooperation and Development (IICD) is a nonprofit inspired by a Scandinavian folk education idea: "education for common people independent of their skills or schooling." The learning takes place for the sole purpose of gaining knowledge and experience, not for fame or credit. IICD trains volunteers to work with people who are in need through community development projects in Africa, Latin America, and India.

The Experience: Volunteers participate in three components of the program: (1) the preparation period, which takes place in Massachusetts and includes regional and lan-

guage studies, practical training, and fund-raising; (2) the international period, when volunteers travel to Africa, India, or Latin America and work in community projects ranging from construction of a new school to educating new teachers; and (3) the follow-up period in the United States, where participants spend time creating educational materials and giving presentations to schools, organizations, and the general public. Becoming a part of IICD means expecting the unexpected and learning new things with others and by yourself. You definitely won't be the same person when you return home.

Commitment: Programs last anywhere from six to twenty months, which includes preparation and follow-up periods in the United States.

Perks: Program fees range from $3,600 to $4,900 (with limited financial aid available). This fee covers the expenses for training, room and board, international health insurance, and airfare. Volunteers participate in extensive fund-raising efforts in support of the institute.

Ideal Candidate: Applicants must be at least eighteen years of age. Applications are encouraged from those who are ready to accept the challenge of undertaking new and demanding tasks, working in a group, and opening themselves to new understandings of the world—and of their own potential.

Getting In: Call for application materials (which are evaluated on a rolling basis).

INSTITUTE OF INTERNATIONAL EDUCATION—LATIN AMERICA

Embassy Education • Mexico • 3 Months
www.iie.org/latinamerica

Coordinator for Educational Services
AmEmbassy Educational Center
P.O. Box 3087
Laredo, TX 78044-3087
(525) 703-0167 • (525) 535-5597 (fax)
iie@solar.sar.net

••

THE INSTITUTE OF International Education's Regional Office for Latin America functions as an integral part of the U.S. Information Service in Mexico, providing information about U.S. education to more than forty thousand people per year. The institute maintains close ties with the American Embassy, Mexican government offices, and universities and schools both in Mexico and the United States.

The Experience: Working in the regional office in Mexico, interns will have the opportunity to work as student advisors, providing information about U.S. educational

A mind that has been stretched by a new experience can never go back to its old dimensions. —OLIVER WENDELL HOLMES

opportunities. Interns also participate in various projects, such as college fairs and the editing of publications.

Commitment: Internships are generally offered for three months throughout the year. Longer assignments can be arranged during the fall and winter.

Perks: A $300 per month stipend is provided. Interns are required to cover travel, lodging, meals, and personal expenses while on assignment. Perks include a great cultural experience and contacts with U.S. Embassy and Mexican institutions.

Ideal Candidate: Applicants must have an interest in international education and Latin America, the ability to communicate well in Spanish and English, and have a general knowledge of Mexican history and culture.

Getting In: Call for application materials. There is no formal deadline; however, applications should be sent at least three months before the desired start date.

INTEREXCHANGE

International Exchange • Europe • 1–12 Months
www.interexchange.org

Casey Slamin, Program Manager
161 Sixth Ave.
New York, NY 10013
(800) 479-0907 • (212) 924-0446 • (212) 924-0575 (fax)
info@interexchange.org

IN ADDITION TO HELPING to arrange for any necessary work and residence permits, InterExchange prearranges work abroad experiences for both U.S. and non-U.S. citizens. The security of a prearranged job and accommodation allows participants to integrate into their new life more easily, without the stress of having to find a position and a place to live. Living and working in another culture enables participants to develop foreign language skills, gain greater insight into another way of life, all while earning money to help offset living and traveling expenses.

The Experience: Have you ever enjoyed a real Finnish sauna, dreamed about ordering a croissant and café au lait in Paris, or wanted to become part of a real Italian family? If so, InterExchange might be the program for you. They have dozens of positions in dozens of countries all over Europe. Typical jobs include picking rhubarb and blackberries, tending livestock, teaching English, being a camp counselor or an au pair, or working at a resort.

Commitment: Placements vary from one month to one year depending on program: Teaching and au pair positions range from six months to a year; farm programs, two to four months; and internships range from summer positions to yearlong ventures.

Perks: A program placement fee ranges from $400 to $450. Along with a self-sustaining work salary, housing is offered with some programs.

Ideal Candidate: Participants must be at least eighteen years of age; some programs have an upper-age limit or language and degree requirements. Additionally, all participants must be covered by health and accident insurance.

Getting In: Applicants are required to purchase a country kit for $2, which explains the details of the programs available. After the proper paperwork is completed, most participants receive word of placement anywhere from four to eight weeks before their requested departure date.

INTERNATIONAL CHRISTIAN YOUTH EXCHANGE

International Exchange • Germany • 6–12 Months
www.icye.org

International Office
Große Hamburger Str. 30
D-10115 Berlin
Germany
(011) 49 30 2839055-0/-1
icye@icye.org

IN 1949, with the world still recovering from the horrors of war, fifty courageous German teenagers ventured across the Atlantic and were welcomed into American host families as ICYE exchangees—and ICYE was born. Building bridges of peace, justice, and understanding through personal encounters has been their goal throughout the past fifty years, with the program now reaching more than thirty countries around the globe.

The Experience: Participants have the opportunity to live with a family or in a shared living situation, and work as volunteers in local projects. Typical assignments include working on a farm in Iceland, helping youth-at-risk in Belgium, coordinating health development projects in Ghana, working and living with disabled people in Italy, or teaching environmental education projects in Costa Rica.

Commitment: ICYE offers six-month and yearlong programs; however, in some countries, such as Belgium, France, and Costa Rica, summer work camps are also offered.

Perks: For programs that extend six months or longer, there is program fee ranging from $3,000 to $6,000. This fee covers room and board and a monthly stipend.

Ideal Candidate: Participants need to be flexible, emotionally mature, motivated to learn about new lifestyles and to become more conscious about their own culture. For six-month and yearlong programs, participants must be between sixteen and thirty years of age (although some programs have an upper age limit of twenty-five). Summer work camps are open to those sixteen and older.

THE INTERNATIONAL PARTNERSHIP FOR SERVICE-LEARNING

Service Learning • Worldwide • 1–12 Months
www.studyabroad.com/psl

Howard Berry, President
815 Second Ave., Suite 315
New York, NY 10017-4594
(212) 986-0989 • (212) 986-5039 (fax)
pslny@aol.com

••

THE INTERNATIONAL PARTNERSHIP FOR SERVICE-LEARNING, a consortium of colleges, universities, and service agencies, develops programs of service-learning that unite college-level academic studies with volunteer service in international and intercultural settings. Programs are offered in the Czech Republic, Ecuador, England, France, India, Israel, Jamaica, Mexico, Philippines, Scotland, and South Dakota (in the U.S.).

The Experience: The International Partnership fully integrates participants in a new culture through service, academics, and living arrangements. Participants work in a community service project fifteen hours per week in schools and orphanages, health care and education institutions, recreational centers, or community development projects. The rest of the week is filled with an academic component, integrating studies and service that range from education and sociology to anthropology and philosophy at a local university. Finally, living arrangements are provided with a host family or college housing, providing a unique way to interact and learn from the new culture. Also inquire about their master's degree in international service.

Perks: There is a program fee of $4,500 to $16,000 (depending on country and time frame), which includes room, board, orientation, field trips, instruction, placement, and administrative costs. Housing is arranged in either dorms, flats, or homestays.

Ideal Candidate: Candidates—from mature high school graduates to retirees—should be open to learning about new cultures and dedicated to service.

INTERNATIONAL VOLUNTEER EXPEDITIONS

Volunteer Service • Worldwide • 2–8 Weeks
www.espwa.org

Dawn Moorhead, Executive Director
2001 Vallejo Way
Sacramento, CA 95818
(916) 444-6856
ivex@email.com

••

INTERNATIONAL VOLUNTEER EXPEDITIONS conducts short- and medium-term volunteer projects in California, Africa, the Caribbean, and Latin America. Most work projects range from construction to reviving agriculture fields over a two-week period, with an emphasis placed on sustainable development, the environment, and outdoor activities. Those with professional skills might engage in architecture, education, web site design, and the like. Participants are recruited internationally and all ages are welcome. Curiosity, adaptability, an adventurous spirit, and a sense of humor are indispensable volunteer attributes. Costs range from $450 to $1,500, which includes vegetarian meals, simple lodging (ranging from a self-contained tent in the rain forest to dormitory-style facilities), and project materials during the service component. (Airfare is additional.)

INTERNATIONAL YMCA

Camp • Worldwide • 1–6 Months
www.ymcanyc.org/international

Jennifer Holt, Special Programs Director
71 W. 23rd St., Suite 1904
New York, NY 10010
(888) 477-9622 • (212) 727-8800 • (212) 727-8814 (fax)
jholt@ymcanyc.org

••

THE INTERNATIONAL CAMP COUNSELOR PROGRAM ABROAD allows those over the age of eighteen, who are involved in their local YMCA and community, to volunteer for international YMCA programs around the world. Volunteers typically work up to three months in the summer and winter in projects related to resident or day camps, with activities including sports, arts and crafts, swimming, hiking, and sailing. In exchange for your volunteer service, room and board is provided. There is a fee of $155, and airfare and health insurance are additional. YMCA also offers work opportunities from six weeks to six months in West Africa for a fee of $500. Some countries have language proficiency requirements.

The slower one travels, the more enriching the experience. —SHEILA CUNNINGHAM

FINDING A PLACE IN THE WORLD

Twenty years ago, we had what my husband, Bud Philbrook, wryly refers to as "a properly balanced honeymoon." We spent five days at theme parks in Orlando, followed by five days in an impoverished Guatemalan village. This curious blending of Disney World and "the real world" was, I believed then, a statement of our commitment to keep our marriage balanced and focused on human values. But more, it was a harbinger of our work to afford others a new perspective on their place in the world.

The first week in Orlando was predictably captivating as we explored all the area attractions. At the week's end, I was eager, but also apprehensive, about the next leg of our journey.

One thought dominated my mind as we embarked on our journey to Conacaste, Guatemala: I was writing a new, significant chapter of my life. Our act of service would define who we were as individuals and as a couple in a world where humanity struggles to maintain human relationships. Bud's vision was clearer than mine. He believed it was each person's moral responsibility to work for human justice and equality. As a former state legislator, he often challenged me to question my personal role in waging world peace. But I felt ill-equipped to make a real difference outside my immediate area of influence. How would I make sense of the poverty and struggles of a life I knew nothing about?

Our warm welcome into Guatemala assuaged my worries. We were greeted by the American program directors and the local community leaders. One of my first thoughts was: "They're just like us." While we toured the village, I felt progressively comforted by the openness and hospitality of the villagers.

The little mountain hamlet housed some two hundred families, many descendants of indigenous Indian tribes. They opened their homes to us, welcomed us into their fields, and included us in their friendly conversations, allowing us a glimpse into their daily lives. I was awestruck by how utterly normal—albeit difficult—life here seemed. With minimal electricity, no running water, few books, and no stores for daily necessities, the villagers accepted their formidable challenges not with resignation, but with pride. A nature-dominated flow of daily life seemed to guide their gentle spirits. Life was to be celebrated.

My comfort level in my temporary "home" grew as I became familiar with local residents. We were eager to become as much a part of the community as possible. Bud, with his background in human and economic development, was asked to help write a grant proposal, and I, with my journalism background, began work on a brochure explaining the community's needs to potential benefactors.

Every evening Bud and I joined project leaders to reflect on the day. The goals of their work were explained to us: Conacaste was a "demonstration" village for neighboring communities. The hope was to develop strategies in farming, health care, education, and commerce that other villages could replicate to improve their subsistence-level standard of living. Over several years, several innovations had been developed, including a bread-baking "industry" and basket-weaving center.

The project leaders explained that progress was slow, because as a demonstration project, the construction techniques used must be replicable with locally available resources. The American program directors knew that the initiative, as well as the strategies, must be the local people's themselves if the community's efforts would remain long term. Therefore construction practices that to me had first seemed awkward and unnecessarily labor-intensive, gained greater relevance as I began to understand the meaning of "appropriate technology."

As I scanned the village square, I tried to imagine what this place would look like in twenty years. Would one-room, thatched-roofed homes be replaced by more spacious dwellings? Would the village build the educational and medical facilities needed to ensure its children's health and development? Would farmers develop agricultural techniques to raise the families' subsistence-style of life? My heart swelled with hope and optimism.

Now, twenty years later, I have personally witnessed what is possible when local initiative and community self-determination join with catalytic assistance from committed "outsiders."

Like most people, Global Volunteers' team members are at first motivated to make a difference, to "give back" some of what they are grateful for in their own lives, and to know that in a small, personal way, they have altered the course of world history in a positive way. It is upon reflection they often realize, perhaps as they are packing their bags to return home, that they are the ones who have truly benefited from their act of service. Life will never be the same. They have their own story to tell.

—Contributed by Michele Gran, codirector of Global Volunteers (see listing page 269)

Photo Credit: Global Volunteers

Over twenty years ago, Global Volunteers' cofounders Bud Philbrook and Michele Gran discovered their life's work on their honeymoon in Guatemala.

INTERNSHIPS INTERNATIONAL

Experiential Learning • Worldwide • 6 Weeks
www.rtpnet.org/~intintl

Judy Tilson, Director
1612 Oberlin Rd.
Raleigh, NC 27608
(919) 832-1575 • (919) 834-7170 (fax)
intintl@aol.com

INTERNSHIPS INTERNATIONAL, a program for college grads and seniors, offers the opportunity to add a foreign dimension to your college or graduate degree through carefully chosen placements in major international cities, including Bangkok, Budapest, Cologne, Dublin, Florence, Glasgow, London, Melbourne, Nairobi, Paris, Saigon-Ho Chi Minh, and Santiago. These quality internships, covering all disciplines and fields, provide valuable exposure to the foreign market. Participants are placed in a nonpaying, full-time internship for a minimum duration of six weeks, and the $700 placement fee ($800 for London; $1,000 for Dublin) is well worth the cost. Many students have found ways to moonlight to bring in a little money.

> *You must be very specific about what you want in an internship. We help you to focus so that by the time you are through with your internship, you are viewed as a professional in your field.*

JAPAN EXCHANGE AND TEACHING PROGRAM

Teaching • Japan • 1–3 Years
www.jet.org

Program Coordinator
Embassy of Japan
2520 Massachusetts Ave., NW
Washington, DC 20008
(800) 463-6538 • (202) 238-6772
eojjet@erols.com

THE JAPAN EXCHANGE AND TEACHING PROGRAM (commonly known as JET) seeks to enhance internationalization in Japan by promoting mutual understanding between Japan and other countries, including the United States. The program's aims are to intensify foreign language education in Japan and to promote international contacts at the local level by fostering ties between Japanese youth and young foreign college/university graduates. More than five thousand participants are currently involved in the JET Program, approximately half of whom come from the United States.

The Experience: Assistant Language Teacher (ALT) participants are assigned to local schools and boards of education in various cities, towns, and villages throughout Japan as team teachers and engage in foreign language instruction. They may also be involved in language clubs, teachers' seminars, and judging speech contests. Coordinator for International Relations (CIR) participants engage in international activities carried out by local governments throughout Japan. These activities include receiving guests from abroad, editing and translating documents, interpreting during international events, assisting with the language instruction of government employees and local residents, assisting with international exchange programs, and various other activities.

Commitment: The duration for an individual contract is one year, beginning in late July. JET contracts are generally renewable for up to three years, upon consent of both the participant and the host institution.

Perks: An annual remuneration of approximately $33,000 per year is provided to cover the cost of accommodations, living expenses, and mandatory health insurance. Round-trip airfare is provided, although only from designated points within the United States. The host institution in Japan will assist participants with accommodations.

Ideal Candidate: ALT applicants must have an interest in Japan and excellent English communication skills. Japanese language ability or teaching experience is not required. CIR applicants must have a functional command of Japanese and excellent communication skills. All candidates must have a bachelor's degree and U.S. citizenship.

Getting In: Applications for the following year's JET Program will be available beginning in late September. Call 1-800-INFO-JET for an application. Completed application packets must be received by the Japanese Embassy in Washington, DC, by the first week of December. (Call for exact dates.)

KIBBUTZ PROGRAM CENTER

Kibbutz • Israel • 2–12 Months
www.kibbutz.org.il

Milka Eliav, Program Coordinator
633 3rd Ave., 21st Floor
New York, NY 10017
(800) 247-7852 • (212) 318-6118 • (212) 318-6134 (fax)
ulpankad@aol.com

THOSE WANTING TO PARTICIPATE in a unique kibbutz way of life have a chance to work, study, and live side by side with Israelis. The Kibbutz ulpan program is a combination of language study and strenuous work (generally agricultural) on various kibbutz branches over a five-month period; the Hebrew and work program offers the opportunity to learn Hebrew while living and working within the communal kibbutz environment over a three-month period; and the volunteer program allows participants to live and work on a kibbutz from two to twelve months. Program fees range from $150 to $800 (medical insurance is additional), which includes food, lodging, and an educational component. Participants must be between the ages of eighteen and twenty-eight (thirty-two maximum for the volunteer program). Note that there are centers around the world for those who live outside the U.S. and would like to apply to the program.

LATIN AMERICAN LANGUAGE CENTER

**Language/Community Service • Costa Rica
• 1–4 Weeks**
www.madre.com/~lalc

Susan Shores, Registrar
PMB 122
7485 Rush River Dr., Suite 710
Sacramento, CA 95831-5260
(916) 447-0938 • (916) 428-9542 (fax)
lalc@madre.com

AFTER BEING WELCOMED by staff and teachers at Juan Santamaria International Airport, Intensive Spanish Immersion Program participants are transported to their new home in Costa Rica. Host families are typically middle-class professional people and, like most Costa Ricans, are very family-oriented. Living with a local family who speaks little or no English is one of the best ways to learn Spanish, make new friends, and begin to understand Costa Rican culture all at the same time. Throughout the week, participants engage in Spanish language classes (of all levels) for $5^1/2$ hours per day at the Centro Linguistico Latinoamericano. Teachers provide the two to five students in each class with highly individualized instruction with conversations focused on the student's instructional needs. Beyond learning Spanish, participants also share in Costa Rican dance and cooking classes as well as a three-hour cultural trip once per week. Those who have completed at least two weeks of Spanish immersion classes can also participate in volunteer projects, which may include assisting ESL and computer teachers or spending time with social service projects. The program extends from one to four weeks, with tuition ranging from $355 to $1,405. Tuition includes homestay (with private room), three meals each day, and laundry service. (Airfare is additional.)

LOS NIÑOS

Service Learning • Mexico • 1 Week
www.electriciti.com/~losninos

David Cox, Program Director
287 G St.
Chula Vista, CA 91910-3927
(619) 426-9110 • (619) 426-6664 (fax)
losninos@electriciti.com

LOS NIÑOS is a nonprofit organization dedicated to long-term community development projects along the Mexico/U.S. border that encourages education and self-sufficiency. Development Education Program volunteers work together on weeklong community projects in Tijuana, as they learn about Mexico from Mexican nationals themselves. Participants take part in seminars with guest speakers (including topics such as NAFTA, human rights issues, and immigration) to learn more about the unique culture and issues surrounding this region. The experience is completed with cultural excursions to different locations in Tijuana and neighboring cities. These tours will show the relevance, past and present, of the history of Mexico. Volunteers must be at least sixteen years of age; Spanish-speaking ability is not necessary. The fee of $285 includes all programming, local transportation, lodging, and two to three meals per day. Also inquire about summer teaching internships.

MAR DE JADE

Language/Community Service • Mexico • 3 Weeks
www.mardejade.com

Work/Study Program Director
1605-B Pacific Rim Ct., MX 78-344
San Diego, CA 92173
(011) 52-322-2.1171 (phone/fax) • info@mardejade.com

SURROUNDED BY tropical forests, palms, and mango groves, Mar de Jade is a tropical beachfront retreat center in a small fishing village $1^1/2$ hours north of Puerto Vallarta. Mar de Jade's three-week work/study program provides participants with the opportunity to partake in community health care, local construction, organic gardening, or teaching projects, along with the chance to study Spanish in small groups with native teachers. The $950 fee includes a shared room, board, twelve hours per week of Spanish, and fifteen hours per week of community work. To receive more information, the preferred method of communication is through e-mail.

The world only exists in your eyes—you can make it as big or as small as you want. —F. SCOTT FITZGERALD

MIDDLEBURY COLLEGE LANGUAGE SCHOOLS

Language • Vermont • Summer
www.middlebury.edu/~ls

Program Director
Sunderland Language Center
Middlebury, VT 05753-6131
(802) 443-5510
languages@middlebury.edu

A MIDDLEBURY summer prepares people of all ages for a much more successful study-abroad experience by dramatically improving their language skills, deepening their cultural understanding, and strengthening their confidence and learning strategies. With a formal commitment of "No English Spoken Here," Middlebury students use their target language exclusively—in classes, dining halls, dormitories, and throughout a range of cocurricular activities over a course of seven to nine very full weeks of intensive language learning! Whether students are studying Arabic, Chinese, French, German, Italian, Japanese, Spanish, or Russian, participants literally live the language at all hours of the day. One summer at Middlebury equals at least one full academic year of conventional language study. Tuition begins at $4,485, which includes room and board, for the seven-week summer program.

MONTEVERDE FRIENDS SCHOOL

Teaching • Costa Rica • 1–2 Years

Jenny Rowe, Program Coordinator
Codigo Postal 5655
Monteverde, Puntarenas
Costa Rica
mfschool@racsa.co.cr

MONTEVERDE FRIENDS SCHOOL is an English-dominant, bilingual school in Costa Rica's rural mountains. Tuition is kept low for the seventy-five students (in multigrade levels) so that no child will be denied an education. Challenging one- to two-year teaching assignments allow North American teachers, who lovingly share their knowledge and skills, to serve as role models for these children. Classes are small (generally eight to twelve students) with a curriculum based on the sciences, math, social studies, history, English, Spanish, and religion, along with special awareness to the environment, community, and peace issues. An interest or experience with bilingual education, conversational Spanish, and a willingness to develop curriculum while living in

a rustic tropical setting is required. Benefits include a modest salary, rustic housing, health insurance, and visa costs.

NANNIES PLUS

Au Pair • USA • 1 Year
www.nanniesplus.com

Joy Wayne, Director
520 Speedwell Ave., Suite 114
Morris Plains, NJ 07950
(800) 752-0078 • (973) 285-5100 • (973) 285-5055 (fax)
nannies@nanniesplus.com

NANNIES PLUS places U.S. citizens into nanny positions throughout the United States. Over a one-year period, nannies are responsible for the care and development of the children of busy professional parents. Salaries range from $300 to $800 per month, and include private room, board, and car use. Nannies generally work ten to twelve hours per day (five days per week), with some variation depending on the family needs. There is no program fee.

NEW WORLD TEACHERS

Teaching • Worldwide • 1 Year
www.goteach.com

Neville Fridge, President
605 Market St., Suite 800
San Francisco, CA 94105
(800) 644-5424 • (415) 546-5200 • (415) 546-4196 (fax)
teacherssf@aol.com

NEW WORLD TEACHERS, with headquarters in San Francisco (including their own guest house off Union Square), is the largest teacher-owned school in the United States. They also have schools in three other countries: Turkish baths, an excellent transportation system, and more than two million people provide the backdrop for training facilities in Budapest, Hungary; the University of Guadalajara in Mexico serves as the academic site for the Puerto Vallarta center (where trainees live in "old town," a five-minute walk from the beach); and since many trainees head for destinations in Asia, Phuket, in Thailand, provides an ideal spot to receive training.

The Experience: New World Teachers will train you in a one-month intensive TEFL (Teaching English as a Foreign Language) certificate course, so you will have the ability to teach English overseas. Their methodology is based on learning through doing. Participants work in small groups and learn how to create a dynamic classroom learning environment. Course components include grammar, drama, cross-cultural training, teaching children, video and computers, TOEFL (Test of English as a Foreign Language), and business English. Job placement assistance includes one-on-one consultations, informational seminars, and a resource center filled with employer profiles, contacts, guidebooks, articles, Internet listings, and people to help you through the process.

Commitment: Most teaching contracts are for one year, with work encompassing twenty-five hours a week. Shorter assignments and flexible schedules are also possible.

Perks: The course fee ranges from $2,200 to $3,350 depending on the location you choose. Fees include registration, tuition, books, orientation, Internet access, and lifetime job placement assistance. Overseas locations also include language and culture orientation and site visits to interesting spots (such as a jungle tour or a Turkish bath visit). For an additional fee ranging from $300 to $575, you can opt for their accommodations package, which includes shared housing. Teacher wages overseas vary from a few hundred dollars a month to $3,000 a month, plus housing and airfare in some countries. Teachers often further supplement their income by giving private lessons at rates up to $35 an hour, depending again on the country. The real perks are unlimited self-funded world travel and the opportunity to interact more closely and directly with other cultures than a tourist can ever imagine.

Ideal Candidate: Most course participants have college degrees, although high school graduates are acceptable. The key is fluency in English. (Employers overseas often expect native English speakers.)

Getting In: Call for an information packet and application forms. Courses generally fill one to two months prior to start dates. Applicants are welcome to visit any of the New World schools at any time and sit in on classes if they so desire.

> *Teaching your way around the world will be as much an education for you as it will be for your students. You may be invited to their homes for dinner or perhaps taken to local sites and events that do not appear in the best of travel guides. You can be sure that this will be a big change from the nine-to-five world that is so prevalent around us. It's an education that goes beyond libraries and lecture halls, a way to travel that's as beneficial to you as to the people you meet along the way.*
> —Jeff Darling, New World Teachers

OPERATION CROSSROADS AFRICA

Global Development • Africa/Caribbean • Summer
www.igc.org/oca

Kate Shackford, Program Services Director
475 Riverside Dr., Suite 1366
New York, NY 10015-0050
(212) 870-2106 • (212) 870-2644 (fax)
oca@igc.apc.org

• •

SINCE OPERATION CROSSROADS AFRICA'S founding in 1957, more than ten thousand volunteers have made contributions to development in thirty-five African and twelve Caribbean countries as well as in Brazil. The late President Kennedy paid special tribute to Crossroads for serving as the example and inspiration for the creation of the Peace Corps.

The Experience: After a brief but intense cross-cultural training, Crossroads volunteers are teamed up with eight to ten other men and women and immersed into the culture of their host community (along with a team leader and equal number of local volunteers). All projects are community initiated, and volunteers will live and work with hosts who have designed the project. The project work may entail construction of a school, an inoculation drive, or planting trees—all of which fall under four types of projects: construction of community facilities, community health, agriculture, and education and training. Living conditions only provide the basic amenities and lack many of the modern conveniences many Westerners take for granted (often there is no electricity or running water, and participants eat a modest, high-starch, low-protein diet). Each season Crossroads also hires a handful of team leaders who are responsible for stimulating interest and cooperation among participants and for guiding them in attaining greater contextual understanding of the experience. (Call for the specifics on these positions.)

Commitment: The program runs from mid-June to mid-August and consists of three orientation days in New York City, six workweeks on a rural project, and one travel week in the host country.

Perks: There is a participation fee of $3,500, which covers all program expenses, including round-trip airfare. A majority of volunteers raise all or part of their fee. Crossroads provides the fund-raising how-tos, contacts with others who have successfully raised their fee in the past, and consistent encouragement in the process.

Ideal Candidate: Though most Crossroaders are college students and young professionals, there are no set age or occupation requirements. Fluency in French or Portuguese is a plus, since these are the main languages of many host countries.

Getting In: Call for application materials. Team leader applications must be received by February 1.

> *You will experience Africa from the inside out . . . this is not an African tour.*

PEACE CORPS

Global Development • Worldwide • 2 Years
www.peacecorps.gov

Director,
Volunteer Recruitment and Selection
1111 20th St., NW
Washington, DC 20526
(800) 424-8580
info@peacecorps.gov

SINCE 1961, Peace Corps volunteers have been sharing their skills and energies with people in the developing world, helping them learn new ways to fight hunger, disease, poverty, and lack of opportunity.

The Experience: As a Peace Corps volunteer, you'll travel overseas and make real differences in the lives of real people. Whether you're helping people stay healthy, expand their businesses, or grow more nutritious food, you will help change and improve the human condition at the grassroots level. There is a particular need for certified teachers, French language speakers, and those interested in agriculture, environmental education, business development, and teaching English.

> *Not sure if you want to continue with graduate school or become involved with the Peace Corps?* Now you can do both by participating in the Master's International Program. Through partnerships with more than thirty schools offering master's-level studies in a variety of subjects, individuals become Peace Corps volunteers as partial fulfillment of a graduate degree.

Commitment: Assignments last for two years and begin after the successful completion of an intensive language, cultural, and technical training (which lasts from two to three months).

Perks: "Two years of service, a lifetime of benefits." It is often said that the Peace Corps is not simply something great; it is the beginning of something great. From practical benefits such as student loan deferment to career benefits like fluency in a foreign language to the intangible benefits that come with making a difference in people's lives, there are a variety of rewards for serving. During this "serving" time, volunteers receive a monthly allowance to cover housing, food, clothing, and spending money. Medical and dental care, transportation to and from their overseas sites, and twenty-four vacation days a year are also provided. Upon completion of service, volunteers receive a $6,075 readjustment allowance and job-hunting assistance.

Ideal Candidate: Any healthy U.S. citizen of eighteen years or older is eligible for consideration, with most assignments requiring at least a bachelor's degree or three to five years of substantive work experience. For many assignments, a language other than English is required. Previous knowledge of another language can be very helpful but is not always required. Perseverance, adaptability, creativity in problem solving, and sociability are traits important to volunteers.

Getting In: For more information, call the toll-free number to locate the recruitment office nearest you. Volunteers will be notified where they'll be serving as much as six months before they get on a plane.

PEACEWORK

Work Camp • Worldwide • 1–4 Weeks
www.peacework.org

Stephen Darr, Program Director
305 Washington St., SW
Blacksburg, VA 24060-4575
(800) 272-5519 • (540) 953-1376 • (540) 552-0119 (fax)
sdarr@compuserve.com

PEACEWORK manages and organizes short-term international volunteer projects in developing communities around the world—from Zimbabwe to Vietnam. Through volunteer interaction and cooperation, participants learn about the world's cultures, customs, politics, and problems while contributing their skills and interests to a positive process of international development.

The Experience: Groups of volunteers learn about the dynamics of global hunger and poverty by working together on housing, health, and other development initiatives. Planned and implemented by leaders in the host community, projects typically involve the construction or renovation of schools, houses, orphanages, and clinics, or work on agricultural, educational, and health care projects. Group leaders are uniquely experienced in the host country, languages, and working with volunteer groups. Volunteers live and work in sometimes difficult and demanding conditions.

Commitment: Programs vary in length from one to four weeks. The majority of the programs occur during the summer, spring break, or during other holiday seasons; however, dates depend on the sponsoring group.

Perks: Typical costs range from $450 to $900, plus airfare. Comprehensive orientation materials, planning assistance, in-country arrangements (including housing), visas, supplemental international health insurance, and contributions toward project materials and program administration are included in the program cost. Peacework provides a guide to scholarships and other assistance with fund-raising for those who need additional financial support.

Ideal Candidate: Volunteers range in age from sixteen to seventy-six years old, but in general are college or graduate students. Peacework does not require knowledge of language or construction skills in order to participate in the trips. Acceptance is generally based on one's enthusiasm for international and humanitarian service, academic preparation, volunteer experience or travel, and references that indicate one's ability to work and live in a multicultural and often demanding environment.

PEOPLE TO PEOPLE INTERNATIONAL

**Learning Adventure • Worldwide
• 9 Weeks
www.ptpi.org/studyabroad**

Ines Dähne-Steuber, Internship/Homestay Coordinator
Collegiate and Professional Studies Program
501 East Armour Blvd.
Kansas City, MO 64109-7502
(816) 531-4701 • (816) 561-7502 (fax)
internships@ptpi.org

••••••••••••••••••••••••••••••••••

PEOPLE TO PEOPLE INTERNATIONAL is a nonprofit educational and cultural exchange organization originally founded by President Eisenhower in 1956. Traveling seminars and overseas internships encompass the Collegiate and Professional Studies Abroad Program. Cosponsored by the University of Missouri–Kansas City, interns venture to Australia, Central/South America, or Europe on a nine-week work/learn adventure, with internships available in

practically every conceivable field, along with the option to earn academic credit. The program fee of $1,875 includes tuition, orientation and placement, medical insurance, academic credit, and a one-year People to People membership. A homestay program and airfare is additional; plan on $4,000 for the entire experience. Applications must be sent at least three months prior to departure date. People to People also offers two- to five-week traveling seminars throughout the world for those who want a "live and learn" experience (without the work component).

PROJECT OTZMA

**Kibbutz • Israel • 10 Months
www.projectotzma.org**

Nessa Saltzman, North American Otzma Coordinator
United Jewish Communities
111 8th Ave., Suite 11E
New York, NY 10011
(877) 466-8962 • (212) 284-6721 • (212) 284-6844 (fax)
otzma@cjfny.org

••

A GREAT ALTERNATIVE TO WORK or graduate school, Project Otzma is a ten-month leadership development program in which North American young adults (aged twenty to twenty-four) contribute a year of service to Israel and the Jewish people, and gain an in-depth understanding of the country and their own capacities to lead. Beginning in August, volunteers initially live and work in large groups at immigrant absorption centers, then participate in an "ulpan," a program of intense Hebrew language study. For the next three months, volunteers participate in community service projects, which range from building playgrounds to coordinating events for youth in the community center. The next phase focuses on a diverse range of service opportunities based on personal interest, and the final two months are dedicated to working and living in groups in youth villages or on a kibbutz. Each participant is paired with an Israeli adoptive family to visit and spend holidays with, and special trips, seminars, workshops, and field trips are planned throughout the year. There is a nominal fee of $1,850 that covers most expenses ($5,200 is already subsidized for each participant). Airfare is additional.

> *The intensity of my year on Otzma enabled me to grow in ways which far exceeded my expectations. The opportunities that were presented to me, and those that I sought out for myself, led me to have one of the most rewarding adventures of my life.*
> —Brooke Gardberg, participant

What you do will be insignificant, but it is important that you do it. —MOHANDAS K. GANDHI

Hostelling

Suppose that the thoughtful young people of all countries could be provided with suitable meeting places where they could get to know each other. That could and must be the role of our youth hostels, not only in Germany, but throughout the world, building a bridge of peace from nation to nation.

—RICHARD SCHIRRMANN, father of
the hostelling movement

Short of camping on the roadside, hostels are by far the least expensive places to rest your weary head for the night, with costs ranging from $5 to $40 per night. The six thousand hostels scattered across the globe vary widely, from lighthouses, tree forts, and home hostels to ranch bunkhouses, Victorian buildings, mountain huts, and medieval castles—each with a personality and charm of its own.

One thing is certain about hostels: they are usually crammed with other budget-conscious folks who are looking for the same things that you are—adventure and excitement. They tend to be fun places to meet other happy wanderers. Many hostels are dormitory-style and separated by gender. Others offer private rooms (for a few dollars more) for those traveling together or if you want a good night's rest. Hostels generally supply a bed and a blanket; you just need to bring your own sleepsack (or sleeping bag). Many provide do-it-yourself kitchens, lockers, laundry facilities, and common areas to discuss global events with people from the world over.

Hostelling is perhaps best described as traveling cheaply with an adventurous spirit. You see the world from a perspective that the average tourist will never see. You meet local people, learn customs, eat local food, and often have opportunities to do things you never imagined. Budget hotels, pensions (family-owned inns), university dorms, and bed-and-breakfasts provide alternatives to hostels for the same or slightly higher costs.

The word hostel does not describe a place; it describes attitude, a philosophy, a coming together of culturally diverse people sharing the wonders, high and low, of the traveling adventure.

—Janet Thomas, author of *At Home in Hostel Territory*

FINDING OUT MORE

Hostelling International—American Youth Hostels
733 15th St., NW, Suite 840
Washington, DC 20005
(202) 783-6161 • (202) 783-6171 (fax)
hiayhserv@hiayh.org • www.hiayh.org

An investment in a Hostelling International—American Youth Hostels membership will help get you connected to the hostelling movement. A one-year membership card is $25, which includes a complimentary guide to HI-AYH hostels in Canada and the United States, plus newsletters from a regional office. The membership also allows members to receive discounts while staying at HI-AYH sponsored hostels.

INTERNSHIP OPPORTUNITIES AT THE NATIONAL OFFICE

HI-AYH's relatively small professional staff relies upon interns to complete purposeful and responsible tasks. Internships are available in marketing, hostel services, hostel development, and programs and education, with responsibilities that include special projects as well as routine office duties. Positions are available year-round, with a minimum duration of ten weeks. Additional positions are offered in the summer months, an extremely busy time for HI-AYH. Interns receive free housing at the Washington, DC, International AYH Hostel (or a similar housing arrangement), a stipend of $100 per week for undergraduates ($150 per week for graduate students), and $200 for relocation assistance (paid upon completion of internship). Send resume, transcript, three letters of recommendation, and a cover letter highlighting your personal interest in HI-AYH, your department preference, and your dates of availability.

RECOMMENDED RESOURCES

Backpackers Hostels, Canada

(www.backpackers.ca) provides links to hostels, retreat centers, campgrounds, guest houses, and hostel farms throughout North America.

When Tom Dennard takes a vacation from his day-to-day life, he makes the best of it in adventures that address the testing of self and self-discovery. Stories in his book, **Discovering Life's Trails:**

Adventures in Living (Rainbow Books, $14.95), illustrate how he has managed to accommodate the realities of everyday life but still follow his dreams. The final chapter is a letter to his daughter (to share with her sons), which offers sixteen short essays addressing love, learning, and living (which I recommend to everyone). His own extensive travel experience around the globe introduced him to hostelling, which prompted his desire to build a hostel of his own, A Hostel in the Forest, where guests check in at a geodesic dome and can sleep in a bunkhouse or a private tree-house suite. To get your own copy of his book or to learn more about staying at his hostel, call (912) 264-9738 or write Hostel in the Forest, P.O. Box 1496, Brunswick, GA 31521; www.foresthostel.com.

A must for information on cheap places to sleep in the United States and Canada is Jim Williams's **The Hostel Handbook**. This guide provides contact information and prices for more than six hundred Hostelling International hostels, independent hostels, and backpacker's bungalows. The information is extremely fresh, with a new edition of this pocket-sized guide released early every year. A lifelong traveler and incredible cook, the author keeps busy by running his own hostel, the Sugar Hill International House, in New York City (which is conveniently located off the A-train express near 145th Street). If you do stay

HOT TIP Many travelers have turned their short stay at a hostel into a three- to six-month experience by working for them. For instance, the **Malta Youth Hostels Association** operates a year-round work camp and focuses on helping people who come in need of shelter. Volunteers, aged sixteen to thirty, may receive free lodging and breakfast from two weeks to three months in exchange for three hours of work per day on various projects including hostel maintenance and administration. To apply, send three international reply coupons (which you can get at a local post office) or $2, and detailed information and an application form will be sent to you. Your completed application should be sent at least three months prior to your arrival date. Malta Youth Hostels Association Workcamp, 17, Triq Tal-Borg, Pawla, PLA 06, Malta; (011) 356-693957, myha@keyworld.net

HOSTELLING

The traveler's-eye-view of men and women is not satisfying. A man might spend his life in trains and restaurants and know nothing of humanity at the end. To know, one must be an actor as well as a spectator. —ALDOUS HUXLEY

at his hostel, be sure to ask about the "six barstool" Texas Star, which serves up great food at 1950s prices. His handbook is available at independent hostels, bookstores, or by sending a check or money order for $3 (plus $1 for shipping) directly to the author: Jim Williams, 722 St. Nicholas Ave., New York, NY 10031; (212) 926-7030, www.hostelhandbook.com.

Everything you ever wanted to know about hostelling and the hostel movement can be found at **Hostels.com**. Along with advice, stories, budget travel resources, and a backpacker bookstore, visitors can search for information on any hostel in the world.

From hostels that provide a real family spirit to those you might want to bypass altogether, **Hostels USA** (Globe Pequot Press, $14.95) details more than 340 hostels throughout the country. This comprehensive and witty guide provides engaging descriptions, stories, and guest comments that will assist everyone from the business traveler to those who want a romantic getaway. Author Paul Karr also has an entourage of other hostel guides that will take you beyond North America. If you are planning an adventure to Austria/Switzerland, Benelux, Canada, France, Ireland, Italy, or the U.K., be sure to take his wit and wisdom on the road with you.

BEYOND HOSTELS

If you ever imagined stepping into a simpler lifestyle, without the worry of rent or making a living, you might check out the opportunities listed in **The Caretaker Gazette**. This unique bimonthly newsletter lists more than 125 caretaker and house-sitting positions throughout the U.S. and as far away as Australia or Costa Rica at properties including estates, farms, ranches, resort homes, or even a private island. Duties range from general house and property upkeep to land restoration, cooking, and organic farming. Most caretakers are provided with free housing, while others include meals and salaries. A one-year subscription is available for $27.

The Caretaker Gazette, Gary Dunn, P.O. Box 5887, Carefree, AZ 85377-5887; (480) 488-1970, caretaker@uswest.net, www.caretaker.org

Those looking for unconventional lodging arrangements while traveling might indulge in **Sanctuaries: The Complete United States** by Marcia and Jack Kelly, a guide to accommodations in monasteries, abbeys, and retreat centers. (Bell Tower, $18)

If you are venturing off to England, Wales, Scotland, or Northern Ireland, **The British Universities Accommodation Consortium** provides a free brochure on universities that provide lodging facilities during the summer months. Contact BUAC, Box 1808, University Park, Nottingham, NG7 2RD, England; (011) 44-115-950-4571. The guide is also available on their web site at www.buac.co.uk.

For a moment we smile, striving to pull down barriers quickly. Strangers becoming friends, we only have a small amount of time. Tomorrow . . . you go north, I go south. Adventures in travel, seeking new experiences. This moment is special. Our lives were meant to touch, to share. My life is richer because I have met you. There have been so many people like you in the youth hostels of the world.

—Redwood National Park Youth Hostel journal

SCI—INTERNATIONAL VOLUNTARY SERVICE USA

Work Camp • Worldwide • 2–4 Weeks
www.sci-ivs.org

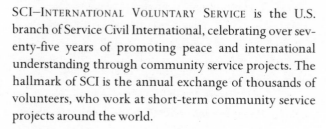

Volunteer Exchange Coordinator
814 N.E. 40th St.
Seattle, WA 98105
(206) 545-6585 • (206) 545-6585 (fax)
sciinfo@sci-ivs.org

SCI–INTERNATIONAL VOLUNTARY SERVICE is the U.S. branch of Service Civil International, celebrating over seventy-five years of promoting peace and international understanding through community service projects. The hallmark of SCI is the annual exchange of thousands of volunteers, who work at short-term community service projects around the world.

The Experience: Eight to fifteen volunteers of various nationalities and backgrounds come together to solve problems, work together, and have fun over a two- to four-week period during the summer. Volunteers might help teach solar technology in Denmark, renovate an ancient church in Russia, or work on an organic farm in the Swiss Alps. SCI-sponsored work camps have a local sponsor in more than fifty countries around the globe.

Perks: The application fee for residents of the United States and Canada is $65 for domestic programs and $125 for most overseas programs. For work camps in Asia, Africa, Latin America, and Eastern Europe, the fees are higher and vary by location. Participation in more than one camp runs an additional $35 to $80 (with a limit of three camps per year). SCI covers room and board and a supplemental health and accident insurance. (Airfare is additional.) Your fee also pays for a year's membership in SCI.

Ideal Candidate: U.S./Canadian volunteers must be sixteen and older for U.S. camps and eighteen or older for overseas camps. (There is no upper age limit and retirees are welcome.) In general, there is no special experience required, except the ability to work in a team environment.

Getting In: Applicants must purchase the *Directory of International Workcamps* (available in early April each year) for a fee of $5, which includes registration and application information. Volunteers are placed in work camps of their choice, beginning in mid-April on a first-come, first-served basis. (After June 15, it becomes more difficult to get your first choice.) Have patience, as applications are processed by a small group of volunteer staff across the country.

SEMESTER AT SEA

Adventure Travel • Worldwide • 4 Months
www.semesteratsea.com

Staff Selection
University of Pittsburgh
811 William Pitt Union
Pittsburgh, PA 15260
(800) 854-0195 • (412) 648-2298 (fax)
shipboard@sas.ise.pitt.edu

WITH SEMESTER AT SEA, you'll live with Chinese students in a dorm at the University of Beijing, stay at an Untouchable village in India, watch twenty-foot waves hit the bow of your "campus" (the SS *Universe Explorer*) walk the crowded byways of Istanbul's 400-year-old covered markets, learn about the life of the Masai while on safari in Kenya, or study tropical rain forests while canoeing down the Amazon River—all of which provides a life-altering learning adventure.

Environment: The spring voyage departs from the Bahamas and travels to Cuba, Brazil, South Africa, Kenya, India, Malaysia, Vietnam, Hong Kong, Japan, and arrives in Seattle, Washington. The fall voyage departs from Vancouver, British Columbia, then sets sail to Japan, China, Hong Kong, Vietnam, Malaysia, India, Suez Canal, Turkey, Croatia, Spain, Cuba, and finishes in Miami, Florida.

The Experience: Staff positions are available as administrative assistant, assistant dean, AV/media coordinator (and assistant), bursar (financial operations), director of student life, field office coordinator (and assistant), information technology coordinator, librarian (and assistant), mental health professional, nurse, photographer, physician, resident staff, secretary, security officer, and senior adult coordinator. In addition to regularly assigned duties, you will be expected to be an integral part of the shipboard community, participating in all aspects of the program as your shipboard work schedule permits. In addition, you will serve on a limited number of in-port duty assignments, which may include serving as a trip leader for some of the field practicums.

Commitment: Spring voyages depart in late January and return mid-May. Fall voyages depart in mid-September and return just before Christmas. Staff is hired on a non-permanent basis for one term only.

Perks: Staff will be paid a small stipend (usually $1,500 to $4,000), depending on the position. In addition, a $700 travel allowance is provided to help defray the cost of travel to/from the ports of embarkation/debarkation. Room and board on ship are provided.

Bloom where you're planted. —MARY ENGELBREIT

Ideal Candidate: The ideal applicants are those who support the concept of academic and personal enrichment through travel and education. Maximum flexibility, cooperation, and adaptability are essential traits of all applicants.

Getting In: Call for application packet. Applying for a single, specific voyage and expecting to be hired is not realistic. While personally it might be the best time for an individual's own needs, applicants are rarely hired right away. For most positions, there are between forty and sixty applications on file; thus, competition is very high. Some applicants wait several years before receiving an interview. Deadlines: spring voyages—March 1; fall voyages—January 1.

UNITED NATIONS ASSOCIATION OF THE USA

Global Development • New York • Year-Round
www.unausa.org

John Gagain, Internship Program Coordinator
801 Second Ave.
New York, NY 10017-4706
(212) 907-1326 • (212) 682-9185 (fax)
jgagain@unausa.org

• •

THE UNITED NATIONS ASSOCIATION (UNA) is the nation's leading center for research and information on the work and structure of the UN system. Through a unique combination of grassroots activism and high-level policy studies, UNA, through its 26,000 members nationwide, pioneers efforts to involve the American public, government, and business leaders in the discussion of foreign policy priorities. Internships are available in these departments: communications, Model UN and education, policy studies, media relations/public affairs, and corporate affairs. Besides important research and writing assignments, UNA interns are given a coveted UN grounds pass with which they may observe UN meetings and briefings. Call or write for application materials. Also inquire about the paid Estelle Linzer fellowship.

UNIVERSITY RESEARCH EXPEDITIONS PROGRAM

Adventure Education • Worldwide • 1–2 Weeks
www.urep.ucdavis.edu

Jean Colvin, Program Director
University of California at Davis
1 Shields Ave.
Davis, CA 95616
(530) 752-0692 • (530) 752-0681 (fax)
urep@ucdavis.edu

• •

THE UNIVERSITY RESEARCH EXPEDITIONS PROGRAM (UREP) invites you to join in the challenges and rewards of field research expeditions around the world. These research teams investigate everything from Costa Rican monkeys that use medicinal plants to excavating medieval castles of Ireland. Whether you choose to study archaeological sites to learn about the past or record the biodiversity of fragile environments, your participation will improve our understanding of the planet and help plan for the future. You don't need special training or experience to participate—your curiosity, adaptability, and willingness to share the costs and lend a helping hand are the most important qualifications. The average cost for a one- to two-week expedition runs about $1,300, which includes meals and shared lodging, ground transportation, camping and field gear, and research equipment and supplies. (Airfare and visas are additional.) More than just contributing to a worthy cause, you will have a unique opportunity to learn new skills, make new friends, and gain insights into other cultures in a way that ordinary travelers rarely experience. It's an adventure with a purpose.

VEN-USA

Language • Venezuela • Year-Round
www.flinet.com/~venusa

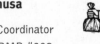

Rosa Corley, U.S. Field Coordinator
6342 Forest Hill Blvd., PMB #308
West Palm Beach, FL 33415
(561) 357-8802 • (561) 357-9199 (fax)
venusa@flinet.com

• •

MÉRIDA is the principal city of the Venezuelan Andes—a clean, safe university town where the weather and people are always warm and the scenery is breathtaking. This intensive and highly individualized program offers four hours of instruction with a qualified teaching professional each weekday. Students and professors work together to tailor schedules, teaching styles, and course content to the specific needs of each student. Obtaining room and board with a Venezuelan family is optional but is highly recommended. Program participants and Venezuelan students of English are invited to social events and activities. The immersion program begins every Monday throughout the year. There is an instruction fee of $540 for the first two weeks (each additional week is $180), and room and board is available for a fee of $75 per week. VEN-USA also offer summer, semester, and academic year programs with fees ranging from $3,125 to $6,180, as well as internships and TESL (Teaching English as a Second Language) programs.

VISIONS INTERNATIONAL

Service Adventures • Worldwide • 6–10 Weeks
www.visions-adventure.org

Joanne Pinaire, Director
P.O. Box 220
Newport, PA 17074-0220
(800) 813-9283 • (717) 567-7313 • (717) 567-7853 (fax)
visions@pa.net

• •

VISIONS INTERNATIONAL is a nonsectarian organization offering teens a summer experience in Alaska, Montana (on Plains Indian reservations), South Carolina, Dominica, the Dominican Republic, the British Virgin Islands, Peru, or Guadeloupe. A Visions summer integrates community service work, outdoor adventure, cross-cultural living, and learning in coed residential programs of up to twenty-five high school students and six staff. Students and staff live in schools or other local buildings in the heart of each host community.

The Experience: Serving as mentors, summer trip leaders and specialists supervise groups of teens in a residential living setting and during community service projects. Leaders also teach participants building techniques, basic carpentry skills, and outdoor activities such as backpacking, rock climbing, and rafting. In addition, leaders introduce participants to cross-cultural activities and experiences.

Commitment: Staff positions are available for either six or ten weeks.

Perks: Stipends for staff positions start at $220 per week (dependent on position and experience) and also include room and board.

Ideal Candidate: All staff applicants must be at least twenty-one years old, have strong interpersonal skills, a safe driving record, current wilderness first aid and CPR certification, experience leading or teaching teenagers, and flexibility and a sense of humor. Carpentry and masonry skills and/or advanced first aid certification are also

required for some positions. Spanish is required for the Dominican Republic and French for Guadeloupe.

Getting In: Send cover letter and resume. Applications are accepted starting in October for the following season.

VOLUNTEERS FOR PEACE

Work Camp • Worldwide • 2–3 Weeks
www.vfp.org

Peter Coldwell, International Workcamps Coordinator
1034 Tiffany Rd.
Belmont, VT 05730-0202
(802) 259-2759 • (802) 259-2922 (fax)
vfp@vfp.org

• •

INTERNATIONAL WORK CAMPS emerged from war-torn Europe back in 1920. More recently, work camps have become an affordable and meaningful way for people of all ages to travel, live, and work in a foreign country. Volunteers for Peace (VFP) coordinate more than fifteen hundred work-camp experiences in seventy countries, including Africa, the Americas, Asia, and Western and Eastern Europe. Hundreds of field volunteers and office staff provide consultation and placement services for work-camp hosts and volunteers.

The Experience: As a fully internationalized short-term "Peace Corps," work camps are a way you can respond positively to the challenges we face in our world. Focusing on cooperation, caring, sharing, and group living, you'll have a fun-filled adventure, building bonds with people from diverse cultural backgrounds. Work camps are sponsored by an organization in the host country and coordinated by people in a local community. In general, ten to twenty volunteers from four or more countries arrive at the community sponsoring the work project. Agricultural, archaeological, construction, environmental, and restoration work camps are common.

Commitment: Programs vary as to their start dates and length but generally run two to three weeks from mid-June to mid-October (although others are offered throughout the year). About twenty percent of the people they place abroad every year register for multiple work camps in the same or different countries and spend several months abroad.

Perks: Most programs cost $195, with room and meals provided. African, Russian, and Latin American programs may cost $300 to $500. You may be housed in a school, church, private home, or community center. Living arrangements are generally family style, with work campers coordinating and sharing the day-to-day activities, food preparation,

The real voyage of discovery consists not in seeking new landscapes, but in having new eyes. —MARCEL PROUST work projects, and recreation. Travel expenses will be left up to the volunteer.

Ideal Candidate: You must be at least eighteen years old, (although there are some work camps for sixteen- and seventeen-year-olds in France and Germany), and there is no upper age limit. (They've placed several folks in their seventies.) The most common age of participants is between twenty and twenty-five. In most areas, foreign language proficiency is not necessary.

Getting In: Each April the *International Workcamp Directory* can be obtained for $15 (deductible from your program fee), which lists more than fifteen hundred opportunities, registration information, and their free newsletter. Volunteers are placed on a first-come, first-served basis and are advised to register as soon as possible after receipt of the directory. Most volunteers register between mid-April and mid-May.

VOLUNTEERS IN ASIA

Teaching • Asia • 7 Weeks–2 Years
www.volasia.org

Kim Yap, Volunteer Coordinator
P.O. Box 4543
Stanford, CA 94309
(650) 723-3228 • (650) 725-1805 (fax)
volasia@volasia.org

VOLUNTEERS IN ASIA (VIA) traces its origins to a 1963 group of Stanford students who saw volunteer work as an appropriate way to enter and better understand the non-Western world. Since its beginnings in the refugee settlements of Hong Kong, VIA has sent more than a thousand volunteers to a wide range of assignments in Asia. Current programs in China, Indonesia, Laos, and Vietnam continue to reflect the organization's original goals: to immerse Americans directly into the workplaces and neighborhoods of contemporary Asia and to provide Asian organizations with volunteer assistance.

The Experience: As a small organization with limited resources, VIA focuses its efforts on one skill Americans can offer Asian organizations without displacing Asian workers—native English-language assistance. Thus, most volunteers teach English at the college level or in community organizations such as the YMCA. Others act as English resource volunteers who assist with translation and editing needs. Between thirty and forty volunteers are sent each year.

Commitment: Long-term volunteers participate in an intensive three-month predeparture training program at Stanford beginning in March, which focuses on cross-

cultural training, Teaching English as a Foreign Language, and language training. Participants generally depart to Asia in late June.

Perks: Participant fees: summer—$1,425; one year—$1,350; and two years—none. This fee represents approximately ten percent of the cost of sending a volunteer to the field. While on assignment, one- to two-year volunteers receive a monthly housing and living stipend. VIA covers the cost of round-trip transportation, basic health insurance, cross-cultural training, and in-country field support. Living arrangements are provided in guest houses, faculty apartment buildings, or dormitories. Scholarships are available.

Ideal Candidate: Applicants must be mature, responsible, native English speakers, and hold a bachelor's degree. VIA does not require any specific educational background, prior language training, teaching, or overseas experience. Volunteers range in age from eighteen to eighty and come from many different walks of life.

Getting In: Applications are available starting in November and are due at the end of January. All prospective applicants are encouraged to attend one of VIA's informational sessions held during this time frame. Staff and former volunteers will be on hand to help you gain a clearer picture of the program and philosophy and whether it meets your needs and interests. Acceptance into the program will be announced in early March.

WILDLANDS STUDIES

Endangered Species • Worldwide • Year-Round
www.wildlandsstudies.com/ws

Crandall Bay, Program Director
3 Mosswood Circle
Cazadero, CA 95421
(707) 632-5665 • (707) 632-5665 (fax)
wildlnds@sonic.net

SPONSORED BY San Francisco State University's College of Extended Learning, Wildlands Studies participants work with field teams searching for answers to important environmental problems affecting endangered wildlife and threatened wildland ecosystems in areas of the mainland U.S., Alaska, Hawaii, New Zealand, Fiji, Canada, Belize, Thailand, or Nepal. Research projects occur entirely in the field and involve extensive on-site experiences in wildlife preservation, resource management, conservation ecology, and cultural sustainability with experts in the field. Prior fieldwork experience is not necessary and academic credit can be arranged. There is a program fee that ranges from $425 to $1,900.

WORLDTEACH

Teaching • Worldwide • 2–12 Months
www.worldteach.org

Jodi Hullinger, Director of Recruiting and Admissions
Harvard Institute for International Development
14 Story St.
Cambridge, MA 02138-5705
(800) 483-2240 • (617) 495-5527 • (617) 495-1599 (fax)
info@worldteach.org

WORLDTEACH provides opportunities for individuals who want to make a meaningful contribution to international education by living and working as volunteer teachers in developing countries. Academic year opportunities exist in Africa, Asia, and Latin America, as does an eight-week Summer Teaching Program in China. Some volunteers opt for the six-month Mexico Nature Guide Training Program, with responsibilities that include the development and implementation of a curriculum combining English-as-a-foreign-language instruction and natural history, which will train local people for work in nature tourism and environmental education. Fees range from $3,800 to $5,950, which include housing, a small stipend, round-trip international airfare, health insurance, training, a teaching position, and field support. To help with fund-raising efforts, WorldTeach produces a useful pamphlet called *Fundraising Suggestions*. Candidates must have a bachelor's degree and have a sincere interest in education, international development, and/or cultural exchange. The ability to speak a foreign language or teaching experience is not necessary to participate in the program.

Recommended Work and Volunteer Resources

Alternatives to the Peace Corps (Food First Books, $9.95) offers many options for those who want to volunteer their time (almost anywhere in the world) for a good cause. The guide provides listings of voluntary service organizations, work brigades, and study tours that work to support development as defined by the local people. A must for anyone dedicated to grassroots work in their own backyard and in the Third World. Food First also offers internships at their headquarters in California, with work dedicated to eliminating the injustices that cause hunger and poverty. Food First, Marilyn Borchardt, Development Director, Institute for Food and Development Policy, 398 60th St., Oakland, CA 94618; (510) 654-4400, (510) 654-4551 (fax), foodfirst@ foodfirst.org, www.foodfirst.org

For anyone interested in teaching English as a Second Language or working abroad, head to **Dave's ESL Café** (www.eslcafe.com). Most visitors explore the café's Job Center, which lists postings of hundreds of teaching and administration jobs throughout the world, or the ESL Web Guide, which provides literally thousands of links sorted by category.

Friends of World Teaching maintains updated listings of American community schools, international schools, church-related and industry-supported schools, private or government schools, and colleges where American and Canadian educators may seek employment. Opportunities in more than one hundred countries are uncovered, with positions lasting anywhere from three months to two years. For a fee of $20, they will send you a list of addresses for three countries of your choice. (Each additional country is $4.) Send a self-addressed, stamped envelope to receive a free descriptive brochure. Friends of World Teaching, Dr. Louis Bajkai, Director, P.O. Box 84480, San Diego, CA 92138-4480; (800) 503-7436, (619) 224-2365, (619) 224-5363 (fax), fowt@fowt.com, www.fowt.com

Are you interested in international volunteer positions, teaching positions around the world, or jobs, internships, or study programs abroad? **GoAbroad.com** (www.goabroad.com) has a lot of options to explore.

Written by two seasoned American journalists who lived and worked in Italy, **Living, Studying, and Working in Italy** is brimming with candid insider tips and practical advice on experiencing Italy as

RESOURCES

Though we travel the world over to find the beautiful, we must carry it with us or we will find it not. —RALPH WALDO EMERSON

the locals might. Geared toward Americans, Travis Neighbor and Monica Larner provide information on volunteer opportunities, internship programs, and language schools as well as information about freelance and professional employment opportunities. Essential for anyone interested in making Italy their home—at least for awhile. (Henry Holt, $16)

Can you teach without any experience? Author Don Best says you can. Most foreigners who teach conversational English in Japan's language schools start with little or no teaching experience. **Make a Mil-¥en: Teaching English in Japan** is a great starter guide for everything you need to know and do to get a job teaching English in Japan. (Stone Bridge Press, $14.95)

Published electronically on a biweekly basis, **O-Hayo Sensei: The Newsletter of (Teaching) Jobs in Japan** (www.ohayosensei.com) provides listings of seventy to eighty teaching and other language-related positions, writing/editing jobs, and current travel information for Japan. Single issues are free (with subscriptions available). Their web site also features more than sixteen hundred Japan-related books, links, and resources.

StudyAbroad.com provides listings for thousands of study-abroad programs throughout the world as well as a special page of links dedicated to internship and volunteer programs overseas.

Anyone making plans to travel abroad should stop in first at **Transitions Abroad**. Along with their companion web site (www.transitionsabroad.com), they publish a handful of resources and directories that will have you fully engrossed in planning your new adventure. For those who need a constant stream of knowledge throughout the year, you might indulge in their bimonthly magazine. Topics include short-term jobs, special interest and language vacations, an overseas travel planner, work abroad, and adventure travel ($24.95 per year, or $6.25 for a single issue or back issues). For those who want the whole kit and kaboodle in one book, the *Alternative Travel Directory* focuses on travel, study, and living overseas ($19.95); and their *Work Abroad* guide provides the key contacts on landing an overseas job ($15.95). Stop by their web site and sign up for a monthly e-mail newsletter on overseas news or, for more in-depth discussions, subscribe to *TA NEWS* by sending an e-mail message to listserv@transitionsabroad.com. In the body of the message, type SUBSCRIBE TANEWS-L

Travelers who want to combine a little adventure and personal growth with service to others should include **Volunteer Vacations** by Bill McMillon in their research. The seventh edition (1999) of this classic profiles more than 250 organizations that need volunteers along with vignettes from previous volunteers. (Chicago Review Press, $16.95)

Get the real scoop on working overseas through the eyes of author Susan Griffith. **Work Your Way Around the World** ($17.95), although geared mainly to the U.K. crowd, provides detailed information for the working traveler, with explicit country-by-country overviews that cover everything from picking olives in Greece to working as a tour guide in Peru. And for those who might want to "talk" their way around the world, **Teaching English Abroad** ($16.95) intertwines actual accounts of enjoyable and disappointing experiences by people who have taught abroad. You'll also find specific job vacancy information compiled from language schools from the south of Chile to Iceland. Published by Vacation Work in the U.K. (www.vacationwork.co.uk) and distributed by Peterson's in the United States (www.petersons.com).

Recommended Travel Guides and Resources . . . .

Travel on the cheap and down-to-earth! **Big World** provides such inspiring destination articles that you'll find yourself on the next train to some remote village to celebrate the simple thrill of exploration. Each issue includes regular columns on adventuring, biking, cyber-traveling, hostelling, and dozens of budget travel tips. Subscriptions for this quarterly travel magazine are $13.50 for one year (single copies are $4). More information can be found at their companion web site (www.bigworld.com), which includes everything from pages of travel links to information on becoming a travel writer.

Connecting is a nonprofit, international organization of individuals interested in sharing going-solo tips and news about single-friendly trips as well as promoting hospitality and goodwill among solo travelers everywhere. *The Single-Friendly Travel Directory* lists over two hundred travel-related organizations (including volunteer vacation and learning adventures) that have been designated sensitive to the needs of people who travel alone. The publication is free for members ($25 per year for memberships, or $7.95 just for the directory). Also included with membership is *Connecting: Solo Travel News*, a twenty-page, bimonthly newsletter that includes newsy items about single-friendly tours, alternative holiday ideas, going-solo tips, and educational and volunteer opportunities. Connecting: Solo Travel Network, P.O. Box 29088, Vancouver, BC V6J 5C2, Canada; (800) 557-1757, (604) 737-7791 (fax), info@cstn.org, www.cstn.org

Izon's Backpacker Journal is the perfect travel journal designed to compliment budget travel guidebooks while you trek about the world. The journal includes 160 pages to record your adventures, including three hundred tips and helpful quotes throughout. How else would you know not to blow your nose in public in Japan or not to pick up food with your left hand in Indonesia? With your scintillating entries alongside the author's, you'll have more than just memories of your adventure (Ten Speed Press, $9.95). Izon's Backpacker News Wire at www.izon.com provides the latest line on backpacking around the world.

The classic Europe handbook, **Let's Go Europe** (St. Martins Press, $21.99), has been the bible for a generation of student travelers. Over the years Let's Go (www.letsgo.com) has added in-depth regional and country guides to most of Europe and North America.

Lonely Planet (www.lonelyplanet.com) publishes down-to-earth, comprehensive, and practical guidebooks for independent travelers who "have an interest in things." There are over two hundred books in print, all written in a straightforward, readable style with lots of firsthand tips and recommendations. Highly recommended. Call them at (800) 275-8555 to receive their free quarterly newsletter.

For more than two decades, **Moon Travel Handbooks** (www.moon.com) have been guiding independent travelers to the world's best destinations. The guidebooks are adventures in themselves, providing coverage of off-the-beaten-path destinations, fascinating accounts of the region's history and varied cultures, insight into political and environmental issues, street-savvy advice, language glossaries, accommodations and transportation information—everything travelers need for an extraordinary travel experience. Whether you are headed for the Hawaiian surf, the Colorado Rockies, or the streets of Tokyo, Moon probably has the guide to get you there. For U.S. travelers, a must is Road Trip USA, ($24), which covers eleven cross-country routes, providing practical information and entertaining sidebars.

Author Rick Steves takes a lighthearted, personal approach to sharing with you everything you need to know to have a great trip in Europe. **Rick Steves' Europe Through the Back Door** ($19.95, John Muir Publications) is full of practical travel advice—a must for anyone venturing to Europe who desires a more intimate feel for the places that locals patronize, rather than hitting the main tourist stops. You can receive a free quarterly travel newsletter or monthly e-mail dispatch, which also explains and promotes his other travel guidebooks, tours, and other great stuff. They're also known for having the best deals on Eurail passes. Contact Rick at (425) 771-8303; P.O. Box 2009, Edmonds, WA 98020-2009; www.ricksteves.com.

Rough Guides (www.roughguides.com) are aimed squarely at independent-minded travelers of all kinds, on all budgets—whether vacationers, business travelers, or backpackers. Thoughtful writing, painstaking research, and conscientiously prepared maps are fundamental to their commitment to provide you with the best possible guides.

Traveling alone need not mean lonely. How about taking a cooking and language workshop in France? What about a three-week cycling tour in the Grand Canyon or hiking the hills of Tuscany? In **Traveling Solo**, Eleanor Berman provides advice and ideas for more than 250 learning adventures for travelers without a companion, along with plenty of advice on how to plan the perfect solo vacation. (Globe Pequot Press, $16.95)

You don't have to be a travel agent or flight attendant to get amazing deals on airfares. You just need to know the right places to call. **The Worldwide Guide to Cheap Airfares** by Michael McColl provides the essentials on flying cheaply anywhere in the world. (Inside Publications, $14.95)

RESOURCES

Once we believe in ourselves we can risk curiosity, wonder, spontaneous delight, or any experience that reveals the human spirit. —e.e. cummings

About the Author . . . .

With over ten years of experience in the career and life planning field (and considered an internship guru in job adventure circles), Michael Landes believes there is room for every person to "find their place in the world" and meaning in their work. At age 35 (and a kid at heart), Landes has worked in literally hundreds of short-term job experiences over the course of his life, including stints with Gallo Winery, Apple Computer, MTV, Yellowstone National Park, California State University, Chico, Harvard University, the American Institute of Wine and Food, and many other places. Just recently, he split his work week between Boston and New York City, working as a career consultant for Pace University and developing his companion web site, Backdoorjobs.com. And as the book went to print, Landes decided to take a "sabbatical" from the career field to connect more with the earth by participating in Michaela Farm's internship program in Indiana (see their listing on page 192).

12

yOUR COMPASS TO THE GUIDE

Alphabetical Listing of Programs   293

Category

Geographical Listing of Programs

Program Length

General

INDEXES

Alphabetical Listing of Programs. . . . .

Here you will find all the programs in the book listed in alphabetical order. Use this index when you know the name of the program you are looking for.

A

Academic Study Associates, 204
Academy of Television Arts and Sciences, 204
Adirondack Mountain Club, 110
The Adventure Centre at Pretty Lake, 44
Adventure Connection, 44
Adventure Pursuits, 45
Adventures Cross-Country, 45
Advocacy Institute, 234
Alabama Sports Festival, 45–46
Alaska State Parks, 110
Alaska Wildland Adventures, 46
Alliances Abroad, 260
Alpine Meadows, 98
Amelia Island Plantation, 78
American Adventures, 46
American Dance Festival, 204–205
American Hiking Society, 110–111
American Horticultural Society, 144
American Institute for Foreign Study, 260
The American-Scandinavian Foundation, 260
American Theatre Works, 205
American Youth Foundation—Miniwanca, 46–47
AmeriCorps, 234–235
Amigos de las Américas, 260–261
Amity Institute, 261
Amizade, 261
Ananda Marga, 179
Angelic Organics, 179
Anasazi Heritage Center, 111
Angel Fire Resort, 102
Angelic Organics, 179
Anita Purves Nature Center, 144–145
Aperture Foundation, 205–206
Appalachian Mountain Club, 111–112
Appalachian Mountain Teen Project, 47
Appalachian Trail Conference, 112
Appel Farm Arts and Music Center, 206
Aprovecho Research Center, 179–180
Arcosanti, 180
Arctic Organics, 180
Arena Stage, 206–207
Arrowmont School of Arts and Crafts, 180–181
Art Workshops in Guatemala, 207
Aspen Center for Environmental Studies, 145
Aspen Lodge Ranch Resort, 78
Aspen Skiing Company, 99
Astors' Beechwood Mansion, 207
Atlantis Youth Exchange, 181

Attitash Bear Peak Resort, 102
Au Pair in Europe, 262
Audubon Ecology Camps and Workshops, 78
Audubon Naturalist Society, 145
Augusta Heritage Center, 181
Aullwood Audubon Center and Farm, 146

B

Backroads, 55
Badlands National Park, 112
The Banff Centre for the Arts, 208
Barrier Island Environmental Education Center, 146
BCT.TELUS Employee Fitness Program, 47
Bear Valley Ski Company, 98
Beaver Run Resort, 99
Berkeley Repertory Theatre, 208
Berlitz International, 262
Berry Botanic Garden, 146
Big Mountain Ski and Summer Resort, 101
Big Sky Ski and Summer Resort, 101
Bike–Aid, 55–56
Bikes Not Bombs, 56
The Biking Expedition, 56
Blue Moon Farm, 185
Boarshead: Michigan's Public Theater, 208
Bombard Balloon Adventures, 47–48
Boojum Institute for Experiential Education, 48
Boreal Mountain Playground, 98
Boston Mobilization for Survival, 235
Bradford Woods, 79
Bradley Wellness Center, 48
Breckenridge Outdoor Education Center, 48–49
Brethren Volunteer Service, 235–236
Brukner Nature Center, 147
BUNAC USA, 262
Bureau of Land Management, 113–114

C

Callaway Gardens, 147
Camp Chatuga, 79
Camp Counselors/Work Experience USA, 79
Camp Courage, 79–80
Camp Courageous of Iowa, 80
Camp Friendship, 80–81
Camp High Rocks, 81
Camp Highland Outdoor Science School, 81
Camp La Jolla, 81

Camp McDowell Environmental Center, 147–148
Camp Woodson, 81–82
Campaign to Save the Environment, 148
Canadian Border Outfitters, 49
Canyonlands National Park, 112
Career Discovery Program, Harvard University, 209
Carlsbad Caverns National Park, 115
The Carter Center, 236
Casa Xelajú, 262–263
Cascadian Home Farm, 185–186
CDS International, 263
Center for American Archeology, 209
Center for Global Education, 263
The Center for Health, Environment, and Justice, 148
Center for Investigative Reporting, 209–210
Center for Photography at Woodstock, 210
Center Stage, 210
Central City Opera House Association, 211
Central Wisconsin Environmental Station, 148–149
Centre for International Mobility, 266
Challenge Alaska, 49
Château de Jean d'Heurs, 266
Chesapeake Wildlife Sanctuary, 149
Chicago Botanic Garden, 149–150
Children's Defense Fund, 240
China Teaching Program, 266
Chingachgook YMCA Outdoor Center, 50
Choate Rosemary Hall, 240
Christian Appalachian Project, 240
A Christian Ministry in the National Parks, 234
Christodora-Manice Education Center, 82
Chuck Richards' Whitewater, 50
Ciclismo Classico, 56–57
City Year, 241
Claymont Farm CSA, 186
The Clearing, 211
Clearwater, 50–51
Clearwater Canoe Outfitters and Lodge, 82
Clipper Cruise Line, 51
Club Med, 51
Co-op America, 241
Coffee Creek Ranch, 82–83
College Settlement—Kuhn Day Camps, 83
Colonial Williamsburg Foundation, 211
The Colorado Mountain Ranch, 83
Colorado Outward Bound School, 67
Colorado Trail Foundation, 115
Colorado Trails Ranch, 84
Colvig Silver Camps, 84
Concern America, 266–267
Confrontation Point Ministries, 241–242
Congressional Youth Leadership Council, 242
Contiki Holidays, 52
Copper Mountain Resort, 99
Costa Azul Adventure Resort, 84–85

Costa Rica Rainforest Outward Bound School, 68
Coulter Lake Guest Ranch, 85
Council on International Educational Exchange, 267
Crater Lake Company, 115
Crater Lake National Park, 115
Creede Repertory Theatre, 211
Crested Butte Mountain Resort, 99–100
Cross-Cultural Solutions, 267–268
Crow Canyon Archaeological Center, 211–212
Custer State Park Resort Company, 116

D

Dahlem Environmental Education Center, 150
Davis Family Farm, 186
Deep Portage Conservation Reserve, 150
Delaware Nature Society, 151
Delta Queen Steamboat Company, 52
Denali National Park and Preserve, 116
Denali Park Resorts, 116–117
Denali Raft Adventures, 58
Diamond Peak Ski Resort, 101
Directors Guild—Producer Training Plan, 212–213
Dodge Nature Center, 186
Dorset Colony for Writers, 205
Dow Jones Newspaper Fund, 213

E

Eagle Bluff Environmental Learning Center, 151
Eagle's Nest Foundation, 85–86
Ebner Camps, 86
Educational Concerns for Hunger Organization, 242
Elderhostel, 237
ElderTreks, 237–238
Emandal—A Farm on a River, 186–187
Epley's Whitewater Adventures, 58
Esalen Institute, 183

F

Fairview Lake YMCA Camps, 87
Farm and Wilderness Foundation, 87
Farm Sanctuary, 242
Fernwood Nature Center, 151
Five Rivers MetroParks, 152
Flagg Ranch Resort, 117
Flagstaff Area National Monuments, 117
Flamingo Lodge in Everglades National Park, 117
Flat Rock Playhouse, 213
Florissant Fossil Beds National Monument, 117–118
Food Service Management Internship, 88
Foothill Horizons Outdoor School, 152
Four Corners Rafting, 58
Four Corners School of Outdoor Education, 59
4-H Environmental Education Program, 144
Fredericksburg and Spotsylvania National Military Park, 118

It is better to fail at something new than to succeed at the same old thing. —FRANK BUTTERFIELD

Friends of the Earth—U.S., 153
Frontiers Foundation, 243
Fulbright Teacher Exchange Program, 243
Furnace Creek Inn and Ranch Resort, 118

G

Garden Harvest, 187
Garden in the Woods, 153
George Washington's Mount Vernon, 188
Geva Theatre, 213
The Glacier Institute, 121
Glacier Park, 121–122
Glacier Park Boat Company, 122
Glen Helen Outdoor Education Center, 153–154
Global Citizens Network, 268
Global Exchange, 243
Global Routes, 268–269
Global Service Corps, 269
Global Volunteers, 269–270
Global Works, Inc., 270
Good Earth Farm School, 188
Gould Farm, 243–244
Grand Canyon National Park Lodges, 122
Grand Targhee Ski and Summer Resort, 103
Grand Teton Lodge Company, 122–123
Gray Line of Alaska, 59–60
Great Smoky Mountains Institute, 154
Greek Dances Theater—Dora Stratou, 214
Green Chimneys Children's Services, 244
Green Gulch Farm and Zen Center, 188
Green Valley Recreation, 60
Greenbrier River Outdoor Adventures, 60
Guided Discoveries, 60–61
Gunflint Lodge and Outfitters, 88

H

Habitat for Humanity International, 244
Hartford Food System, 244
Harvard University, Career Discovery Program, 209
Hawk Mountain Sanctuary Association, 154
Hawthorne Valley Farm, 189
Headlands Institute, 154–155
Heartwood School, 189
Heavenly Ski Resort, 102
Heifer Project Ranch, 245
Henry Crown Sports Pavilion, 61
Henry Ford Museum and Greenfield Village, 214
The Hermitage, 214–215
Hidden Creek Ranch, 88–89
Hidden Villa Environmental Education Program, 189–190
Hilton Oceanfront Resort, 89
HIOBS—Southern Lands Programs, 61–62
The History Factory, 215
Holden Arboretum, 155

Hollyhock, 183
The Home Ranch, 89
Hoodoo Ski Area and Recreation Services, 102
Hopewell Furnace National Historic Site, 123
Horizon Camps, 90
Horizons, 215
Horizons for Youth, 155
Hostelling International—American Youth Hostels, 282–283
Howell Living History Farm, 190
Hulbert Outdoor Center, 62
Humane Society of the United States, 156
Hunewill Guest Ranch, 90
Hungarian Association for Organic Farming, 199
Hurricane Island Outward Bound School, 67

I

Incline Village General Improvement District, 90
Inn of the Seventh Mountain, 102
Innisfree Village, 245–246
The Institute for Academic Advancement of Youth (IAAY) Summer Programs, 245
Institute for Central American Development Studies (ICADS), 270–271
Institute for International Cooperation and Development, 271
Institute of International Education—Latin America, 271–272
InterExchange, 272
Interlocken International, 62–63
International Agricultural Exchange Association, 190–191
International Bicycle Fund, 57
International Christian Youth Exchange, 272–273
International Crane Foundation, 156
International Field Studies, 63
The International Partnership for Service-Learning, 273
International Volunteer Expeditions, 273
International YMCA, 273
Internships International, 276
Isle Royale National Park, 123–124

J

Jacob's Pillow Dance Festival, 215
Japan Exchange and Teaching Program, 276
Juilliard School, 216
Just Act—Youth Action for Global Justice, 246

K

Kalamazoo Nature Center, 156
Kalani Oceanside Retreat, 91
Keewaydin Environmental Education Center, 156–157
Kellogg Child Development Center, 246

The Kennedy Center, 216
Kewalo Basin Marine Mammal Laboratory, 157
Kibbutz Program Center, 276–277
Kirkwood Resort, 98
The Kitchen, 217
Kripalu Center for Yoga and Health, 183–184

L

La Sabranenque, 217
Lake County Forest Preserve, 157
Lake Powell Resorts and Marinas, 124
Lake Tahoe Basin Management Unit, 124
Land Between the Lakes, 157–158
Landmark Volunteers, 247
Lassen County Youth Camp, 158
Latin American Art Resource Project, 217–218
Latin American Language Center, 277
Legacy International, 91
Life Adventure Camp, 92
Little Brothers—Friends of the Elderly, 247
Little Children of the World, 247–248
Loch Arthur Community, 248
Long Lake Conservation Center, 158
Longacre Expeditions, 63–64
Longwood Gardens, 158–159
Lookout Pass Ski Area, 101
Loon Mountain Resort, 102
Los Niños, 277
Losang Dragpa Buddhist Centre, 184
Lost Creek Ranch, 92
Lost Valley Educational Center, 191
Lutheran Volunteer Corps, 248–249

M

Maho Bay Camps, 92–93
Maine Appalachian Trail Club, 124–125
Maine Organic Farmers, 197
The Maine Photographic Workshops, 218
Maine State Music Theatre, 218–219
Make-A-Wish Foundation, 249
Malta Youth Hostels Association, 283
Mammoth California, 98
Mar de Jade, 277
Mast International Experience, 191
Merck Forest and Farmland Center, 192
Mercy Ships, 249
The Metropolitan Museum of Art, 219
Michaela Farm, 192
Mickey Leland Hunger Fellows Program, 249–250
Middlebury College Language Schools, 278
Minnesota Conservation Corps, 125
Mission Springs Conference Center, 159
Mobility International USA, 250
Monterey Bay Aquarium, 159–160

Monteverde Friends School, 278
Montshire Museum of Science, 160
Mote Marine Laboratory, 160
Mt. Bachelor Ski and Summer Resort, 102
Mt. Hood Meadows Ski Resort, 102
Mt. Rushmore National Memorial, 125
Mount Vernon, 188
Mountain Trail Outdoor School, 93
My Sister's Place, 251

N

Nags Head Woods Preserve, 160–161
Nannies Plus, 278
The Nation Institute, 219
National Building Museum, 219
National Civilian Community Corps, 235
National 4-H Council, 251
National Future Farmers of America Center, 192–193
National Outdoor Leadership School, 64–65
National Park Service, 127–129
National Service Corps, 238
National Wildlife Federation, 161
The Nature Conservancy, 161
Nature's Classroom Atop Lookout Mountain, 161–162
Naval Historical Center, 222
NCCC, 235
Network: A National Catholic Social Justice Lobby,
    251–252
New Canaan Nature Center, 162
New Stage Theatre, 222–223
New World Teachers, 278–279
Newfound Harbor Marine Institute, 162
Norfolk Chamber Music Festival, 223
Norlands Living History Center, 223
North Carolina Outward Bound School, 67
North Cascades Institute, 163
North Country Farms, 193
North Fork Guest Ranch, 93
North Pacific Fisheries Observer Training Center, 163
Northeast Organic Farming Association of Vermont, 197
Northstar-at-Tahoe, 98
Northwest Youth Corps, 125–126
NYS Department of Environmental Conservation,
    163–164

O

Oakland House Seaside Inn and Cottages, 94
Offshore Sailing School, 65
Okemo Mountain Resort, 103
Old Mill Farm School of Country Living, 193
Olympic National Park, 126
Omega Institute for Holistic Studies, 184
Operation Crossroads Africa, 279–280
The Option Institute, 184

If you improve in one talent, God will give you more. —Mother Ann Lee

Oregon Dunes National Recreation Area, 126
Outdoor Adventure River Specialists, 65
Outdoors Wisconsin Leadership School, 68–69
Outward Bound, 66–68
Overland Travel, 69

P

Pacific Crest Outward Bound School, 68
Pacific Crest Trail Association, 129
Park City Mountain Resort, 102
Parks Canada Research Adventures, 129
Peace Corps, 280
Peace Valley Nature Center, 164
Peacework, 280–281
The Pearl Theatre Company, 223
People to People International, 281
Phillips Cruises and Tours, 69
Pine Ridge Adventure Center, 69–70
Pocono Environmental Education Center, 164–165
Point Reyes National Seashore Association, 94
The Population Institute, 252
Potomac Appalachian Trail Club, 130
Priest Lake State Park, 130
Project Otzma, 281
Purgatory Resort, 100
Putney Student Travel, 70

R

Rainforest Action Network, 165
Ramapo Anchorage Camp, 94–95
Reachout Expeditions, 70
Redfish Lake Lodge, 95
Reporters Committee for Freedom of the Press, 224
Resort at Squaw Creek, 98
Richardson Bay Audubon Center and Sanctuary, 165
River Bend Nature Center, 165
River Network, 166
River Odysseys West, 70–71
Riverbend Environmental Education Center, 166
The Road Less Traveled, 71
Roads Less Traveled, 71
Rocky Mountain Village, 95
The Rodale Institute Experimental Farm, 193–194
Rose Resnick Lighthouse for the Blind, 95
Royal Gorge Cross Country Ski Resort, 98–99
Royal Palm Tours, 72

S

Sagamore Institute, 130–131
Sail Caribbean, 72
St. Elizabeth Shelter, 253
St. Mary Lodge and Resort, 132
St. Vincent Pallotti Center for Apostolic Development, 253–254

Salish Sea Expeditions, 166–167
Sarett Nature Center, 167
The School for Field Studies, 167
Schuylkill Center for Environmental Education, 168
SCICON, 168
SCI—International Voluntary Service USA, 285
The Scott Arboretum of Swarthmore College, 169
Sea Turtle Restoration Project, 169
Seacamp, 95–96
Seattle Repertory Theatre, 224
Semester at Sea, 285–286
Seniors Abroad, 238–239
Shakespeare Sedona, 224
Shaver's Creek Environmental Center, 169–170
Shenandoah National Park, 131
Signal Mountain Lodge, 131
Silver Creek Resort, 100
Ski Homewood, 99
Slide Ranch, 194
Smithsonian Institution, 225
Snow Mountain Ranch, 96
Snow Summit Mountain Resort, 99
Snowbird Ski and Summer Resort, 103
Sol Duc Hot Springs, 104
Southern Lands Programs, 61–62
Special Expeditions Marine, 72–73
Spoleto Arts Symposia, 225
Spoleto Festival USA, 226
Spring Lake Ranch, 252–253
Squam Lakes Natural Science Center, 170
Squaw Valley USA, 99
Stage One, 226
Stagedoor Manor Performing Arts Center, 226–227
Stanford Sierra Camp, 104
Starr Ranch Sanctuary, 170–171
Staten Island Zoological Society, 171
Steamboat Ski and Resort Corporation, 100
Stevens Pass Ski Area, 103
Stowe Mountain Resort, 103
Stratton Mountain, 103
Student Conservation Association, Inc., 132–133
Student Hosteling Program, 57
Student Pugwash USA, 254
Sugar Bowl Ski Resort, 99
Sugarbush Resort, 103
Sugarloaf/USA, 101
Sun Valley Resort, 101
Sunday River Ski Resort, 101
Sunriver Resort, 105
Supercamp, 105–106
Surfrider Foundation, 171
Sustenance Farm, 194–195

T

Tassajara Zen Mind Temple, 185
Teach for America, 254
Telluride Ski and Golf Company, 100
The Theater at Monmouth, 227
Theodore Roosevelt National Park, 133
Third World Opportunities, 254–255
Tillers International, 195
Timberline Lodge, 102
Topnotch Resort and Spa, 103
Touch of Nature Environmental Center, 73
Trailmark Outdoor Adventures, 73
Tree of Life Rejuvenation Center, 195
Trees for Tomorrow, 172

U

United Nations Association of the USA, 286
University of California at San Francisco AIDS Health
    Project, 255
University Research Expeditions Program, 286
Up With People Worldsmart, 227–228
Upham Woods 4-H EE Center, 172
U.S. Adaptive Recreation Center, 73–74
U.S. Army Corps of Engineers, 133
U.S. Fish and Wildlife Service, 134–135
U.S. Forest Service, 137–138
U.S. Olympic Committee, 74

V

Vail/Beaver Creek, 100
Vega State Park, 135
VEN-USA, 286–287
Vermont Youth Conservation Corps, 136
Village at Breckenridge Resort, 100
Virginia Robinson Gardens, 172–173
Visions International, 287
VISTA, 235
Volunteers for Peace, 287–288
Volunteers in Asia, 288
Voyageur Outward Bound School, 68

W

Walden Farm, 195
Walking the World, 239
Washington Performing Arts Society, 228
Westport Country Playhouse, 228
Widgiwagan's Environmental Education Program, 173
Wilderness Canoe Base, 106
Wilderness Inquiry, 74–75
Wilderness Trails Ranch, 106
Wilderness Way Experiential Learning Program, 75
Wildlands Studies, 288
Wildlife Prairie Park, 173
Williamstown Theatre Festival, 229
Willing Workers on Organic Farms, 196–199
Wind Cave National Park, 136
Winter Park Resort, 100–101
Wolf Creek Outdoor School, 136
Wolf Ridge Environmental Learning Center, 173–174
Wollam Gardens, 195
Women's Studio Workshop, 229
Woods Hole Sea Semester, 75
World Teach, 289
WWOOF, 196–199
Wyman Center, 75–76

Y

Yellowstone National Park Lodges, 139
Yellowstone Park Service Stations, 140
YMCA Camp Surf, 107
YMCA Willson Outdoor Center, 107
Y.O. Adventure Camp, 107
Yosemite Concession Services Corporation, 140
Yosemite National Park, 140–141
Youth Enrichment Services, 76

Z

Zion and Bryce Canyon National Park Lodges, 141

*Life would be infinitely happier if we could only be born at the age of eighty
and gradually approach eighteen.* —MARK TWAIN

Category Index. . . . .

From Adventure Travel to Yoga Centers (and everything in between), this index provides you with a "buzz word" associated with each program. And although each has been assigned a particular category, some of the programs cover such a wide spectrum of opportunities that they could be listed under many categories. So become an explorer while perusing this index.

Active Travel
Backroads, 55

Adventure Education
The Adventure Centre at Pretty Lake, 44
Adventure Pursuits, 45
Adventures Cross-Country, 45
Costa Rica Rainforest Outward Bound School, 68
Greenbrier River Outdoor Adventures, 60
Outdoors Wisconsin Leadership School, 68–69
Outward Bound, 66–68
University Research Expeditions Program, 286

Adventure Travel
American Adventures, 46
Club Med, 51
Four Corners School of Outdoor Education, 59
Gray Line of Alaska, 59–60
Interlocken International, 62–63
Longacre Expeditions, 63–64
The Outdoor Network, 76
Overland Travel, 69
Roads Less Traveled, 71
Semester at Sea, 285–286
Wilderness Inquiry, 74–75

Aging
Little Brothers—Friends of the Elderly, 247

Agriculture
American Horticultural Society, 144
International Agricultural Exchange Association, 190–191
Mast International Experience, 191
National Future Farmers of America Center, 192–193

AIDS Education
University of California at San Francisco AIDS Health Project, 255

Alternative Farming
Alternative Farming Systems Information Center, 200
Old Mill Farm School of Country Living, 193

Alternative Transportation
Bikes Not Bombs, 56

Animal Rights
Farm Sanctuary, 242

Aquarium
Monterey Bay Aquarium, 159–160

Arboretum
American Association of Botanical Gardens and Arboreta, 174
Holden Arboretum, 155
The Scott Arboretum of Swarthmore College, 169

Archaeology
Archaeological Institute of America, 230–231
Center for American Archeology, 209
Crow Canyon Archaeological Center, 211–212
The Hermitage, 214–215

Art Discovery
The Banff Centre for the Arts, 208
The Clearing, 211

Art Education
Academic Study Associates, 204
Latin American Art Resource Project, 217–218

Art Museum
The Metropolitan Museum of Art, 219

Art Studio
Women's Studio Workshop, 229

Art Workshop
Art Workshops in Guatemala, 207

Arts Administration
Spoleto Arts Symposia, 225
Washington Performing Arts Society, 228

Au Pair
Atlantis Youth Exchange, 181
Au Pair in Europe, 262
Nannies Plus, 278

Ballooning

Bombard Balloon Adventures, 47–48

Bicycle Advocacy

International Bicycle Fund, 57

Birding

American Birding Association, 174
International Crane Foundation, 156
Massachusetts Audubon Society, 175

Botanical Garden

American Association of Botanical Gardens and
    Arboreta, 174
Berry Botanic Garden, 146
Callaway Gardens, 147
Chicago Botanic Garden, 149–150
Virginia Robinson Gardens, 172–173

Buddhist Center

Losang Dragpa Buddhist Centre, 184

Camp

American Camping Association, 108
Camp Chatuga, 79
Camp Friendship, 80–81
Camp High Rocks, 81
College Settlement—Kuhn Day Camps, 83
Colvig Silver Camps, 84
Ebner Camps, 86
Farm and Wilderness Foundation, 87
Horizon Camps, 90
International YMCA, 273
Point Reyes National Seashore Association, 94
Seacamp, 95–96
Supercamp, 105–106
YMCA Camp Surf, 107
Y.O. Adventure Camp, 107

Canoe Outfitter

Canadian Border Outfitters, 49
Gunflint Lodge and Outfitters, 88

Castle

Château de Jean d'Heurs, 266

Caving

Carlsbad Caverns National Park, 115

Child Advocacy

Children's Defense Fund, 240

Child Development

Kellogg Child Development Center, 246

Community Service

Amizade, 261
Casa Xelajú, 262–263
Frontiers Foundation, 243
Global Citizens Network, 268
Latin American Language Center, 277
Mar de Jade, 277

Conservation Education

Adirondack Mountain Club, 110
Appalachian Mountain Club, 111–112
Bureau of Land Management, 113–114
Minnesota Conservation Corps, 125
Nags Head Woods Preserve, 160–161
Northwest Youth Corps, 125–126
Parks Canada Research Adventures, 129
Potomac Appalachian Trail Club, 130
Student Conservation Association, Inc., 132–133
U.S. Army Corps of Engineers, 133
Vermont Youth Conservation Corps, 136

Cruise Ship

Clipper Cruise Line, 51
Phillips Cruises and Tours, 69

Cycling, 53–57

Bike-Aid, 55–56
The Biking Expedition, 56
Ciclismo Classico, 56–57
Student Hosteling Program, 57

Dance Festival

American Dance Festival, 204–205
Jacob's Pillow Dance Festival, 215

Design Discovery

Career Discovery Program, Harvard University, 209

Disability Awareness

Mobility International USA, 250

Domestic Violence

My Sister's Place, 251

Dude Ranch

Aspen Lodge Ranch Resort, 78
Coffee Creek Ranch, 82–83
Colorado Dude and Guest Ranch Association, 108
The Colorado Mountain Ranch, 83
Colorado Trails Ranch, 84
Coulter Lake Guest Ranch, 85

*Unless we fully give ourselves over to our endeavors, we are hollow,
superficial people and we never develop our natural gifts.* —Epictetus

Dude Ranchers' Association, 108
Hidden Creek Ranch, 88–89
The Home Ranch, 89
Hunewill Guest Ranch, 90
Lost Creek Ranch, 92
North Fork Guest Ranch, 93
Wilderness Trails Ranch, 106

Ecology

Audubon Ecology Camps and Workshops, 78
Starr Ranch Sanctuary, 170–171

Ecotourism

Eco-Source Network Center, 76
Kalani Oceanside Retreat, 91
Sea Turtle Restoration Project, 169

Education

Aullwood Audubon Center and Farm, 146
Congressional Youth Leadership Council, 242
The Institute for Academic Advancement of Youth
    (IAAY) Summer Programs, 245

Educational Travel

American Institute for Foreign Study, 260
Camp Counselors/Work Experience USA, 79
Center for Global Education, 263
Global Service Corps, 269
Putney Student Travel, 70
Up With People Worldsmart, 227–228
Woods Hole Sea Semester, 75

Embassy Education

Institute of International Education—Latin America,
    271–272

Endangered Species

Wildlands Studies, 288

Environmental Advocacy

Campaign to Save the Environment, 148
The Center for Health, Environment, and Justice, 148
Friends of the Earth—U.S., 153
Rainforest Action Network, 165
Surfrider Foundation, 171

Environmental Education

Barrier Island Environmental Education Center, 146
Brukner Nature Center, 147
Central Wisconsin Environmental Station, 148–149
Deep Portage Conservation Reserve, 150
Eagle Bluff Environmental Learning Center, 151

Fairview Lake YMCA Camps, 87
4-H Environmental Education Program, 144
Glen Helen Outdoor Education Center, 153–154
Great Smoky Mountains Institute, 154
Headlands Institute, 154–155
Horizons for Youth, 155
Kalamazoo Nature Center, 156
Keewaydin Environmental Education Center, 156–157
Lake County Forest Preserve, 157
Land Between the Lakes, 157–158
Massachusetts Audubon Society, 175
NYS Department of Environmental Conservation,
    163–164
Pocono Environmental Education Center, 164–165
River Bend Nature Center, 165
Riverbend Environmental Education Center, 166
Schuylkill Center for Environmental Education, 168
Shaver's Creek Environmental Center, 169–170
Squam Lakes Natural Science Center, 170
Upham Woods 4-H EE Center, 172
Widgiwagan's Environmental Education Program, 173
Wolf Creek Outdoor School, 136
Wolf Ridge Environmental Learning Center, 173–174

Environmental Studies

The School for Field Studies, 167

Experiential Education

American Youth Foundation—Miniwanca, 46–47
Association for Experiential Education, 76
Boojum Institute for Experiential Education, 48
Hulbert Outdoor Center, 62
Long Lake Conservation Center, 158
Nature's Classroom Atop Lookout Mountain,
    161–162
North Cascades Institute, 163
Wilderness Way Experiential Learning Program, 75
Wyman Center, 75–76

Experiential Learning

Eagle's Nest Foundation, 85–86
Legacy International, 91

Experimental Farm

The Rodale Institute Experimental Farm, 193–194

Family Resort

Snow Mountain Ranch, 96

Farm Education

Dodge Nature Center, 186
Hidden Villa Environmental Education Program, 189–190

Farming

The American-Scandinavian Foundation, 260
Aullwood Audubon Center and Farm, 146
Appropriate Technology Transfer for Rural Areas, 200
Atlantis Youth Exchange, 181
Ohio Ecological Food and Farm Association, 200

Fire Fighting

Bureau of Land Management, 113–114

Fish Observer

North Pacific Fisheries Observer Training Center, 163

Flower Farm

Wollam Gardens, 195

Food Service

Food Service Management Internship, 88

Forest Service

Oregon Dunes National Recreation Area, 126
U.S. Forest Service, 137–138

Gas Station

Yellowstone Park Service Stations, 140

Global Development

Institute for International Cooperation and
    Development, 271
Operation Crossroads Africa, 279–280
Peace Corps, 280
United Nations Association of the USA, 286

Global Justice

Just Act—Youth Action for Global Justice, 246

Golden Years, 237–239

Elderhostel, 237
ElderTreks, 237–238
National Service Corps, 238
Seniors Abroad, 238–239
Walking the World, 239

Guest House

Oakland House Seaside Inn and Cottages, 94

Happiness Center

The Option Institute, 184

Health & Fitness

BCT.TELUS Employee Fitness Program, 47
Bradley Wellness Center, 48
Camp La Jolla, 81
Henry Crown Sports Pavilion, 61

Historic Site

Hopewell Furnace National Historic Site, 123
Sagamore Institute, 130–131

History

The History Factory, 215
Naval Historical Center, 222

Holistic Learning, 182–185

Esalen Institute, 183
Hollyhock, 183
Omega Institute for Holistic Studies, 184

Home Building

Heartwood School, 189

Homeless Shelter

St. Elizabeth Shelter, 253

Horse-Powered Farm

Davis Family Farm, 186
Good Farming Apprenticeship Network, 200

Horticulture

American Association of Botanical Gardens and
    Arboreta, 174
Garden in the Woods, 153
Longwood Gardens, 158–159

Hospitality Services

Crater Lake Company, 115
Custer State Park Resort Company, 116
Denali Park Resorts, 116–117
Flagg Ranch Resort, 117
Flamingo Lodge in Everglades National Park, 117
Furnace Creek Inn and Ranch Resort, 118
Glacier Park, 121–122
Grand Canyon National Park Lodges, 122
Lake Powell Resorts and Marinas, 124
Mt. Rushmore National Memorial, 125
Shenandoah National Park, 131
Yosemite Concession Services Corporation, 140

Hunger Awareness

Mickey Leland Hunger Fellows Program, 249–250
Third World Opportunities, 254–255

Intentional Community

Lost Valley Educational Center, 191

International Education

CDS International, 263
Centre for International Mobility, 266
Internships International, 276

Success is the ability to go from one failure to another with no loss of enthusiasm. —WINSTON CHURCHILL

International Exchange

InterExchange, 272
International Christian Youth Exchange, 272–273

Journalism

Center for Investigative Reporting, 209–210
Dow Jones Newspaper Fund, 213
The Nation Institute, 219
Reporters Committee for Freedom of the Press, 224

Kibbutz

Kibbutz Program Center, 276–277
Project Otzma, 281

Language

Berlitz International, 262
Casa Xelajú, 262–263
Institute for Central American Development Studies (ICADS), 270–271
Latin American Language Center, 277
Mar de Jade, 277
Middlebury College Language Schools, 278
VEN-USA, 286–287

Learning Adventure

People to People International, 281

Living History

Association for Living History, Farm, and Agricultural Museums, 231
Astors' Beechwood Mansion, 207
Colonial Williamsburg Foundation, 211
George Washington's Mount Vernon, 188
Norlands Living History Center, 223

Lodge

Clearwater Canoe Outfitters and Lodge, 82
Redfish Lake Lodge, 95
St. Mary Lodge and Resort, 132
Signal Mountain Lodge, 131
Zion and Bryce Canyon National Park Lodges, 141

Marine Science

Guided Discoveries, 60–61
Kewalo Basin Marine Mammal Laboratory, 157
Mote Marine Laboratory, 160
Newfound Harbor Marine Institute, 162
Salish Sea Expeditions, 166–167

Media

Academy of Television Arts and Sciences, 204

Military Park

Fredericksburg and Spotsylvania National Military Park, 118

Monastery

Tassajara Zen Mind Temple, 185

Museum

American Association of Museums, 230
Anasazi Heritage Center, 111
Henry Ford Museum and Greenfield Village, 214
National Building Museum, 219
Smithsonian Institution, 225

Music Festival

Norfolk Chamber Music Festival, 223
Spoleto Festival USA, 226

National Monument

Flagstaff Area National Monuments, 117
Florissant Fossil Beds National Monument, 117–118

National Park

Badlands National Park, 112
Canyonlands National Park, 112
Carlsbad Caverns National Park, 115
Crater Lake National Park, 115
Denali National Park and Preserve, 116
Isle Royale National Park, 123–124
National Park Service, 127–129
Olympic National Park, 126
Theodore Roosevelt National Park, 133
Wind Cave National Park, 136
Yosemite National Park, 140–141

National Park Ministry

A Christian Ministry in the National Parks, 234

Natural History

Audubon Naturalist Society, 145
Five Rivers MetroParks, 152

Natural Resources

Badlands National Park, 112
The Glacier Institute, 121
Lake Tahoe Basin Management Unit, 124
Lassen County Youth Camp, 158
Trees for Tomorrow, 172

Natural Science

The Nature Conservancy, 161
Richardson Bay Audubon Center and Sanctuary, 165

Nature Center

Anita Purves Nature Center, 144–145
Aspen Center for Environmental Studies, 145
Dahlem Environmental Education Center, 150
Delaware Nature Society, 151
Fernwood Nature Center, 151
New Canaan Nature Center, 162
Peace Valley Nature Center, 164
Sarett Nature Center, 167

Opera Festival

Central City Opera House Association, 211

Organic Farming

Angelic Organics, 179
Arctic Organics, 180
Cascadian Home Farm, 185–186
Claymont Farm CSA, 186
Good Earth Farm School, 188
Green Gulch Farm and Zen Center, 188
Hungarian Association for Organic Farming, 199
Maine Organic Farmers, 197
Michaela Farm, 192
North Country Farms, 193
Northeast Organic Farming Association of Vermont, 197
Sustenance Farm, 194–195
Walden Farm, 195
Willing Workers on Organic Farms, 196–199

Organic Garden

Seattle Tilth Association, 201
Tree of Life Rejuvenation Center, 195

Outdoor Adventure

Trailmark Outdoor Adventures, 73
YMCA Willson Outdoor Center, 107

Outdoor Center

Camp Highland Outdoor Science School, 81
Mountain Trail Outdoor School, 93

Outdoor Education

Camp McDowell Environmental Center, 147–148
Chingachgook YMCA Outdoor Center, 50
Foothill Horizons Outdoor School, 152
The Outdoor Network, 76
SCICON, 168

Outdoor Education Ministry

Mission Springs Conference Center, 159
Reachout Expeditions, 70
Wilderness Canoe Base, 106

Peace

Boston Mobilization for Survival, 235

Performing Arts

Appel Farm Arts and Music Center, 206
Greek Dances Theater—Dora Stratou, 214
The Kennedy Center, 216
The Kitchen, 217
Stagedoor Manor Performing Arts Center, 226–227

Photography

Aperture Foundation, 205–206
Center for Photography at Woodstock, 210
The Maine Photographic Workshops, 218

Population Awareness

The Population Institute, 252

Public Advocacy

Advocacy Institute, 234

Recreation

Green Valley Recreation, 60

Refugee Aid

Concern America, 266–267

Resort

Amelia Island Plantation, 78
Costa Azul Adventure Resort, 84–85
Grand Teton Lodge Company, 122–123
Hilton Oceanfront Resort, 89
Incline Village General Improvement District, 90
Sol Duc Hot Springs, 104
Stanford Sierra Camp, 104
Sunriver Resort, 105
Yellowstone National Park Lodges, 139

Restoration

La Sabranenque, 217

River Conservation

River Network, 166

River Outfitter

Adventure Connection, 44
Chuck Richards' Whitewater, 50
Denali Raft Adventures, 58
Epley's Whitewater Adventures, 58
Four Corners Rafting, 58
Outdoor Adventure River Specialists, 65
River Odysseys West, 70–71

*We must be willing to get rid of the life we've planned, so as to have
the life that is waiting for us.* —Joseph Campbell

Safari

Alaska Wildland Adventures, 46

Sailing

American Sailing Association, 76
Clearwater, 50–51
Offshore Sailing School, 65
Sail Caribbean, 72

Sailing Adventure

International Field Studies, 63
Special Expeditions Marine, 72–73

Science Museum

Montshire Museum of Science, 160

Service Adventures

Global Routes, 268–269
Global Volunteers, 269–270
Global Works, Inc., 270
Visions International, 287

Service Learning

AmeriCorps, 234–235
Amigos de las Américas, 260–261
Brethren Volunteer Service, 235–236
City Year, 241
Cross-Cultural Solutions, 267–268
Habitat for Humanity International, 244
The International Partnership for Service-Learning, 273
Los Niños, 277
Lutheran Volunteer Corps, 248–249
St. Vincent Pallotti Center for Apostolic Development, 253–254

Ship Ministry

Mercy Ships, 249

Skiing, 97–103

Alpine Meadows, 98
Angel Fire Resort, 102
Aspen Skiing Company, 99
Attitash Bear Peak Resort, 102
Bear Valley Ski Company, 98
Beaver Run Resort, 99
Big Mountain Ski and Summer Resort, 101
Big Sky Ski and Summer Resort, 101
Boreal Mountain Playground, 98
Copper Mountain Resort, 99
Crested Butte Mountain Resort, 99–100
Diamond Peak Ski Resort, 101
Grand Targhee Ski and Summer Resort, 103
Heavenly Ski Resort, 102
Hoodoo Ski Area and Recreation Services, 102

Inn of the Seventh Mountain, 102
Kirkwood Resort, 98
Lookout Pass Ski Area, 101
Loon Mountain Resort, 102
Mammoth California, 98
Mt. Bachelor Ski and Summer Resort, 102
Mt. Hood Meadows Ski Resort, 102
Northstar-at-Tahoe, 98
Okemo Mountain Resort, 103
Park City Mountain Resort, 102
Purgatory Resort, 100
Resort at Squaw Creek, 98
Royal Gorge Cross Country Ski Resort, 98–99
Silver Creek Resort, 100
Ski Homewood, 99
Snow Summit Mountain Resort, 99
Snowbird Ski and Summer Resort, 103
Squaw Valley USA, 99
Steamboat Ski and Resort Corporation, 100
Stevens Pass Ski Area, 103
Stowe Mountain Resort, 103
Stratton Mountain, 103
Sugar Bowl Ski Resort, 99
Sugarbush Resort, 103
Sugarloaf/USA, 101
Sun Valley Resort, 101
Sunday River Ski Resort, 101
Telluride Ski and Golf Company, 100
Timberline Lodge, 102
Topnotch Resort and Spa, 103
Vail/Beaver Creek, 100
Village at Breckenridge Resort, 100
Winter Park Resort, 100–101

Social Justice

Co-op America, 241
Global Exchange, 243
Institute for Central American Development Studies (ICADS), 270–271
Network: A National Catholic Social Justice Lobby, 251–252

Social Service

Christian Appalachian Project, 240
Make-A-Wish Foundation, 249

Sports

Alabama Sports Festival, 45–46
U.S. Olympic Committee, 74

State Park

Alaska State Parks, 110
Priest Lake State Park, 130
Vega State Park, 135

Steamboat

Delta Queen Steamboat Company, 52

Sustainable Agriculture

Hartford Food System, 244

Sustainable Education

Hawthorne Valley Farm, 189
Slide Ranch, 194

Sustainable Farm

Blue Moon Farm, 185
Emandal—A Farm on a River, 186–187
Garden Harvest, 187
Howell Living History Farm, 190
Merck Forest and Farmland Center, 192

Sustainable Living

Aprovecho Research Center, 179–180
Arcosanti, 180

Sustainable Resort

Maho Bay Camps, 92–93

Teaching

The American-Scandinavian Foundation, 260
Amity Institute, 261
China Teaching Program, 266
Choate Rosemary Hall, 240
Friends of World Teaching, 289
Fulbright Teacher Exchange Program, 243
Japan Exchange and Teaching Program, 276
Monteverde Friends School, 278
New World Teachers, 278–279
Teach for America, 254
Volunteers in Asia, 288
World Teach, 289

Technology

Student Pugwash USA, 254

Television

Directors Guild—Producer Training Plan, 212–213

Theatre

Arena Stage, 206–207
Berkeley Repertory Theatre, 208
Boarshead: Michigan's Public Theater, 208
Center Stage, 210
Creede Repertory Theatre, 211
Flat Rock Playhouse, 213
Geva Theatre, 213
Juilliard School, 216

Maine State Music Theatre, 218–219
New Stage Theatre, 222–223
The Pearl Theatre Company, 223
Seattle Repertory Theatre, 224
Shakespeare Sedona, 224
Stage One, 226
The Theater at Monmouth, 227
Theatre Directories, 232
Westport Country Playhouse, 228

Theatre Festival

American Theatre Works, 205
Williamstown Theatre Festival, 229

Therapeutic Camp

Camp Courage, 79–80
Camp Courageous of Iowa, 80
Camp Woodson, 81–82
Life Adventure Camp, 92
Ramapo Anchorage Camp, 94–95
Rocky Mountain Village, 95
Rose Resnick Lighthouse for the Blind, 95

Therapeutic Community

Gould Farm, 243–244
Green Chimneys Children's Services, 244
Innisfree Village, 245–246
Loch Arthur Community, 248
Spring Lake Ranch, 252–253

Therapeutic Recreation

Bradford Woods, 79
Breckenridge Outdoor Education Center, 48–49
Challenge Alaska, 49
U.S. Adaptive Recreation Center, 73–74

Think Tank

The Carter Center, 236

Tour Boat Outfitter

Glacier Park Boat Company, 122

Tourism

Contiki Holidays, 52
Royal Palm Tours, 72

Traditional Crafting

Arrowmont School of Arts and Crafts, 180–181
Augusta Heritage Center, 181
Horizons, 215

Traditional Farming

Tillers International, 195

There are two ways of spreading light—to be the candle or the mirror that reflects it. —EDITH WHARTON

Trail Maintenance

American Hiking Society, 110–111
Appalachian Trail Conference, 112
Colorado Trail Foundation, 115
Maine Appalachian Trail Club, 124–125
Pacific Crest Trail Association, 129

Volunteer Service

International Volunteer Expeditions, 273
Landmark Volunteers, 247
Little Children of the World, 247–248

Wilderness Adventures

National Outdoor Leadership School, 64–65
Pine Ridge Adventure Center, 69–70
The Road Less Traveled, 71

Wilderness Education

Christodora-Manice Education Center, 82
HIOBS—Southern Lands Programs, 61–62
Outward Bound, 66–68
Touch of Nature Environmental Center, 73

Wildlife

Chesapeake Wildlife Sanctuary, 149
Hawk Mountain Sanctuary Association, 154
Humane Society of the United States, 156
National Wildlife Federation, 161
U.S. Fish and Wildlife Service, 134–135
Wildlife Prairie Park, 173

Work Abroad

Council on International Educational Exchange, 267

Work Camp

Malta Youth Hostels Association, 283
Peacework, 280–281
SCI—International Voluntary Service USA, 285
Volunteers for Peace, 287–288

Work/Travel

Alliances Abroad, 260
BUNAC USA, 262

World Hunger

Educational Concerns for Hunger Organization, 242
Heifer Project Ranch, 245

Writing

Dorset Colony for Writers, 205

Yoga Center

Kripalu Center for Yoga and Health, 183–184

Yoga Farm

Ananda Marga, 179

Youth Development

Appalachian Mountain Teen Project, 47
Confrontation Point Ministries, 241–242
Internships in Youth Development, 257
National 4-H Council, 251
Youth Enrichment Services, 76

Zoo

Staten Island Zoological Society, 171

Geographical Listing of Programs . . . .

Are you looking for a particular program in a specific locale? This index gives you the tools to narrow your search to a specific state, country, or region. The United States is broken down by state, with the rest of the world grouped by country. You'll also find programs that are offered in more than one state grouped under the heading "USA" and those offered in more than one country grouped under "Worldwide." The programs under these headings are not listed separately by their respective state or country, so you'll have to get the specifics by referring to each listing.

Alabama

Alabama Sports Festival, 45–46
Camp McDowell Environmental Center, 147–148
Nature's Classroom Atop Lookout Mountain, 161–162

Alaska

Alaska State Parks, 110
Alaska Wilderness Recreation and Tourism Association, 76
Alaska Wildland Adventures, 46
Arctic Organics, 180
Bureau of Land Management, 114
Challenge Alaska, 49
Denali National Park and Preserve, 116
Denali Park Resorts, 116–117
Denali Raft Adventures, 58
Gray Line of Alaska, 59–60
National Park Service, 128
North Pacific Fisheries Observer Training Center, 163
Phillips Cruises and Tours, 69
U.S. Fish and Wildlife Service, 134
U.S. Forest Service, 137–138

Arizona

Arcosanti, 180
Bureau of Land Management, 114
Flagstaff Area National Monuments, 117
Grand Canyon National Park Lodges, 122
Green Valley Recreation, 60
Lake Powell Resorts and Marinas, 124
Shakespeare Sedona, 224
Tree of Life Rejuvenation Center, 195

Arkansas

Heifer Project Ranch, 245

California

Academy of Television Arts and Sciences, 204
Adventure Connection, 44
Alpine Meadows, 98
Ananda Marga, 179
Bear Valley Ski Company, 98
Berkeley Repertory Theatre, 208
Boojum Institute for Experiential Education, 48
Boreal Mountain Playground, 98
Bureau of Land Management, 114
Camp Highland Outdoor Science School, 81
Camp La Jolla, 81
Center for Investigative Reporting, 209–210
Chuck Richards' Whitewater, 50
Coffee Creek Ranch, 82–83
Directors Guild—Producer Training Plan, 212–213
Emandal—A Farm on a River, 186–187
Esalen Institute, 183
Farm Sanctuary, 242
Foothill Horizons Outdoor School, 152
Furnace Creek Inn and Ranch Resort, 118
Global Exchange, 243
Green Gulch Farm and Zen Center, 188
Guided Discoveries, 60–61
Headlands Institute, 154–155
Heifer Project Ranch, 245
Hidden Villa Environmental Education Program, 189–190
Hunewill Guest Ranch, 90
Just Act—Youth Action for Global Justice, 246
Kirkwood Resort, 98
Lake Tahoe Basin Management Unit, 124
Lassen County Youth Camp, 158
Mammoth California, 98
Mission Springs Conference Center, 159
Monterey Bay Aquarium, 159–160
Northstar-at-Tahoe, 98
Old Mill Farm School of Country Living, 193
Outdoor Adventure River Specialists, 65
Pacific Crest Trail Association, 129
Point Reyes National Seashore Association, 94
Rainforest Action Network, 165
Resort at Squaw Creek, 98
Richardson Bay Audubon Center and Sanctuary, 165
Rose Resnick Lighthouse for the Blind, 95
Royal Gorge Cross Country Ski Resort, 98–99
SCICON, 168
Ski Homewood, 99
Slide Ranch, 194
Snow Summit Mountain Resort, 99

A smile on your face is like a window to your heart that lets people know you are home. —PAULA LESLIE

Squaw Valley USA, 99
Stanford Sierra Camp, 104
Starr Ranch Sanctuary, 170–171
Sugar Bowl Ski Resort, 99
Tassajara Zen Mind Temple, 185
University of California at San Francisco AIDS Health
    Project, 255
U.S. Adaptive Recreation Center, 73–74
U.S. Olympic Committee, 74
Virginia Robinson Gardens, 172–173
Wolf Creek Outdoor School, 136
YMCA Camp Surf, 107
Yosemite Concession Services Corporation, 140
Yosemite National Park, 140–141

Colorado

Anasazi Heritage Center, 111
Aspen Center for Environmental Studies, 145
Aspen Lodge Ranch Resort, 78
Aspen Skiing Company, 99
Beaver Run Resort, 99
Breckenridge Outdoor Education Center, 48–49
Bureau of Land Management, 114
Central City Opera House Association, 211
The Colorado Mountain Ranch, 83
Colorado Outward Bound School, 67
Colorado Trail Foundation, 115
Colorado Trails Ranch, 84
Colvig Silver Camps, 84
Copper Mountain Resort, 99
Coulter Lake Guest Ranch, 85
Creede Repertory Theatre, 211
Crested Butte Mountain Resort, 99–100
Crow Canyon Archaeological Center, 211–212
Florissant Fossil Beds National Monument, 117–118
Four Corners Rafting, 58
The Home Ranch, 89
Kellogg Child Development Center, 246
North Fork Guest Ranch, 93
Purgatory Resort, 100
Roads Less Traveled, 71
Rocky Mountain Village, 95
Silver Creek Resort, 100
Snow Mountain Ranch, 96
Steamboat Ski and Resort Corporation, 100
Telluride Ski and Golf Company, 100
U.S. Olympic Committee, 74
Vail/Beaver Creek, 100
Vega State Park, 135
Village at Breckenridge Resort, 100
Volunteers for Outdoor Colorado, 142
Wilderness Trails Ranch, 106
Winter Park Resort, 100–101

Connecticut

Audubon Ecology Camps and Workshops, 78
Choate Rosemary Hall, 240
Ebner Camps, 86
Hartford Food System, 244
New Canaan Nature Center, 162
Norfolk Chamber Music Festival, 223
Westport Country Playhouse, 228

Delaware

Delaware Nature Society, 151

Florida

Amelia Island Plantation, 78
Educational Concerns for Hunger Organization, 242
Flamingo Lodge in Everglades National Park, 117
HIOBS—Southern Lands Programs, 61–62
Mote Marine Laboratory, 160
Newfound Harbor Marine Institute, 162
Royal Palm Tours, 72
Seacamp, 95–96

Georgia

Bradley Wellness Center, 48
Callaway Gardens, 147
The Carter Center, 236
4-H Environmental Education Program, 144
Habitat for Humanity International, 244

Hawaii

Kalani Oceanside Retreat, 91
Kewalo Basin Marine Mammal Laboratory, 157
North Country Farms, 193

Idaho

Bureau of Land Management, 114
Epley's Whitewater Adventures, 58
Hidden Creek Ranch, 88–89
Lookout Pass Ski Area, 101
Priest Lake State Park, 130
Redfish Lake Lodge, 95
River Odysseys West, 70–71
Sun Valley Resort, 101

Illinois

Angelic Organics, 179
Anita Purves Nature Center, 144–145
Blue Moon Farm, 185
Center for American Archeology, 209
Chicago Botanic Garden, 149–150
Henry Crown Sports Pavilion, 61
Lake County Forest Preserve, 157
Little Brothers—Friends of the Elderly, 247

Touch of Nature Environmental Center, 73
Wildlife Prairie Park, 173

Indiana

Bradford Woods, 79
Michaela Farm, 192

Iowa

Camp Courageous of Iowa, 80

Kentucky

Christian Appalachian Project, 240
Land Between the Lakes, 157–158
Life Adventure Camp, 92
Stage One, 226

Louisiana

Delta Queen Steamboat Company, 52

Maine

Appalachian Trail Conference, 112
Audubon Ecology Camps and Workshops, 78
Horizon Camps, 90
Hurricane Island Outward Bound School, 67
Maine Appalachian Trail Club, 124–125
Maine Organic Farmers, 197
The Maine Photographic Workshops, 218
Maine State Music Theatre, 218–219
Norlands Living History Center, 223
Oakland House Seaside Inn and Cottages, 94
Sugarloaf/USA, 101
Sunday River Ski Resort, 101
The Theater at Monmouth, 227

Maryland

Audubon Naturalist Society, 145
Center Stage, 210
Chesapeake Wildlife Sanctuary, 149
Garden Harvest, 187
National 4-H Council, 251

Massachusetts

Bikes Not Bombs, 56
Boston Mobilization for Survival, 235
Career Discovery Program, Harvard University, 209
Garden in the Woods, 153
Gould Farm, 243–244
Heartwood School, 189
Heifer Project Ranch, 245
Horizons, 215
Horizons for Youth, 155
Jacob's Pillow Dance Festival, 215
Kripalu Center for Yoga and Health, 183–184
Massachusetts Audubon Society, 175

The Option Institute, 184
Williamstown Theatre Festival, 229
Youth Enrichment Services, 76

Michigan

The Adventure Centre at Pretty Lake, 44
American Youth Foundation—Miniwanca, 46–47
Boarshead: Michigan's Public Theater, 208
Dahlem Environmental Education Center, 150
Fernwood Nature Center, 151
Henry Ford Museum and Greenfield Village, 214
Isle Royale National Park, 123–124
Kalamazoo Nature Center, 156
Sarett Nature Center, 167
Tillers International, 195

Minnesota

Camp Courage, 79–80
Canadian Border Outfitters, 49
Clearwater Canoe Outfitters and Lodge, 82
Deep Portage Conservation Reserve, 150
Dodge Nature Center, 186
Eagle Bluff Environmental Learning Center, 151
Gunflint Lodge and Outfitters, 88
Long Lake Conservation Center, 158
Minnesota Conservation Corps, 125
River Bend Nature Center, 165
Voyageur Outward Bound School, 68
Widgiwagan's Environmental Education Program, 173
Wilderness Canoe Base, 106
Wolf Ridge Environmental Learning Center, 173–174

Mississippi

New Stage Theatre, 222–223

Missouri

Wyman Center, 75–76

Montana

Big Mountain Ski and Summer Resort, 101
Big Sky Ski and Summer Resort, 101
Bureau of Land Management, 114
The Glacier Institute, 121
Glacier Park, 121–122
Glacier Park Boat Company, 122
River Odysseys West, 70–71
St. Mary Lodge and Resort, 132

Nevada

Bureau of Land Management, 114
Diamond Peak Ski Resort, 101
Heavenly Ski Resort, 102
Incline Village General Improvement District, 90

*That which we obtain too easily, we esteem too lightly. It is dearness only which gives everything its value.
Heaven knows how to put a proper price on its goods.* —THOMAS PAINE

New Hampshire

Appalachian Mountain Club, 111–112
Appalachian Mountain Teen Project, 47
Attitash Bear Peak Resort, 102
Davis Family Farm, 186
Loon Mountain Resort, 102
Squam Lakes Natural Science Center, 170

New Jersey

Appel Farm Arts and Music Center, 206
Fairview Lake YMCA Camps, 87
Howell Living History Farm, 190

New Mexico

Angel Fire Resort, 102
Bureau of Land Management, 114
Carlsbad Caverns National Park, 115
St. Elizabeth Shelter, 253

New York

Adirondack Mountain Club, 110
Aperture Foundation, 205–206
Center for Photography at Woodstock, 210
Chingachgook YMCA Outdoor Center, 50
Christodora-Manice Education Center, 82
Clearwater, 50–51
Farm Sanctuary, 242
Geva Theatre, 213
Green Chimneys Children's Services, 244
Hawthorne Valley Farm, 189
Horizon Camps, 90
Juilliard School, 216
The Kitchen, 217
The Metropolitan Museum of Art, 219
The Nation Institute, 219
NYS Department of Environmental Conservation, 163–164
Omega Institute for Holistic Studies, 184
Outward Bound USA, 67
The Pearl Theatre Company, 223
Ramapo Anchorage Camp, 94–95
Sagamore Institute, 130–131
Spoleto Arts Symposia, 225
Stagedoor Manor Performing Arts Center, 226–227
Staten Island Zoological Society, 171
United Nations Association of the USA, 286
U.S. Olympic Committee, 74
Wilderness Way Experiential Learning Program, 75
Women's Studio Workshop, 229

North Carolina

American Dance Festival, 204–205
Camp High Rocks, 81
Camp Woodson, 81–82
Eagle's Nest Foundation, 85–86
Flat Rock Playhouse, 213
Mountain Trail Outdoor School, 93
Nags Head Woods Preserve, 160–161
North Carolina Outward Bound School, 67
Sustenance Farm, 194–195

North Dakota

Theodore Roosevelt National Park, 133

Ohio

Aullwood Audubon Center and Farm, 146
Brukner Nature Center, 147
Five Rivers MetroParks, 152
Glen Helen Outdoor Education Center, 153–154
Holden Arboretum, 155
Ohio Ecological Food and Farm Association, 200
YMCA Willson Outdoor Center, 107

Oregon

Aprovecho Research Center, 179–180
Berry Botanic Garden, 146
Bureau of Land Management, 114
Crater Lake Company, 115
Crater Lake National Park, 115
Hoodoo Ski Area and Recreation Services, 102
Inn of the Seventh Mountain, 102
Lost Valley Educational Center, 191
Mobility International USA, 250
Mt. Bachelor Ski and Summer Resort, 102
Mt. Hood Meadows Ski Resort, 102
Northwest Youth Corps, 125–126
Oregon Dunes National Recreation Area, 126
Pacific Crest Outward Bound School, 68
Pacific Crest Trail Association, 129
River Network, 166
Sunriver Resort, 105
Timberline Lodge, 102

Pennsylvania

Appalachian Trail Conference, 112
College Settlement—Kuhn Day Camps, 83
Hawk Mountain Sanctuary Association, 154
Hopewell Furnace National Historic Site, 123
Horizon Camps, 90
Longwood Gardens, 158–159
Peace Valley Nature Center, 164
Pocono Environmental Education Center, 164–165
Riverbend Environmental Education Center, 166
The Rodale Institute Experimental Farm, 193–194
Schuylkill Center for Environmental Education, 168
The Scott Arboretum of Swarthmore College, 169
Shaver's Creek Environmental Center, 169–170

Rhode Island

Astors' Beechwood Mansion, 207

South Carolina

Barrier Island Environmental Education Center, 146
Camp Chatuga, 79
Hilton Oceanfront Resort, 89
Spoleto Festival USA, 226

South Dakota

Badlands National Park, 112
Custer State Park Resort Company, 116
Mt. Rushmore National Memorial, 125
Wind Cave National Park, 136

Tennessee

Arrowmont School of Arts and Crafts, 180–181
Confrontation Point Ministries, 241–242
Great Smoky Mountains Institute, 154
The Hermitage, 214–215
Walden Farm, 195

Texas

Y.O. Adventure Camp, 107

Utah

Bureau of Land Management, 114
Canyonlands National Park, 112
Four Corners School of Outdoor Education, 59
Park City Mountain Resort, 102
Snowbird Ski and Summer Resort, 103
Zion and Bryce Canyon National Park Lodges, 141

Vermont

American Theatre Works, 205
Appalachian Trail Conference, 112
Dorset Colony for Writers, 205
Farm and Wilderness Foundation, 87
Hulbert Outdoor Center, 62
Keewaydin Environmental Education Center, 156–157
Merck Forest and Farmland Center, 192
Middlebury College Language Schools, 278
Montshire Museum of Science, 160
Northeast Organic Farming Association of Vermont, 197
Okemo Mountain Resort, 103
Pine Ridge Adventure Center, 69–70
Spring Lake Ranch, 252–253
Stowe Mountain Resort, 103
Stratton Mountain, 103
Sugarbush Resort, 103
Topnotch Resort and Spa, 103
Vermont Youth Conservation Corps, 136

Virgin Islands

Maho Bay Camps, 92–93

Virginia

American Horticultural Society, 144
Appalachian Trail Conference, 112
Camp Friendship, 80–81
The Center for Health, Environment, and Justice, 148
Colonial Williamsburg Foundation, 211
Fredericksburg and Spotsylvania National Military Park, 118
George Washington's Mount Vernon, 188
Good Earth Farm School, 188
The History Factory, 215
Innisfree Village, 245–246
Legacy International, 91
The Nature Conservancy, 161
Potomac Appalachian Trail Club, 130
Shenandoah National Park, 131
Wollam Gardens, 195

Washington

Cascadian Home Farm, 185–186
Gray Line of Alaska, 59–60
International Bicycle Fund, 57
North Cascades Institute, 163
Olympic National Park, 126
Pacific Crest Trail Association, 129
Reachout Expeditions, 70
Salish Sea Expeditions, 166–167
Seattle Repertory Theatre, 224
Seattle Tilth Association, 201
Sol Duc Hot Springs, 104
Stevens Pass Ski Area, 103

Washington, DC

Advocacy Institute, 234
Arena Stage, 206–207
Children's Defense Fund, 240
Co-op America, 241
Congressional Youth Leadership Council, 242
Friends of the Earth—U.S., 153
Hostelling International—American Youth Hostels, 282–283
Humane Society of the United States, 156
The Kennedy Center, 216
Mickey Leland Hunger Fellows Program, 249–250
My Sister's Place, 251
National Building Museum, 219
Naval Historical Center, 222
Network: A National Catholic Social Justice Lobby, 251–252
The Population Institute, 252
Reporters Committee for Freedom of the Press, 224

The significant problems we face cannot be solved at the same level of thinking we were at when we created them. —ALBERT EINSTEIN

Smithsonian Institution, 225
Student Pugwash USA, 254
Washington Performing Arts Society, 228

West Virginia

Augusta Heritage Center, 181
Claymont Farm CSA, 186
Greenbrier River Outdoor Adventures, 60

Wisconsin

Central Wisconsin Environmental Station, 148–149
The Clearing, 211
International Crane Foundation, 156
Outdoors Wisconsin Leadership School, 68–69
Trees for Tomorrow, 172
Upham Woods 4-H EE Center, 172

Wyoming

Audubon Ecology Camps and Workshops, 78
Bureau of Land Management, 114
Flagg Ranch Resort, 117
Grand Targhee Ski and Summer Resort, 103
Grand Teton Lodge Company, 122–123
Lost Creek Ranch, 92
Signal Mountain Lodge, 131
Yellowstone National Park Lodges, 139
Yellowstone Park Service Stations, 140

USA

Adventure Pursuits, 45
American Adventures, 46
American Hiking Society, 110–111
AmeriCorps, 234–235
Amizade, 261
Appropriate Technology Transfer for Rural Areas, 200
Bike-Aid, 55–56
The Biking Expedition, 56
Bureau of Land Management, 113–114
Campaign to Save the Environment, 148
A Christian Ministry in the National Parks, 234
City Year, 241
Contiki Holidays, 52
Dow Jones Newspaper Fund, 213
Food Service Management Internship, 88
Good Farming Apprenticeship Network, 200
The Institute for Academic Advancement of Youth (IAAY) Summer Programs, 245
Landmark Volunteers, 247
Lutheran Volunteer Corps, 248–249
Make-A-Wish Foundation, 249
Mickey Leland Hunger Fellows Program, 249–250
Nannies Plus, 278
National Park Service, 127–129
National Service Corps, 238

National Wildlife Federation, 161
Offshore Sailing School, 65
Overland Travel, 69
The Road Less Traveled, 71
Special Expeditions Marine, 72–73
Student Conservation Association, Inc., 132–133
Student Hosteling Program, 57
Surfrider Foundation, 171
Teach for America, 254
Trailmark Outdoor Adventures, 73
U.S. Army Corps of Engineers, 133
U.S. Fish and Wildlife Service, 134–135
U.S. Forest Service, 137–138

Africa

Concern America, 266–267
Cross-Cultural Solutions, 267–268
Institute for International Cooperation and Development, 271
Operation Crossroads Africa, 279–280

Asia

Volunteers in Asia, 288

Australia

Amizade, 261
BUNAC USA, 262
Camp Counselors/Work Experience USA, 79

The Bahamas

International Field Studies, 63

Canada

Adventure Pursuits, 45
Appropriate Technology Transfer for Rural Areas, 200
The Banff Centre for the Arts, 208
BCT.TELUS Employee Fitness Program, 47
Frontiers Foundation, 243
Good Farming Apprenticeship Network, 200
Hollyhock, 183
Parks Canada Research Adventures, 129
Student Hosteling Program, 57

Caribbean

Operation Crossroads Africa, 279–280
Sail Caribbean, 72

China

China Teaching Program, 266

Costa Rica

Costa Rica Rainforest Outward Bound School, 68
Institute for Central American Development Studies (ICADS), 270–271

Latin American Language Center, 277
Monteverde Friends School, 278
The Road Less Traveled, 71
Sea Turtle Restoration Project, 169

Denmark

Alternative Travel Club—Denmark, 199

Europe

Au Pair in Europe, 262
Bombard Balloon Adventures, 47–48
European Centre for Ecological Agriculture and
    Tourism, 199
InterExchange, 272
Overland Travel, 69
Student Hosteling Program, 57

Finland

The American-Scandinavian Foundation, 260
Centre for International Mobility, 266

France

Château de Jean d'Heurs, 266
La Sabranenque, 217

Germany

CDS International, 263
International Christian Youth Exchange, 272–273

Greece

Greek Dances Theater—Dora Stratou, 214

Guatemala

Art Workshops in Guatemala, 207
Casa Xelajú, 262–263

Haiti

Educational Concerns for Hunger Organization, 242

Honduras

Latin American Art Resource Project, 217–218

Hungary

Hungarian Association for Organic Farming, 199

India

Cross-Cultural Solutions, 267–268
Institute for International Cooperation and
    Development, 271

Israel

Kibbutz Program Center, 276–277
Project Otzma, 281

Italy, 289–290

Ciclismo Classico, 56–57
La Sabranenque, 217

Japan, 290

Japan Exchange and Teaching Program, 276

Kosovo

Cross-Cultural Solutions, 267–268

Latin America

Amigos de las Américas, 260–261
Amity Institute, 261
Amizade, 261
Concern America, 266–267
Institute for International Cooperation and
    Development, 271

Malta

Malta Youth Hostels Association, 283

Mexico

Adventure Pursuits, 45
Costa Azul Adventure Resort, 84–85
Institute of International Education—Latin America,
    271–272
Los Niños, 277
Mar de Jade, 277
Third World Opportunities, 254–255

Nepal

The Road Less Traveled, 71

New Zealand

Camp Counselors/Work Experience USA, 79

Norway

Atlantis Youth Exchange, 181

Peru

Cross-Cultural Solutions, 267–268

Philippines

Little Children of the World, 247–248

Russia

Camp Counselors/Work Experience USA, 79

Scotland

Loch Arthur Community, 248

To acquire knowledge, one must study; but to acquire wisdom, one must experience. —Sue Schmid

United Kingdom

The British Universities Accommodation Consortium, 284
BUNAC USA, 262
Losang Dragpa Buddhist Centre, 184

Venezuela

Camp Counselors/Work Experience USA, 79
VEN-USA, 286–287

Worldwide

Academic Study Associates, 204
Adventures Cross-Country, 45
Alliances Abroad, 260
American Institute for Foreign Study, 260
Backroads, 55
Berlitz International, 262
Brethren Volunteer Service, 235–236
Center for Global Education, 263
Clipper Cruise Line, 51
Club Med, 51
Council on International Educational Exchange, 267
Elderhostel, 237
ElderTreks, 237–238
Fulbright Teacher Exchange Program, 243
Global Citizens Network, 268
Global Routes, 268–269
Global Service Corps, 269
Global Volunteers, 269–270
Global Works, Inc., 270
Interlocken International, 62–63
International Agricultural Exchange Association, 190–191

The International Partnership for Service-Learning, 273
International Volunteer Expeditions, 273
International YMCA, 273
Internships International, 276
Longacre Expeditions, 63–64
Mast International Experience, 191
Mercy Ships, 249
National Future Farmers of America Center, 192–193
National Outdoor Leadership School, 64–65
New World Teachers, 278–279
Peace Corps, 280
Peacework, 280–281
People to People International, 281
Putney Student Travel, 70
St. Vincent Pallotti Center for Apostolic Development, 253–254
The School for Field Studies, 167
SCI—International Voluntary Service USA, 285
Semester at Sea, 285–286
Seniors Abroad, 238–239
Supercamp, 105–106
University Research Expeditions Program, 286
Up With People Worldsmart, 227–228
Visions International, 287
Volunteers for Peace, 287–288
Walking the World, 239
Wilderness Inquiry, 74–75
Wildlands Studies, 288
Willing Workers on Organic Farms, 196–199
Woods Hole Sea Semester, 75
World Teach, 289

Program Length Index . . . .

Here are the programs divided up based on program length. Some programs appear in
multiple categories. You will find seasonal programs at the end of the index, followed
by programs whose length varies. Don't forget to investigate those!

Less than 1 month (1–3 weeks)

American Hiking Society, 110–111
Amizade, 261
Appalachian Trail Conference, 112
Art Workshops in Guatemala, 207
The Banff Centre for the Arts, 208
Berlitz International, 262
Camp Courageous of Iowa, 80
Center for Global Education, 263
Clearwater, 50–51
Council on International Educational Exchange, 267
Cross-Cultural Solutions, 267–268
Elderhostel, 237
ElderTreks, 237–238
Global Citizens Network, 268
Global Service Corps, 269
Global Volunteers, 269–270
Heartwood School, 189
The Hermitage, 214–215
Horizons, 215
Interlocken International, 62–63
International Volunteer Expeditions, 273
Kripalu Center for Yoga and Health, 183–184
La Sabranenque, 217
Landmark Volunteers, 247
Latin American Language Center, 277
Los Niños, 277
Malta Youth Hostels Association, 283
Mar de Jade, 277
National Outdoor Leadership School, 64–65
Pacific Crest Trail Association, 129
Parks Canada Research Adventures, 129
Peacework, 280–281
Potomac Appalachian Trail Club, 130
SCI—International Voluntary Service USA, 285
Sea Turtle Restoration Project, 169
Seniors Abroad, 238–239
Supercamp, 105–106
Third World Opportunities, 254–255
University Research Expeditions Program, 286
Volunteers for Peace, 287–288
Walking the World, 239
Wilderness Canoe Base, 106

1 month (4–5 weeks)

Appalachian Trail Conference, 112
Arcosanti, 180
The Banff Centre for the Arts, 208
Berlitz International, 262
Camp Courageous of Iowa, 80
Clearwater, 50–51
Council on International Educational Exchange, 267
Elderhostel, 237
Esalen Institute, 183
Farm Sanctuary, 242
Global Routes, 268–269
Global Service Corps, 269
The Hermitage, 214–215
International Volunteer Expeditions, 273
Keewaydin Environmental Education Center, 156–157
Kripalu Center for Yoga and Health, 183–184
La Sabranenque, 217
Latin American Art Resource Project, 217–218
Latin American Language Center, 277
Little Children of the World, 247–248
Malta Youth Hostels Association, 283
National Outdoor Leadership School, 64–65
Peacework, 280–281
SCI—International Voluntary Service USA, 285
Seniors Abroad, 238–239
Spoleto Festival USA, 226
Supercamp, 105–106

1¹/₂ months (6–7 weeks)

Appalachian Trail Conference, 112
The Banff Centre for the Arts, 208
Berlitz International, 262
Camp Courageous of Iowa, 80
Career Discovery Program, Harvard University, 209
Farm Sanctuary, 242
Fulbright Teacher Exchange Program, 243
Global Routes, 268–269
Interlocken International, 62–63
International Volunteer Expeditions, 273
Internships International, 276
Keewaydin Environmental Education Center, 156–157
Kripalu Center for Yoga and Health, 183–184
La Sabranenque, 217
Little Children of the World, 247–248
The Maine Photographic Workshops, 218
Malta Youth Hostels Association, 283
Omega Institute for Holistic Studies, 184
Supercamp, 105–106
Visions International, 287

*A life spent in making mistakes is not only more honorable but
more useful than a life spent in doing nothing.* —George Bernard Shaw

2 months (8–10 weeks)

Aprovecho Research Center, 179–180
Atlantis Youth Exchange, 181
The Banff Centre for the Arts, 208
Berlitz International, 262
Bike-Aid, 55–56
Camp Courageous of Iowa, 80
Carlsbad Caverns National Park, 115
Casa Xelajú, 262–263
Challenge Alaska, 49
Children's Defense Fund, 240
Clearwater, 50–51
Crater Lake Company, 115
Dodge Nature Center, 186
Farm and Wilderness Foundation, 87
Farm Sanctuary, 242
Fernwood Nature Center, 151
The Glacier Institute, 121
Global Exchange, 243
Global Routes, 268–269
Global Service Corps, 269
Green Valley Recreation, 60
Hollyhock, 183
Interlocken International, 62–63
International Volunteer Expeditions, 273
Keewaydin Environmental Education Center, 156–157
The Kitchen, 217
Kripalu Center for Yoga and Health, 183–184
La Sabranenque, 217
Latin American Art Resource Project, 217–218
Little Children of the World, 247–248
Malta Youth Hostels Association, 283
Oakland House Seaside Inn and Cottages, 94
The Option Institute, 184
Peace Valley Nature Center, 164
People to People International, 281
Royal Palm Tours, 72
Visions International, 287
Wollam Gardens, 195
Woods Hole Sea Semester, 75

3 months (11–14 weeks)

Advocacy Institute, 234
Angelic Organics, 179
Appel Farm Arts and Music Center, 206
Atlantis Youth Exchange, 181
Audubon Naturalist Society, 145
Aullwood Audubon Center and Farm, 146
The Banff Centre for the Arts, 208
Brukner Nature Center, 147
Camp Courageous of Iowa, 80
Canyonlands National Park, 112
The Carter Center, 236
Casa Xelajú, 262–263

Center for Photography at Woodstock, 210
Challenge Alaska, 49
Children's Defense Fund, 240
Council on International Educational Exchange, 267
Deep Portage Conservation Reserve, 150
Dodge Nature Center, 186
Fairview Lake YMCA Camps, 87
Farm Sanctuary, 242
Fernwood Nature Center, 151
Flagstaff Area National Monuments, 117
Four Corners School of Outdoor Education, 59
4-H Environmental Education Program, 144
Friends of the Earth—U.S., 153
Frontiers Foundation, 243
The Glacier Institute, 121
Global Exchange, 243
Global Service Corps, 269
Green Chimneys Children's Services, 244
Henry Crown Sports Pavilion, 61
HIOBS—Southern Lands Programs, 61–62
Hopewell Furnace National Historic Site, 123
Howell Living History Farm, 190
Institute of International Education—Latin America, 271–272
Kalani Oceanside Retreat, 91
The Kennedy Center, 216
The Kitchen, 217
Kripalu Center for Yoga and Health, 183–184
La Sabranenque, 217
Latin American Art Resource Project, 217–218
Little Children of the World, 247–248
Long Lake Conservation Center, 158
Malta Youth Hostels Association, 283
Mobility International USA, 250
National 4-H Council, 251
National Outdoor Leadership School, 64–65
Nature's Classroom Atop Lookout Mountain, 161–162
North Pacific Fisheries Observer Training Center, 163
NYS Department of Environmental Conservation, 163–164
Oakland House Seaside Inn and Cottages, 94
Peace Valley Nature Center, 164
Reporters Committee for Freedom of the Press, 224
Richardson Bay Audubon Center and Sanctuary, 165
Royal Palm Tours, 72
Shaver's Creek Environmental Center, 169–170
Starr Ranch Sanctuary, 170–171
Telluride Ski and Golf Company, 100
Tillers International, 195
U.S. Olympic Committee, 74
Wildlife Prairie Park, 173
Wind Cave National Park, 136
Woods Hole Sea Semester, 75

4 months (15–18 weeks)

Advocacy Institute, 234
Alaska Wildland Adventures, 46
Amelia Island Plantation, 78
American Youth Foundation—Miniwanca, 46–47
Amity Institute, 261
Angelic Organics, 179
Callaway Gardens, 147
Camp Courageous of Iowa, 80
Camp McDowell Environmental Center, 147–148
Camp Woodson, 81–82
Canyonlands National Park, 112
Casa Xelajú, 262–263
Center for Photography at Woodstock, 210
Clearwater, 50–51
Council on International Educational Exchange, 267
Crater Lake Company, 115
Creede Repertory Theatre, 211
Deep Portage Conservation Reserve, 150
Denali Raft Adventures, 58
Fairview Lake YMCA Camps, 87
Four Corners School of Outdoor Education, 59
Frontiers Foundation, 243
Fulbright Teacher Exchange Program, 243
The Glacier Institute, 121
Glen Helen Outdoor Education Center, 153–154
Global Exchange, 243
Global Service Corps, 269
Green Chimneys Children's Services, 244
Headlands Institute, 154–155
Henry Crown Sports Pavilion, 61
Hilton Oceanfront Resort, 89
Hopewell Furnace National Historic Site, 123
The Kennedy Center, 216
Lake County Forest Preserve, 157
Long Lake Conservation Center, 158
Mobility International USA, 250
Montshire Museum of Science, 160
National 4-H Council, 251
North Fork Guest Ranch, 93
Royal Palm Tours, 72
Schuylkill Center for Environmental Education, 168
Semester at Sea, 285–286
Shaver's Creek Environmental Center, 169–170
Tillers International, 195
U.S. Olympic Committee, 74
Wilderness Inquiry, 74–75
Wind Cave National Park, 136
Women's Studio Workshop, 229

5 months

Angelic Organics, 179
Breckenridge Outdoor Education Center, 48–49
Camp Courageous of Iowa, 80
Casa Xelajú, 262–263
Center for Photography at Woodstock, 210
Council on International Educational Exchange, 267
Deep Portage Conservation Reserve, 150
Denali Park Resorts, 116–117
Frontiers Foundation, 243
The Glacier Institute, 121
Glen Helen Outdoor Education Center, 153–154
Global Exchange, 243
Global Service Corps, 269
Green Chimneys Children's Services, 244
Headlands Institute, 154–155
Hidden Villa Environmental Education Program, 189–190
Hunewill Guest Ranch, 90
Long Lake Conservation Center, 158
Mobility International USA, 250
National 4-H Council, 251
North Fork Guest Ranch, 93
Phillips Cruises and Tours, 69
Shaver's Creek Environmental Center, 169–170
Tillers International, 195
U.S. Olympic Committee, 74
Wilderness Inquiry, 74–75

6 months

Alabama Sports Festival, 45–46
Angelic Organics, 179
Aperture Foundation, 205–206
Appel Farm Arts and Music Center, 206
Arctic Organics, 180
Breckenridge Outdoor Education Center, 48–49
Brukner Nature Center, 147
Callaway Gardens, 147
Casa Xelajú, 262–263
Cascadian Home Farm, 185–186
Center for Investigative Reporting, 209–210
Center for Photography at Woodstock, 210
Christodora-Manice Education Center, 82
Council on International Educational Exchange, 267
Crater Lake Company, 115
Deep Portage Conservation Reserve, 150
Friends of the Earth—U.S., 153
Frontiers Foundation, 243
Garden in the Woods, 153
The Glacier Institute, 121
Global Exchange, 243
Global Service Corps, 269
Gould Farm, 243–244
Hilton Oceanfront Resort, 89
Institute for International Cooperation and Development, 271
International Christian Youth Exchange, 272–273
Lake County Forest Preserve, 157
Long Lake Conservation Center, 158

If you want to be successful, know what you are doing, love what you are doing, and believe in what you are doing. —WILL ROGERS

Lost Creek Ranch, 92
Mobility International USA, 250
North Country Farms, 193
Old Mill Farm School of Country Living, 193
The Pearl Theatre Company, 223
Pocono Environmental Education Center, 164–165
The Population Institute, 252
Sagamore Institute, 130–131
Shaver's Creek Environmental Center, 169–170
Signal Mountain Lodge, 131
Special Expeditions Marine, 72–73
Spring Lake Ranch, 252–253
Tillers International, 195
Women's Studio Workshop, 229

7 months

Alabama Sports Festival, 45–46
Angelic Organics, 179
Backroads, 55
Blue Moon Farm, 185
Brukner Nature Center, 147
Chingachgook YMCA Outdoor Center, 50
Deep Portage Conservation Reserve, 150
The Glacier Institute, 121
Gould Farm, 243–244
Green Gulch Farm and Zen Center, 188
Hilton Oceanfront Resort, 89
Institute for International Cooperation and
    Development, 271
Long Lake Conservation Center, 158
Pocono Environmental Education Center, 164–165
Slide Ranch, 194
Tillers International, 195
Vermont Youth Conservation Corps, 136

8 months

Alabama Sports Festival, 45–46
Amigos de las Américas, 260–261
Brukner Nature Center, 147
Custer State Park Resort Company, 116
Deep Portage Conservation Reserve, 150
Fernwood Nature Center, 151
Gould Farm, 243–244
Hilton Oceanfront Resort, 89
Institute for International Cooperation and
    Development, 271
Long Lake Conservation Center, 158
Pocono Environmental Education Center, 164–165
The Rodale Institute Experimental Farm, 193–194
Shenandoah National Park, 131
Slide Ranch, 194
Tillers International, 195

9 months

Alabama Sports Festival, 45–46
Appel Farm Arts and Music Center, 206
Atlantis Youth Exchange, 181
Barrier Island Environmental Education Center, 146
Brukner Nature Center, 147
Camp Courage, 79–80
Center Stage, 210
Costa Azul Adventure Resort, 84–85
Deep Portage Conservation Reserve, 150
Eagle Bluff Environmental Learning Center, 151
Five Rivers MetroParks, 152
4-H Environmental Education Program, 144
Fulbright Teacher Exchange Program, 243
Gould Farm, 243–244
Hidden Villa Environmental Education Program, 189–190
Hilton Oceanfront Resort, 89
Institute for International Cooperation and
    Development, 271
Juilliard School, 216
Long Lake Conservation Center, 158
Michaela Farm, 192
Mountain Trail Outdoor School, 93
New Canaan Nature Center, 162
New Stage Theatre, 222–223
Pocono Environmental Education Center, 164–165
The Rodale Institute Experimental Farm, 193–194
Seattle Repertory Theatre, 224
Slide Ranch, 194
Stage One, 226
Tillers International, 195
Trees for Tomorrow, 172

10 months

AmeriCorps, 234–235
Amity Institute, 261
Atlantis Youth Exchange, 181
Berkeley Repertory Theatre, 208
Center Stage, 210
China Teaching Program, 266
City Year, 241
Costa Azul Adventure Resort, 84–85
Foothill Horizons Outdoor School, 152
Good Earth Farm School, 188
Gould Farm, 243–244
Hilton Oceanfront Resort, 89
Institute for International Cooperation and
    Development, 271
Pocono Environmental Education Center, 164–165
Project Otzma, 281
SCICON, 168
Slide Ranch, 194
Sustenance Farm, 194–195
Wolf Ridge Environmental Learning Center, 173–174

11 months

Arrowmont School of Arts and Crafts, 180–181
Atlantis Youth Exchange, 181
Costa Azul Adventure Resort, 84–85
Gould Farm, 243–244
Hilton Oceanfront Resort, 89
Institute for International Cooperation and
     Development, 271
Network: A National Catholic Social Justice Lobby,
     251–252
Slide Ranch, 194
Up With People Worldsmart, 227–228

1 year

AmeriCorps, 234–235
Atlantis Youth Exchange, 181
Brethren Volunteer Service, 235–236
Cascadian Home Farm, 185–186
Clipper Cruise Line, 51
Costa Azul Adventure Resort, 84–85
Davis Family Farm, 186
Five Rivers MetroParks, 152
Geva Theatre, 213
Gould Farm, 243–244
Great Smoky Mountains Institute, 154
Hilton Oceanfront Resort, 89
Howell Living History Farm, 190
Innisfree Village, 245–246
Institute for International Cooperation and
     Development, 271
International Christian Youth Exchange, 272–273
International Field Studies, 63
Japan Exchange and Teaching Program, 276
Lake County Forest Preserve, 157
Little Brothers—Friends of the Elderly, 247
Loch Arthur Community, 248
Lutheran Volunteer Corps, 248–249
Mickey Leland Hunger Fellows Program, 249–250
Monteverde Friends School, 278
My Sister's Place, 251
Nannies Plus, 278
New World Teachers, 278–279
River Network, 166
The School for Field Studies, 167
The Scott Arboretum of Swarthmore College, 169
University of California at San Francisco AIDS Health
     Project, 255
Volunteers in Asia, 288

More than 1 year

Brethren Volunteer Service, 235–236
Concern America, 266–267
Directors Guild—Producer Training Plan, 212–213
Educational Concerns for Hunger Organization, 242

Institute for International Cooperation and
     Development, 271
Japan Exchange and Teaching Program, 276
Monteverde Friends School, 278
Peace Corps, 280
Teach for America, 254
Volunteers in Asia, 288

Spring

Arrowmont School of Arts and Crafts, 180–181
Camp Highland Outdoor Science School, 81
Lassen County Youth Camp, 158
Nature's Classroom Atop Lookout Mountain, 161–162
Newfound Harbor Marine Institute, 162
Salish Sea Expeditions, 166–167
Stanford Sierra Camp, 104
Wolf Creek Outdoor School, 136
Women's Studio Workshop, 229
Wyman Center, 75–76

Summer

Academy of Television Arts and Sciences, 204
Adventure Pursuits, 45
Adventures Cross-Country, 45
Alaska State Parks, 110
American Adventures, 46
American Dance Festival, 204–205
American Theatre Works, 205
Anasazi Heritage Center, 111
Appel Farm Arts and Music Center, 206
Arrowmont School of Arts and Crafts, 180–181
Aspen Center for Environmental Studies, 145
Astors' Beechwood Mansion, 207
Audubon Ecology Camps and Workshops, 78
Berry Botanic Garden, 146
Big Mountain Ski and Summer Resort, 101
Big Sky Ski and Summer Resort, 101
The Biking Expedition, 56
Boreal Mountain Playground, 98
Breckenridge Outdoor Education Center, 48–49
Camp Chatuga, 79
Camp Courage, 79–80
Camp High Rocks, 81
Camp La Jolla, 81
Campaign to Save the Environment, 148
Canadian Border Outfitters, 49
Central City Opera House Association, 211
Choate Rosemary Hall, 240
Chuck Richards' Whitewater, 50
Clearwater Canoe Outfitters and Lodge, 82
The Colorado Mountain Ranch, 83
Colorado Trail Foundation, 115
Colorado Trails Ranch, 84
Colvig Silver Camps, 84

The secret of success is to do the common duty uncommonly well. —JOHN D. ROCKEFELLER, JR.

Confrontation Point Ministries, 241–242
Dow Jones Newspaper Fund, 213
Ebner Camps, 86
Epley's Whitewater Adventures, 58
Five Rivers MetroParks, 152
Flagg Ranch Resort, 117
Flat Rock Playhouse, 213
Florissant Fossil Beds National Monument, 117–118
Food Service Management Internship, 88
Four Corners Rafting, 58
George Washington's Mount Vernon, 188
Glacier Park, 121–122
Glacier Park Boat Company, 122
Glen Helen Outdoor Education Center, 153–154
Global Works, Inc., 270
Grand Targhee Ski and Summer Resort, 103
Gray Line of Alaska, 59–60
Greenbrier River Outdoor Adventures, 60
Guided Discoveries, 60–61
Gunflint Lodge and Outfitters, 88
Hartford Food System, 244
Headlands Institute, 154–155
Holden Arboretum, 155
Horizon Camps, 90
Horizons for Youth, 155
Incline Village General Improvement District, 90
The Institute for Academic Advancement of Youth
    (IAAY) Summer Programs, 245
Institute for Central American Development Studies
    (ICADS), 270–271
International Christian Youth Exchange, 272–273
Isle Royale National Park, 123–124
Jacob's Pillow Dance Festival, 215
Kalamazoo Nature Center, 156
Lake Powell Resorts and Marinas, 124
Legacy International, 91
Life Adventure Camp, 92
Little Brothers—Friends of the Elderly, 247
Longacre Expeditions, 63–64
The Maine Photographic Workshops, 218
Maine State Music Theatre, 218–219
The Metropolitan Museum of Art, 219
Middlebury College Language Schools, 278
Minnesota Conservation Corps, 125
Monterey Bay Aquarium, 159–160
Mt. Bachelor Ski and Summer Resort, 102
Mt. Rushmore National Memorial, 125
Nags Head Woods Preserve, 160–161
National Wildlife Federation, 161
The Nature Conservancy, 161
New Canaan Nature Center, 162
Norfolk Chamber Music Festival, 223
Northwest Youth Corps, 125–126
Operation Crossroads Africa, 279–280

Overland Travel, 69
Pine Ridge Adventure Center, 69–70
Point Reyes National Seashore Association, 94
Potomac Appalachian Trail Club, 130
Priest Lake State Park, 130
Putney Student Travel, 70
Ramapo Anchorage Camp, 94–95
Redfish Lake Lodge, 95
River Odysseys West, 70–71
Riverbend Environmental Education Center, 166
The Road Less Traveled, 71
Rocky Mountain Village, 95
Rose Resnick Lighthouse for the Blind, 95
Sagamore Institute, 130–131
Sail Caribbean, 72
St. Mary Lodge and Resort, 132
The Scott Arboretum of Swarthmore College, 169
Seacamp, 95–96
Shakespeare Sedona, 224
Snowbird Ski and Summer Resort, 103
Sol Duc Hot Springs, 104
Spoleto Arts Symposia, 225
Squam Lakes Natural Science Center, 170
Stagedoor Manor Performing Arts Center, 226–227
Staten Island Zoological Society, 171
Student Hosteling Program, 57
Sunriver Resort, 105
Tassajara Zen Mind Temple, 185
The Theater at Monmouth, 227
Trailmark Outdoor Adventures, 73
U.S. Adaptive Recreation Center, 73–74
Virginia Robinson Gardens, 172–173
Volunteers in Asia, 288
Westport Country Playhouse, 228
Wilderness Trails Ranch, 106
Wilderness Way Experiential Learning Program, 75
Williamstown Theatre Festival, 229
Yellowstone Park Service Stations, 140
Yosemite National Park, 140–141

Fall

Astors' Beechwood Mansion, 207
Camp Highland Outdoor Science School, 81
Lassen County Youth Camp, 158
Nature's Classroom Atop Lookout Mountain, 161–162
Newfound Harbor Marine Institute, 162
Sagamore Institute, 130–131
Salish Sea Expeditions, 166–167
Stanford Sierra Camp, 104
Wolf Creek Outdoor School, 136
Women's Studio Workshop, 229
Wyman Center, 75–76

Winter

Alaska State Parks, 110
Alpine Meadows, 98
Angel Fire Resort, 102
Aspen Skiing Company, 99
Attitash Bear Peak Resort, 102
Bear Valley Ski Company, 98
Beaver Run Resort, 99
Big Mountain Ski and Summer Resort, 101
Big Sky Ski and Summer Resort, 101
Boreal Mountain Playground, 98
Breckenridge Outdoor Education Center, 48–49
Copper Mountain Resort, 99
Crested Butte Mountain Resort, 99–100
Diamond Peak Ski Resort, 101
Flagg Ranch Resort, 117
Grand Targhee Ski and Summer Resort, 103
Gunflint Lodge and Outfitters, 88
Heavenly Ski Resort, 102
Hoodoo Ski Area and Recreation Services, 102
Incline Village General Improvement District, 90
Inn of the Seventh Mountain, 102
Kirkwood Resort, 98
Lookout Pass Ski Area, 101
Loon Mountain Resort, 102
Mammoth California, 98
Mt. Bachelor Ski and Summer Resort, 102
Mt. Hood Meadows Ski Resort, 102
Northstar-at-Tahoe, 98
Okemo Mountain Resort, 103
Park City Mountain Resort, 102
Purgatory Resort, 100
Resort at Squaw Creek, 98
Royal Gorge Cross Country Ski Resort, 98–99
Silver Creek Resort, 100
Ski Homewood, 99
Snow Summit Mountain Resort, 99
Snowbird Ski and Summer Resort, 103
Squaw Valley USA, 99
Steamboat Ski and Resort Corporation, 100
Stevens Pass Ski Area, 103
Stowe Mountain Resort, 103
Stratton Mountain, 103
Sugar Bowl Ski Resort, 99
Sugarbush Resort, 103
Sugarloaf/USA, 101
Sun Valley Resort, 101
Sunday River Ski Resort, 101
Telluride Ski and Golf Company, 100
Timberline Lodge, 102
Topnotch Resort and Spa, 103
U.S. Adaptive Recreation Center, 73–74
Vail/Beaver Creek, 100
Village at Breckenridge Resort, 100
Widgiwagan's Environmental Education Program, 173
Winter Park Resort, 100–101

Variable length

Academic Study Associates, 204
Adirondack Mountain Club, 110
The Adventure Centre at Pretty Lake, 44
Adventure Connection, 44
Alliances Abroad, 260
American Horticultural Society, 144
American Institute for Foreign Study, 260
The American-Scandinavian Foundation, 260
Ananda Marga, 179
Anita Purves Nature Center, 144–145
Appalachian Mountain Club, 111–112
Appalachian Mountain Teen Project, 47
Arena Stage, 206–207
Aspen Lodge Ranch Resort, 78
Au Pair in Europe, 262
Augusta Heritage Center, 181
Badlands National Park, 112
BCT.TELUS Employee Fitness Program, 47
Bikes Not Bombs, 56
Boarshead: Michigan's Public Theater, 208
Bombard Balloon Adventures, 47–48
Boojum Institute for Experiential Education, 48
Boston Mobilization for Survival, 235
Bradford Woods, 79
Bradley Wellness Center, 48
BUNAC USA, 262
Bureau of Land Management, 113–114
Camp Counselors/Work Experience USA, 79
Camp Friendship, 80–81
CDS International, 263
Center for American Archeology, 209
The Center for Health, Environment, and Justice, 148
Central Wisconsin Environmental Station, 148–149
Centre for International Mobility, 266
Château de Jean d'Heurs, 266
Chesapeake Wildlife Sanctuary, 149
Chicago Botanic Garden, 149–150
Christian Appalachian Project, 240
A Christian Ministry in the National Parks, 234
Ciclismo Classico, 56–57
Claymont Farm CSA, 186
The Clearing, 211
Club Med, 51
Co-op America, 241
Coffee Creek Ranch, 82–83
College Settlement—Kuhn Day Camps, 83
Colonial Williamsburg Foundation, 211
Congressional Youth Leadership Council, 242
Contiki Holidays, 52
Coulter Lake Guest Ranch, 85

*Obstacles are placed in our way to determine whether we truly wanted
something or just thought we did.* —Harold Smith

Crater Lake National Park, 115
Crow Canyon Archaeological Center, 211–212
Dahlem Environmental Education Center, 150
Delaware Nature Society, 151
Delta Queen Steamboat Company, 52
Denali National Park and Preserve, 116
Dorset Colony for Writers, 205
Eagle's Nest Foundation, 85–86
Emandal—A Farm on a River, 186–187
Flamingo Lodge in Everglades National Park, 117
Fredericksburg and Spotsylvania National Military Park, 118
Furnace Creek Inn and Ranch Resort, 118
Garden Harvest, 187
Grand Canyon National Park Lodges, 122
Grand Teton Lodge Company, 122–123
Greek Dances Theater—Dora Stratou, 214
Habitat for Humanity International, 244
Hawk Mountain Sanctuary Association, 154
Hawthorne Valley Farm, 189
Heifer Project Ranch, 245
Henry Ford Museum and Greenfield Village, 214
Hidden Creek Ranch, 88–89
The History Factory, 215
The Home Ranch, 89
Horizons for Youth, 155
Hostelling International—American Youth Hostels, 282–283
Hulbert Outdoor Center, 62
Humane Society of the United States, 156
Hungarian Association for Organic Farming, 199
InterExchange, 272
International Agricultural Exchange Association, 190–191
International Bicycle Fund, 57
International Crane Foundation, 156
The International Partnership for Service-Learning, 273
International YMCA, 273
Just Act—Youth Action for Global Justice, 246
Kellogg Child Development Center, 246
Kewalo Basin Marine Mammal Laboratory, 157
Kibbutz Program Center, 276–277
Lake Tahoe Basin Management Unit, 124
Land Between the Lakes, 157–158
Longwood Gardens, 158–159
Losang Dragpa Buddhist Centre, 184
Lost Valley Educational Center, 191
Maho Bay Camps, 92–93
Maine Appalachian Trail Club, 124–125
Maine Organic Farmers, 197
Make-A-Wish Foundation, 249
Mast International Experience, 191
Merck Forest and Farmland Center, 192
Mercy Ships, 249
Mission Springs Conference Center, 159
Mote Marine Laboratory, 160

The Nation Institute, 219
National Building Museum, 219
National Future Farmers of America Center, 192–193
National Park Service, 127–129
National Service Corps, 238
National Wildlife Federation, 161
Naval Historical Center, 222
Norlands Living History Center, 223
North Cascades Institute, 163
Northeast Organic Farming Association of Vermont, 197
Offshore Sailing School, 65
Olympic National Park, 126
Oregon Dunes National Recreation Area, 126
Outdoor Adventure River Specialists, 65
Outdoors Wisconsin Leadership School, 68–69
Outward Bound, 66–68
Rainforest Action Network, 165
Reachout Expeditions, 70
River Bend Nature Center, 165
Roads Less Traveled, 71
St. Elizabeth Shelter, 253
St. Vincent Pallotti Center for Apostolic Development, 253–254
Sarett Nature Center, 167
Smithsonian Institution, 225
Snow Mountain Ranch, 96
Student Conservation Association, Inc., 132–133
Student Pugwash USA, 254
Surfrider Foundation, 171
Theodore Roosevelt National Park, 133
Touch of Nature Environmental Center, 73
Tree of Life Rejuvenation Center, 195
United Nations Association of the USA, 286
Upham Woods 4-H EE Center, 172
U.S. Army Corps of Engineers, 133
U.S. Fish and Wildlife Service, 134–135
U.S. Forest Service, 137–138
Vega State Park, 135
VEN-USA, 286–287
Walden Farm, 195
Washington Performing Arts Society, 228
Widgiwagan's Environmental Education Program, 173
Wildlands Studies, 288
Willing Workers on Organic Farms, 196–199
World Teach, 289
Yellowstone National Park Lodges, 139
YMCA Camp Surf, 107
YMCA Willson Outdoor Center, 107
Y.O. Adventure Camp, 107
Yosemite Concession Services Corporation, 140
Youth Enrichment Services, 76
Zion and Bryce Canyon National Park Lodges, 141

General Index. . . . .

Consult this index to find general information on the application process or to find books and other resources. If you want to find a particular program—whether by name, category, location, or program length—the previous four indexes will be able to help you.

A

About.com, 39
Aboutjobs.com, 39
Action Without Borders, 257
Adventure Cycling Association, 54
The Adventures of Tom Sawyer (Twain), 36
Aging, 237–239
Airfares, 291
Alaska Wilderness Recreation and Tourism Association, 76
The Alchemist (Coelho), 36
Alta Vista, 40
Alternative Farming Systems Information Center, 200
Alternative Travel Club—Denmark, 199
Alternative Travel Directory, 290
Alternatives to the Peace Corps, 289
American Association of Botanical Gardens and Arboreta, 174
American Association of Museums, 230
American Association of Retired Persons (AARP), 239
American Association of Snowboard Instructors, 97
American Birding Association, 174
American Camping Association, 108
American Sailing Association, 76
Applications
 requesting, 23–24
 filling out, 25
 following up, 27
Appropriate Technology Transfer for Rural Areas, 200
Archaeological Fieldwork Opportunities Bulletin, 230–231
Archaeological Institute of America, 230
Arcology, 180
The Art of Living (Epictetus), 37
Art Papers Magazine, 231
Artists Communities, 231
Ask for the Moon—and Get It (Ross), 37
Association for Experiential Education, 76
Association for Living History, Farm, and Agricultural Museums, 231
AVISO, 230

B

Bach, Richard, 36
Back to Basics, 201
Backpackers Hostels, Canada, 283
Backyard Market Gardening (Lee), 188
Balance, 8–13
 emotional, 12–13
 mental, 8–9

physical, 9–10
 spiritual, 11–12
Beginning to Pray (Bloom), 37
Berman, Eleanor, 291
Big World, 290
Biodynamic Agriculture, 178
Biodynamic Farming and Gardening Association, 178
Bloom, Anthony, 37
Bode, Richard, 36
Bolles, Richard, 42
The Book of Qualities (Gendler), 37
Borrie, Bill, 119–120
Bridges, William, 42
The British Universities Accommodation Consortium, 284
Bus 9 to Paradise (Buscaglia), 39
Buscaglia, Leo, 39

C

Camp SARK, 41
Career change, 18–19, 42
The Career Guide for Creative and Unconventional People (Eikleberry), 37
Career Opportunities News, 36
Career resources, 36
The Caretaker Gazette, 284
Carter, Jimmy, 236, 239
Carter, Rosalynn, 239
Casey, Karen, 42
Catholic Network of Volunteer Service, 258
Center for Interim Programs, 36
Chadwick, Alan, 201
Change, requirements for, 14
Choices, making, 17
CityFarmer.org, 197
Coalition for Education in the Outdoors, 176
Coelho, Paulo, 36
Colorado Dude and Guest Ranch Association, 108
Combs, Patrick, 40
Community Supported Agriculture (CSA), 178
The Complete Tightwad Gazette (Dacyczyn), 33
Connecting, 290–291
Connecting: Solo Travel News, 290–291
Contact names, 23
Cover letters, 25–26, 27
Covey, Stephen, 41
Creating the Work You Love (Jarow), 38
Creative Whack Pack (von Oech), 38

You can only give away what you have. That's the miracle. If you have love, you can give it. If you don't have it, you don't have it to give. —Leo Buscaglia

D

Dacyczyn, Amy, 33
Dave's ESL Café, 289
de Saint-Exupéry, Antoine, 36
Decision-making, 17
Denial, 19
Dennard, Tom, 12, 283
Discovering Life's Trails: Adventures in Living (Dennard), 12, 283
Dlugozima, Hope, 41
Do What You Love, the Money Will Follow (Sinetar), 38
Dreams, listening to, 12
Dude Ranchers' Association, 108
Dunkin, Craig, 18–19
Dynamic Cover Letters for New Graduates (Hansen), 27

E

Each Day a New Beginning: Daily Meditations for Women (Casey), 42
Earth Work Annual, 133
Earth Work Magazine, 133
Earth Work Online, 133
Eating habits, healthy, 10
Eco-Source Network Center, 76
Eight Weeks to Optimum Health (Weil), 10
Eikleberry, Carol, 37
E-mail, 24
Emotional balance, 12–13
Environmental Career Opportunities, 175
Environmental Careers Organization, 175
Environmental Opportunities, 175
Epictetus, 37
European Centre for Ecological Agriculture and Tourism, 199
Exercise, 9–10

F

Falter-Barns, Suzanne, 39
Fear, pushing past, 38
Feel the Fear and Do It Anyway (Jeffers), 38
Fiction, life-changing, 36–37
First Year Focus, 39
First You Have to Row a Little Boat (Bode), 36
Fodor's Great American Learning Vacations, 231
F-1 Student Visa, 25
Food First, 289
Ford, Henry, 214
4Anything Network, 40
Friends of World Teaching, 289
Funding, 32–33

G

Gallagher, Winifred, 41
Garage sales, 33

Gardner, Elizabeth, 232
Geese, lessons from, 15–16
Gendler, Ruth, 37
Gitka, Robert, 220
The Giver (Lowry), 36
Global Work, 257
Go Network, 40
GoAbroad.com, 289
Good Farming Apprenticeship Network, 200
Government jobs, 119–120
Gran, Michele, 275
Grants, 33
Griffith, Susan, 290
Growing a Business (Hawken), 38
The Guide to Internet Job Searching, 40

H

Hall, Colin, 42
Hansen, Katharine, 27
Happiness Is a Choice (Kaufman), 38–39
Happy box, creating, 12
Hawken, Paul, 38
Health, 9–10
Herrin, Betty, 176
Herriott, Joy, 176
Hirsh, Sandra Krebs, 39
Hoff, Benjamin, 37
Home
    leaving, 16–17
    meaning of, 39
Hope for the Flowers (Paulus), 36
The Hostel Handbook (Williams), 283–284
Hostelling, 282–284
Hostels USA, 284
Hostels.com, 284
House as a Mirror of Self (Marcus), 39
How Much Joy Can You Stand? (Falter-Barns), 39
How to Become a Teacher, 258
How to Grow More Vegetables, 201

I

I Could Do Anything If I Only Knew What It Was (Sher), 39
Icons, key to, 3
Idealist.org, 257
Illusions: The Adventures of a Reluctant Messiah (Bach), 36
Information gathering, 21–22
Inspiration Sandwich (SARK), 41
InterAction, 257
Intercristo, 257
International applicants, 25
International Reply Coupons, 196
Internships in Youth Development, 257
Interviews
    practicing for, 27–28

questions for, 28–29
    following up, 30
Introduction to Permaculture, 201
IRC, 196
Izon's Backpacker Journal, 291

J

Jackson, Andrew, 214
Jarow, Rick, 37–38
Jeavons, John, 201
Jeffers, Susan, 38
Jensen, Jens, 211
Job Bulletin—Opportunities for Musicians Worldwide, 231
The Job Seeker, 174–175
JobHuntersBible.com, 42
Job-Hunting on the Internet (Bolles), 42
Jobweb.org, 39
J-1 Exchange Visitor's Visa, 25
Journal, keeping a, 9
The Joy of Not Working (Zelinski), 39

K

Kaufman, Barry, 38–39
Kelly Services, 33
Kidscamps.com, 108
Kruempelmann, Elizabeth, 264–265
Kummerow, Jean, 39

L

Larner, Monica, 290
Learning Disabilities Association of America, 108
Lederman, Ellen, 185
Lee, Andy, 188
Leisure time, 39
Let's Go Europe, 291
Letters of recommendation, 26–27
Lieber, Ron, 42
Lifetypes (Hirsh and Kummerow), 39–40
The Little Prince (de Saint-Exupéry), 36
Living, Studying, and Working in Italy (Neighbor and Larner), 289–290
Living conditions, 29
Living Juicy: Daily Morsels for Your Creative Soul (SARK), 41
Loans, 33
Lonely Planet, 291
Loompanics, 37
Lore, Nicholas, 40
Love (Buscaglia), 39
Lowry, Lois, 36
Luhrs, Janet, 14
Lyman, David, 220–221

M

Magic Museletter, 41
Major in Success (Combs), 40

Make a Mil-¥en: Teaching English in Japan, 290
Making a Living Without a Job (Winters), 40
Management, 40–41
Manpower, 33
A Manual for Living (Epictetus), 37
Marcus, Clare Cooper, 39
Marzetta, John, 40–41
Maslow's hierarchy of needs, 13
Massachusetts Audubon Society, 175
McColl, Michael, 291
McMillon, Bill, 290
Mental balance, 8–9
Mentors, seeking out, 15
Mollison, Bill, 201
Monday Developments, 257
Money issues, 32–33
Moon Travel Handbooks, 291
Myers-Briggs personality test, 39

N

The National Assembly, 257
National Association for Interpretation, 142
National Audubon Society, 78, 146
National Ski Patrol, 97
Needs, understanding your, 13
Neighbor, Travis, 290
Nelson, Portia, 17
The New England Conservatory of Music, 231
Nuanaarpuq, 64

O

Oh, the Places You'll Go! (Seuss), 37
O-Hayo Sensei: The Newsletter of (Teaching) Jobs in Japan, 290
Ohio Ecological Food and Farm Association, 200
Olson, Milton, 15
The 100 Best Small Art Towns in America, 231
Opportunities in Arts and Crafts Careers (Gardner), 232
Organization, 24
Outdoor Network, 76
Over the Rainbow, 250

P

Parker, Yana, 27
Passport in Time Clearinghouse, 142
The Pathfinder (Lore), 40
Paulus, Trina, 36
PCC: How to Survive in Management, or Just Another Fish Story (Marzetta), 40–41
Permaculture: A Designers' Manual (Mollison), 201
Personhood: The Art of Being Fully Human (Buscaglia), 39
Philbrook, Bud, 274, 275
Physical balance, 9–10
Place, power of, 16–17, 41
Possession downsizing, 33

Many of life's failures are people who did not realize how close they were to success when they gave up. —THOMAS A. EDISON

The Power of Place (Gallagher), 41
Prayer, power of, 37
Professional Ski Instructors of America, 97

Q

Quaker Information Center, 257
Quintessential Careers, 27

R

Recruiting New Teachers, 258
Regional Theatre Directory, 232
Rejection, dealing with, 30–31
Response, 258
Resume Catalog: 200 Damn Good Examples (Parker), 27
Resumes, 25–26, 27
Rick Steves' Europe Through the Back Door, 291
Rileyguide.com, 40
Risking (Viscott), 41
Ross, Percy, 37
Rough Guides, 291
RVs, 239

S

Sanctuaries: The Complete United States, 284
SARK, 41
Scott, James, 41
Seattle Tilth Association, 201
Self-actualization, path of, 13
Self-development, 6–8
Self-employment, 32, 40
Seuss, Dr., 36–37
The 7 Habits of Highly Effective People (Covey), 41
ShawGuides.com, 232
Sher, Barbara, 39
The Simple Living Guide (Luhrs), 14
Simplicity, 14
Sinetar, Marsha, 38
The Single-Friendly Travel Directory, 290
Six Months Off (Dlugozima and Scott), 41
Skeptics, examples of, 31
Soleri, Paolo, 180
Solo travel, 290–291
Sparklett's jug theory, 33
Spirituality, 11–12
Steves, Rick, 291
Stratou, Dora, 214
Stretching, 10
StudyAbroad.com, 290
Summer Opportunities in Marine and Environmental Science (Herriott and Herrin), 176
Summer Theatre Directory, 232

T

TA NEWS, 290
Take This Job and Love It!, 258

Taking Off, 37
Taking Time Off (Hall and Lieber), 42
The Tao of Pooh (Hoff), 37
Taproot, 176
Teachers, seeking out, 15
Teaching English Abroad, 290
Temp jobs, 32–33
Thank-you notes, 22
Theatre Directories, 232
Touchstones: A Book of Daily Meditations for Men (Spohn), 42
Training, 28
Transitions Abroad, 290
Transitions (Bridges), 42
Travel guides, 290–291
Traveling Solo (Berman), 291
Twain, Mark, 36

U

United States Information Agency, 243

V

Vacations That Can Change Your Life (Lederman), 185
Villani, John, 231–232
The Virtues of Aging (Carter), 239
Visas, 25
Viscott, David, 41
Volunteer adventures, 256
Volunteer America.com, 142
Volunteer Vacations (McMillon), 290
Volunteers for Outdoor Colorado, 142
von Oech, Roger, 38

W

Wants, 13
Washington, George, 188
Web sites, 35, 39–40. *See also individual organizations*
Weil, Andrew, 10
What Color Is Your Parachute? (Bolles), 42
Whole Work Catalog, 37
Williams, Jim, 283–284
Williams, Michael and Dorrie, 53–54
Winning Ways, 40
Winters, Barbara, 40
Work Abroad, 290
Work Your Way Around the World (Griffith), 290
Workamper News, 239
Working Options, 239
A World of Options, 250
The Worldwide Guide to Cheap Airfares (McColl), 291

Z

Zelinski, Ernie, 39